On Trial

There were two men in one city; the one rich, and the other poor. The rich man had exceeding many flocks and herds: But the poor man had nothing, save one little ewe lamb, which he had bought and nourished up: and it grew up together with him, and with his children: it did eat of his own meat, and drank of his own cup, and lay in his bosom, and was unto him as a daughter. And there came a traveler unto the rich man, and he spared to take of his own flock and of his own herd, to dress for the wayfaring man that was come unto him; but took the poor man's lamb, and dressed it for the man that was come to him.

—Nathan to David

We ask, not what this man meant, but what those words would mean in the mouth of a normal speaker of English, using them in the circumstances in which they were used.

—Oliver Wendell Holmes Jr.

On Trial

From Adam & Eve to O. J. Simpson

George Anastaplo

LEXINGTON BOOKS
Lanham • Boulder • New York • Toronto • Oxford

LEXINGTON BOOKS

Published in the United States of America
by Lexington Books
An imprint of The Rowman & Littlefield Publishing Group, Inc.
4501 Forbes Boulevard, Suite 200, Lanham, Maryland 20706

PO Box 317
Oxford
OX2 9RU, UK

British Library Cataloguing in Publication Information Available

Library of Congress Cataloging-in-Publication Data

Anastaplo, George, 1925–
  On trial : from Adam & Eve to O. J. Simpson / George Anastaplo ; foreword by Abner J. Mikva.
     p. cm.
  ISBN 0-7391-0779-8 (cloth : alk. paper) — ISBN 0-7391-0780-1 (pbk. : alk. paper)
  1. Trials. 2. Rule of law. 3. Law and politics. 4. Social justice. I. Title.
K540.A53 2004
340'.11—dc22   2003022688

Printed in the United States of America

⊗™ The paper used in this publication meets the minimum requirements of American National Standard for Information Sciences—Permanence of Paper for Printed Library Materials, ANSI/NISO Z39.48–1992.

To the Memory
of
my Law School teachers (1948–1951)
who,
with a few noble exceptions,
preached (and hence taught)
far better than they could practice.

Contents

Foreword

To say that George Anastaplo has eclectic interests is to state the obvious. One need only look at the table of contents for this book to become aware of his fascination with everything. But it is not only the diversity of his interests that make him unusual. It is the way he pursues those interests—the combinations, the variations, the mutations—that accounts, at least in part, for why he is such a prolific writer. One is reminded of Thomas Jefferson's "perpetually active and inquisitive mind."

This is his twelfth book—everything from Lincoln to Shakespeare to the Constitution to Homer to the classics of non-Western thought. The subjects are not only in his sights but relate to each other in ways that other writers do not see. Again, the table of contents says it eloquently: George Anastaplo starts with the serpent in the Garden of Eden and ends with another visit to the O. J. Simpson trial. But books are only a part of the trove.

There are the law reviews and the scholarly journals. George did not go to law school by accident or simply because the postwar G.I. Bill of Rights made it financially easy for our generation to take on all the education we could digest. He came to the University of Chicago Law School with the notion that being a wordsmith was the most useful calling around, and that law school allowed one to use wordsmithing in so many ways. Writing for the journals, for others to pick over, criticize, and elaborate on is a worthy end in itself. It is a special kind of writing. One of the premises is that nothing should be said that can't be verified in a footnote (in progressive journals they sometimes use endnotes). Sometimes the footnotes allow a wandering into pastures only vaguely related to the subject matter being footnoted, but that is part of the game. I suspect that George Anastaplo would defend the results of the famous footnote 4 of a case that has become obscure as to its own subject matter, but footnote 4 has developed an entire branch of jurisprudence.[1]

And then there is the potpourri. A few weeks ago, I found a letter to the editor from George Anastaplo questioning the usefulness of the president of the United States weighing in on the merits of a threatened baseball strike. I was only surprised that he didn't also express himself on why the Chicago teams never live up to expectations.

George Anastaplo was an iconoclast from the time he was in law school. He would enter his class and pay studious attention to the opening words of the professor, and if they stimulated his thought process, he would become engaged. His contributions were vigorous and stimulated the Socratic dialogue that most of our pedagogues used. If, on the other hand, the subject matter or the delivery was dull, George would often pull out a copy of the *Wall Street Journal*, or the *Daily Worker*, and read. George never intended that this conduct should be construed as any kind of a "statement"—he was always very respectful—but it was simply his decision not to waste time by daydreaming or whatever else students do when the class doesn't stimulate them. He never did that in any of William Winslow Crosskey's classes. Crosskey was one of George Anastaplo's academic heroes, and engagement was never a problem in those classes. Some of the other professors weren't happy with this practice, but it confirmed the fact that the grading of exams was on a blind basis: George graduated first in our class of over one hundred.

The iconoclasm showed up more dramatically when he graduated and took the bar exam. He passed, of course, but refused to answer questions about his political beliefs before the "character and fitness" committee that interviewed him. It wasn't that he had anything to hide, as anyone examining his background could have figured out in a New York minute. This time he did want to make a statement: that a free society ought to have reasons for prying into a person's beliefs. He could not see what relevance the questions had to his fitness to be a member of the bar. The 1950s were not an enlightened period in our political society, and the courts would not reverse the decision that kept George Anastaplo from practicing law.

That forced a career choice that certainly turned out well for George Anastaplo's itch to write. He went into teaching—and writing. Even with his distinctive habit of picking and choosing where to spend his time and intellect, it is doubtful that practicing law would have allowed him the breadth of interests that he has indulged in his career. Briefs have page limits, oral arguments have time limits, and those limits are incompatible with the way George Anastaplo uses wordsmithing. To him, words are the way we describe our interest in what's going on. If you really are interested, then why would you want to place artificial limits on your description?

I am not sure that George would agree, but I think a part of his curiosity, his eclecticism, has to do with growing up in a small town. Those of us who grew up in larger cities always had our interests channeled and cabined. There would be a one-hour field trip to the museum and a thirty-minute exposure to the public library. There is more flexibility in scheduling and a more leisurely budgeting of time in the smaller towns. Even though there are not quite as many things to see, not quite as many cultural opportunities, there is greater time to indulge what interests one has. And in George Anastaplo's case, his curiosity was boundless.

On Trial is a prime example of how George Anastaplo can take a landscape as broad as all of civilization and use his wordsmithing to relate Adam not only to Eve but also to O. J. Simpson.

ABNER J. MIKVA

NOTE

1. *United States v. Carolene Products*, 304 U.S. 144 (1938).

Author's note: The text Abner Mikva had when he prepared this foreword did not yet include the dedication, introduction, or four appendixes. See, on Judge Mikva, preface, notes 7–9. See as well the recollection by him incorporated in note 1 of the introduction to the appendixes in this book.

Preface

It is now half a century since the publication of the best-known works of my most important University of Chicago teachers, William W. Crosskey and Leo Strauss.[1] I have borrowed from their two books the epigraphs for this occasion, epigraphs that remind us of enduring standards implicit in the virtue of justice and in the art of reading.[2] I attempt, with such invocations, to suggest how one should deal with the stories that interest us, stories that are, for the most part, quite familiar.[3] The collection in this volume of exercises in disciplined reading and prudential judgment offers *not* the last word but (it is hoped) a reliable first word (as well as "a good read") for the general reader with respect to a score of well-known matters, ancient and modern, historical and fictional.[4] These are introductions that academic specialists should also find useful here and there, and not only because of the notes in which some of the relevant scholarly literature is noticed.[5]

It is difficult here, as in several other works of mine, to overestimate the importance of the circumstances in which these discussions (originally oral essays) were first developed. A reliable awareness of such circumstances is useful for appreciating what is offered by me from time to time and how this is done. Again and again, therefore, indications are provided of what the circumstances invited and required. These discussions, often in response to invitations, were developed with a view to eventual publication in projected collections of my explorations.[6]

The fist introduction to this particular collection has been provided by Abner J. Mikva, a law school classmate.[7] He is perhaps the most successful member professionally of our class, having served with distinction in the legislative, judicial, and executive branches of the national government.[8] He and I have collaborated, one way or another, on several "projects" over the years, projects in which I have played minor roles.[9] I have yet to meet anyone who, knowing him well, speaks ill of him, which is a tribute to that happy conjunction in him of a considerable talent and an obvious good will.

Another introduction to this collection of discussions is provided by a thoughtful political scientist who has done substantial work both in classical thought and in the philosophy of Alfarabi.[10] He can refer to my discussions as samples of what I have called "constructive provocations."[11] Although *On Trial* has been considerably reworked since the original publication of much of it in a law journal,[12] our political scientist's observations about this collection, such as the following, continue to be instructive:

> Students of these trials—in the extended sense of the word according to which Abraham and Jonah also undergo trials—will hardly find a better place to begin thinking about them than Anastaplo's essays. Central to each essay is a concern with what we can know and how much we have to know in order to make a responsible judgment. . . . *On Trial* provides us with a way into what one is tempted to call Anastaplo's philosophy of history. Perhaps it is misleading to use the phrase "philosophy of history" in order to describe the thought of an author who always places nature above history. Nature is the standard by which Anastaplo intends to judge and to be judged. [13]

Our political scientist continues his generous introduction to *On Trial* with these observations:

> The connections [among freedom, nature, and community in the Anastaplo essays] can be anticipated by three questions. In the first two of these questions, the reader will see that we are in a way asking about Anastaplo's philosophy of history. Does nature limit human freedom in the construction of a political community? Does nature serve as a standard in guiding the affairs of the community? Can a community be true to its own standards while remaining open to the standards of other communities, or to what extent is it feasible to have a community within a community? The emergence of human freedom is one of the . . . themes of *On Trial*.[14]

Further on it is observed,

> *On Trial* is an advocacy of . . . decent reasonability as natural and proper in the affairs of men. Is the effort to be reasonable and to see all sides of a question not sometimes either debilitating or corrupting? "Has reason been good for man?" This is Anastaplo's question, but, of course, it is also [Friedrich] Nietzsche's. Nietzsche's answer is complicated by the fact that truth often (always?) destroys the limited or closed horizon that sustains life. It is from Nietzsche that we have heard that the truth can be deadly. Anastaplo could claim the authority of Nietzsche to sustain the point that "the natural understanding sometimes may even

be taken to suggest that there really is no meaning to the cosmos." It is easy to see how speculation along these lines could be destructive of political life. Notwithstanding such speculations, Anastaplo . . . takes the view that reason and enlightenment, albeit perhaps only moderate enlightenment, have been good for man and for political life, even though he notes that reason makes some men, Oedipus or Socrates, vulnerable. Reason is both a moderating influence *and* a political good.[15]

We are then told,

I have spoken of Anastaplo as an advocate of moderate enlightenment, by which I mean nothing more than that he sees the influence of reason on human life and political life as a salutary one. This may seem a harmless assertion, an obvious truism about reason. But it is a truism that has been disputed, for example, by Nietzsche. Reason can be seen as destroying the faiths by which men live, the hopes without which life would not be possible, the necessary love of one's own just because it is one's own. Anastaplo puts reason on trial. He tries to make the case for the goodness of reason without falling into the extreme hopes that characterized the Enlightenment. Those hopes assumed the possibility of radical change in human circumstances, change so radical that it would obliterate a nature that, in its immutability, would leave some problems irresolvable. The moderate enlightenment that tries to steer between the Scylla of Enlightenment and the Charybdis of irrationalism seems, if I may be judgmental, not only noble but essentially correct.[16]

Additional introductions to this collection are provided in effect in the thirteen chapters that follow. Since the two dozen talks incorporated in these chapters had originally had to stand alone, my general approach and routine presuppositions had to be drawn upon, sometimes explicitly, in each instance of delivery over several decades. It is this reliance upon talks tailored to circumstances, even as they depend upon abiding principles, which permits work such as this to take on the character of a series of dialogues that can reinforce one another.[17]

The four appendixes to this collection, illuminating aspects of my career and suggesting thereby the general background for my reflections, can be said to be related somewhat to the Four Causes drawn upon in Aristotle's treatises.[18] These appendixes indicate responses, in a variety of circumstances, to my Illinois bar admission litigation (1950–1961).[19] There is in my first appendix an account that sketches the climate of opinion nationwide that that litigation had to work with, suggesting thereby the material cause of this personally fateful controversy.[20] Then there is an account of my 1960 oral argument before the United States Supreme Court, indicating how I shaped my position in the circumstances in which I happened to find myself.

This can suggest the efficient cause in this matter.[21] Then there is the account of my career as a whole, in which bar admission litigation has been only a part. This can suggest the formal cause in this matter.[22] Then there is my response to a law student's questions about my litigation, "Why did you do it?"—which does seem to be the kind of question that the final cause is associated with.[23]

It is well, as we look to nature for guidance in what follows in this book, to be reminded of that understanding of nature recorded in the preface to my 2002 collection of seven introductions to non-Western thought: "*Nature* is not simply that which we often mean when we refer to material properties, climate, mortality, passions, mental capacities, and the like. It includes, as particularly significant, that principle of constancy and change in things, a principle of order that is independent of a superintending Intelligence."[24]

The concluding passage in my preface for the non-Western collection, *But Not Philosophy*, can also serve to illuminate this *On Trial* collection:

> This collection is offered . . . as a set of useful introductions to long-established and otherwise impressive traditions around the world. Even more important, perhaps, are the reminders available here of that which Westerners can learn from non-Westerners about what the West itself is like, particularly with respect to its grasp of and reliance upon the divine, its reliance upon nature and causality, and its reliance upon philosophy. It usually contributes to one's self-knowledge to secure a reliable sense of what one is *not*.
>
> Critical to all of this exercise, as well as to much else that I have studied, is an emphasis upon the vital importance of *truly reading* those texts that do permit, require, and reward careful study.[25]

Related to these observations is what our political scientist has said in his preliminary assessment, almost a decade ago, of my *On Trial* collection:

> Anastaplo himself says that he has been shielded by his temperament from "an apocalyptic view of things" of the sort that he ascribes to [Martin] Heidegger. Perhaps it is this temperament that allows him to promote reason in politics without fostering the utopian expectations that have played havoc with both our theory and our practice over the last two centuries and longer. To point the way to a more prudent course is no small achievement.[26]

NOTES

1. See William W. Crosskey, *Politics and the Constitution in the History of the United States* (Chicago: University of Chicago Press, 1953); Leo Strauss, *Natural*

Right and History (Chicago: University of Chicago Press, 1953). Mr. Crosskey drew on his *Politics and the Constitution* manuscript in the Constitutional Law courses I took in 1949–1950. I attended, in 1949, the lectures expanded thereafter by Mr. Strauss into his *Natural Right and History* book.

See, on these teachers, George Anastaplo, "Leo Strauss at the University of Chicago," in Kenneth L. Deutsch and John A. Murley, eds., *Leo Strauss, the Straussians, and the American Regime* (Lanham, Md.: Rowman & Littlefield, 1999), p. 3; Anastaplo, "Mr. Crosskey, the American Constitution, and the Natures of Things," 15 *Loyola University of Chicago Law Journal* 181 (1984). See, also Malcolm P. Sharp, "Crosskey, Anastaplo, and Meiklejohn on the United States Constitution," *University of Chicago Law School Record* (Spring 1975): 3; appendix C, note 49.

2. The epigraph taken by me from the Strauss book had been taken by him from *2 Samuel* 12:1–4. It was supplemented by another passage, taken by Mr. Strauss from *1 Kings* 21:1–3. It is significant that Mr. Strauss uses, in a study of natural right, epigraphs taken from the Bible. See, on natural right, as distinguished from the natural law tradition influenced by religious doctrines, George Anastaplo, *But Not Philosophy: Seven Introductions to Non-Western Thought* (Lanham, Md.: Lexington Books, 2002), p. 323.

The epigraph taken by me from the Crosskey book had been taken by him from Oliver Wendell Holmes Jr., *Collected Legal Papers* (New York, 1921), p. 204. One can begin to assess Justice Holmes's limitations as a constitutional scholar when one considers his opinion in *Schenck v. United States*, 249 U.S. 47 (1919), and in *Missouri v. Holland*, 252 U.S. 416 (1920), and Justice Louis Brandeis's Holmesian opinion in *Erie Railroad Company v. Tompkins*, 304 U.S. 64 (1938). (The Constitutional contortions that "had" to be resorted to in *Missouri v. Holland* should have provoked questions about the sensibleness of the then-prevailing interpretation of the Commerce Clause.) See, on the limitations of Justice Holmes, George Anastaplo, *The Constitutionalist: Notes on the First Amendment* (Dallas: Southern Methodist University Press, 1971), p. 824.

3. Or they were familiar until fairly recently. Be that as it may, we are often unable really to look at the things most familiar to us. The stories examined in this book are drawn from ancient literature and history (sacred and profane), from modern literature and history, and from contemporary events.

4. The matters reviewed are arranged in a plausible chronological order. Of course, the order in which these accounts are read need not be that which I have provided.

5. I have not attempted to "update" the literature drawn upon in the notes, although I do notice some recent things here and there. There is, for the benefit of the reader interested in pursuing relations among the parts of this book, considerable cross-referencing in the notes.

The notes reinforce what is said in the text about how to read the kind of materials examined in this book. See, for example, chapter 7, note 101; chapter 9, note 49; chapter 12, notes 117, 128; and the conclusion, note 1. See also preface, note 13.

6. See, for a catalogue of my "Explorations" genre, "George Anastaplo: Tables of Contents for His Books and Published Collections (1950–2001)," 39 *Brandeis Law Journal* 219–87 (2000). See also preface, note 17.

See, for an emphasis upon "circumstances," the epigraph for this book taken from Justice Holmes. A consideration of circumstances with respect to my published work is aided by the detailed inventory of sources provided in "George Anastaplo: An Autobiographical Bibliography (1947–2001)," 20 *Northern Illinois University Law Review* 581–710 (2000). See also Kenneth L. Deutsch and John A. Murley, eds., *Leo Strauss, the Straussians, and the American Regime* (Lanham, Md.: Rowman & Littlefield, 1999), George Anastaplo entry.

7. This was the University of Chicago Law School Class of 1951. See, on that class, appendix C, note 64, appendix D, note 14. See, on the faculty of the law school, the dedication for this book. The "noble exceptions" referred to there include Harry Kalven Jr., Wilbur G. Katz, Roscoe T. Steffen, and Malcolm P. Sharp.

8. Abner J. Mikva was in the United States House of Representatives from 1968 to 1972 and from 1974 to 1979, on the United States Court of Appeal for the District of Columbia Circuit from 1979 to 1994 (serving as Chief Judge from 1991 to 1994), and White House Counsel from September 1994 to November 1995. He had, before going to Congress, served in the General Assembly of the State of Illinois.

Other members of our law school class with distinguished political careers were Ramsey Clark and Patsy T. Mink.

9. Thus, we have served together as speakers on panels for which he was the principal attraction. Thus, also, he was Co-Chair of Citizens for the Constitution (A Project of The Century Foundation) (I was one of the seventy or so "Members"). This organization was responsible for publication of the booklet, *"Great and Extraordinary Occasions": Developing Guidelines for Constitutional Change* (New York: The Century Foundation Press, 1999). See Anastaplo, "Constitutionalism and the Good: Explorations," 70 *Tennessee Law Review* 737, 812–25 (2003) (Part 10: "On Amending the Constitution"). See, on Representative Mikva's insertion of my articles on modern Greek affairs in the *Congressional Record*, appendix C, note 64.

10. See, e.g., Chrisotpher A. Colmo, *Ancient Communism* (University of Chicago doctoral dissertation, 1979); Colmo, *Alfarabi as Founder: Human Action and the Quest for Certainty* (forthcoming).

11. Christopher A. Colmo, "Freedom, Nature, and Community," 26 *Political Science Reviewer* 164 (1997). This is one of seven articles that were contributed to the symposium, "The Scholarship of George Anastaplo," which was published in the 1997 volume of the *Reviewer*. My immediate response was published in that issue; my more extended response was published in the 1998 volume of the *Reviewer*. See, for another article in the symposium, preface, note 16.

12. See Anastaplo, "On Trial: Explorations," 22 *Loyola University of Chicago Law Journal* 765 (1991). The considerable reworking of the 1991 collection for this book was supplemented by altogether new chapters, 7 and 13, and the addition of the four appendixes.

13. Colmo, "Freedom, Nature, and Community," p. 16. Here, as usually elsewhere in this book, references and notes in the quotations are omitted. See, on what is "central to each essay," preface, note 5.

14. Colmo, "Freedom, Nature, and Community," p. 166. See, on history and on nature, Anastaplo, *The American Moralist: On Law, Ethics, and Government* (Athens,

Ohio: Ohio University Press, 1992), pp. 611, 616. See, also, Anastaplo, *But Not Philosophy*, pp. 383, 387.

15. Colmo, "Freedom, Nature, and Community," p. 180. See, on Friedrich Nietzsche, Anastaplo, *The American Moralist*, p. 616; Anastaplo, *But Not Philosophy*, p. 387.

The Enlightenment can look rather good when one considers some manifestations of Islam today. See, on Islamic thought, Anastaplo, *But Not Philosophy*, p. 175. And it looks even better when one considers the ferocious European (that is, "Christian") witch-trials epidemic of a few centuries ago. See Anastaplo, "Church and State: Explorations," 19 *Loyola University of Chicago Law Journal* 61, 65 (1987). See also chapter 12-A.

16. Colmo, "Freedom, Nature, and Community," p. 192. Stephen Vanderslice draws on my *On Trial* collection in his survey of a dozen of my publications in his article, "George Anastaplo on Religion," 26 *Political Science Reviewer* 114 (1997). He begins his conclusion in this fashion (p. 162):

> George Anastaplo, working within a long, thoughtful tradition, recognizes and proclaims the importance of religion for communities of men and for men's souls. From the statesman's perspective he sees both the importance of sensible collaboration of Church and State, and the serious obstacles to such collaborations, especially in the United States, and especially these days. From the perspective of the human being he acknowledges that there are plausible ontological hints of the divine, and he appreciates the great religions' reach for the true and their various contributions toward the good and the useful for man. He acknowledges this, even as he also notes certain implausibilities or flaws in the original conceptions of, or "revelations" of, several of the world's great religions, flaws perhaps developing unavoidably as the ineffable struggles to find its way into logos.

17. It can be salutary for authors to keep in mind the caution in Plato's *Phaedrus* about the limitations of writings when compared to oral exchanges. See, on my "Explorations" genre, preface, note 6.

18. See, e.g., Aristotle, *Physics*, bk. II, chaps. 1–3. See also Joe Sachs, trans., *Aristotle's "Physics": A Guided Study* (New Brunswick, N.J.: Rutgers University Press, 1995), p. 257 (on "causes"); Book Review, 26 *Interpretation* 275 (1999).

19. See *In re George Anastaplo*, 366 U.S. 82 (1961). See also John A. Murley, "In re George Anastaplo," in Deutsch and Murley, eds., *Leo Strauss, the Straussians, and the American Regime*, p. 159.

20. See appendix A, "Subversion, Then and Now (1987)."

21. See appendix B, "On Representing Oneself (2001)."

22. See appendix C, "Chance and the Good Life (2001)."

23. See appendix D, "Why Did You Do It? (2003)." See also *In re Anastaplo*, 366 U.S. 82, 104 (1961); Jon Bauer, "The Character of the Questions and the Fitness of the Process," 49 *University of California at Los Angeles Law Review* 93 (2001).

Clues to why I did what I have done with my career, beginning with my fateful encounter with the Committee on Character and Fitness in November 1950, may be found in the recollections supplied by a gifted law school classmate, Abner J. Mikva. (See foreword; also, note 1 of the introduction to the appendixes.) These clues include the determined independence exhibited from time to time in my response to the conventions of law school student life a half century ago. No doubt, I was somewhat immature at times. I could be unconventional in other ways as well in that highly competitive milieu. See, for example, appendix D, note 14.

24. Anastaplo, *But Not Philosophy*, p. xxi, note 13.

25. Anastaplo, *But Not Philosophy*, pp. xviii–xix.

26. Colmo, "Freedom, Nature, and Community," pp. 210–11. See, on Martin Heidegger, Anastaplo, *The American Moralist*, p. 611; Anastaplo, *But Not Philosophy*, p. 383.

Several members of the secretarial staff of Loyola University of Chicago School of Law have contributed to the preparation of these materials for publication, including Elaine Gist, John Connolly, and Cora Ortiz, as has the editorial board of volume 22 of the *Loyola University of Chicago Law Journal*, especially Thomas J. Pauloski and William E. Meyer Jr. Sherman Lewis, of the Loyola Law Library, has been of considerable help for many years now.

Introduction

Having thus briefly spoken of the Naturall Kingdome of God, and his Naturall Lawes, I will adde onely to this Chapter a short declaration of his Naturall Punishments. There is no action of man in this life, that is not the beginning of so long a chayn of Consequences, as no humane Providence, is high enough, to give a man a prospect to the end. And in this Chayn, there are linked together both pleasing and unpleasing events; in such manner, as he that will do any thing for his pleasure, must engage himselfe to suffer all the pains annexed to it; and these pains, are the Naturall Punishments of those actions, which are the beginning of more Harme than Good. And hereby it comes to passe, that Intemperance, is naturally punished with Diseases; Rashnesse, with Mischances; Injustice, with the Violence of Enemies; Pride, with Ruine; Cowardise, with Oppression; Negligent government of Princes, with Rebellion; and Rebellion, with Slaughter. For seeing Punishments are consequent to the breach of Lawes; Naturall Punishments must be naturally consequent to the breach of the Lawes of Nature; and therefore follow them as their naturall, not arbitrary effects.

—Thomas Hobbes[1]

The cases and controversies I happen to discuss here include some that I have dealt with elsewhere.[2] Students of literature and of politics should recognize in this book plots and issues that have long challenged the Western student. Students of law should recognize various matters that are addressed in law school courses in law and literature, in jurisprudence (or philosophy of law), in criminal law, in evidence, in civil procedure, in constitutional law, and in legal history. Simplifications of the plots, issues, and cases reviewed have been required for some of the audiences I have addressed. I draw upon nonlegal materials that were once much more familiar to legislators, judges, lawyers, and other students of law, as well as to the educated generally, than they are now.

This collection brings together talks and essays prepared by me across three decades, the earliest going back to 1974. These have been supplemented by the four, much more personal, talks in the appendixes. Each of the discussions collected here should be able to stand alone: I assume in most instances the general knowledge among us of the matter at hand. (The original independence of each discussion accounts for some overlapping between parts of this book.) Extensive notes have been provided that reinforce the argument in each chapter and that relate the discussions to one another, especially as common topics and principles become apparent. Just as recorded trials can often be seen as literary, so the crises in literature can often be seen as trials.[3]

Literary sources (going back to the Garden of Eden) as well as historical records provide materials for these discussions of what justice, prudence, and the rule of law mean. The reader is challenged to see what sense there is to the judgments I presume to make, judgments that again and again draw upon and refine principles and standards that invite thoughtful criticism. I judge in order that I in turn may be properly judged, hoping to learn thereby what more I need to know in order to understand better the matters I presume to discuss here. It should be evident that one may be helped in thinking about these matters by getting what guidance one can from the best thinking available in the greatest works of the mind offered us by our tradition.[4]

NOTES

1. Thomas Hobbes, *Leviathan*, chap. 31 (1651). See conclusion, note 3.

The reader is urged, as with my other publications, to begin by reading the text of this book without reference to its notes, except for the note at the beginning of each of the chapters. The opening note for each chapter indicates the occasion for which that chapter was originally prepared—and an awareness of the occasion may bear both on what is said and on how it is said.

An earlier version of this collection may be found in George Anastaplo, "On Trial Explorations," 22 *Loyola University of Chicago Law Journal* 765 (1991). Some of the 1991 *Loyola Law Journal* material dropped from this volume is cited here and there in this collection. See, e.g., chapter 1, notes 51, 75. See, on my "Explorations" genre, the text at note 59 of appendix C.

See, for citations to my bibliographies, conclusion, note 2. See also appendix C.

2. See, e.g., George Anastaplo, *The Constitutionalist: Notes on the First Amendment* (Dallas: Southern Methodist University Press, 1971), pp. 798 n. 32 (Antigone and Oedipus), 294–305 (*Schenck Case*), 312–23 (*Chicago Conspiracy Trial*), 824 (*Dennis Case*), 825 (*Rosenberg Case*) (1971).

Other published discussions by me of cases are noticed in chapter 1, notes 2, 95, chapter 12, notes 153, 173, 193. See, for references to still other cases that could usefully be discussed: chapter 1, notes 23, 71, 102, 117; chapter 4, notes 20, 29; chapter 5, note 1; chapter 7, notes 25, 26, 58; chapter 9, note 14; chapter 12, notes 29, 139, 165.

Litigation in which I have been personally involved is discussed in the appendixes. See also Anastaplo, *The Constitutionalist*, pp. 331–418; 35 *DePaul Law Review* 551–647 (1986); chapter 12, note 146.

3. See, e.g., the text at note 91 of chapter 7. Consider also John Milton's *Areopagitica*:

> He that can apprehend and consider vice with all her habits and seeming pleasures, and yet abstain, and yet distinguish, and yet prefer that which is truly better, he is the true warfaring Christian. I cannot praise a fugitive and cloistered virtue, unexercised and unbreathed, that never sallies out and sees her adversary, but slinks out of the race where that immortal garland is to be run for, not without dust and heat. Assuredly we bring not innocence into the world, we bring impurity much rather: *that which purifies us is trial*, and trial is by that which is contrary.

John Milton, *Complete Poems and Major Prose*, ed., Merritt Y. Hughes (Indianapolis: The Odyssey Press, 1957), p. 728 (emphasis added). Someone such as Socrates might take issue with what is implied here about human nature and original sin. See, e.g., chapter 10, section V. Would not Thomas More, on the other hand, have found such talk congenial? See Milton, *Complete Poems*, p. 728. See also, for what can be said about the trials to which Abraham was subjected, the text at note 52 of chapter 5. See, on nature, conclusion, note 2. See, on original sin, chapter 1, notes 45, 91.

Judges, too, are themselves put to decisive tests, as may be seen in about half of the cases and stories discussed in this collection. See, e.g., chapter 12, note 123. The judges can include a goddess and the citizens of Athens, as may be seen in Aeschylus's *Oresteia*. See chapter 2. Consider, on the relation between what goes on in everyday life and what is presented by the artist, this introduction to this great Aeschylean trilogy:

> No one knows for sure when human beings first gathered together to watch their fellows stage a play. And no one knows when formal trials became regular events in the lives of civilized communities. There is not evidence that these institutions developed together. But the watching of trials seems to have much in common with the watching of plays. Speech, action, and props are arranged to display events that are not really occurring as they are watched. In each case, a staged representation imitates past or possible events, and elicits the passions and judgments of the assembled spectators. Perennial interest in accounts of "dramatic" trials, the continual popularity of courtroom dramas and movies, and recent interest in televised crimes and trials, all suggest that dramatic reenactment and judicial judgment are fundamentally related to each other.
>
> Perhaps it is no accident that the first and foremost drama of the Western world [the *Oresteia*] is about the establishment of institutional public justice. Presented in a city where, at different times, the same citizens are required to constitute themselves as

collective spectator in the theatre and collective jury in a court of law, community come to look together to see that justice is done. As such, it is one of the deepest meditations on human beings as moral and law-abiding beings, and on what is necessary to heal individuals, families, and communities when they have been violated. But it is even more than a meditation on justice and punishment, even more than a guide for those who make institutional arrangements for handling such matters. The trilogy itself, staged for citizen-spectators, contributes, as the courts do, to making justice visible. No wonder Aeschylus wanted to tell this story in the theatre.

Mera Flaumenhaft, "Seeing Justice Done: Aeschylus' *Oresteia*," *Interpretation*, Fall 1989, p. 69. See also pp.105–7.

4. I return, however briefly, to these general considerations in my conclusion to this collection. An extensive discussion by me of the themes and arguments drawn upon here, including the relation of justice to freedom and that wisdom on which true freedom depends, is offered in another collection: Anastaplo, "On Freedom: Explorations," 17 *Oklahoma City University Law Review* 465 (1992).

It is important that the reader recognize that an awareness of the date and of the occasion of the original development of each discussion in this book can be critical for understanding what is said and how it is said.

Unless otherwise indicated, all references in the notes to chapters, appendixes, and notes are to materials in this book.

1

From Adam and Eve to Faustus

1-A.   ADAM, EVE, AND THE SERPENT[1]

I.

The account in the opening chapters of *Genesis*, once generally known as the *First Book of Moses*, is dismissed by some today as "just a story." Much that we may discover in that account may not have been noticed by its author: we know that artists often say more than they are consciously aware of.[2] Even so, the author may have had a hold of something substantial, which accounts for the durability and appeal of *Genesis* to this day.

Included here in *Genesis* is the story of Adam and Eve in the Garden of Eden, of the trials they endure. Multiple trials can be discerned:

1. there is the trial of Adam and Eve, in the sense of their being tested;
2. there is the trial of Adam and Eve, in the sense of the experiment that they conducted;
3. there is the trial of Adam and Eve, in the sense of the experiment that God conducted, in His effort to give mankind an opportunity to develop or maintain perfection in the Garden;[3]
4. there is the trial of Adam and Eve, in the sense of God's quasi-judicial examination of them, and to a far less extent of the Serpent, after their transgressions;
5. and there is the trial of Adam and Eve, in the sense that they were imposed upon, if not used, by the Serpent and perhaps even by God.

5

All these senses of *trial* may be seen in our discussion on this occasion of what happened in the Garden and how that bears on our notions of where human beings came from and of what they want to go to or to return to.

Eden is depicted in the opening chapters of *Genesis* as a definite place on earth: for example, it is located in relation to certain rivers. (2:10–14)[4] It seems, also, to have been definitely placed in time. The name *Eden* is used a half-dozen times in *Genesis* (2:8, 2:10, 2:15, 3:23, 3:24, 4:16); it is used seven more times in the Hebrew Bible, or the Old Testament (thirteen times altogether).[5] The later references to Eden are, for the most part, by way of comparison, not with a view to reconsidering the original story. It is said that the word *Eden* itself means *delight*, which suggests (as may be seen repeatedly in the Bible) that there can be a reliable correspondence between a thing, including a place, and its name.

It is from the word *Garden*, it seems, that we get our word *Paradise* (by way, perhaps, of the Persian language). *Paradise* is literally an enclosure or park.[6] The Garden is considered by some as that paradise in which we, as human beings, have already been and to which we long to return in some form. This may be the orthodox Jewish view. The word *paradise*, in its Greek form, may be found at three places in the Greek Bible, or the New Testament, as a perhaps new place for mankind to which one can hope to go.[7] The most emphatic New Testament use may be what Jesus says to the penitent thief crucified with him, "Truly, I say to you, today you will be with me in Paradise."[8]

II.

Differences between Jewish and Christian emphases with respect to these matters may be seen also in responses to such notions as "the Fall of Man" and "Original Sin." Jewish writers insist that these notions are foreign to them—that is, to the Hebrew Bible. Thus, one such commentator has argued,

> Strange and somber doctrines have been built on this chapter of the Garden of Eden, such as the Christian doctrine of Original Sin (e.g., "In Adam's fall, we sinned all"—New England Primer. "The condition of man after the fall of Adam is such that he cannot turn and prepare himself by his own natural strength and good works to faith and calling upon God"—Art. X, Free Will, of the Thirty-nine Articles). This Christian dogma of Original Sin is throughout the Middle Ages accompanied by an unbelievable vilification of Woman, as the authoress of death and all our earthly woe. Judaism rejects these doctrines. Man was mortal from the first, and death did not enter the world through the transgression of Eve. Stray Rabbinic utterances to the contrary are merely homiletic, and possess no binding authority in Judaism. There is no loss of the God-likeness of man, nor of man's ability to do right in the eyes of God; and no such loss has been

transmitted to his latest descendants. Although a few of the Rabbis occasionally lament Eve's share in the poisoning of our human race by the Serpent, even they declare that the antidote to such poison has been found at Sinai; rightly holding that the Law of God is the bulwark against the devastations of animalism and godlessness. The Psalmists often speak of sin and guilt; but there is never a reference to this chapter or to what Christian Theology calls "The Fall." One searches in vain the Prayer Book, of even the Days of Penitence, for the slightest echo of the doctrine of the Fall of man. "My God, the soul which Thou hast given me is pure," is the Jew's daily morning prayer. "Even as the soul is pure when entering upon its earthly career, so can man return it pure to his Maker" (Midrash).[9]

This commentator observes elsewhere, "Only as long as Adam lived was the earth under a curse."[10]

The Christian approach to these matters, on the other hand, may be seen in such passages as the following from Cardinal Newman's *Apologia Pro Vita Sua*: the world and man's condition in it are such that "the human race [must be] implicated in some terrible original calamity."[11]

We can see here, therefore, two quite divergent responses to "the human condition." Does the response to which one inclines depend, in part, upon what one sees, or has been taught to see, the world to be like? The response to which one inclines, influenced perhaps by one's natural temperament, may bear on whether one believes a special divine redeemer (other than God Himself) to be necessary for the salvation of the human race.

We will return to these general considerations after we review the story of what is reported to have happened in the Garden.

III.

Whatever the differences between Jews and Christians, they do seem to agree in principle with respect to the proper status of revelation as against reason. Thus, Rabbi Hamina ben Dosa is reported to have said, some two thousand years ago, "Whosesoever fear of sin precedes his wisdom, his wisdom stands; and whosesoever wisdom precedes his fear of sin, his wisdom stands not."[12] One commentator has added this observation upon this saying:

Different meanings are assigned to the precedence of the fear of sin to "wisdom." The saying is taken to denote either that a man's fear of sin should be instinctive, rather than a result of calculation; or that the fear of sin should be a motive urging him to the acquisition of knowledge as a safeguard against transgressions into which his ignorance might betray him. The former interpretation is to be preferred: a man should build upon the foundation of religious feeling, rather than of philosophy.[13]

Emphasis is placed here *not* upon what one figures out about the good but rather upon obedience to the rules or law laid down through revelation. It is not one's judgment, or wisdom, that is ultimately decisive but rather one's submissiveness, or surrender, before the divine command.

Of course, it *is* predicted in *Deuteronomy* that nations that shall hear all the statutes laid down for the Israelites will say, "Surely this great nation is a wise and understanding people."[14] But the wisdom that the Torah represents is, for most observant Jews, rooted in, and primarily devoted to, subordination under the Law, a Law for which no reasons are given for most of its particulars.[15]

There may even be a danger in making much of the reasons for the rules, since (as we all know from experience) it is tempting to rationalize devoting ourselves to what we anticipate pleasure in doing: an excuse can almost always be found, if there is something we want "bad enough" to do. What human beings need, then, is not permission to "figure out" ways to satisfy their desires, calling their calculations *wisdom*. Rather, what they need is practice in doing what they are blessed enough to have had God tell them to do.

The tension between fear of sin, on the one hand, and wisdom, on the other, may be seen in one Biblical commentator's observation:

> The will of God, revealed in His Law, is the one eternal and unfailing guide as to what constitutes good and evil—and not man's instincts, or even his Reason, which in the hour of temptation often calls light darkness and darkness light.[16]

A critical difference remains, then, between reason and revelation, however much each of them does make use of the other.[17]

IV.

These general observations have prepared us for our examination of the story of what happened, once upon a time, in the Garden of Eden. I do not intend a systematic commentary upon the story, but rather brief considerations of a series of points raised by that story.

i.

The temptation to rationalize (that is, to excuse if not even to justify) one's disobedience of the law applies to law made by human beings as well as to law handed down through revelation. When God's law is involved, however, the human being is asked for unquestioning compliance. What unquestioning compliance means, in counterdistinction to what happened in the Garden, may be seen once and for all in the story of Abraham and Isaac. Indeed, it can be said, only *he* could be the founder of a holy nation who would, like Abraham, exhibit so radical a faith in, and obedience to, God as to "make up" (so to speak) for what had happened in the Garden, where it had proved too much for human beings (in the midst of plenty) to comply with one seemingly modest prohibition.[18] The Christian can even see Abraham as an anticipation of Jesus in this respect.

Consider how the Biblical story of God, Abraham, and Isaac can be commented on in our day:

> The election of the holy nation begins with the election of Abraham. Noah was distinguished from his contemporaries by his righteousness; Abraham separates himself from his contemporaries and in particular from his country and kindred at God's command—a command accompanied by God's promise to make of him a great nation. The Bible does not say that this primary election of Abraham was preceded by the fact of Abraham's righteousness. However this may be, Abraham shows his righteousness by obeying God's command at once, by trusting in God's promise whose fulfillment he could not possibly live to see, given the short lifespan of postdiluvian man: only after Abraham's offspring would have become a great nation would the land of Canaan be given to them forever.
>
> The apparent contradiction between the command to sacrifice Isaac and the divine promise to the descendants of Isaac is disposed of by the consideration that nothing is too wondrous for the Lord. Abraham's supreme trust in God, his simple, singleminded, childlike faith was rewarded although, or because, it presupposed his entire unconcern with any reward, for Abraham was willing to forgo, to destroy, to kill the only reward with which he was concerned: God prevented the sacrifice of Isaac. Abraham's intended action needed a reward although he was not concerned with a reward because his intended action cannot be said to have been intrinsically rewarding. The preservation of Isaac is as wondrous as his birth. These two wonders illustrate more clearly than anything else the origin of the holy nation.[19]

Did not God prevent the sacrifice of Isaac in as casual a way as he had first requested it, in so casual a way as perhaps to make one wonder whether all of this depended upon Abraham's peculiarly sensitive openness to God? Are we not to understand that this kind of devotion is in marked contrast to the conduct seen in the Garden?

ii.

We can understand Abraham's obedience to have been with respect to that upon which his survival depended: in a sense, he was being asked to sacrifice his life, at least as the father of a nation. In a sense, too, he was giving up the privilege of thinking for himself, of wondering if an impossibility (or self-contradictory course of action) had been charted for him by the God who had promised him a multitude of descendants through the very child he was asked to sacrifice. Should this remind us of the prohibition laid down for Adam and Eve in the Garden? Certainly, we can wonder why that prohibition took the form it did, with respect to acquiring knowledge of good and bad. We sense that this bears upon qualities that distinguish the human being from the other animals.

Perhaps, indeed, this is why the decisive command, which somehow accounts for the human condition, should have been put in terms of the knowledge of good and bad. Tragedy reminds us that our very strength can sometimes lead to our downfall. This decisive command is directed to that which we treasure as making us deeply human.[20]

Only three episodes in the Garden are recorded for us, once man is created. (We do not see man gardening, although we are told he is to do some.) The third, and final, episode consists, of course, of the eating of the forbidden fruit and the responses to that. But the first episode also bears on that which is distinctively human, for we see man naming the animals. (2:20) It has been suggested by some readers that this naming is more or less arbitrary on Adam's part, whereas the naming that God had done earlier had not been arbitrary. Still, when Adam comes to give the woman a name, it is hardly arbitrary, for he calls her *Eve*, "because she was the mother of all living." (3:20) Besides, it seems, it is after the animals have been named that it becomes evident that the woman must be created as a helper for the man (this is the second Garden episode to which I have referred). The naming by Adam was a kind of searching—and no helper was found.

The naming episode suggests that man did know something before eating of the fateful tree. But to know some things is hardly the same as knowing good and bad, even though some commentators have suggested that "knowledge of good and bad" may also mean knowledge of all things, or omniscience.[21] This may be going too far. Still, one does need to know some things, perhaps even something about the good, in order to be able to comply at all with the command that one not eat of the tree.[22] At least, one needs to be able to grasp the good enough to want to obey; also, one needs enough knowledge to be able to distinguish among the trees.[23]

Perhaps knowledge of good and bad is somehow different from being aware of the good (or of the right thing to do) as the result of God's commands and provisions for one. Does to *know* good and bad mean, among other things, to know something about the tentative character of the good in some respects? Does this mean that one does *not* accept and do the good fully? The problem with any questioning is suggested by the fact that the first question asked in the Bible is put by the Serpent. (3:1) But is it possible to learn, or to learn fully, without questioning, without calling into question that which has been revealed and commanded even by God?

Besides, to know both good and bad may mean that one is to some extent tainted by the bad: is not one thus exposed to it and to some extent affected by it? Does knowledge imply a unity between the knower and the known?[24] To know good and bad means, then, that the bad does exist, or comes to exist, for the human being, especially if knowing should be primary in one's soul. Certainly, we have all had the experience of being to some extent shocked, if not even wounded (and permanently scarred), upon learning about the awful things that others have done. Such things then become *thinkable* for us. Do not they somehow become a part of us? At the very least, it can be said, the prohibition in the Garden was designed to shield human beings from dangerous exposure to the bad until they were prepared to receive it properly.

iii.

I have implied that some kind of knowledge of good and bad would have had to come eventually if the first human being was to live a full life, just as it is essential for us, if we are to conduct ourselves properly, especially in our social capacity.[25] Certainly, God as ruler must distinguish between the good and the bad or, in the first instance, between the good and the not good. The explicit prohibition by God to Adam with respect to the tree of the knowledge of good and bad is followed immediately by God's making a judgment as to what is good for man (that he not be alone). (2:18)[26] But mere knowledge, or knowledge for its own sake, seems to be suspect. Consider, also, the ambiguous status of the arts in *Genesis* and elsewhere in the Bible.

Another way of putting all this is to say that Adam and Eve were wrong in their timing: they should have been more concerned first with the tree of life.[27] Preparation for proper assimilation of the knowledge of good and bad depends upon training, experience, and maturation. We have all seen the bad effects of premature exposure to learning. One is apt to be released from unwelcome moral restraints before one comes to appreciate the reasons for such restraints.[28]

We notice also that the Serpent is the first interpreter of Biblical language. This, too, should warn us against what can happen when unbridled cleverness is let loose upon the world. Moral attainment, we have heard, follows upon discipline and testing.[29] The truth, we have also heard, can be deadly.

In any event, to say, later in the Bible, that someone has no knowledge of good or bad is to indicate that he is not yet of an age to incur communal responsibility.[30] This is not to suggest that once one does come of age, whether in the Garden or in "real life," one's problems are over. Commentators have suggested that more prohibitions would have followed in the Garden had Adam and Eve successfully passed the first test imposed upon them.[31]

Even so, it can be said that the failure of Adam and Eve foreclosed the possibility of an enduring good for mankind until after the Flood. Thus, from the time of man's expulsion from the Garden until after the Flood, the word *good* is not used in the Bible. It had been used fourteen times (and one more time in the phrase, "not good") during the first three chapters of *Genesis*. It is not used again until Abraham appears on the scene.[32]

iv.

There have been differences of opinion for thousands of years now as to whether human beings would have been immortal in the Garden had they not eaten of the forbidden fruit. Moses Maimonides, it seems, believed that they would not have been immortal; others believe that the man and the woman were intended to live in the Garden forever.[33]

Did death come into the world only after the disobedience in the Garden? We are told that God made "coats of skins" with which to clothe Adam and Eve after they had fallen. (3:21) Had He had to kill animals in order to get the skins? Or, at least, had some animals died, whose skins could be used? (Some commentators, in order to postpone death's appearance, have suggested that the sloughed-off skins of serpents had been used, but that does not seem likely.) Why had not God used, if not the leaves of other trees, cotton, or linen (that is, the products of vegetation) with which to make clothing? Would this have made too much of art? (It is possible, of course, that an omnipotent Creator of the world could have simply created skins of the kind associated with animals.)

What was the purpose of the tree of life? Had there even been an implied command to eat of all the trees of the Garden? Some so argue, that there is a *mitzvah*, or duty, to sustain oneself with what is permitted.[34] Would one meal from the tree of life have sufficed for eternal life? That seems to be suggested by what God says in *Genesis* 3:22: "[A]nd now, lest he put forth his hand and take also of the tree of life, and eat, and live for ever." It is this concern by God that triggers the expulsion from the Garden, a garden already radically changed in character, it seems, by what human beings had done. At the very least, perhaps it can be said, to deprive human beings of the tree of life was to allow their innate mortality to assert itself.

A recent commentator on these matters has raised the question, "One may wonder why man, while he was still in the Garden of Eden, had not eaten of the tree of life of which he had not been forbidden to eat."[35] He goes on to suggest, "Perhaps he did not think of it because, lacking knowledge of good and evil, he did not fear to die and, besides, the divine prohibition drew his attention away from the tree of life to the tree of knowledge."[36] That is, he had not recognized, while in the Garden, that death is clearly a bad thing, something to be avoided. *Is* it?[37]

Proper training for life would have prepared human beings for exposure to the bad. The tree of life and the tree of the knowledge of good and bad are brought together in this fashion by a recent commentator:

> For almost all purposes the word of God as revealed to His prophets and especially to Moses became *the* source of knowledge of good and evil, the true tree of knowledge which is at the same time the tree of life.[38]

It has even been suggested that eternal life would be an intolerable burden for anyone who has sinned.[39]

v.

Man, we are reminded, "was denied knowledge of good and evil, i.e., the knowledge sufficient for guiding himself, his life. Though not being a child, he was to live in childlike simplicity and obedience to God."[40] Is only the innocent truly durable? Purity means that a thing is unalloyed, that it is not a vulnerable composite. There *is* an inherent tendency of composites to disintegrate into their elements. Death, then, is linked to the change toward which all composites tend.[41]

Is there already a compromise with the most durable unity when the human being becomes male and female? God, as eternal, is one and unchanging. Man, like God, may have been originally a complete whole, containing both male and female, but he was unaware of that perfection.[42] Is God (in whose image the human being is made) compromised also, if only by implication, in that both male and female are contained in Him? Is *He* somehow dual in nature?[43] Or should we teach ourselves that God simply cannot be understood according to *our* rules and our "chemistry" or "biology"?

Is the impurity of humanity, reflected in its duality, evident in sexuality? It does seem appropriate that the first offense should have been sex-linked, if only in that it should have at once led to a recognition by human beings of their nakedness. Had they, although unclothed, not been "naked" theretofore? We do not consider the animals to be naked.[44]

Sexuality does imply inadequacy, imperfection, a lack of a self-sufficient oneness. It reminds us of our vulnerability and mortality, and hence of the need for procreation.[45] Does any questioning expose one's ignorance and hence one's vulnerability? Consider how Maimonides speaks of shamefulness when he responds to the query about whether Adam's disobedience had been a good thing for mankind.[46]

Related to the significance of sexuality is the observation that Adam and Eve, once they are created, continue as if they had been generated in the ordinary way. They are like others after them, as if they, too, had had predecessors. We, like them, do not "know" our origins, except by hearsay?

vi.

God, of course, knows our origins. Is He responsible for all this? Is there reflected, in the provision in *Genesis* 1:28 ("God blessed them and said to them, be fruitful and multiply; fill the earth and master it; have dominion over the fish of the sea and the fowl of the sky and all the living things that creepeth on the earth")—is there here an anticipation of the fact that man would not be permanently confined to the Garden or, at least, that the Garden would, because of human conduct, change in character?

As for God's responsibility, these things can be said: He did make the Serpent (about whom, more later). Also, He gave to Adam the woman who, in turn, gave Adam the forbidden fruit, something that Adam points out to God when he is judged. (3:12) Indeed, we have seen that the original prohibition with respect to the tree was immediately followed by God's becoming concerned about a helper for Adam—as if to *help* him deal with that tree! (2:17–18) And, of course, God "caused to grow" the tree of the knowledge of good and bad. (2:9)

Would the world have been incomplete without such a tree, without the occasion for sin in the world? We do know that there *are* in the world numerous occasions for sin. Thus, it has been suggested, "Perhaps creation as a whole cannot be 'very good' if it does not contain some evils."[47] Or, "[E]verything that God had created would not be very good if it did not include something congenitally bent on mischief."[48] Certainly, it can be said, the world would be incomplete if there were not in it beings capable of doing bad, and exposed to temptations to do bad, who nevertheless choose to do good.

Was the fall of Adam and Eve inevitable? The answer to this question depends, in part, upon what one means by *inevitable*. If one says that God "had" to act as He did against man, is not one suggesting that God merely reflects the human condition and that He is limited in what He could have done?

God's command does appear arbitrary to many readers, just as do various laws laid down later in the Torah.[49] Is it a reflection of our ignorance, if not of our innate willfulness, that we should consider any of God's prohibitions arbitrary? Have we not seen that there must be a reason why this particular fruit was forbidden?[50] That is, the fruit was forbidden because it was wrong, at least at this stage of human development; it was not wrong merely because it happened to be forbidden.[51]

We can hardly expect to understand fully the reasons for the various prohibitions that God lays down. Similarly, it is hard for us to understand why Moses' sin (striking the stone or chastising the people?) should have been as severely punished as *it* was.[52] Certainly, we should not have expected God to guard access to the tree of the knowledge of good and bad as He was later to guard access to the tree of life. (3:4) To have done so would have denied man his humanity.[53]

Is God (or, at least, one popular opinion about God) implicitly rebuked in the Lord's Prayer, which asks, among other things, that we not be led into temptation? Or is that request merely a concession to the limited view of man as to what is indeed responsible for what happens to him? Is this, moreover, primarily a Christian view of things, not a Jewish one? Even so, Maimonides does conclude his chapter on the significance of the disobedience of Adam (and whether that was a good thing for man)—he concludes this discussion with the observation, "Praise be to the Master of the *will* whose aims and wisdom cannot be apprehended!"[54]

vii.

God's motives are, it can be said, difficult, if not simply impossible, to fathom. But what about human motivation with respect to eating of the tree?

We must concern ourselves, in the first instance, with the motives of the woman. They seem to be summed up in the observation that "the woman saw that the tree was good for food, and that it was pleasant to the eyes, and a tree to be desired to make one wise." (3:6) Only the third item, that it was "to be desired to make one wise," is new here, since it had been said earlier, "And from the ground [in the Garden of Eden] the Lord God caused to grow every tree that was pleasing to the sight and good for food." (2:9) The woman saw what *was* there with respect to the eyes and the appetite.[55] As for her desire for wisdom: some see her to have been moved primarily by *pride*; others see her as having been moved primarily by *naïveté*.[56]

So much, then, for the woman's motivation. What about the man's? Is it not essentially the same as the woman's, with one significant addition, perhaps, the desire he might have had not to lose her? (This is suggested in Milton's *Paradise Lost*.) Does this desire conform to the divine plan?[57] Of course, it could even have been that he ate the fruit, not knowing where it came from, once she offered it: this would indeed be an instance of connubial compliance. Maimonides, on the other hand, sees Adam to have been moved by greed.[58]

Womankind has been sometimes vilified for what happened in the Garden. Thus, "Eve's flesh" can mean *erring woman*, as in Shakespeare's *Twelfth Night*.[59] Perhaps much more significant than the fact that it was the woman who first fell is the fact that she is shown to be fully human, that she can, in effect, act for, and be taken to act for, all humankind. We do not need to be given Adam's motivation in the detail that hers is given: we can assume that he is moved pretty much the way she is, except for the fact that he *is* second rather than first. And, we can see, Adam ratifies what she does.[60] *Adam*, we are told, does mean *mankind* or *human being*, someone who is made of earth, who is earth bound.[61] In a sense, of course, Eve was to Adam what the Serpent was to Eve. Even so, her motivation may suffice, in that they are "one flesh." (2:24) Certainly, both man and woman are human. After the expulsion from the Garden their similarity is emphasized (5:1–2):

> This is the book of the generations of Adam. In the day that God created Man, in the likeness of God made He him: male and female created He them; and blessed them, and called their name Man, in the day when they were created.

It *has* been noticed that "the woman does not explicitly speak of the tree of knowledge; she may have had in mind the tree of life."[62] Even so, she did take and eat from the tree that she somehow knew was forbidden to them. *Did* she consider it the tree of life? Certainly, this "misconception" would conform with that which distinguishes her from man, that she is to be, as her name indicates, "the mother of all living." (3:20) Is she intrinsically more inclined to be concerned with life and hence with the family, while man is more inclined to be concerned with the political order and hence with the knowledge of good and bad?

viii.

There is one puzzling feature about the prohibition as Eve reports it to the Serpent, "But the fruit of the tree which is in the midst of the garden, God hath said, Ye shall not eat of it, neither shall ye touch it, lest ye die." (3:3) Whether it *was* "in the midst of the garden" *is* a question: *that* had been said explicitly of the tree of life (2:9); the tree of knowledge of good and bad *was* spoken of immediately thereafter, perhaps as if next to it. Besides, is she not a valuable witness to where the tree indeed was?[63] Also, she may soften God's injunction, "[F]or in the day that thou eatest thereof thou shalt surely die" (2:17), making it instead, "lest ye die." This, too, we can understand, especially from someone whose very name reflects life.

But what of the addition, "neither shall ye touch it"? Thus, it has been observed, "There was no word concerning 'touching' in the original prohibition. This exaggeration on the part of the woman, says the Midrash, was the cause of her fall."[64] Was such an addition by her presumptuous? Did it thereby make the fruit even more alluring? Did it make the rule even more difficult to obey?[65]

But why should it be assumed (as the commentators all do, so far as I can tell) that it was Eve who made this perhaps fatal addition to the prohibition? (It can be noticed in passing that Eve does assume, both at the outset and during her "trial," that a command made by God to Adam is essentially a command to her also: that is, she recognizes herself to be as human as he is.) Could not the addition have been made by Adam, to impress upon her the seriousness of the prohibition, especially if he knew that she had not had the advantage of exposure to the "personality" of God to impress upon her the seriousness of the prohibition? Thus, the questionable addition, if it *was* questionable, could have been Adam's.

Besides, could not *she* have gotten the word herself directly from God, who had adjusted it to her tastes and circumstances? We are not told that, it will be said, but neither are we told that Adam told her. If we are to assume that someone told her *something*, why not assume God, and not Adam? And why not assume that it was God who added the prohibition with respect to touching? Or are we to assume that we are told, in the Old Testament, every instance that God speaks to man?

At the very least, we have raised here the question of the significance of the silences one encounters upon reading a book.[66]

ix.

We see in the Serpent how *one* mind reads, or misreads, a "book"—for, among other things, it "interprets" what God has said.

We are not told why the Serpent approaches Eve and not Adam. Did it sense that the further one is from direct contact with God, the more fallible one is likely to be? Does *this* speak to the question of whether God did command Eve directly?[67]

Nor are we told where the Serpent got *its* information. Had it overheard God speaking to Adam, or to Adam and to Eve? Or had the Serpent otherwise heard of what God had said, and if so, how? Or had it figured out the prohibition from the nature of things, just as we can try to figure out God's reasoning (or just as, it might be said, some poet did)?[68] Is there something presumptuous, if not also deceitful, in the Serpent's assigning a reason to God's command when God had not done so?

Nor are we told what the Serpent's motivation was in tempting Eve. The following suggestion has been made over the centuries:

> Nothing is mentioned about the motives which the Serpent had for beginning the following dialogue. He is, however, the cleverest of the beasts and the only one, so far as we know, capable of speech. God, after realizing the insufficiency of Man, formed the animals in the hope that one of them might do as Man's helper. Perhaps the Serpent, thinking himself the most likely candidate, intended to show Man the foolishness of his choice by causing Eve's downfall.[69]

Is the Serpent moved, then, primarily by jealousy?

The first recorded sin seems to be the Serpent's.[70] The Serpent probably would not have been persuasive if *everything* it said had been wrong. Even so, is there not something fundamentally irrational, or purposeless, in wickedness?[71] If so, this would make the Serpent's doings beyond understanding or accounting for, whether the Serpent is seen as a separate being or as "the personification of the sinful tendencies in man."[72]

Is something like the Serpent inevitable in a world where there is to be found the supreme beauty of a deliberate preference for the good over the bad? His crawling ever after suggests that he looks somewhat like he is, low and sneaky and unreliable?[73] "Should" the forbidden fruit also have looked somewhat like it is and thus have put man on notice? Or would that have obscured the genuine attractions of the knowledge of good and bad?

God's final word in the Garden about the Serpent reminds us that the deadly temptation thus represented will always face the mortal human being (3:15):

> And I will put enmity between thee and the woman and between thy seed and her seed; it shall bruise thy head, and thou shalt bruise his heel.

The Serpent will "always" be there to strike?[74]

V.

We return now to some general observations, having concluded our consideration of a series of points raised by the story of the Garden of Eden. My general observations at the beginning of these remarks included comments on the relation of reason to revelation, of wisdom to the fear of sin, in determining how one should conduct oneself. This can be seen as a distinction between the way of philosophers such as Socrates and the way of the prophets. Thus, it has been said by a recent student of these matters, "According to the Bible, the beginning of wisdom is fear of the Lord; according to the Greek philosophers, the beginning of wisdom is wonder."[75] This student concludes his reflections thus:

> Finally, the perfectly just man, the man who is as just as is humanly possible, is, according to Socrates, the philosopher; according to the prophets, he is the faithful servant of the Lord. The philosopher is the man who dedicates his life to the quest for knowledge of the good, of the idea of the good; what we would call moral virtue is only the condition or by-product of that quest. According to the prophets, however, there is no need for the quest for knowledge of the good: God "hath shewed thee, O man, what is good; and what doth the Lord require of thee, but to do justly, and to love mercy, and to walk humbly with thy God" (*Micah* 6:8).[76]

Is it not from Socrates' point of view, then, that one asks whether Adam was better off for his expulsion? It is Socrates who understands evil to be rooted in ignorance.[77] Still, if God is taken (as He must be, if the general account in the Torah is reliable) to represent goodness and wisdom, must not we say that man should not have disobeyed God, that he was not better for having done so?[78] If it was truly God who gave the prohibition in the Garden, then we can hope to do no more than to try to understand *something* of the rationale of what was ordered: we cannot presume to question the command, to be superior to it—since God, if the story is otherwise correct, is omnipotent, omniscient, and surpassingly righteous. Certainly, we cannot safely second-guess a perfect God. Would not something more have been provided eventually for man, to complete his humanity, if he had withstood the early temptation(s) confronting him in the Garden?

Still, we are told, the Rabbis have argued that Adam and Eve, once they were expelled from the Garden, discovered repentance—and that they thereby came nearer to God outside of Eden than in Eden.[79] Knowledge of good and bad does seem to be needed if man is to find his way, as Solomon did, through the world as it now is for him. The question still remains, at least for us in the West, whether or not *that* way is best indicated by the prophets or by someone such as Socrates?

VI.

No doubt, there are prophets and prophets—of which we are reminded when we consider what the influence has been of this story both among the Jews and among the Christians. Any examination of their differences can be still another way of asking about the significance of "Original Sin" and of "the Fall of Man."

As for the Jews: we have seen what it is that distinguishes Abraham: an unquestioning obedience that counteracts, so to speak, Adam's lack of obedience in a critical respect. Consider, also, how much is made by the Jews of dietary laws. Does this reflect a concern with mistaken *eating*? (Does the Christian concern with *sexuality* emphasize another aspect of the Garden story?) The body and one's earthly existence seem to be made less of by the Christians, who tend to regard all food as clean.[80]

The Christians do make more of Adam (in the New Testament and in works such as Milton's) than do the Jews (who make very little of him, once they get past the opening chapters of *Genesis*).[81] Jesus can be seen by Christians as the second Adam (and his mother as the second Eve).[82] This is related to the Christian opinion that "sin came into the world through one man and death through sin, and so death spread to all men because all men sinned."[83]

Christians are, we have noticed, more apt than Jews (at least, Orthodox Jews) to speak of man's fallen nature and a broken world.[84] Should it be added that to speak of a fall not only implies there was once a golden age but also assumes that progress is something to which one can aspire? If one does not consider humankind to be fallen, then one's primary concerns may be to become and to remain as righteous as human beings have been known to be. This means, among other things, that there is, as the Midrash says, "no generation without its Abraham, Moses or Samuel."[85] May the Garden of Eden itself, once spoiled by Adam and Eve, become again a place of delight for the righteous human being?

VII.

How one answers such questions depends, in part, upon how one understands the story of the Garden of Eden. Do we see there, and in subsequent chapters of *Genesis*, God repeatedly experimenting with man, trying out first this dispensation and then that one? Or, rather than talk of God experimenting, should the sequence that is recorded in the Bible be understood as a series of opportunities offered man to work out the best possible destiny of which he is capable?[86] Did human nature change decisively because of the disobedience in the Garden? Or have only the circumstances of the human being changed, for which adaptations are required?

Is there now a "way back" or a "way out" for mankind? Are Jews more apt to think of a way *back* and Christians of a way *out*? Is "paradise" still available on earth, in a rehabilitated Garden, for the human being who attains (or retains) a purity of heart, for the truly pious? Indeed, some Jews seem to have argued, death will disappear (even on earth) once mankind again achieves (under the leadership of the Messiah?) the closeness to God intended at the Creation.[87] Christians, on the other hand, make much more of the immortal soul, a soul that is not confined to the body and hence to the earth. A different kind of paradise is anticipated. Is the consideration of these alternatives still another way of asking whether the expulsion of Adam and Eve from the Garden was indeed good for human beings?

Another kind of paradise anticipates neither a conquest of death on earth nor removal to another sphere of existence, but rather depends upon the highest use of the powers of the human mind with respect to moral questions and, perhaps even more, with respect to the study and grasp of eternal things. One is reminded here of philosophers such as Aristotle, who tended to see life as, by and large, a good thing, as something to be cherished. It is best for the human being to do good, knowing good and bad and preferring (that is, choosing and delighting in) the good.[88] Is not this an approach that takes its bearings from the nature and hence the end of human beings, not (as the Bible might seem to do) from their beginnings. This anticipates the sentiment in Shakespeare's *King Lear*, "Ripeness is all."[89]

In any event, paradise, however it is conceived, is presented by various authorities as eminently attractive—as a place of delight. The extent to which the story of the Garden has captured the imagination of mankind is suggested by the inscription carried by one of the rooms of the fabulous Red Fort in India, "If on earth there be an Eden of bliss, it is this, it is this, it is this."[90] But, we have also been told, paradise (at least the first time human beings were exposed to it on earth) did turn out to be a rather dangerous place. Does the prospect of a trial make the delight even more intense? Does the prospect of eternal bliss seem somewhat tamer than adventurous human beings (at least as we know them) can be content with? But this, too, may reflect our ignorance and our misshapen passions.[91]

The story of the Garden of Eden does strike home for us—even as what our true home is, which may depend in part upon what we truly are, remains for us a matter of wonder.

1-B. LUCIFER AND FAUSTUS[92]

I.

Not is the opening word of Christopher Marlowe's *The Tragical History of the Life and Death of Doctor Faustus*. This negative at the beginning of the first

clause is echoed at the beginning as well of the second and third clauses of
the introductory sentence of the play.[93] We are initiated thereby to the negativity that can be expected wherever the Devil prevails.

And yet the Devil, however much he stands for the spirit of negation,
depends for his effectiveness, if not for his very existence, upon something
positive—upon an affirmation of an enduring principle. At a critical moment
in the career of Doctor Faustus, when he tries to turn to Christ to save his distressed soul from the consequences of the bargain he had made with one of
the Devil's agents, Lucifer appears for the first time before Faustus and us.
Lucifer's opening words, offered in a successful effort to maintain the hold he
has on Faustus's soul, are these (p. 374):

> Christ cannot save thy soul, for he is just.
> There's none but I have interest in the same.

Thus, even Lucifer cannot do without recourse to the eternal principles that
Christ represents and that Lucifer himself has made a career of desperately
denying. We are reminded at the outset of this play, therefore, of the profound
limitations of the Devil: he can do no more than affirm nay saying.

The play in and through which we are reminded of what the Devil tries to
be and to mean draws upon the medieval story of a German scholar, Johannes
Faustus, who made a pact with the Devil, giving up his soul to him in exchange for twenty-four years of remarkable magical powers. At the end of the
allotted time, the Devil claimed his prize, leaving behind the dismembered
body of the distinguished scholar.

Such bargaining may be a distinctively Christian phenomenon. There does
not seem to be in Classical Greece or Rome, for example, any comparable supernatural being of an evil disposition who is out to collect human souls. Nor
is such a being important in traditional Judaism. The Faustus story, which has
been reworked by artists down to our day, is peculiarly appealing to moderns
who see themselves obliged to challenge long-accepted norms in their pursuit
of the knowledge of good and bad.

We are familiar with the "Faustian bargains" of modern men who aspire to
know and to do unprecedented things on a grand scale. Reworkings of the
Faustus story culminate in Goethe's masterpiece, *Faust*, which leaves the
hero saved at the last moment from the dreadful fate he had bargained for.[94]

Perhaps Marlowe, in his *Doctor Faustus*, came close to expressing the
thought and mood of his own troubled character and turbulent life, which
ended with his murder in 1593 at the age of twenty-nine. An irreligious man,
at least in reputation, Marlowe nevertheless bore himself the name of Christ
(in Christopher). His reputed ambivalence toward Christianity is evident in
the play he fashioned from the old Faustus story.

The intriguing character of this old story is reflected in anecdotes associated with it. For example, it was said, in the German sources, that at the end of the original Faustus's ill-spent life, his corpse was found facedown on the earth. Nothing could be done to turn it over so as to leave its face looking up.

Marlowe's play, too, has intriguing anecdotes connected with it. It is reported, for example, that during a performance at Exeter in Elizabethan times, in a scene in which Faustus called up devils, the actors counted on stage one more devil than the scene called for and realized that Satan himself was in their midst. In terror, they stopped the play; the audience bolted from the theatre; and the actors quit the town next morning.[95]

II.

Marlowe's plot is an old-fashioned one, whatever rearrangements and innovations in episodes he may rely upon. We cannot know for sure what parts, in the texts that we happen to have, were done by Marlowe and what by other hands. The Marlowe play itself comes down to us in more than one uncertain version; it is obviously incomplete and otherwise altered, making it difficult to read with care.

It is said that some, perhaps even many, of the things originally provided by Marlowe were censored out as theologically, perhaps also politically, questionable. It is also said that various of the comic scenes were provided by others. If so, perhaps that was done in order to try, in the playing time that had to be filled, to compensate for some of the things that had been cut.

Although we may now have little more than a rough version of the original play, we can still get from it glimpses of the modern movement that had its inception in Elizabethan times, if not before in Italy. Even if various scenes are spurious, they are additions that the interpolators probably believed their audiences would consider consistent with the play as a whole. What we know of Marlowe's tempestuous career is consistent, in turn, with the spirit of this play.

The Marlowe play, we should notice, represents Faustus as clearly lost at the end, unlike what is later done on his behalf by Goethe. Even so, Marlowe's Faustus continued to be respected by his fellow scholars and is to be given a proper funeral by them.

Two particularly modern features of Faustus's career should be noticed. He rises from humble origins to his achievements as a scholar. (p. 358) He is not *tempted* by the Devil; instead, *he* seeks out the help of the Devil, help that is consistent with his way of life or at least with his ambitions. (pp. 360–65) (If he *is* tempted, it is by two of his fellow Germans. [p. 361]) The fame he seeks, and in some measure secures, seems to be a substitute for that immortal life on earth that he recognizes is simply not available for human beings.[96]

III.

One odd feature of this story, at least as told by Marlowe, is that the uses to which Faustus puts his magic-derived powers are not intrinsically wicked. (The exception is what he tries to do, in desperation at the end, to the pious Old Man who had tried to save Faustus's soul—and even that episode may be provided by someone other than Marlowe.) Faustus spells out to Mephistophilis at the outset what he expects during his years of empowerment by the Devil (p. 366):

> Say he [Faustus] surrenders up to him [the Devil] his soul,
> So he will spare him four and twenty years,
> Letting him live in all voluptuousness,
> Having thee [Mephistophilis] ever to attend on me,
> To give me whatsoever I shall ask,
> To tell me whatsoever I demand,
> To slay mine enemies, and aid my friends,
> And always be obedient to my will.

Further on Faustus says he wants to be "cloyed with all things that delight the heart of man" and that he will enjoy "four and twenty years of liberty." (p. 380) Both *delight* and *liberty* are important to him. His liberty includes that of being able to "walk invisible to all and do what'er I please unseen of any." (p. 384)[97]

It can be argued that Faustus is moved ultimately by pleasure. He does want beautiful things, but evidently without appreciating the excellence that beauty represents. His final gift from the Devil, or by the use of his powers, is his dalliance with Helen of Troy. (His first request for action, from Mephistophilis, had been for a wife, which Mephistophilis had refused to provide him. (pp. 371–72) Had the sacramental aspect of securing a wife troubled or threatened, or at least called upon powers beyond those of, Mephistophilis?) Faustus is ecstatic about the encounter with Helen. Thereafter his disintegration, with its final debacle, sets in. When the Seven Deadly Sins were paraded by Lucifer for Faustus's edification, the first was Pride, the last was Lechery—that is, Lucifer began and ended with Faustus's distinctive failings.

By and large, though, the pleasures that Faustus resorts to are not perverse or otherwise questionable. Nor does he indulge himself in sadistic or other enormities, aside from what happens to the Old Man. Thus, he slays no enemies. Some of the uses to which he puts the powers borrowed from the Devil are prosaic; others are whimsical; still others are those of the courtier out to please and to impress his social betters, as by providing grapes out of season for a pregnant duchess. (p. 400) We can see reflected here as well modern restlessness and the liberty to which that is intimately related. Also modern is the constant experimentation, the desire for novelty, perhaps even a desire to run "unnecessary" risks.

Then there are the grander projects, political and religious (with religion itself being politically oriented), that Faustus undertakes on behalf of Germany and, it seems, the Protestant Reformation. Rome and the Pope are thwarted in their projects by this patriotic German. Faustus contributes as well to various worthy public-spirited enterprises; he serves as an effective medical doctor; and he instructs scholars about the heavens and other subjects in the physical sciences.[98]

Mixed in with these more serious endeavors are low-down magic tricks and the conjuring up of historical personages for the edification of noble audiences. Some of the scenes in the play show plebeian characters exercising, or trying to exercise, on their own base level, various of the powers that Faustus uses. Perhaps this is intended by the playwright as a commentary upon what the more impressive-looking exploits by Faustus really come down to.

A related commentary may be seen in how Faustus himself mixes the cosmic with the trivial, perhaps another symptom of modernity. Thus, the Emperor is very much impressed by what Faustus does in conjuring up Alexander the Great. But, it turns out, what the Emperor *really* wants to see is whether there is, as there has long been said to be, a mole on the neck of Alexander's paramour, and in this desire he is gratified to his great delight. (pp. 390–91)

One must wonder, indeed, whether one difficulty with the way of life embarked upon by Faustus is that the trivial cannot be truly distinguished from the cosmic. That is, a deeply-flawed judgment may be at the core of such a career as that chosen by Doctor Faustus.

IV.

The deeds that Faustus does, I have been suggesting, may not be critical to his condemnation. Certainly, most of these deeds seem innocent enough and could be accomplished today with the help of modern technology.

On the other hand, the opinions he has—the allegiance he is willing to show to the Devil, the great Naysayer—can be seen as treason toward the Divine Governor of the universe. Is it not an acceptance of the negativity of the Devil that can even lead Faustus at the very end to curse his parents and his very existence? (pp. 409–10) Nor is this allegiance mere youthful folly on Faustus's part, for he ratifies his pact with the Devil on more than one occasion during his career.

Fateful negativity may be seen as well in how Faustus moves into his alliance with the Devil: he exhibits a determined denial of the Trinity and a philosophic disbelief in an afterlife. (p. 365) The first and last things that Faustus gets from Mephistophilis are revelations about Hell and about the afterlife implied by that institution. (pp. 370–71, 406f)

That it is Faustus's ideas that make him vulnerable is suggested by the opening and closing passages of the play. His bookishness is critical; he has risen by scholarship and he wants, as is often seen in scholars, to go ever further in his studies, even beyond prudent limits. At the end, the last thing Faustus says is that he would destroy his books if he should be spared.[99]

Vital to Faustus's fate, then, is the issue of his Faith. (That is the way the pious Christian would put it, whereas the Classical thinker would have preferred to put it in terms of his Judgment.) Faustus's faith, or lack of it, reflects his character, his passions. Early on, Mephistophilis, although pressed by Faustus who reminds him of their pact, refuses to say who made the world. (p. 374) This refusal by Mephistophilis is related to Pride being the first of the sins: the Devil and his minions are constitutionally unable to recognize the primacy of God. (p. 378) Similarly, Lechery as the last of the sins portrayed anticipates the Helen episode (a *succubus* episode?) being last, and perhaps most critical, in the career of Faustus before his final fall. (p. 376)

The refusal of Mephistophilis to say who made the world leads to the great crisis of the soul for Marlowe's Faustus, that crisis that in turn leads to the dramatic appearance of Lucifer with his threats and cajolements. Faustus can talk of Paradise and the Creation—but Lucifer will have none of that. Instead, he provides the show, for Faustus, of the Seven Deadly Sins. (pp. 375–76) These Sins seem to be the devilish counterparts to the attractions of Paradise—and such a show, if not art in general, is the Devil's counterpart to Divine Creation.[100]

True, the Sins as presented here do not appear to *us* as attractive. But Faustus is evidently impressed, perhaps by the very fact that such things can be conjured up in this fashion. The Sins offer to satisfy here on earth the desires legitimately satisfied in Paradise—and to do so when and where the accomplished man wills.

Evidently, Faustus's desires are such that he cannot appreciate the folly of his undertaking, even though he had made at the outset the right inquiry, "Now tell me who made the world." (p. 374)[101] Why does not Faustus turn away from the Devil when he fails to get his vital question answered? Lucifer does threaten him; he also reminds him of Faustus's great promise—but Faustus could have countered with a reminder of the Devil's original promise to answer all inquiries.

Perhaps at the heart of Faustus's response here (and earlier, when he first sees Mephistophilis in his native ugliness) is that he simply wants to go with the Devil, which is to say that his character is seriously flawed. (This determination may be seen also in Faustus's refusal to adjust, in time, his opinions about the afterlife, a refusal that does not make sense in the light of what he learns from Lucifer and Mephistophilis about their existence and interests.) Did Marlowe want us to consider these issues as we have been considering them here, including the issue of what Christianity has come to when someone as gifted and respected as Faustus can deliberately turn away from it despite the revealing equivocations of the Devil?

Faustus wants to be God-like in his powers. (pp. 359, 362, 375) But, it turns out, he is Devil-like—and that may mean, most of all, presumptuousness. Does it not also mean foolishness? Is it not odd, moreover, that Lucifer should want damaged, or inferior, souls—or that people believe that there *is* someone who wants and gets such "prizes"?[102]

Is it truly in Lucifer's (or anyone else's) interest to collect, and then to torment, the souls he does? Indeed, does the very "concept" of Lucifer make sense, especially as a being who had once known God and still was able to defy Him? Certainly, there is something deeply dubious about someone who must rely upon a just ordering of the universe if he is to be able to secure the things *he* is "entitled" to as a result of his subversion of justice and the other virtues.

Some would argue that to question the existence of Lucifer is, in effect, to question as well the existence of God. Or is it instead to see God in His perfection?

V.

Although we do see Lucifer in this play, we do not see God. The closest we come to Him is in the form of the Good Angel who appeals to Faustus to save himself, while the Bad Angel encourages him to continue in the self-destructive path he has chosen for himself.

There are five encounters by Faustus with the Good and Bad Angels, four of them early in the play, the fifth at the very end after there is no further possibility of repentance by Faustus.[103] There is a struggle among Angels for Faustus's soul during the first third of the play. After the fourth encounter, Lucifer appears on stage to move Faustus to confirm his allegiance. The remainder of the play, about two thirds of it, depicts the notorious career of Faustus. After that comes the fifth encounter with the Good and Bad Angels, ratifying Faustus's impending collapse. Shortly thereafter the play ends.

Some scholars suggest that the depictions of the Angels are not Marlowe's. But they do serve to accentuate, or dramatize, Faustus's character and interests. For most if not all of the play, it should again be noticed, Faustus *is* on his own.

In the first encounter, the Good Angel warns Faustus against being tempted by books of magic, lest he have "God's heavy wrath upon [his] soul." He is counseled to read the Scriptures instead. (p. 360) The Bad Angel counters with a prospect that can serve as the motto for the enterprising modern (p. 360):

> Go forward, Faustus, in that famous art
> Wherein all nature's treasury is contained.
> Be thou on earth as Jove is in the sky,
> Lord and commander of these elements.

In the second encounter, the Bad Angel again urges Faustus to go forward "in that famous art" that the Good Angel characterizes as that "execrable art." He is urged by the Good Angel to "think of heaven and heavenly things," while the Bad Angel urges him to "think of honor and wealth." (pp. 368–69)

In the central encounter, Faustus is assured by the Good Angel that if he repents, God will pity him. The Bad Angel, on the other hand, both denies that God would pity him if he did repent and correctly predicts that, in any event, Faustus never would repent. (p. 372)

In the fourth encounter, the Bad Angel insists that it is too late for Faustus to repent, while the Good Angel insists that it is never too late. If he repents, the Bad Angel warns Faustus, devils will tear him to pieces. No, the Good Angel assures him, only if he repents will he be safe. There seems to be here still the possibility of repentance—and this is when Lucifer, *invoking justice*, threatening punishments, and offering blandishments, arrives to take a firm, and permanent, hold of Faustus. (p. 374)

The career of Faustus follows—and then we have his fifth encounter with the Good and Bad Angels at the end of the play. The Angels are by then agreed that Faustus is hopelessly lost, with the Good Angel finally leaving him. Shortly thereafter Faustus, after bitter and fearful lamentations, is dead, having been shown the various tortures awaiting him. (pp. 408–9) This is knowledge of good and bad "in spades."

The key question in these angelic encounters is whether Faustus is going to be saved. That depends upon whether he will renounce his alliance with the Devil and sincerely repent. The Bad Angel offers immediately the pleasures of the world. The Good Angel, in urging Faustus to repent, is exhibited as preeminently obedient.

It is again and again noticed in the play that pride, or presumptuousness, led to the fall of Lucifer and his lieutenants.

VI.

Perhaps the most disturbing thing about the entire play, as well as about Faustus's encounters with the Angels, is that virtue is not presented as something good in itself. This is not unrelated to Mephistophilis's last remarks to Faustus (p. 408):

> What, weep'st thou? 'Tis too late. Despair! Farewell!
> Fools that will laugh on earth must weep in hell.

This, too, suggests that virtue is not conducive to human happiness on earth, that it is not truly or fully good in itself but rather for its consequences.[104]

Of course, it is never said that virtue is bad in itself. But it *is* presented as requiring the surrender of pleasures and other such goods here.[105]

Virtue is offered, or advocated, as something good, if at all, for its long-term rewards—in the forms of the enjoyment of heavenly pleasures and bliss and of the avoidance of perpetual pains. When Virtue is presented thus, it is not surprising that it is keyed especially to Faithfulness (as it is in the pious Old Man), while Vice is keyed to Infidelity (or to allegiance to Lucifer).

At no point, then, is it said in the play that virtue is in itself attractive or noble or otherwise choiceworthy for its own sake, that it exhibits an excellence that should be desired, no matter what the external consequences may be. Indeed one may wonder—perhaps, even, Marlowe wants us to wonder—whether the virtues of antiquity are, from the Christian perspective, little more than the splendid vices that St. Augustine called them, especially if they divert man from a recognition of his complete dependence upon God. When this approach is taken, is there not the tendency to reduce all of the virtues to that of obedience to God, or piety?[106]

But, we should at once be reminded, vice *is* shown as ugly in this play. Both Mephistophilis and Lucifer, when not disguised, are painfully ugly (just as Satan is in Dante's *Inferno*). The logical extension of this is not developed, however, which would display virtue as intrinsically beautiful. Rather, the most beautiful thing presented in the play is the apparition of Helen—and that is, to say the least, morally ambiguous in these circumstances. (pp. 403, 405) The fallen angels are described in one fashion or another at a dozen places in the play.[107] Much is made of their pride, their self-centeredness, and their self-pleasing. In short, the negative, or what is to be avoided, may be more effectively presented in the play than the affirmative, or what is to be sought. This, too, may be a modern propensity.

Yet the inherent integrity of virtue is assumed in the play, even though the implications of this assumption are not spelled out. The fact that Faustus is literally dismembered at the end, however, does point up the destructive, or disintegrating, effect of vice. Even the Devil himself must depend upon justice as the basis of his claims on Faustus. That is, we have seen that he and his cohorts can become indignant when Faustus threatens to deny them what is owed them: another soul that they have earned and that had been counted upon to enlarge their domain.[108] Faustus, too, sees himself as just, or at least as not unjust.[109] He also sees himself as entitled to the powers that he seeks and exercises.

For the wicked, whether devils or humans, to rely on justice reveals a profound self-contradiction in them, in their very being. They truly do not know what they are doing. The learning that they may have cannot be recognized as *wisdom* or *prudence* but rather as *cunning*, a term that is applied on several occasions to Faustus, including by Faustus himself.[110]

Granted, it may be difficult to show virtue as always choiceworthy for its own sake, especially in dramatic productions. There can be something salutary in a reminder of the practical consequences of vice, including the consequences of punishment here or elsewhere for one's misconduct, however well that misconduct seems to be hidden from public view.[111]

Philosophy, properly understood, has always argued for the intrinsic choiceworthiness of virtue. But that which Faustus calls philosophy, and which he has presumably mastered, easily becomes an emphasis upon natural philosophy, or the natural sciences—and it is tempting to harness those sciences to technology. This is related to the tendency in the play to equate *virtue* with effectiveness.[112]

It is nature, at the foundation of genuine philosophy, which holds the secret of the status of virtue. But it is evident in this play that nature does not provide a guide. Thus, in the five angelic encounters, only the Bad Angel uses the word *nature* (that speech has been quoted by me). The Bad Angel's use of *nature* is the first, and decisive, use of the term in the play. For that Angel, as for much of modernity, nature is something to be exploited, not something by which to take one's bearings. (p. 360) Later, technology, in the form of fire, is used to overcome nature (in the form of the reluctance of Faustus's blood to flow for him to use in signing his fateful pact with the Devil; the term *nature* is not used there). (p. 370) Perhaps nature would have asserted herself in a salutary manner for Faustus if he could have taken a proper wife—but that was not to be.[113]

Philosophy is not seen in the play as an aid to virtue. In fact, it is related to Faustus's dangerous bookishness. One can be reminded here of Saint Augustine's criticism of an ancient philosopher:

> It was, no doubt, difficult for so great a philosopher either to acknowledge all this society of demons or to censure them with confidence, whereas any Christian old

woman would have had no hesitation about the fact of their existence, and no reserve about denouncing them.[114]

VII.

However much Faustus and the Devil rely upon justice and the sanctity of
promises and compacts, they are ultimately not moved by them. They cannot
truly rely upon justice: that would be against their nature, or inclinations.

Rather, much is made by them instead of *resolution*.[115] The fallen angels
were resolute: they simply would not submit to God; presumably, they persist
in their original disobedience. Resolution is thus intimately related to willfulness.

Faustus is explicitly concerned with resoluteness. In a way, resoluteness is
for Faustus the distillation of all the virtues. It can be contrasted by him to
baseness or base despair. (p. 373) Is there not, in such an emphasis upon resoluteness, something distinctively modern? It has found expression in Existentialism, providing a respectable way of dressing up self-assertiveness. Is
not this the contemporary response to the desperate awareness of abandonment?

Socrates could be resolute, of course, but not simply for the sake of resoluteness. Winston Churchill can include Resolution in the epigraph for his
history of the Second World War—but it is linked by him explicitly to war.
His complete epigraph reads,

> In War: Resolution
> In Defeat: Defiance
> In Victory: Magnanimity
> In Peace: Good Will.

Is there any place for Good Will in the Faustian scheme of things? Does the
modern emphasis upon resoluteness work from a perspective that sees
mankind as essentially at war all the time?[116] The Old Man, too, is shown as
resolute—but that can be understood as commendable, considering the faith
that he is determined to hold on to. (p. 406)

Perhaps, indeed, it is because *the* Faith had meant so much for so long, and
hence the determination to stand by it, that resoluteness has become so important in modernity. This steadfastness mimics, in a way, that of the Christian martyr. Thus, this can become the modern virtue, the new virtue in place
of the old ones: it exhibits something of the appearance of the old virtues as
things that are attractive for their own sake. But the hollowness of resoluteness as an end in itself is exposed by the stark, even unseemly, terror to which

Faustus is reduced at the end. There is nothing at his center around which he can "collect" himself. The dismemberment of Faustus's body is the physical counterpart to the collapse of his soul in the face of his final adversity.[117]

All this reflects the pervasive sense of the play, however muted, that the virtuous man is a whole, someone reliably consistent, and hence truly self-sufficient, which self-sufficiency is something for which the ambitious scholar may strive in a misguided manner. Does the restless playwright thereby acknowledge in his work as an artist something that he cannot bring himself to live up to as a man?

Perhaps, that is, Christopher Marlowe was astute (or inspired) enough, and man enough, to recognize that his uncompromising play properly called his own tempestuous life into question. We can be reminded here of Faustus's parting from his fellow scholars the night of his immediately impending death, the last contact he has on earth with other human beings. One of his colleagues asks, "O, what may we do to save Faustus?" To this Doctor Faustus generously replies, "Talk not of me, but save yourself and depart." (p. 408)

We can be reminded as well of Mephistophilis's honest outburst when he is asked by Faustus, during their first encounter, how it comes that he is here on earth if he has been (as he reports) condemned perpetually to hell—an eloquent (however despairing) outburst by a fallen angel that can teach us more than it evidently did the ill-fated Faustus (p. 366):

> Why this is hell, nor am I out of it.
> Think'st thou that I who saw the face of God
> And tasted the eternal joys of heaven
> Am not tormented with ten thousand hells
> In being deprived of everlasting bliss?
> O Faustus, leave these frivolous demands
> Which strike a terror to my fainting soul.

NOTES

1. This talk was given at the University of Chicago Basic Program Weekend conference on "The Idea of Paradise," Alpine Valley Resort, East Troy, Wisconsin, May 16, 1981. The original title of this talk was "The Trials of Adam and Eve in the Garden of Eden."

The parenthetical citations in the text are to the *Book of Genesis*. The translation of *Genesis* used here is that found in Robert Sacks, *The Lion and the Ass: A Commentary on the Book of Genesis*. The Sacks commentary was published in *Interpretation*, beginning in volume 8 (May 1980), and thereafter by the Edwin Mellen Press (1991).

2. See, e.g., Plato, *Apology of Socrates* 22B–C. See also George Anastaplo, *Human Being and Citizen: Essays on Virtue, Freedom, and the Common Good* (Chicago:

Swallow Press, 1975), pp. 15, 17. (Swallow Press has been acquired by the Ohio University Press.)

3. Can there be true justice without divine rule or providence? See Leo Strauss, *Natural Right and History* (Chicago: University of Chicago Press, 1953), p. 150 n. 24. See also chapter 9, note 41. See as well chapter 1, note 68.

4. See Sacks, *The Lion and the Ass*, commentary on *Genesis* 2:10–14.

5. See *Isaiah* 51:3; *Ezekiel* 28:13, 31:9, 31:16, 31:18, 36:35; *Joel* 2:3.

6. See J. H. Hertz, *The Pentateuch and Haftorahs* (London: Soncino Press, 1952), p. 7.

7. See *Luke* 23:43; *2 Corinthians* 12:4; *Revelation* 2:7. See, on *Revelation,* Anastaplo, "Law & Literature and the Bible: Explorations," 23 *Oklahoma City University Law Review* 515, 841 (1998).

8. *Luke* 23:43.

9. Hertz, *The Pentateuch and Haftorahs*, p. 196.

10. Hertz, *The Pentateuch and Haftorahs*, p. 12 (commenting on *Genesis* 3:17 and citing *Genesis* 5:29, 7:21).

11. Modern Library edition (1950), p. 241. See also pp. 247–48. Newman can speak of "the great evil" against which the infallible Christ is marshaled.

12. *Chapters of the Fathers*, III, 13.

13. *Sayings of the Jewish Fathers* (Cambridge: Cambridge University Press, 1897), p. 49 n. 22.

14. *Deuteronomy* 4:5–6. See the text at note 70 of chapter 5, at note 89 of chapter 7, and at note 65 of chapter 10 of this collection. See also Anastaplo, "Law & Literature and the Austen-Dostoyevsky Axis: Explorations," 46 *South Dakota Law Review* 712, 751 (2001).

15. Consider Maimonides's effort, in *The Guide of the Perplexed*, to suggest the rationale for *some* of the rules laid down by God. See Moshe Greenberg, "Some Postulates of Biblical Criminal Law," in *Yehezkel Kaufmann Jubilee Volume* (Jerusalem: Magnes Press, 1960), p. 11. See also the text at note 68 of chapter 1, and at note 65 of chapter 10 of this collection. See as well chapter 1, note 65, conclusion, note 3.

16. Hertz, *The Pentateuch and Haftorahs*, p. 8.

17. See, e.g., Plato, *Phaedrus* 229B–230A.

18. See chapter 2, part B, section III, and chapter 5 of this collection. See also George Anastaplo, *The American Moralist: On Law, Ethics, and Government* (Athens, Ohio: Ohio University Press, 1992), pp. 66–69.

19. Leo Strauss, "Jerusalem and Athens," *Commentary*, June 1967, pp. 51–52.

20. Consider, for example, what made both Oedipus and Socrates vulnerable. See chapters 4 and 6 of this collection. See also Moses Maimonides, *The Guide of the Perplexed* (Chicago: University of Chicago Press, 1963), pp. 635–61 (on the ultimate perfection of man: "through it man is man"). See as well chapter 1, notes 77, 78, the text at note 35 of chapter 4 of this collection.

21. See Hertz, *The Pentateuch and Haftoral*, p. 8 (commentary on *Genesis* 2:9).

22. See Strauss, "Jerusalem and Athens," p. 50.

23. Cain, it seems, could distinguish right from wrong enough to be held accountable for what he did. See Sacks, *The Lion and the Ass*, commentary on *Genesis* 4:6,

4:8, and 4:14. But then Cain did come after mankind had partaken of the fruit from the tree of the knowledge of good and bad. See Mera Flaumenhaft, "Seeing Justice Done: Aeschylus' *Oresteia*," p. 104. See, on how one begins to learn anything, Plato, *Meno* and *Phaedo*. See also chapter 6–A. See as well appendix C, note 65.

24. See Sacks, *The Lion and the Ass,* commentary on *Genesis* 4:1.

25. See Maimonides, *The Guide of the Perplexed*, p. 23 (part I, chapter 2, paragraph 1); Sacks, *The Lion and the Ass*, commentary on *Genesis* 3:5, 3:16, and 4:8.

26. See, on the good and the bad, ibid., commentary on *Genesis* 3:5.

27. See *Deuteronomy* 30:15: "therefore choose life." See also the text at note 9 of chapter 9 of this collection.

28. See, e.g., Plato, *Republic* 494A sq.; Plato, *Apology* 39C–D; Anastaplo, *Human Being and Citizen*, pp.19–20, 206–13.

29. See *Genesis, Art Scroll Tanach Series* (New York: Mesorah Publications, 1977), I, 101n.

30. See *Deuteronomy* 1:39; Hertz, *The Pentateuch and the Haftorahs*, p.742.

31. See *Genesis, ArtScroll Tanach Series*, I, 113.

32. See, e.g., *Genesis* 18:7. Compare *2 Samuel* 12:4.

33. See Hertz, *The Pentateuch and Haftorahs*, p. 8; Sacks, *The Lion and the Ass*, commentary on *Genesis* 2:25.

34. *Genesis, ArtScroll Tanach Series*, I, 110.

35. Strauss, "Jerusalem and Athens," p. 50.

36. Strauss, "Jerusalem and Athens," p. 50.

37. See "On Death: One by One, Yet Altogether," in Anastaplo, *Human Being and Citizen*, p. 214. See also chapter 1, notes 41, 53.

38. Strauss, "Jerusalem and Athens," p. 53.

39. *Genesis, ArtScroll Tanach Series*, I, 102.

40. Strauss, "Jerusalem and Athens," p. 49.

41. Did death come for the animals only through human beings? Should it be said, at least, that animals have no sense of time and hence can truly know neither life nor death? See Aristotle, *De Anima* 433b5 sq. See also the commentary on Edwin Muir's "The Animals" in George Anastaplo, *The Artist as Thinker: From Shakespeare to Joyce* (Athens, Ohio: Ohio University Press, 1983), pp. 357–63; chapter 1, note 37 above.

42. See Sacks, *The Lion and the Ass*, commentary on *Genesis* 2:21–23.

43. See Sacks, *The Lion and the Ass*, commentary on *Genesis* 1:26–27. See also the text at note 49 of chapter 4 of this collection.

44. Is to be free from passion also to be free from understanding as well as from vice and virtue? Socrates refers again and again to the erotic element in the philosopher. Consider also *Upanishads*, II, 24. Compare *Upanishads*, II, 63. Compare also chapter 5, note 32. See introduction, note 3.

God, it seems, did not need to say anything to Adam and Eve in order for them to become aware of their nakedness. That is, the sin of Adam and Eve evidently had its effect "automatically." This suggests that a sense of how one should respond to right and wrong (whether or not stimulated by the proscribed fruit?) is innate in human beings. See chapter 12–A. See also chapter 1, note 71, conclusion, note 2.

45. See Sacks, *The Lion and the Ass*, commentary on *Genesis* 2:25. See also Søren Kierkegaard, *The Concept of Dread*, which is concerned with sexuality as a critical element in the concept of original sin. See also chapter 5, note 32. References to Adam are frequent in the work of Kierkegaard.

Is such sexuality, or sensuality, "romanticized" in the *Song of Songs*? See *Interpreter's Bible* (New York: Abingdon-Cokesbury Press, 1951), p. 98: "It began in the Garden of Eden . . ." Does it continue but under a cloud, into the New Testament, even to the *Book of Revelation*? See *Interpreter's Bible*, p. 141n. See also p. 100. See as well chapter 1, note 7 above.

46. See Maimonides, *The Guide of the Perplexed*, pp. 23–25. Central to the inquiry in this chapter is this caution from Maimonides:

> O you who engage in theoretical speculation using the first notions that may occur to you and come to your mind and who consider withal that you understand a book that is the guide of the first and the last men while glancing through it as you would glance through a historical work or a piece of poetry . . . collect yourself and reflect, for things are not as you thought following the first notion that occurred to you, but rather as is made clear through reflection upon the following speech.

Maimonides, *The Guide of the Perplexed*, p. 24. See also chapter 1, note 48; chapter 7, note 101; chapter 9, note 49.

47. Strauss, "Jerusalem and Athens," p. 48.

48. Strauss, "Jerusalem and Athens," p. 49. This problem, it is suggested, is at the "heart of being." Do vital ineluctable necessities thus assert themselves? See also Sacks, *The Lion and the Ass*, commentary on *Genesis* 1:25, 3:17–19.

49. *Law* is avoided in the early chapters of *Genesis*. See Sacks, *The Lion and the Ass*, commentary on *Genesis* 2:1–2.

50. Compare Anastaplo, *The Artist as Thinker*, p. 82 (drawing on John Bunyan's *The Pilgrim's Progress*).

51. Consider the discussion of piety to this effect in Plato's *Euthyphro*. See George Anastaplo, "On Trial: Explorations," 22 *Loyola University of Chicago Law Journal* 765, 873 (1991).

52. See *Genesis, ArtScroll Tanach Series*, I, 13.

53. Is not the keeping of man from immortality less of a problem for the nature of man? That is, would an indefinite extension of life have added anything essential to what human nature is capable of (especially since human beings sometimes, if not even usually, do have the sense that they are not mortal)? On the other hand, why does God take care that Adam and Eve not eat of the tree of life? How, for example, would the virtue of courage be affected? See chapter 1, note 37, above; the text at note 96 of this collection. See also Plato, *Seventh Letter* 334E.

54. Maimonides, *The Guide of the Perplexed*, p.26 (emphasis added).

55. Compare *Encyclopedia of Religion and Ethics* (New York: Charles Scribner's Sons, 1908), I, 85. Compare also Strauss, "Jerusalem and Athens," p. 49. Did Eve, having already eaten of the tree, know more than Adam did when she offered him fruit of that tree? Could she notice, already, that she and he were naked?

56. See, e.g., William Shakespeare, *Two Gentlemen of Verona*, III, i, 327; Sacks, *The Lion and the Ass*, commentary on *Genesis* 3:6.

57. See Sacks, *The Lion and the Ass*, commentary on *Genesis* 3:12.

58. See Maimonides, *The Guide of the Perplexed*, p. 26.

59. Shakespeare, *Twelfth Night*, I, v, 26.

60. Consider the use of Pandora, in the Greek story, to account for miseries having been let loose upon the world. But *there*, it seems, no human male ratifies what the enterprising woman does.

61. See Hertz, *The Pentateuch and Haftorahs*, p. 684.

62. Strauss, "Jerusalem and Athens," p. 49.

63. Compare, on the placement of the tree, Strauss, "Jerusalem and Athens," pp. 49–50.

64. Hertz, *The Pentateuch and the Haftorahs*, p. 10.

65. See, on *not* adding to the commandments and prohibitions, *Leviticus* 10:1–3; *Deuteronomy* 13:1; Moses Maimonides, *The Book of Knowledge,* Moses Hyamson, ed. (Jerusalem: Boys Town Publisher, 1962), pp. 17a–b. Would being able to add sensibly to God's directives imply the primacy of reason over revelation? Compare chapter 1, note 15 above, conclusion, note 3. See also chapter 8, note 51.

Even so, does not some sensibleness have to be used in choosing among the many purported revelations that one may be offered? Be that as it may, some mystics have argued that there is a limited understanding of that Divine that can come to human beings only by revelation, not by the use of the unaided reason. See, e.g., Pseudo-Dionysius, *The Complete Works* (New York: Paulist Press, 1987), pp. 49f, 65 ("The most evident idea in theology, namely, the sacred incarnation of Jesus for our sakes, is something that cannot be enclosed in words nor grasped by any mind, not even by leaders among the front ranks of the angels. That he undertook to be a man is, for us, entirely mysterious"). Yet it can be noticed that the remarkable insights offered by mystics often resemble those delivered by poets—that is, by artists who may draw upon a kind of reasoning that has ostensibly been liberated from conventional restraints and routine tests. (Still, does the human mind somehow grasp, "enclose in words," and perhaps even develop that which is identified as "mysterious"?) See Plato, *Apology* 22A–C. See also appendix C, note 29. See, on *the* Incarnation and its reception by evidently uninspired men, chapter 7. See, on the limitations of any human understanding of the mysterious and of the spiritual, Mortimer J. Adler, *A Second Look in the Rearview Mirror* (New York: Macmillan Publishing Co., 1992), pp. 278f.

66. See Aristotle, *Metaphysics* 984a4 sq. See also Leo Strauss, *Persecution and the Art of Writing* (Glencoe, Illinois: The Free Press, 1952).

67. Does Eve first encounter God when she is judged by Him? This is not unrelated to the Annunciation story in the Greek Bible (the New Testament). Mary, the mother of Jesus, can be known by Christians as "the second Eve." See the text at note 84 of chapter 1 of this collection.

68. See Leo Strauss, *Thoughts on Machiavelli* (Glencoe, Illinois: The Free Press, 1958), pp. 136–37, 148–49, 165–66. See also chapter 1, note 15 above; chapter 2, note 9; the text at note 10 of chapter 2 of this collection.

69. Sacks, *The Lion and the Ass*, commentary on *Genesis* 3:1.

70. Compare, on the earth as the first sinner, Sacks, *The Lion and the Ass*, commentary on *Genesis* 1:11. See chapter 3, note 12.

71. See chapter 12–A. There is no "trial" for the Serpent: the other two involved in this disobedience *were* given an opportunity to say something. Had any divine prohibition been provided to the Serpent? See chapter 1, note 44 above; chapter 1, note 73.

72. See Hertz, *The Pentateuch and Haftorahs*, p. 196.

73. Did the Serpent "always" crawl? Did he "always" look ominous? But see *Genesis* 3:14–15. Had the Serpent already "fallen"? See Hertz, *The Pentateuch and Haftorahs*, pp. 11–12.

74. See Sacks, *The Lion and the Ass*, commentary on *Genesis* 3:15. Consider also the sexual implications of both the snake and its seed.

75. Strauss, "Jerusalem and Athens," p. 46. See Anastaplo, "On Trial"(*Loyola Law Journal*), p. 1052 n. 309.

76. Strauss, "Jerusalem and Athens," p. 57. See chapter 7, note 101.

77. See, on whether the disobedience in the Garden was good for man, Maimonides, *The Guide of the Perplexed*, pp. 23–26. Is not Maimonides's display of indignation somewhat suspicious? See chapter 1, note 20 above. Compare Dietrich Bonhoeffer, *Creation and Fall* (New York: Macmillan, 1959); *Piers Plowman*, XVIII, 208f; and an essay by Hermann Weigand in Johann W. von Goethe, *Faust* (New York: Norton Critical Edition, 1976), pp. 447–49. See also the text at note 35 of chapter 4 of this collection.

78. *Has* reason been good for man? See Cicero, *On the Gods* (Penguin edition), pp. 221f. See also chapter 1, note 20 above.

79. See Hertz, *The Pentateuch and Haftorahs*, p. 13.

80. See, e.g., *Mark* 7:19.

81. See the genealogy in *1 Chronicles* 1. See also, on a misreading in the Authorized Version in *Deuteronomy* 32:8, *Encyclopedia of Religion and Ethics*, I, 84.

82. See *I Corinthians* 15:22, 15:45. See also *Luke* 3:38, *Romans* 5:14 (twice), *I Corinthians* 15:22, 15:45 (twice), *I Timothy* 2:13, 2:14, *Jude* 14. See, on Eve, *2 Corinthians* 11:3, *I Timothy* 2:13, chapter 1, note 69 above. See, on the Serpent, *Revelation* 12:9, 20:2.

83. *Romans* 5:12.

84. See, e.g., "Homosexuality and the Church," lines 108–33 (position paper of the Presbyterian Church in the United States, 1979).

85. Hertz, *The Pentateuch and Haftorahs*, p. 196. In Christianity, however, there is but one hero. See the text at note 18 of chapter 1 of this collection.

86. See Sacks, *The Lion and the Ass, passim*. See especially commentary on *Genesis* 5:1. Are the first two accounts of the Creation "hypothetical," with the true beginning to be seen in *Genesis* 5:1? Have there been at least three attempts to "settle" human beings upon the earth: in the Garden of Eden, in the pre-Flood dispensation, and in the post-Flood dispensation? Then there is, according to Christians, the dispensation because of the career of Jesus? Still another dispensation awaits mankind upon the Second Coming (or, for the Jews, upon *the* coming of the Messiah)? (The

distinctive secular "prophets" in the Western World of the first three stages can be said to have been Jean-Jacques Rousseau, Thomas Hobbes, and Plato, respectively.)

87. See *Genesis, ArtScroll Tanach Series*, I, 102.

88. See Aristotle, *Politics* 1452b1 sq.

89. William Shakespeare, *King Lear*, IV, ii, 11.

90. Ved Mehta, *Portrait of India* (New York: Farrar, Straus and Giroux, 1970), p. 12. The Red Fort is at Delhi.

91. See, on what "the pursuit of happiness" does and does not mean, Anastaplo, "The Constitution at Two Hundred: Explorations," 22 *Texas Tech Law Review* 967, 989–94 (1991). Compare Emily Dickinson, "Success Is Counted Sweetest."

We return to the differences between Jews and Christians with respect to "the way" (whether a way back or a way out) by noticing that *way* is used some 1,700 times in the Hebrew Bible (which we know as the Old Testament), whereas it is used only about 80 times in the Greek Bible (which we know as the New Testament). Is *way* more apt to suggest *a way of life*, a continuing existence on earth, something that Jews are more apt to make much of than are Christians? See chapter 1, note 106; chapter 3, note 21; the text at note 11 of chapter 3 of this collection; chapter 9, note 9. See also chapter 5, note 18.

Notice that *nature* is not used at all in the Old Testament or in the Gospels; but it is used thirteen times by Paul and five more times elsewhere in the New Testament. Are Christians more apt than Jews to speak today of nature as a problem and of the nature of man as having been somehow changed by The Fall? See, on nature, Anastaplo, *The American Moralist*, pp. 410–11; conclusion, note 3.

The Old Testament use of *way* can remind one of what is to be found in Chinese thought. See, e.g., George Anastaplo, *But Not Philosophy: Seven Introductions to Non-Western Thought* (Lanham, Md.: Lexington Books, 2002), pp. 22 (on Confucian Thought), 303 (on nature). (At p. xix of *But Not Philosophy*, the second note 25 should be note 26.) See also Anastaplo, "The Constitution at Two Hundred," pp. 980–91.

92. This talk was given in the First Friday Lecture Series, The Basic Program of Liberal Education for Adults, The University of Chicago, at the Cultural Center, Chicago Public Library, Chicago, Illinois, March 3, 1989. The original title of this talk was "Negation and Affirmation: Some Perhaps Salutary Lessons From Christopher Marlowe's *Doctor Faustus*."

The parenthetical citations in the text and notes are to the version of *Doctor Faustus* found in Irving Ribner, ed., *The Complete Plays of Christopher Marlowe* (New York: Odyssey Press, 1963).

See, on Christopher Marlowe, George Anastaplo, "Law & Literature and the Christian Heritage: Explorations," 40 *Brandeis Law Journal* 192, 357 (2001).

93. The introductory sentence of the play, recited by the Chorus, reads (p. 357),

> Not marching in the fields of Trasimene
> Where Mars did mate the warlike Carthagens,
> Nor sporting in the dalliance of love
> In courts of kings where state is overturned,

Nor in the pomp of proud audacious deeds
Intends our muse to vaunt his heavenly verse.

94. Roger Bacon, who is mentioned in the Marlowe play (p. 362), and others are called to mind as leaders in this great adventure. Is not the Ulysses in the twenty-sixth canto of Dante's *Inferno* another such adventurer? See, on Marlowe and Machiavelli, Leo Strauss, *Natural Right and History*, p. 177.

95. See *The Tragedy of Doctor Faustus*, ed. Louis B. Wright (New York: Washington Square Press, 1962), p. xx. See, on the once widespread belief in witchcraft and the many trials of witches, George Anastaplo, "Church and State: Explorations," 19 *Loyola University of Chicago Law Journal* 61, 65–86 (1987).

96. See *Doctor Faustus*, pp. 359, 362, 380, 388, 390, 411. See also p. 405: "make me immortal with a kiss." See as well chapter 1, note 53 above.

97. See Plato, *Republic* 359C sq., 612B.

98. One can be reminded by Faustus's civic-mindedness of Raskolnikov in Fyodor Dostoyevsky's *Crime and Punishment*. Faustus *is* a German patriot: that lends some meaning to his life; it cannot be all desire and voluptuousness. See, on the relation of Faustus to Adam and Eve, conclusion, note 2.

99. Compare Shakespeare's Prospero and his giving up of his potent books when his compassion-guided project on behalf of justice in *The Tempest* is completed. See chapter 9, note 10.

100. Does an artist create a "world" that he peoples with his own fancies? Is there something divine in this? See the text at note 20 of chapter 3 of this collection. I have argued, in *The Artist as Thinker*, that it is critical, in order to understand the typical story, to determine how the character one is interested in *should* have acted. See chapter 4, note 6. Still, one should consider the implications of a comment by Paul Sérusier (quoted by Scribner Ames in her unpublished autobiography), "One says of an apple painted by the ordinary painter, 'It looks good enough to eat.' Of an apple painted by Cezanne, one says, 'It's beautiful.'"

101. This is the inquiry that the Bible deals with at its outset, thereby legitimating the authority of the Creator who directs thereafter the people of Israel. That basis for authority is invoked in other places, such as in the *Book of Job* (even though its hero is not an Israelite). See chapter 3, note 16. See also conclusion, note 3.

102. How seriously can one take the notion that misery loves company? What makes Lucifer in Dante's *Inferno* "want" to chew—for he does most vigorously chew—Judas Iscariot, Brutus, and Cassius in his three massive jaws?

103. These five encounters with the Angels are in *Doctor Faustus*, pp. 360, 368–69, 372, 374, and 408–9.

104. Its principal, if not only significant, consequences are after one's life on this earth. See chapter 1, note 91 above.

105. Consider the equivocations with respect to such matters by Thrasymachus in the first book of Plato's *Republic*.

106. See, as bearing on these matters, Augustine, *The City of God* (New York: Penguin Books edition, 1972), pp. 247 ("it is, strictly speaking, for the sake of eternal life

alone that we are Christians"), 252–53, 287, 293, 415, 498, 589–90, 891, 991, 995, 1005. Compare p. 567. See chapter 1, note 91 above.

107. See *Doctor Faustus*, pp. 445–47, 449–50, 477, 479f, 482, 551–52, 568–69, 572–73.

108. See *Doctor Faustus*, pp. 374–75, 394, 395, 405, 407, 408, 409.

109. See, e.g., *Doctor Faustus*, pp. 394–95, 403. Compare pp. 404–5.

110. *Cunning*, although it once had in common usage a broader meaning than it does now, could be somewhat questionable in character. Compare *Dictionary of National Biography* 13:891 (1917). See, for various uses, *Doctor Faustus*, pp. 358, 362, 380, 386, 392, 398, 407. This may not be unrelated to Faustus's low origins. See pp. 358, 393. Compare p. 395. These observations apply as well to another notorious German, Martin Heidegger. See Anastaplo, *The Constitutionalist*, p. 815; Anastaplo, *The Artist as Thinker*, p. 269; Anastaplo, *The American Moralist*, pp. 144–60. Heidegger has been identified as "the only major thinker to opt for Nazism, the main example of absolute evil in our time, possibly of any time," Victor Farias, *Heidegger and Nazism* (Philadelphia: Temple University Press, 1989), p. ix. See also chapter 1, note 116; chapter 5, note 69; chapter 12, note 71.

111. See Leo Strauss, *The Rebirth of Classical Political Rationalism* (Chicago: University of Chicago Press, 1989), pp. 65–66.

112. See *Doctor Faustus*, p. 365. See, on philosophy, *Doctor Faustus*, pp. 358, 361, 365 (atheism?).

113. See, for uses of *nature*, *Doctor Faustus*, pp. 360, 363 (twice), 374, 403–4, 409 (twice). See also chapter 1, note 91 above.

114. *The City of God*, p. 387. See also pp. 1027–28, 1068.

115. See, for uses of *resoluteness* in the play, *Doctor Faustus*, pp. 362, 364, 366, 368, 373, 393, 406. Related to this is *fortitude*. See *Doctor Faustus*, p. 366. *Despair* is what has to be counteracted. See, e.g., *Doctor Faustus*, pp. 393, 397, 401, 403–4, 408. See also the text at note 67 of chapter 10 of this collection.

116. Is resoluteness somehow derivative from the Kantian emphasis upon doing one's duty, in the formal sense, regardless of consequences? See Anastaplo, *The American Moralist*, pp. 27, 144–48. See also chapter 9, note 23. The Heideggerian emphasis on the importance of strife is significant here. See Farias, *Heidegger and Nazism*, pp. 91–92, 99, 103; chapter 12, note 75. See also Plato, *Laws* 625D sq. Compare chapter 10, note 70.

117. Faustus's final terror should be compared with the fortitude displayed by several of the perpetually condemned men in Dante's *Inferno*. Faustus's dramatic dismemberment is anticipated by that of Pentheus in Euripides' *The Bacchae*: both victims suffered in part because of an unbridled curiosity. See chapter 2, note 5.

2

Clytemnestra, Electra, and Orestes

2-A. THE CHORUSES IN AESCHYLUS' *ORESTEIA*[1]

I.

Aeschylus' trilogy, the *Oresteia*, is, according to A. C. Swinburne, perhaps "the greatest achievement of the human mind."[2] I consider on this occasion the question of motivation in the *Oresteia*, primarily that of the Chorus of slave-women in *The Libation Bearers*, the second play of the trilogy.

But one cannot properly talk about what happens in one play in this trilogy without at least touching upon the other two. An awareness of the whole is essential for proper consideration of any part.

Consider the end of the *Agamemnon* the first play of the trilogy. The Chorus there disparage Aegisthus when he parades before them as one of the murderers of Agamemnon. They taunt him as a "woman," skulking at home while real men fought at Troy. (*Ag.*, 1625) The Chorus cannot, will not, believe that Aegisthus can be their master. (*Ag.*, 1633–35) Aegisthus explains himself by saying that the woman's role was needed in the killing of Agamemnon if he was to be safely snared. (*Ag.*, 1636–37) Even so, that role in the slaying continues to be stressed, in disparagement, by the Chorus. (*Ag.*, 1643–45)

Perhaps the Chorus speak as they do, in the *Agamemnon*, partly because they *are* ineffectual old men: after all, they had been, even ten years before, too old to go to Troy. Their age and lowly status are sneered at by Aegisthus. (*Ag.*, 1619–20) Clytemnestra intervenes to try to moderate the struggle between Aegisthus and the Chorus. (*Ag.*, 1654) She speaks more respectfully to them as Elders. (*Ag.*, 1657–61) She counsels acceptance of what she says, labelling her counsel as womanly. (*Ag.*, 1661) In this role she can remind us somewhat of Athena at the end of *The Eumenides*, the third play of the trilogy.

The reconciliation that Clytemnestra seeks is at best partial. Aegisthus still resents what he considers the Chorus's insolence. (*Ag.*, 1663–65) And the Chorus insist that it is not like Argives to cringe before a knave. The Chorus's last word in the *Agamemnon* is that of disparagement of Aegisthus as a cockerel beside his hen, not as someone independent and truly manly. (*Ag.*, 1671) We are challenged, in many (if not in all) of the Greek plays, to consider essential differences between male and female (both among human beings and among divinities).

II.

The Chorus of Argive elders in the *Agamemnon* did sense correctly, one can say, that their status under a rule other than Agamemnon's would be dubious. They can be understood to have been transformed, by the time of *The Libation Bearers*, into a Chorus of subjugated slave-women serving the household of Clytemnestra and Aegisthus.

Women are referred to by each of the first three speakers in *The Libation Bearers*. Orestes, at the very beginning of this second play in the trilogy, sees a throng of women coming out to the tomb of Agamemnon (*Lib. B.*, 10–11); he wants to learn what this band of suppliant women are up to. (*Lib. B.*, 11–20) The Chorus are thereupon heard to consider themselves mistreated women; and they refer to Clytemnestra as a godless woman, as they invoke still another female, Mother Earth. (*Lib. B.*, 21–46) Electra begins her first speech in the play, immediately thereafter, by addressing the women of the household. (*Lib. B.*, 84)

The ambiguous status of women is to be seen throughout the play. The women in this play have far more lines than the men. They figure very much in the action, far more in a sense than does even Orestes. And yet they are repeatedly put in their place, as can be seen in the disparagement by Orestes (*to* women: the Chorus and his sister)—his disparagement of Aegisthus and Clytemnestra as "this brace of women." (*Lib. B.*, 304)

III.

One can see throughout the play, as well as throughout the trilogy, the tension between male and female. Clytemnestra and Orestes can debate the contributions of, and the impositions upon, men and women in the community. (*Lib.*

B., 911–21) And, of course, Clytemnestra can invoke the natural respect a son has for his mother. (*Lib. B.*, 896–98) The Chorus had anticipated this invocation: they had made much more of the Olympian gods, who tend to be male in their stance, than of the primitive earth divinities, who tend to be female; they had made more of fathers than of mothers, of the male than of the female. (*Lib. B.*, 783 sq.) They had counseled Orestes that if Clytemnestra should plead "Son" to him, he was to shout "Father" in response to her. (*Lib. B.*, 826–30)

Clytemnestra, I have already indicated, can be thought of as the one character in the trilogy, before the efforts of Athena in *The Eumenides*, who attempts to bridge somewhat the gulf between male and female. She *is* a wife (the Greek word for *wife* is also the word for *woman*); but whether she can be thought of as a loving wife, which is what women are supposed to be, is, to say the least, questionable. (*Lib. B.*, 89–90) She does seem to speak to and of Aegisthus with affection, both in the *Agamemnon* and in *The Libation Bearers*.

Even so, Clytemnestra does seem more manly than Aegisthus. True, she defers to Aegisthus when she first talks to Orestes after he appears in the guise of a stranger: that is, she defers to the man of the household if there is serious business to be discussed with outsiders. (*Lib. B.*, 668–73) But one suspects that she is playing a role here, just as she had done in the *Agamemnon* when she had welcomed her husband home and just as she is to do later when she laments upon hearing of Orestes' supposed death. (*Lib. B.*, 691–99)[3]

Clytemnestra *is* more manly than Aegisthus. We hear shrieks when Aegisthus is killed by Orestes. (*Lib. B.*, 869) Not so when Clytemnestra is killed: in fact, when she recognizes what is happening, she calls for a battle-ax. (*Lib. B.*, 887–89)

IV.

The play is half over before the Chorus of slave-women are given a conventional choral speech to deliver. Much is made by them in that speech of the consequences of the conduct of *overbold* men and of *passionate* women. (*Lib. B.*, 585 sq.) After the Chorus recount the vivid stories of various women who went wrong, especially in marriage, the action can proceed. (*Lib. B.*, 653) This recollection serves to remind us that the proper sphere for men is the city, that for women is the household—with overreaching a serious failing of men and undue passion a serious failing of women.[4]

It may be because this chorus of women do "know" the proper place of women, in subordination to men, that they can resent as much as they do the rule of Clytemnestra and Aegisthus, which is for them really the rule of Clytemnestra, even though Aegisthus *is* the one who carries in his veins the blood of the royal house of Pelops.

Various things the women say indicate their Eastern origins. (E.g., *Lib. B.*, 423–24) Perhaps they come from Persia or elsewhere in the East. Perhaps they even come from Troy: if so, they are part of the booty of Agamemnon, that wealth brought home from Troy that is referred to in the play. (*Lib. B.*, 135–38) If they were brought to Argos from Troy, they may have aroused in Clytemnestra the resentment that she seems to have had all along toward anything connected with the Trojan expedition. (Consider, for example, how the captive Cassandra was regarded and treated by Clytemnestra in the *Agamemnon*.)

Wherever the Chorus came from, they claim that both West and East share the same law. (*Lib. B.*, 400–404) This is so if the law is generally what *they* say it is, a system that makes much of retribution. This means, among other things, that the Chorus can speak of the just retribution that came to Priam and his sons, which retribution is now visited upon Clytemnestra and Aegisthus. (*Lib. B.*, 935–71)

V.

It is late in the play when the Chorus speak thus of Troy. When Orestes had mentioned the overcoming of Troy as a mark of Agamemnon's spirit, they in their response did not mention Troy but emphasized hate returning for hate, and this is called justice. (*Lib. B.*, 297–314)

The Chorus do seem reconciled to their fate: they can recognize "Almighty Destinies." (*Lib. B.*, 306) This, it seems, accounts for *their* situation. They are somewhat reconciled to their fate only if they have an appropriate master. The male is preferred by them to the female, just as they recognize Zeus as "father of the Olympian gods." (*Lib. B.*, 783–84) They do not consider themselves to have been treated kindly by their current mistress. (*Lib. B.*, 22 sq.) Besides, Orestes, if he is supported by them, would owe them special consideration.

Generally, the Chorus seem to say, a woman is not a fit ruler. They seem to assume that a city thus ruled is not of sufficient stature to dignify their subjugation enough to make it endurable. Otherwise their lot is simply a bitter one. (*Lib. B.*, 76–84) Agamemnon can be referred to by them as a *king*. (*Lib. B.*, 354 sq.) A royal title is never given by them to Clytemnestra (nor, of course, to Aegisthus). Orestes can ask, when he appears as a stranger at the palace, for the lord of the house. (*Lib. B.*, 658–67: *Kyriosi domato*) Agamemnon is referred to by the Chorus as their fallen *lord*. (*Lib. B.*, 153: *despoti*) The Chorus refer to Clytemnestra and Aegisthus as those who *hold* them (*Lib. B.*, 264: *kratountas*); strangely, the same term, that of *holder*, can be used by Clytemnestra when she refers to Aegisthus. (*Lib. B.*, 716: *kratousi domaton*) Does this reveal what she really thinks of him? One cannot help but wonder whether this pair always doubted their legitimacy. Did they *hold* only by sufferance, so to speak? (*Lib. B.*, 535–37, 942–45)

The Chorus, it would seem, consider themselves *held* by unnatural masters—and this contributes to their frenzy, a frenzy that is perhaps grounded in the fact that they are *foreign* women.[5] The Chorus's central speeches in the play (#30 and #31 of sixty speeches) have them telling Orestes how his father's corpse had been mutilated before burial and then urging Orestes and Electra to be firm and hard in what lies ahead. (*Lib. B.*, 439 sq.) It is the Chorus who use the most brutal and provocative language in the play. Certainly, they are less restrained than Orestes, and they reinforce the tendency in Electra to let herself go. (*Lib. B.*, 181–82) Again and again they insist that the key to justice is revenge. (*Lib. B.*, 123) Orestes, too, can come to speak of justice as dependent upon reciprocity. (*Lib. B.*, 556–59) But he can also make much of justice as obedience to a god's command (in this case, Apollo's), especially since he believes that it is better for one to hurt another human being than to be hurt oneself by that god. (*Lib. B.*, 269 sq.)

But it should be noticed about the Chorus that they do respond in a more restrained way than does Electra to Orestes' wish that his father had died a hero's death at Troy. (*Lib. B.*, 354 sq.) Electra does not go along with him: *she* wishes that her father had come home to kill his enemies before they killed him. (*Lib. B.*, 363 sq.) The Chorus, on the other hand, imagine how the great king would have been received in Hades by his fallen companions if he *had* died at Troy. Perhaps their uncharacteristic preference here for the milder alternative is moved by their awareness (never made explicit) that if Agamemnon *had* been killed at Troy, that city might never have fallen and they might not now be enslaved (whether they were taken at Troy or elsewhere during the long campaign abroad by Agamemnon).

One must wonder whether the Chorus ever appreciate Orestes' motives in his attack on his mother. Theirs is bound to be, it seems, a bitterer, pettier, more limited view of things. One should expect women and especially foreign women, we seem to be told, to be more family-minded, less political, in their interests and allegiances.[6]

Much is made by the Chorus of *order*, an order firmly grounded in a kind of justice. (*Lib. B.*, 783 sq.) Such an order can lead to what they call *liberty*, a liberty that they can share as beneficiaries of orderly rule. After Orestes has killed Clytemnestra and Aegisthus, the Chorus can assure Orestes that he has done well, liberating Argos and so forth. (*Lib. B.* 1043)

VI.

The Chorus had been instructed by Orestes, as he proceeds to execute his plan, that they should speak only "in the way that will help"; otherwise they are to remain silent. (*Lib. B.*, 580–84) He does not seem to expect much, if anything, from them. He does not even allude to their grievances when he lists the grievances against Clytemnestra and Aegisthus. (*Lib. B.*, 246 sq.) Nor are their grievances noticed later by Electra when she prays to her father. (*Lib. B.*, 332 sq.) Similarly, when the Chorus counsel Electra on what to say when she is to pour the libation at her father's tomb, she is to ask for someone "to kill them [Clytemnestra and Aegisthus] for the life they took." (*Lib. B.*, 121) Of course, the slain Cassandra does not figure in anyone's reckoning on this occasion.

Even so, this Chorus does get involved in the action. Few if any other Choruses in Greek tragedy *do* as much as the Chorus does in *The Libation Bearers*. For it is they who, on their own, improvise the strategy that will induce Aegisthus to return without his armed retinue to the palace upon being bidden by Clytemnestra. That is, it is they who instruct the nurse, another foreign slave-woman, to alter significantly the message she is to carry from Clytemnestra to Aegisthus. (*Lib. B.*, 770–73)

Perhaps it should even be said that this decisive intervention by them is indeed a blow for liberty: for they have affected, or at least they seem to have affected, the course of events in Argos more than ordinary citizens there have done. To act thus is to be, if only for a moment, rulers and not mere slaves, and hence free.

Their boldness takes them only so far, however. The Chorus stand aside, after Aegisthus' death, lest *they* be blamed. (*Lib. B.*, 870–74) But this may be only "realistic" on their part: they did what they *could* do, and there is no sense in now courting trouble for its own sake. Surely one cannot be free if one does not sense the limits of one's powers.

It may be the Chorus, more than the others in *The Libation Bearers*, who sense that there are likely to be troubles after the killing of Clytemnestra. This may be seen early in the play; but they seem to suppress their foreboding. (*Lib. B.*, 463 sq.) They do say after the killing of Clytemnestra that the House of Atreus is now free from the afflictions it had suffered. (*Lib. B.*, 961–71) But this may be due to the euphoria following immediately upon the successful execution by Orestes of his plot. After they see the bloody robe of Agamemnon, from many years before, they observe that no one may escape unscathed, that one tribulation follows another. (*Lib. B.*, 1018–20) It is immediately after this that Orestes begins to see the threatening Furies.

The Chorus seem, by the end of the play (which is shortly thereafter), to have been somewhat tamed. Certainly, they sum up, in a rather sober manner, the threefold tempest that has shaken the House of Atreus.[7]

VII.

It does seem fitting that Orestes should first "see" the Furies as he is talking to the Chorus at the end of *The Libation Bearers*. The Chorus in this play do not see the Furies; neither do we on this occasion. What *we* can see are the Chorus—and, it can be said, it is really the Chorus that Orestes can see as the Furies. After all, the Furies, too, are female (more or less), garbed in black, "foreign," and implacable or fierce. They too can be referred to as the women who "serve" this house. (*Lib. B.*, 10–11, 84, 719, 1048)

The Chorus of slave-women *are* more like Electra than they are like Orestes—or, rather, Electra is more like them than is Orestes. They, unlike Orestes, are more interested in family and "personal" matters than in political, including dynastic and property, matters.

Electra does not have anything to say in *The Libation Bearers* after the killings. Nor do we ever hear either Electra or the Chorus speaking with Clytemnestra. Are Electra and the Chorus counterparts, so to speak, of Clytemnestra? Do they represent the Clytemnestra element on Orestes' side of this conflict? *Aeschylus*'s Electra, it can even be said, existed only in her hatred of her mother. She never expressed any of the reservations about the killing by a child of its parent that Orestes did. She is not permitted to exult over the corpses as Clytemnestra had done in *Agamemnon*. She dies, so to speak, along with Clytemnestra.

The importance of the Chorus is pointed up not only by all they have said and done, and especially by their timely intervention in the action, but also by the very fact that they replace Electra in the second half of the play.

VIII.

There is something enduring about this Chorus of slave-women. The successors to the Chorus of slave-women in *The Libation Bearers* are, in the structure of this trilogy, the Furies in *The Eumenides*. Thus, there is a movement (a sort of decline) from the Chorus of Argive elders in the *Agamemnon* to the Chorus of slave-women in *The Libation Bearers* to the Chorus of Furies in *The Eumenides*.

Perhaps, indeed, one can say that the motivation of the slave-women in *The Libation Bearers* cannot properly be understood without a probing of the psyche of the Furies. But that, too, must be reserved for another occasion. We can notice, however, that there *is* a second chorus that emerges in *The Eumenides*, a silent chorus of Athenians, both men and women. This mixed chorus points to what may be needed to resolve, or at least to ameliorate, the struggle evident throughout the *Oresteia*.

IX.

The male-female struggle, we have noticed, runs throughout the trilogy, if not throughout much of Greek tragedy. It is reflected here in the distinction between the Olympian and the earth divinities, between the new and the old, and between the city and the family.

It takes Athena—who is (and considers herself to be) peculiarly, perhaps even uniquely, associated with both the male and the female—to resolve this struggle as well as it can be among human beings. Male dominance seems to be recognized. (It may even be suggested by the very name of the trilogy, *Oresteia*.) But there is still a significant place recognized for the female element.

The Furies are eventually transformed, with their consent (however much the decisive persuasion was reinforced by judicious threats), into benevolent females serving the household. The Furies in *The Eumenides*, like the slave-women in *The Libation Bearers*, seem to be sobered by their experience, by their need to come to terms with the new order.

Perhaps it can be said of both sets of females in the two plays that they are eventually liberated from implacable passions that, however vital to humanity at one time, have outlived their usefulness, at least in their most primitive form.

2-B.   THE CHARACTER OF A MATRICIDE[8]

I.

In *The Libation Bearers* of Aeschylus, we have noticed, Clytemnestra and Electra never appear on stage at the same time. In the *Electra* plays of Sophocles and Euripides, on the other hand, mother and daughter do appear together and talk to one another. How is Aeschylus' distinctive arrangement of things to be understood?

Clytemnestra and Electra seem to be, we have also noticed, quite similar women in critical respects that distinguish them from Orestes (their son and brother, respectively). Orestes does appear with each of them—and perhaps may best be understood as in fundamental opposition to both of them, so much so as to make it plausible that he should be singled out for a fate radically different from that suffered theretofore in the House of Atreus.

Electra, it is true, does not exhibit in *The Libation Bearers* as bitter a vindictiveness as is evident in the Sophoclean and Euripidean versions of this story. Even so, there is a decisive difference between Electra and her brother. Orestes addresses his murdered father thus (*Lib. B.*, 345–53):

> If only at Ilium, father, and by some Lycian's hands
> you had gone down at the spear's stroke,
> you would have left high fame in your house,
> in the going forth of your children
> eyes' admiration; founded the deep piled bank of earth
> for grave by the doubled water
> with light lift for your household . . .

The Chorus (of slave-women) pick up Orestes' theme and seem to endorse it. Electra, however, wishes a different fate for her father (*Lib. B.*, 363–71):

> No, but not under Troy's ramparts, father, should you have died,
> nor, with the rest of the spearstruck hordes
> have found your grave by Scamandrus' crossing.
> Sooner, his murderers should have been killed, as he was,
> by those they loved, and have found their death,
> and men remote from this outrage
> had heard the distant story.

The Chorus dismiss Electra's sentiments here as "dreaming"—and remind both of them of the killing to be done.

Early in the play, Electra *had* expressed the prayer, "And for myself, grant that I be more temperate of heart than my mother; that I act with purer hand." (*Lib. B.*, 140–41) But this was when she was most conscious of her helplessness. She speaks in a different vein when she is united with Orestes and can look forward to the revenge she longs for (*Lib. B.*, 420–22):

> So let her [Clytemnestra] fawn if she likes.
> It softens not, For we are bloody like the wolf
> And savage born from the savage mother.

Although Electra portrays both Orestes and herself like "the savage mother," what she says applies more to herself than to him, as is evident upon comparing the passages from each that I have quoted about the wished-for fate of Agamemnon.

Orestes seems to see all this from the man's viewpoint: a hero's death and burial are much to be preferred—and thereby the avoidance (for himself included) of bloody business at home. But Electra is very much her mother's daughter: would not Clytemnestra, too, have genuinely mourned the death of Agamemnon at Troy, a death that would have deprived her of revenge?

Clytemnestra and Electra are so much alike that only one of them need appear on stage at a time. The fact that there is not even a reference to Electra after she leaves the stage suggests that she "dies" with Clytemnestra. Or, put another way, this Electra has no meaning after Clytemnestra dies. Thus we see Orestes dealing not only with Clytemnestra as victim but also with Clytemnestra as ally, in the form of Electra.

II.

All this bears upon the conduct and fate of Orestes. He may, we have seen, share some of Electra's passions and motives—but they are not decisive with him. He may even sense that Electra needs to be protected from further participation in the matricide to which he is dedicated. He directs her to go indoors and to keep watch. (*Lib. B.*, 554, 579) She is not involved later in the manner that the Chorus is. A matricide by Electra might have been impossible to purge: *she* had not been commanded, in the manner that Orestes was, by Apollo; rather, she relied only on what we may call "human reasons," reasons of the kind her mother had had in killing Agamemnon. Another way of putting the difference between sister and brother may be to say that Electra has been corrupted by having lived in Argos with Clytemnestra and with the curse of the House of Atreus, whereas Orestes has been fortunate to have lived elsewhere (and, indeed, in the vicinity of Apollo's shrine?) during his formative years.

The Chorus counsel Orestes (*Lib. B.*, 826–30):

> Be not fear struck when your turn comes in the action
> but with a great cry *Father*
> when she cries *Child* to you
> go on through with the innocent murder.

But when the decisive moment comes—a moment that leads to Orestes' only hesitation and to Pylades' only speech in the play—recourse is had by Orestes not to the "Father" counseled by the Chorus but to the name of Apollo (*Lib. B.*, 896–903):

Clytemnestra:
Hold, my son, oh take pity, child, before this breast
where many a time, a drowsing baby, you would feed
and with soft gums sucked in the milk that made you strong.

Orestes:
What shall I do, Pylades? Be shamed to kill my mother?

Pylades:
What then becomes thereafter of the oracles
declared by Loxias [Apollo] at Pytho? What of sworn
oaths? Count all men hateful to you rather than the gods.

Orestes:
I judge that you win. Your advice is good.

Thus, Apollo is set above whatever tie Orestes may have not only to his mother but also to his father and sister. When Orestes comes to begin his justification of the matricide, he stresses the command given to him by Apollo. (*Lib. B.*, 1030)

III.

I have observed that human reasons cannot suffice for matricide. Perhaps the same can be said about what Agamemnon did to Iphigenia (albeit with some degree of divine sanction), about what Clytemnestra did in turn to Agamemnon, and about what Electra would like to do to Clytemnestra. Such reasons are "understandable"—but they leave a pollution that cannot be cleansed but (if anything) may be somewhat expiated. Only a god's command can justify matricide, just as only a divine command can justify what Abraham was prepared to do to Isaac. (No other Jew, no matter how pious, is expected to do on his own what Abraham tried to do to *his* son.)

That is to say, one cannot reason to the conclusion that one's parent should be killed: this highly questionable act cannot be arrived at by analysis and calculation. Therefore, one can argue, Apollo's reason (or Zeus', if Apollo is primarily his agent) must remain mysterious. Otherwise, men too can reach, or can believe they reach, such conclusions on the same basis.[9]

Orestes' deed is not a precedent for the generality of men thereafter: a son can (should?) insist, the next time such a problem arises, "Apollo, or Someone comparable, must speak to me as he did to Orestes! Otherwise, I will commit no matricide." That is, the obviously impious act of matricide (or patricide) can be excused only by the piety of conforming to a god's decree—to the decree of a god with authority to govern the affairs of human beings. The

Oresteia can even be said to confirm, if not also to reinforce, the ancient prohibition of parent killing. Or, put another way, it has always been recognized
by the thoughtful that the rule of the truly wise is superior to the mere rule of
law, however much the rule of law has to be routinely relied upon.

One wonders why Apollo insisted upon having Clytenmestra killed and
why she should have had to be killed by Orestes (and not, say, by Pylades).
Perhaps we are meant to notice both that Apollo does not give reasons and
that Orestes does not ask why *he* should have been chosen. Perhaps we are
also meant to notice that Orestes is, Abraham-like, truly a pious man in that
he does not question the divine message, except in what he says to Pylades.

Human beings cannot help but wonder about why the gods move as they
do, if only to assure themselves that the manifestations that are said to be the
movements of gods are indeed so. The poet, at least, claims to know something critical about how the gods can be expected to act. We must reserve for
another occasion, however, whatever speculations we may dare to entertain
about why it is that Apollo moves as he does to bring to a close in this manner the curse of the House of Atreus. It suffices to notice here both that
Orestes *is* in many ways a stranger to Clytemnestra (with his nurse more of a
mother to him in some ways) and that he can say in response to Clytemnestra's observation, "I think, child, that you mean to kill your mother," "No. It
will be you who kill yourself. It will not be I." (*Lib. B.*, 923–24)[10]

2-C.   THE HUNTING OF ORESTES[11]

I.

In *The Eumenides*, the final play in Aeschylus' *Oresteia* trilogy, there are to
be found a few lines that make up one of the richest passages in ancient dramatic literature. These are the lines about Orestes addressed by the Ghost of
Clytemnestra to the sleeping Furies in the Temple of Apollo at Delphi (*Eum.*,
111–13):

> [H]e is out and gone away like any fawn
> so lightly, from the very middle of your nets,
> sprung clear, and laughing merrily at you.

To speak as I have of these lines may only mean that I have been infected by
the extremism that Clytemnestra represents in this play. Even so, to speak
thus is to be, as with her, not without effect. At the very least, we can work
from this passage, and from the speech in which it is found, to some perhaps
useful suggestions about the entire play, if not about the trilogy as a whole.

II.

In the first play of the trilogy (*Agamemnon*), it will be remembered, the conqueror of Troy returns to his native Argos, after a decade at war, to be greeted ceremoniously by his wife Clytemnestra and thereafter to be slaughtered in his bath by her and her lover, Aegisthus. The sacrifice by Agamemnon of his daughter Iphigenia, at the outset of the Trojan War campaign, had driven his wife to take revenge on him.

In the second play of the trilogy (*The Libation Bearers*), Orestes, the son of Agamemnon and Clytemnestra, returns home in disguise, makes common cause with his sister Electra, and thereupon (with the assistance of his comrade, Pylades, and of the Chorus of slave-women) slaughters his mother and her lover. It is insisted throughout the play that this matricide is ordained by Apollo.

The action of the third play (*The Eumenides*) is conveniently summarized for us in the argument provided in the Loeb Classical Library edition of the trilogy:

> The priestess of Apollo discovers Orestes as a suppliant in the inner shrine of the god at Delphi, and fronting him the Erinyes [Furies] of his mother, a band of fearsome creatures who, wearied with the pursuit of the fugitive, have fallen on sleep. Under promise of his support, Apollo bids Orestes flee to Athens, where he shall submit his case to judgment and be released from his sufferings. The ghost of Clytemnestra rises to upbraid the sleeping Erinyes because of their neglect, whereby she is dishonored among the other dead. Awakened by her taunts, they revile Apollo for that he has given sanctuary to a polluted man whom they rightly pursue by reason of their office—to take vengeance on all who shed kindred blood.
>
> The scene shifts to Athens, whither [Orestes'] pursuers have tracked their prey. Orestes, clasping the ancient image of Pallas [Athena], implores her protection on the plea that the blood upon his hands has long since been washed away by sacred rites and that his presence has worked harm to none who have given him shelter. The Erinyes chant a hymn to bind the soul of their victim with its maddening spell. In answer to Orestes' call, the goddess [Athena] appears and with the consent of the Erinyes undertakes to judge the case, not by herself alone but with the assistance of a chosen number of her best [Athenian] citizens who are to constitute the jury.
>
> The trial opens with Apollo present as advocate of his suppliant and as representative of Zeus, whose commands he has merely to set forth in all his oracles. Orestes, he declares, slew his mother by his express behest. The accused confesses to the deed but urges in his defense that in killing her husband Clytemnestra killed his father and that his accusers [the Erinyes] should justly have taken vengeance upon her. On their rejecting this argument on the ground that the

murderess was not blood kin to him she murdered, Orestes denies blood kinship
with his mother; in which contention he is supported by Apollo, who asserts that
the father alone is the proper parent of the child, the mother being only the nurse
of the implanted seed.

Athena announces that the court, the first to try a case of homicide, is now
established by her for all time to come. The jury cast their ballots; and the
goddess, declaring that it is her duty to pronounce final judgment on the case,
makes known that her vote is to count for Orestes, who is to win if the ballots are equally divided. Proclaimed victor by the tie, Orestes quits the scene;
his antagonists threaten to bring ruin on the land that has denied the justice
of their cause. It is the part of Athena by promises of enduring honors to
assuage their anger; and now no longer Spirits of Wrath but Spirits of Blessing, they are escorted in solemn procession to their sanctuary beneath the Hill
of Ares.[12]

III.

Our concern on this occasion will be in large part with what Clytemnestra had
to say, through her Ghost, to the sleeping Furies. Orestes has fled to Athens,
where (it is said in the Loeb summary) "he shall submit his case to judgment
and be released from his sufferings." It is thereupon said in the summary,
"The ghost of Clytemnestra rises to upbraid the sleeping [Furies] because of
their neglect, whereby she is dishonored among the other dead." The thing
that matters most, it seems, is what happens on earth. (This is, in effect, what
Achilles in Hades says to Odysseus in Book Nine of Homer's *Odyssey*.)

What we have here is Clytemnestra's petition for redress of grievances.
This petition, addressed by the Ghost of Clytemnestra to the sleeping Furies,
consists of some forty lines. These lines have been rendered in this fashion
(*Eum.*, 94–139):

> *Clytemnestra:*
> You would sleep, then? And what use are you, if
> you sleep? It is because of you I go dishonored thus
> among the rest of the dead. Because of those I
> killed my bad name among the perished suffers no
> eclipse but I am driven in disgrace. I say to you
> that I am charged with guilt most grave by these.
> And yet I suffered too, horribly, and from those
> most dear, yet none among the powers is angered
> for my sake that I was slaughtered, and by
> matricidal hands. Look at these gashes in my heart,
> think where they came from. Eyes illuminate the

sleeping brain, but in the daylight man's future
cannot be seen.

Yet I have given you much to lap up, outpourings
without wine, sober propitiations, sacrificed in
secrecy of night and on a hearth of fire for you, at
an hour given to no other god. Now I watch all
these honors trampled into the ground, and he is
out and gone away like any fawn so lightly, from
the very middle of your nets, sprung clear, and
laughing merrily at you. Hear me. It is my life
depends upon this spoken plea. Think then,
O goddesses beneath the ground. For I, the dream of
Clytemnestra, call upon your name.

(*The Furies stir in their sleep and whimper.*)

Clytemnestra:
Oh, whimper, then, but your man has got away and
gone far. He has friends to help him, who are not
like mine.

(*They whimper again.*)

Clytemnestra:
Too much sleep and no pity for my plight. I stand,
his mother, here, killed by Orestes. He is gone.

(*They moan in their sleep.*)

Clytemnestra:
You moan, you sleep. Get on your feet quickly, will
you? What have you yet got done, except to do evil?

(*They moan again.*)

Clytemnestra:
Sleep and fatigue, two masterful conspirators, have
dimmed the deadly anger of the mother-snake.

(*The Chorus start violently, then speak in their sleep.*)

Chorus:
Get him, get him, get him, get him. Make sure.

Clytemnestra:
The beast you are after is a dream, but like the
hound whose thought of hunting has no lapse, you
bay him on. What are you about? Up, let not work's
weariness beat you, nor slacken with sleep so you
forget my pain.

> Scold your own heart and hurt it, as it well
> deserves, for this is discipline's spur upon her own.
> Let go upon this man the stormblasts of your
> bloodshot breath, wither him in your wind, after
> him, hunt him down once more, and shrivel him in
> your vital's heat and flame.

Only after the Ghost concludes her protest and exhortation and then disappears do the Furies awake, revile Apollo for his intervention, and leave in pursuit of the fleeing Orestes.

IV.

At the heart of Clytemnestra's forty-some lines are to be found the lines that make up, I have suggested, one of the richest passages in ancient dramatic literature (*Eum.*, 111–13):

> [H]e is out and gone away like any fawn
> so lightly, from the very middle of your nets,
> sprung clear, and laughing merrily at you.

One interesting feature of these lines is that they direct attention to the *hubristic* character of what Orestes is seen to have done and to be doing. Clytemnestra here is particularly sensitive to what constitutes insolence in such circumstances. Her perceptiveness (or, if you will, Aeschylus') may be confirmed by Aristotle's discussion of anger in the *Rhetoric*. *Hubris*, he says,

> consists in doing or saying things that cause shame to the victim, not in order that anything may happen to you, nor because anything has happened to you, but merely for your own gratification. *Hubris* is not the requital of past injuries; that is revenge. As for the pleasure in *hubris*, its cause is this: men think that by ill-treating others they make their own superiority the greater.[13]

Aristotle concludes his discussion of anger with a long series of instances of the kind of persons with whom men grow angry. "First," he says, "come those who laugh at them, or sneer at them, or make scornful jests about them; for such persons insult them [commit *hubris*]."[14] Indeed most, if not all, of the other instances in this long list can be understood as forms (some concealed, others implied, still others in variant forms) of the open laughing and mocking described in the first instance I have just noticed. This is, it can be said, the crudest (and hence, in a way, the purest) form of *hubris*. It is precisely this form that is to be found at the heart of Clytemnestra's petition. It is bad enough for Orestes to escape, but for him to treat the Furies so cavalierly is (Clytemnestra suggests) insufferable.

It is no wonder then that this image of the mocking Orestes should be central to Clytemnestra's account. But it is not this alone that justifies my suggestion that this is one of the richest passages in ancient dramatic literature, but something else vital to these lines: this description is not really of Orestes but rather of Clytemnestra herself! Orestes is doing anything but laughing merrily at his escape; he is certainly not mocking the Furies. Rather, he is still what he was at the conclusion of *The Libation Bearers*, a man suffering from the inevitable torments of his matricide, a man who is haunted and desperate. Clytemnestra's description of Orestes is, I have suggested, a description of Clytemnestra herself—that is to say, it is a description of an Orestes fashioned in Clytemnestra's image: *she* would laugh merrily and skip derisively whenever she can have her revenge and escape. She thus sees others through her vengeful psyche.

Consider, for example, Clytemnestra's remarkable exultation, in the first play of this trilogy, upon killing Agamemnon. (*Ag.*, 1372 sq.) She "lives" for and in such revenge. Later, she can urge the Furies (we are back at the center of her petition in *The Eumenides*), "Hear me. It is my life [that] depends upon this spoken plea." (*Eum.*, 113–14) These lines reveal Clytemnestra's character most graphically, illuminating thereby everything she has said and done in the trilogy.

Clytemnestra is completely self-centered in her petition to the Furies. She is concerned only for herself. She does not care at all for Orestes as a son, at least so long as he is alive and a threat to her. She never refers either to Agamemnon (except perhaps by implication, in the opening lines of her petition) or to Aegisthus her lover. She wants self-gratification primarily in the form of revenge. Critical to her petition is the fact that a woman has been slain by her child. Even so, there is something monstrous in her: her affront, when Iphigenia (who is not mentioned either) was sacrificed for a political cause, has led her into a career that finds her pursuing relentlessly another child of hers for a personal cause. Only her suffering matters: those who thwart her self-gratification are seen to be scorning and challenging her, thereby inviting even more of her enmity.

V.

Orestes' matricidal deed has unleashed primitive forces, which are seen not only in Clytemnestra's passion but also in the physical forms of those to whom she looks as allies. There are various indications, even in Clytemnestra's petition, of the primitiveness of the Furies and their concerns. No wine is used in their sacrifices, it seems, perhaps because their sacrifices are very old, dating back before human beings developed agriculture and cultivation of the grape.[15] The darkness of the hour of sacrifice for the Furies is indicated, perhaps also the secretiveness. Elsewhere in the play, the Furies invoke their mother, Night. (*Eum.*, 322) These divinities are to be contrasted to the divinities around Zeus, such as Apollo and Athena. The Furies are more or less female, very old, ugly, dark; the Olympians are male in their inclinations, young, beautiful, shining. There is about the Furies something unreasoning, unrelenting, instinctive (even if, at times, self-defeatingly so?). The mother snake, which burrows into the ground, is connected with them. Something of their primitiveness may also be indicated by their lack of inventiveness: they are the only ones in *The Eumenides* who repeat speeches. (*Eum.*, 778 sq., 807 sq.) The upper gods, it can be noticed, were often worshipped on "high places"; the way to reach the lower powers was by scooping out a hollow in the ground to receive the offerings for them.

The primitiveness of the Furies' concern may be seen as well in the insistence throughout the play on hunting motifs, on the almost instinctual hunting dogs that Orestes' deed has unleashed. We have already seen that Clytemnestra has likened Orestes to an escaping fawn. The Furies see themselves as the hound pursuing a bleeding fawn. (*Eum.*, 245 sq.) Even while they sleep, their moans represent the whining and growling of hounds.[16] Perhaps it should also be said that such primitiveness can be expected to continue to manifest itself in the dreams of human beings long after it has had to be repudiated in everyday life.

The strength of the primitive forces here may be seen in Apollo's rationalization during the course of Orestes' trial: he suggests that the true parent of a child is the father, that the female merely nourishes the seed planted by the male. (*Eum.*, 608, 658, 736) Still, Aeschylus and his contemporaries must have observed what we see all the time, that there are some children who very much favor their mothers or their maternal grandparents. The Furies do see themselves as assigned to deal with those men of proud thoughts who flaunt themselves. (*Eum.*, 368) (This again reminds us of the central lines of Clytemnestra's petition.) Whether Orestes is such a man is another question. Certainly he, in his reliance on Apollo, is confident. (*Eum.*, 596 sq.) But does Clytemnestra misread such confidence (if not even piety) as arrogance, because of the condition of her own soul?

Arrogant men do have to be guarded against. Consider the jurisdiction of the Furies: the irreverence exhibited toward the divine, the stranger, or a parent. (*Eum.*, 270–72) Stranger and parents are obviously quite vulnerable to the assaults of the arrogant. Are they not in need, then, of special protection?

Violence, the Furies argue during the trial of Orestes in Athens, "is the child of vanity; but out of health in the heart issues the beloved and the longed-for prosperity." (*Eum.*, 532–37) They plead for a kind of moderation, as does Athena. (*Eum.*, 527, 696) To recognize the virtue of moderation is to encourage reasonableness.

VI.

There is in Clytemnestra's petition no reasonableness, no recognition of any justification or right on Orestes' part. No doubt, a good deal can and should be said for mothers generally. But Clytemnestra's case does seem to be special, as is evident in that Apollo did issue, presumably on the authority of Zeus, an explicit command that her son kill her. The dubiousness of her case is even recognized at the outset of her petition, when she reports that she is "dishonored . . . among the rest of the dead." (*Eum.*, 95–96) She is correct about what her reputation had become and was to be. Thus, a Roman lady in Cicero's time could be disparaged as a "fourpenny Clytemnestra," for having murdered her husband.[17] In any event, Clytemnestra's fellow-dead evidently regard what she had done to Agamemnon as worse than either what Agamennon had done to Iphigenia or what Apollo and Orestes had done to Clytemnestra. Does not this anticipate the final disposition of the controversy?

Still, that there *is* something to Clytemnestra's complaint may be seen in the fact that a place has to be found for the Furies in Athens, once Orestes has been vindicated.[18] I have noticed various conflicts—or one conflict with multiple facets—in the relations between the Furies and the Olympians. (*Eum.*, 149 sq.) In conflict here are the old and the new, the indoor and the outdoor, the female and the male, the dark and the light, the underground and the aboveground.[19]

It can never be a question of completely eliminating either side of any of these pairs. Rather, it is a question, in each instance, of dominance. We see here the ascendancy of the city—the city and its gods, the Olympians—over the family. Apollo was indignant with Clytemnestra over the killing of Agamemnon, a highborn man invested by the gods with the scepter of rule. That he was done in at the hands of a woman using nets made matters worse. (*Eum.*, 625 sq.) But the city in its ascendancy is generous, as well as apprehensive, in dealing with the Furies. Indeed, one can say, the city is generous because it (guided by Athena) is properly apprehensive, aware of the primitive elements in the soul that the Furies minister to. So a place does have to be found for the Furies in Athens, with the transformation of the primitive forces of vengeance into supports for institutionalized love. Certainly, the new gods stress, more than the Furies did, the benefits and privileges of spouses and of love connections. (*Eum.*, 209 sq.) The Olympians themselves did marry and beget children, unlike the repulsive Furies. The political context of these generative activities is stressed. Much more is generally made by the Olympians of political life, of the "outdoor" life of men, so to speak—and of the civic virtues related to such a life. It is not inconsequential in the *Oresteia* that Orestes is recovering his royal patrimony and that his Argos will ever after have a special regard for Athens.[20]

The Furies, in their traditional role, remind us of passions and disruptions that precede the city and upon which the city is built. Still another set of reservations, also useful to keep in mind, is generated not by the primitive Furies who precede the city but by cosmopolitan men who consider themselves to have transcended the city. I can do no more than to indicate here another complaint against Orestes, Apollo, and the like, or at least their natural successors. It is not a complaint that Clytemnestra can make, considering her temperament, but still it should be kept in mind in evaluating what is presented in the *Oresteia*. This complaint is conveniently found presented for us, albeit from the perspective of Descartes, in an essay on political philosophy:

> While the pagan writings [the moral teachings of the Stoics, but also those of Platonic and Aristotelian political philosophy] contain many "exhortations to virtue which are most useful," the "superb and magnificent palaces" of virtue are "built on sand and mud." What the pagans "called by such a beautiful name," i.e., "virtue," is "often only insensibility, or pride, or despair, or parricide." Pagan virtue which claimed to be a mean, and the excellence of man, is therefore often an extreme, and an inhumane, presumptuous, poor-spirited, and even criminal extreme.[21]

Such sentiments should be kept in mind, I have suggested, in assessing and hence truly seeing what Orestes has and has not done.

VII.

Now, a final word, for the time being, about Clytemnestra. I have suggested that she cannot be rehabilitated. She is, by the time of *The Eumenides*, no more than a ghost, a kind of dream for the Furies. In the first play of the trilogy, she (in her full strength) scorns dreams; in the second play, she is (on the eve of her death) terrified of her dreams; and in the third, she has become a dream. In *The Eumenides* the Furies do not begin to speak and act until Clytemnestra goes. They replace her—or, rather, they are always, and she is replaced by them in this situation. Clytemnestra disappears, sinking into the ground, it seems, once her grievances are vented. A place can be found for the Furies, properly reconstructed. But Clytemnestra can only be herself.[22]

She is never referred to by name after her ghost disappears. Agamemnon *is* named by Orestes, when he identifies himself in Athens; and Orestes himself is several times referred to by name. But Clytemnestra's name is used only once in the play, and that once by herself in the petition we have examined. (*Eum.*, 116) One consequence of such a desire for revenge as possessed her, it seems, is that the desire for revenge becomes dominant and her personality becomes secondary or virtually nonexistent. Thus, she becomes almost incoherent in her passion. Everything is seen by her in terms of her desire for revenge, including, as we have seen, the depiction of Orestes as merrily fleeing retribution.[23]

Clytemnestra as a "personality" has no just claim, only Clytemnestra as a mother. But is it the personality (or individual *psyche*) that wants revenge, not truly the mother? Is she virtually destroyed because of what she did to her husband and what she wants to do to her son? Is not everything in the world reduced by her to a hunt, to the demands of the chase, first against her husband, later against her son? All that which is not hunting—including, it would seem, those things for the sake of which one ordinarily hunts, those things that are at rest, the things that endure—all that which is not hunting is forever beyond her aim.

2-D.   QUERIES ABOUT THE *ORESTEIA*[24]

I.

The *Oresteia* of Aeschylus was first performed in Athens in the spring of 458 B.C., a couple of years before the playwright's death. Ever since then, we are told, this trilogy "has been regarded by all sensitive critics as one of the most (if not the most) magnificent and powerful achievements of man in drama."[25] The complexities of the trilogy—the only trilogy that has survived intact from ancient Greece—are testified to by its repeated references to nets, hearkening back to the nets in which Agamemnon was enmeshed so that he could be safely killed by his wife Clytemnestra with the aid of her lover Aegisthus. All of the characters in the trilogy, it seems, are caught in a complicated web, which has been generations in the weaving, which it will take considerable skill and patience to unravel.

An initial inquiry, which could be instructive to consider but which we will do little more than touch upon here, is what Aeschylus had to work with in fashioning his trilogy. His purpose, or understanding of things, might be better grasped by us if we knew the various accounts he had received about the House of Atreus. Related to this approach are what historians suggest about the political circumstances of Athens at the time this trilogy was first presented and what anthropologists suggest about the centuries-long movement there had been in the Mediterranean world from matriarchy to patriarchy. We can do little more than notice to the extent we have, however, the first of the queries that suggest themselves here, What did Aeschylus have to work with in preparing this trilogy?

II.

Our overall concern on this occasion, which presupposes earlier discussions of the *Oresteia*, is with the trial of Orestes for matricide. Our second query here is, Why does not Apollo, who had ordered the matricide, suffice to protect Orestes permanently from the Furies evoked by his mother's blood?

Apollo *is* a party to the dispute in *The Eumenides*: it is his decision that is being judged. If he should undertake to settle Orestes' fate, it would be (or at least it would appear to be) merely another exercise of superior force by the new gods in subduing further the old divinities that the Furies represent. Force is evident in the harsh way that Apollo talks to the Furies in his temple at Delphi, where Orestes had gone for ritual purification. (*Eum.*, 181 sq.)

The new gods make much of *the city* and of *political rule*, or of the life "outdoors." The Furies, on the other hand, make much of *blood* and *the family*, or of the life "indoors." For Apollo, Clytemnestra's primary offense seems to be not that she killed her husband but rather that she had destroyed a king established by Zeus.[26]

Clytemnestra's destruction of a king is carried out when she has him once more indoors—that is, in the bosom of his family. She must resort to stratagem and a private killing because of his vastly superior strength outdoors. But even outdoors she conquers him to the extent of "making" him walk a purple carpet against his will, thereby leading him in the most dramatic fashion possible for her to the bloody sacrifice she plans. (*Ag.*, 905 sq.) In this and other ways she so challenges political rule that Apollo must take offense, even though Apollo is not remembered as a champion of Agamemnon at Troy.[27] The kind of subversion of the political order practiced by Clytemnestra seems to trouble Zeus.

III.

Our next query is, What is the role of Electra in the trilogy? Hers is, we note at the outset, a role quite different in Aeschylus' work from the roles of Electra in the variations upon this story provided by Sophocles and Euripides.

We have seen that Electra is kept out of the way for the actual killing. Neither Electra nor Clytemnestra before her (in killing Agamemnon) is ever Apollo's agent. Electra's motives are "human," not divine. Her longtime hatred of her mother is independent of whatever Orestes had been commanded by Apollo to do. Orestes is moved ultimately by that command, however much he is moved also by a desire for the throne belonging to him as heir in the House of Atreus. Electra has nursed various grievances against her mother over the years.

When the brother and sister invoke their father's spirit at his grave, Orestes addresses Agamemnon more as a king, Electra addresses him more as her father. (*Lib. B.*, 345 sq., 332 sq.) Similarly, in the preceding generation, Agamemnon, in what he had done in sacrificing his daughter, had been moved primarily by political concerns, while Clytemnestra, in killing her husband, had been moved primarily by personal concerns.

Both Electra and the spirited Chorus of slave-women in *The Libation Bearers* are counterparts to Clytemnestra in their fierceness. The fierceness of Clytemnestra had been expressed, it seems, in her mutilation of Agamemnon's corpse and in her killing of Cassandra, which can be seen as a mixing of blood lust and sexuality. (*Lib. B.*, 439–43, *Ag.*, 1444–47) Such a mixing may underlie the resentment of a father-worshipping Electra who has long been suppressed by her domineering mother.

The troubling correspondence between Clytemnestra and Electra may be reflected in the fact that the two women never speak to each other, or even appear together on stage, in Aeschylus' version of the story. Electra is well out of the way before Orestes acts against his mother. (Electra leaves at line 584. Orestes first sees Clytemnestra at line 668 and prepares to kill her at line 930.) Electra is not heard of again after the death of Clytemnestra: it is as if she has no further reason for "existence" once Clytemnestra is killed.[28]

IV.

We must next consider, Why is Athens the site of the great trial to which Orestes and, in effect, Apollo are subjected? In the oldest tradition known to us upon which Aeschylus drew, that of Homer, Athens did not figure as much

of a city. Argos (that is, Mycenae), as the source of the commander of the
Acheans at Troy, was much greater. This was several centuries before the time
of Aeschylus. Some scholars, in attempting to explain the emphasis placed
here upon Athens, make much of the political situation in Athens toward the
end of Aeschylus' life, a life that had had as its most dramatic event the great
victory of the Greeks, under Athenian leadership, against the Persians. The
Oresteia was first produced at a time when it seems to have been very much
in Athens' interest to cement its relationship with Argos.

But there are indications enough within the trilogy itself to account for the
recourse to Athens by the contending parties. Argos, the city of Agamemnon,
is where the pollution of matricide had occurred. Besides, there had been in
that city generations of strife within the House of Atreus. Delphi, another possible site for the trial of Orestes, is Apollo's place, and he is a party to the dispute. Also, Delphi was more "religious" than "political" in its orientation.
Athens, on the other hand, is identified as the place where speeches, or rhetoric, can make a difference. (*Eum.*, 80–82) And it is rhetoric that, for all of its
deviousness, is particularly concerned with the pursuit of justice, giving that
pursuit its vitality. Athena, in her efforts at reconciliation, invokes Zeus of the
Assembly. (*Eum.*, 970 sq.) This can remind us of the workings of the Athenian assembly in a democratic era, the era of Aeschylus.[29]

Rhetoric is also seen in the uses made of persuasion in *The Eumenides*. The
only substantial persuasion in the trilogy theretofore had been when
Clytemnestra had prevailed upon Agamemnon to submit to the purple carpet.
(*Ag.*, 905 sq.) Later, Clytemnestra came close enough to persuading Orestes
not to kill his mother that Pylades had to remind Orestes of Apollo's mandate.
(*Lib. B.*, 896–903)

The specialness of Athens is also suggested by the evenly divided votes
cast by the Athenian jury in the trial of Orestes. The Athenians seem to appreciate what can be said on each side of this momentous conflict. Is the prudence of the Athenians reflected in the fact that they "deliberately" leave this
matter, finally, for Athena to decide? (*Eum.*, 707 sq.)

The choice of Athens as the site of the trial may turn ultimately upon the
need to have Athena herself resolve this conflict. Athena, by the fifth century,
is made as much of in Athens as she is anywhere else in the Greek world.

V.

Our next query is, Why is Athena needed? The simple answer may be, Because only she among the gods, with the possible exception of Zeus, can do
what is needed and do it in the way it is done here. It is instructive how Apollo

and Athena in turn speak of and to the Furies when they first confront them in *The Eumenides*. Apollo is consistently harsh, unable to say a civil word to them. Athena is struck by their bizarre appearance, but she is still open to what they have to say for themselves. (*Eum.*, 405–14, 644) She can, in talking with them, both cajole and threaten. Apollo can only threaten, and it is not clear whether his threats can restrain the Furies to the extent or in the way that Athena wants to restrain them. (*Eum.*, 794 sq.)

The reliance upon Athena is related to the superiority of rule by the truly wise.[30] Also, she reminds the Furies that she has access to Zeus' thunderbolts, an access that may follow naturally from her wisdom. (*Eum.*, 826–29) Is the female, implacable though the Furies first appear to be, shown to be intrinsically more moderate than the male in *talking* to others? (*Eum.*, 881 sq., 970 sq.) Even the "mannish" Clytemnestra is shown, at the end of the first play, to be better than Aegisthus in talking with the angry Chorus of Argive elders. Athena knows that there are at least two sides to every controversy. (*Eum.*, 428) The Furies seem to be challenged, in turn, by Athena's suggestion that they should want to act justly as well as to be called just. (*Eum.*, 430–31)[31]

However much Athena identifies herself with the male cause, she does have a female aspect. She can bridge, therefore, the gulf between male and female in a way that no one else in the trilogy can. Eventually, Athena can even offer to share with the Furies some of her sovereignty in Athens. (*Eum.*, 832 sq.)

VI.

Our next query is, Why does Athena vote as she does? The simplest answer may be, Because this is in accordance with the will of Zeus himself, who has ordained all these matters. She certainly will not, perhaps cannot, defy that will as she understands it. Even the willful Clytemnestra had, in the first play of the trilogy, invoked Zeus as "accomplisher." (*Ag.*, 973–74)[32]

Athena's disavowal of the female element in herself can strike us as somewhat forced, if not even as bizarre. (*Eum.*, 734 sq.)[33] But however she repudiates the female element, she cannot simply do without it—and so she secures a place in the city for the Furies, who are representatives of the female element in its most primitive form. If there is to be a city, the political or male element must be dominant; but it cannot be exclusive, without risking the very foundations of human life and hence the city itself.

Judicious balancing is needed for a proper resolution of that conflict in the House of Atreus that had seen political rule undermined by intrafamily passions in one generation after another. Athena's vote in the trial of Orestes is more complicated than the *yes* or *no* of which a jury is capable. She can *say* more than the jury can, both warning and enticing the Furies as she finds a place for them in the theological-political order that is to replace the old order in which blood ties and bloody feuds had been dominant.[34]

VII.

Our final query about the *Oresteia* on this occasion is, How *are* things left at the end? That is, what does Aeschylus really expect for the long run? Does he work from the fact, if fact it be, that there is no further intrafamily killing in the tradition from which he took his story?[35]

Aeschylus knows that it is folly to attempt to eliminate the Furies altogether from the life of a community. In fact, Orestes himself promises, in effect, that he will play a Furies-like role if any future generation of Argives should ever repudiate the debt that he now owes to the Athens that secured his salvation. (*Eum.*, 762–77) This is in his last speech of the trilogy.[36]

We can endorse here what some anthropologists suggest about the movement evident in this trilogy—the centuries-long movement from *feud* to *law*, from *family* to *city*, from *old* to *new*. We add the suggestion that what Agamemnon and Clytemnestra did in turn—one acting for the political order, the other for the family order—are deeds of a fundamental character, pursued regardless of the consequences to themselves personally.

However astutely Athena worked things out on this occasion, such matters do have to be reworked as circumstances change. Further study of these plays is required in order to determine what hope Aeschylus truly held out for mankind, and what reservations he had about both human beings and gods, in the age of the Olympians, an enlightened age that is still with us in critical respects. *Have* the eternal Furies, the dark recesses of the human soul being what they are, been adequately provided for as well as guarded against by the wisdom of Athena in the service of the will of Zeus?

NOTES

1. This talk was given at a Staff Seminar of the Basic Program of Liberal Education for Adults, The University of Chicago, Chicago, Illinois, February 13, 1982.

The Richmond Lattimore translation of the *Oresteia* is used here and in Parts B, C, and D of this chapter. The parenthetical citations in the text (except when Greek terms are commented upon) are to lines in the Lattimore translation of this trilogy as published by the University of Chicago Press (with *The Agamemnon* abbreviated as *Ag.*, *The Libation Bearers* as *Lib. B.*, and *The Eumenides* as *Eum.*). A translation for the theater by David Grene and Wendy Doniger O'Flaherty has also been published by the University of Chicago Press. See chapter 4, note 55. See, for useful introductions to the trilogy, David K. Nichols, "Aeschylus' *Oresteia* and the Origin of Political Life," *Interpretation*, Autumn 1980, p. 83; Mera Flaumenhaft, "Seeing Justice Done: Aeschylus' *Oresteia*," *Interpretation*, Fall 1989, p. 69.

Summaries of the three plays of the *Oresteia* are provided in section II of Part C of chapter 2 of this collection. See also chapter 2, note 7.

2. Gilbert Murray, *Aeschylus: The Creator of Tragedy* (Oxford: Clarendon Press, 1940), p. 179. See the text at note 25 of chapter 2 of this collection.

3. If Orestes is considered dead by Clytemnestra, he can then be for her, naturally enough, someone to be mourned, however much she had feared (if not even hated) him earlier. See Sophocles, *Oedipus Tyrannos* 707–25, 849–57. See also the text at note 8 of chapter 4 of this collection.

4. See, on the proper spheres of men and woman respectively, Plato, *Meno* 71E. See also the text at note 49 of chapter 4 of this collection. Compare Plato, *Republic* 455D sq., 458C sq., 466C sq., 540C. See, on the *Meno*, chapter 6-A.

5. The frenzied Dionysian cult, in which women figured prominently, was also from the East. See, e.g., Euripides, *The Bacchae*. See also chapter 1, note 117. See, on the femaleness of the Furies, as well as of Clytemnestra, Flaumenhaft, "Seeing Justice Done," p. 88. See, on Apollo's preference for the paternal, Flaumenhaft, p. 96.

6. Much is made in the *Oresteia* of family relations. We hear in *The Libation Bearers* from no citizens of Argos aside from Clytemnestra and her children. The choral place occupied in *Agamemnon* by elders of the city is taken in *The Libation Bearers* by foreign slave-women. Is there any sign visible to everyone that something is wrong in Argos because of the usurpation by Clytemnestra and Aegisthus? Compare the effects of a most palpable plague in the Thebes of Sophocles' *Oedipus Tyrannos*. See chapter 4. Apollo *is* concerned in both instances, but his displeasure is indicated in quite different ways in Thebes and in Argos, establishing (if not even reflecting) fundamental differences between those two cities. (Thebes and Argos/Mycenae dominate the thirty-two extant Greek tragedies.)

7. Here, in the final lines of *The Libation Bearers* (1065–76), is the Chorus's account of the House of Atreus:

Here on this house of the kings the third storm has broken, with wind from the inward race, and gone its course. The children were eaten: there was the first affliction, the curse of Thyestes. Next came the royal death, when a man and lord of Achaean armies [Agamemnon] went down killed in the bath. Third is for the savior. He [Orestes] came. Shall I call it that, or death? Where is the end? Where shall the fury of fate be stilled to sleep, be done with?

8. This talk was given at a Staff Seminar of the Basic Program of Liberal Education for Adults, The University of Chicago, Chicago, Illinois, December 6, 1975.

See, on the translation of the *Oresteia* used here and on the parenthetical citations in the text, chapter 2, note 1.

Summaries of the three plays are provided in section II of Part C of chapter 2 of this collection. See also chapter 2, note 7.

9. Does not a poet do so, but in a different sense, in describing what the gods order? See the text at note 10 of chapter 2 of this collection. See also chapter 1, note 65; chapter 4, note 54.

10. I am reminded, by the use of the mother-nurse relation here, of how the incestuous relationship is made somewhat palatable in the Louis Malle movie, *Murmur of the Heart*. See also the text at note 22 of chapter 4 of this collection; chapter 4, note 11. See, on the poet's knowing how the gods act, chapter 2, note 9. See, on the rule of the truly wise being superior to the rule of law, Plato, *Republic* 294A. See also Plutarch, *Pelopidas*, XXI, Murray, *Aeschylus*, p. 202. Compare chapter 12, note 189.

11. This talk was given at a Staff Seminar of the Basic Program of Liberal Education for Adults, The University of Chicago, Chicago, Illinois, December 8, 1979.

See, on the translation of the *Oresteia* used here and on the parenthetical citations in the text, chapter 2, note 1.

Summaries of the three plays are provided in section II of this talk. See also chapter 2, note 7.

12. Aeschylus, *Oresteia*, pp. 270–71 (Loeb Classical Library, 1926). The archaic-sounding language used in this summary is appropriate for Aeschylus. Nothing is ever said (or has to be said?) in the trilogy as to why Agamemnon is not pursued by the Furies for his sacrifice of his daughter, Iphigenia. See Aeschylus, *The Libation Bearers* 242.

13. Aristotle, *Rhetoric*, II, 2. See, on the *Rhetoric* generally, Larry Arnhart, *Aristotle on Political Reasoning* (DeKalb: Northern Illinois University Press, 1981). See also the text at note 29 of chapter 2 of this collection.

14. Aristotle, *Rhetoric,* II, 2. See Plato, *Greater Hippias* 291E–292A.

15. See George Thomson, *The Oresteia of Aeschylus* (Cambridge: Cambridge University Press, 1938), notes to lines 106–9.

16. See Thomson, *The Oresteia of Aeschylus*, notes to line 117. See also Aeschylus, *The Eumenides* 131–32, 147, 327.

17. The "fourpenny" came from the fact that this lady charged men four pence for admission to her presence. See *Basic Works of Cicero* (New York: Modern Library edition, 1951), p. 295.

18. Clytemnestra, we have noticed, cannot be personally rehabilitated. What she *is* continues: she cannot be reasoned with, even to the extent that the Furies can be, encouraged as they are by Athena's reminders that *she* has access to Zeus' thunderbolts. See chapter 2, note 34. See also conclusion, note 3.

19. The critical female-male conflict was anticipated, on the Areopagus, by the battle of the Amazons and Theseus. See Aeschylus, *The Eumenides* 628, 685 sq.

20. See section VII of Part D of this chapter.

21. Richard Kennington, *René Descartes*, in Leo Strauss and Joseph Cropsey, eds., *History of Political Philosophy* (Chicago: University of Chicago Press; 3rd ed., 1987), p. 423. See also, on Descartes, George Anastaplo, *The American Moralist: Essays on Law, Ethics, and Government* (Athens, Ohio: Ohio University Press, 1992), p. 83; George Anastaplo, "The Forms of Our Knowing: A Somewhat Socratic Introduction," in Douglas A. Ollivant, ed., *Jacques Maritain and the Many Ways of Knowing* (Washington, D.C.: The Catholic University Press of America, 2002), pp. 1, 13.

22. See Thomson, *The Oresteia of Aeschylus*, notes to lines 130–39, 155–58. See also Aeschylus, *The Eumenides* 155; chapter 1, note 20.

23. See Thomson, *The Oresteia of Aeschylus*, notes to lines 95–102. Does the hunting motif here go back to the sacrifice of Iphigenia to the offended goddess, Artemis, the huntress? If so, the story of the House of Agamemnon comes full circle, with Apollo (the twin brother of Artemis) restraining the hunting of Iphigenia's brother, Orestes.

24. This talk, sponsored by the Department of Government, was given at the University of Texas, Austin, Texas, March 26, 1991. The original title of this talk was "Queries About the *Oresteia* and the Pursuit of Justice."

See, on the translation of the *Oresteia* used here and on the parenthetical citations in the text, chapter 2, note 1. See, on the relations between Orestes and Pylades, George Anastaplo, "Constitutionalism and the Good: Explorations," 70 *Tennessee Law Review* 737, 765 (2003).

Summaries of the three plays are provided in chapter 2–C, section II. See also chapter 2, note 7.

25. Rex Warner, introduction, *Aeschylus, The Oresteia* (Edmund. D. A. Morshead, trans.) (New York: A. Colish; Limited Editions Club, 1961), p. ix. See the text at note 2 of chapter 2 of this collection.

26. See Aeschylus, *The Eumenides* 625f. Apollo's enmity toward Cassandra is different. See Aeschylus, *Agamemnon* 1072 sq. Apollo had been cheated of love by Cassandra. See, on the relation of prophecy to character, the text at note 3 of chapter 3 of this collection. Had Cassandra avoided giving Apollo the love she had promised, in exchange for the gift of prophetic powers, because she divined that that would have been even worse than what did happen to her? Is it not instructive to assume, that is, that Cassandra already had the gift of prophecy from Apollo at the time she refused him? On the other hand, why did not Apollo (as god of prophecy) anticipate what Cassandra would do to him? See the text at note 7 of chapter 3 of this collection. Does not Apollo conduct himself with respect to Cassandra somewhat as Clytemnestra conducts herself with respect to Orestes: he uses Clytemnestra as his agent just as Clytemnestra uses the Furies as her agents? These are side queries as we pursue our principal line of inquiry on this occasion.

27. Compare Aeschylus, *The Eumenides* 456–58, for Athena's championing of Agamemnon at Troy.

28. See chapter 2–A, section VII, and chapter 2–B, section I. It should again be noticed that Electra is dealt with differently in versions of this story by other poets.

29. See, on rhetoric, chapter 2, note 14. See also chapter 2, note 13.

30. See, e.g., chapter 1, notes 3, 44, 65. See also Plato, *Republic* 473C–D, Plato, *Letters* VIII, 336A–B. Compare chapter 2–B, section VI.

31. See, on the universal desire for the good, the opening sentences of Aristotle's *Nicomachean Ethics* and *Politics*. Compare chapter 1–A. Compare also the text at note 60 of chapter 5 of this collection. Compare as well the text at note 75 of chapter 5 of this collection. See chapter 12, note 46, where this proposition about the pervasiveness of the good is put to a severe test. See, for even a Clarence Darrow's apprehension of the divine, chapter 11, note 19. See also conclusion, note 3.

32. See Aeschylus, *Agamemnon* 1035 sq., 1481 sq., Aeschylus, *The Eumenides* 614 sq., 794 sq., 972–73, 1045–46. See also Aeschylus, *Agamemnon* 1577 sq.

33. This is anticipated by Apollo in Aeschylus, *The Eumenides* 657 sq.

34. See the text at note 52 of chapter 4 of this collection. Clytemnestra gets all that *she* gets, such as it is, through her surrogates, the Furies. She remains unchanged. Death does not make her (or anyone else?) more thoughtful than they were in life, it seems; death may only make one's character more apparent. See Plato, *Apology* 40B–41C; Dante, *Inferno*. See chapter 2, note 18.

35. Consider the alternative versions of this story, as in Euripides, one that can have Orestes finding a still-living Iphigenia (who was not sacrificed by her father after all!). But then there are also versions of the Trojan War story that have only an image of Helen taken to Troy by Paris. This is, in one sense, true of Homer's account also. That is, to whom is the divine Helen truly available? See George Anastaplo, "On Trial: Explorations," 22 *Loyola University of Chicago Law Journal* 765, 1053 n. 337 (1991).

36. See the text at note 20 of this collection. See also Aeschylus, *The Eumenides* 696 sq., 824 sq.

3

Jonah and the Ninevites[1]

I.

The *Book of Jonah*, a particularly vivid Biblical account of repentance, is read as part of the service on the afternoon of Yom Kippur, the annual Day of Atonement for Jews. It is said in a famous sermon on *Jonah*—by a preacher in Herman Melville's *Moby Dick*, "Shipmates, I do not place Jonah before you to be copied for his sin, but I do place him before you as a model for repentance. Sin not; but if you do, take heed to repent of it like Jonah."[2]

One may wonder, of course, how much Jonah truly repents. Much more striking, perhaps, is the repentance by the Ninevites after hearing the preaching of Jonah. (The other characters in this story had nothing, so far as we know, to be penitent about aside, of course, from the problem of the divinities they had happened to worship.) Contributing to the remarkableness of this Israelite story of Ninevite penitence is the fact that the Ninevites (or Assyrians) were enemies of Israel. Is there an indication that Jonah did not want to serve enemies thus? Or that he longed for their destruction? Or should we simply say that he did not understand how he was serving Israel by ministering to the Ninevites?

It is indicative of the "ecumenical" character of God's concern that this book should be used as it is at the Yom Kippur service. Do the Jews, as well as God, mean for this to be noticed?

II.

One can wonder what moves Jonah both at the beginning and at the end of this book. He evidently wants God to be more implacable, or less available, for the Ninevites than he had wanted Him to be for himself. (Had he ever really thought he could escape God's command and sanctions?)

But Jonah's intriguing character or career is *not* our primary concern on this occasion. Rather, we are much more concerned about what is said, or at least what is taken for granted, in the *Book of Jonah* about rules and standards (or "the rule of law") and about the consequences of disregarding such rules and standards.

Since the character and career of Jonah do seem critical concerns of the author, one cannot fully understand the book as a whole (or any important facet of it, such as what is said there about rules) without taking Jonah himself into account. In any event, one cannot help but wonder what character is presupposed by the gift of prophecy that Jonah evidently exercised.[3]

III.

"Everyone" knows the story of Jonah: many more people "know" the story than have read the *Book of Jonah*. Even so, what the story "says" depends in large part upon the preconceptions one brings to it.

Christians (including the earliest Christians, if not Jesus himself) see the *Book of Jonah* primarily as a prefiguration of the story of the Crucifixion, Burial (for three days), and Resurrection of Jesus. So massive may such an interpretation, or later development, be that the original intention of the author (at least as his original readers understood it) can be lost sight of.

Some Christians even go so far as to see the story as literally true. Arguments are heard from time to time about what kind of fish this would have had to have been (to have had a large enough mouth, throat, and stomach) and what the physical effects would ordinarily be upon a man thus swallowed and held.[4]

Where the early Christians saw the story primarily in terms of *their* faith, and where medieval Jews such as Maimonides saw it primarily in terms of *their* way of life, cannot we consider what it says to and (more important for our purposes) *about* all mankind?

IV.

Nineveh is judged by God to be wicked—and the Ninevites themselves are moved by Jonah's preaching to recognize their evil ways and to turn away from them. (3:3–9) Does not genuine wickedness require that one sense, at least before one becomes altogether hardened, that one is not acting as one should? Violent madmen or fierce animals may not be truly wicked, however dangerous and destructive they may be. The same may be said of tornadoes or earthquakes. An element of understanding is required if wickedness is to be diagnosed—and certainly if preaching is to be resorted to.[5]

The Ninevites were held accountable by standards that most of the rest of the world respected as well. But the rest of the world is usually not dramatically threatened with destruction for *its* offenses: there does seem to be something distinctive about the moral condition of the Ninevites. Do most other peoples, most of the time, conduct themselves better than the Ninevites did in the time of Jonah?

All this suggests that most people most of the time do have access to the moral standards by which they should live. This access seems to come more or less naturally for them, certainly not by means of any genuine revelation of the kind provided on a systematic basis through Moses and the other prophets recorded in the Bible. Is it not even implied by the Bible that there are moral standards generally available to human beings that reason can discern, at least to some degree?[6]

V.

In the ordinary course of things, it can be said, wickedness brings its own punishment (that is, its own deprivation) with it. This, too, is natural—as is the ability of reason to perceive the connections between wickedness and punishment.

But wickedness can so distort one's understanding as to conceal from one the harm one is doing to oneself as well as to others. Besides, the fruits of wickedness may be so plentiful and attractive, at least in the short run, as to beguile both the reasoning of the wicked and the judgment of observers. In this and in other ways the wicked can harm not only themselves but also others, if only as bad examples. Especially is this so when wickedness is practiced on a large scale. The community is usually a moral teacher, in that it is a visible manifestation of the law. But the authority of the law, when devoted to the cause of wickedness, can be particularly pernicious. And so the dramatic destruction of a city is sometimes called for, destruction that does not wait for nature to take its course. That is, something dramatic may be required when a widely-known city is remarkably wicked, especially when its destruction can serve to instruct others about the perils of wickedness.

The destruction of Sodom and Gomorrah not only saved the people of those two cities from further wickedness but also served the rest of mankind, especially when the story of their destruction was perpetuated and explained in an authoritative manner.[7] Books of revelation, which report divine doings that are not otherwise apparent to the reason of most men, can be said to transcend nature. Without such revelation, it can also be said, most men could not appreciate the full effects either of wickedness or of virtue.

The full scope of revelation for people may be seen in accounts of what is yet to come, along with accounts of what has already happened. That is, both prediction and explanation (or "history") are to be seen in revelation. The natural understanding rarely provides such dramatic accounts.[8]

Still, it may seem only fair, before dramatic (or supernatural) means are resorted to in response to wickedness, that some extraordinary effort be made on behalf of those about to be destroyed. And so, the "forty days" warning is sent by God to the Ninevites. This is the kind of direct and explicit information that nature does not supply.[9] Not only may it seem fair that such an extraordinary development should be predicted, but its prediction and fulfillment do tend to make a considerable impression upon others who hear about what has happened.

But, someone might ask, why was not a special warning also issued to the people of Sodom and Gomorrah? The answer could be that they too had had a sufficient dramatic effort made on their behalf—in the form of the plea made to God by Abraham to spare the city, a plea that depended for its success upon the existence there of a saving remnant among the people.[10] Perhaps prophecy depends as well upon such a saving remnant—upon a few who can be receptive to the divine word. If there is not a receptive element in the community, the efforts of an Abraham or of a Jonah can have no effect. If, on the other hand, the Abraham test is passed by a people, then the Jonah effort can usefully be made.

These are determinations made by God or by His prophets. That there should have to be such determinations suggest the limits of ordinary reasoning and hence of nature in the everyday world. From the Christian point of view, it can be said that the world needed to be prepared, through a proper development of the people of Israel, before Jesus could usefully appear to perform *his* mission.[11]

One way or another, people need to be taught that there *is* available a punishment to fit each crime. Consider, by way of illustration, a sign I saw in a Mennonite shop in an Ontario small town a couple of days ago:

> Notice to Shoplifters:
> His eye is on the sparrow—and you can be sure
> He is watching you, too.

This, too, can be considered prophecy of sorts, in however low a key.

It should be evident from these observations how prophecy can be useful for deterring misconduct, even though it may not be absolutely needed for good conduct. Does not the Bible itself, especially the Hebrew Bible, or the Old Testament, recognize that there have been, and still can be, *good* men and women who have not had the benefit of genuine revelation? But the Bible does seem to raise the question of whether the very best human being is possible without genuine revelation, whatever the lawgivers and poets of pagan peoples have relied upon for their guidance. This is, in effect, a question about the status among us of *piety*.

Is revelation needed, then, primarily for the "extreme" cases—for the most complete piety and for the most disturbing wickedness?

VI.

The limits of ordinary reasoning in extreme cases and the attractions of divine intervention may also be seen in the sort of "situation" faced by the sailors on the ship with which the fleeing Jonah had booked passage. These sailors are confronted by a terrible storm. (1:4–5) So far as they can see, we are told, it is not for anything they had personally done. Should they have noticed that something was wrong with Jonah? Should they have investigated him more carefully? The author does not suggest this, although Melville's preacher seems to do so in his effort to make sense of everything.[12]

The sailors, when all their efforts seem about to fail in the face of an im-placable (if not even determined) storm, resort to prayer (each man to his own god) and thereafter to the casting of lots. (1:5–7) The prayers prove in-effective, unless it is understood that such prayers were a necessary prelude to a useful recourse to lots, which recourse may be considered a kind of revelation-on-demand.[13]

The lots proved most revealing—and Jonah, upon having been thus pointed to, confirms that *he* is indeed the target of the storm. (1:7–10) He rec-ommends that he be thrown overboard. (1:10–11) These sailors, however, are remarkably restrained: they refuse to act at once on what Jonah reveals; rather, they turn again to vigorous rowing, in order to save the ship without recourse to the desperate measure recommended by Jonah. (1:13–14) These sailors have long intrigued me. They seem such a decent, reasonable crew. Even so, must not the author of the *Book of Jonah* implicitly regard them as impious—or, at least, as *not* pious—in their desperate efforts to avoid the harsh necessity evidently imposed upon them by the divine will?[14]

The sailors are much moved by the cessation of the storm upon the "sacri-fice" of Jonah to the sea. They are at once converted, it seems, to the worship of the God of Israel. (1:15–16) We are not told how this changes them: would they, for example, be more prompt thereafter in despatching a Jonah?[15]

We can see in the experiences of the sailors the uses of revelation in making sense of what is today called "the human condition," that state of existence that finds terrible (and even seemingly inexplicable) things happening to good people. Revelation was needed both in order to permit the sailors to understand what was happening to them and in order to guide them as to how to act to save themselves. The salvation of oneself in such circumstances, the pious man would add, need not be considered limited to securing access to physical survival: it may suffice that one is permitted to understand, by virtue of revelation, that there is an overall purposefulness to the world that one should accept on faith. An undue concern for one's physical survival, which can be no more than temporary in any event, can deflect one from the kind of understanding that is available to the truly pious man who submits himself completely to the divine will.

But all this is not to deny what is also apparent from the story of Jonah: there is available what we would call a natural understanding that suffices for much of human activity in this world and provides a useful guide to decent conduct. Most ships do sail successfully: most sailors know how to conduct themselves properly most of the time, just as most cities do promote morality. Yet extreme situations are bound to arise that make many wonder, if not even despair, about the overall sense and sensibleness of things.

VII.

Prophets such as Jonah, and perhaps even more those who choose to write about them, do seem to help reassure mankind about the ultimate sense and sensibleness of things. This they do by proclaiming an "understanding" of a God who is omniscient, omnipotent, just and yet merciful, and radically inscrutable—in short, a God who is not truly to be understood but *is* to be obeyed and relied upon.[16]

The inscrutability of God is reflected even in the fact that someone such as Jonah should be His instrument, along with a storm, a fish, a gourd, and a worm. (1:4, 17; 4:6–7) Why should Jonah happen to have had access to the critical (indeed precise) information he had—say, about the circumstances of the sailors and thereafter of the Ninevites? Why did not the Jonah who knew so much about things know even more than he apparently did about himself, about the limits of his power to avoid God's demands, and about what would happen to him if he did embark on efforts of evasion and recrimination?[17]

All this reminds us of a question suggested by students of the Bible such as Maimonides, who insisted upon the moral character as well as the high level of intelligence required in the prophet.[18] Must Jonah, despite his evasiveness and his recriminations, be considered, at heart, a good man, indeed even a very good man? This may perhaps be seen in the prayer he is given to recite while still in the belly of the fish, a prayer that anticipates his deliverance. (2:2–9) One may see in this anticipation the confidence of the truly pious man?[19]

Who should we say is the author of this book? Is it Jonah himself, or at least someone instructed as to critical details by a prophet such as Jonah if not by God Himself? Do even the evasiveness and recriminations of Jonah reflect a desire on his part to see the world as a coherent and predictable whole?[20] But does he not come to recognize that God is always able to go one step further than even Jonah can anticipate? Is Jonah silenced, but not necessarily fully persuaded, by what is done and said to him at the end of the story?

Thus, that which had required a great storm earlier, and a great fish, can be taught again later in an unexpected way (even for Jonah?) by means of a gourd and a worm, especially if a story is made using such experiences. (4:2–11) All this suggests that the great and the small, the past, the present, and the future—in short, the world—are all bound together in ways that no man can *know* but that everyone can be taught *is* somehow so.

One can see in this story the difficulty of fathoming the depths of God's understanding of things, a difficulty evident in any effort to grasp why it is that Jonah should be the one used as he is here. This reminds us, in turn, that other difficulties await us when these are solved, even more serious difficulties that point up the specialness of the truly pious man and the profound difference between him and any human being who relies upon the natural understanding alone.[21]

VIII.

How was it that Jonah proved so effective with the Ninevites. I have suggested that there must have been a receptive element among them.[22] What might have Jonah said to appeal to that receptive element among the Ninevites? It is difficult to see that a threat of impending destruction would suffice, with nothing more.

What more could Jonah have said to the them? Why not *that* which is so interesting to us, as it has been to the millennia of readers—the story of the call that had come to Jonah from God, the efforts Jonah had made to run away from God, the storm, the sailors, and the fish, and finally Jonah's submission

to his unavoidable God? "All this has just happened to me," he could well testify, "and I have been forced to warn you, even though I did not (and still do
not) want to do so." This kind of sermon could very well have had a salutary
effect on the Ninevites. An audience would certainly be likely to notice this
kind of message.

With these observations in mind we can begin to answer one of the questions we have been asking, Why was Jonah chosen as the prophet to the
Ninevites? Perhaps he was chosen, at least in part, because he could be depended upon to respond as he did—and all with a view to having, at the end,
the story he can tell the Ninevites (and the even more subtle story, which includes Jonah's experience with the gourd, that can eventually be told to generations of readers of the Bible).

Jonah's effectiveness in these circumstances—his usefulness both to the
Ninevites and to us—may depend in part, therefore, upon his misconduct.
Similarly, it can be said, the full force of Oedipus' conduct, with respect to
his father and his mother, depended upon the vigorous efforts made by
Oedipus (after hearing the dreadful oracle) to avoid the fate that was said to
await him.[23]

Do not these observations, in turn, reflect a view of the whole not altogether susceptible to the natural understanding? Do poets and prophets alike
report on things that they do not themselves truly understand?

IX.

And yet, poets and prophets can be understood to support, by their inspired
sayings, the conclusions arrived at otherwise by the natural understanding.

Among the things that the natural understanding is aware of is the importance in human affairs of a reliance upon divine providence. How else are we
to explain the fact that each of the sailors on the ship has some divinity to pray
to, or the fact that it is generally believed among them, as later among the
Ninevites, that prayer and repentance can have a good effect,[24] or the fact that
human affairs are widely believed to be somehow keyed to the divine will?
The captain on the troubled ship can even arouse the sleeping Jonah so that
he might add his prayers and divinity to the others. (1:6)

Faith in the God of Israel is not required for many of the salutary effects
that the natural understanding associates with various religious opinions. On
the other hand, a genuine divinity would seem to be needed if there are to be
miracles of the kind exhibited in the career of Jonah in this story.

Still, *tales* of miracles are not infrequent, and can be persuasive, even in
circumstances where it is clear to others that no true divinity is involved.

Aside from all this there is the Maimonidean query as to whether even God ever acts through miracles as ordinarily understood.[25]

Thus, the story of Jonah can have a salutary effect, even if it should not be "literally" true. Of course, our understanding might be served by probing into what "really happened" on that occasion. But this may be virtually impossible, perhaps absolutely impossible, to determine conclusively. This may be true with respect to any other highly unusual event in history. This may be another way of indicating that there is an unbridgeable gulf between reason and revelation—that is, between one approach that makes much of general propositions about nature and another approach that makes much of dramatic particulars.

The Ninevites *are* moved to repentance by an Israelite prophet, more so it seems than Jonah is himself thus moved. Indeed, Nineveh, in repenting, did something that is never said about Jerusalem in the Bible. The repentance of Nineveh was not permanent, however dramatic it was on this occasion. That is, was not Nineveh eventually destroyed by the Lord?[26]

But, in another sense, Nineveh's repentance was permanent—in that it has been so graphically recorded as to provide a reminder to the people of Israel and to their successors (Jews, Christians, and Muslims across the centuries and in many lands)—a constant reminder of what the God of Israel is capable of and how limited, and yet somehow exalted, His people can be.

In this way, then, the enemies of Israel were permitted to be of service to the Chosen People of God. That the God of Israel should thus make use, for the good of His people, of even their enemies is something well worth remembering on Yom Kippur, with its call to repentance. The people of Israel are thereby raised up, even as they humble themselves before their God.

Even those who can rely on no more than a natural grasp of these matters can see how this story contributes to an understanding of not only the nature of piety but also of the nature of nature and hence of the nature of understanding itself. Is it not fitting and proper therefore, that the *Book of Jonah* should end with a question?

NOTES

1. This talk, sponsored by the Office of Continuing Legal Education, was given at the School of Law, Loyola University of Chicago, Chicago, Illinois, October 28, 1984. The original title of this talk was "The Book of Jonah and the Rule of Law."

The parenthetical citations in the text are to the *Book of Jonah*. A general familiarity with the story is assumed.

2. See Herman Melville, *Moby Dick*, chap. 9. Does Jonah ever fully repent? See the text at note 26 of chapter 3 of this collection.

3. See the text at note 18 of chapter 3 of this collection. See also chapter 2, note 34.

4. There was a lively exchange about these matters, and about the nature of miracles, between Clarence Darrow and William Jennings Bryan in the course of the Scopes Trial in 1925. Is not this sort of public speculation something that Maimonides would avoid, using *Jonah* instead primarily as a moral tale? See chapter 3, note 19.

5. See chapter 1–A.

6. The Old Testament does not use the term *natural* in describing this state of affairs. See chapter 1, note 91. See also chapter 1, notes 24, 44, 71; chapter 3, notes 9, 21; conclusion note 2. See as well *Judges* 21:25, *Romans* 2:14.

7. See *Genesis*, chaps. 18 and 19.

8. The natural understanding may sometimes even suggest that there really is no meaning to the cosmos. See chapter 3, note 21. Compare conclusion, note 3 below. See also appendix C, note 29.

9. Compare the passage from Hobbes's *Leviathan* set forth in the text at note 1 of the introduction to this collection. Consider, also, President Lincoln's use of a hundred-days warning period before he issued the Emancipation Proclamation. See, on the Emancipation Proclamation, George Anastaplo, *Abraham Lincoln: A Constitutional Biography* (Lanham, Md.: Rowman & Littlefield, 1999), p. 197. (My preferred title for this book is *Thoughts on Abraham Lincoln*. Its sequel should be entitled *Further Thoughts on Abraham Lincoln*.)

10. See *Genesis* 18:16–33.

11. See chapter 1, note 91.

12. See chapter 3, note 2.

13. Lots were also used to fill the place of Judas Iscariot among Jesus' twelve apostles. See *Acts* 1:24–26. Lots were used on many other occasions as well. See, e.g., *Joshua* 18:8, 59. Compare, on the conquest of fortuna, Niccolo Machiavelli, *The Prince*, chap. 25. See the text at note 37 of chapter 4 of this collection.

See, for my suggestion of November 10, 2000 that the deadlocked Year 2000 Presidential Election be immediately decided by lot, Letters to the Editor, *Chicago Daily Law Bulletin*, November 13, 2000, p. 2; *Chicago Tribune,* November 15, 2000, sec. 1, p. 20; *University of Chicago Maroon*, November 17, 2000, p. 7. See also George Anastaplo, "*Bush* v. *Gore* and a Proper Separation of Powers," *Loyola University of Chicago Law Journal* 131, 132 (2002).

14. Are they somewhat like the Abraham of the Sodom and Gomorrah story in this respect? See the text at notes 7 and 10 of chapter 3 of this collection.

15. Consider how Abraham responds to what God said about the Sacrifice of Isaac. See chapter 5.

16. One is reminded of the *Book of Job* as well. See chapter 1, note 101.

17. See chapter 2, note 26.

18. See Moses Maimonides, *The Guide of the Perplexed* (Chicago: University of Chicago Press, 1963), pp. 369–73. See also the text at note 3 of chapter 3 of this collection. See as well chapter 2, note 26.

19. Some scholars consider Jonah's prayer a much later interpolation in the text. But is it not useful and hence integral to the story in that it shows us the hopeful way in which Jonah could see his own dire circumstances, especially if he has genuine prophetic powers? In any event, if the prayer *is* interpolated, it was done by someone

of talent who evidently believed that this kind of prayer followed from the character of Jonah and from the story.

20. See chapter 1, note 100. Consider, as bearing on how we might approach the story about Jonah, the following exchange between Socrates and Euthyphro in Plato, *Euthyphro* 6C (Thomas G. West and Grace Starry West, trans.):

Socrates:
Shall we assert that these things [about the gods] are true, Euthyphro?

Euthyphro:
Not only these, Socrates, but as I said just now, I will also explain many other things to you, if you wish, about the divine things; and when you hear them, I know well that you will be astounded.

See chapter 3, note 4. See also George Anastaplo, "On Trial: Explorations," 22 *Loyola University of Chicago Law Journal* 765, 873 (1991).

21. Consider what is said about God in that He acts only through such instruments as Jonah, storms, fishes, gourds, and worms, rather than "directly." Is this all, or almost all, that is ever clearly observed by human beings? Does this, too, point up the importance of the natural, and of the natural seeming, in human affairs? Thus, natural developments may be seen in supernatural terms by the particularly intuitive. See chapter 1, note 91, conclusion, notes 2, 3.

22. With the possible exception of St. Francis, human preaching to animals—that is, to nonrational beings—is not likely to be effective, at least in the Western World. Compare chapter 1, note 70.

23. See chapter 4–A.

24. It is a nice question, however, what the status of "repentance" is in the *Nicomachean Ethics* of Aristotle.

25. See Maimonides, *The Guide of the Perplexed*, pp. liv–lvi, 407f.

26. It is said that Nineveh gained a respite of two hundred years from the time of Jonah. The city is believed to have been destroyed in 612 (or 606) B.C.E. See *The Zondervan Pictorial Dictionary,* ed. Merrill C. Tenney (Grand Rapids, Mich.: Zonderman Publishing House, 1963), pp. 588–89.

Could the Ninevites ever have been "certain" about the workings of God from only such episodes as those described in the *Book of Jonah*? That is, could they have ever been certain that they had in fact been saved from anything? (What if they learned about what happened to Jonah at sea?) Compare, on the other hand, the Israelites who had (among other things) a spectacular deliverance from Egypt to build upon. See also chapter 4–A.

4

Oedipus, Creon, and Antigone

4-A.   SOPHOCLES' *OEDIPUS TYRANNOS*[1]

I.

There is no hope either that one can, on such an occasion as this, add much to what has already been said many times about Sophocles' *Oedipus Tyrannos* or that one can exhaust any important aspect of this subject. Every talk on this play can reasonably hope to be no more than an introduction, which may be true as well of all talks on any great text. What one says about a great text can be less than an introduction—it may even obscure the text—if one (like Oedipus himself?) tries to do too much.[2]

Oedipus Tyrannos is perhaps the greatest tragedy ever written, at least among the plays to which we in the West have reliable access. Certainly, it is one of the most influential, serving as a wonders-filled reservoir for playwrights, theater goers, and critics for more than two thousand years. It is a play everyone knows something about, and not only because (as some would have it) it deals with psychic forces to be found in us all. It is also a play that bristles with puzzles, questions, and problems, only a few of which we can touch upon here—but touch upon, it is hoped, in a way that is useful for one's understanding of the entire play.

The story of Oedipus is an old one. The first literary account we have is that found in Homer, where we hear Odysseus reporting what he saw during his visit to Hades:

> I saw the mother of Oedipus, lovely Epicaste, who did an enormous deed in the ignorance of her mind and married her son. He slew his own father and married

her. The gods soon made these things known to men. But he suffered pains in his much-beloved Thebes, and ruled the Cadmeians through the destructive plans of the gods; and she went to the place of the mighty gatekeeper Hades. She hung up a high noose from the lofty roofbeams, possessed by her grief. For him she left many pains behind her, the kind a mother's Furies bring to pass.[3]

Odysseus' account put the emphasis on Epicaste (another name for Oedipus' mother; Jocasta is the name *we* are more familiar with). Nothing is said of Oedipus' eventual fate in Odysseus' account except that he had "many pains." Nor does Homer say anything about Oedipus' presence in Thebes being a pollution upon the land or about Oedipus' blinding himself. These differences are touched upon in the *Encyclopedia Britannica* entry on Oedipus, an entry that reports on the mythological as well as the Homeric accounts about the man:

Oedipus, in Greek mythology, the king of Thebes who unwittingly killed his father and married his mother. Homer related that Oedipus' mother hanged herself when the truth of their relationship became known, though Oedipus apparently continued to rule at Thebes until his death. In the post-Homeric tradition, most familiar from Sophocles' *Oedipus [Tyrannos]* and *Oedipus Colonus*, there are notable differences in emphasis and detail.

Traditionally, Laius, king of Thebes, was warned by an oracle that his son would slay him. Accordingly, when his wife, Jocasta (Iocaste; in Homer, Epicaste), bore a son, he exposed the baby on Mt. Cithaeron, first pinning his ankles together (hence the name Oedipus, meaning Swell-Foot). A shepherd took pity on the infant, who was adopted by King Polybus of Corinth and his wife and was brought up as their son. In early manhood Oedipus visited Delphi and, upon learning that he was fated to kill his father and marry his mother, he resolved never to return to Corinth.

Travelling toward Thebes, he encountered Laius, who provoked a quarrel in which Oedipus killed him. Continuing on his way, Oedipus found Thebes plagued by the Sphinx, who put a riddle to all passersby and destroyed those who could not answer. Oedipus solved the riddle, and the Sphinx killed herself. In reward, he received the throne of Thebes and the hand of the widowed queen, his mother, Jocasta. They had four children: Eteocles, Polyneices, Antigone, and Ismene. Later, when the truth became known, Jocasta committed suicide, and Oedipus (according to another version), after blinding himself, went into exile, accompanied by Antigone and Ismene, leaving his brother-in-law Creon as regent. Oedipus died at Colonus near Athens, where he was swallowed into the earth and became a guardian hero of the land.

Although the Oedipus legend may have originally been based on a core of historical truth, it is impossible to isolate it from its folktale elements. Oedipus appears in the folk traditions of Albania, Finland, Cyprus, and Greece. The ancient story has intense dramatic appeal; through Seneca the theme was transmitted to a long succession of playwrights, including Pierre Corneille, John Dryden, and Voltaire. It has had a special attraction in the 20th Century, motivating Igor Stravinsky's secular oratorio *Oedipus Rex*, André Gide's *Oedipe*, and Jean Cocteau's *La Machine infernale*. Sigmund Freud chose the term *Oedipus complex* to designate a son's feeling of love toward his mother and jealousy and hate toward his father, although these were not emotions that motivated Oedipus' actions or determined his character in any ancient version of the story.[4]

It would be helpful, before turning to a discussion of some points in Sophocles' version of this story, to be reminded of what is in that version, which is in several respects different both from the Homeric account and from the general tradition of antiquity reported by the *Encyclopedia Britannica*:

Years ago, as [Sophocles'] audience already knew, Apollo through an oracle declared to Oedipus' parents, Laius and Jocasta, that a son born to them was destined to kill his father and marry his mother; it is not said that they were warned against having a child, although that is perhaps to be inferred. Thinking to circumvent the oracle, Laius and Jocasta had their new-born son abandoned at Mt. Cithaeron to die, its feet pinned together. The infant was rescued by a herdsman who took it back with him to Corinth. There the child grew to manhood, supposing himself to be the son of Polybus, King of Corinth, and his wife Merope, and called "Oedipus" because of the deformity to his feet. Taunted at a banquet with being no son of Polybus and Merope, he journeyed to [Delphi] to learn the truth of this; and the god [Apollo] gave him no answer to his question but stated that he was doomed to kill his father and marry his mother. Determined therefore never again to set foot in Corinth, Oedipus went onward and in a sudden quarrel at a cross-road killed an elderly man—his father—with all his retinue excepting one man who fled. He then came to Thebes and, on solving the riddle of the Sphinx, was hailed by that city as its deliverer from plague, and was made king; and the former king's wife—his mother—became his consort. When he learned the truth, he put out his own eyes.[5]

In my discussion of the play on this occasion, I should like to see what does happen in the Sophocles play primarily in the light of what the characters should have done. The characters I am particularly concerned about here are Laius, Jocasta, and of course Oedipus himself. What should each of them have done at various stages of the careers indicated in this play?[6]

II.

What *should* Laius and Jocasta have done when they learned of the oracle that their son would kill his father and marry his mother?

We cannot be sure from this Sophocles play, although it does seem to be indicated, that Laius and Jocasta may have been given their warning before the conception of Oedipus, if not even before they decided to marry.[7] Were Laius and Jocasta, or at least Laius, overcome by passion, so much so that they could not resist coming together? Is Jocasta discreet about this, perhaps because she is ashamed of her passion, just as she is about precisely how the infant was disposed of when it was born? Certainly, if they were warned in advance, and if they took the warning seriously enough to have the child killed, the conception of Oedipus should have been prevented. That, presumably, would have been the end of the story.

Suppose, however, that the warning came only after the child had been conceived, if not even born. There is no indication given us *in this play* of a family curse, extending back to prior generations. We do learn that Laius has a temper, which is exhibited at the fatal crossroads when he meets Oedipus and where Oedipus exhibits his own temper in turn. Perhaps Laius' temper reflects his passion, perhaps indeed the very passion that had made him unable to keep away from Jocasta. She, it might be added, is said by some—but not in this play—to have been irresistible as a very young woman. Evidently, she was still attractive as the middle-aged woman that Oedipus came to know and to marry, reinforcing thereby his political power as an outsider.

Laius, we have noticed, has a remarkable temper. He, like Oedipus, seems to have been used to having his way. Is there not something presumptuous, or *hubristic*, in the effort made by Laius and Jocasta (as well as later, by Oedipus) to thwart the presumed will of the gods? We will return to these considerations later.

What, then, should Laius and Jocasta have done if they had in hand both a baby son and the ominous prophecy? Are we not taught by the play to notice that the first, and indispensable, step in such circumstances is to become as clear as one can possibly be about the meaning of the prophecy? Laius and Jocasta should have tried to understand the prophecy thoroughly. Or, put another way, in such matters it *is* generally desirable to be prudent.

Prudence should have instructed these royal parents about one simple fact on which everything depended and in the light of which their conduct should have been shaped both then and thereafter: the simple fact is that any baby they *could* kill should not, and need not, have been killed by them.[8] Indeed, one could argue, the *attempt* to kill the baby only made matters worse, and not only because of its presumptuousness. In this case the attempt meant, among other things, that the parents would become estranged from (strangers to) their son and hence more vulnerable with respect to him.

I say that the simple fact is that any baby they *could* kill need not have been killed by them, since he obviously was not destined to kill his father and marry his mother. But my statement should be qualified, for it could also be said that a successful killing of the infant *could* mean that Laius and Jocasta *had* managed thereby to kill off Laius' line, and hence Laius himself. And could it also be said that Jocasta, if childless thereafter, would have been as if married to her dead son, a sterile marriage?

We shall see, now that we turn to a consideration of what Oedipus himself should have done in response to the oracle, that there are indeed various ways to understand the prophecy that so shook Laius, Jocasta, and Oedipus.

III.

When Oedipus learned of the oracle—that he would kill his father and marry his mother—what *should* he have done?[9]

Again it can be said that the first, and indispensable, step was to become as clear as one could be about the meaning of the prophecy, including if possible an awareness of the cause of this fate. One recalls how Socrates responded to another oracular report from Delphi, to the effect that no man was wiser than Socrates: Socrates claimed that he spent much of his life thereafter trying to understand what the god had meant.[10] But, alas, Sophocles' Oedipus did not believe that there was anything he had to investigate, even though he *had* gone to consult Apollo originally because of the doubts aroused by a drunken man in Corinth about Oedipus' parentage. (775–82) (Was that drunken man exhibiting a different kind of "inspiration"?) Of course, Oedipus' supposed mother and father in Corinth, King Polybus and Queen Merope, had assured a troubled Oedipus about his parentage—but he had not been satisfied, and hence had gone to Delphi. (783–98) What the Delphic oracle said about his future immediately drove out of Oedipus' mind, it seems, the question he had had about his past—although his past and future were obviously connected—and so he did not do what he should have done in order to be clear about the meaning of the prophecy. (I notice, in passing, that the incident with the drunken man in Corinth *seems* to have been added by Sophocles—and, if so, it suggests that Sophocles wanted his more thoughtful readers, whatever may be said of the typical audience, to reflect upon what it meant that Oedipus did not try to make use of all the information he did have.)

What should a thorough, even a Socratic, investigation of the oracle have included? Should not Oedipus have gone back to the man he believed to be his father, Polybus, reporting what he had been told at Delphi and asking for advice? He could have added what he no doubt believed, "Obviously, I don't want to kill you!" That is, an awareness by Oedipus of his limitations was in order. Instead, his efforts were immediately aimed at overcoming the oracle, as he immediately understood it—and he persisted in this attitude and response for more than a decade. It is generally true, I suppose, that children who refuse to discuss "personal matters" with their parents make themselves even more vulnerable than they would naturally be.

Had Oedipus gone back to Polybus, he could have been reassured by him about blood ties. The obvious advice would then have been, "Stay here!"[11] But, it seems, the prophecy received by Oedipus himself at Delphi was evidently too horrible for him to contemplate; the most he could do was to *react* to it—and that meant to *run*.

There *are* things to be usefully talked about in such cases. No matter how dark things look, it usually helps to discuss them with a sensible counselor who has one's interests at heart.[12] One may need help to spell out properly the implications of such a prophecy. To keep it to oneself may make it far more insidious in its consequences than it need be. But, it seems, Oedipus had never discussed the prophecy with anyone until the day of terrible revelations that we see unfold on the stage—and by then it was probably too late, although even then (as we shall see) there were better and worse ways of responding to the grim revelations.

As for the possible meanings of the oracle, in addition to the frightful (and likely?) meaning that Oedipus immediately assumed and reacted to, several others can be suggested. We are encouraged to conjure up such alternatives when we notice that Oedipus himself devised an alternative when he learned that his supposed father Polybus had died in Corinth: for Oedipus *then* suggested that perhaps the oracle was indeed fulfilled in that Polybus had died pining for his absent son. (964–73) If *that* qualified as a sufficient fulfillment of the prophecy—and, it should be noticed, this too is a touch added by Sophocles, so far as we know—if death by pining qualified, in Oedipus' opinion, as an adequate (but not for him a horrible) fulfillment of the prophecy that Oedipus would kill his father, then any one of the following half dozen similarly equivocal fulfillments should have qualified as well:[13]

Thus, Oedipus could have "killed Laius" by staying in Corinth and thereby cutting off Laius' known line (in Thebes); Oedipus could have killed his father (whoever he may have been) by not conforming to the model or guidance provided him by his father; Oedipus could have killed his father, in a more literal sense, by providing him, at his request, a mercy killing when he was old and in great pain; Oedipus could have killed his father by killing himself, cutting off the line in that way also; Oedipus could have killed his father, again in the more literal sense, in an accident; and Oedipus could have killed his father by not marrying at all, cutting off the line in still another way.[14] Of course, one or more of these might have been considered polluting, however innocent Oedipus' intention. But this observation reminds us of still another response that Oedipus did *not* make to the oracle's dire warning, and that is a determined recourse to prayers and sacrifices.

But what, someone might ask, could be considered an adequate fulfillment of the prophecy with respect to the incest, that incest that it is evident that Sophocles' Oedipus dreaded even more than he did the patricide?[15] Can the incest prophecy be similarly compiled within a more or less innocent fashion? No doubt, plausible fulfillments can be conjured up here as well, such as the following: Oedipus could have married his mother in his imagination; or Oedipus could have married his mother in a play or game or mock marriage, a play in which he acted as the groom and she as the bride; or (and this *is* quite common to this day) Oedipus could have married a woman very much like his mother; or Oedipus could have married his mother, so to speak, by always siding with her against his father in family differences; or Oedipus could have married his mother in a dream (as, indeed, Jocasta says to him that men often do). One might even argue that Oedipus, by declining to marry because of the fear of incest, could in effect be marrying his mother. But one need not go that far in order to show that what Oedipus required was to think long and carefully about what this prophecy too could mean and how best to deal with it.

Instead, Oedipus, like Jocasta and Laius before him, believed himself to know more than he could be sure of—and hence did not protect or conduct himself as well as he could have. By responding as he did to the oracle, he made it more likely that the prophecy would be fulfilled in perhaps the worst possible way.

Does Oedipus' reaction to the original prophesy, as well as the reactions by Laius and by Jocasta, suggest that there *is* something deep in the soul that makes such prophecies plausible? Do we sense in ourselves tendencies in the directions prophesied? Otherwise, would we not laugh off such "threats"? Or is it that deeds of this character are so terrible, and so far from our desires, that we cannot even hear of them without shuddering? Besides, it can be argued, one should not simply ignore what the gods say, or seem to say.

Of course, one must wonder what kind of gods these are and whether *they* in any way arrange for or endorse what is prophesied? And if they do, what should be said and done about such gods? To ask such questions *is* to seek genuine understanding about the world on the basis of which to conduct one's life—and this seems to be something that Oedipus never disciplined himself to seek. Instead, as we have noticed, Oedipus resorted to immediate and direct action, as his parents had evidently done at the time of his birth: he must rule, wherever he is; he must prevail with whomever he is dealing, be it the old man at the crossroads, the Sphinx, a blind seer, old men who have information he wants, or (it can be said) even the gods.

But ruling is hardly the same as understanding—unless, of course, one is talking about genuine rule, which depends upon true understanding.[16]

IV.

All this raises the question whether oracles are of any use at all. This question is raised aside from the problem, evident in various remarks by Jocasta, as to whether any particular purported oracle is sound. (707–25) It is aside, as well, from the problem I have already referred to: if the baby *could* be killed, if Oedipus' parents *could* be fled by him, then the oracle in its conventional interpretation could not have been sound.

As for the usefulness of oracles: it *can* be said that the oracle secured by Creon at Delphi, about the cause of this most recent plague in Thebes, *was* useful, in that it evidently induced Oedipus, who had sought the cause of the plague, to take the measures needed to lift it. But is this the only oracle dealt with in the play that we know to have been sought for, in its own terms, by human beings? That is, there is no indication that Laius and Jocasta sought the oracle *they* got. (707–25) And we do know that Oedipus did not seek the oracle *he* got; rather, it was gratuitously given to him in place of the one he did seek (that is, about his parentage).[17]

Are unsought oracles of any use? What would the lives of these people have been like if they had never had any oracles to contend with or to be guided (or misguided) by? Would their lives have merely seemed senseless or perhaps only ordinary? Do oracles help to make sense of things?

In any event, we should notice, the terrible things Oedipus feared most, and about which he received oracles—the patricide and the incest—were done before the play begins. Just as they were in his future once (and to be run away from), so they are in his past now (and to be run away from in still another way, by Oedipus' blinding himself). The terrible deeds he is most concerned about are never in his *present*: is *this* what comes from indulging in oracles or taking them too seriously, that one never deals properly with the present?

It can even be said that the worst thing Oedipus did, his self-blinding, he was perhaps never *fated* to do (even though Tiresias did predict it). (370–77, 1265–79) Does this self-mutilation reflect a deep anger at himself and at things in general? Is this an act striking out against nature, against the gods, against the very order of things if not against being itself, as well as against learning and knowing?

It may well be, then, that fate does not exist, or have its worst effects, until men somehow know of it. Things, including terrible events, are explained otherwise if fate is not made explicit: for a man to know of his fate may be critical to *suffering* that fate fully. On the other hand, to attempt to avoid one's prophesied fate *is* to avoid the truth—and hence to make oneself more vulnerable than one might otherwise be. The more vigorous one's efforts to avoid one's fate, the more ignorant or impassioned one is apt to become—and that may be essential to the fulfillment of one's fate in the worst possible way.

I have suggested that the personal characteristics of Laius, Jocasta, and Oedipus made it likely that the prophecies would indeed be fulfilled in the worst possible ways—and that is, in part, because they did not properly address themselves to the question of the possible meanings and usefulness of the oracles they received. One is not likely ever to be told or to know the future in any reliable detail, however sound one's oracle may be. One needs, in such circumstances, to inquire, to think, and to respond carefully.

How one conducts oneself depends, in part, upon what one considers the world and the divine to be like.[18] For example, are the truly virtuous pursued by a malignant fate (whatever may be the effects of chance)? With or without an oracle, should not prudence and right conduct be one's guide and one's way?

Prudence is to be differentiated both from too much calculation and from not enough. Too much calculation may be seen in the *hubristic*, which is evident in one's belief that one can circumvent a genuine prophecy (as may be seen in the attempted infanticide). Not enough calculation may be seen in panic, such panic as Oedipus exhibited when he was told at Delphi what he would do: he wanted to put more and more distance between himself and Corinth—but his flight led him immediately to his natural father. (794–800)[19]

We can also see in this play how one's strengths can contribute to one's undoing. Thus, Oedipus' ability to solve riddles first established him (so much so that men called him "the Great") and then toppled him. And, it can be said, his exalted ability to uncover secrets is seen, in its most extreme form, in the dreaded incest. Not only that, but an improper response to what one is able to learn may mean that one's very knowledge of a particular prophecy may itself contribute to one's downfall.

V.

But enough, for now, of these more general observations. Let us return to the particulars of Oedipus and his parents.[20]

We have considered what might have been thought and done by Laius and Jocasta and later by Oedipus in response to the oracles of patricide and incest that they received. We should now consider what they should have done afterwards—that is, after they learned what they did about the dreadful outcome of their efforts. First, let us consider Laius and Jocasta in turn.

Laius, after having done what he believed he had done to his infant son, still goes to Delphi—and is killed on the way, by Oedipus. Why did he go? To seek advice, it seems, about the Sphinx, which was plaguing his city,

Thebes. (128–32) He did find an answer on the way to Delphi, but not the one he believed he was looking for. Should Laius have been a "believer" in Delphi or in oracles once he had, as he believed, needlessly killed his only son?

Why was the Sphinx plaguing Thebes? Perhaps because of what had been done to the infant Oedipus, a generation before, or because Laius and Jocasta had been pitiless, completely selfish and *hubristic*? Are we to understand—is it salutary to believe—that such afflictions as plagues often have moral causes?[21] Again, we are asking, what kind of a world *is* it? The infection from the exposure of the infant Oedipus took a generation to fester into the affliction of the Sphinx; the infection from the patricide (or is it only the regicide?) took another generation to fester into the affliction of the plague. Was it appropriate, then, that the king who had thought he could circumvent an oracle (by the infanticide) should be killed on his way to take advantage of Apollo once again?

What about Jocasta? How should *she* have conducted herself upon learning of the patricide and incest? She, at least, had accepted, more than Laius had, the implications of the attempted infanticide: she no longer believed in oracles, or so she said. (707–25) At least, she had not believed enough to wonder before marrying a younger second husband—someone young enough to be her son, with scarred feet yet, and with the same build as her first husband. (742–44)

How should Jocasta have responded to the dreadful revelation in this play about her second marriage? Was suicide by hanging called for? Should she have regarded Oedipus as her *son*? After all, the most intimate relations, as mother and child, had not existed between them, whatever blood ties they happened to have—and so the more serious moral blame and self-recrimination should not follow, it can be argued.[22]

Besides, we have noticed, the oracle about the Theban plague had mentioned only the killer of Laius, not the incest at all.[23] The gods themselves engage in incest; it can be acceptable to them. Besides, this Theban incest did produce so remarkable a child as the noble Antigone.[24] Did not both Oedipus and Jocasta, as well as others, overreact to the revelation of incest *in these circumstances*? Was pride, even more than piety, offended here? Did their pain come as much from the recognition of their presumptuous self-confidence and yet ignorance as from anything else? They were exposed as not controlling what they had believed they controlled, as not understanding what they had been certain they understood.

VI.

Let us now consider Oedipus himself and how he should have responded to the unexpected revelations about both the patricide and the incest. To do this, let us first return to the problem of the Sphinx. Sophocles does not report the traditional riddle put by the Sphinx, which inquires as to what walks on four feet in the morning, on two feet at noon, and on three feet in the evening.[25] Is Sophocles silent about this because he did not want it—or because it was too well known to need repetition?

The traditional Sphinx' riddle does seem connected with Oedipus himself, the man whose very name refers to his *feet*. And, of course, the blinded Oedipus ends up with a cane, if he does not have one at the outset because of his feet? But then, he would never have walked on two feet.[26] Thus, there are two great questions that Oedipus becomes occupied with. The first question, put by the Sphinx, is, "What is the thing that walks, etc.?" The answer is "Man." The second question, put by the anxious Oedipus, is, "Who is *this* man?" This question has, for Oedipus, two related forms: "Who am I?" and "Who killed Laius?" The answer to both forms of this question is that Oedipus is the man—the man who is not only the killer of Laius but also the child of Laius and Jocasta.

Should not Oedipus have sensed that the Sphinx episode, in its bizarreness and in its subtle connection with *his* own name, was especially significant for him?[27] Was not he being thoughtless in not wondering how *this* could be connected with the prophecy he feared (and that he had just gotten at Delphi)? Certainly, the handling by him of the Sphinx looms large in his career: it is mentioned many times in the play.

We have seen that Oedipus is not really a man of reflection, but rather a man of action: he seems inclined to respond to every crisis with blows, either physical or verbal. Oedipus' gift, such as it was, lay in answering questions *put to him* in public circumstances, not in identifying and pursuing properly those questions of a somewhat private character he should have pursued.

Oedipus' responses to the two revelations that mattered most to him can now be assessed. When Oedipus discovers he has killed Laius, he seems more concerned about the penalty due him as the cause of pollution in the city (the exile he had ordered for the killer of Laius)—he seems more concerned about *that*, about the consequences for him personally, that is, than he is about patricide itself. And in the *Oedipus at Colonus*, the play that shows Oedipus as a very old man, much is made by him of having had to act in self-defense at the crossroads.[28] Certainly, he does not ever seem to take seriously the notion that he had killed his *father*, if only because he had never known Laius.

Should not Oedipus have been bothered more by the killing of Laius and the others at the crossroads than by the incest? In that seemingly chance encounter, he forgot all considerations of humanity. (801–13) To kill any other man, and certainly someone appreciably older than one is, *is* to try to kill one's father in one's self. But Oedipus is rather self-centered about these matters. Thus, he had never wondered about his predecessor as king or as husband (just as

Thebes had ignored the fate of Laius and thus invited its most recent plague?). By the time Oedipus discovers who he is, he seems to lose interest in the city, its fate, or its needs.[29]

Much, much more is made by Oedipus of the incest—even though, as we have noticed, the oracle about the plague had ignored the incest and even though this mother and this child were attached, as such, by blood alone. What kept Oedipus from acting sensibly in response to the revelation about the incest was, at least in part, the fact that he had conducted all his inquiries in public, thus making the element of shame and of injured pride much greater. Creon had indicated, upon returning from Delphi, that he could report to Oedipus in private. But Oedipus insisted he had "nothing to hide." (91–94) Is incest, too, one consequence of an insistence that there is nothing to hide? Does Oedipus have a natural inclination to uncover that which should remain hidden?

It is perhaps significant that, as we are told in *Oedipus at Colonus*, there is to be no monument over Oedipus' grave: he became a fully private man at his death (whatever may be the "magic" power of his presence at Colonus), with his body simply gone.[30] Is this a counterpoint to *his* uncovering of his birthplace? The last thing said by Oedipus to his daughters in the *Colonus* play includes this admonition, "You must not wish to see what is forbidden, or hear what may not be told. "[31] Oedipus' self-blinding may also be seen as a way of going private, of withdrawing from the world—of compensating, so to speak, for having not known what to look at and how?

In any event, one should be able to "walk away" from certain situations, when they have gotten distorted and there is no reasonable prospect of clearing them up—to walk away and thereby to allow other people to work out their lives as best they can. Certainly, it often does not do much good to publicize such situations and thus intensify and worsen them, especially when family relations are involved.

A "way out" *is* provided to Oedipus in *his* disturbed situation: that is, fate, or the gods, who had "set up" Oedipus also provided him a graceful way out that he did not appreciate, the opportunity to go to Corinth and to rule. Corinth *does* expect him to come. (1000-1005) Should not Oedipus have long before recognized that everything about him was special and that, consequently, he should wonder about anything that he took for granted, looking to see how things all fit together (especially if the gods are considered essentially, or eventually, just)? The remarkable string of coincidences here should have made him wonder. Thus, for example, he should have wondered why the Corinthian opportunity came when it did. True, the messenger's coming led to the unraveling of things, but this was necessarily harmful (I repeat) only because it was all done in public. (91–94)

The Socrates we are familiar with from Plato's dialogues would have regarded all this as curious, to say the least. He certainly would not have blinded himself upon discovering what he had blundered into. This self-blinding may have been, I have suggested, Oedipus' greatest offense, reflecting a blind, and blinding, rage.[32] This is related, I have also suggested, to his delusion, now exposed, that he had indeed been in control. What *would* he have done to the devastated Jocasta in his rage if he had found her alive? Would he have added an intentional matricide to his unintentional patricide? (1254–63) This points up the foolishness of his immediate responses.[33]

Oedipus' best conduct may have been after he blinded himself. Does he act then—in the closing scene of the *Oedipus Tyrannos* and throughout much of the *Oedipus at Colonus*—better than he had done while still able to see? The blinding, and his resulting helplessness and suffering, may have been critical to his transformation into a *daemonic* power of sorts, which we see at the end of the *Colonus* play.[34]

Did Oedipus have any reason to believe that blinding himself was at all sensible in the circumstances. Was it an almost instinctive reaction to having seen, in the incest, what he should not have seen? Was it even a desire to become "wise" as the blind Tiresias was? Had Tiresias, in effect, suggested this to Oedipus, in the form of a prediction? (372–74) Once Oedipus *is* blinded, he becomes (at least for awhile) somewhat more passive, less obviously in control—whatever the daemonic power may be that he is aware of (or becomes aware of, or remembers) as associated with the place of his death.

VII.

We should not conclude this introduction to *Oedipus Tyrannos* without at least touching upon the question of whether it was good for Oedipus that he learned the truth about himself.[35] How one responds to the bitter truth may suggest whether one truly grasps it *as* the truth—as something that reveals the world and not merely as something that deals with oneself primarily and that one must "personally" respond to and be pained and challenged by.

There is a presumption in favor of the truth, it has again and again been noticed by thoughtful human beings. But we can all think of instances in which a noble lie may be kind, prudent, or otherwise useful.[36] Would a Socratic counselor, who alone learned the truth about this family, have told either Jocasta or Oedipus what had happened and how they were related? Does what a counselor should do depend, in large part, upon whether it is likely that the counseled would be able to "handle" the truth sensibly? Certainly, he would want to separate them physically—and the Corinthian summons is convenient (even a godsend?) for that purpose. But what more should he do? A Socratic counselor would probably recognize something that Oedipus was perhaps naturally incapable of grasping, that one cannot truly control things unless one truly understands—and even then, there may be, because of chance and mortality, limits to one's effective control.[37]

To talk about the *Oedipus Tyrannos* as I have done on this occasion *is* to step outside the character and hence the perspective of an Oedipus or of a Jocasta. To talk about the play thus may even seem monstrous to some, if only because it might seem to rob the story of some of the drama that appeals to playgoers. But even though I have not been talking about what most playgoers are apt to notice, the things I have noticed may help one *see* the text and what contributes to the power of the drama better than one otherwise might.

Perhaps the most telling criticism to be made of what I have said here is that I have failed to appreciate the horror aroused in the Greeks by both patricide and incest. Even an innocent, or accidental, killing of a parent would have been considered deeply polluting. Still, I have suggested that Oedipus was not without choices in responding to the various crises he faced. If he had truly had no choice, this powerful story would be far less interesting than it is. That is, one must have choices, even though what happens may appear to be inevitable—or else the story cannot continue to challenge us. Even if one's critical acts were inevitable, one might still have choices in how one responds to them when they do come.

To suggest that a reader can be reasonable in identifying and discussing the passions and choices in this play is not to expect most people—whether as readers or as men of action—to be reasonable most of the time. Is it not the mark of the truly reasonable human being to be aware of the limits of reason for most, if not for all, people. Thus, the prudent Odysseus once had himself tied to the mast of his ship, so that he could listen safely to the dangerously beguiling music of the Sirens while his men, with wax in their ears, rowed him past that deadly but instructive place.[38]

Such a man as Odysseus, who understood the risks as well as the enticements of discovery and who was almost always aware of the limits of human power, would never blind himself in a rage or in despair upon learning that the world is in important respects different from what he as a youth had believed. Rather, it was *he*, the wily Odysseus, who blinded the bloodthirsty Cyclops and then devised a use of the four feet of a sheep so that he could escape from the Cyclops' cave to walk freely again on his own two feet and thus to return home to his father, wife, and son.[39]

That is, of course, another story for another occasion, a story that is a healthy and most welcome counterpart to the story of Oedipus, that misconceived and misconceiving man who killed his father, took his mother as his wife and (to round out his perverse instincts with respect to family obligations) eventually cursed his own sons and thus left his most faithful daughter with a deadly legacy.

4-B.   SOPHOCLES' *ANTIGONE*[40]

I.

Sophocles' *Antigone* opens with its heroine's outburst to her sister (1–5):

> My sister, my Ismene, do you know of any suffering from Oedipus sprung that Zeus does not achieve for us survivors? There's nothing grievous, nothing free from doom, not shameful, not dishonored, I've not seen.

One translator has referred to these opening lines as made up of "confused and contradictory negative."[41] A decided negativity is intended, something that is reflected in Antigone's very name.[42]

But what is it that induces such negativity, a negativity that takes on the proportions of nobility in its single-mindedness? The noble considers actions superior to explanations, deeds superior to words—but it may, in its own good time, attempt to explain itself. When Antigone *is* moved to do so, she uses an argument that seems to suffer from the confusion seen in her opening lines (903–13):

> Polyneices knows the price I pay for doing final service to his corpse. And yet the wise will know my choice was right. Had I had children or their father dead, I'd let them moulder. I should not have chosen in such a case to cross the city's decree. What is the law that lies behind these words? One husband gone, I might have found another, or a child from a new man in first child's place, but with my parents hid away in death, no brother, ever, could spring up for me. Such was the law by which I honored you.

On the surface, this argument does seem irrational.[43] Perhaps it was thus regarded by Creon and his entourage as well as by the typical Greek audience.

What does a closer examination of Antigone's argument reveal? First, there is an implicit exclusion of concern for the corpses of anyone outside the family: dead fellow citizens would not find Antigone defying the city's decree on their behalf. (It is even implied that her defiance of the city would come only in the service of the dead, not of the living.) What she does applies to the family, the dead of the family, if at all. The critical distinction even among family members is between a dead husband or child, on the one hand, and a dead brother (or, at least, a dead brother, with parents being dead), on the other hand. What is the basis of such a distinction?

Antigone puts it in terms of irreplaceability. A husband or child can always be replaced, but not a brother if their common parents are dead.[44] Why should such a distinction be decisive? Does not the irreplaceability criterion point to another element, that of whether one has any control over the relation? One has no control over the initial existence of one's brother: it is one of the "givens" of this world. Not so with a husband or a child: one's own doing helps determine their existence. Not only does one choose the status of spouse or parent, but one chooses it (if one lives in a city) pursuant to, or in conformity with, the laws of the city. The city has, to some degree, taken a part in the making of one's spouse or child.[45]

Of course, the very same laws have played a similar role in the determination of one's parents or brothers—but that is not evident to the child. One's parents, and hence one's brothers, seem much more by nature; they are among the natural, even inevitable, things of the world that one finds oneself confronted by. Such relations are natural, inevitable, even shrouded in awesome mystery. In the relation with one's spouse or child, one looks up and out and to the future; in the relation with one's parents or brother, one looks down and inward and to the past—and it is appropriate that these primitive, seemingly irrational, attachments should include invocations of the gods under the ground, the gods hidden away from human view, the gods of the distant past and of dark places. (460–62, 1068–77)

It is also appropriate that Antigone's argument—if it can be called that—should appear to defy analysis, should appear to be the outburst of hidden, inarticulate passion.[46]

II.

Creon, on the other hand, invokes the gods of the city, the gods of the heavens. Both Creon and Antigone recognize that Zeus is Creon's ally, that it is Zeus to whom he looks. Antigone had spoken in her opening words of the suffering that Zeus had achieved for Oedipus' survivors. (1–5) Indeed, Creon can argue that the city (not the family) is fundamental to human existence, that even the family relies upon it for its effectiveness. It is on behalf of the city, a particular city, that Creon had issued his decree forbidding the burial of Polyneices, in order that citizens may learn to respect the city and not attempt to overthrow it. (162–210) The city and all that it makes possible require that severe measures be taken to punish and thereby to deter treason.

But the claim for the city, for the political, cannot be as exclusive as Creon regards it. This is evident as he talks to his son. (639 sq.) He first appeals to his son as a father. That is, he wants to take advantage of the family tie that he had, in effect, disparaged in condemning Antigone's action. In this speech, the Zeus who had been theretofore regarded as the guardian of political life and associated with Creon's action is for the first time referred to as the "Zeus who guards the kindred." (658–59) Thus, not even the gods of the upper world are as single-minded as Creon has taken them to be: even those gods recognize the claims, and the role, of the family, however much the family tends to look to the underworld. And, of course, it is through his family that Creon is struck down. (1191 sq., 1279 sq.)[47]

Before this happens, Creon is "converted" to Antigone's view. He is frightened by Tiresias. (1094 sq.) He asks the Chorus what he should do. They respond (1100–01),

> Go free the maiden from that rocky house.
> Bury the dead who lies in readiness.

It remains one of the mysteries of the play what would have happened if Creon had followed this advice. Instead of freeing Antigone first, he turns to the burial of Polyneices. The messenger describes what they had done (1203–5):

> [W]e gave the final purifying bath,
> then burned the poor remains on new-cut boughs,
> and heaped a high mound of his native earth.

How long *did* all this take—to bathe the body, cut boughs, build a proper fire, burn flesh and bone, and then pile up a high mound? When the royal party finally gets to Antigone's tomb, they hear Haemon's outburst. (1207 sq.) How long had Antigone been dead? Could not the dead have waited a little longer—or, at least, could not two parties have been dispatched to perform the two tasks?

One is tempted to say that Creon moves from one extreme to the other—to the consequent destruction of his family and against the best interests of the city entrusted to his care. Had he remained dedicated primarily to the realm of the living—with his primary concern for life and with an openness to political advice from the living—things might have turned out differently. But then, he would never have been in the terrible situation he was if he had not attempted to extend the jurisdiction of the city to include the realm of the dead.

III.

There is in Antigone, too, something of an unreflecting mixture of elements from two disparate realms.[48] Her opening speech, with its insistence on the negative, is followed almost immediately by the declaration, commenting on Creon's decree to the citizens about Polyneices' body (31–32),

> Such orders they say the worthy Creon gives
> to you and me—yes, yes, I say to *me*. . . .

Her concern is with the rites due to the gods of the world below; but her nobility—her style, so to speak—reminds of the heroes who look up to Olympus. It is no wonder that what she does is regarded as manly, and that Creon fears that he would be taken as womanish if he yields. (484–85) Creon discovered too late that there is concealed even in a king that female element that underlies and thus sustains human existence.[49]

Antigone's final act, her suicide, also reflects this nobility.[50] She *will* insist upon some control over her fate—we remember that she considers herself obliged to safeguard the rights of relatives (parents and brothers) over which she has no control. She will not either try to survive in a prison cave or wait upon nature to take its toll of her through starvation. She will, to the degree possible, be master of her fate—with the result that she not only forestalls the aid of a chastened city but also draws into the underworld with her anyone who may be immoderately attracted by her noble but deadly eminence.

Even Antigone's name suggests that her dedication to the family looks to the past, not to the future.[51] We are again reminded that the heroic in this somehow attractive woman, unlike in the heroes dedicated to the gods of light and the upper world, is in the service ultimately of the dark, hidden and even primitive forces found in human beings.[52]

4-C.   ANOUIHL'S *ANTIGONE*[53]

I.

Genuine tragedy recognizes something of what can be said "for each side" in the most serious conflicts. It teaches us, among other things, that the moderating of extreme positions is necessary if there is to be both life and a humane life; it avoids both sensationalism and sentimentality in its effort to grasp fundamentals. Whether Jean Anouihl's *Antigone* is truly a tragedy is one of the questions to be considered by us. It is said at one point, by the Chorus, that in a tragedy "[t]he least little turn of the wrist will do the job. Anything will set it going" (p. 23). Is this intended to suggest that trivial happenstance can be decisive? Does this do justice to the great, contending forces one associates with tragedy?

Or, to put all this another way, can tragedy concern itself as much as modern plays do with the personal and intimate? Does not this concern move us toward the legitimation of sentimentality as well as of sensationalism, with either paralysis or grotesqueness the ultimate result? Anouihl's play very much devotes itself to the private lives of Antigone, of her family, and even of the guards who deal with her.

II.

This play is to be seen against the backdrop of the great past of the *story* of Antigone, especially as we know that story in the timeless form provided it by Sophocles. The Sophoclean version is much shorter—it must have less than one half the words of Anouihl's. But Sophocles' is a version that demands much more from us, in that it is less dependent upon its circumstances and more concerned with questions that are intrinsic to human life and to serious thought about that life.

I will return in a moment to the Sophoclean backdrop of the play. Also of significance for Anouihl's version, even though not (so far as we know) for Sophocles', are the immediate circumstances of the play's initial production, the circumstances provided by the occupation of a decadent France by Nazi Germany during World War II. What are we to make of the fact, if fact it is, that the Creon of this play may have the better of the argument, an argument for law and order as well as for the futility of nobility? Was this a healthy argument for the French to have thrust before them at a time when collaboration with the Nazis was offered them? Should Antigone's position be reducible to the virtual willfulness—a kind of selfishness—that is depicted here? Consider, by comparison, the Declaration of Independence, with its insistence that there are by nature standards in the light of which the doings of governors and of regimes might be judged. Was not 1944 the wrong time—is it still so today—to make so much of official power and so little of individual nobility, to say nothing of a vigorous piety? Whatever is wrong with the resistance offered by an Antigone, does it not pale into insignificance against the enormity of that parody of law and order provided by the Nazis, no matter how Creon is presented? Put another way, must not a Creon who can make an argument for law and order in the circumstances of this play be a man who is, whatever his pretensions to culture, a hollow man?

III.

It may be useful to recapitulate in this context the Sophoclean version that cannot help but provide the backdrop of any *Antigone* written in our time. (1) Sophocles' *Antigone* opens with Antigone informing her sister Ismene of

Creon's impending decree forbidding the burial of their fallen brother, Polyneices. This is the first of a half dozen major scenes in the play, scenes that are separated by extended choral statements. Antigone expresses her deep resentment, and Ismene her helplessness, in the face of Creon's decree. (1–98) (2) We then hear from Creon himself his decree—a decree in the wake of a terrible civil war—and thereafter the report from a guard that the dishonored body has nevertheless had a ritual burial administered by an unknown party. Creon is furious and the guard is threatened. (154–331) (3) The next scene shows Antigone brought in to Creon, apprehended when she returned to repeat the ritual burial that, she seems to have thought, had somehow been counteracted by the guards' removing the earlier dust. Antigone and Creon engage in an extended exchange, part of which Ismene joins, all of which assumes that Antigone will indeed be executed for her act of defiance. (373–581) (4) After Antigone is taken away, Creon's only surviving son, Haemon, comes to plead with his father for his fiancée's life, but to no avail. (628–780) (5) Thereafter, Antigone is brought back to Creon, for her final condemnation and her removal for execution. (801–943) (6) Now, for the first time, we see Tiresias (the blind, old seer) who rebukes Creon for what he has done, who is then reviled by Creon, and who in turn shakes Creon with a terrible prophecy that moves Creon to rush out to bury Polyneices and to save Antigone. (1088–1114) (7) The final scene shows a messenger returning with the tale of the prophesied catastrophes that have befallen Creon: not only is Antigone dead, but so also are Haemon and Creon's wife. Creon, at the end, is little more than a walking corpse himself. (1152–342)

IV.

Central to Sophocles' *Antigone* is the scene between Creon and Haemon. It has been said, and I believe with some justice, that "Haemon does not know how to argue; he knows only how to be right."[54] One sees here the decisive responses, made somewhat in political terms, to the political argument Creon makes and stands for. Central to the Sophocles play as a whole are the lines, found in Creon's speech here to Haemon, that civilization depends upon discipline. (660–80) The merits of this argument should be evident, whatever one may think of Creon's distortion of them by his extremism.

This confrontation of father and son—a confrontation that has the son trying to bridge the gulf between his city-based father and his family-based fiancée—this confrontation is not central, however, to Anouihl's *Antigone*. Central to Anouihl's play is the early part of the extended conversation between Creon and Antigone. One can, by comparing Anouihl and Sophocles in their accounts of the father-son confrontation, notice one of the critical differences between the two plays. In Sophocles, Haemon reports that the (pious?) people of Thebes are deeply disturbed by the condemnation of Antigone; they see what she has done on behalf of her brother to be noble, worthy of praise, not of death. In Anouihl, the people, in the form of a mob, is seen as demanding Antigone's death, with Creon trying to save her both from the mob and from herself. Anouihl's Haemon is urged by his father to grow up, to put away his childish dependence upon his fiancée. His Creon alone is presented as knowing that the things others yearn for, howl for, even die for—whether the others be Antigone, the mob, or his son—are childish things, not to be taken seriously. (One must wonder if *this* Creon is momentarily out of character when he desperately attempts to save his son's life at the end.) Maturity, for Creon, seems to require considerable deceit and to presuppose, as well as to produce, cynicism.

V.

Thus, Anouihl's Creon "has" to do what he does. His private inclinations are against what the others, particularly Antigone and the mob, force him to do. Somebody has to do the "dirty business" of governing. Why it is considered "dirty business" is never indicated with clarity. Anouihl's Antigone seems to believe that every government is demeaning. That is not assumed in Sophocles' version of the story, where Antigone is proud of her royal blood. (38, 941) Perhaps all government is suspect wherever so much is made, as in our time and in Anouihl's play, of private lives.

One consequence of (or reason for?) the emphasis upon, and interest in, private lives is the radically diminished role of the gods in the Anouihl version. The gods have very little to do with either side in this great conflict, virtually making the question of a proper burial pointless. In the Sophoclean version, on the other hand, the gods are invoked on both sides: the Zeus of kinship, with his underground allies, by Antigone, the Olympian and celestial Zeus by Creon.[55] Antigone looked inward and to the primeval past associated with the family; Creon looked outward and to the future, and to a kind of happiness associated with the city. In Anouihl, also, kinship and politics provide the points of departure for the protagonists—but these are soon left behind as each is reduced to little more than self-expression (especially Antigone, since Creon is almost too cynical to take even himself seriously). Such self-centeredness leads to an emphasis upon self-consciousness, upon the sense that one is performing in a theatrical production—something that one notices again and again in the Anouihl play and (I believe) hardly at all in the Sophocles play.

VI.

Without the divine for the characters to draw upon, and to be illuminated by, we *are* left with hollow men on the stage. It is no accident, then, that Tiresias does not appear in the Anouihl play. The page who is introduced by Anouihl provides something of a substitute for Tiresias, perhaps, as well as a tentative assurance of the future. The hollowness of Anouihl's men, at least of the more sophisticated men (such as his Creon, and to some extent his Chorus?), is revealed upon comparing the conclusions of the two plays. In Anouihl, Creon prepares to continue with the business of state; a Cabinet meeting is now on the agenda. (p. 52) In Sophocles, Creon's last words are (1340–42),

> Take me away at once, the frantic man who killed my son, against my meaning.
> I cannot rest. My life is warped past cure. My fate has struck me down.

The response of Creon (whether Anouihl's Creon or Sophocles' Creon) is not that of the philosopher, of the truly thoughtful man. But certainly, the response of Sophocles' Creon is more "human," less "mechanical" or banal.

VII.

I have suggested that both sides in Sophocles' *Antigone* stand for something vital to human existence, however distorted and hence distorting each side may be in advancing its claims. But what about in Anouihl's *Antigone*? *Does* either side there stand for anything enduring? Two major figures in Anouihl's play are "at their best" (if "best" it can be called) not in what they respectively stand for but in their devastating critiques of what "the other side" stands for.

That is, one must wonder whether modernity has perfected (if "perfected" it can be called) the destructive capacity of mankind, that dreadful power we have for negation. I trust, however, that what I have said on this occasion has not been simply negative: I have attempted to suggest the greatness that Sophocles' *Antigone* represents and that even Anouihl's *Antigone*, properly viewed, can remind us of and perhaps reinforce in us.

NOTES

1. This talk was given in the Works of the Mind Lecture Series, The Basic Program of Liberal Education for Adults, The University of Chicago, Chicago, Illinois, May 9, 1982 (Mother's Day).

The parenthetical citations in the text are to the David Grene translation of Sophocles' *Oedipus Tyrannos* as published in the *Complete Greek Tragedies* by the University of Chicago Press. See chapter 4, note 55. The use here of *tyrannos* is the technical one: it refers to whether the ruler is regarded as the legitimate successor, not to the quality of his rule. One of the critical revelations in this play is that Oedipus is indeed the legitimate successor to Laius, not the outsider (and hence "tyrant") that he had been regarded. See Plato, *Letters* VIII, 352C–E, 354A–357D. See, on tyranny, chapter 4, note 14.

2. I have touched upon *Oedipus Tyrannos* on other occasions. See, e.g., George Anastaplo, *The Constitutionalist: Notes on the First Amendment* (Dallas: Southern Methodist University Press, 1971), pp. 642 n. 77, 783 n. 9, 798–99 n. 33 (chapter 4, note 14); *The American Moralist: Essays on Law, Ethics, and Government* (Athens, Ohio: Ohio University Press, 1992), pp. 6–8; "Law, Literature, and Judge Posner" 23 *Loyola University of Chicago Law Journal* 199 (1992).

3. Homer, *Odyssey*, X1, 271–80, Albert Cook translation, (New York: W.W. Norton, 1974). See chapter 4, note 32.

4. *Encyclopedia Britannica,* VIII, 879 (1988).

5. S. M. Adams, as reprinted in Sophocles, *Oedipus* (New York: Norton Critical Edition, 1970), p. 110.

6. I draw here on the approach developed in my book, *The Artist as Thinker: From Shakespeare to Joyce* (Athens, Ohio: Ohio University Press, 1983). That book has been described as "establishing a genre of literary interpretation, in which the critic judges what happens primarily in the light of what the actors should have done." Catalogue, Ohio University Press/Swallow Press, Spring/Summer 1982. See also John Alvis, "Moral Criticism," *Claremont Review of Books*, October 1983, p. 1 (reprinted in John A. Murley, Robert L. Stone, and William T. Braithwaite, eds., *Law and Philosophy: The Practice of Theory* [Athens, Ohio: Ohio University Press, 1992], I, 559) See as well chapter 1, note 100.

7. Oedipus in the *Oedipus at Colonus*, written by Sophocles many years after his *Oedipus Tyrannos*, says to Creon (968–73):

> And tell me this: if there were prophecies
> Repeated by the oracles of the gods,
> That father's death should come through his own son,
> How could you justly blame it upon me?
> On me who was yet unborn, yet unconceived,
> Not yet existent for my father and mother?

See chapter 4, note 42.

8. See chapter 2, note 3.

9. We learn in *Oedipus at Colonus* (e.g., 624–29) that there was more than this in the oracles available to Oedipus—more about his last days and the consequences of his burial. But did the Sophocles of *Oedipus Tyrannos* assume such things?

10. See Plato, *Apology* 20E sq. See also chapter 1, note 2.

11. An Oedipus enlightened about his adoptive status might have been curious to seek out his parents and thus might still have made his way to Thebes and to encounters there with Laius (if Laius had not already been killed by him) and with Jocasta. Or, perhaps, Laius would have gone to Corinth on a state visit. Besides, might not

one's adoptive parents serve as parents for the purpose of the prophecy? See George Anastaplo, "On Trial: Explorations," 22 *Loyola University of Chicago Law Journal* 765, 1052 n. 325 (1991). See also chapter 2, note 10.

12. See, "Of Counsel—and the Limits of Politics," in Anastaplo, *The American Moralist*, p. 484. See also chapter 4, note 17.

13. This inventory, to which more could be added, points up the need for Oedipus to have thought, at the outset, both about what the prophecy *could* mean and about which forms of its fulfillment were particularly to be avoided.

14. The complexities here are suggested by a comment I had occasion to make in *The Constitutionalist* (p. 798 n. 32):

> [Seth] Benardete says of the Oedipus ("Sophocles' *Oedipus Tyrannos*," [in Joseph Cropsey, ed., *Ancients and Moderns* (New York: Basic Books, 1964)], pp. 2–3): ". . . The play therefore moves from the question of who killed Laius to that of who generated Oedipus. It moves from a political to a family crime, which is, paradoxically, from the less comprehensive to the more comprehensive theme (cf. 635 ff.). Oedipus' discovery of his parents *silently discloses his murder of Laius*, but to discover himself as the murderer of Laius would not have disclosed his origins. Sophocles indicates this shift from one theme to the other by the absence of the word *polis* after its twenty-fifth occurrence at 880, the context of which is the denunciation of tyranny. Tyranny links the political and family crime. [Italics in quotation added]"
>
> Consider the shifting back and forth in the play between "one" and "many" murderers of Laius. See Benardete, ibid., pp. 5, 7, 14, n. 13. It is useful to notice that, although both Oedipus and the audience are convinced he did kill Laius, the evidence is not brought forth to support this conclusion; that inquiry is abandoned when Oedipus gets on the track of who he is. Sophocles leaves this vital question [of the killer of Laius] technically (legally?) open. (An identification of Oedipus as the killer at the crossroads could easily have been brought in to round out the case if the author had so desired.) May not this be because the question remains essentially open? Who *did* kill Laius? One or many? Oedipus, alone, at the crossroads? Or Oedipus as an instrument of the gods, of the "fates," perhaps even of Laius and Jocasta, to say nothing of the city itself? The audience cannot help moving (without perhaps being conscious of it) from one assessment to the other (as does Oedipus himself in *Oedipus at Colonus*?). Does not this contribute to the timeless fascination, and even terror, of the play? One is responsible—and yet again one is not?

See the text at note 96 of chapter 7 of this collection. See also chapter 4, note 32, 33. Is it not to speak somewhat dramatically, and hence loosely, to refer to the "murder of Laius"?

15. The Delphic oracle about the Theban plague, as reported by Creon to Oedipus, did not refer at all to the incest.

16. See the text at note 30 of chapter 2 of this collection.

17. Consider here the advice given by Machiavelli in chapter 23 of *The Prince* (Leo Paul S. de Alvarez translation [Irving, Texas: University of Dallas Press, 1980]):

> A prince, therefore, ought always to take counsel, but only when he wishes to do so and not when others wish; indeed he ought to take the heart out of anyone counseling him on anything, when he does not ask for it. But he ought very much to be an asker-at-large,

and then a patient hearer of the truth about the things asked; indeed, when he understands that someone, because of some reservation, does not speak the truth, he should be disturbed by it.

See also chapter 4, note 12, chapter 10, note 68. Compare chapter 10, note 3. See as well George Anastaplo, "Law, Judges, and the Principles of Regimes: Explorations," 70 *Tennessee Law Review* 455, 459 (2003).

18. Consider, on what the world is like, the problem of "one murderer or many," chapter 4, note 14. See also, on patricide and being, chapter 4, note 20.

19. Did Sophocles know that Oedipus was, both at the fatal crossroads and in Thebes, actually *closer* to Corinth than he had been in Delphi, whatever his frantic intention may have been (upon leaving Delphi) to get as far away from Corinth as possible?

20. See, on the significance of patricide (as distinguished from fratricide), Robert Sacks, *The Lion and the Ass: A Commentary on the Book of Genesis* (chapter 1, note 1), commentary on *Genesis* 4:8:

> The theme of brother killing brother is a common beginning for many peoples. The most famous is the story of Romulus and Remus. It is by no accident that in this case we are more familiar with the Roman myth than with any corresponding Greek myth. The political, in the most common usage of the word, played a higher role in Rome than it did in Athens. In the Bible, too, the fratricide is committed by [Cain] the founder of the first city. The myth or account is an essentially political account, though the fratricide itself is an essentially prepolitical act. The founding of a city requires a leader, and yet there is a natural equality among brothers. The awareness of this difficulty seems to lie behind both accounts. Greek myth, on the other hand, deals more with patricide, which ultimately means the attempt to become one's own father by replacing him. Motivations for erasing one's own origins, or rather becoming one's own origins, lie in the attempt to assert one's own complete independence of being. In that sense patricide is essentially an apolitical act.

See chapter 4, note 23.

21. See the text at note 1 of the introduction to this collection.

22. See chapter 2, note 10.

23. Why does this regicide lead to these consequences? Is it because it is also a patricide? Is patricide a repudiation of fertility itself, something that incest is not by *its* very nature? See chapter 2, note 6, chapter 4, note 20. Besides, the gods themselves sometimes engage in incest, but not in patricide.

24. See chapter 4–B.

25. The traditional answer, it will be remembered, is *Man*.

26. Cane or no cane, Oedipus is physically powerful in his encounter with Laius and his party at the crossroads.

27. See Benardete, "Sophocles' *Oedipus Tyrannos*," pp. 5–6.

28. See Sophocles, *Oedipus at Colonus* 988–99.

29. One can be reminded here of King Hamlet in Shakespeare's *Hamlet*: he is so bent on revenge that he is not concerned about the welfare either of Denmark or of his son, Prince Hamlet. See, e.g., George Anastaplo, "Law & Literature and Shake-

speare: Explorations," 26 *Oklahoma City University Law Review* 1, 220 (2001). See also chapter 9, note 14.

30. See Sophocles, *Oedipus at Colonus* 1640–65, 1725–31, 1755–69.

31. See Sophocles, *Oedipus at Colonus* 1642–44.

32. It does not seem that the Homeric Oedipus blinded himself. Rather, he continued to rule in Thebes. See the text at notes 4 and 5 of chapter 4 of this collection. Is the blinding something "sentimental" as well as "symbolic" that is added later? Did the Homeric version reflect the opinion that Oedipus had not been personally blameworthy? See chapter 4, note 14.

33. This also points up a tendency to something like patricide that may be in Oedipus when he is provoked, especially by someone who is older. Did the Delphic oracle simply "read" what Oedipus might be like in his passion? Did Jocasta's hanging herself spare her son/husband from doing still another dreadful thing? That is, did she hang herself, partly for his sake? Did she attempt thereby to "solve" their problem (riddle?) by doing to herself what Laius and she had tried to do to the infant Oedipus?

34. See Sophocles, *Oedipus at Colonus* 576f, 647, 760–67.

35. See the text at note 77 of chapter 1 of this collection. See also chapter 1, note 20.

36. See, e.g., Plato, *Republic* 414B sq.; Plato, *Letters VIII* 332D–E, 341C–E, 344C–E. See also chapter 7, note 67. Compare the text at note 34 of chapter 7 of this collection. See as well Anastaplo, "On Trial" (*Loyola Law Journal*), p. 881.

37. See chapter 3, note 13.

38. Homer, *Odyssey*, XII, 36–54, 153–200.

39. Homer, *Odyssey*, IX, 116–566.

40. This talk was given at a Staff Seminar of the Basic Program of Liberal Education for Adults, The University of Chicago, Chicago, Illinois, October 3, 1964.

The Elizabeth Wychoff translation of *Antigone* (with an occasional correction by me) is used here and in part C of this chapter. The parenthetical citations in the text are to the Wychoff translation of *Antigone* as published by the University of Chicago Press in *Sophocles I* (1954).

A recapitulation of the plot of the Sophoclean play is provided in section III of part C of this chapter. See also chapter 10, note 26.

41. Elizabeth Wychoff, trans., Sophocles, *Antigone*, in *Sophocles I*, p. 206. See also chapter 8, note 33, chapter 10, section II.

42. Antigone's name represents a negation of generation. It is said that her family's "original crime consists in generation itself." What *does* that mean? Is the conception of Oedipus himself thus referred to? It is also said, "Laius was held to be the first homosexual." Seth Benardete, "A Reading of Sophocles' *Antigone, II*," *Interpretation,* summer 1975, p. 28 note 84. See the text at note 7 of chapter 4 of this collection. See also the text at note 51 of chapter 4 of this collection.

43. In fact, some scholars have tried to cut these lines from the text, but unfortunately for them (and fortunately for us) they are in all of the manuscripts and were known to Aristotle as Antigone's. Our translator observes,

> For those, like myself, who are sure the lines are Antigone's, there is drama in her abandoning her moralities and clinging to her irrational profundity of feeling for her lost and irreplaceable brother, devising legalistic arguments for her intellectual justification.

Wychoff, in *Sophocles I*, p. 206. I hardly believe that Antigone "abandon[ed] her moralities" on this occasion, whatever tension may be exhibited, in her awareness of things, between the just and the noble. See Anastaplo, *The Constitutionalist*, p. 651 n. 91. See, on the noble and the just, George Anastaplo, *The Thinker as Artist: From Homer to Plato & Aristotle* (Athens, Ohio: Ohio University Press, 1997), p. 182. Consider the "irrationality" of Athena in the text at note 33 of chapter 2 of this collection. See also chapter 4, note 44.

44. Would Antigone really want still another brother from the incestuous marriage of her parents? See Benardete, "A Reading of Sophocles' *Antigone, III*," *Interpretation*, winter 1975, pp. 151f.

45. See Plato, *Crito* 50D.

46. See Anastaplo, *The Constitutionalist*, p.798 n. 32:

Thus, the lines which scholars dismiss as distracted, perhaps even as spurious, point not (as some say) merely to irrationality on her part but rather to her awareness of both her strength and her vulnerability. But awareness is not the same as understanding: and so she challenges a new convention (Creon's decree) in the name of an older one (which some mistakenly see as either natural or divine in its origin). And yet the city does depend on the very family that it legitimates: it is appropriate that Creon is destroyed through his family.

Compare Plato, *Republic* 457C sq., 469C–E.

47. See chapter 4, note 48.

48. See Anastaplo, *The Constitutionalist*, p 798 n. 32:

Creon, invoking the claim of the city against the family, fails to discern that his authority comes to him through his family; Antigone, invoking the claim of the family against the city, fails to discern that her pride of family has been nurtured by the political role of her family in the city. Agamemnon is greeted on his return home as "king, sacker of Troy's citadel, and issue of Atreus." *Agamemnon* 783–84. But what he had to do to become the sacker of Troy (as well as to remain king?) corrupted his family relations and led to his destruction. (This juxtaposition is seen as well in the conflict in *The Eumenides* between the family-linked old divinities and the city-linked new ones.)

See also chapter 4, note 50.

49. See the text at notes 42 and 43 of chapter 1 of this collection. See also chapter 2, note 4; chapter 2–D, sections V and VI.

50. Her mother, Jocasta, had also hung herself. Antigone's last speech in Sophocles' play is heard as she is led to her entombment (937–43):

> O town of my fathers in Thebe's land,
> O gods of our house.
> I am led away at last.
> Look, leaders of Thebes,
> I am last of your royal line.
> Look what I suffer, at whose command,
> Because I respected the right.

She can proclaim herself the last of the Theban royal line, whether or not her sister survives her. See Sophocles, *Antigone* 38.

51. See chapter 4, note 42.

52. See chapter 2–D, sections VI and VIII.

53. This talk was given for the Basic Program of Liberal Education for Adults, The University of Chicago, Chicago, Illinois, March 4, 1979.

The parenthetical citations in the text to Jean Anouihl's *Antigone* are to the Lewis Galantière translation as published by Hill and Wang as a Mermaid Dramabook (1958). The parenthetical citations in the text to Sophocles' *Antigone* are to the Wychoff translation. See chapter 4, note 40.

54. Benardete, "A Reading of Sophocles' *Antigone, II*," p. 32. May the same be said about Orestes? See, e.g., section II of chapter 2–B; the text at notes 9 and 29 of chapter 2 of this collection.

55. See Benardete, "A Reading of Sophocles' *Antigone, II*," p. 33. It should be evident, upon a careful reading of the Benardete analysis, how much one's grasp of the Greek plays can be enhanced by that knowledge of the language that permits the most precise translations, however tempting it may sometimes be in such circumstances to overinterpret. I have been using here, and in my discussions of the *Oresteia*, the English translations that are generally available. See chapter 7, note 24.

5

Abraham and Kierkegaard[1]

I.

We have been told, for thousands of years now, the following story (in chapter 22 of the *Book of Genesis*) about the patriarch Abraham, the founder of a great people:

1. And it came to pass after these things, that God did test Abraham, and said unto him,"Abraham"; and he [Abraham] said, "Behold, here I am."
2. And He [God] said, "Please take thy son, thine only son, whom thou lovest, even Isaac, and get thee into the land of Moriah; and offer him there for a burnt offering upon one of the mountains which I will tell thee of."
3. And Abraham rose up early in the morning, and saddled his ass, and took two of his young men with him, and Isaac his son, and clave the wood for the burnt offering, and rose up, and went unto the place of which God had told him.
4. Then on the third day Abraham lifted up his eyes, and saw the place afar off.
5. And Abraham said unto his young men, "Sit yourselves down here with the ass; and I and the lad will go yonder and bow down and return to you."
6. And Abraham took the wood of the burnt offering, and laid it upon Isaac his son; and he took the fire in his hand, and a knife; and they went both of them together.
7. And Isaac spake unto Abraham his father, and said, "My father"; and [Abraham] said, "Here am I, my son," and [Isaac] said, "Behold the fire and wood: but where is the lamb for a burnt offering?"

8. And Abraham said, "My son, God will provide Himself a lamb for a burnt offering": so they went both of them together.

9. And they came to the place that God had told him of; and Abraham built an altar there, and laid the wood in order, and bound Isaac his son, and laid him on the altar upon the wood.

10. And Abraham stretched forth his hand, and took the knife to slay his son.

11. And the angel of the Lord called unto him out of Heaven, and said, "Abraham, Abraham," and he said, "Here am I."

12. And [the angel] said, "Lay not thine hand upon the lad, neither do thou anything unto him; for now I know that thou fearest God, seeing thou hast not withheld thy son, thine only son from Me."

13. And Abraham lifted up his eyes, and looked, and behold behind him a ram caught in a thicket by his horns: and Abraham went and took the ram, and offered him up for a burnt offering in the stead of his son.

14. And Abraham called the name of that place Jehovah-jireh: as it is said to this day, in the mount of the Lord it shall be seen.

15. And the angel of the Lord called unto Abraham out of Heaven the second time.

16. And said, "'By Myself have I sworn,' saith the Lord, 'for because thou hast done this thing, and hast not withheld thy son, thine only son:

17. 'That in blessing I will bless thee, and in multiplying I will multiply thy seed as the stars of the heaven, and as the sand which is upon the sea shore; and thy seed shall possess the gate of his enemies;

18. 'And in thy seed shall all the nations of the earth be blessed; because thou hast obeyed my voice.'"

19. So Abraham returned unto the young men, and they rose up and went together to Beer-sheba; and Abraham dwelt at Beer-sheba.[2]

This story—the story of what is most tellingly referred to among Jews as "The Binding"—has been retold (and in the way of retelling, commented upon) again and again. Consider, for example, what the twelfth-century Jewish scholar, Moses Maimonides, had to say about it:

As for the story of *Abraham* at the *binding* [*of Isaac*], it contains two great notions that are fundamental principles of the Law. One of these notions consists in our being informed of the limit of *love* for God, may He be exalted, and *fear* of Him—that is, up to what limit they must reach. For in this story he was ordered to do something that bears no comparison either with sacrifice of property or with sacrifice of life. In truth it is the most extraordinary thing that could happen in the world, such a thing that one would not imagine that human nature was capable of it. Here there is a sterile man having an exceeding desire for a son, possessed of great property and commanding respect, and having the wish that his progeny should become a religious community. When a son comes to him after his having lost hope, how great will be his attachment to him and love for him! However, because of his fear of Him, who should be exalted, and because of his love to carry out His command, he holds this beloved son as little, gives up all his hopes regarding him, and hastens to slaughter him after a journey of days. For if he had chosen to do this immediately, as soon as the order came to him, it would have been an act of stupefaction and disturbance in the absence of exhaustive reflection. But his doing it days after the command had come to him shows that the act sprang from thought, correct understanding, consideration of the truth of His command, may He be exalted, love of Him, and fear of Him. No other circumstance should be put forward, nor should one opt for the notion that he was in a state of passion. For *Abraham our Father* did not hasten to slaughter *Isaac* because he was afraid that God would kill him or make him poor, but solely because of what is incumbent upon the Adamites—namely, to love Him and fear Him, may He be exalted—and not, as we have explained in several passages, for any hope of a reward or for fear of punishment. Accordingly the *angel* said to him: *For now I know that thou fearest God*: meaning that through the act because of which the term *fearing God* is applied to you, all the Adamites will know what the limits of *the fear of the Lord* are. Know that this notion is corroborated and explained in the *Torah*, in which it is mentioned that the final end of the whole of the *Torah*, including its commandments, prohibitions, promises, and narratives, is one thing only—namely, fear of Him, may He be exalted. This is referred to in its dictum: *If thou wilt not take care to observe all the words of this Law that are written in this book, that thou mayest fear this glorious and awful Name, and so on.* [*Deut.* 28: 58] This is one of the two notions aimed at in the *binding*.[3]

II.

Seven centuries after Maimonides a Danish writer published, from the Christian perspective, what has become a celebrated discussion of this story of Abraham and Isaac. That discussion has been described in these terms, from a Jewish perspective, by a contemporary American scholar:

> Soren Kierkegaard wrote a book called *Fear and Trembling*. It is the story of an old man who had spent many years thinking about the present chapter [*Genesis* 22]. He looks at it from many sides and his final thoughts were something like this: Abraham had been promised the seed, and that seed could only come through his chosen son, Isaac. On the other hand, God has commanded that the boy die. Abraham, in order to maintain his faith in God, must believe both that the promise would be kept and that the son would die. The old man reaches the conclusion that it is human reason itself that was placed on the altar that day so many years ago in the land of Moriah.[4]

Another contemporary of ours, a German scholar, has had this to say about Kierkegaard's book:

> In *Fear and Trembling* faith is depicted as a major human passion, affecting daily life at every point, its content being the reality of the individual's existence. Faith is heroic and absurd, for it transcends the calculations of worldly wisdom. It implies an infinite resignation with respect to finite goods. Only after such resignation the religious experience lives again in the finite, but in virtue of an absolute relation to the Absolute or Eternal. The main theme, which stands for Kierkegaard's own act of renunciation, is Abraham's sacrifice of Isaac.[5]

Our German scholar, writing some thirty years ago, observed,

> [T]here is a distinct possibility for Kierkegaard's influence, for a recollection of the basic principle of Christianity. This will become apparent when we realize that the conventionally Christian habit of mind has suffered the corrosion of three centuries of liberalism, and that the final breakup of the Victorian age is inevitable. The language and outlook upon life, where to be a Christian was practically the same as to be a gentleman and to live in a civilized world, became a foreign tongue. In this atmosphere the radical distinction between Greek wisdom and Christian faith by men like Kierkegaard and Nietzsche may restore once more the original condition of Christianity to its true significance.[6]

Still another contemporary of ours, a Jewish scholar in this country, has written of Kierkegaard in this manner:

> Under [his] influence, many contemporary thinkers have stressed the decisive importance of religious commitment, of self-engagement. They consider faith primarily a matter of will and decision.
>
> Reminiscent of Tertullian and Pascal, Kierkegaard maintained that what the individual did was conditioned by what he willed, not by what he understood.[7]

That Kierkegaard's influence extends beyond what may sometimes seem a limited circle of theologians may be seen in an observation by Leo Strauss, in his *Natural Right and History*, in the course of his description of the importance attached in modernity to history and the philosophy of history:

> By becoming the highest theme of philosophy, practice ceased to be practice proper, i.e., concern with *agenda*. The revolts against Hegelianism on the part of Kierkegaard and Nietzsche, in so far as they now exercise a strong influence on public opinion, thus appear as attempts to recover the possibility of practice, i.e., of a human life that has a significant and undetermined future. But these attempts increased the confusion, since they destroyed, as far as in them lay, the

very possibility of theory. "Doctrinairism" and "existentialism" appear to us as the two faulty extremes. While being opposed to each other, they agree with each other in the decisive respect—they agree in ignoring prudence, "the god of this lower world." [Edmund Burke, *Works*, II, 28] Prudence and "this lower world" cannot be seen properly without some knowledge of "the higher world"—without genuine *theoria*.[8]

Consider the terms that stand out in the various passages I have quoted from thus far in providing the contemporary intellectual setting for our discussion of Kierkegaard and Abraham: *individuality, resignation, commitment, absurdity, will, self-engagement,* and now *existentialism. Existentialism* is a likely, if not even the natural, response to the sense of the *absurdity* of life that the modern *individual* has come to experience. It may well be, then, that Kierkegaard's principal interest for us may come from what a study of him helps us see about the Existentialist movement, a movement that can be traced from Kierkegaard (in reaction to Kant and to Hegel) to the more serious (and perhaps even more influential) developments in Nietzsche and Heidegger.[9]

The sense of the absurd, upon which so much seems to depend for Existentialism, is perhaps dealt with for someone such as Kierkegaard by the story of Abraham and Isaac. One sees in that story, Kierkegaard argues, the diametrically opposed positions one is led to take: everything depends upon Isaac's long life and yet everything depends as well upon Isaac's immediate death. This kind of argument may be anticipated in works such as a sixteenth-century commentary on *Genesis* by John Calvin:

> For God, as if engaging in personal contest with [Abraham], requires the death of the boy, to whose person He himself had annexed the hope of eternal salvation. So that this latter command was, in a certain sense, the destruction of faith. . . .
> God, in a certain sense, assumes a double character [in his dealings here with Abraham], that, by the appearance of disagreement and repugnance in which He presents Himself in his word, he may distract and wound the breast of the holy man. For the only method of cherishing constancy of faith, is to apply all our senses to the word of God. But so great was then the discrepancy of the word, that it would wound and lacerate the faith of Abraham. Wherefore, there is great emphasis [in the passage] on the word, "said," because God indeed made trial of Abraham's faith, not in the usual manner, but by drawing him into a contest with his own word.[10]

An editor of the Calvin text explains, at this point,

> God's usual manner of trying the faith of his people is, by causing the dispensations of his providence apparently to contradict his word, and requiring them

still to rely upon that word, notwithstanding the apparent inconsistency. But in Abraham's trial, He proposed a test far more severe. For His own command, or word, was in direct contradiction to what he had before spoken; His injunction respecting the slaying of Isaac could, by no human method of reasoning, be reconciled to his promises respecting the future destinies of Abraham's family, of the Church, and of the world.[11]

The stage had been set, then, for our discussion of Kierkegaard—and, whatever the failings may be of my own observations about him, you will at least have had, for your reflections hereafter, indications of what various scholars and commentators of note have had to say about Abraham and Isaac and about Abraham and Kierkegaard. One cannot reasonably expect in such matters to add much that is both original and valid.

III.

The Kierkegaard I presume to talk about on this occasion is, I must emphasize, a limited one. I am more concerned to examine certain problems, or rather to suggest how those problems might be considered, than to present a reliable account of Kierkegaard as a whole.

In order to understand Kierkegaard here, one must try to deal with the account in *Genesis* of The Binding of Isaac. Only if one *begins* to understand the account of The Binding may one learn something vital about Kierkegaard, how he reads a serious text that he takes seriously. One might also learn thereby what to expect from his reading of other texts, such as the Platonic dialogues.[12] This would not be a critical point for one's efforts to understand an author who merely uses a text as an occasion or as a point of departure— but it is stressed in *Fear and Trembling* that the *Genesis* story had been much thought about.

Our effort is complicated in this instance, as in dealing with a Platonic dialogue,[13] because of the various interpreters of the story evident in the book: there is the old man who has pondered long about the story;[14] there is the man under whose name (Johannes de Silentio) the account of the old man and of Abraham is issued;[15] and there is, of course, Kierkegaard himself. A further complication is indicated by the name of the man to whom this book is assigned by Kierkegaard: what is left unsaid in the book may be more significant than, or at least as significant as, what is made explicit.

One must distinguish, however, between that which is deliberately left unsaid and that which is left unsaid because of ignorance or inadvertence. The first contemporary Jewish American from whom I quoted—the one who reported that "the old man reaches the conclusion that it is human reason itself which was placed on the altar that day"[16]—added this comment to his summary of *Fear and Trembling*:

> Kierkegaard, who considers himself a master of irony, at one point says, "If the old man had known Hebrew perhaps he would have understood the chapter better." It is a pity for the modern world that Kierkegaard did not understand the true irony of that statement. If he had, he would have seen that the old man's lack of Hebrew was indeed the cause of his misunderstanding of the text. The irony of the statement lies not in its falsity, as Kierkegaard thought, but rather in its truth.[17]

Hebrew, I take it, includes not only the language, and hence how the text is to be read, but also (among other things) the opinions, expectations, and practices both of those writing and of those expected to read this text.

I can do no more than put you on notice about these things, for my knowledge of Hebrew (however understood) is virtually nonexistent. But the importance of such things can be suggested by two illustrations, one taken from the Greek Bible, or the New Testament, the other from the Hebrew Bible, or the Old Testament. Consider, for example, the *Gospel of Matthew*, where there are recorded, as the last words of Jesus on the Cross, "My God, my God, why hast thou forsaken me?"[18] Despair, a sense of abandonment, perhaps even a loss of faith are suggested by these words, standing alone. But, one must remember, *Matthew* may be the most Jewish of the Gospels (in the way it is written, in the readers addressed);[19] and, I am told, a Jewish reader would have recognized Jesus' recourse to his last words as an instance of the pious practice of invoking an entire Psalm (in this case, the twenty-second) by proclaiming its opening line. The Psalm in this case is one that moves from a cry of anguish to a song of praise of God, that is, to an enduring reliance upon Him.[20]

My Old Testament illustration, suggesting what knowledge of the Hebrew can provide one, is taken from the twenty-second chapter of *Genesis*, from our story, where God says to Abraham, "Please take thy son, thine only son, and so forth."[21] Most translations into English do not notice the "please" here but rather say such things as, "Take your son, thine only son, and so forth." A Jewish commentator has observed about this usage, "The Hebrew is peculiar: the imperative 'take' is followed by the Hebrew particle . . . which means, 'I pray thee'—God was speaking to Abraham 'as friend to friend.'"[22]

Another commentator, the one who had said what I have quoted about Kierkegaard's irony in connection with this very passage, goes on to say (perhaps to begin to explain how the lack of Hebrew can mislead one),

> The word *please* in Hebrew is a short word and is often ignored by translators, but when it appears in the words of God spoken to a human being it certainly

cannot be overlooked. God uses the word in four other places, but in all of them it is used in the sense of inviting someone to accept a gift (*Gen.* 13:14; 15:5; and 31:12). To no other person aside from Abraham does God say *please* in the whole of the Bible.

God and Abraham had made a Covenant. God would give Abraham a son and make his name great if Abraham were willing to devote that seed to the establishment of the New Way. He asked Abraham whether he would be willing to give up that seed and the Covenant. The question is whether Abraham would be willing to relinquish the seed while remaining perfect in the sense discussed in the beginning of chapter 17 [of *Genesis*].

God's request was dangerous on both sides. But suppose Abraham had refused? Killing Abraham would have been of little help, and yet how could the two of them ever face each other again? Could God have nullified the Covenant? Perhaps, but then God's word would be meaningless, and what man could ever trust Him again?

So long as there was no command there was no contradiction, and Kierkegaard, in his sacrifice of reason [in his argument, that is, that a sacrifice of reason had been required of Abraham?], became more like the followers of Moloch than like Abraham.

The present chapter [chapter 22] appears in sharp contrast to God's discussion with Abraham prior to the destruction of Sodom and Gomorrah. In that case Abraham was willing to argue with God as any man might argue with another, but here he says nothing.

These two poles may not be so different as first appears. God may have the right to request that which He has no right to demand. If God had commanded the death of Isaac it is by no means clear that Abraham would have complied. The most that can be said is that Abraham is willing to argue with God in order to save the lives of men whom he does not know while he is willing to be silent when the destruction touches him personally. In the whole of the discussion about Sodom and Gomorrah, Lot's name was never mentioned. In a strange way the present passage speaks more about God's faith in Abraham than Abraham's faith in God. If Abraham had refused, God would still be forced to keep His promise, but the relationship between Him and Abraham would have become unbearable. As it is Abraham and God will never speak with each other again after the present chapter.[23]

Was Kierkegaard aware of such considerations? Was he equipped to become aware of them? Did he really *read* the Biblical (or Platonic) texts? Or did he merely *use* them?[24] Let us consider further the story of The Binding and what Kierkegaard does with it. We can thus see what more can be said in support of the proposition that Abraham was not truly faced by contradictory commands, that there was no *sacrifice of reason* required of him. Perhaps we can also see why Kierkegaard may have wanted to believe a sacrifice of reason *is* required from the man of faith (that is, the man of action)—and how all this bears upon, among other thing, the psychic underpinnings of contemporary Existentialism.

IV.

Should it not be understood that there is something fierce, even monstrous, about the attempted sacrifice of Isaac, and this is so independent of the promise associated with Abraham's seed through Isaac?

There may be, in the Old Testament stories, other deaths and other sacrifices (or attempted sacrifices) as troubling (at least at first glance) as what is seen here. The destruction of Job's family comes to mind as does the sacrifice by Jephthah of his innocent daughter.[25] But those people—the family and the daughter—do not become known as human beings to the reader. Of course, Isaac might not have become *as* known as he has to us if he had been sacrificed. But the desire by Abraham and Sarah for him is vivid and his birth is remarkable.[26] To assess these matters thus *is* to work from the impression made upon us; it is to treat these matters somewhat as one would a play. But should not this be expected in thinking about accounts that were written to achieve particular effects, to put across particular teachings, in the community at large?

The fierceness, if not monstrousness, of what Abraham seems to have been asked to do is recognized, it would seem, by the author of the *Book of Genesis*. God Himself is shown as acknowledging this as the supreme test. Yet it is also shown as something Abraham should be willing to do, that it is almost "natural" that he should be willing to do it, however unnatural the deed might have been.

But, we notice, this episode, partly because of its fierceness, raises for us questions that are not explicitly addressed by the author of *Genesis*.[27] How did Abraham learn that he should do this? How could he know that the request came from God? Abraham, it would seem, is a man who, by this time, has had well-established contacts with God. This particular message, it would also seem, came to him during the night, perhaps in a dream, for he is reported to have risen early in the morning and to have gone about complying with God's request. Maimonides had spoken of the story of Abraham and The Binding containing "*two* great notions that are fundamental principles of the Law."[28] One of those notions, as we have seen, "consists in our being informed of the limit of *love* for God, . . . and *fear* of Him—that is, up to what limit they must reach."[29] The other notion contained in the story of The Binding is one that bears on our immediate problem, that of how Abraham could have known that the fateful request truly came from God. Maimonides can say,

The second notion consists in making known to us the fact that the prophets consider as true that which comes to them from God in a prophetic revelation. For it should not be thought that what they hear or what appears to them in a parable is not certain or is commingled with illusion just because it comes about *in a dream and in a vision*, as we have made clear, and through the intermediary of the imaginative faculty. Accordingly [Scripture] wished to make it known to us that all that is seen by a prophet in *a vision of prophesy* is, in the opinion of the prophet, a certain truth, that the prophet has no doubts in any way concerning anything in it, and that in his opinion its status is the same as that of all existent things that are apprehended through the senses or through the intellect. A proof for this is the fact that [Abraham] hastened to slaughter, as he had been commanded, *his son, his only son, whom he loved*, even though this command came to him *in a dream* or *in a vision*. For if a dream of prophecy had been obscure for the prophets, or if they had doubts or incertitude concerning what they apprehended *in a vision of prophecy*, they would not have hastened to do that which is repugnant to nature, and [Abraham's] soul would not have consented to accomplish an act of so great an importance if there had been *a doubt* about it.[30]

The primary consideration, it would seem, is not the form in which the "prophetic revelation" appears but rather "that the prophet has no doubts in any way concerning anything in it." This certainty, it would also seem, depends primarily upon one's overall relations with God. The intimate relation between prophetic insight and genuine poetic inspiration seems to be evident here. In a sense, then, the most reliable revelation consists of the best insight into the highest things—and the inspired man reflects this either in his words or in his deeds.[31]

The question remains, however, as to the immediate source of such insight. (I say *immediate* since everything, including the workings of what we call *nature*, can be considered by the believer to be ultimately derived from God.) Does not the absurdity that Kierkegaard insists upon depend upon a particular view of the world and of the constant involvement of God in the things of this world? Does not his positing of absurdity somehow depend upon interventions from time to time by God, interventions at least in the form of messages?

What *is* God like? Does He move, change, or act? What can man know about God? If God does not change, the world may be such as to provide guidance to people even about God, if they but look and then think about what they see.

Dare one add that if God is indeed changeless—and does not this follow from perfection?—may not the place one has to look to understand what happened on the occasion of The Binding be not into the unfathomable mind of God but in the all-too-human soul of Abraham?[32]

V.

A critical question remains: What should Abraham have known about God? The answer to this question affects one's judgment as to whether this was a case of overwhelming absurdity and as to whether absurdity is at the roots of seriousness, with "commitment" (which is essentially arbitrary, in appearance) the only way out.[33]

What *should* Abraham have known about God? A man, for example, who is told (as Socrates was) that a god had identified him as among the wisest of men would be wise to examine that identification for what it truly means.[34] A man who is told, or asked, by God to undertake an apparently questionable mission might well wonder whether he understands precisely what is to happen. Was there, on the occasion of The Binding, a case of absurdity, with a leap of faith by Abraham across the dreadful abyss thereby revealed?[35]

Does a miracle represent a kind of absurdity in the concrete, something that obliges us to accept contradictory propositions? But, one is again obliged to ask, does a perfect God act? Does He change? St. Augustine argues that the Biblical accounts of God's anger do not mean that His changeless tranquility had been, or can be, disturbed.[36] He can say, in a passage that reminds one of how philosophy can regard poetry,

> Now God's anger is not an agitation of his mind; it is a judgment by which punishment is inflicted on sin. And his consideration and reconsideration are his unchanging plan applied to things subject to change. For God does not repent of any action of his, as man does, and his decision on any matter whatsoever is as fixed as his foreknowledge is sure. But if Scripture did not employ such words, it would not strike home so closely, as it were, to all mankind. For Scripture is concerned for man, and it uses such language to terrify the proud, to arouse the careless, to exercise the inquirer, and to nourish the intelligent; and it would not have this effect if it did not first bend down and, as we may say, descend to the level of those on the ground.[37]

Perhaps another way of asking what Abraham should have known about God is to address the question, What should Abraham have expected to happen on this occasion? What should one, who perhaps knew as much as any living man can about what God is like,[38] expect God to do or to allow—that is, to want or to call for? Should Abraham have known[39] what even we know, that God would not permit Isaac to be killed? How do we know it? From the story, it will be said. But how did the writer of the story know it? Abraham himself did not write the story. The writer had been moved to believe this story; it had somehow been told to him. Why did he believe this story, this version of the story, among the many versions that may have been available to him? Is it because it fit in with, or reflected, what he otherwise knew to be the truth about God and about His dealings with human beings?[40]

In principle, then, did not the original writer of the story have to make the same decision we must make, or that Abraham had to make, as to what God truly wants of human beings? Should one, without having to be told, be able to figure out, in the words of the Psalmist, "All the paths of the Lord are mercy and truth"?[41] *Should* not Abraham have sensed, therefore, that he would not have to go through with the sacrifice of his son if he was truly acting in accordance with the divine will?

It can be argued—and with this argument Kierkegaard's absurdity is further questioned—that Abraham was in fact somehow aware that he would *not* have to sacrifice Isaac. You will recall that Abraham did say to the servants accompanying him and his son, "Sit yourselves down here with the ass; and I and the lad will go yonder and bow down and return to you."[42] "The Rabbis [of old?] declare that at [this] moment the Spirit of Prophecy entered into [Abraham], and he spoke more truly than he knew."[43] Consider, also, Abraham's answer to the inquiring Isaac, "God will provide Himself a lamb for a burnt offering."[44] True, Abraham did draw his knife—but with what expectation? We would speak today of a conflict (or shall we say a difference of opinion?) between the conscious and the unconscious parts of Abraham. One commentator has observed of the language, "and offer him there for a burnt offering," that this is literally, " 'lift him up' (upon the altar)," adding, "God, in His command, did not use the word which signifies the *slaying* of the sacrificial victim. From the outset, therefore, there was no intention of accepting a human sacrifice, although Abraham was at first not aware of this."[45] Or would it be better to say, "Abraham was at first not *fully* aware of this"?

After all, it seems to me, *far less* is required to stop Abraham from completing the sacrifice than had happened up to this point to bring Isaac to the point of being sacrificed. What does happen now is something quite ordinary—and if not this ordinary thing, would not another have appeared and sufficed? I refer to the appearance of a ram caught by his horns in a thicket. Abraham sees a ram and sacrifices it instead of his son. He did not insist upon the lamb earlier anticipated (prophesied?) by him![46] What other compromises might he have made if properly directed?

To ask this question about proper direction is to remind ourselves that an angel also speaks to Abraham on this occasion.[47] Does Isaac hear this angel? We are not told. In what form does the angel appear to Abraham? Can this be understood as a second thought—perhaps as the culmination of the thinking he had been doing for three days? In a sense, then, there is nothing truly extraordinary about the intervention of such an angelic message. Does it not make sense? Is Abraham's *binding* of Isaac as he did the only extraordinary thing that takes place in the entire episode?

If one considers this matter in this manner, the issue of absurdity need not arise. Nor *did* it arise, I should add, for many, perhaps most, Jewish as well as Christian believers over the centuries.[48] Not that most of them would have spoken of all this as I just have. But neither would they have been reduced to Kierkegaard's mode of reasoning about the sacrifice. For example, Augustine writes (echoing his Jewish predecessors),

> Abraham, we can be sure, could never have believed that God delights in human victims; and yet the thunder of a divine command must be obeyed without argument. However, Abraham is to be praised in that he believed, without hesitation, that his son would rise again when he had been sacrificed. . . . The devout father therefore clung . . . faithfully [to the promise] that had to be fulfilled through the son whom God ordered to be slain, he did not doubt that a son who could be granted to him when he had ceased to hope [because of age] could also be restored to him after he had been sacrificed.[49]

Augustine adds, "This is the interpretation we find in [St. Paul's] *Epistle to the Hebrews*. . . ."[50] One is reminded of the (also fundamentally unJewish?) observation by John the Baptist that God could raise children out of stones to provide descendants for Abraham.[51]

To say that the believer has not, over the centuries, usually conceived of himself as somehow accepting an absurdity is *not* to say that faith is not required. But faith has long been regarded as supplementing, not as contradicting, the truths arrived at by natural reason. Some moderns, on the other hand, almost seem to welcome the appearance of absurdity: this seems to characterize for them the whole (or, perhaps we should say, the divergent wholes) they perceive. But before we turn to these moderns and their inclinations, we must notice something else about Abraham.

VI.

Another way of approaching all this is to ask, What was Abraham trying to do, to prove, to be, or to find out? Was Abraham's understanding of God faulty, perhaps too much influenced by the child-sacrifice practices of his neighbors? Was he somehow challenged by the extent of devotion evident among such idolators?

Is there also reflected in this story Abraham's recognition that he had made, or was in danger of making, too much of his son or of the ambition to be realized through that son? All this, he seems to say, he is willing to put entirely in God's hands to dispose of as *He* wishes. But it is still left to Abraham to listen for, and to respond to, the divine wish.

And so, like the dreamer or the poet, Abraham controls what happens—what he is inspired or moved to say or to do. It does not matter, for our purposes, whether control of events rests in Abraham or in the author of *Genesis* (who may have had, we have noticed, several accounts to choose among, accounts distilled over many years in the memory of the Jewish people).

The rabbis speak of this as the tenth and the greatest of the trials to which Abraham was exposed.[52] "Exposed" by whom or by what? If God does not move—if He does not intervene in particular cases—must not one's *understanding* of the divine will be decisive? That understanding may be faulty or limited, depending upon one's training, one's capacities, and one's character and passions.

We thus return to our question, What is Abraham like? What did he truly want? Is it a sense of himself, or of what we might even call self-expression, rather than any dedication to God, that he is moved by? Something of this may be discerned in a somewhat romantic interpretation of The Binding that one Jewish scholar has provided us (adapting, it seems, ancient accounts to his tastes):

> Abraham stood the test twice: first when he placed Isaac on the altar, then when he helped him down from it. The second trial exacted greater strength than the first. God Himself had told him to sacrifice his son. Then an angel came and called out, "Stop, don't touch him." How could he listen to an angel and disobey God? It took great self-control to miss such a marvelous opportunity to make a supreme sacrifice, and to yield to the angel.[53]

Or is it that Abraham—or the author of Abraham—wanted to impress indelibly upon Isaac and his descendants what fidelity to this faith can mean, what it can look and feel like? Is Abraham's deed a founding act, an act that defies the past and is not to be repeated (but "only" admired) in the future?[54]

A Jewish colleague has told me that he remembers having been profoundly moved as a child by the story of The Binding—and that his own child (a girl), upon first hearing the story as a ten-year old, simply turned white. What do children sense about this story, that it reflects the vulnerability that draws them to even as it makes them wary of their parents, if not also of God?

VII.

My deliberations and conclusion seem, for the most part, alien to Kierkegaard's approach. He wants, or at least recognizes, man to be on his own. Not even reason is to be of much help, except to point up the aloneness and vulnerability of man. Kierkegaard seems to *want* absurdity, one might even suspect, so as to magnify the role of faith and the required leap. At any rate he surely wants to draw out the full implications of an absurd premise and to show that an awareness of that premise does not dissolve the mysteries that reason finds for or by itself.

The community, ecclesiastical as well as political, is systematically depreciated by Kierkegaard in his magnification of faith. In this respect—in his willingness to give up all to God—Abraham is for Kierkegaard *the* Old Testament model of the devout Christian. One must wonder, of course, whether it distorts the Abraham story to see it primarily as a model for, or in terms of, Christianity? One should remember that the story does teach that Judaism in itself offers something that is worth giving up *everything* one cherishes for.

But even to have this story—to be able to read it and to think about it and thereby to take it seriously—depends upon a canon of sacred texts, upon language, and hence upon a community and tradition. It is to depend upon those associations, of believers and of citizens, that Kierkegaard again and again disparages, those associations for whom prudence is indeed "the god of this lower world."[55]

To enter into an absolute relation with God would require, it would seem, that the human being be stripped of all these chance influences (the influences of family, political community, and church). Only thus, Kierkegaard seems to say, is man to be left as a *willing* self. Is this state of affairs, in which the roots of Existentialism may be detected, somehow regarded as creative?[56] For such self-assertion, passion, not reason, is critical—and requires to be deepened.[57] Kierkegaard observes that dread lures forth the obscure *libido* (emotion).[58] This, it would seem, permits one really to confront oneself, to live. And, Kierkegaard also suggests, when one delves into oneself, one first of all discovers the disposition to evil.[59] Compare the ancient teaching that all actions and all pursuits naturally aim at the good.[60]

One might dismiss much that appeals to Kierkegaard as due merely to his own temperament. No doubt, problems in his personal life may have encouraged him to believe that the truly sensitive person is torn by an overwhelming conflict of alternatives. Some of the stories in *Fear and Trembling*[61] exhibit a sickly sentimentality—and may seem to some to suggest that there may be here instances of oddness that should be traced back to the artist's character.

But it will not do to dwell upon Kierkegaard's quirks. The considerable appeal, especially in intellectual circles, of Kierkegaard's opinions, especially the emphasis upon the role of the will, should be taken into account. Has Christianity discovered, invented, or elevated the will, making of it what it never was in antiquity? Has this transformation of the will become particularly critical because of what has happened to the status of nature among us? Is this partly because of the somewhat successful effort to conquer nature? Has nature, that is, somehow been turned against nature?[62]

VIII.

What *is* the status of nature? What is the relation between nature and the good? That is, can the good be *discovered*? Is it somehow rooted in nature? And does not this mean that one's bearings should be taken by universals that exist independent of our will and are knowable?

Kierkegaard's faith, on the other hand, may rest on the opinion that the particular is higher than the universal. This would be seen by him in his acceptance of what *he* would consider the unreasonable (even absurd?) conclusion that Jesus could be both God and man. When one thus places the emphasis upon the particular, one must consider oneself as a witness, not as a teacher.[63] Witnessing points to particulars; it does not rest, as teaching does, on a common good, on a community, or indeed on universals or the ideas.

Put another way, one can say that there is involved here the distinction, for the achievement of the best, between sacrifice and discipline. To emphasize sacrifice, as Kierkegaard does, is perhaps to make much of the will, at the expense of reason and of nature. On the other hand, to emphasize discipline is to assume that there are standards to which one can aspire and from which freedom follows. This means, among other things, that prudence should be brought to bear upon human affairs. When prudence is at work, there is not the teleological suspension of the ethical of which Kierkegaard makes so much, but rather that proper interpretation and application of the ethical pursuant to the dictates of prudence.[64]

Kierkegaard sees the tragic hero as sacrificing everything for the universal; he is the beloved son of ethics.[65] But is not this a misunderstanding? Does not the tragic hero sacrifice the universal for the particular, the whole for a part? Prudence, on the other hand, permits one to see the whole properly. Kierkegaard's insistence upon the ultimate primacy of the absurd, however, makes prudence a futile exercise.

The act of will, and hence of faith, is relied upon by him. One can *know* it *is* the will, it seems to be said, only if one has to resist desires. Pleasure is suspect.[66] But from the perspective of the natural, it can also be said, one takes pleasure, if one is properly trained, in doing what one discerns to be truly good.

Nature is seen by us at bottom in the human awareness of, and the inevitable reliance upon, the principle of contradiction. To talk meaningfully even about absurdity may be to assert a fundamental congruity between reason and the natural order. Do not Kierkegaard and his successors call into question the ground of the natural understanding? Do they question that which human beings have always regarded as somehow immediately apparent to them, their natural awareness of critical things?[67]

All this, it seems, is called into question to a radical extent by what can be called the Existentialist movement. Of course, Kierkegaard himself happened to have something of a way out—in the form of a kind of Christianity. But his successors do not have this way out, especially since they may have sensed, better than did he, how much any body of religious opinions and practices depends upon institutions and upon other opinions (of an epistemological character) that have been undermined by rhetorical positions such as Kierkegaard's.

All this may also represent a reaction against Hegel with his apparent collectivization of thought.[68] Kierkegaard wanted to make it clear, and for this he should be given credit, that the most important things cannot be collectivized. The culmination of the development advanced by Kierkegaard can be seen, perhaps, in Heidegger: God is gotten rid of altogether, leaving only Being—and, in Heidegger's case, the crudest of particulars (a resurgent Germany!) is depended upon to supply a body for his denatured universals. That bodies *are* needed it would not be prudent to deny, but surely we can do better than this.[69]

So, we can again ask, what does nature teach? What is the status of nature? What can human beings, using their natural faculties, learn and know about divinity?

IX.

To raise these questions—to examine these matters as we have—is to approach these things from a perspective far older than that which Kierkegaard provides. It is from that older perspective that one is inclined, in thinking about Old Testament thinking, to make much of that always-challenging passage in *Deuteronomy* that has Moses counseling his people,

> Behold, I have taught you statutes and ordinances, even as the Lord my God commanded me, that you should do so in the midst of the land whither you go in to possess it. Observe therefore and do them; for this is your wisdom and your understanding in the sight of the peoples, that, when they hear all these statutes, shall say, "Surely this great nation is a wise and understanding people."[70]

Should one make more of fear and trembling than of the questioning and perplexity that can lead to wisdom? "With fear and trembling," the Apostle Paul wrote, "work out your own salvation."[71] It has been noticed that the good for Kierkegaard is not to compel a man to recognize his urgent need for knowledge, but his urgent need for a leap of faith.[72] Do fear and trembling encourage one to leap, that fear and trembling that philosophy was once thought to discourage? It is said of the old man in the Kierkegaard story that his enthusiasm for the Abraham story grew and grew as he understood it less and less.[73]

Is too much made by the philosopher of reason? It is argued, in another work by Kierkegaard, that the Greeks failed to notice the will, the defiant will, as a determinant in determining what sin is.[74] He says there,

> The Greek intellectualism was too happy, too naive, too aesthetic, too ironical, too witty . . . too sinful to be able to get it into its head that a person knowingly could fail to do the good, or knowingly, with knowledge of what was right, do what was wrong. The Greek spirit proposes an intellectual categorical imperative.[75]

Does Kierkegaard say what he does because he fails to see the considerable role recognized among the Greeks, for example in the Platonic dialogues, for the passions—for irrepressible if not ultimately ungovernable passions that make vulnerable any concrete manifestation of the works of the mind? Should not the emphasis be put *not* upon defiance as the cause of troubles but rather upon opinions and desires determined by chance instead of by understanding?[76]

The critical role of understanding, even in the man of faith, may be seen in Maimonides's warning against anyone who, even if by recourse to miracles, "issues a call to believe in impossible things."[77] Does Kierkegaard's interpretation of the Binding of Isaac amount to an illegitimate call "to believe in impossible things"?

Kierkegaard, like many before him, did recognize that it is in adversity that one may be obliged to recognize the deeper meaning of one's faith in God. Thus, the Talmud says, "When Nebuchadnezzar, the mighty King of Babylonia, wanted to sing praises to God, an angel came and slapped him in the face." A famous rabbi once asked, "Why did he deserve to be slapped, if his intention was to sing God's praises?" The rabbi answered himself, "You want to sing praises [to God] while you are wearing your crown? Let me hear how you praise [Him] after having been slapped in the face."[78]

To praise God properly in such circumstances, as well as to conceive of this story, to frame the appropriate question, and to develop a telling answer—in order to do all these things, and thereby make the act of faith both meaningful and salutary, is there not needed a sound awareness of the nature of things?

NOTES

1. This talk was given at Rockford College, Rockford, Illinois, May 11, 1977. The original title of this talk was "Kierkegaard, Abraham, and Socrates: Illusions of the Absurd." An epigraph was provided from a speech by Don Quixote: "If I were to show [Dulcinea] to you, what merit would there be in your confessing a truth so self-evident? The important thing is for you, without seeing her, to believe, confess, affirm, swear, and defend the truth." Miguel de Cervantes Saavedra, *Don Quixote* (New York: Viking Press, 1949), p. 45. See chapter 8, note 37. Consider also Augustine, *The City of God* (New York: Penguin Books, 1972), p. 436: "We cannot understand what happened as it is presented to us [in the *Genesis* creation story]; and yet we must believe it without hesitation." Consider as well pp. 1027f. One can be reminded here of Tertullian.

I have found very useful the comments on my original manuscript made by Christopher A. Colmo of Dominican University. His influence is particularly to be noticed in chapter 5, notes 24, 27, 48, 62, and 67. See George Anastaplo, *The American Moralist: Essays on Law, Ethics, and Government* (Athens, Ohio: Ohio University Press, 1992), pp. 139–44. Also useful has been Jules Gleicher of Rockfort College.

2. The translation of *Genesis* used here is that found in Robert Sacks, *The Lion and the Ass: A Commentary on the Book of Genesis,* first published in *Interpretation,* vol. 8f (1980). See chapter 1, note 1. (What can "only son" mean?)

3. Moses Maimonides, *The Guide of the Perplexed* (Chicago: University of Chicago Press, 1963), pp. 500–501 (III, 24). The "absurdity" argument of Kierkegaard can be said to have been anticipated by Maimonides's observation, "In truth it is the most extraordinary thing that could happen in the world, such a thing that one would not imagine that human nature was capable of it." See, on Maimonides, Anastaplo, *The American Moralist,* pp. 58–82; chapter 1, notes 15, 20, 46, 65, and 77; the text at note 54 of chapter 1 of this collection.

4. *Sacks, The Lion and the Ass,* commentary on *Genesis* 22:2. See, on placing "human reason itself . . . on the altar," the discussion of absurdity in chapter 5 of Thomas Hobbes's *Leviathan.* See chapter 7, note 58. See also George Anastaplo, "On Trial: Explorations." 22 *Loyola University of Chicago Law Journal* 768, 879 (1991). See, on Thomas Hobbes and madness, George Anastaplo, "Samplings," 27 *Political Science Reviewer* 345, 389 (1998). See also chapter 8, note 11.

5. Karl Löwith, "Recent Kierkegaard Literature," *Philosophy and Phenomenological Research,* vol. 4, p. 577 (1943–1945).

6. Löwith, "Recent Kierkegaard Literature," p. 578.

7. Abraham Heschel, *A Passion for Truth* (New York: Farrar, Straus, and Giroux, 1973), p. 120.

8. Leo Strauss, *Natural Right and History* (Chicago: University of Chicago Press, 1953), pp. 320–21. See also Leo Strauss, *What Is Political Philosophy?* (Glencoe,

Ill.: The Free Press, 1959), pp. 241–42, 268–69. See, on Edmund Burke, chapter 7, note 33.

9. See, on Kant, Nietzsche, Existentialism, and Heidegger, Anastaplo, *The American Moralist*, pp. 27–36, 125–34, 139–50, 144–60.

10. John Calvin, *Commentaries on the First Book of Moses Called Genesis*, ed. John King (Edinburgh: Calvin Translation Society, 1844), I, 560–62.

11. Calvin, *Commentaries*, I, 562 n. 2.

12. Kierkegaard's reading of Platonic texts includes his book, *The Concept of Irony—with Constant Reference to Socrates*. See also chapter 5, notes 24, 57.

13. Consider, for example, the complicated fashion in which the account in Plato's *Symposium* is introduced. Consider also Plato's *Theaetetus*.

14. Søren Kierkegaard, *Fear and Trembling*, trans. Walter Lowrie (Princeton: Princeton University Press, 1954), p. 26.

15. Kierkegaard, *Fear and Trembling*, p. 21.

16. Sacks, *The Lion and the Ass*, commentary on *Genesis* 22:2.

17. Sacks, *The Lion and the Ass*, commentary on *Genesis* 22:2.

18. *Matthew* 27:46. To speak, as I do in this talk, of the Old and New Testaments is to speak out of the Christian tradition. See chapter 1, note 91.

19. See chapter 7–A. See, on the original language of *Matthew*, chapter 7, note 13.

20. Various incidents in *Matthew's* account of the Crucifixion seem to be keyed to this psalm. See also *Psalms* 10, 13, and 74.

21. *Genesis* 22:2.

22. J. H. Hertz, *The Pentateuch and Haftorahs* (London: Soncino Press, 1952), p. 74.

23. Sacks, *The Lion and the Ass*, commentary on *Genesis* 22:2. One might well wonder what the relations between Abraham and Sarah were after she learned what "almost" happened to her (not his!) only child. Do they ever "speak with each other again" after that?

It is asked here, "Could God have nullified the Covenant? Perhaps, but then God's word would be meaningless, and what man could ever trust Him again?" But would there have even been *any* account (whether disturbing or reassuring) of God's dealings with Abraham if this Covenant had not been kept? See Anastaplo, *The American Moralist*, pp. 5–6, 10–11.

Compare, on the significance of *please*, chapter 5, notes 30, 49.

24. Did Kierkegaard bring to the Abraham story (as perhaps Robert Sacks has done) questions that he learned from Plato, such as may be seen in the discussion in the *Euthyphro* of whether the gods love a thing because it is pious or whether a thing is pious because the gods love it? (See Anastaplo, "On Trial" [*Loyola Law Journal*], p. 873.) Would the latter position here, but not the former, vindicate Abraham?

See, on using discussion of an author merely as an occasion for developing one's own thoughts, the opening paragraph of section III of this talk.

25. See *Job* 1:18–19; *Judges* 11:29–40. See also Kierkegaard, *Fear and Trembling*, pp. 68f.

26. See *Genesis*, chaps. 16, 17, 18, and 21. Maimonides spoke of Abraham, not of Sarah, as sterile. See the text at note 3 of chapter 5 of this collection. (But Abraham is

reported to have had children both before and after Isaac [by other women].) What is the significance, in this connection, of the episode described in the twentieth chapter of *Genesis*? See Augustine, *The City of God*, pp. 692–93. See also chapter 7, note 4.

27. I have been told that Kierkegaard raises the principal question here in the appendix to chapter III of the *Philosophical Fragments*. All of his *Fear and Trembling* may be regarded as an explication of the difficulties (absurdities?) that arise if one tries to assume that the request with respect to Isaac did come from God or that Abraham could "know" this.

28. Maimonides, *The Guide of the Perplexed*, p. 500 (emphasis added).

29. Maimonides, *The Guide of the Perplexed*, p. 500. See the text at note 3 of chapter 5 of this collection.

30. Maimonides, *The Guide of the Perplexed*, pp. 501–2. Maimonides here, and in the passage set forth in the text at note 3 of chapter 5 of this collection, makes more of God's *order* and *command* to Abraham than of any request (*please*). Compare the text at note 23 of chapter 5 of this collection. See chapter 5, note 51.

31. See, on the relation between prophecy and philosophy, Augustine, *The City of God*, pp. 811–12 ("The prophetic authority antedates the beginnings of pagan philosophy"). See also the text at note 83 of chapter 7 of this collection. Compare Søren Kierkegaard, *Philosophical Fragments*, trans. Howard V. Hong and Edna H. Hong (Princeton: Princeton University Press, 1985), p. 53: "[I]s not that what philosophers are for—to make supernatural things ordinary and trivial?" See chapter 8, note 51, conclusion, note 3. Compare chapter 5, note 71. See, on the relation between prophesy and poetry, chapter 1, note 100; chapter 2, notes 9, 10; chapter 3, note 21; chapter 5, note 39; the text at note 35 of chapter 5 of this collection. See also chapter 7, note 101; chapter 10, note 78. See as well George Anastaplo, *But Not Philosophy: Seven Introductions to Non-Western Thought* (Lanham, Md.: Lexington Books, Rowman & Littlefield, 2002), p. 131, n. 38.

32. "Faith is a miracle, and yet no man is excluded from it; for that in which all human life is unified is passion, and faith is a passion." Kierkegaard, *Fear and Trembling*, p. 72. See chapter 1, notes 44, 45; chapter 5, note 62; the text at note 33 of chapter 7 of this collection. See, on miracles, chapter 3, note 4; chapter 5, notes 1, 3; chapter 5, note 41; chapter 8, notes 51, 54, 60.

33. I say *in appearance* because the desire for "commitment," as well as the forms that commitment is likely to take, suggests something natural at work, including perhaps a natural awareness of being. See, on being, chapter 1, note 48; chapter 4, note 18; chapter 10, note 26; conclusion, note 2.

34. See Plato, *Apology* 20E sq.

35. Or are we meant to see that any great trust in God is an instance of an absurdity being accepted?

36. See, e.g., Augustine, *The City of God*, pp. 642–43, 1023–25.

37. Augustine, *The City of God*, pp. 642–43. The same is said by Augustine about reports of God seeing or descending or otherwise acting. See, e.g. pp. 658–59. See also the opening chapters of Maimonides's *The Guide of the Perplexed*. Things do seem somewhat different for Augustine when there is an instance of an incarnation of God. See, e.g., Augustine, *The City of God*, pp. 691–92. But would not Maimonides have

asked Augustine, albeit prudently, whether he really wanted to make an exception of The Incarnation? See *Acts* 14:11–18. See also the text at note 5 of chapter 7 of this collection; Anastaplo, "On Trial" (*Loyola Law Journal*), p. 1053 n. 333. Compare Thomas Aquinas, *Summa Theologiae* 3a. 39, 7. Compare also chapter 7, note 43.

38. See, e.g., *Genesis* 18:17: "Shall I hide from Abraham that which I am doing?"

39. What *knowing* means in the case of Abraham may be at the heart of our inquiry here. See chapter 8, note 65. In a sense, perhaps, Abraham in his relations with God (or in his responses to and dependence upon God) knows "how things will turn out" much as does the typical dreamer who is (I believe) ultimately in control of his dream. Or, put another way, Abraham may be understood to be the poet (the maker-discoverer) of his most critical relations with God. See conclusion, note 3. See also chapter 8, notes 47, 55.

40. See, e.g., Plato, *Republic*, Books II and III.

41. *Psalms* 25:10.

42. *Genesis* 22:5.

43. Hertz, *The Pentateuch and Haftorahs*, p. 74.

44. *Genesis* 22:8.

45. Hertz, *The Pentateuch and Haftorahs*, p. 74.

46. *Genesis* 22:8.

47. *Genesis* 22:11–12, 15–18.

48. But see chapter 5, note 1. Kierkegaard was not the first to notice the element of irrationality (or, at least, that which is not susceptible to reason) at the core of religion. In pointing this out, he appears as a son of the Enlightenment. On the other hand, he does present himself as an advocate of religion, if not even as an informed enemy of the Enlightenment. Did he see in the Enlightenment a "religion of reason" that posed a greater threat to philosophy than any posed by the established revealed religions of the West? See chapter 5, note 23; chapter 5, notes 67, 71; the text at note 56 of chapter 7 of this collection. See also, chapter 10, note 26. Consider the reported unsettling effect upon the Pythagoreans of their discovery of incommensurability.

49. Augustine, *The City of God*, p. 694. See on "the thunder of a divine command," the text at note 23 of chapter 5 of this collection. Compare chapter 5, note 30.

50. Augustine, *The City of God*, p. 694. See *Hebrews* 11:17–19. Augustine provides a Christian symbolic interpretation of the ram, the thicket, etc. Were not Augustine and Paul more inclined to rely on resurrection than most Jews (including Abraham?) have been inclined to do? See chapter 7, note 43.

51. See *Matthew* 3:9. See also the text at note 27 of chapter 7 of this collection.

52. See Hertz, *The Pentateuch and Haftorahs*, p. 74.

53. Heschel, *A Passion for Truth*, p. 227.

54. See Leo Strauss, *Thoughts on Machiavelli* (Glencoe, Ill.: The Free Press, 1958), pp. 13–14.

55. See the text at note 8 of chapter 5 of this collection.

56. Does all this lead, in Nietzsche, to an emphasis upon the will to power? See Werner Dannhauser, *Nietzsche's View of Socrates* (Ithaca: Cornell University Press, 1974), pp. 271–72. See chapter 5, note 62.

57. See Raymond L. Weiss, "Kierkegaard's 'Return' to Socrates," 45 *The New Scholasticism* 573, (1971).

58. See Kierkegaard, *Fear and Trembling*, p. 110. The translator (Walter Lowrie) says, in a note to this passage, "[Kierkegaard] uses here the word 'emotion,' but it is clear that he has in mind what modern psychology has called *libido*." (p. 269 n. 78)

59. See Kierkegaard, *Fear and Trembling*, p. 110n.

60. See chapter 2, note 31.

61. Such are the variations on the legend of Agnes and the Merman and the comments on the story of Sarah and Tobias. See Kierkegaard, *Fear and Trembling*, pp. 103f, 111f.

62. See Anastaplo, *The American Moralist*, pp. 412–15. Is the emphasis upon the role of the will ultimately subverted (or is it merely disguised) by the definition of faith as a passion? See chapter 5, note 32; the text at note 52 of chapter 7 of this collection. See also chapter 10, note 26.

63. See Kierkegaard, *Fear and Trembling*, pp. 85, 90.

64. Consider, for example, the difficulties that Cephalus faces in Book I of Plato's *Republic*. See, on the status of prudence for Kierkegaard, Weiss, "Kierkegaard's 'Return' to Socrates," pp. 578–79, 582.

65. See Kierkegaard, *Fear and Trembling*, p. 122.

66. See Kierkegaard, *Fear and Trembling*, pp. 84, 103. See also Anastaplo, *The American Moralist*, pp. 27–32 (on Kant, at least as he is generally understood).

67. Is such an awareness of things, and the capacity thus to become aware, reflected in the recollection story of Plato's *Meno*? See chapter 6–A. Does a serious examination of the principle of contradiction oblige us to raise the questions that Kierkegaard does? Was the restoration by Kierkegaard of the difference between revealed religion and philosophy ultimately a defense of the principle of contradiction and hence also of nature? See Anastaplo, "On Trial" (*Loyola Law Journal*), p. 1059 n. 407. A thorough study of Kierkegaard would have to address such questions. One purpose of *Fear and Trembling* may be to encourage thoughtful men to see the passions for what they are. See Anastaplo, *The American Moralist*, pp. 125–34 (on Nietzsche). See also chapter 5, notes 32, 48; the text at note 46 of chapter 7 of this collection. See, on the relation of revelation to reason, George Anastaplo, "Constitutionalism and the Good: Explorations," 70 *Tennessee Law Review* 737, 843 (2003).

68. See, on Hegel, the essay by Pierre Hassner in *History of Political Philosophy*, p. 732.

69. See Anastaplo, *The American Moralist*, pp. 148–49, 154–545 (with comments on Heidegger's observation, "Only a god can save us," an observation from a thinker who grievously mistook the worst possible political leader in his own country as a savior). See chapter 12–A. See also chapter 1, note 110.

70. *Deuteronomy* 4:5–6. See the text at note 14 of chapter 1 of this collection. See also the text at note 89 of chapter 7 of this collection; Anastaplo, "Law & Literature and the Austen-Dostoyevsky Axis: Explorations," 46 *South Dakota Law Review* 712, 751–57 (2001).

71. *Philippians* 2:12. Compare Leo Strauss, *The Rebirth of Classical Political Realism* (Chicago: University of Chicago Press, 1989), p. 206: "For the beginning of

philosophy as the philosophers understood it is not the fear of the Lord, but wonder."
See chapter 10, note 61; conclusion, note 3. See also the text at note 75 of chapter 1
of this collection; chapter 5, note 31.

72. See Weiss, "Kierkegaard's 'Return' to Socrates," p. 575.

73. See Kierkegaard, *Fear and Trembling*, p. 27.

74. See Kierkegaard, *The Sickness unto Death* (in the same volume as *Fear and Trembling*), pp. 218f.

75. Kierkegaard, *The Sickness unto Death*, pp. 220–21. (The dots in the quotation are Kierkegaard's.) Compare chapter 2, note 31. Does not Kierkegaard deliberately say "sin" where the Greeks would have said "vice"? See, on how sin might be regarded, chapter 9, note 41.

76. See chapter 5, note 67; Plato, *Crito* 44D. Consider also the ancient Greek saying that one's character is one's fate.

77. Maimonides, *The Guide of the Perplexed*, p. 499. See also George Anastaplo, *The Artist as Thinker: From Shakespeare to Joyce* (Athens, Ohio: Ohio University Press, 1983), p. 13.

78. Heschel, *A Passion for Truth*, p. 191.

6

Socrates of Athens

6-A. PLATO'S *MENO*[1]

I.

Plato's *Meno* includes an exhibition of the kind of inquiry that can be said to have gotten Socrates killed. Particularly provocative on this occasion is his handling of an influential Athenian politician (Anytus), who became one of the three accusers of Socrates. This is in the course of a discussion of virtue and its teachability. A classic discussion, as well as a series of illustrations, of teaching may be found in this dialogue. It opens with an inquiry put to Socrates by Meno, a visitor from Thessaly, as to how virtue is acquired by human beings. The emphasis is placed, in Socrates' immediate response, upon the question of whether virtue is teachable. Meno's inquiry develops (or, from the acquisitive Meno's point of view, degenerates?) into an inquiry as to what virtue is and what it means to teach or to learn. The dialogue concludes with the revelation (or is it a teaching?) that those men who are generally recognized as virtuous, such as the leading statesmen of Athens for at least two generations, became what they were because of divine dispensation, not because anyone had taught them to be good. Thus it is reported, in textbooks and elsewhere, that Plato concluded in the *Meno* that virtue cannot be taught, that it comes to human beings in a mysterious way attributable to divinity. Does Plato want this conclusion taught? Is this good for a city to believe? If virtue depends upon divine dispensation, what does vice depend upon? Does it, too, depend somehow upon some divine allocation, or is vice what human beings are "naturally" inclined to when there is no divine provision for virtue?

We recall, however, that the same Plato (again using Socrates as his principal character) argues in the *Republic* that a properly ordered city could produce virtuous citizens, including rulers, generation after generation. The role of the gods is muted in that dialogue, however much divine intervention may help account for the opportunity that philosophers have to shape and govern a city. The *Republic* ends with the Myth of Er, which somehow accounts for the lives that human beings lead, lives chosen by them a thousand or so years after their preceding lives had consigned them to the millennium of rewards or purgations that serve as prelude to their next stint of life on earth. But, it seems, however much one's earlier life affected the life one has chosen for oneself "this time around," little if anything is remembered of one's previous life. The waters of Lethe see to that.

This account in the *Republic* is somewhat at variance with what we seem to be told by the *Meno*, where human learning is put emphatically in terms of recollecting. According to the *Meno*, there is neither teaching nor learning, but rather a recalling of what we have known before, if not even "always" (that is, "naturally"?). The spirit here is quite different from that evident in the *Republic* where systematic teaching and habituation, for those properly equipped and prepared, are arranged by astute rulers. So different an approach to the development of virtuous citizens and rulers, elaborated in such a massive work as the *Republic*, and thereafter in the *Nicomachean Ethics* of Aristotle (Plato's best student), obliges us to reconsider what the *Meno* seems to say.

Here is Meno's opening speech (as set forth in the venerable Benjamin Jowett translation of this Platonic dialogue):

> Can you tell me, Socrates, whether virtue is acquired by teaching or by practice; or if neither by teaching nor by practice, then whether it comes to man by nature, or in what other way?

We notice that Meno has an array of four possible answers to his question that, it turns out, he has evidently heard proposed in discussions of these matters back home in Thessaly: teaching, practice, nature, and some "other way." We also notice that Meno assumes that these ways are to be considered as alternatives. Perhaps this, too, reflects the discussions he has heard elsewhere. This assumption may be important, if not decisive, for the course that this conversation follows.

Socrates' immediate response to the opening speech in the *Meno* (as seen in a recent translation) emphasizes critical disclaimers:

> Meno, it used to be that Thessalians were well-reputed among the Greeks and were admired both for horsemanship and for wealth, but now, it seems to me, for

wisdom also; and not least of them the fellow citizens of your comrade, Aristippus, the Larissians. And the one responsible for this happening to you is Gorgias. For when he came to the city, he captivated the foremost men among the Aleudai as lovers of wisdom, of whom your lover Aristippus is one, and the foremost of the other Thessalians too. And in particular this is the habit to which he has habituated you, namely, of answering both fearlessly and magnificently whenever anyone asks you anything, as is fitting for those who know; inasmuch, indeed, as he makes himself available to any Greek who wants to question him about whatever one might wish to ask, and there is no one whom he does not answer. But hereabouts, dear Meno, the opposite condition prevails: it's as if some sort of drought of wisdom has come about, and there seems to be a danger that wisdom has left these parts for yours. And so, if you are willing to ask anyone hereabouts such a question, there is no one who will not laugh and say, "Stranger, I seem to be in danger of your thinking me to be someone who is blessed—to know about virtue, whether it is something teachable or in what way it comes about. But I am so far from knowing about virtue, whether it is something teachable or not teachable that I happen not to know at all what that thing virtue itself is."

And I myself, Meno, am in this condition, too. I share the poverty of my fellow citizens in this matter and blame myself for not knowing about virtue at all. And how could I know what sort of thing something is, if I do not know what it is? Or does it seem possible to you that someone who has no cognisance of Meno at all, who he is, could know whether he is handsome or rich or well-born, or the opposite of these? Does it seem possible to you?

This response is disappointing to Meno, who had hoped to acquire from Socrates an answer, perhaps even a novel argument, to take north with him. This is how Meno understands what Socrates has just said about his own lack of knowledge concerning virtue:

> But do you, Socrates, truly not know what virtue is, and is this really what we should report about you back home?

Thus, what is decisive for Meno here is that Socrates has presented himself as not knowing what virtue is. And yet, we not only suspect that Socrates knows more about virtue than he admits, but we also see him talk again and again in this dialogue as if he has a reliable enough grasp of what virtue is to make the observations and arguments that he makes.

We must consider again what Socrates does say in his first speech. That he cannot be taken completely at face value there is suggested by what he predicts about all Athenians professing themselves to be as ignorant as Socrates says he himself is about what virtue is. Whatever suspicions we have about this are reinforced by how so prominent a politician as Anytus conducts himself when he, later on, joins the conversation in the *Meno. He* certainly does not profess ignorance of such matters.

We return to Meno's opening speech, which has him asking (in a more precise translation of the dialogue):

> Can you tell me, Socrates, whether virtue is something teachable? Or is it not
> teachable, but something that comes from practice? Or is it something neither
> from practice nor from learning, but comes to human beings by nature, or some
> other way?

The illustration with which Socrates thereafter ends his own opening speech
to Meno is instructive:

> Or does it seem possible to you that someone who has no cognizance of Meno
> at all, who he is, could know whether he is handsome or rich or well-born, or
> the opposite of these? Does it seem possible to you?

We notice that the attributes of Meno are put in the alternative by Socrates
(handsome or rich or well-born or their opposites), just as had been Meno's
list of the four ways that virtue is acquired (teaching or practice or nature or
in some other way). Yet we are shown in the course of the dialogue that Meno
himself is indeed handsome *and* rich *and* well-born (in the conventional sense
of these terms), not "the opposite of these." Should virtue, then, be understood to be acquired by human beings through a combination of teaching and
practice for those who are naturally equipped to be receptive? This would be
consistent with the illustrations used later by Socrates about the young men
trained in horsemanship, gymnastics, and the like. We would expect there,
also, a necessary combination of elements for the emergence of the best
horsemen and gymnasts.

Meno, we recall, had a fourth way: "some other way." It is that, it can be
said, which happens to leave a place in his scheme of things for the "divine
dispensation" finally resorted to in this dialogue. We see that Socrates, too,
has a fourth element in his inventory (of Meno's attributes): "the opposite
of these." Is there a sense in which divine dispensation should be considered somehow critically different from, if not the opposite of, the three
modes that Meno had listed? Also, is there a sense in which Meno's being
handsome, rich, and well-born depends upon something other than, if not
the opposite of, these? Indeed, does Meno merely appear to be handsome,
rich, and well-born?

When we return to the *Republic* we notice a reliance upon knowledgeable
leaders who identify the various natural capacities among the young and
who thereafter provide the appropriate teaching and practice required to
produce virtuous citizens in the service of the city. Even in ordinary cities,
good men and women arise—and we can see, upon examining those situa-

tions, the combination of nature, teaching, and practice needed to secure that end. But, in the ordinary city, chance—or, if one prefers, divine intervention—seems to have much more to do with whether the youngsters who are naturally equipped for virtue happen to be provided the required teaching and habituation.

Perhaps more important than the lessons offered in the *Meno* as to how virtue is acquired are the lessons about teaching itself. Socrates both says and does not say what we have found him to indicate in his opening speech in the dialogue. Or, rather, Meno does not recognize that Socrates, in his opening speech, indicates what we have found him to indicate. What Socrates does indicate, albeit quietly, affects how the rest of this dialogue should be read. We can see that however much may be offered by a would-be teacher, it is not likely to "register" with a student unless he is both disposed and prepared to receive it. In this sense, it can be said, teaching, as a sovereign activity, is not possible—and this opens the way to the "recollection" made so much of in the *Meno* and in textbook accounts of that dialogue.

Does talk about recollection become an inspired or poetic way of talking about that which is natural to the reasoning capacity of human beings? The development of virtuous human beings who understand themselves depends, in part, upon circumstances. It is useful, as one reads the *Meno*, to be aware of differences between Athens and Thessaly. Instructive inquiries into virtue can be expected in democratic Athens, just as successful efforts on behalf of horsemanship can be expected in oligarchic Thessaly.

The Socrates of the *Meno* resorts to a reliance upon divine dispensation only after it becomes clear that the limitations of Meno and Anytus make it impossible for him to develop an account of any systematic training for virtue that works from a reliable definition of virtue and from a dispassionate recognition of natural differences among human beings. Would the fierce democrat, Anytus, be tamed only if he could be induced to believe that there are vital differences between those who know, such as Socrates, and those who do not, just as the covetous oligarch, Meno, would be restrained only if he could be induced to believe that there are powerful gods who truly prefer just human beings to those who look out for themselves alone?

Meno's limitations are reflected in his assumption that virtue must come by only one of the three or four ways he proposes in his acquisitively abrupt opening speech. As we have seen, it is indicated in the dialogue, beginning with the way an anything but abrupt Socrates ends his first response to Meno, that virtue may come by a *combination* of the alternatives listed disjunctively by Meno. That is, the virtues can be expected to develop in a human being naturally receptive to them only after the establishment of proper habits prepares one to be taught. Whether those naturally receptive to virtue have the opportunity to be habituated and taught properly may depend upon the gods, or upon chance.

Meno, whatever *his* nature, will not practice. This is evident throughout the dialogue. The habits he has already happened to acquire have become second nature to him. Meno's "instinctive" avoidance of practice may be confirmed in a late restatement by him of his opening inquiry, after Socrates had several times tried to discipline him: he drops "practice" from the alternatives he then lists. Indeed, Meno can be recognized as a man devoted to "freedom"—to the tyrannical desire to have power himself, while not being subject at all to the power or standards of others.

Meno's general position can be said to have been made explicit, in the first book of Plato's *Republic*, by Polemarchus and Thrasymachus. Both of these men, despite their limitations, are more receptive to serious arguments than Meno could ever be. The groundwork is laid there for Socrates' elaboration in the *Republic* (with even more gifted interlocutors) of a system of education, for teachers and students alike, which should make the development of virtuous men and women far more likely than it is apt to be in the ordinary city, in the kind of city that can inadvertently condemn its most virtuous citizen.

6-B.   XENOPHON'S *APOLOGY OF SOCRATES*[2]

I.

The trial of Socrates, in 399 B.C.E., has intrigued the Western world for two and a half millennia, partly because it took place in the most cultured city of antiquity, one of the greatest democracies in history (but by then a much-battered democracy). The trial can be understood to have been triggered by the troubles at the end of the disastrous Peloponnesian War between Athens, on one side, and Sparta and her allies, on the other. But the passions unleashed against Socrates at that time (in part because of the wartime conduct of some of his former students) can be understood to have been aroused by the challenges always posed by philosophy (or, at least, by some philosophers) in any ambitious community. Pericles had managed to protect a great thinker, Anaxagoras, when *he* came under attack in Athens several decades earlier. But, it seems, there was in Athens no political figure of comparable stature to do the same for Socrates when he happened, after the great war, to become most vulnerable.[3]

The account of the trial of Socrates that is most familiar to us, and that is virtually authoritative, is the account provided by Plato, probably Socrates' most important student.[4] The official indictment, as set forth in Plato's account, charges Socrates with being "guilty of corrupting the youth and of acknowledging not the gods that the city acknowledges but other new daemonic things."[5]

Five hundred citizens were evidently empaneled to pass on the charges made against Socrates, who was then in his seventieth year. It is reported that a switch of thirty votes would have won him an acquittal on that occasion. This information is provided by Plato.[6]

II.

Another gifted student of Socrates, Xenophon, provides an account of the trial of Socrates, a sketch that emphasizes one intriguing feature of the Socratic position that can challenge us on this occasion. The conventional scholarly attitude toward Xenophon may be gathered from the following entry in a reference book of our time:

> Greek historian and moralist (c. 430–c. 354), a member of a prominent Athenian family. In his youth he was a none too loyal pupil of Socrates. [It is not clear what this assessment is based on.] In 401 he joined the expedition of Cyrus the Younger as an observer, and after most of the Greek commanders had been treacherously murdered after the Battle of Cunaxa, he led the retreat of the "Ten Thousand" (about 10,000 Greek mercenaries hired by Cyrus) as commander of the rear guard. [It was while Xenophon was on this Persian expedition that the trial and execution of Socrates took place.[7]] After 396 Xenophon served under the Spartan king Agesilaus, with whom he fought against his own native city [Athens] at Coronea in 394; for this he was banished from his city (after Athens and Sparta had made peace in 369, this decree was revoked). Sparta gave him an estate at Scillus near Olympia, which he left in about 371, when Elis, after the Battle of Leuctra, again took possession of Scillus. He then settled in Corinth, where he died.[8]

The relatively low opinion of Xenophon as a thinker held by many scholars today (but *not* in the eighteenth century and before[9]) may be gathered from the continuation of the entry from which I have just been quoting:

> Xenophon's works do not possess great literary value, but they are written in pure Attic in a simple style, often fresh and lively; for this reason Xenophon is usually required reading for students of Greek. In addition to the description of his campaign with Cyrus and the Ten Thousand, the *Anabasis*, his works are: (a) *Hellenica*, a history of Greece from 411–362, a continuation of the history of Thucydides; (b) *Memorabilia*, memoirs of Socrates, a rather unreliable portrait

of the great philosopher; (c) *Cyropedia*, an idealized biography of Cyrus the Elder. He also wrote lesser works on politics, horsemanship, finances, and other subjects.[10]

I deal here only with the account of the trial presented in Xenophon's *Apology*, not that found in Xenophon's *Memorabilia*.[11]

Xenophon's portrait of Socrates has been called "unreliable" partly, it seems, because Socrates is presented as giving advice to all kinds of people on various practical matters.[12] There is, moreover, the intriguing, if not even startling, feature of Xenophon's account to which I have referred (whether or not Xenophon had evidence to support it)—and that is the insistence, touched upon by him a half-dozen times in an account of Socrates' trial that runs to only about ten pages, the insistence that Socrates welcomed death at this time.[13] Socrates' longest comment to this effect (in Xenophon's *Apology*) is the following (5–6):

> Do you know that I would refuse to concede that any man has lived a better life than I have up to now? For I have realized that my whole life has been spent in righteousness toward God and man—a fact that affords the greatest satisfaction; and so I have felt a deep self-respect and have discovered that my associates hold corresponding sentiments toward me. But now, if my years are prolonged, I know that the frailties of old age will inevitably be realized,—that my vision must be less perfect and my hearing less keen, that I shall be slower to learn and more forgetful of what I have learned. If I perceive my decay and take to complaining, how could I any longer take pleasure in life? Perhaps God in his kindness is taking my part and securing me the opportunity of ending my life not only in season but also in the way that is easiest.[14]

The divine intervention noticed here follows, at least in part, upon Socrates' having reported that twice he had tried to meditate on his defense for the trial, but that his divine sign (his daemonic thing) had interposed to stop him from doing so. (4–5)

We notice in passing that it is assumed by Socrates that suicide is not a proper remedy to be resorted to by anyone in order to head off "the frailties of old age."[15] (In this respect Socrates is closer to the traditional Jewish and Christian responses to suicide with which we are familiar than he is to, say, the ancient Roman and the modern Japanese responses, which make so much of honor.[16]) We should also notice that Socrates is reported here by Xenophon to have made far more of the body, in effect, than may be seen in various Platonic dialogues, where the philosopher is presented as oblivious of the body.[17]

Xenophon himself seems to endorse, or at least to respect, the Socratic desire to head off the "frailties of old age." The Xenophonic response is particularly significant in that it comes from a man of action who had (a decade or two before) distinguished himself, in Asia Minor, by having been effective in saving not only his own life but the lives of thousands of others who found themselves in the most miserable and threatening circumstances. Some scholars who have great respect for Xenophon play down, when they do not virtually dismiss, the "frailties of old age" argument attributed by him to Socrates.[18] But so important a reader of Xenophon as Søren Kierkegaard recorded this reservation about what had been said by Xenophon in the *Memorabilia*, but that applies to Xenophon's *Apology* also:

[Xenophon's Socrates'] conception of death is equally impoverished, equally small of heart [as the notion of prudence attributed to Socrates by Xenophon]. This appears in Xenophon where Socrates rejoices, now that he shall die, because he will be free from the burdens and infirmities of old age (*Mem.* IV, 8, 8).[19]

III.

What does all this say about campaigns to prolong life? This is a question dramatized for us these days by political campaigns to finance more and more medical care, including very expensive prescription drugs, for the elderly. It is taken for granted that ever more people among us will live to a very old age and with markedly diminished capacities. It is also taken for granted that such people ought to be catered to.

Just this week, when I put to a gifted law school classmate the "frailties"-avoidance doctrine of Xenophon's Socrates, it was soundly rejected by him. My seventy-five-year-old classmate recognizes that his own energies are already substantially diminished, and even that his thinking processes have been somewhat impaired, but he has discovered that he can now make up with good judgment what he has lost in mental capacity. He expects that he will have to cut back more and more in what he tries to do—he already spends his winters in Florida—but he believes that he has an *obligation* to continue to do what he can in his community, and in this he has the support of a loving family and of admiring friends. This response, which I would expect to be also the response of most if not even all of my audience this evening, is very much opposed to what Xenophon's Socrates says again and again in anticipating (almost with relish) his impending death. Thus, Socrates argues, in effect, that just as life should not be held onto at all costs, neither should it be voluntarily ended (while many among us today would, on the other hand, be open to a voluntary end when everyday living becomes a torment).

We must wonder whether the divine intervention reported by Socrates in Xenophon's *Apology* should be interpreted as Socrates said he did. We must also wonder, of course, how much of what Socrates is recorded as saying here, about death as a timely release, was said for the benefit of his grieving friends. Perhaps Socrates' daemonic thing did stop him from defending himself, but was it primarily for the reason that this Socrates seems to read out of the situation?

Sympathy for a soon-to-be-enfeebled Socrates may not have been the principal concern of Socrates' guardian spirit—for we have all known elderly people who provided us impressive guidance well into their very old age, even as their bodies were collapsing all around them, so to speak. Perhaps we are left to surmise that the daemonic thing recognizes that Socrates, during the decade or two that may still be available to him, will not be able to end his life as well as he can now in the service of philosophy. The essential Socrates, *we* can see (and why not the daemonic thing also?) could live on, in an undiminished, if not even in an enhanced, condition by permitting his life to be ended when *and how* it was ended after seven decades.

We are reminded by this observation that it can be very difficult to determine what any particular divine sign in our lives might mean, even more difficult perhaps than it may be to determine whether it is indeed a divine sign that one is dealing with.[20] Certainly, Xenophon's account of the trial of Socrates has a higher density of references to the divine than does Plato's account. What Xenophon himself truly thinks of the divine is well worth our study.[21]

IV.

But, first, we should study—or, at least, speculate about—how Xenophon, the preeminent man of action among the ancient Socratics, would have responded if he had found himself in Athens at the time of the trial of Socrates. It is one thing for Socrates to argue that it was time for him "to go." It would have been quite another thing for Xenophon to stand by while vicious men undertook to kill or to banish his teacher. (I notice in passing that Alcibiades, another student of sorts of Socrates, may have been more of a "man of action," but less of a "Socratic," than Xenophon.)

I have long believed that if Xenophon had been in Athens at that time, Socrates' would-be accusers, such as Anytus, would have been personally advised by Xenophon that they ran considerable personal risk by proceeding with a prosecution. A *Godfather*-like hint from someone such as Xenophon might have sufficed. We see in Plato's *Apology* that Plato and others offered to pay a fine as a sufficient punishment for Socrates upon his conviction. Xenophon's contribution to an effort to save Socrates would, I suggest, have been more vigorous. Would he not have regarded such an attack upon Socrates as both an affront and a threat to Socrates' closest students? Neither Xenophon nor Plato, it can be argued, believed that it *was* time for Socrates to die, whatever Socrates himself believed it useful to say now and then.

In short, Xenophon could have been heard saying, "Socrates may have his standards—but I have mine also, and no teacher of mine is going to be killed in these circumstances, if I can do anything, with or without his consent, to save him." In all this Xenophon would have been a more efficient Crito.[22] Earlier, before Xenophon embarked on his Persian campaign, he had made a different use of the Delphic Oracle from that which Socrates had wanted him to make—and Socrates had thereafter acquiesced, reluctantly, in what Xenophon had done. Another way of putting all this is to say that Xenophon is more "political" than Socrates.[23]

V.

It does not seem, in Xenophon's account of the trial, that Socrates informed the men who would judge him that he welcomed a death sentence. Is it fair to permit, if not even to encourage, others to do a monstrous act against oneself if one can say or do something honorable that might head off such misconduct?

How, for example, *would* the Five Hundred have responded if they *had* known that Socrates was looking forward to, if not even courting, his death?[24] Were they entitled to be told what Socrates' friends had been told about Socrates' readiness, if not even eagerness, for death? Does his failure to talk about this with the Five Hundred suggest that this kind of talk *was* only something conjured up to comfort his friends? We are wondering, with such questions, what the truly just course of action would be here not only for those passing judgment but also for anyone who is being judged in such circumstances.

At the core of the long-standing distrust of, if not even hostility toward, Socrates on the part of many, if not of most, of his fellow citizens was their awareness that he did not care much if at all for the things that they cared so deeply about. Particularly threatening could have been his obvious unconcern about the things that mattered most for them, beginning with the preservation of one's life. To show disdain for whatever another human being treasures can indeed be an affront. This is something we usually tend to be careful about when we encounter, for instance, the questionable religious opinions of others.

The troublesome distinctiveness of Socrates is revealed in what seems to be the literally central passage in Xenophon's account of the trial, a passage that includes this observation by Socrates, recalling what had happened during the fatal blockade of Athens by the Spartans in the last year of the Peloponnesian War (18): "[D]uring the siege, while others were commiserating their lot, I got along without feeling the pinch of poverty any worse than when the city's prosperity was at its height."[25]

Socrates, the Athenians were thus reminded, did not care for the things that others desperately cared for and very much missed. Such a man, people can be provoked to say, is not really "one of us." Particularly irksome for them (except perhaps when they are somehow taught to regard him as a saint) can be the perception that someone is "showboating" and otherwise displaying his superiority.[26]

VI.

A city, and particularly one in which democratic doctrines of liberty and equality reign, can find offensive the truly superior man who does not trouble to appear to humble himself from time to time. Such a man is, to say the least, rather impolitic, if not even dangerously provocative.[27] Plato's Socrates could be exasperating by showing up those who claimed to know various important things, even as he himself insisted that he knew that he knew nothing.[28] Xenophon's Socrates, on the other hand, could be exasperating by claiming to know far more than others did. Both Plato and Xenophon, I daresay, would have considered Hugh, a twelfth-century Bishop of Lincoln (*now* known as Saint Hugh), to be possessed of qualities that could infuriate others (especially those in authority) in the way that Socrates could. Consider this account of the dying Hugh:

> Archbishop Hubert came once [to visit Hugh on his deathbed]; he did not care, perhaps, to return a second time.
>
> The archbishop, sitting by his bed, after the usual condolences, suggested that the Bishop of Lincoln might like to use the opportunity to repent of any sharp expressions that he had occasionally been betrayed into using. As the hint was not taken, [the archbishop] referred especially to himself as one of those who had something to complain of.
>
> "Indeed, your Grace," replied Hugh, "there have been passages of words between us, and I have much to regret in relation to them. It is not, however, what I have said to your Grace, but what I have omitted to say. I have more feared to offend your Grace than to offend my Father in heaven. I have withheld words that I ought to have spoken, and I have thus sinned against your Grace and desire your forgiveness. Should it please God to spare my life I purpose to amend the fault."[29]

The democratically minded Five Hundred "raised a clamor" at hearing Xenophon's Socrates talk about that daemonic thing that routinely advised him, primarily by somehow impeding a proposed course of action that was not good for him. Some of the Athenians, Xenophon reports, disbelieved Socrates' statements, while others were jealous at his having received greater favors from the gods than they had. (13–14) It is curious, and indicative of how the democratic spirit works, that those who did believe Socrates here were not intimidated into respecting him because of the divine favor that had evidently been shown to him.

Socrates made matters even worse, it seems, by reminding the Five Hundred of what had happened when one of Socrates' enthusiastic followers went to Delphi to consult Apollo (14):

> Once on a time when Chaerephon made inquiry of the Delphic Oracle concerning me, in the presence of many people Apollo answered that no man was more free than I, or more just, or more prudent.

Upon hearing this we learn, "the jurors naturally enough made a still greater tumult." (15) Socrates "tried" to calm them down by saying that Apollo had *not* spoken of him as he had long ago spoken of Lycurgus, when he had said, "I am pondering whether to call you god or man." (15) But this still left Socrates high in the god's estimation—and it probably did not help that the person elevated by Socrates even higher in the divine judgment, Lycurgus, was the founder of the Spartan regime, a regime very much in opposition to what Athens stood for.

Further on in his account, Xenophon sums up these repeated provocations by saying (31–32):

> As for Socrates, by exalting himself before the court, he brought ill-will upon himself and made his conviction by the jury all the more certain.

We have been taught by Plato's *Apology* that Socrates never addressed the Five Hundred as *Court* or *Jurors* (that is, as *Judges*) until he had learned who among them had voted for him and who against.[30] Only those who had voted for him, Socrates explained, were truly *Judges*. This kind of distinction is not likely to endear a speaker to most people, including perhaps some who may be disposed (for whatever reason) to be sympathetic to him. In Xenophon's *Apology*, also, when Socrates is *quoted* as addressing all of the Five Hundred, he does what he does in Plato's *Apology*, addressing them as *Men*, not as *Court* or *Judges* or *Jurors*.

That is, Xenophon seems to be aware of Socrates' precision here, conforming thereby to what is reported by Plato. But Xenophon himself, when he refers to the Five Hundred, calls them *Court* or *Jurors*. He does not point out how Socrates' usage differs from his own. Rather, he allows the careful reader to notice this, reminding him thereby not only of Xenophon's greater respect for political protocol but also of Xenophon's subtlety, a subtlety deeper than what would be ordinarily expected in the kind of literate soldier and articulate outdoorsman Xenophon is often taken to be.

VII.

Although there are, in Xenophon's *Apology*, many references to the gods and to Socrates' daemonic thing, there is nothing at all said about the immortality of the soul, or about what (if anything) can reasonably be expected to happen to Socrates after his death. (This matter is explicitly left, at the end of Plato's *Apology*, an open question.)

Perhaps this is partly because Socrates is, by the time Xenophon writes, already on the way to a kind of immortality. For Xenophon begins by noticing that others have already written about Socrates' defense and about his end. Xenophon offers his own account as a supplement to what is already available. Thus, it can be said, Socrates was living on in the souls of others—and how long that would continue depended, in part, upon how thoughtful (and hence how thought-inspiring and thought-shaping) the surviving accounts were. Is there not reassurance for us in the fact that one is more likely to gain immortality if one does not try to survive physically at all costs?

Socrates, when the trial was over, said to those citizens (the majority of the Five Hundred) who had condemned him (26):

> It seems astonishing to me how you could ever have been convinced that I had committed an act meriting death. But further, my spirit need not be less exalted because I am to be executed unjustly, for the ignominity of that attaches not to me but to those who condemned me.

Here, it does seem, Socrates is *not* welcoming the fate awaiting him: after all, the corruption of his fellow citizens had been required in order for him to get what he is *said* to want, that is, to be spared the frailties of old age. Even so, would *we* (unlike Xenophon perhaps) have wanted Socrates either to escape from prison or to die a natural death in his circumstances? If not, why should not Socrates and his daemonic thing have "felt" as we do?

Socrates continues thus in his closing remarks to the Five Hundred before he is led away to await execution (26):

> I get comfort from the case of Palamedes, who, died in circumstances similar to mine; for even yet he affords us far more noble themes than does Odysseus, the man who unjustly put him to death.[31]

Perhaps Socrates refers here to the theater of his days, which may have tended to present Odysseus as a conniving character. Even so, it should have been evident to Socrates that Odysseus, an adventurous and even noble Odysseus, lived on in the great (and immensely influential) Homeric epics. Such an Odysseus, and not the unjustly condemned Palamedes, would have been the hero that Xenophon himself would have taken as a model. And Socrates can elsewhere bestow very high praise indeed upon Odysseus—as when he has him anticipating, in Book Ten of Plato's *Republic*, that Odysseus would, in his next incarnation on earth, choose not a public life but rather the kind of life that would *permit* him to become a philosopher.[32] Here, as elsewhere, we can see the friendly and often subtle rivalry between Socrates' two greatest students, Plato and Xenophon.[33]

NOTES

1. See, for the source of this discussion of *Meno* and Plato's *Republic*, George Anastaplo, "Teaching, Nature, and the Moral Virtues," 1997 *The Great Ideas Today* 4–9 (Encyclopedia Britannica, 1997). Consider Aristotle, *Nicomachean Ethics*, X, 9 (in a translation by Laurence Berns):

> Some suppose that people become good by nature, some that it is by habit, and some that is by teaching. Now then it is clear that what is from nature does not belong to those things that are in our power, but that it belongs to those who are truly fortunate through some divine cause. Argument and teaching, I am afraid, are not effective with all, but what is needed is for the soul of the hearer to be cultivated before by habits so as to both enjoy and to hate nobly. . . . To hit upon the right training for virtue from youth on is difficult if one has not been brought up under the right kind of laws.

See, on Plato's Socrates, chapter 6, note 4; chapter 10, note 46 below. See also chapter 11, section V below.

The translation of Plato's *Meno* primarily drawn on here is that prepared by Laurence Berns and George Anastaplo for the Focus Publishing Company (2004).

2. This talk was given in a program presented by the Hellenic Group of the International Women Associates, Chicago, Illinois, May 4, 2001. The original title of this talk was "Xenophon, the Trial of Socrates, and the Proper Response to the Prospect of Death." An epigraph was provided from Edmund Burke, *Reflections on the Revolution in France* (Penguin Classics, 1986), p. 373:

> What is liberty without wisdom, and without virtue? It is the greatest of all possible evils; for it is folly, vice, and madness, [if it is] without tuition or restraint. Those who know what virtuous liberty is, cannot bear to see it disgraced by incapable heads, on account of their having high-sounding words in their mouths. Grand, swelling sentiments of liberty, I am sure I do not despise. They warm the heart, they enlarge and liberalize our minds; they animate our courage in a time of conflict. . . . Neither do I wholly condemn the little arts and devices of popularity. They facilitate the carrying of many points of moment, they

keep the people together; they refresh the mind in its exertions; and they diffuse occasional gaiety over the severe brow of moral freedom. Every politician ought to sacrifice to the graces; and to join compliance with reason.

3. Anaxagoras of Clazomenae (c. 500–428 B.C.E.) is believed to have been attacked for "godlessness" by political enemies of Pericles as a way of attacking Pericles himself. It can be said that the conduct, during the Peloponnesian War, of Pericles' gifted ward, Alcibiades, contributed to making Socrates as vulnerable as he became. See also Aeschines (c. 389–314 B.C.E.) on the notorious postwar career of Critias and its effect on Socrates' fate. See as well chapter 10, note 46 below.

See, on Thucydides and his account of the Peloponnesian War, George Anastaplo, *The Thinker as Artist: From Homer to Plato & Aristotle* (Athens, Ohio: Ohio University Press, 1997), p. 253.

4. See, on Plato's *Apology of Socrates*, George Anastaplo, *Human Being and Citizen: Essays on Virtue, Freedom and the Common Good* (Chicago: Swallow Press, 1975), p. 8. See, on Plato's *Meno* and on Plato's *Crito*, Anastaplo, *Human Being and Citizen*, pp. 74, 203.

5. See, on Socrates' daemonic thing, Anastaplo, *Human Being and Citizen*, p. 325 (index).

6. See Plato, *Apology* 36A. Some of this information (with variations) may be found elsewhere as well.

7. Xenophon's best-known work, *Anabasis*, recalls the remarkable Retreat of the Ten Thousand. See chapter 6, note 33 below.

8. *The Encyclopedia of the Classical World* (Englewood Cliffs, New Jersey: Prentice-Hall, Inc., 1965), p. 236. The bracketed sentences in this quotation are my insertions.

9. Niccolo Machiavelli, for example, evidently held Xenophon in high regard. See chapter 6, note 33 below.

10. *The Encyclopedia of the Classical World*, p. 236. Foremost among the scholars who have spoken highly of Xenophon, a most subtle Xenophon, has been Leo Strauss. See Leo Strauss, *On Tyranny* (Glencoe, Illinois: The Free Press, 1963); Leo Strauss, *What Is Political Philosophy?* (Glencoe, Illinois: The Free Press, 1959), p. 95; chapter 6, notes 18, 19, 31 below. See also George Anastaplo, *The American Moralist: On Law, Ethics, and Government* (Athens, Ohio: Ohio University Press, 1992), p. 51. See as well chapter 6, note 25 below. See, for a highly favorable biographical sketch of Xenophon, chapter 6, note 33 below.

11. See George Anastaplo, "Constitutionalism, the Rule of Rules: Explorations," 39 *Brandeis Law Journal* 17, 84 (2000–2001).

12. Consider what Aristophanes, in his *Clouds*, makes of Socrates as advisor. See Anastaplo, *The Thinker as Artist*, pp. 157f, 199f, 209f.

13. It should again be noticed that this is not in the spirit of Plato's *Apology*. See, e.g., 41C.

14. All citations in the text are, unless otherwise indicated, to Xenophon's *Apology of Socrates*.

15. See, on suicide, George Anastaplo, "Law & Literature and the Christian Heritage: Explorations," 40 *Brandeis Law Journal* 191, 493 (2001).

16. These matters have been revived for our consideration by the recent series of suicide bombings by Muslims. See, on Islamic thought, George Anastaplo, *But Not Philosophy: Seven Introductions to Non-Western Thought* (Lanham, Md.: Lexington Books, 2002), p. 175. See also conclusion, note 3 below. See as well appendix A, note 15 below.

17. Consider, for example, "the bridle of Theages" referred to by Socrates in Plato's *Republic* (496B–C). The only time Plato's Socrates refers in the *Apology* to his vulnerability because of his age is in the remarks he made immediately *after* he was condemned to death (38C):

> For the sake of a little time, men of Athens, you will get a name and be charged with the responsibility, by those wishing to revile the city, for having killed Socrates, a wise man. For those wishing to reproach you *will* assert that I am wise, even if I am not. At any rate, if you had waited a short time, this would have come about for you of its own accord. For you see that my age is already far advanced in life and close to death. I say this not to all of you, but to those who voted to condemn me to death.

See, on the distinction Socrates makes between those who voted to condemn him ("men of Athens") and the others of the five hundred, the concluding paragraphs of section VI of this talk.

18. See, e.g., Thomas L. Pangle, "On the *Apology* of Socrates to the Jury," in Robert C. Bartlett, ed., *Xenophon—The Shorter Writings* (Ithaca: Cornell University Press, 1996), p. 20. See also Leo Strauss, *Xenophon's Socrates* (Ithaca: Cornell University Press, 1972), pp. 137–38.

19. Søren Kierkegaard, *The Concept of Irony* (Bloomington: Indiana University Press, 1968), p. 62. See, on Kierkegaard, chapter 5 above.

20. See, e.g., *Judges* 6:36–40.

21. See, on the subtlety of Xenophon, Anastaplo, *The American Moralist*, p. 51. See also chapter 6, note 18 above; chapter 10, note 43 below.

22. See, on Plato's *Crito*, Anastaplo, *Human Being and Citizen*, p. 203. I suspect that Alcibiades, if alive at the time (and in Athens), would also have acted to save Socrates.

23. I prepared, for the May 4, 2001 presentation of this talk in Chicago, the following comment at this point in my remarks:

> Similarly, to go to a much lower plane of activity and discourse, it can be observed that my own University of Chicago Law School classmates were much more "political" than I have been for five decades now, which may be reflected in the fact that I am privileged (if only by chance) to be pursuing with you here tonight this inquiry into the teachings of Xenophon rather than sharing with them, elsewhere in this city, the fiftieth anniversary gathering of our class graduation.

See appendix C of this collection.

24. See, on the Five Hundred, the text at note 6 of chapter 6 of this collection.

25. See Strauss, *Xenophon's Socrates*, p. 132:

> It must have been particularly galling to [Socrates' listeners at the trial] to hear that during the siege (when Athens was starved into submission) "the others" pitied themselves

while he was no way in greater straits than when the city was at the height of her prosperity. He draws the conclusion that he is justly praised by both god and men.

26. See, on "showboating," the quotation relayed by Frank Kruesi in Cornelia Grumman, "Wrong Question," *Chicago Tribune Magazine*, November 26, 2000, pp. 14, 24. See also appendix C, note 21 below.

27. Compare, for example, the care with which Abraham Lincoln dealt with explosive issues. See George Anastaplo, *Abraham Lincoln: A Constitutional Biography* (Lanham, Md.: Rowman & Littlefield, 1999), pp. 149f, 157f, 197f. See also appendix C, note 42 below. See as well chapter 10, note 46 below.

28. See, on what Socrates *did* know, George Anastaplo, "Freedom of Speech and the First Amendment: Explorations," 21 *Texas Tech Law Review* 1941, 1945 (1990) See also chapter 10, note 46 below.

29. Maurice Powicke, "Introduction," in *Saint Hugh of Lincoln*, Lincoln Minster Pamphlets, Second Series No. 1 (Published by The Friends of Lincoln Cathedral, 1959), p. 3. See also chapter 8, note 31 below.

30. See Plato, *Apology* 40A. Compare 26D (for Meletus' use of *Judges*).

31. Consider, on Palamedes, the following entry in *The Encyclopedia of Classical Mythology* (Englewood Cliffs, Prentice-Hall, Inc., 1965), p. 109:

Palamedes. Son of Nauplius and Clymen, a wise and noble man. He was regarded as the inventor of the lighthouse, measures, the balance, dice, and some letters of the Greek alphabet. He took part in the expedition against Troy and was given the task of forcing the unwilling Odysseus to take part. When Odysseus feigned madness, Palamedes was able to expose his deceit. From then on Odysseus plotted revenge, until he falsely accused Palamedes of treason during the siege of Troy. He caused a compromising letter, allegedly from Priam, to be intercepted and secretly hid a sum of money in Palamedes' tent to make it look as if Palamedes had accepted a bribe from the enemy. The ruse succeeded, and Palamedes was unjustly executed [by stoning]. (Virgil, *Aeneid*, ii, 82; Ovid, *Metamorphoses*, xiii, 56f.)

See also the "Nauplius" entry, *The Encyclopedia of Classical Mythology*, p. 94. See as well Strauss, *Xenophon's Socrates*, pp. 134–35. See, on Odysseus, chapter 8, sections I and IX below.

32. See Plato, *Republic* 620C.

33. We can now appreciate another account of Xenophon that is not limited by the conventional opinions of our day. It begins:

Born in Athens, Xenophon was in his youth a companion of Socrates. While still a young man he became an accomplished military leader, then in later life, a distinguished prose author. He wrote two major historical works. The *Hellenica* covers political and military events from the late 400s down to the 360s. The autobiographical *Anabasis* is a pseudonymous account of his own greatest military success. It tells the story of how, although Socrates warned him of the trouble ahead, Xenophon left Athens in 401 to join a Greek mercenary force hired by Cyrus, the younger brother of the king of Persia, for a campaign to take over the throne. (This Cyrus must not be confused with Cyrus the Great, founder of the Persian empire.) When Cyrus and the Greek generals were defeated and killed, the still youthful and inexperienced Xenophon was elected to take over the leadership of the desperate Greek remnant, trapped in the middle of Asia Minor. He proved a brilliant commander, and saved the mercenaries by leading them to the Black Sea, where they met up with a Spartan force. His account of this expedition shows him a great tactician and skillful rhetorician. For obscure reasons, perhaps involving his Spartan connections, Xenophon was banished from Athens in the 390s, and subsequently served with distinction under the Spartan king Agesilarus. He did not return to Athens until the banishment was lifted shortly before his death in the later 350s.

Xenophon's thoughts and writings were deeply influenced by his military experiences. He was also a devotee of the vigorous outdoor entertainments of Greek gentlemen, and wrote influential practical treatises on hunting and horsemanship. Perhaps because of these influences and interests, scholarly opinion in the twentieth century tended to cast him as rather conventional and simple, lacking in the gifts of intellect and imagination necessary for original philosophical thought, or for a real appreciation of Socrates. But Xenophon was clearly a very brilliant and charismatic young man, in talents if not in tastes a rival of Alcibiades, to judge from their achievements. His moral wisdom was esteemed by the Romans (Cicero recommended Xenophon to his brother as the best writer on effective political leadership), as well as by moral thinkers such as Montaigne and Rousseau, who shared his lack of interest in more theoretical areas of philosophy. His intellectual interests and achievements are perhaps best compared to those of Machiavelli, who made much use of Xenophon. Both excel at thoughtful observation rather than theory construction, and both are model writers of clear, vivid and discreet prose, which often leaves their readers to draw out the lessons left implicit in their presentations of conversations and events.

David K. O'Connor, "Xenophon," *Routledge Encyclopedia of Philosophy* (1998), vol. 9, p. 810. See also chapter 6, note 10 above. See as well George Anastaplo, "Law & Literature and the Austen-Dostoyevsky Axis: Explorations," 46 *South Dakota Law Review* 713 (Leo Strauss quotation) (2001); chapter 10, note 43 below.

See, on old age and the easiest of deaths, Plato, *Timaeus* 81D–E. See, on Socrates' death scene, Plato, *Phaedo.*

7

Jesus of Nazareth

7-A.   *THE GOSPEL OF MATTHEW*[1]

I.

I have found, in preparing for this talk, that many of my Jewish friends know little about the life, to say nothing of the trial, of Jesus. When I have asked them what questions I should address here at Hillel House, they have said that they themselves would like to have, among other things, an elementary account of the career of Jesus. Few of them know anything about the trial itself except that Jesus was killed as one result of it. This is, in some ways, a curious phenomenon: whatever Jesus' shortcomings may be in Jewish eyes, he is certainly one of the most famous Jews of all times, perhaps the most famous. Thus, he is known of and highly regarded in many places where Abraham, Moses, and David, for example, either are hardly known or are known only as figures in the background of the story of Jesus, a story that may be known in considerable detail worldwide.

Abraham, Moses, and David, on the other hand, *are* known much more, I would guess, to Christians than Jesus is to Jews today. But then, one might say, Christians must accept as valid the Biblical accounts of those three men if they *are* to be Christians, whereas Jews in order to be Jews do not have to accept (perhaps "should not" accept) as valid the New Testament accounts of Jesus. My remarks thus far, however, have not been directed to "acceptance" but rather to "acquaintance"—to knowledge among Jews generally of the principal features of Jesus' life. Perhaps there is seen here, on the part of Jews, something of a defensive reaction: they would just as soon put out of mind Jesus and all he stands for, including the misery long associated, for Jews, with his

worship. But safety, if not curiosity, should incline one to learn something reliable about one's adversary, if adversary he or his movement truly is.[2]

Perhaps, the skeptic might reply, there is nothing reliable to be know here:
the story of Jesus is largely mythological, certainly highly improbable. But it
should be said that that story is no more improbable, in some respects less so,
than many stories in the Hebrew Scriptures.[3] The most dramatic events in Jesus' life, as recounted in the Gospels, are duplicated again and again in the
Hebrew Scriptures. But what about the account of divinity assuming human
form? One does not *see* that happen in the Gospels. Rather, someone who is
shown as a man is said to be somehow divine. What he is shown to be *doing*
(say, by walking on water or by healing) may be seen in the Hebrew Scriptures, if not in the same form, at least in comparable if not even more august
forms. For example, nothing is portrayed on the part of Jesus or associated
with him comparable in grandeur to the plagues visited upon Egypt or to the
opening and then the most timely closing of the Red Sea, to say nothing of
the Creation of the World that makes the resurrections of both the Old and the
New Testaments pale by comparison.[4]

One *can* add that the *claim* that divinity has assumed human form is, in
principle, far more extreme than anything found in the Old Testament.[5] One
can find in the philosophers—for example, the *Republic* of Plato—support
for such a criticism.[6] But that, I repeat, is not part of the *action* in the New
Testament accounts before the reader but is rather an interpretation of action.
It is certainly conceivable that someone made such a claim or had it made
about him. Whether such a claim was in fact made about a mere human being, and how it was understood if made by him or by his followers, would be
of some use in assessing him as a leader.

When I referred to the prudence of learning something reliable about Jesus,
I was not concerned primarily about the reliability of the New Testament accounts themselves but rather about the accuracy of one's information about
what is in these accounts. Truly to know such accounts would include, of
course, a sound judgment about the reliability of such accounts[7]—but short of
that deeper knowledge is the acquisition of preliminary information about
what someone else *is* saying.

II.

I turn now to Jesus, his life, and his trial. I draw, at the outset of my account
here, on the *Encyclopedia Judaica* for information about Jesus' life that can
serve as the setting for what I in turn will have to say:

JESUS (D. 30 C.E. [Common Era = A.D.]), whom Christianity sees as its founder and object of faith, was a Jew who lived toward the end of the Second Commonwealth period. The martyrdom of his brother James is narrated by Josephus (*Ant.* 20:200–3), but the passage in the same work (18:63–64) speaking about the life and death of Jesus was either rewritten by a Christian or represents a Christian interpolation. The first Roman authors to mention Jesus are Tacitus and Seutonius. The historicity of Jesus is provided by the very nature of the records in the New Testament, especially the Four Gospels: *Matthew, Mark, Luke,* and *John.* The Gospels are records about the life of Jesus. . . . The picture of Jesus contained in [*Matthew, Mark,* and *Luke*] is not so much of a redeemer of mankind as [it is] of a Jewish miracle maker and preacher. The Jesus portrayed in these three Gospels is, therefore, the historical Jesus.

The Gospels. The precise day of the composition of the Gospels is not known, but all four were written before 100 C.E. and it is certain that *Matthew, Mark,* and *Luke* are interdependent. . . . It is generally accepted that the main substance of [these] Synoptic Gospels comes from two sources: an old account of the life of Jesus which is reproduced by *Mark,* and a collection of Jesus' sayings used in conjunction with the old account by *Matthew* and *Luke.* . . .

Both of the chief sources of the Synoptic Gospels, the old account, and the collection of Jesus' sayings, were produced in the primitive Christian congregation in Jerusalem, and were translated into the Greek from Aramaic or Hebrew. The present Gospels are redactions of these two sources, which were often changed as a result of ecclesiastical tendentiousness. This becomes especially clear in the description of Jesus' trial and crucifixion in which all Gospel writers to some degree exaggerate Jewish "guilt" and minimize Pilate's involvement. . . .

The Name, Birth, and Death Date of Jesus. Jesus is the common Greek form of the Hebrew name Joshua. Jesus' father, Joseph, his mother, Mary (in Heb., Miriam), and his brothers, James (in Heb., Jacob), Joses (Joseph), Judah, and Simon (*Mark* 6:3) likewise bore very popular Hebrew names. Jesus also had sisters, but their number and names are unknown. Jesus Christ means "Jesus the Messiah" and according to Jewish belief, the Messiah was to be a descendant of David. Both *Matthew* (1:2–16) and *Luke* (3:23–28) provide a genealogy leading back to David, but the two genealogies agree only from Abraham down to David. Thus, it is evident that both genealogies were constructed to show Jesus' Davidic descent, because the early Christian community believed that he was the Messiah. *Matthew* and *Luke* set Jesus' birth in Bethlehem, the city of David's birth. This motif is made comprehensible if it is assumed that many believed the Messiah would also be born in Bethlehem. . . .

According to *Luke's* data, Jesus was baptized by John the Baptist either in 27/28 or 28/29 C.E., when he was about the age of thirty. On the evidence of the first three Gospels, the period between his baptism and crucifixion comprised no more than one year; although according to *John* it ran to two or even three years.

It seems that on the point of the duration of Jesus' public ministry, the Synoptic Gospels are to be trusted. Most probably, then, Jesus was baptized in 28/29 and died in the year 30 C.E.

Jesus' Family and Circle. Jesus' father, Joseph, was a carpenter in Nazareth and it is almost certain that he died before Jesus was baptized. All the Gospels state that there was a tension between Jesus and his family, although after Jesus' death his family overcame their disbelief and took an honorable place in the young Jewish-Christian community. . . .

John the Baptist, who baptized Jesus in the river Jordan, was an important religious Jewish personality; he is recorded in Josephus (*Ant.* 18:116–9) as well as in the New Testament. From Josephus it is seen that John's baptismal theology was identical with that of the Essenes. . . . From his closest disciples, [Jesus] appointed twelve apostles to be, at the Last Judgment, judges of the twelve tribes of Israel. After the death of Jesus the twelve apostles provided the leadership for the Jerusalem Church.

The Arrest of Jesus. Meanwhile, Herod Antipas, who had beheaded John the Baptist, also wanted to kill Jesus, whom he saw as the heir of the Baptist, but Jesus wanted to die in Jerusalem, which was reputed for "killing the prophets" (*Luke* 13:34). With Passover drawing near, Jesus decided to make a pilgrimage to the Temple at Jerusalem. There he openly predicted the future destruction of the Temple and the overthrow of the Temple hierarchy. According to the sources, he even tried to drive out the traders from the precincts of the Temple . . . these actions precipitated the catastrophe. The Sadducean priesthood, despised by everyone, found its one support in the Temple, and Jesus not only attacked them but even publicly predicted the destruction of their Temple. . . .

After the festive meal, Jesus left the city together with his disciples and went to the nearby Mount of Olives, to the garden of Gethsemane. There, although he had foreseen the danger of his death, he prayed for his life (*Luke* 22:39–46). One of the twelve apostles, Judas Iscariot, had already betrayed him from unknown motives. . . . The Temple guard, accompanied by Judas Iscariot, arrested Jesus and took him to the high priest.

The "Trial" and Crucifixion. The Gospels in their present form contain descriptions of the so-called "trial" of Jesus rewritten in a way to make them improbable from the historical point of view. Nevertheless, a literary analysis of the sources is capable of revealing a closer approximation of the reality. . . . Thus it seems very probable that no session of the Sanhedrin took place in the house of the high priest where Jesus was in custody and that the "chief priests and elders and scribes" who assembled there were members of the Temple committee (see also *Luke* 20:1): the elders were apparently the elders of the Temple and the scribes were the Temple secretaries. The deliverance of Jesus into the hands of the Romans was, it seems, the work of the Sadducean "high priests," who are often mentioned alone in the story. A man suspected of being a messianic pretender could be delivered to the Romans without a verdict of the Jewish high court. In addition, the high priests were interested in getting rid of Jesus, who had spoken against them and had predicted the destruction of the Temple. The Roman governor Pontius Pilate ultimately had Jesus executed in the Roman way, by crucifixion. All the Gospels indicated that on the third day after the crucifixion Jesus' tomb was found empty. According to *Mark* an angel announced that Jesus had risen, and the other Gospels state that Jesus appeared before his believers after his death.[8]

The learned author of this entry in the *Encyclopedia Judaica* then turns to an assessment of those sayings and doings of Jesus that had contributed to the tension between him and the Jewish authorities.[9] But I must pass this by—some of you will want to read the entire article—and quote for you only a dozen more lines from this useful article:

> *Jesus as the Messiah.* The early Christian Church believed Jesus to be the expected Messiah of Israel, and he is described as such in the New Testament; but whether Jesus thought himself to be the Messiah is by no means clear. . . . [After examining various passages:] Thus Jesus' understanding of himself as the Messiah was probably inconsistent, or at first he was waiting for the Messiah, but at the end, he held the conviction that he himself was the Messiah.[10]

This author concludes his article,

> If, as Christians believe, the martyr was at the same time the Messiah, then his death has a cosmic importance. Through the teachings of Jesus, as well as through other channels, the Jewish moral message entered Christianity. Thus, the historical Jesus has served as a bridge between Judaism and Christianity, as well as one of the causes for their separation.[11]

I supplement this account with a few sentences from a Jewish lawyer, Bernard Weisberg, a Chicagoan active in civil liberty causes, who has written me in these terms about his understanding of Jesus:

> The priests viewed him as one who threatened their hierarchy, but the Romans, whose rule must have been very repressive of all liberties of expression and association, wanted him tried by natives and killed by Romans to avoid any threat to their exploitation of the colony. His views, his preaching, and his fathering of non-priestly apostles to form an organization guaranteed the fatal reprisal. The Romans have plenty of modern successors.

III.

I venture to add some opinions of my own, not to contradict what has been said by others who are much more learned in these matters than I ever will be but rather to suggest ways of beginning to think about what is known about the trial of Jesus. Perhaps, we can all acquire thereby what the *Encyclopedia Judaica* author called "a closer approximation of the reality."[12]

I draw, on this occasion, primarily on the *Gospel of Matthew*, noting in passing that one or another of the *written* gospels may have been all that many Christians ever had to draw upon in the early Church, if they had even that. *Matthew* seems to be the most Jewish of the Gospels;[13] it is traditionally placed first in the compilation of the New Testament. The *Columbia Encyclopedia* includes the following observations:

> [T]here are more allusions to the Old Testament in [the *Gospel of Matthew*] than in the others. . . . Its composition is assigned to the latter half of the [first century]. The Gospel was written for Jewish Christians; its purpose was to prove that Jesus was the Messiah foretold in the Old Testament. The traditional ascription [of this Gospel] to St. Matthew (doubted by many) dates from the [second century].[14]

This Gospel, it seems to be agreed by scholars, was written by Jews for Jews (but not necessarily written originally in Hebrew); it was probably passed on by and to Jewish-Christians in an effort to settle what had become an intrafamily struggle. The author of this Gospel does not say that he knew Jesus personally. Nor does he say that he reports all he had heard about him. But he may well have believed that he told all that needed to be said.

The Jewishness of Christianity, not of *Matthew* alone, is reflected in the reference by a distinguished Roman Catholic priest to his faith as "the new order of salvation, whose roots were in Judaism and not in Hellenism."[15] This opinion goes back to the earliest days of Christianity. Consider, for instance, the concern by the Gentile craftsmen who routinely made the offerings to be taken to the great Temple of Diana at Ephesus—the concern recorded in the *Book of Acts*, about the teachings of Jewish (that is Christian) missionaries against the pagan worship of idols. We are told that a multitude, "when they knew that [a missionary who was about to speak] was a Jew, all with one voice cried for about the space of two hours, 'Great is Diana of the Ephesians.'"[16]

As for *Matthew* itself, it is filled with Jewish things: a dozen prophecies of old (which are spelled out here and there) are said to have been fulfilled, confirming thereby Jesus' Messiahship; miracles abound among a people that regarded them as unusual but *not* as highly improbable events (and this includes miracles of resurrection).[17] It is assumed throughout *Matthew* both that God is active in the affairs of men and that this is a time of wickedness *and* of divine intervention on a grand scale. Jesus turns against official Judaism its own doctrines and presuppositions. He can even exploit a Jewish complaint against the authorities, to the effect that the prophets have always been persecuted, especially in Jerusalem. (5:12)[18]

The text is so Jewish that it is difficult for the typical modern reader to understand much of it. It is obvious, for instance, that John the Baptist's "Repent ye" (3:2) draws on Jewish doctrines and standards. But we are not told—the original readers, it seems, did not have to be told—what those standards were. Similarly, Jesus is reported as speaking in Galilee's synagogues, "preaching the gospel of the kingdom." (4:23) This, too, obviously meant something to the original readers.[19]

The Jewishness of this Gospel is anticipated by the way it opens with a genealogy that connects Jesus to King David. (*Luke* has its genealogy in its third chapter.) The opening verse of *Matthew* reads, "The book of the generation of Jesus Christ, the son of David, the son of Abraham." (1:1) The series of *begats* is so arranged that it can be said, "So all the generations from Abraham to David are fourteen generations; and from David until the carrying away into Babylon are fourteen generations; and from the carrying away into Babylon unto Christ are fourteen generations." (1:17) The history of the Jewish people is thereby so organized as to set up everything for Jesus: all that went before is to be seen as preparation for the coming of Jesus. Three names seem to matter most in this list: Abraham, David, and Jesus; only two names in the sequence have titles assigned to them: "David the king" and "Jesus, who is called Christ." There had been, since the founding of the people by Abraham, the high point represented by the royal rule of David and then fourteen generations later the low point represented by the Babylonian captivity. Now a new high point—the very highest point—is to be reckoned with: that of the Messiah.

Abraham established the necessary people; David established the relevant royal line. Moses is not mentioned here: he (or his Law?) does not matter for the immediate purpose of the genealogist. There is no need to go earlier than Abraham: it seems that Jesus comes primarily for the Jews. Nor is there any need to have any lineage after Jesus. Not only is family life disregarded by Jesus,[20] but we are to understand that with the coming of Jesus (as the Messiah) there is an end to significant Jewish (perhaps even human) history. This is anticipated in what is said by John the Baptist, in disparaging those who proudly invoked "Abraham as their father": "God is able of these stones to raise up children unto Abraham." (3:9)[21]

A further indication of Jewishness, if I may call it that, is the arrangement of the generations so as to have forty of them. In thirty-nine of the generations, *begat* is used; for Jesus a different formulation is used: "And Jacob begat Joseph the husband of Mary, of whom was born Jesus, who is called Christ." (1:16) (Later, the wise men who call on the infant seem to have their attention directed only to the child and its mother. [2:11]) Of course, if Joseph is not the father, that might seem to cut the vital connection with David. But that is hardly an objection that someone who believes Mary was impregnated by the Holy Ghost would be concerned about. Besides, it can be said that not only is Joseph the putative father (as under the common law) but also that this is still another indication that blood ties are to be superseded. (It is believed by some, however, that Mary too was of the line of David.)

Once *Matthew* is done, Jewishness can be forgotten as a vital source for the future development of Christianity. But within *Matthew*, the heritage of Judaism is exploited. The forty generations (13 plus 14 plus 13) are followed, in the fourth chapter of this Gospel, by an account of Jesus' *forty* days in the wilderness and the resulting temptations by Satan.[22] Is there not about all this symmetry, and the importance of critical numbers, something Jewish as well?[23]

IV.

The trial of Jesus was, in a way, to be expected: it was the culmination of all that had gone before. What had gone before included fierce polemics, which seemed then to be generally taken for granted as the appropriate form of public discourse! One must wonder, living in a tamer place (if not a tamer age), where the fervor came from for such polemics. One suspects that it must be related to the sense both of righteousness and vulnerability on all sides.

The language of the trial itself, however, is much milder than one finds elsewhere in the Gospel. I propose now to provide you an account of Jesus' trial, from which I can proceed and upon which our discussion can be based. In doing so I draw on the seventeenth-century King James translation, which is not as accurate as some English translations of the Bible since then but which is unmatched in beauty and in the sense it conveys of pious grandeur.[24] We begin in the Garden of Gethsemane (26:45–47, 49–50, 57, 59–68; 27:1–2, 11–26):

> Then cometh [Jesus] to his disciples, and saith unto them, "Sleep on now, and take your rest: behold, the hour is at hand, and the Son of man is betrayed into the hands of sinners.
>
> "Rise, let us be going: behold, he is at hand that doth betray me."
>
> And while he yet spake, lo, Judas [Iscariot], one of the twelve, came to Jesus, and said, "Hail, Master;" and kissed him.
>
> And Jesus said unto him, "Friend, wherefore art thou come?" Then came they, and laid hands on Jesus, and took him. . . .
>
> And they that laid hold on Jesus led him away to Caiaphas the high priest, where the scribes and the elders were assembled. . . .
>
> Now the chief priests, and elders, and all the council, sought false witness against Jesus, to put him to death;

But found none: yea, though many false witnesses came, yet found they none. At the last came two false witnesses.

And said, "This fellow said, I am able to destroy the temple of God, and to build it in three days."

And the high priest arose, and said unto him, "Answerest thou nothing? What is it which these witness against thee?"

But Jesus held his peace. And the high priest answered and said unto him, "I adjure thee by the living God, that thou tell us whether thou be the Christ, the Son of God."

Jesus saith unto him, "Thou hast said: nevertheless I say unto you, Hereafter shall ye see the Son of man sitting on the right hand of power, and coming in the clouds of heaven."

Then the high priest rent his clothes, saying, "He hath spoken blasphemy; what further need have we of witnesses? Behold, now ye have heard his blasphemy.

"What think ye?" They answered and said, "He is guilty of death."

Then did they spit in his face, and buffeted him; and others smote him with the palms of their hands,

Saying, "Prophesy unto us, thou Christ, Who is he that smote thee?" . . .

When the morning was come, all the chief priests and elders of the people took counsel against Jesus to put him to death:

And when they had bound him, they led him away, and delivered him to Pontius Pilate the governor. . . .

And Jesus stood before the governor: and the governor asked him, saying, "Art thou the King of the Jews?" And Jesus said unto him, "Thou sayest."

And when he was accused of the chief priests and elders, he answered nothing.

Then said Pilate unto him, "Hearest thou not how many things they witness against thee?"

And he answered to him never a word; insomuch that the governor marveled greatly.

Now at that feast the governor was wont to release unto the people a prisoner, whom they would.

And they had then a notable prisoner, called Barabbas.

Therefore when they were gathered together, Pilate said unto them, "Whom will ye that I release unto you? Barabbas, or Jesus which is called Christ?"

For [Pilate] knew that for envy they had delivered [Jesus].

When he was set down on the judgment seat, his wife sent unto him, saying, "Have thou nothing to do with that just man: for I have suffered many things this day in a dream because of him."

But the chief priests and elders persuaded the multitude that they should ask Barabbas, and destroy Jesus.

The governor answered and said unto them, "Whether of the twain will ye that I release unto you?" They said, "Barabbas."

Pilate saith unto them, "What shall I do then with Jesus which is called Christ?" They all say unto him, "Let him be crucified."

And the governor said, "Why, what evil hath he done?" But they cried out more, saying, "Let him be crucified."

When Pilate saw that he could prevail nothing, but that rather a tumult was made, he took water, and washed his hands before the multitude, saying, "I am innocent of the blood of this just person: see ye to it."

Then answered all the people, and said, "His blood be on us, and on our children."

Then released he Barabbas unto them: and when he had scourged Jesus, he delivered him to be crucified.

One can regret that more detail is not provided about the trial itself. But the slimness of the record can be understood. Few trials of the time would have been recorded. There were, we gather, a lot of trials around.[25] Indeed, two other men were crucified with Jesus—and nothing at all is said about *their* trials. We do not even know their names. Although it happens that the trial of Jesus is the one that has come to matter, we have to be satisfied with what is almost a stylized rendering of it.[26]

It should be noticed that there is nothing that is reported to have happened at this trial that does not happen every day. Nothing miraculous, or remarkably unusual, is offered up to us. Pontius Pilate's equivocal attitude is all too familiar. This is not to say, however, that whatever is plausible *must* have happened. Jewish scholarship today seems to agree that the account of the trial, insofar as it touches on Jewish legal procedures and standards, is either fragmentary or distorted. But if God *was* involved (as, for example, in the story of the Binding of Isaac[27]), then things could have been done for the first, perhaps only, time *this* way. I myself do not know enough about how things were done then to know whether this trial departed from standard procedure and hence was unjust in this respect also.[28]

The case, as presented in the *Matthew* account, may not be of much interest in itself without consideration of the significance of the claim of divinity associated with Jesus. Can one pass on all this without passing judgment first on the claim of divinity? Does *that* rest, in turn, on the issue of the Resurrection? Certainly, the belief of the author of *Matthew* in the Resurrection very much shapes the account he presents. We can see, here as elsewhere, that what we today call "facts" and "values" cannot be readily separated. Truly to describe—that is, fully to understand—the career of Jesus, one has to pass upon the soundness of the claims made on his behalf as well as upon the soundness of the presuppositions on which such claims may be based.[29]

V.

But, as I have indicated, our efforts on this occasion will be much more modest: the truly serious questions we must leave to others. Even so, we do venture to say something more about the career of Jesus.

Matthew, alone of the Gospels, has the Herod problem at the outset of its account (after the genealogies). Herod the King (maintained in power by the Romans, it seems) seeks to destroy the infant Jesus when he learns, from the "wise men from the East," that someone had been born in Bethlehem who would be "King of the Jews." (2:1–20) From his very birth, therefore, Jesus "confronts" political authority, in the form of a king who is apprehensive about his temporal power. Jesus, at his death, confronts political authority in the form of a governor who is apprehensive that *his* temporal power may be compromised by disturbances due to the religious beliefs of his restless subjects. That is, the final (and perhaps decisive) phase of Jesus' trial—that held before Pilate—concerns explicitly only his supposed kingship. (27:11) This is seen, also, when he is given up to be crucified, in the mockery of him as a king by the Roman soldiers and in the inscription placed over his head on the cross, "THIS IS JESUS THE KING OF THE JEWS." (27:37) On the other hand, the Jewish authorities, when they had mocked him the night before, had addressed him as a prophet. (26:68)

What we may call the spiritual mission of Jesus is framed in *Matthew* by the political challenges he faced: at birth from Herod, at death from Pilate. (It is a later Herod who has John the Baptist killed, etc.) The challenge at birth can remind the reader of similarities in the infancy of Moses. Both infants were unusually vulnerable at birth; they both came to the attention of an unfriendly local ruler; both survived while many other babies were said to have been killed; and special efforts had to be made to save them by removing them from where they otherwise would have been.

No doubt, some would regard Jesus as a Jew with what could be called a Moses Complex—just as Sigmund Freud seems to have seen Moses and Judaism in Christian terms, with a decisive emphasis upon a sacrificed leader.[30] But whereas Moses was very much concerned with a law that would govern one's temporal (including family) affairs, Jesus can be said to have been un-Jewish both in his relative lack of concern about his physical survival and in his casualness about family ties.

But, it should be added, Jesus' principal accusers may not have been concerned ultimately about physical survival either, but rather about the body (and the community that is made up of and serves bodies) primarily as means for the proper development of spiritual life. Certainly, Jesus and his accusers seem to have agreed that his spiritual manifestations were more important than his political manifestations. Or, put another way, both Jesus and his Jewish enemies would have agreed that what happened to the soul was far more important than what any Herod or Pilate could do to anyone's body.

How souls should be ministered to is implied, in *Matthew*, by the account of the genealogy that precedes the Herod-and-the-infants' story and by the account of the Resurrection that follows the Pilate story. Critical to the trial of Jesus was conduct by him in the very last years of his life that could be plausibly associated by some with blasphemy.

VI.

Blasphemy has been taken to include, at least in Anglo-American law, the denial to God of something that belongs to Him.[31] And, it would seem, to arrogate to oneself a divine attribute *is* to deny God something that may be regarded as exclusively His. But, scholars say, a claim to Messiahship was *not* blasphemous, but an "invocation of the divine name" *was.*[32]

Insofar as blasphemy consists also of offending the religious sensibilities of the community, then Jesus can certainly be considered to have raised doubts about the propriety of what he was doing. (This is not to say that the sensibilities of a particular community may not themselves be questionable.) Consider the following illustrations drawn from *Matthew* of how troublesome Jesus could be. Wonder is aroused early in his recorded ministry: "For he taught them as one having authority, and not as the scribes [do]." (7:29) Some scribes, upon observing how Jesus healed, believed him to have blasphemed when he said, "Son, be of good cheer; thy sins be forgiven thee." (9:2–3) That is, he conducted himself as if *he* had the power to forgive sins. Less serious questions were raised about Jesus' eating with publicans and sinners. (9:11) More serious, of course, was his healing on the Sabbath of a man with a withered hand. (12:10–13) It is at this point that *Matthew* notes, "Then the Pharisees went out, and held a council against him, how they might destroy him." (12:14) His hungry disciples (but not Jesus himself, it should be noticed) had troubled the Pharisees by plucking corn on the Sabbath. (12:2) Before and after this the Pharisees had concluded, "This fellow doth not cast out devils, but by Beelzebub the prince of the devils." (9:34, 12:24) Finally, in this array of a half-dozen illustrations of what bothered Jesus' critics, there is the query, "Why do thy disciples transgress the tradition of the elders, for they wash not their hands when they eat bread?" (15:2) His critics were concerned about his repeated defiance of Jewish law, that law that reflected and protected the core of the revelation made available to their people.

All of these episodes are outside Jerusalem. By the time Jesus got to the great city, packed with visitors and excited by the impending Passover, he had established himself as incorrigible in the eyes of some of the authorities. His reception in the city as a prophet, his conduct in the Temple, and his preaching disturbed his critics. They returned to the questions he had encountered at the outset of his career: "By what authority doest thou these things? And who gave thee this authority?" This is what "the chief priests and the elders of the people" asked of him "as he was teaching." (21:23) Jesus avoided an answer by exploiting the equivocal status among them of John the Baptist. (21:24–27) He then spoke scathingly, but in parables, about questioners who were astute enough to perceive that he referred to them. But we are further told, "When they sought to lay hands on him, they feared the multitude, because they took him for a prophet." (21:46)

VII.

All sides to this controversy acted in the spirit of the declaration that Jesus had considered himself obliged to make: "Think not that I am come to send peace on earth: I came not to send peace, but a sword." (10:34) That is, they all considered themselves at war.

Jesus and his critics talked at, but not to, each other. Their vigorous exchanges (with "generation of viper" a mild epithet, it sometimes seems) cannot be readily considered rational discourse. (3:7) Such exchanges do remind us both of the seriousness of the pursuit of truth for human beings and the folly to which one's passions can lead one.[33] Something of the imprudence of the times may be seen in Jesus' promise (or is it a threat?) after a series of parables, "I will utter things which have been kept secret from the foundation of the world." (13:35)[34]

Who *is* most at fault here? (I set aside for the moment the question of which side, if either, expressed the divine will.) In such "confrontations," which do display features of a civil war, he is most at fault who should have been superior. The superior, in such circumstances, should be able to step back, assess what is happening, and resolve differences, or at least avoid adding to the turmoil. Certainly, each of the parties should have made allowances for the shortcomings of the other. There is little indication in this account that such allowances were made. Certainly, also, both parties, assessed in human terms, suffered mightily from allowing this conflict to proceed to its bitter conclusion.

A good man, we are taught by Socrates, prefers to be harmed than to harm another.[35] We are taught in another Platonic dialogue that complete virtue is a condition for immunity from suffering harm as well as protection against doing harm to another.[36] That is to say, the truly good man can take care of himself in the proper fashion. His courage, for example, discourages many would-be attackers; his prudence anticipates the follies of others. Thus, moral virtue is seen as productive of good; suffering is not seen as a desirable means to happiness.[37]

Consider, in this connection, the story of the young man who had kept all the commandments since his youth. He was then told by Jesus, "If thou wilt be perfect, go and sell that thou hast, and give to the poor, and thou shalt have treasure in heaven: and come and follow me." (19:16–21) At this the young man went away sorrowful, for he had great possessions. (19:22) The old way, it seems, was no longer sufficient, nor perhaps yet the new.[38]

VIII.

We return to our immediate concern, the trial of Jesus, and the charge of blasphemy. The fatal statement, made in response to the high priest's insistence, seems to have been, "Hereafter shall ye see the Son of man sitting on the right hand of power, and coming in the clouds of heaven." (26:64)

This evident claim by Jesus of divine powers for himself seems to have been considered an obvious blasphemy by almost everyone else present. Their response indicates that Jesus was not regarded as simply mad. Should what he said have been taken in the way that, or as seriously as, they did take it?

Most of us, I dare say, cannot appreciate the seriousness of this matter. It can seem to us that the crime here consists of a mere difference of opinion. (This is aside from the political consequences that might have been anticipated from Jesus' ministry—but then, could he not have been isolated for a while, so as not to provoke the Romans during the Passover Season?) Our inability to appreciate all this, if only as an excuse for disposing of Jesus, again suggests our distance from such things. Neither can we understand the competition among the disciples when they vie for privileged positions in Heaven or when some try to say who Jesus really is: John the Baptist, Elijah, and Jeremiah are conjured up. (16:13) Even someone as sophisticated as Herod, we are told, could be moved by a prophecy that a threat to his rule would be born in Bethlehem. (2:46)

Most of us, I have said, do not feel as Jesus, his supporters, and his enemies did. We must wonder whether we are liberated and thus enriched? Or are we poorer for our sophistication? It is evident that the responses to Jesus' claims—the responses of enemies and enthusiasts alike—suggests that he was addressing, in his own way, a vital issue, perhaps even a profound need in the human soul.

IX.

It can be instructive to notice in *Matthew* how each side to the controversy accounts for the other side's doings and sayings. The chief priests and Pharisees are shown saying to Pilate, "Sir, we remember that that deceiver [Jesus] said, while he was yet alive, 'After three days I will rise again.'" (27:63) They suggest that precautions to be taken lest Jesus' disciples steal the body and then claim that he had risen. This accounts for a guard being at the tomb. (27:64–66) Later, the Jewish authorities say that the body was stolen and the Christians say that the authorities bribed the guards to conceal the Resurrection. (28:11–15) Thus, each side has its explanation for the other side's account of the evidently missing body.

The alertness of the Jewish leaders, we are in effect told, is in some ways superior to that of the disciples, for the disciples never seemed to hear, or to take much account of, Jesus' indication on more than one occasion that he would rise again. In a curious way, Jesus and his principal adversaries understood and respected each other more than either of them respected most of their own followers. Did "the better men" in the community *tend* to be among the authorities, rather than among the followers of Jesus, and did they continue thus until Christianity became established?[39]

Of course, one might wonder why, if one accepts the Gospel account, the chief priests did not become Christians if they knew what really happened.[40] This is a complicated problem, and not only because it must have been difficult in those trying days to find out what had "really happened," including what the authorities learned and believed.

X.

The Gospel itself recognizes the problem of establishing the believability of anything. One of the twelve disciples, despite intimate contact with Jesus, is said to have betrayed him. (26:47–50) The betrayer evidently did not believe all that he had heard from Jesus himself. After the Resurrection, most of the remaining eleven worshiped Jesus when they met in Galilee, "but some doubted." (28:17) Earlier, Jesus had complained about those cities "wherein most of his mighty works were done, because they repented not." (11:20) Consider, also, the later Herod: he is willing to believe,

almost matter-of-factly, that Jesus is the beheaded John the Baptist resurrected—and yet Herod continues to conduct himself as he had. (14:2) But,
then, consider as well the Jews in the Desert who repudiated Moses' teaching not long after having witnessed the great miracles of the Exodus.[41] Is
there not, in such accounts, an honest recognition that not all who see do
believe, just as many who do not see may come to believe. In short, the
eyes may be informed, or misled, by the mind or the will.[42]

The last that is seen of Jesus in *Matthew*—the very end of the Gospel, in
fact—consists of Jesus commissioning his disciples to go out and teach all
nations. He promises that he will be with them "even unto the end of the
world." This is a long way and a long time from the quite particular genealogy (in quite particular times and places) with which the *Matthew* account opens and upon which all that follows seems to depend. (1:1–18,
28:16–20)

XI.

How successful was Jesus in what he did? Does this bear on the validity of
that which he claimed? What was he truly after? Was there something wrong
among the Jews (or, at least, among the Romans and Jews in their collaboration) upon which Jesus worked? Was Jesus (whatever he may have been)
somehow correct, for instance, in what he had to say, in his fatal blasphemy,
about his coming glory? After all, how many others, at least in the Western
world, have had such elevation as he has been accorded for almost two thousand years now?

Did Jesus, in what he said, adapt for and broadcast to the world the old
Jewish teaching? Was such eventual worldwide dissemination intended from
the outset by the founder(s) of that teaching? Is the form that this dissemination took a distortion of Judaism, a dilution of it? Or is it a salutary transformation of it? Was that teaching, before transformation, dependent upon a people, preferably a people in its own land, a relatively small people?[43]

The Gospels replace genealogy: affirmations of the Word (or of an idea) replace ties of blood. Such a proposed replacement could well have been taken
as the end of Jews as Jews—and so naturally many, perhaps most, Jews resisted. In the same way, love can pose a threat to law, as may be seen in the
resistance encountered by routine recourse to healing on the Sabbath.

Both Jesus and his adversaries, one can say, sensed that Roman power was
hollow at its core, that it was bound to be replaced by a vital faith.[44] The new
Jewish teaching, somewhat modified by Greek thought, was not primarily
that of a community but rather that of individuals.[45]

XII.

What determines who happens to be moved by what faith? Is it due to chance—whether in one's circumstances or in one's passions or in one's capacities? What is the status in these matters of reasonableness?[46]

There are, throughout the *Gospel of Matthew*, displays of remarkable intelligence: apt responses, shrewd evasions, and extended sermons drawing on a sensitive grasp of human nature. But, it can sometimes seem to the modern reader, there is not much emphasis upon rationality itself. I can recall only two important instances where someone persuades another (not silences him, not parries him, not overwhelms him, but *persuades* him). In both instances, the one persuaded by an argument is Jesus himself; in neither instance is the persuader a Jew.

The first instance is found in 8:5–10, 13:

And when Jesus was entered into Capernaum, there came unto him a centurion, beseeching him, and saying, "Lord, my servant lieth at home sick of the palsy, grievously tormented." And Jesus saith unto him, "I will come and heal him." The centurion answered and said, "Lord, I am not worthy that thou shouldest come under my roof: but speak the word only, and my servant shall be healed. For I am a man under authority, having soldiers under me: and I say to this man, 'Go,' and he goeth: and to another, 'Come,'" and he cometh; and to my servant, "Do this,' and he doeth it." When Jesus heard it, he marvelled, and said to them that followed," Verily I say unto you, I have not found so great faith, no, not in Israel. . . ." And Jesus said unto the centurion, "Go thy way; and as thou hast believed, so be it done unto thee." And his servant was healed in the selfsame hour.

The second instance is in 15:22–28:

And, behold, a woman of Canaan came out of the same coasts, and cried unto him, saying, "Have mercy on me, O Lord, thou Son of David; my daughter is grievously vexed with a devil." But he answered her not a word. And his disciples came and besought him, saying, "Send her away; for she crieth after us." But he answered and said, "I am not sent but unto the lost sheep of the house of Israel." Then came she and worshiped him, saying, "Lord, help me." But he answered and said, "It is not meet to take the children's bread, and to cast it to dogs." And she said, "Truth, Lord: yet the dogs eat of the crumbs which fall from their masters' table." Then Jesus answered and said unto her, "O woman, great is thy faith: be it unto thee even as thou wilt." And her daughter was made whole from that very hour.

That an outsider should be involved in each case suggests (and I grant this may be rather fanciful) that the Jews of that time may not have been able really to *talk* to one another, especially when critical differences were involved. But notice also—I believe this is less likely to be fanciful—that Jesus speaks of the great faith evident on both of these occasions. No doubt, faith *is* involved, but may not that which makes these two exchanges so effective be what I have called their rationality, rationality that is expressed (in each case) in a kind of metaphor?[47]

XIII.

Jews and Christians, despite their millennia-old differences, have much more in common than either group has with most of the rest of the world. I have suggested that the struggle between them, especially in the early generations of their common era, was like a civil war, with the special bitterness of which such war is capable. Since one's brother is likely to know where one's weaknesses lie, one is particularly threatened. One is also disturbed at having to strike out at part of oneself. Does not each faction continue to remind the other of their common origins, failings, and aspirations?

The Socratic dialogues, it should be evident from what I have said, *are* clearer (in one sense) than a gospel addressed to one's faith, perhaps in part because such dialogues are devoted more to questions than to answers. We must not forget, however, the importance in Greek life of the Eleusinian mysteries,[48] the rituals of an old faith that had matured and become responsible as well as satisfying. What is there in the human being, or at least in most human beings, that cannot otherwise be reliably ministered to in a civilized way?[49]

7-B.   *THE GOSPEL OF MARK*[50]

I.

I do not believe it would be prudent for either you or me to expect anything truly new to be said on this occasion about the life, the trial, or the death of Jesus. When as much has been written about any subject as there has been about Jesus, it would be folly to expect anyone to be able to say anything new.[51] On the other hand, when this much had been written about any subject, it is almost as if nothing has been written—and so one can presume to share one's impressions with others.

It is no doubt significant that there *has* been the worldwide response there has been to the story of Jesus.[52] His story seems, at the very least, to satisfy—

perhaps to develop and to satisfy—a natural need in the human being. That which is natural is something that can be examined afresh again and again, or at least can be observed for what it is. One's understanding of divine, as well as of human, things may be thereby enhanced.

I do believe that something useful can be said on this occasion, not necessarily about the life of Jesus but about how one might begin to think about matters related to that life. Thus, one can make suggestions about how to read a text, even a sacred text, if only in a preliminary fashion, and how to deal with it once it is read—how to begin to think about what one reads and how to speak responsibly about what one might learn. At the very least one can, as a student of these matters, suggest questions, perhaps clarified questions, to be answered by partisans who are more confident than the genuine student is likely to be about the answers to other, perhaps even prior, questions.[53]

II.

When there has been as much partisan effort as there has been with respect to Jesus, the inquiring mind is driven back to the original texts—and, in this case, to the Gospel accounts in the form that they happen to have come down to us. That form is itself open to question—but we must have a point from which to begin on this occasion here at Rosary College.

Once one turns to the Gospels, one must start from the fact that their hero is a Jew. Jesus of Nazareth was born a Jew; he lived a Jew; he died a Jew. One cannot begin to understand him without taking into account the fact of his pervasive Jewishness. One cannot otherwise understand him, his disciples, his multitude of followers, his enemies, or his fate.[54] We today—and this includes many if not even most contemporary Jews—necessarily come to Jesus and his story from a Gentile view of things. Even so, someone who is truly a Christian today is in large part Jewish, in some ways perhaps even more Jewish in his devoutness than any Jew who has become thoroughly secularized.

The Jewishness of Jesus is a massive fact that the sensitive reader of the Gospels cannot help but notice.[55] Much of what Jesus says would not be comprehensible otherwise. His teaching, standing alone—that is, independent of its Jewish context and expectations—is hardly coherent. Allusions are made by him to a long, and evidently well-known, Israelite tradition. Virtually everyone with whom Jesus deals (at least among his Jewish countrymen) is what we today would call a believer. Intense struggles were waged among Jesus' countrymen, it seems, not about whether the God of Abraham, Isaac, and Jacob existed and was entitled to single-minded devotion but rather about what form that devotion should take and what in turn could be expected from God for the people of Israel, if not also for the world.

Any speaker about the Gospels today addresses an audience vastly different from that which originally confronted the authors of the Gospels. One must, in what one says today, accommodate oneself to believers and unbelievers alike—to the doctrines of one sect and the sensibilities of the other. Unbelievers are quite varied in their opinions—they are as varied as believers and as much shaped as they by the "faith" of their fathers.[56] Temperament and chance do seem to play a considerable role in these matters, as some insist upon their freedom while others upon their salvation—and all, one way or another, very much want and need the truth, so that they may truly be saved, so that they may truly be free.

III.

It is convenient to settle for our discussion on this occasion primarily upon one of the Gospels. The *Gospel of Mark* is the shortest of the four Gospels. It is often said to be the oldest of the Gospels, even though *John* has in it details about the trial of Jesus that are not found in *Mark* or in the other two Synoptic Gospels.[57] Those gospels, *Matthew* and *Luke*, are fairly close to *Mark* in their descriptions of the trial of Jesus. *Mark* seems not only the oldest but also the simplest and the most naive of the four accounts. (It is also the one in which the Resurrection barely figures.) *Mark* is said to have been written a half-century or so after the death of Jesus, whose death was about 30 A.D.

Most early Christians, it seems to me, probably knew only one *written* Gospel, if they knew any at all. One might wonder whether there has ever been a time when what most people learned about Jesus was exclusively, or even primarily, from written Gospels. Still, I will assume knowledge here of the Gospel stories, at least in outline, stories that have been retold in so many different ways.[58]

Believers and unbelievers alike *can* be brought together in a joint effort to think through the implications of the Gospel accounts of the trial of Jesus. There is nothing miraculous on the face of the standard account *of that trial*, as it appears in *Mark*. This is not to say that there is nothing that would not be questioned by informed readers. Some scholars, for example, question the emphasis placed upon the role of a Jewish council in the effort to move Pilate to pronounce a sentence of death for Jesus. But the reader is not asked to take much if anything on what is called faith. Men, in the natural order of things, could have acted as the participants in the trial are reported to have acted.

IV.

It is remarkable that there should be, in a Gospel, so many pages as there are in the account of the trial without a miracle in it. Is this because of the nature of legal proceedings? That is, things are done more or less in the open during a trial, with official witnesses and, perhaps, official reporters. In addition, the circumstances tend to be controlled and routine—and so things tend to get "down to earth" and hence to be prosaic, even when life-and-death matters are at stake. Besides, there are what we can call theological reasons why there should have been no miracles during this trial, no extraordinary deliverance of Jesus from the fate in store for him.[59] Thus, between the Last Supper (14:12) and the Crucifixion (15:24) there are no miracles recorded in the *Gospel of Mark*. Before the Last Supper there were numerous healings; after the Crucifixion there is, of course, the Resurrection.

This absence of miracles at the time of Jesus' arrest, trial, and execution is not characteristic of the *Gospel of Mark* alone: the same can be said of the other three Gospels, except for an incident that has Jesus healing (restoring?) the ear of one of the men who had come to seize him, the ear cut by the sword of one of Jesus' companions.[60] This healing is found only in *Luke* and little is made of it even there.

Spectacular healing, or other miracles of note, might have deterred the enemies of Jesus from proceeding against him as they did if they had personally witnessed them. No important miracle takes place in Jerusalem during Jesus' fatal visit there prior to the Resurrection, which can be thought of as the miracle of miracles. Why this should be so—why miracles are reserved for the more credulous countryside rather than for sophisticated Jerusalem—may be left as something of a mystery. In any event, the distribution of miracles in the Gospels may be worthy of note.

The story of the trial is, I have suggested, plausible enough as a human story. Whatever doubts scholars may have about it (based on what they know about Jewish and Roman history, law, and practices), there is nothing in that story that is difficult to believe, humanly speaking. One's questions need be only as to human passions and motivations. We all know that such things as are reported in the Gospel accounts of Jesus' trial can do and happen, that there is nothing miraculous or extraordinary about *them*. No one has to be persuaded that an innocent man can be convicted and punished. So routine, from a Christian point of view, is what happens to Jesus that it shows what is wrong with the world and how someone such as Jesus fits in as a radically redemptive element. What is wrong with the world can have the human Jesus both somehow guilty and yet clearly innocent: man is fallen and yet worthy and capable of being saved.

V.

It has been suggested by some scholars that the Passion story—the story of the arrest, trial, and execution of Jesus—may have been the first part of the Christian tradition set in a continuous narrative.[61] Jesus *does* first come to view to the Gentile world (in a sense, to "us"; certainly, to the Romans) as a defendant in a trial. Whatever happened to him theretofore happened among the Jews. He is very much rooted, it seems, in his time, people and place—and those roots may always have been very difficult for Gentiles to make out. Jesus does seem to have had a meteoric rise among the Jews—but something about his preaching and his doctrine among them doomed him, if the Gospel story is to be believed.

Thus, for us as Gentiles, it is through Pilate that we make "our" first substantial contact with Jesus. The accounts of his trial in the Synoptic Gospels are more consistent, however different they may be in critical details, than, say, the birth or the resurrection accounts in those same Gospels. But it should be emphasized, it is not the truth or the comprehensiveness of any trial account that is critical for us on this occasion. Rather, our concern is more with the implications for us of a career that somehow is most critically determined by the facts and effects of a prosecution.

What *have* been the effects of a long-accepted story that is built around what is taken to be a radically unjust condemnation? May not one effect, if not moderated by venerable religious institutions, be that of calling into question among us the laws of men and the human administration of justice, even calling into question all political authority, lawful or otherwise? The tension between the way of Jesus and the way of authority is prefigured from the earliest days of his life, as may be seen in the story in *Matthew* of the slaying by Herod of all infants under the age of two, slayings said to have been ordered in the hope of killing one particularly threatening infant.[62] Jesus is shown, again and again during his life, as challenging constituted authority, as questioning established interpretations and practices of the law. Much of what he stands for—and here his trial and condemnation are the culmination of his lifetime encounters with authority—is seen in vital opposition to the rule of law, perhaps even to the life and the people of the law. Thus, how one thinks about the *trial* of Jesus may well affect much of what one thinks about the *life* of Jesus and of the authority from which he can be said to have rebelled.

What does it mean that an unjust trial should be as critical as it is to the West? What *does* it say about, or do to, the status of community and of politics among us? What does it do to legitimate among us whatever natural inclination there may be to self-development, to self-fulfillment, even to a kind of selfishness? The overriding concern for personal salvation—that, in temporal terms, easily takes the form of a comfortable self-preservation—*is* something to be reckoned with. One must wonder whether a fear of death and a concern for self permeate the Gospels, legitimated and reinforced as they may be by the individuality of salvation, and all this in defiance of, or at least apart from, the community.

VI.

I have been speaking thus far of *the* trial of Jesus as reported in *Mark*. But, it can be said, there were two trials, the one before the Jewish council (the Sanhedrin) in which Jesus was found guilty of blasphemy, the other before the Roman governor (Pontius Pilate) in which Jesus was found guilty of, or at least condemned for, sedition. (14:53–65, 15:1–15) The accounts of both trials are fragmentary, perhaps even grossly distorted, partly because of the lack of legal skills on the part of the narrator, partly because of the immediate polemical interests of the narrator and of his associates. But let us consider the accounts as we find them.

The two trials, if two there be, seem to be intimately related to one another. The Jewish authorities evidently do not have the last word: they must go before Pilate for his decision. (15:1) Crucifixion was a peculiarly Roman form of punishment, not one to which the Jews on their own ever had recourse. (Compare, for example, the stoning of Stephen by Jews recorded in chapter 7 of the *Book of Acts*.) It is clear from the account in *Mark*, as that account is apt to be read and as it is likely that it was intended to be read, that the principal drive for the condemnation of Jesus came from the Jewish authorities. (15:10–11)

We are given to understand by this account (and, for that matter, by the other three Gospel accounts as well) that the Romans really did not care much, one way or another, about Jesus. He was not known to them, it would seem; Pilate had not had soldiers out looking for him; perhaps, even, Pilate had never heard of Jesus before he was brought in by his Jewish enemies. Nor is *this* Pilate (as distinguished from his wife) sympathetic toward Jesus, at least not so sympathetic toward someone he says is an innocent man that he can resist executing him at the insistence of his enemies. Pilate can even be seen to be mocking those enemies of Jesus, the Jewish authorities, obliging them to take what may have been the unusual position of pressing a Roman governor to be harsher than he was inclined to be toward one of their coreligionists.

VII.

It is the animosity of the local Jewish authorities to which, we are told in *Mark*, Pilate is pressed to defer. (15:10–11) What are we to understand to have been the cause of that deadly animosity on the part of Jesus' accusers? It can be argued that his persistent criticism of established practices and his condemnation of the hypocrisy of established practitioners was fiercely resented. The language he used in berating his opponents was not designed to endear him to them. In fact, one is startled to notice how much harsher[63] Jesus' language is than that of his opponents, reflecting perhaps the ardor of youthful righteousness.

But *Mark* is somewhat more precise than this in singling out the causes of a deadly animosity toward Jesus on the part of the Jewish authorities. There are, I believe, only two occasions in *Mark* on which it is said that Jesus' enemies took counsel among themselves "how they might destroy him." The first may be found following his insistence upon healing on the Sabbath; the second may be found following his assault upon the money exchangers and other businessmen in or near the Temple (in Jerusalem). (3:6, 11:18) Concerns *were* expressed by Scribes and Pharisees on other occasions, but the two responses I have singled out seem to be particularly strong. How can these two responses be understood? One cannot discount altogether the role of envy and of the desire that men may have to retain their privileged positions. But to make too much of these elements, important as they may have been, is to fail to appreciate what is special about the two "overt acts" that *are* singled out by the Gospel narrator, however he himself understood them.

The healing episode was preceded by the concern expressed by the Pharisees about the plucking of grain on the Sabbath by Jesus' followers. (2:23–24) Jesus stoutly defends what his followers have done, citing a precedent (but not a Sabbath-day precedent?) from David, and observing that "the Sabbath was made for man, not man for the Sabbath." (2:25–28) He then heals a man who had a withered hand. (3:1–5)[64] The plucking of the grain, and the way that that was justified by Jesus, had alerted the Pharisees here to see whether he would heal the withered hand on the Sabbath, so "that they might accuse him." (3:2) Jesus, before healing the hand, asked, "Is it lawful to do good on the Sabbath days, or to do evil? To save life, or to kill?" "But," we are told, "they held their peace." Jesus, we are further told, "looked round on them with anger, being grieved for the hardness of their hearts," and then healed the man. (3:4–5) It should be noticed that any criticism of a man for healing on the Sabbath does concede the genuineness of the healing. Jesus' enemies *are* prepared to concede *that*, just as they are evidently prepared to believe that others can heal as well. (Similarly, the author of *Exodus* conceded that Pharoah's magicians had *some* magical powers, however inferior they were to Moses in this and other respects.)

Is the narrator correct in endorsing both the anger of Jesus and his grief at "the hardness of their hearts?" (3:5) *Were* the Pharisees hard of heart? What *is* to be made of the Sabbath prohibition? It was a prohibition that *did* allow exceptions for emergencies. Thus, it had long been recognized that one could pull one's ox out of a ditch on the Sabbath, lest it perish while one waited for the first day of the week to come. But what emergency is there for a man born with a withered hand? Cannot *he* wait one more day? Should not a proper compassion take due account of the Law that is seen, in its outward and routine manifestation, in the respect of the community for the Sabbath? The deep respect for the Sabbath may even be reflected in the evident suspension of the efforts to anoint Jesus' body when he was removed from the cross. It seems to be indicated in *Luke* that the women had had to postpone, until after the Sabbath, their preparation of the body for burial.[65] It was when they went to the tomb to finish the work they evidently had not been able to finish before the Sabbath began that they were very much surprised to learn of the Resurrection.[66]

A religion, to be effective, must be to some degree simple-minded, if not even ruthless. The prerogative generously exercised by Jesus in healing on the Sabbath may have threatened Israel no less than did those Israelites in the Sinai who selfishly worshiped the Golden Calf. So it might have seemed to the more thoughtful of those numbered among the critics of Jesus: they saw their people, and the community that shaped that people, as very much dependent upon a Law that inevitably appeared inflexible at times and even callous. Jesus rarely acknowledges the usefulness of temporal authority, and then it is a grudging acknowledgment designed, it would seem, to avoid immediate serious consequences. He does seem aware of his vulnerability, and takes precautions, lest he be killed before what he considers to be his time.[67]

Jesus' apparent casualness about authority is evident throughout *Mark*. Thus, he is never portrayed as *consulting* with men in authority in an effort to modify their behavior. The Gospel narrators do not think it is necessary to show Jesus trying to correct things by normal means. Rather, he is again and again shown to be acting on his own authority, sure of his prerogatives and determined to have his way. At least, that is the way it must have seemed to the authorities, to men who may have been very much concerned lest outbreaks of political rebellion bring down upon the entire community the ferocious wrath of the Romans. At no time does Jesus seem to be concerned about this threat to the community. The Jewish authorities probably saw him as in uncertain control of a number of volatile followers, and so as someone who could be dangerous. The more farsighted among them might have anticipated the destruction brought down upon Jerusalem and the Temple a generation later, in 70 A.D., when the Romans decided once and for all to try to rid themselves of particularly troublesome subjects.[68] There must have been, prior to this, for several decades some very apprehensive, if not desperate, men among the Jewish authorities in Jerusalem.

On the other hand, some of Jesus' followers must have considered the spiritual life of Israel so deteriorated that radical measures had to be taken. Perhaps the very presence of the Roman occupiers could be taken by the more sensitive Jews as a sign of deep-rooted sinfulness on the part of their people. How bad *were* things at the time of Jesus? Were the Jews of his day particularly sinful? *Were* things too far gone to permit the constituted community to proceed as it had for generations—to permit the normal processes of grievances and reform, such as they were, to operate? From one perspective, Jesus' actions in cleansing the Temple could be seen as out-and-out usurpation by an impulsive zealot, unused to city ways, who did not appreciate the accommodations that human beings must make in order to live with one another, especially when they are constantly vulnerable to outside forces. (11:15–17)[69]

The Temple authorities would have seized Jesus after his single-handed cleansing of the Temple, we are told, except that the multitudes around him in effect protected him. (12:1–12) It is evident that those multitudes expected more of Jesus than he, with his pacifist inclinations, was prepared to deliver. They would continue to support and hence protect him so long as it seemed to them that he, as the Messiah, did not need to be protected. The concerns of the Jewish authorities are easy to minimize, but we should remember that there have always been far more false prophets than true ones even among the Jews and, so far as the authorities could see, there was nothing special about this one.[70] Christian charity, to say nothing of political science, should lead us to appreciate the concern that responsible leaders might have. Thus, we find in *John* the sound of desperate men (whatever the narrator himself believed to be the case), when Jewish leaders are recorded to have said, "If we let him thus alone, all men will believe in him; and the Romans shall come and take away both our [holy] place and nation."[71] To this the high priest is recorded as adding that it is expedient "that one man should die for the people, and that the whole nation perish not."[72]

VIII.

Since the Jewish authorities could not get to Jesus—since they themselves could neither dissuade him nor permanently seize him—they tried to make use of Roman power. They attempted, therefore, to trap him with their question about whether taxes should be paid to Caesar. If Jesus answered that taxes *should* be paid, he might lose some of the popular support that made him dangerous and that protected him; if he answered that taxes should not be paid, he would commit a criminal offense of which Rome might be induced to take notice. Jesus escaped the trap set for him by calling for a coin, noting thereon Caesar's inscription, and saying that one should render unto Caesar the things that are Caesar's, and unto God the things that are God's. (12:13–17) This kind of evasiveness obliged the Jewish authorities to seize Jesus by night—and, we can imagine, they were able to do so by making use (with Judas Iscariot) of some of the very coin about which Jesus had spoken so equivocally. (14:10–11) (*Were* the legendary thirty pieces of silver Roman?)

The concerns and motives of the Jewish authorities had to be transformed into formal charges in the course of the two trials I have referred to. When Jesus was taken before the authorities, there was false testimony brought against him, but the witnesses did not agree. (14:55–59) Does not this suggest, by the way, that the case against him may not have been simply a deliberate fabrication? Had the case been well-organized, would there have been the confusion that seems evident here? The testimony brought against Jesus, which failed to hold up, seems to have been with respect to what he might have said (as if somehow divine?) about destroying and rebuilding the Temple. Throughout this part of the proceedings, Jesus stood silent. (14:57–61) He was then asked by the high priest, "Art thou the Christ, the Son of the Blessed?" He is said to have answered, "I am: and ye shall see the Son of man sitting at the right hand of power, and coming in the clouds of heaven." (14:61–67) This is then said to have been identified by the high priest as blasphemy—"and they all condemned him to be guilty of death." (14:63–64)

Scholars differ as to whether this was indeed blasphemy under Jewish law.[73] I am not able to assess the validity of this charge. Nor am I sure that the Gentile (?) narrator of this Gospel was in a position to assess it either. But I suspect that that narrator *was* prepared to concede that if what Jesus said was not true, then it was blasphemy—and it is this that readers of the Gospel were probably intended to concede as well. That is to say, Jesus is evidently shown to have claimed for himself divine powers even though the Synoptic Gospels may never have him explicitly claiming to be other than human. It is not made clear how those who heard him were supposed to know that the remarkable powers and the privileged status he claimed were indeed his. Certainly, those who heard him on trial did not know about him the many things that the reader of the Gospel has been told by the time he comes to the account of the last days. On the other hand, readers of the Gospel outside Palestine were hardly likely to be as aware as the Jewish authorities might have been about the dangerous prevalence of false prophets and of false but plausible messiahs and about the criteria to be taken account of in judging the claims that were presumptuously, if not insanely, made from time to time.

The Christ (or Messiah) charge is transformed, when Jesus is brought before Pilate, into a form intended to be of immediate concern to the Romans. Pilate evidently understood the Messiah to be a Jewish king, and so he greeted Jesus with the question, "Art thou the King of the Jews?" (15:2) This is the only *Roman* question about which we are told by *Mark*, even though the chief priests are said to have accused Jesus of many things. (15:3) Although Jesus is evidently taken to acknowledge his claim of kingship, Pilate is not shown to have taken this charge and admission seriously. (15:14) Even so, the formal justification for the Crucifixion, on the basis of this Gospel account, must have been that Jesus claimed royal power. This sedition[74] on his part is recognized in the announcement placed by the Romans on his cross. It is said in *Mark* that "the superscription of his accusation" on the cross read, "THE KING OF THE JEWS." (15:26)

IX.

The mockery Jesus received at the hands of the Jews and Romans respectively reflected the two sets of charges, or the two sets of interests being guarded, which I have mentioned. Thus, after Jesus had been condemned as a blasphemer, we are told, "some began to spit on him, and to cover his face [that is, to blindfold him], and to buffet him, and to say unto him, 'Prophesy' [that is, 'Although he cannot see, a prophet should be able to identify who strikes him']." (14:65) And when he is on the cross, "they who passed by railed on him, wagging their heads, and saying, 'Ah, thou that destroyest the Temple, and buildest it in three days, save thyself, and come down from the cross.'" (15:29–30) All this is the "Jewish" response. The Roman soldiers, on the other hand, "clothed him with purple, and platted a crown of thorns, and put it about his head. And they began to salute him, 'Hail, King of the Jews!' And they smote him on the head with a reed, and did spit upon him, and bowing their knees worshiped him." (15:29–30)

The two sets of charges to which Jesus was subjected suggest that the people involved did have divergent interests, which are reflected in the two kinds of mockeries to which he was subjected. The Roman soldiers saw Jesus as a political usurper (and hence presumptuous); the Jewish people, those few who joined in the mockery, saw him as a religious imposter (and hence blasphemous). Pontius Pilate, as presented here, can be said not to have been seriously concerned about Jesus in either capacity. The Jewish authorities, on the other hand, can be said to have been concerned about the political consequences of Jesus' religious pretensions, which consequences could in turn very much affect the spiritual life of their people, a people that they conceived to depend very much upon a land of their own. A blending of Jewish and Roman concerns may be heard in what the mocking chief priests said among themselves with the Scribes, "He saved others; himself he cannot save. Let Christ the King of Israel descend now from the cross, that we may see and believe." (15:31–32) Thus, in their private conversation, and there alone, "the Christ" of the first trial (or arraignment) and the "King of Israel" of the second trial can be said to have been brought together.

These two realms—that which we call political and that which we call religious—had never been separated, at least not for the Jewish authorities. Neither was it separated for the narrator of this Gospel or for Jesus himself. There may be, in various circumstances, practical reasons for separating the two realms—but that can be done in a sensible, and hence flexible, manner only by those who appreciate how intermingled the concerns of the two realms may naturally be.[75]

X.

The relations between the realms of politics and of religion are suggested by a brief consideration here of the *Gospel of Matthew*. That Gospel has essentially the same account of the trial of Jesus as does *Mark*.[76] But *Matthew* has also an extended account of Jesus' temptations in the wilderness, whereas *Mark* does no more than note that episode. (1:12–13) The parallels in *Matthew* between the temptations account and the trials account are striking and hence instructive. There were, for Jesus in the wilderness, three temptations: the first, to turn stones into bread; the second, to dare hurl himself off the pinnacle of the Temple; the third, to become ruler of all the kingdoms of the earth shown him from a high mountain.[77] Notice the order of the latter two temptations: one has to do with the Temple as the point of departure, so to speak; the other, with the kingdoms of the earth. This order, religious and political, is the same as that in the trials of Jesus, first before the Jewish authorities, then before the Roman authorities.[78] When one considers the temptations-parallel, one realizes that there can be said to have been three trials as well. Comparable to the first temptation (the temptation for a man who has fasted forty days, of turning stones into bread) is the agony for Jesus, prior to his arrest, as he prays in Gethsemane.[79]

Consider also the circumstances of and sequels to these two sets of challenges. The temptations are preceded by forty days of fasting; the trials are preceded by a feast, evidently the Passover (what we now know as the Last Supper). In the former, Jesus is alone; in the latter, Jesus is with many. This contrast may be seen in the respective sequels as well: the temptations are followed by angels ministering to Jesus; the trials are followed by the Crucifixion. But then, of course, there is the Resurrection to be taken account of: it is that which breaks the pattern, providing the basis, it can be said, for a new ordering of things.[80]

The temptations in the wilderness (at the outset of the account in *Matthew* of Jesus' ministry) and the trial and condemnation of Jesus (at the end of that ministry) bracket the story of his career. Are we to understand thereby that Jesus always, and necessarily, confronted the challenges of the temptations story. He must always wrestle with himself; he must wrestle with spiritual traditions; he must wrestle with political ambitions. These concerns exist together for him: the devil (or perhaps God) brings the three together. It takes self-confidence, with a soul tempered by the first temptation, by the first trial, if one is to be able effectively to challenge constituted authority, whether spiritual or political. Do not we see here, again, that the trials are somehow primary, that everything else in Jesus' life is seen and explained as anticipating that final set of challenges?

We can also see that Jesus could have given into the final set of challenges in Jerusalem and thereby "saved" himself, just as he could have, at the peril of his mission as it is here presented, given into the first set of challenges in the wilderness. He could have, in Gethsemane, decided to flee to Galilee, where he would have been relatively safe; he could, thereafter, have tried to come to terms with the Jewish authorities or thrown himself at the mercy of the Roman governor. Finally we see, upon examining these two sets of three challenges, that the spiritual concern is central to each: that which we call *spiritual* helps shape the human being, on the one hand, and helps guide the community, on the other.

The most critical difference between Jesus and the Jewish authorities may have come down to the question of the extent to which enduring spiritual power depends upon a political community with its discipline and rituals. Certainly, we once again see the importance of moderation in human matters. This seems to depend, in turn, upon understanding.

We began by speaking of the trial of Jesus. We moved to a consideration of his two trials. The parallels to the *Matthew* temptations in the wilderness moved us to notice in turn that there could be said to have been not one, not two, but six trials. And all of these point to a seventh trial, an overarching trial, so to speak—that trial, or challenge, which comes to us in the form of a question, How should a man live?

Saint Augustine observes in his passionate *Confessions*, "Is not the life of man upon earth all trial?"[81] Elsewhere in that book he observes that Jesus had done nothing worthy of death, and yet he was killed.[82] This awareness of the deep injustice among unredeemed men is not to be found, he suggests, in the Platonic (that is, the philosophic) scheme of things.[83] Does not this call somewhat into question the parallels often drawn between Socrates and Jesus? It should be evident from what I have said on this occasion that the differences between these two influential teachers are perhaps more striking than their similarities. Jesus' death is presented as a necessary one: the very nature of things demands his death. This is not so with Socrates: he lived twice the age of Jesus—and had he died, naturally, a few years before he was brought to trial, he still would have lived a full life. If the Peloponnesian War had come out differently or lasted a little longer, Socrates probably would never have been indicted at all.[84] The Platonic Socrates, as is evident from the *Republic*, had an extensive political teaching; Jesus evidently did not. Whatever the natural tension between philosophy and the city, it is neither necessary nor inevitable that the philosopher be killed by the city.

XI.

It is difficult to garner from the Gospels precisely what Jesus' character or teachings are, spiritual as well as political. He does seem to question the established order and, in a sense, life itself.[85] But what *does* he stand for? Consider, by contrast, not only the detailed arguments in the Platonic dialogues (and in Xenophon and Aristotle as well) but also the detailed prescriptions and, in effect, arguments in the Old Testament. Jesus sees the human being in critical need of redemption but capable of it only with God's help. It is far from clear that Socrates sees matters thus. Certainly, Socrates does not consider *his* teaching to be designed for the many.[86] Jesus' offer, on the other hand, is held out to all: everyone is asked to have faith, to believe in him, to join him.

Thus, a Gospel—the good news of salvation—is primarily an account of deeds, illuminated by preaching and capped by the miracle of the Resurrection. It is far less, than is a Platonic dialogue, an account of teachings that make sense on their own. The slimness of the appendage to the Hebrew Testament that the New Testament represents testifies that it *is* a message (very much dependent upon deeds) to be preached to all nations. (13:10) Jesus warns his disciples that there will be false Christs and false prophets—but there is, so far as I can tell, no reliable guidance given as to what constitutes genuineness in prophecy.

An emphasis is placed in the Gospels upon watchfulness: a state of constant anxiety seems to be called for. (13:21–37) The serenity of a Socrates, apparently unconcerned about mistreatment or death, is in marked contrast.[87] From the Christian point of view, such serenity is unwarranted prior to finding oneself in and with the resurrected Christ.

We return to the story in *Mark* of the rich young man. It is not enough, he was told, to obey scrupulously the various commandments, the old teaching; he was also told to sell all his goods, give his wealth to the poor, and follow Jesus. (10:17–22) What *does* following Jesus consist of? A life of poverty *is* indicated and the abandonment of other attachments, even those family and communal attachments that have always meant so much to Jews. It is not for nothing that the Old Testament divinity is seen as the God of Abraham, Isaac, and Jacob: God is, in some critical respect, the God of a family.[88]

To have faith in Jesus means, ultimately, that there must be a decisive act of will, not a sustained activity of the reason. Compare, on the other hand, the passage in *Deuteronomy* that has Moses anticipating that other peoples will come, evidently on the basis of reason alone, to recognize the wisdom of the statutes taught to and obeyed by the people of Israel.[89] All this is not to say that there are *no* teachings emanating from Jesus: one is enjoined to love God and man; the elevated are to be humbled; the lowly and afflicted are to be shown compassion. Beyond that, one might say, religious institutions will provide guidance that includes, perhaps because of the emphasis upon will, rigorous curtailment of the passions. Man is to be kept in his place.[90]

The Christian emphasis upon the will confirms the critical role of the trials of Jesus that we have seen in the Gospels. *The* test of a man is whether he will stand firm, whether he will resist the temptation to succumb. His faith, not his understanding, is what is ultimately appealed to. "All things are possible to him who believes." (9:23) One result of an approach that makes so little of the ways of this world and so much of death as something to be conquered and surpassed is that when its otherworldly expectations begin to fade, human beings are apt to be left in far deeper despair than they would have been if they had had to rely all along "merely" upon a natural understanding of things.

The will is critical—and hence the good will—and this is seen in terms primarily of a determined allegiance to one who calls upon everyone to follow him. Those who are not with him are against him—for they are left, unattended, in the valley of the shadow of death where human life is condemned by a fallen nature to remain. It is necessary to *repent* and have faith. It does not suffice simply to correct one's behavior. Correction implies that human beings can both know and acquire the good; repentance and faith suggest that the human being must, in his helplessness, surrender his will to a higher power.

XII.

When so much depends upon the testing of the human being, of which the trial of Jesus is taken to be the great example, one is obliged to consider where the responsibility lies for the outcome of that testing. Who, indeed, is responsible for the miscarriage of justice that the outcome of Jesus' trial is generally taken to be?

For many years—for many centuries now—the primary responsibility has been assigned to the Jews, to the leaders of the Jews at least, if not to the Jewish people at large. Jesus is regarded as entirely blameless, which is understandable, considering the divine status traditionally accorded him. But Pilate's guilt, too, has been curiously minimized: he is shown, in one Gospel after another, as making repeated efforts to release a man whom he found to be innocent.[91] It is sometimes said by scholars that the Gospels present Pilate thus so as to make the story of Jesus acceptable to the Gentile world.[92] It was not rhetorically useful to picture Jesus as a man condemned for rebellion against *Roman* authority. But the narrator's motives must be distinguished here from their effects—and one effect of the Gospels certainly is that of presenting a Roman governor who did not want to do what he was somehow forced by the Jews to do.

But should it not be said that, of the three parties involved—Jesus, the Jews, and Pilate—the Jews had by far the most difficult task and the most serious duty? The Jewish authorities had a quite vulnerable community to look out for. Their lack of faith in Jesus, someone whom they did not truly know but who seemed to pose a serious threat to the community, was in the circumstances not surprising. In a sense, they were far more realistic about Jesus than were his immediate disciples, for many of those disciples seem to have expected him to be able to protect himself from execution. It is difficult to see that Jesus did or said anything in the presence of the Jewish authorities in Jerusalem that entitled them to believe both that he *was* an extraordinary prophet and that they need not continue to remain vigilant in defense of the old way. The devout Christian is fortunate, in judging the Jewish authorities in Jerusalem, to have the advantage of hindsight, including his critical faith in Jesus' Resurrection.[93]

We have assumed throughout our discussion that the Gospels are intact and that they are substantially accurate in recording the sentiments and activities of the men of that time. Even so, is it not salutary for us to regard Pontius Pilate as far more contemptible in his conduct than the Gospel writers seem to regard him?[94] Pilate should have known that if the Jewish authorities had really believed that Jesus was a genuine threat to Roman political power in Palestine, they probably would have been delighted. Instead, we are in effect told, Pilate killed an innocent man accused of sedition in order to keep that man's enemies from themselves *becoming* seditious.

The principles of natural right would seem to question the justice of the conviction of Jesus. But, it can be said, natural right was overridden, in the case of the more zealous Jewish enemies of Jesus, by their faith. But no such influence excuses Pilate. At the very least he should have acquitted Jesus, if not out of compassion, at least out of a desire not to be personally tainted by an injustice, whatever Jesus himself may have "wanted." An inspired judge could perhaps have acquitted a helpless Jesus in such a way as to diminish his political influence and hence danger.

What Jesus himself truly wanted is difficult to determine. It is far from clear, even from the Gospel accounts, that Jesus *was* important in Israel at the time of his execution. We have noticed that no popular effort was made to interfere with his public execution. Had he been important, rather then merely troublesome and potentially dangerous, it is likely that his trial would have been longer and more carefully recorded than it was.[95] Jesus *can* be said to be responsible for the verdict in the case, at least in the sense of having knowingly provoked a particular response to his conduct. Do not the faithful, curiously enough, regard the charges against Jesus as essentially valid? That is, what does *innocence* mean here? Who is really responsible for what happened?[96] May there not be, in the life of Jesus, the peculiar phenomenon of *the form* but *not the substance* of an *unfair* trial? Suppose Jesus had been acquitted, what then? Would still another challenge by him, still another provocation, have been necessary, until at last the necessary redemptive sacrifice could be made?

How much should we assume Jesus to have foreseen and to have ordained? Is it not more charitable to assume that he did not, that he could not, anticipate the dreadful persecutions visited upon Jews for some two thousand years in large part because of their supposed responsibility for the execution of the Christian God?

I do not mean to suggest that Jews and Judaism were not at all responsible for what happened to Jesus. They *were* deeply responsible—responsible for the life and thought of Jesus much more than for his death. One might even add that Jews and Judaism were responsible for the very best in Jesus, for whatever in him has made him properly attractive to this day and in many lands. The gross misconduct of Jesus' trial—whether by Gentiles or by Jews, whether by the accusers or by the governor—can be understood by recourse to what we know about human nature. Insofar as Judaism was at fault—with its determined righteousness and its provocative self-assurance—it was a fault it has generously shared for two millennia now with millions of Jesus' followers. On the other hand, that Pilate should have had such a good press, that millions of innocent Jews should have suffered as they have, and that the State of Israel should remain as vulnerable as it is today does suggest that there indeed may be something deeply wrong with the world of affairs.[97] That, I am afraid, is nothing new but rather something one has to learn to live with. One should not, however, make matters worse than they need be by expecting too much.

I leave to you to consider what light, if any, this analysis of the trial of Jesus and its aftermath casts on the enduring question of the truth of the miracles recorded in the Gospels, especially that critical miracle of the Resurrection.

XIII.

I conclude by addressing further a question upon which I have repeatedly touched in the course of this talk: What *should* have been done with Jesus? It should not require an argument to establish that good men should not be killed. Certainly, Jesus should have been talked to—again and again and again. It is far from clear that Jesus himself *was* receptive to serious discussion with the skeptical and the unrepentant: his vigorous responses to what he considered hypocritical questions were not such as to encourage patient inquiry on the part of others.[98] Still, more efforts should have been made by all of the parties involved. Delay was on the side of justice, if only because mellowing usually does come with age and experience. Even a few years might have made a considerable difference in Jesus himself and in the responses of others to him. A few days delay, until the passions of the Passover season had cooled and Jerusalem could return to its normal life, might have helped restore a sense of proportion to all the parties involved. (Whether a redemptive sacrifice on behalf of humankind was either needed or inevitable I do not presume to discuss on this occasion.)

To ask what should have been done about Jesus is to ask, in effect, what *we* should do. The desire to pay homage to such a man as Jesus is taken to be is natural enough. But one cannot pay homage to Jesus without paying homage as well, whether or not one recognizes it, to the people who made him possible and to whom he will always belong. One appropriate form of such homage today [1976], I venture to suggest, is that we here in this country take care not to play the demoralizing part of Pontius Pilate. We should take care, as a nation under the pressures now mounting, not to permit a misguided world opinion, and mundane considerations of security and of petroleum, to crucify a beleaguered Israel, however difficult that country may appear to be at times.[99]

What *should* one do in moments of sustained crisis? Perhaps the most prudent thing one can do in such circumstances as the Jewish authorities, Pontius Pilate, and Jesus found themselves comforting—circumstances not altogether unlike those in which we find ourselves from time to time—is to remind the partisans involved in such deadly controversies of the highest aspirations in their heritage. Old-fashionedness, rather than innovation, is very much to be preferred in such matters.

We in the West are the privileged heirs to both the Romans and the Jews of antiquity. For the Roman in us, there is the matter-of-fact dedication to the rule of law evident in the report by a Roman officer to his superior on the disposition of the Apostle Paul. This report may be found in the *Book of Acts*:

> Claudius Lysias to his Excellency the governor Felix, greeting. This man was seized by the Jews, and was about to be killed by them, when I came upon them with the soldiers and rescued him, having learned that he was a Roman citizen. And desiring to know the charge on which they accused him, I brought him down to their council. I found that he was accused about questions of their law, but charged with nothing deserving death or imprisonment. And when it was disclosed to me that there would be a plot against the man, I sent him to you at once, ordering his accusers also to state before you what they have against him.[100]

For the Jew in everyone of us, there is the ageless prescription recorded in the *Book of Micah* and transmitted to us all, in effect, by the ministry of Jesus:

> And what doth the Lord require of thee, but to do justly, and to love mercy, and to walk humbly with thy God?[101]

Thus, we need Socratic prudence—or, if it should happen to be obviously available, divine wisdom—to teach us how to weave together, in practical affairs, these two strands from our complex heritage, the mundane requirements of the rule of law, the eternal demands of the call to purity. Neither the usefulness nor the vulnerability of our necessarily imperfect and yet necessary institutions, both civil and spiritual, should be underestimated by those among us who happen to yearn for the very best and are nobly determined to get it at all costs.

NOTES

1. This talk was given at the Hillel Foundation Jewish Student Center, The University of Chicago, Chicago, Illinois, November 19, 1976.

The parenthetical citations in the text and in the notes of chapter 7-A are to the *Gospel of Matthew*. See, for a comparison of that account with the *Gospel of Mark*, section X of chapter 7–B of this collection. See also chapter 1, note 65.

2. I was invited to give this talk at Hillel House after it became known that a talk on the trial of Jesus that I had given earlier that year at Rosary College (in a Chicago suburb) drew so large an audience as to require moving everyone into a much bigger auditorium on that campus. The earlier Rosary College talk is set forth later in this book, inasmuch as *Mark* does follow *Matthew* in the Bible.

3. See, on the Old Testament-New Testament nomenclature, chapter 5, note 18.

4. See, e.g., *Genesis* 1:1–31, *Exodus* 14:5–31. The virgin birth associated with Jesus was evidently not something that impressed itself upon the people with whom he associated: *they* routinely identified him as the son of Joseph. See *Luke* 3:23, 4:22. Compare *Genesis* 2:21–22, 18:9–15. See also chapter 5, note 26.

5. See chapter 5, note 37.

6. See George Anastaplo, "On Trial: Explorations," 22 *Loyola University of Chicago Law Journal* 765, 1053 n. 3893 (1991).

7. Useful introductions to the relevant literature and history are provided by Samuel Sandmel, *We Jews and Jesus* (New York: Oxford University Press, 1965), pp. 154–58, and by Robert M. Grant, "The Trial of Jesus in the Light of History," 20 *Judaica* 37 (1971).

8. "Jesus," 10 *Encyclopaedia Judaica* 10–12 (1971). "C.E." refers to "Common Era" or "A.D." "The three Gospels of *Matthew, Mark*, and *Luke* are called *synoptic* from the Greek word *synoptikos*, which means to see the whole together, to take a comprehensive view. They present similar views of the career and teaching of Christ, and resemble each other closely in content and in phraseology." *Zondervan Pictorial Bible Dictionary*, Merrill C. Tenney, ed., (Grand Rapids: Zondervan Publishing House, 1963), p. 320. See chapter 7, note 45.

Roman Catholics do *not* regard James and the others sometimes referred to as brothers and sisters of Jesus to have been his siblings.

9. See "Jesus," 10 *Encyclopaedia Judaica* 12–13. "No trial in the long and tragic annals of mankind has had more momentous consequences than that of an obscure Jewish religious leader who came into Jerusalem with a small band of followers and was arrested, convicted, and executed over nineteen hundred years ago." Robert Gordis, "Foreword," 20 *Judaica* 6 (1971).

10. "Jesus," 10 *Encyclopaedia Judaica* 13–14.

11. "Jesus," 10 *Encyclopaedia Judaica* 14.

12. "Jesus," 10 *Encyclopaedia Judaica* 12.

13. "It takes but a moment's thought to glimpse some of the inferences that would follow from the [traditional] view that *Matthew* and *Luke* utilized *Mark* as a source. For one thing, if *Matthew* used *Mark*, and in passage after passage copied or rewrote what is in *Mark*, the great coincidences in the Greek rule out the opinion of Papias that *Matthew* was originally written in Hebrew, for this is scarcely possible in the case of a Greek writing based on an earlier Hebrew writing." Sandmel, *We Jews and Jesus*, p. 59. Compare the ancient story about the miraculous translations that produced the Septuagint. See *Zondervan Pictorial Bible Dictionary*, p. 770.

14. "Matthew, Gospel According to Saint," *Columbia Encyclopedia* (3d. ed., 1963), p. 1331. See, on the "Gospel According to St. Paul," chapter 7, note 101 below.

15. John Courtney Murray, *We Hold These Truths: Catholic Reflections on the American Proposition* (New York: Sheed & Ward, 1960), pp. 175–76.

16. *Acts* 19:34.

17. *Matthew* 9:24–25. See also *2 Kings* 4:32–37; *John* 11:1–12, 19.

18. But, of course, not all who are persecuted are prophets. See Plato, *Crito* 44D.

19. This "gospel of the kingdom" may be spelled out in the long Sermon on the Mount that follows (5:3f), but it is not clear that that *is* what was meant.

20. Is not Jesus "un-Jewish" in this respect? See *Matthew*, chap. 4. See also Anastaplo, "On Trial" (*Loyola Law Journal*), p. 1052 n. 325.

21. See the text at note 51 of chapter 5 of this collection.

22. Thomas Aquinas suggests that the three temptations of Jesus in the wilderness have parallels in the temptations of Adam. See *Summa Theologiae* 3. 42, 4. Origen is quoted as saying that Satan showed Jesus "how, by means of the various vices, he may be the lord of the world." (Aquinas, *Summa Theologiae* 3. 42, 4) See further, on the temptations, section X of chapter 7–B of this collection.

23. See, e.g., Leo Strauss, "How to Begin to Study *The Guide of the Perplexed*," in Moses Maimonides, *The Guide of the Perplexed* (Chicago: University of Chicago Press, 1963), p. xxx; George Anastaplo, "Jacob Klein of St. John's College," *Newsletter*, Politics Department, The University of Dallas, Spring 1979, p. 1.

24. In these matters it is useful to be aware of the form in which critical texts in one's tradition are usually available. A salutary moderation, useful for pedagogical purposes, is likely to be encouraged thereby. See chapter 4, note 55.

25. See, e.g., S. G. F. Brandon, "The Trial of Jesus," 20 *Judaica* 43 (1971). Is there, to go to a much earlier age, any record of the "trials" attending the identification and punishment by Moses of those who worshipped the Golden Calf? See *Exodus* 32:26–28. See also George Anastaplo, "Law & Literature and the Bible: Explorations," 23 *Oklahoma City University Law Review* 515, 604 (1998).

26. Compare the detail provided in various other stories in the Gospels. Is the killing of John the Baptist, for example, told more clearly elsewhere?

27. See chapter 5.

28. *Due process* respects what has come to be expected in the community. But we know from our own experiences that unprecedented, if not even bizarre, things can be done by respectable officials in times of great passion. See, e.g., chapter 12, notes 134, 142, 143. See also appendix A.

29. See Anastaplo, "On Trial" (*Loyola Law Journal*), p. 1054 n. 344; chapter 5, notes 3, 37.

30. See Sigmund Freud, *Moses and Monotheism*. See also chapter 7, note 54. Was Isaac, in a sense, a sacrificed leader? See chapter 5.

31. "Blasphemy," in English law, has been defined as "the offense of speaking matter relating to God, Jesus Christ, the Bible, or the Book of Common Prayer, intended to wound the feelings of mankind or to excite contempt and hatred against the church by law established, or to promote immorality." *Black's Law Dictionary*. It has been defined, in American law, as "any oral or written reproach maliciously cast upon

God, His name, attributes, or religion." *Black's Law Dictionary*. Blasphemy can at times be regarded as treason in the spiritual realm. See, for the Roman law of sedition, chapter 7, note 74, See also the text at note 145 of chapter 12 of this collection. See as well chapter 8, note 28.

32. See Gerard S. Sloyan, *Jesus on Trial: The Development of the Passion Narratives and Their Historical and Ecumenical Implications* (Philadelphia: Fortress Press, 1973), p. 61. See also Haim Cohn, "Reflections on the Trial of Jesus," 20 *Judaica* 15 (1971); Morton S. Enslin, "The Temple and the Cross," 20 J*udaica* 28–29 (1971); the text at note 73 of chapter 7 of this collection. In his article Judge Cohn, of the Supreme Court of Israel, presented "the novel and striking thesis that at the hearings—not the trial—of Jesus before the High Priest and his court, the Jewish authorities were seeking to find a way to save [Jesus] from execution at the hands of the Romans. It was Jesus' insistence upon proclaiming his views that rendered their attempt of no avail and led to his death." Gordis, "Foreword," 20 *Judaica* 7 (1971). See chapter 7, note 74.

33. See chapter 5, notes 32, 67. One can be reminded here of the impassioned rhetoric of Edmund Burke during the French Revolution. Compare the text at note 8 of chapter 5 of this collection. See also chapter 6, note 2.

34. Compare the text at note 36 of chapter 4 of this collection.

35. See Plato, *Gorgias* 467C–476A.

36. See *Plato, Laws* 829A.

37. See Plato, *Apology* 30A–B, 31C–32A; Plato, *Laws* 829A.

38. See the text at note 88 of chapter 7 of this collection.

39. See, on "the better men" who supported Stephen A. Douglas against Abraham Lincoln, George Anastaplo, "Slavery and the Constitution: Explorations," 20 *Texas Tech Law Review* 677, 783 (1989).

40. It is reported, in *Acts* 6:7, that later on "a great company of the priests" in Jerusalem did become Christians. It is known that almost all of the earliest Christians were Jews. But is it known what proportion of the Jews in Palestine allied themselves with the Christian movement within Judaism? See chapter 7, note 68. For a Jew to become what is now known as a Christian in the first quarter-century after Jesus' death was probably regarded as a far less (if at all) traumatic break with his heritage and family than it often is today. Such a move today, except perhaps when marriage and children are anticipated, can be regarded as akin to treason, or at least as suicidal in its implications, by those who are thus "betrayed" or "abandoned." It can also seem in some instances to be "provocative" or otherwise childish and hence a temporary aberration. See chapter 7, note 31, chapter 7, note 49. Is it akin to the betrayal that Plato's Euthyphro practiced, which we can sometimes see presumptuous children resort to? See Anastaplo, "On Trial" (*Loyola Law Journal*), p. 873. See also chapter 7, note 49. Compare chapter 8, note 43.

41. See *Exodus* 32. See also chapter 7, note 25.

42. See the text accompanying note 68 of chapter 5 of this collection.

43. In what ways, if at all, does Judaism depend for its significance (if not even for its survival) *in the modern world* on the influence of Christianity? What has Judaism learned about the divine and about *religion* (*not* a Hebrew term) from the massive intellectual,

political, and artistic efforts devoted to Christianty? In any event, the American support of Israel, which has been so critical to the very existence of that country, does seem to be nourished by Christian sentiments in the United States. See George Anastaplo, *Human Being and Citizen: Essays on Virtue, Freedom and the Common Good* (Chicago: Swallow Press, 1975), p. 155. See also chapter 12, note 126.

44. Lucretius, for instance, can show us the decay of the pagan gods. So can Augustine in *The City of God*. Perhaps that can also be seen in the career of Socrates. See, e.g., Anastaplo, *Human Being and Citizen*, p. 15.

45. Is not this reflected in the fact that there is, in the Torah, only one authoritative version of the founding of the Jewish people, whereas there are, in the Gospels, at least four more or less authoritative accounts of the founding of the Christian faith? See Anastaplo, "On Trial" (*Loyola Law Journal*), p. 1024. See also chapter 7, note 8.

46. See John Locke, *The Reasonableness of Christianity*. See also chapter 5, note 67.

47. See chapter 7, note 43.

48. See, e.g., Plato, *Meno* 76E; Thucydides, *History of the Peloponnesian War,* VI, 27–29, 53, 60–61; Xenophon, *Hellenica,* IV, 20–21.

49. Is there not much to be said for not explicitly repudiating, even as a "nonbeliever," one's people's own civilized way of doing things? See chapter 7, note 40; chapter 8, note 43. Consider how Leo Strauss, in a lecture at the University of Chicago Hillel House in 1962 ("Why We Remain Jews"), addressed this question:

> But here we are up against a difficulty which underlies the very title of this lecture and everything I said before. What shall those Jews do who cannot believe as our ancestors believed? So while religious Zionism is the only clear solution, it is not feasible, humanly speaking, for all Jews. I repeat: it is impossible to get rid of one's past. It is necessary to accept one's past. That means that out of this undeniable necessity one must make a virtue. The virtue in question is fidelity, loyalty, piety in the old Latin sense of the word *pietas*. The necessity of taking this step appears from the disgraceful character of the only alternative, of denying one's origin, past, or heritage. A solution of a man's problem which can be achieved only through a disgraceful act is a disgraceful solution. But let us be detached; let us be objective or scientific. Is this universally true? We must bust the case wide open in order to understand the difficulty. I am not interested in preaching up any solution; I try to help myself and, if I can, some of you in understanding our difficulty. Let us take a man by nature very gifted for all excellences of man, of the mind and of the soul, who stems from the gutter. Is he not entitled to run away from the gutter? Surely one could even say that by being silent about his gutter origins he acts more decently than by displaying them, and thus annoying others with a bad smell. Yet, however this may be, that interesting case—which deserves all our compassion, I think—is surely not our case. Our worst enemies admit this in one way or another.

Leo Strauss, *Jewish Philosophy and the Crisis of Modernity*, ed. Kenneth Hart Green (Albany: State University of New York Press, 1997), p. 320. In the course of the discussion that followed this very instructive lecture, Mr. Strauss was asked,

> Well, if I were to try to draw a general principle from what you have said—I do not know if this is right—but I would say something like this: a man is being dishonorable if he chooses to disagree with, to break away from, his origins, what his family believes.

Mr. Strauss's response was,

> I qualified that. I said that I could visualize a man stemming from absolute degradation and simply having a nobler thing in himself tending away, as it were, in this way. And I could only say he acts wisely. . . . But what I said is that this is not the case of the Jews. However degraded we had to live for centuries in various countries, we were not degraded. Surely we were maltreated; all kinds of things were inflicted upon us. But for the *average* Jew it was perfectly clear that we did *not* deserve it at the hands of these people. Perhaps we deserved it at the hand of God—that is another matter—but not at the hands of the people as such. I could give you some childhood stories, which are illustrative, and older people (or people of my age here) could also give examples, of what the traditional posture was. I remind you of only one essay which is still worthy of being read by everyone who is interested in this. That is an essay by Ahad Ha'am. (You know who he was? Asher Ginsberg.) I mean an essay by Ahad Ha'am that he called "In External Freedom and Internal Slavery," and in which he compared the situation of the Jews in the Russian ghetto to the chief rabbi of France, who was also the head of the Sanhedrin—you know, an institution founded by Napoleon himself. The chief rabbi was highly respectable, with badges and all. . . . And then Ahad Ha'am showed him, on the basis of what this man said—this chief rabbi—that he was a slave, not a free man. Externally he was free, he could vote, and do many other things, acquire property, whatever kind he liked. But in his heart he was a slave. Whereas the poorest Polish Jew (if he did not happen to be an individual with a particularly lousy character, which can happen in any community) was externally a man without rights and in this sense a slave, but he was not a slave in his heart. And that is of crucial importance in this matter.

Strauss, *Jewish Philosophy*, pp. 340–41. What the Jewish heritage can be taken to mean may be seen by considering an earlier comment by Mr. Strauss in the course of his 1962 Hillel House lecture:

> I draw a conclusion. It is impossible not to remain a Jew. It is impossible to run away from one's origins. It is impossible to get rid of one's past by wishing it away. *There is nothing better than the uneasy solution offered by liberal society*, which means legal equality plus private "discrimination." We must simply recognize the fact, which we all know, that the Jewish minority is not universally popular, and we must recognize the consequences which follow from that. We all know that there is in this country an entirely extralegal but not illegal, what we can call "racial hierarchy" coming down from the Anglo-Saxons, down to the Negroes; and we are just above the Negroes. We must face that. And we must see that there is a similarity between the Jewish and the Negro question; there are quite a few Jewish organizations that are very well aware of this. But also, in order to keep the record straight, we must not forget the difference. When we Jews fight for something that we may fairly call justice, we appeal to principles ultimately that, (if I may say so), were originally our own. When the Negroes fight for justice, they have to appeal to principles that were not their own, their ancestors' in Africa, but that they learned from their oppressors. This is not an altogether negligible difference, which should be stated by someone who does not want to beat around the bush.

Strauss, *Jewish Philosophy*, p. 317 (emphasis added). Is there a historicist cast to Mr. Strauss's principal argument in this lecture? For further indications of what Judaism meant to Mr. Strauss, see Anastaplo, "On Trial" (*Loyola Law Journal*), p. 1054 n. 349;

chapter 9, notes 3, 4, 24, 141; chapter 11, note 61; chapter 12, note 78. Perhaps it should be added that as African Americans have fought for justice in their country they could appeal not only (1) to the principles that came to them ultimately from Judaism by way of Christianity, but also (2) to the principles of the American regime that they learned as Americans just as most other immigrants here have learned them, and (3) to the principles of natural right that, we must believe, various of their ancestors were also naturally aware of here and there in Africa. See George Anastaplo, *The Artist as Thinker: From Shakespeare to Joyce* (Athens, Ohio: Ohio University Press, 1983), pp. 254–55, 269–71, 275; Anastaplo, *Human Being and Citizen*, pp. 46, 74; chapter 2, note 31; chapter 6–B, section V; chapter 7, note 40; chapter 7, note 101; chapter 9, note 49; chapter 12, note 46; conclusion, note 3. See also George Anastaplo, *But Not Philosophy: Seven Introductions to Non-Western Thought* (Lanham, Md.: Lexington Books, 2002), chapter 7 (on African thought); George Anastaplo, "'Racism,' Political Correctness, and Constitutional Law: A Law School Case Study," 42 *South Dakota Law Review* 108 (1997); George Anastaplo, "'McCarthyism,' the Cold War, and Their Aftermath," 43 *South Dakota Law Review* 103 (1998); George Anastaplo, "Law & Literature and the Bible," pp. 758, 778; George Anastaplo, "Legal Education, Economics, and Law School Governance: Explorations," 46 *South Dakota Law Review* 102, 304 (2001). See as well Anastaplo, *The Artist as Thinker*, p. 249; chapter 8, note 14; Rod Liddle, "Opinion [on Africa]," *Guardian Weekly*, February 21–27, 2002, p. 21; appendix C, note 15.

50. This talk was given in the Law Lecture Series at Rosary College (now Dominican University), River Forest, Illinois, April 1, 1976. See chapter 7, note 2.

The parenthetical citations in the text are to the *Gospel of Mark*. See, on the King James translation, the text at note 24 of chapter 7 of this collection.

51. See, e.g., Haim Cohn, *The Trial and Death of Jesus* (New York: Harper & Row, 1971), p. xi.

52. It has been said that some sixty thousand books on Jesus were published in the nineteenth century alone.

53. A note of caution is in order for any endeavor at Biblical exegesis among us. My wife was once the principal research "authenticator" for the questions used on the *College Bowl* television-quiz program. There were, she was told, several subjects about which one had to be particularly careful in framing questions and validating answers, lest the National Broadcasting Company switchboard in New York City light up immediately with corrections from indignant viewers all over the United States. Those sensitive subjects included the Irish, the Hungarians, the American Civil War, and, of course, the Bible.

54. "This must be distinctly understood, or nothing wonderful can come of the story I am going to relate." Charles Dickens, *A Christmas Carol*, Stave One. Or, as Leopold Bloom put it, "Christ was a Jew like me." James Joyce, *Ulysses* (Modern Library, 1942), p. 336. Compare John Bush Jones, ed., *W. S. Gilbert: A Century of Scholarship and Commentary* (New York: New York University Press, 1970), p. 23: "Toynbee goes so far [in *A Study Of History*] as to show no less than seventy-eight points of similarity between the life of Christ and the lives of a number of pagan heroes." See chapter 7, note 30.

55. This is evident also upon reading the extended *Encyclopaedia Judaica* entry on the life of Jesus drawn on in the text at note 8 of chapter 7 of this collection.

56. See chapter 5, note 48.

57. See, on the Synoptic Gospels, chapter 7, note 8. See also chapter 7, note 45.

58. I am, in these explorations of the Gospel stories, reconsidering issues I first examined in a systematic fashion in a play I wrote more than thirty years ago. That play, in which the always troublesome character of Jesus' betrayer was critical, was originally entitled *The First Christian*. Upon further reflection, however, I changed its title to *The Last Christian*. This shift in titles suggests how elusive this subject can be. See chapter 5, notes 4, 6, 7. See also Anastaplo, "Law & Literature and the Bible," pp. 830–31.

59. Compare, for example, an angel's deliverance of apostles from prison. *Acts* 5:17–20. See also *Acts* 16:25–40.

60. See *Luke* 22:50–51. Compare *Matthew* 26:51–52; *Mark* 14:47; *John* 18:10–11.

61. See, e.g., Sloyan, *Jesus on Trial*, p. 44 n. 12.

62. A Greek Orthodox monk, at the Church of the Nativity in Bethlehem in 1989, was kind enough to show us a collection of bones ascribed to the infants killed pursuant to Herod's order. Are comparable collections available for viewing in Egypt (perhaps in a Coptic church or in some Jewish institution) from the effects of the anti-Israelite infanticides and then of the plagues in Moses' time? See, on those plagues, Anastaplo, "Law & Literature and the Bible," p. 521.

63. Jesus' gentleness toward inferiors (such as little children and the ill) and harshness toward "equals" and "superiors" can remind one of the proud man in Aristotle's *Nicomachean Ethics*. Consider, also, the *superba* of Joan of Arc. See the text at note 43 of chapter 8 of this collection.

64. Is it the same Sabbath? We are not told, but this does follow immediately in the text.

65. See *Luke* 23:54–56.

66. See *Luke* 24.

67. "Behold, I send you forth as sheep in the midst of wolves: be ye therefore wise as serpents, and harmless as doves." *Mark* 10:16. See chapter 4, note 36. Compare Thomas Aquinas, *Summa Theologiae*, 3a. 42, 3.

68. "The small band of those faithful to Jesus' memory who awaited his return in power to complete his messianic (i.e. kingly) role was virtually wiped out when the Jerusalem church perished in the catastrophe of the year 70." Gerard S. Sloyan, "The Last Days of Jesus," 20 *Judaism* 58 (1971). See chapter 7, note 40.

69. See, on prudence as "the god of this lower world," the text at note 8 of chapter 5 of this collection. See also George Anastaplo, *The Constitutionalist: Notes on the First Amendment* (Dallas: Southern Methodist University Press, 1971), p. 783; chapter 6, note 1.

70. None of Jesus' more spectacular miracles theretofore, I have noticed, had been performed in Jerusalem.

71. *John* 11:48.

72. *John* 11:50.

73. See chapter 7, note 32.

74. The relevant Roman law is said to have been this: "Persons who cause sedition or upheaval or who incite the mobs are, depending upon their civic status, liable to crucifixion, or to be thrown to the wild beasts, or to be banished to an island." Enslin, "The Temple and the Cross," p. 29 (citing *Digesta* xxxxviii, 19, 83, 2, of the Justinian *Pandects*).

75. See, e.g., George Anastaplo, "Church and State: Explorations," 19 *Loyola University of Chicago Law Journal* 61 (1987).

76. See section IV of chapter 7–A of this collection.

77. See *Matthew* 4:1–11.

78. See *Matthew* 26:57f, 27:2f.

79. See *Matthew* 26:36f. Compare the text at note 87 of chapter 7 of this collection. See, on temptation, *Genesis* 3:6, *Matthew* 6:13.

80. See *Matthew* 4:11, 27:26f, 28:20.

81. Augustine, *Confessions* (Mentor Edition, 1963), p. 236.

82. Augustine, *Confessions*, p. 158.

83. Augustine, *Confessions*, p. 158. See chapter 1, note 91; chapter 2, note 31; chapter 5, note 31; the text at note 97 of chapter 7 of this collection.

84. See Anastaplo, *Human Being and Citizen*, pp. 13–14. See also chapter 6.

85. See Plato, *Apology* 40B–E.

86. See Plato, *Crito* 44D. See also Anastaplo, *Human Being and Citizen*, p. 203.

87. See Plato, *Crito* 43B–C. Compare the text at note 79 of chapter 7 of this collection.

88. See the text at note 38 of chapter 7 of this collection. Abraham, we are told, was (and evidently remained) "very rich in cattle, in silver, and in gold." *Genesis* 13:2.

89. *Deuteronomy* 4:6. See the text at note 14 of chapter 1 and at note 70 of chapter 5 of this collection. See also Anastaplo, "Law & Literature and the Austen-Dostoyevsky Axis: Explorations," 46 *South Dakota Law Review* 712, 751 (2001).

90. Consider, by way of contrast, Athena's pleasure in Odysseus' deviousness, Apollo's endorsement of Socrates' wisdom, or even God's praise of Job.

91. See *Matthew* 27:14–26; *Mark* 15:5–15; *Luke* 23:13–25; *John* 18:33–40.

92. See, e.g., Brandon, "The Trial of Jesus," pp. 44–45.

93. See, e.g., *1 Corinthians* 15:12–22.

94. See, e.g., Cohn, "Reflections on the Trial of Jesus," p. 12; Enslin, "The Temple and the Cross," pp. 30–31; David Flusser, "A Literary Approach to the Trial of Jesus," 20 *Judaism* 35–36 (1971); Sloyan, "The Last Days of Jesus," p. 67. Misuse of authority and the abuse of power should be recognized as such. See, e.g., section VII of chapter 12–B of this collection.

95. Compare the way that the trial of Joan of Arc was handled. See chapter 8.

96. See chapter 4, note 14.

97. Compare chapter 1, note 91, chapter 2, note 31.

98. Compare section XII of chapter 7–A of this collection.

99. See Anastaplo, *Human Being and Citizen*, p. 155. See also George Anastaplo, *The American Moralist: On Law, Ethics, and Government* (Athens, Ohio: Ohio University Press, 1992), pp. 506–7; chapter 12, note 126. Compare Marcel Jacques

Dubois, "The Catholic Church and the State of Israel—After 25 Years," *Christian News from Israel*, New Series, vol. XXIII (1973).

100. *Acts* 23:27–30. We can see, in what Claudius Lysias did and said, how Pontius Pilate should have conducted himself. See, on Livy and the Roman regime, George Anastaplo, "The Constitution at Two Hundred: Explorations," 22 *Texas Tech Law Review* 967, 978–87 (1991).

101. *Micah* 6:8. See chapter 7, note 43. Central to most of the controversies reviewed in this collection should be the ability to sense when one knows enough in each set of circumstances to be entitled to be reasonably confident in the judgment one makes. The *humility, justice,* and *mercy* required in each situation may depend upon a reliable thoughtfulness, including an awareness of what the truly divine is and calls for—or at least an awareness, grounded in nature, of what the divine surely does not call for or permit. See, e.g., chapter 1, note 46; chapter 5, note 31; chapter 9, note 49; conclusion, note 3.

The matters discussed in this chapter are examined further in the following talk that I gave at a University of Chicago seminar on the Bible in March 2002:

The Gospel According to St. Paul

I.

Some, if not all, of the Pauline letters are believed by many scholars today to be the oldest part of the New Testament. Some of those letters are said to have been written by Paul as early as a generation after the Crucifixion of Jesus (say, around the year 50). All, or almost all, of them (whether by Paul or by others) are believed to have been written before the destruction of the Temple a generation later (in the year 70). (The first letter to the Thessalonians has been described as the oldest book in the New Testament. See *Harper Collins Study Bible*, p. 2218.) Indeed, some of the letters seem to have been written at a time when the imminent return of the resurrected Christ could still be spoken of by the faithful. (See, e.g., *1 Thess.* 4:1-5:11.)

It has been noticed that the Pauline letters "make up a substantial portion of the New Testament canon." They are identified with what is called "theological radicalism." (*Encyclopedia of Religion*, 11, p. 212) Radical or not, a reading from these letters is a regular part of every service in the Roman Catholic Church.

The letters referred to as Pauline were written either by Paul himself or by authors who were very much influenced by him. The letters now regarded as indisputably written by Paul are *Romans, 1 Corinthians, 2 Corinthians, Galatians, Philippians, Philemon, 1 Thessalonians,* and perhaps *2 Thessalonians.* (Compare how little seems to have survived, from the same period, of the texts associated with that once-robust competitor of early Christianity, the Mithraic cult.)

The term *gospel* is used repeatedly by Paul to designate what is taught by him and by others about the mode of personal salvation available because of the sacrifice of Jesus. But that term is also used, as I do here, to refer to the accounts of the career of Jesus that are attributed to Matthew, Mark, Luke, and John. I consider, on this occasion, what is and is not provided in the Pauline letters about the career of Jesus—and what the implications may be of the selections made and the silences resulting in those letters, letters that seem to have been prepared for recipients who were mostly Gentiles.

II.

A preliminary response to the question of what is and is not explicitly provided in the Pauline letters about the career of Jesus should notice that that career is in the background of whatever *is* said. As much information about the career of Jesus as was needed seems to have been somehow known, or so it would seem upon considering how little is said about that career, at least in the letters.

Information about that career was apt to be in the oral tradition, if not also in early written accounts of the Church, which are now lost. That tradition and those texts could well have been used in the preparation of the four Gospels that we do have. The tradition about Jesus seems to be reflected in the following passage in *Philippians* 2:4–11, which is said to draw upon a hymn of the early Church that is used by Paul in this letter: "Let each of you look not only to his own interests but also to the interests of others. Have this mind among yourselves, which is yours in Christ Jesus, who, though he was in the form of God, did not count equality with God a thing to be grasped, but emptied himself, taking the form of a servant, being born in the likeness of men. And being found in human form he humbled himself and became obedient unto death, even death on a cross. Therefore God has highly exalted him and bestowed on him the name that is above every name, (so) that at the name of Jesus every knee should bow, in heaven and on earth and under the earth, and every tongue confess that Jesus Christ is Lord, to the glory of God the Father." (See, also *Romans* 1:3–4, 3:24–25; *1 Corinthians* 15:3–5; *Galatians* 4:4–5; *1 Timothy* 1:9–10. See, for more liturgical and hymnal fragments, *1 Timothy* 2:5 sq., 3:16 sq.; *2 Timothy* 2:11 sq.) One can see in this early Church hymn the emphasis found in the Pauline letters, that the divine Jesus voluntarily took human form in order to suffer, to die, and to be resurrected for the sake of mankind.

There are, in the Pauline letters, few proper names encountered in the career of Jesus. Those few include Peter (Cephas), James, John (but not the Baptist), and Pontius Pilate. No mention is made, by name, of Joseph or Mary, or of places such as Bethlehem, Nazareth, and Galilee. (Nazareth *is* mentioned in one of the accounts, in the *Book of Acts*, of Saul/Paul's Damascus Road encounter; and John the Baptist is spoken of by Paul in the Antioch speech recorded in *Acts*.)

Although the Crucifixion of Jesus is many times referred to, nothing is said in the Pauline letters about the charges that had been leveled against Jesus in Jerusalem. Those had not been charges (such as treason, murder, or theft) that Gentiles would readily understand, but rather had been charges that were unfamiliar, keyed as they were to Jewish doctrines. It probably would not have mattered to Gentiles which side of the issues *here* that Jesus or his accusers happened to be on.

III.

Many more names are mentioned in the Pauline letters from the history of Israel than from the career of Jesus himself. Abraham, Isaac, Rebecca, Jacob, Moses, David, and Isaiah are among those referred to, but without much being said about them. More is said about the history of Israel, beginning with its departure from Egypt, but this is said to what may have been a primarily Jewish audience. This is in the speech of Paul at Antioch recorded in *Acts*. (Compare Stephen's use of that history in his defense speech in Jerusalem.)

Would Gentiles be less knowledgeable about and less interested in Israel's history, especially if they were not inclined to become fully Jewish in order to become Christian? Later on, of course, Gentiles who had become well-established Christians (especially after a few generations) began to take far greater interest in the history of Israel. It was then "safe" for them to do so, as well as helpful in understanding what they had come to believe.

However that may be, the Israelite approach always seemed to make more of history than Christian Gentiles were inclined to do. That is, Judaism was more the "religion" of a people commanded to conform to a long-established code, whereas Christianity became more a religion depending upon personal choices as to whether to "belong" or not.

IV.

The choice to be made by would-be Christians depended upon a critical message drawn from the career of Jesus. But only a very small part of that career, temporally speaking, mattered for this purpose—or so the Pauline letters indicate.

It can be instructive to try to piece together the career of Jesus from the Pauline letters (and, for that matter, from the speeches by Paul in *Acts*). Very little is recorded there about what Jesus said or did (or had done to him) prior to his last days. That is, if Paul were all that we had, we would have little of the "human interest" aspects of Jesus' career, such as his relations with his twelve companions. Nor would we have much, if anything, in writing about Jesus' miracles or about his encounters with various people, friendly and unfriendly.

Such details about Jesus' career are "build up," which, if the letters are indicative, did not interest Paul much. Or was it that he could not add anything significant to what others were already reporting? It does seem that he did not want merely to repeat what others had said.

Besides, it could well seem to the informed Jew that much of what Jesus said and did during his career was something already familiar to him from the Jewish tradition, however much Jesus varied the emphasis in what he said. If a Jew wanted more of that sort of thing, the Hebrew Bible could seem to provide more than enough material to develop (as Jesus himself could have been considered to have developed, if not redirected, it). As for the receptive Gentile, the tradition of the Jews would have been only of secondary interest.

V.

Of primary interest for the receptive Gentile, it could seem to someone such as Paul, was that the healer/prophet (for which there were several precedents in Judaism) had been physically resurrected after having been killed. And it is this, of course, that is emphasized by Paul in his letters and in the speeches recorded in *Acts* (which do have the career of Jesus anticipated by John the Baptist).

We have seen in the passage quoted from *Philippians* (2:4–11) how Jesus' career can be summed up. What Jesus could mean to Gentiles is put thus by Paul in his first letter to the Thessalonians about what had happened among them as a result of Paul's ministry there: "You turned to God from idols to serve a living God, and to wait for his Son from heaven, whom he raised from the dead, Jesus who delivers us from the wrath to come." (1:9–10)

The emphasis here, as elsewhere, by Paul is upon the sacrifice of completely innocent blood and thereafter the permanent resurrection of the dead. So dominant is this theme that the references to Jesus in the Pauline letters are quite different from the references to him in the four Gospels. In the Gospels he is usually referred to as simply "Jesus." In the Pauline letters, he is usually referred to in a much more elevated way, such as "Lord Jesus," "Jesus the Lord," "Jesus Christ," "Lord Jesus Christ," and "the Lord." Indeed, of the more than four hundred references naming Jesus in the Pauline letters, fewer than one-tenth of them speak of him simply as "Jesus."

Thus, Jesus is not to be regarded as mortal, however exemplary he was as healer/prophet. Rather, he is repeatedly spoken of by Paul as the unique incarnation of the divine in human form, something for which the checkered history of Israel had been the necessary preparation.

VI.

Paul, as I have noticed, is in a position to emphasize the sacrifice and resurrection of Jesus, saying far less about Jesus' career with its day-to-day happenings of a particularly gifted mortal being.

The resurrected Jesus can be testified to by Paul from his own Damascus Road experience. He does not have to rely, as he would have to do for Jesus' day-to-day happenings, upon the testimony of Jesus' long-time companions.

The boldness with which Paul asserts his authority here may be seen in his first letter to the Corinthians (15:3–11):

> For I declared to you as of first importance what I also received, that Christ died for our sins, in accordance with the scriptures, that he was buried, that he was raised on the third day in accordance with the scriptures, and that he appeared to Cephas (Peter), then to the twelve. Then he appeared to more than five hundred brethren at one time, most of whom are still alive, though some have fallen asleep. Then he appeared to James, then to all the apostles. Last of all, as to one untimely born, he appeared also to me [on the Road to Damascus]. For I am the least of the apostles, unfit to be called an apostle, because I persecuted the church of God. But by the grace of God I am what I am, and his grace toward me was not in vain. On the contrary, I worked harder than any of them, though it was not I, but the grace of God that is with me. Whether then it was I or they, so we preach and so you believed.

It can even be said that Paul, in this and like accounts, makes more of the scriptures *anticipating* the coming and doings of a Christ than he does of any accounts about Jesus himself, except of course for accounts of his death and resurrection.

Thus, there is little said in the Pauline letters even about the sayings of Jesus. This is in marked contrast to the so-called *Gospel of Thomas*, which is made up almost entirely of the sayings of Jesus, with little said about the cross and the resurrected Christ. And, also in marked contrast to the Pauline letters, the *Gospel of Thomas* (evidently written down in about 140 AD) repeatedly identifies its hero as simply "Jesus."

VII.

Jesus Christ, in the Pauline letters, stands primarily as *the* means for the abolition of death. Paul can be said to have carried to an extreme the "choose life" commandment that had been issued long before to the Jews.

Paul, as a Pharisee, was of the camp that did believe in some form of resurrection (or immortality of the soul). Jesus' career—or mission—evidently came to be understood by Paul as dedicated to the conquest of death. It may even be that the fearlessness, if not even the exhilaration, of the Jesus-people when threatened by death had demonstrated to Paul that those people had somehow gotten what he was looking for, an escape from a permanent death. Thus, the execution of Stephen, which Paul had witnessed, could have impressed him as at least suggesting the vulnerability of dreaded death itself.

Paul had thereafter his Damascus Road experience, which seemed to inform him that the resurrection hoped for had already happened, and in a decisive manner for everyone willing to take advantage of it, in the person of Jesus. Once this became apparent to Paul, a man who never did anything by half-measures, there was no stopping him. He was off and running, once assigned his mission to the Gentiles in Damascus, soon outstripping worldwide even those men who had actually shared Jesus' life in the Holy Land.

VIII.

Paul's testimony about the resurrected Christ was reinforced by, or opened the way to, the moral lessons that he taught the congregations with which he dealt. He, perhaps more than anyone else among the earliest followers of the resurrected Christ, provided the authoritative guides (perhaps down to this day) as to how Christians should live. Much in his letters is devoted to such guidance.

This moral guidance does not draw explicitly upon the teachings of Jesus: There is not, as we have noticed, much in the way of quotations from Jesus. It draws instead, in large part, upon the moral teachings implicit in Judaism, teachings that Jesus too drew upon insofar as he was human. But Paul also had the Greek tradition to draw upon, some of which is even incorporated in the very language he uses in writing his letters (however much he might warn, as in *Colossians* 8:1, against the allure of philosophy, that philosophy that addresses the prospect of death in a way quite different from Paul's way).

It remains a challenge for the modern reader to determine how much, and in what way, Greek thought influenced Paul's mode of presenting the Jewish heritage to the Gentiles. Does he recognize, for example, that the term *nature*, which he uses, tacitly presupposes a significant shift from the vital presupposition of the Hebrew Bible that an Intelligent Will always governs the continuance of a created world? (Compare, for example, Proclus on the eternity of the world.) Thus, Paul is aware that the Gentiles do some things by nature that the Jews do in accordance with the law.

We can see here something of the rift that may have been developing, independent of the Jesus movement, between the Hellenistic Jews and the Palestinian Jews. Was the Pauline approach more apt to appeal to the Gentiles than to the Jews? But, it can be argued, the Jews themselves, independent of the Jesus movement, may have become more receptive to some aspects of the Pauline approach once the Temple was destroyed and the Palestinian nucleus of the chosen people had been forcibly scattered. (On the other hand, a thriving Jewish community in the Holy Land might have helped sustain a significant Christian sect among the Jews.)

Paul's fascination with the resurrected Christ may have contributed to a mystical strain of Christianity. But, on the other hand, did his familiarity with the idea of nature ever make him suspect that the Israelites had reinforced (or at least had spelled out) with revelations and stories the prescriptions that had been implicitly laid down among them by nature? (Consider here the implications of *Deuteronomy* 4: 6.)

IX.

Although not much is made by Paul, either in *Acts* or in his letters, of the career of Jesus (aside from his death and resurrection), much more is made, in effect, of Paul's own career as a missionary (less so as a persecutor).

Does Paul's relative lack of interest in the human life of Jesus reflect his abandonment of the bodily claims and requirements of Judaism (including circumcision and the elaborate regulations of the law)? Does the lack of a homeland for him influence him here? Is there something Greek, if not even Platonic, in this shift on his part?

The kind of human interest provided in the four Gospels by accounts of Jesus' life tends to be provided in the Pauline letters, as well as in much of the *Book of Acts*, by accounts of Paul's own life. These accounts can include, besides such miracles as those at Lystra, indications of the suffering endured by Paul, so much so that he can even say such things as, "I have been crucified with Christ." (*Galatians* 2: 20. See, also, *Galatians* 3: 1, 6: 12–14.) Insofar as a human biography is needed, to inspire the generations after Jesus, the story of Paul's trials and triumphs will do.

Paul may even be seen as a somewhat counter–Judas Iscariot figure, ending up as a devoted follower of Jesus after having first "betrayed" (that is, persecuted) him. It can be intriguing to speculate what admonitions and guidance Jesus himself might have had to provide if Paul had been in his company in the way that Peter and the others had been.

Do we get, furthermore, from the career of Paul some notion of what the career and teachings of Jesus would have been like among Gentiles—that is, among peoples (unfamiliar with Jewish ways) who would have had to have been *told* about the Resurrection rather than witnessing it? In this and perhaps in other ways, then, Paul can be understood as an exuberant imitator of Christ, confident that Israel had something vital to offer to desperate Gentiles everywhere.

8

Joan of Arc[1]

I.

I can do no more on this occasion than suggest how we can begin to think about and pass responsible judgment upon claims and events, subsequent to Biblical circumstances, that seem to touch on the supernatural—and to do this only with whatever aid is provided us by the light of natural reason and by the guidance of common experience. Those among us who are blessed with more than human wisdom should be looked up to—and it is in the interest of us all, the blessed and the ordinary alike, that systematic efforts be made to use whatever talents we have to identify and cherish those who may happen to be divinely inspired.

Our case in point, for this occasion, is that Medieval treasure, Joan of Arc (Jeanne d'Arc). I anticipate much of what I can say about her and, even more important, about the enduring questions about inspiration that her case can help us examine, by referring you to two instructive stories and by telling you a third. The first story, recorded in the *Book of Jeremiah*, has to do with a struggle between two prophets.[2] The second instructive story, recorded in Shakespeare's *Henry VI, Part 2*, has to do with how a sensible man comes to terms with the miraculous.[3] These are the two stories to which I refer you, bearing as they do on what I will be saying on this occasion. The third instructive story, which Joan of Arc herself (in the lighter moments of which she was capable) would probably have enjoyed as a particularly apt commentary upon her circumstances, goes something like this:

A man who liked to hike across all kinds of terrain fell off a cliff one day but managed to grab a strong branch. Although his arms and shoulders pained him fiercely, he held on desperately. He looked down hundreds of feet and up fifty feet. There was no help in either direction. There was nothing to do but to yell and to hope someone would hear.

"Is anyone up there?" he shouted.

"Yes, I am here," a voice replied.

"Who are you?" the hiker asked.

"I am the Lord," the voice replied again. "Do you need help?"

"I need it badly and at once."

"Do you have faith?"

"I have all the faith in the world."

"Then let go of the branch."

There was a long pause. Then the hiker called out, "Is there anyone else up there?"[4]

Let us turn now to the trial of Joan of Arc, but by way of still another story, a story provided us by a Greek playwright surpassingly alert to the workings of human passions.

II.

Odysseus is shown at the outset of Sophocles' *Ajax* in a kind of conversation with the goddess Athena. It is "a kind of conversation" in that Athena does not appear to him visually; rather, he can (he says) clearly catch her words.[5] That is, he is a man who, insofar as he thinks and is crafty, effectively turns to and relies upon Athena. In a manner of speaking, then, the hardheaded Odysseus hears divine voices, voices that are evidently critical to his plans and activities as a most practical man.

In this respect, it would seem, he is a forerunner, by some two millennia, of Joan of Arc, the teenaged girl who said she heard voices that directed her from a village in the east of France to the court of a king, to glorious exploits both military and political, and eventually to the stake as a heretic. Joan's perceptions of her angels and saints were not limited to voices, however. She could even be moved to say that she saw her visitors, as well, and on occasion touched them and smelled them.[6] But it is as voices that they most significantly affected her—and in that respect, she does resemble the wily Odysseus.

But the Odysseus of Sophocles (or, for that matter, the Odysseus of Homer) is not a "conventional" visionary, either in his temperament or in his effect upon others. The recognized visionary tends to have an unsettling effect upon others as well as, at the outset, upon himself. The oddness of what is happening to such a man, of what he discerns or describes to be happening, can be either exhilarating or intimidating. Sophocles' play does open with instances of such intimidation: Ajax, furious with the leaders of the Greeks (including Odysseus), has that very night gleefully slaughtered many animals, believing them to have been the Greek leaders.[7] He (another visionary, in a sense) had been subjected to this delusion by Athena, the divine protectress of Odysseus and his colleagues. She had, she reports, thrown before Ajax's eyes "obsessive notions, thoughts of insane joy."[8] We can understand how someone of Ajax's fierce temperament, thwarted in his efforts to secure revenge for an affront he has suffered, should have "taken it out" on the animals available to him. We can also understand that Odysseus can regard what Ajax has done as "an act of staggering horror."[9]

Passionate oddness, to use a neutral term, can be intimidating, whether found in a saint, in the insane, or in the diabolically possessed. Consider the following exchange between Athena and Odysseus, when the goddess proposes to show him the afflicted Ajax:

Athena:
Get a grip on your nerves and wait. It's no disaster to see the man. I'll turn his glance away. He'll never see you or know your face. . . .

Odysseus:
Athena, what can you be thinking of? Don't call him out!

Athena:
Quiet, now! No cowardice!

Odysseus:
No, no, for heaven's sake! I'd very much rather he stayed inside.

Athena:
What are you afraid of? He was only a man before.

Odysseus:
Yes, but he was my enemy and still is.

Athena:
But to laugh at your enemies—what sweeter laughter can there be than that?

Odysseus:
It's enough for me if he stays just where he is.

Athena:
You're afraid, then, to see a madman face to face?

Odysseus:
Certainly if he were sane, I should never shrink from him.[10]

This is no idle boast on Odysseus' part: he had always been competent and confident enough to deal with the sane, however powerful, Ajax. But the insane have always aroused in human beings a "reverential awe."[11] There is about them something unnatural, otherworldly, radically irrational. Such people can be more sensitive, more perceptive, as well as far less inhibited in what they say and do. The heightened powers of such people can make others feel more vulnerable. One's soul may even feel unnaturally exposed. One senses that whatever malice there may be in such people is undiluted and thus more likely to be effective, especially because they tend to be oblivious to pain and threats. They can be unsettling even when one recognizes them to be exhibiting a standard mental aberration, such as specific forms of hallucinations. Not only can they not be counted upon to be restrained by prudential considerations and by the typical concern for self-preservation, but they also undermine our reliance upon the possibility of communicating with one another, thereby subverting our own reliance upon rationality.

To be *possessed* is to be like an inspired poet—except that in a poet this sort of thing is held in check, if only barely in some instances. But poetic or otherwise, this kind of manifestation can be beguiling as well as intimidating, depending upon the circumstances and perhaps depending also upon whether it can be harnessed by those who know what they are doing—by those who are aware of the limits of human knowledge of, and control over, events, and by those who are aware as well of the power and limitations of public opinion.

To be possessed is to exhibit a single-mindedness, or to be moved by a mindlessness, that can be wholeheartedly devoted to cosmic purposes. There *can* be something exhilarating as well as eerie about this, perhaps not least because of the risks being run. The career of the visionary can be quite precarious, if only because the visionary stands alone, unable to rely upon anyone else when circumstances change.

III.

An inspired single-mindedness may be seen in the character and career of Joan of Arc. A useful recapitulation of that career is provided us by the entry devoted to her in the *New Catholic Encyclopedia*:

Jeanne la Pucelle, national patroness of France; b. Domremy in Lorraine (Department, Meuse), Jan. 6, 1412; d. Rouen, May 30, 1431 (feast, May 30).

Except for her piety, nothing in 'Jeanette's' early years distinguished her from other children of the countryside. When she was about thirteen, her 'voices,' which she kept a secret for almost five years, revealed her mission, the deliverance of the French kingdom from English control. The treaty of Troyes (May 20, 1420) had made the English king, Henry V, king of France, setting aside the legitimate heir, the future Charles VII. The madness of Charles VI, French military reverses, and the alliance between England and Burgundy had prepared for this shattering event. After the successive deaths of Henry V and Charles VI, the Duke of Bedford, regent of France for his nephew, Henry VI, undertook to complete the conquest of the kingdom by tracking down the Dauphin (Charles VII), who had taken refuge beyond the Loire, and by putting Orleans under siege.

Joan secretly left her home in January of 1429, succeeded in obtaining an escort from the captain of Vaucouleurs, who had remained faithful to the king of France, and was presented to Charles VII at Chinon (Feb. 25, 1429). Having had Joan examined by theologians at Poitiers, Charles consented to follow her advice and reassembled his army. With Joan in command they marched on Orleans and in eight days (May 8, 1429) ended the siege that had lasted eight months. After the brilliant victory of Patay (June 18), she opened the road to Reims, where Charles was crowned in the cathedral on July 17.

The coronation rallied the people of France, who until then had been hesitant in their support of Charles; it marked the end of English victories. But unfortunately the apathetic and ill-advised King opposed Joan's further plans. When at length she again went into action, hoping to relieve Compiegne, besieged by the Burgundians, Joan was taken prisoner (May 25, 1430). She was sold to the English, who, in placing her on trial for heresy, sought at once to remove a formidable adversary and to discredit the King who owed her his crown. The trial was held in Rouen, presided over by the bishop of Beauvais, Pierre Cauchon, the former rector of the University of Paris and a staunch champion of the English. After months of interrogation (Feb. 21–May 24, 1431) and artifice, in which Cauchon tricked Joan into an admission of guilt, the judge sentenced her to death as a relapsed heretic. On May 30, she was excommunicated, turned over to the secular arm, and burned at the stake. Engulfed by flames, Joan protested her innocence and the holiness of her mission.

Even during her lifetime, Joan was hailed as a saint because of both the preternatural character of her deeds and the purity of her life. She was solemnly rehabilitated by the Church after a seven-year trial (1449–56), during which 115 witnesses were heard; she was beatified on April 18, 1909, and canonized on May 9, 1920.[12]

Several immediate qualifications, if not corrections, of this account are called for. There were two judges on this occasion (as seems usually to have been the case in such trials), the Bishop of Beauvais (Pierre Cauchon) and the deputy inquisitor for France (the chief inquisitor himself being occupied elsewhere in another trial).[13] The two judges were advised by dozens of assessors, who commented on the law and the evidence from time to time, and (perhaps more important on this occasion) by the theological faculty of the University of Paris, a body with a European reputation and considerable influence.[14] These proceedings, which extended over several months, were anything but perfunctory.[15] It is, despite what the *New Catholic Encyclopedia* entry says, not useful to consider Joan "tricked . . . into an admission of guilt."[16] Rather, it appears that the fundamental issues were fairly clear by the time the trial ended; it was also fairly clear what each side stood for and required of the other. It is not insignificant that more than a year elapsed between the capture of Joan and her execution. (This was about as long as her military career had been prior to her capture.) Thus, there was no rush to judgment, but rather an extended (sometimes tortured) struggle between troubled churchmen and a troubling, if not troubled, youngster.

Joan seems, in her last days, to have been much disturbed by the prospect of death at the stake.[17] In this she exhibited a normal concern for self-preservation, just as she had been concerned earlier that she not be subjected to the torture often resorted to in the interrogation of defendants in heresy and witchcraft trials.[18] It may well be that she did not fully realize, until almost the very end, that she faced immediate execution upon conviction—and when she did realize this, as the final judgment was being pronounced, she renounced her claims about the divine origins of her voices and formally accepted the authority of the Church with respect to the disputed matters.[19]

But, as it turned out, this was a submission (on May 24, 1431) that she could not really live with. Within a few days, she had repudiated her submission, and thereby invited her condemnation and immediate execution as a relapsed heretic. Her relapse turned around her revival of claims about the voices by which she had been, and continued to be, guided.[20] Thus, her submission in the face of death gained her only a few more days of life. But it might well have contributed immeasurably to her reputation with subsequent generations in that it did reveal her as someone with a healthy desire to live, something that must be naturally wondered about when enthusiasts, especially youthful enthusiasts, are encountered. That is to say, Joan's life-preserving retreat suggests that, however unsettling and distorting her voices might have been, she probably had some notion of what she was letting herself in for when she returned, after her submission, to her original position.

Of course, there can be no assurance that this relapse was anything other than a resurgence of what some today would diagnose as a psychopathic state from which the immediate prospect of death had momentarily shaken her, like a kind of shock treatment. But that is not how this timely assertion and then renunciation by her of the self-preservation instinct strike most people. Such a desperate exhibition of weakness, if weakness it is, can appeal to mankind at large. Certainly, she has an extensive appeal. Thus [I could report in 1977], fifty years ago, an American writer said of her, "It is just five hundred years since Joan of Arc lived her brief life. Her story has been told many times, and will be told oftener in the years to come, for she was, she is, the most interesting human being the world has ever known."[21] And only last year she was voted the "most admired" public figure by the multitudes who visit Madame Tussaud's Wax Museum in London,[22] a tribute particularly touching considering that it was the English who executed her after she had been excommunicated by a tribunal of French Churchmen. It is not without interest to notice that she was followed in this poll by Winston Churchill and, thereafter, by Jesus, John F. Kennedy, and Lord Nelson. Her career resembles in some respects that of Jesus himself. The careers of four of these five favorites are marked by, and perhaps are attractive partly because of, untimely deaths. The exception, of course, is Churchill, whose "glamour" comes not from a "romantic" death, which does seem to have some appeal today, but from his reputation as the savior of Great Britain from the threat posed by Adolf Hitler, who is awarded recognition (in the same poll) as "the most-hated public figure."[23]

It is Churchill himself who has written in his *History of the English-Speaking Peoples* one of the most eloquent (and, in a sense, authoritative) appreciations of the girl whose trial we are considering.[24] He opens and closes his account of the leader he considers the decisive enemy of England during the Hundred Years War with these celebrations of her:

> There now appeared upon the ravaged scene an Angel of Deliverance, the noblest patriot of France, the most splendid of heroes, the most beloved of her saints, the most inspiring of all her memories, the peasant Maid, the ever-shining, ever-glorious Joan of Arc. . . .
>
> Joan was a being so uplifted from the ordinary run of mankind that she finds no equal in a thousand years. The records of her trial present us with facts alive today through all the mists of time. Out of her own mouth she can be judged in each generation. She embodied the natural goodness and valor of the human race in unexampled perfection. Unconquerable courage, infinite compassion, the virtue of the simple, the wisdom of the just, shone forth in her. She glorifies as she freed the soil from which she sprang. All soldiers should read her story and ponder on the words and deeds of the true warrior, who in one single year, though untaught in technical arts, reveals in every situation the key of victory.[25]

IV.

We speak of the trial of Joan of Arc, but it may be more instructive to consider her to have been subjected to three different trials. The first was the examination to which she was assigned upon offering her services to Charles VII; the second was the inquisition undergone upon her capture; the third was the trial for relapse following immediately upon her conviction, her abjuration, and her sentence to life imprisonment by the Inquisition. Let us consider each of these trials in turn.

The examination by Churchmen loyal to Charles VII lasted three weeks.[26] A young girl had appeared before the king, reporting strange experiences and making extraordinary demands. How was she to be understood? The inquiries to which Joan was repeatedly subjected recognized that it is rare to have observable angels and saints visit human beings. This is not to suggest that a visionary may not be sincere in what she reports but rather that alternative explanations must be routinely considered. If Joan's claims had not been outlandish, there would have been no need to examine her; but then, if they had not been outlandish, she probably would not have been (upon establishing herself) as influential as she was, nor would we have come to learn of, and be interested in, her. She was able to persuade her initial examiners that her voices were genuine—or, at least, that there was no spiritual risk in allowing her to advise the king.[27] There does not seem to be a record available of that first examination (although, it seems, some record was made). One must wonder whether Joan was more accommodating in what she said about her voices in that initial effort, upon which everything else depended, than she was in her trial at Rouen, by which time she had (whether or not she recognized it) accomplished much of what she had set out to do.

The trial at Rouen, the second of our three trials, consisted of several stages.[28] There were a preliminary examination, a formal trial on charges drawn from the preliminary examination, consultations with the appropriate advisors (such as the theologians at the University of Paris), and the final confrontation that led to her conviction, abjuration, and sentence.[29] This extended examination, by French Churchmen loyal to the English king, Henry VI, was probably concerned with many of the issues to which the earlier French Churchmen loyal to Charles VII had directed their attention. Of this examination, at Rouen, there is an official transcript available.[30] There are indications, however, that this transcript is not complete; some suggest that it is not strictly fair to Joan, that it may even have been doctored somewhat.[31] But this may not matter for our purposes: enough seems to be said there, and in a plausible fashion, to suggest to us what the issues were, and what standards were applied, in judging Joan.

No doubt, her judges began with prejudice against her. After all, she was a captured enemy leader, *and a woman at that*, who was generally believed to have performed wonders. In such proceedings, it may be virtually impossible to have participants who are without prejudice.[32] Joan, it should be emphasized, was executed not so much because of what she and her court differed on as because of what she and they agreed about. It was crucial that they agreed that both the divine and the diabolical can manifest themselves in appearances among human beings.[33] Of secondary importance was the determination of how claims of particular manifestations are to be regarded and tested. The attitude of her judges can be characterized as that of men who were highly skeptical without being skeptics. They believed, among other things, that her voices were, at best, questionable (reflecting perhaps a "dialogue" within her own disturbed soul), and that in such circumstances she should defer to the judgment of the constituted Church authorities with respect both to the character of her visions and to how she should respond to them. The typical modern observer would no doubt share much of these authorities' skepticism about her voices.

Joan's abjuration leaves one no better off than one would otherwise be in determining the character of her voices. She was quite practical about her abjuration, waiting until the final judgment was actually being read.[34] If they really proposed to *kill* her because of what she reported, she can be understood to have thought, then she would formally unsay what she had said, just as earlier she had warned them that if they tortured her she would say whatever they wanted her to say and then repudiate it afterwards as having been said because of torture.[35] The required recantation, she can also be understood to have thought, would be put by her in a form that was sufficient for her judges, even as it allowed intelligent people to figure out why she had spoken as she had. Thus, she said repeatedly "that inasmuch as the clergy had pronounced that her revelations and apparitions were not to be upheld or believed, she would not maintain them, but would defer in all things to her judges and our Holy Mother Church."[36] This seems to be at the heart of her abjuration, an essentially hypothetical statement that recognizes ("repeatedly") that she is saying this because it is what they evidently want said. There is a longer, even more formal abjuration that follows, but that is not in her style.[37] Nowhere else in the hundreds of pages of record is there so long a statement on her part, I believe, as in this more explicit abjuration. Are we not counted on to recognize that that detailed statement is some Churchman's doing, not Joan's?

Joan learned in short order, however, that her abjuration would not save her from the terribly oppressive conditions in which she was held. She had already had months of that, which provided her a sample of what the life sentence she now received could mean. Once the immediate threat of death was removed, she could assess properly the alternative, imprisonment for life. Perhaps she also came to reflect upon the fact that she had once led men into battle and to their deaths by instilling in them belief in voices that she had just now been intimidated into repudiating.

Did it hurt to deny voices that others could not hear or believe in? What did those voices "want" to happen, and why? Why did they not appear to her judges and tell *them* to leave her alone? Did her voices care what happened to her? If we moderns dismiss the voices, as most of us are probably inclined to do, do we want her to have insisted on a delusion (or a self-deception) at the cost of her life? If we believe in the voices, but voices *we* have not been privileged to have heard ourselves, are we in a position to second-guess her personal relations with the sources of those voices? What she conceived those relations to be is poignantly suggested by the following exchanges during her short trial for relapse (on May 28, 1431):

> As we her judges had heard from certain people that she had not yet cut herself off from her illusions and pretended revelations, which she had previously renounced, we asked her whether she had not since Thursday [May 24] heard the voices of St. Catherine and St. Margaret. She answered yes.
>
> Asked what they told her, she answered that they told her God had sent her word through St. Catherine and St. Margaret of the great pity of this treason by which she consented to abjure and recant in order to save her life; that she had damned herself to save her life. She said that before Thursday they told her what to do and say then, which she did. . . . She said that if she [now] declared God had not sent her she would damn herself, for in truth she was sent from God. She said that her voices had since told her that she had done a great evil in declaring that what she had done was wrong. She said that what she had declared and recanted on Thursday was done only for fear of the fire. Asked if she believed her voices to be St. Catherine and St. Margaret, she answered, "Yes, and they came from God."[38]

V.

Is it not highly likely, in the circumstances, that Joan was sincere in stating her belief that the voices were those of "persons" she had come (perhaps even had been induced) to identify as St. Catherine and St. Margaret?[39] But the duty of the court was not limited to determinations of sincerity: rather, it believed that it had to decide what the origins and character of the voices in fact were. I do not presume to pass judgment on Joan's voices, only (as I have indicated) to suggest how one might begin to think about them. It is important to see that even such matters *can* be systematically examined and assessed, however inconclusive one's assessment might have to be in some circumstances.

In assessing such matters, it is important to separate the critical issues from the secondary. Secondary were such matters as the male clothing Joan wore, the way she conducted herself as a military leader, her uses of incantations, magic, and divination, and even her attitude toward the property of others.[40] Such matters as this may have been important, but mostly as clues to or reflections of deeper problems. The deeper problems in Joan's case were the visitations she claimed and, ultimately, the question of who should assess those supposed visitations.

The key to heresy is, it seems, a stubborn, inflexible will.[41] The question of submission to a Church that had seen a lot of things, including the limits of enthusiasm, became critical.[42] Should not long-established institutions be given the benefit of the doubt, at least in circumstances where one member is claiming revelations that other members simply do not have? Is not the Church entitled, if not even obliged, in such circumstances, to insist upon generally observable confirmations, lest catastrophic delusions and deceptions be let loose upon the world?

Joan's recalcitrance was condemned as *superba* (the word from which we derive *superb*).[43] The superb has its obvious attractions: a kind of gallantry is suggested, among other things. But willfulness may also be suggested, a willfulness that could be said in this instance to have put religion in the service of politics.[44] Joan's judges can be understood to have believed that she cared more for France than she did for God and for God's Church. In this respect the Maid of Orleans can be said to have been the forerunner of that muchmarried English King, Henry VIII.[45]

VI.

This need not mean, however, that Joan of Arc was either a crude nationalist or an early Protestant. Her case was more complicated than that, which is evident in the contending claims made upon Joan to this day in France by clerical and anticlerical factions alike. There are two dates on which she is "officially" remembered in her own country. Some prefer to celebrate her on the second Sunday in May, ordered by Proclamation of the Republic in 1920, to commemorate her relief of Orleans;[46] others prefer to celebrate her Feast Day as a saint, May 30, the date of her death.

I have suggested that Joan's considerable piety was somehow put in the service of her country. This identification of herself with her country may even be seen in her use of the word *pity*. She had reported that her saints had told her, at the very outset of her career, of the pity that was in the Kingdom of France as a result of the English occupation; and she reported that her saints had told her, at the end of her career, that the treason of her abjuration had been a great pity.[47]

The Church's view of these matters had to be that politics should be in the service of religion or, at least, that religion and politics should be separated, not that religion should be subordinated to politics as Joan somehow seemed to do. The subordination of politics to religion had, aside from its spiritual benefits, several temporal advantages as well: nationalism was

subdued; international order was encouraged, with a consequent moderation of war; and natural right was more apt to be generally appealing, as
were various salutary opinions about God and the Good. Such an international order in both society and opinion can be more rational, less expres-
sive of partisan local interests, and hence more civilized.[48]

Patriotism, on the other hand, *can* become single-minded, less thoughtful
and yet more ingenious, in that all is organized for the national effort. The desire for personal salvation can also be single-minded, but not when it is organized as it is apt to be by a long-established Church with worldwide re-
sponsibilities. Such an organization, one might argue, is more apt to be
mistaken about particulars than about general principles—and even in its errors about particulars it will affirm general principles by which its own shortcomings can eventually be gauged and corrected.[49]

VII.

The question remains for us, How does one begin to assess such claims as
Joan made?

There is first the problem of determining what she did claim. Misrepresen-
tation, or misreporting, of her claims has to be guarded against. Let us assume, for purposes of illustration, that the claims here are as to the manifestation before her (and external to her) of angels and saints—of *talking* bodies
as apparent at least to her hearing, if not also to her sight, as I seem to be to
you and as you seem to be to me.

How are her claims to be understood? Several possibilities suggest themselves to account for the things that she claims to have observed:

1. that these were messages sent by God;
2. that these were messages sent by the Devil;
3. that they were hallucinations, reflecting either a pathological mental
   state or powerful passions (such as patriotic passions);
4. that these claims were the result of deliberate deceptions by her or by
   some other human beings;
5. that what she experienced were auditory (if not also optical) illusions or
   were due merely to some other such misperception or misunderstanding.[50]

How does one determine which of the possibilities (whether these or still
others) made the most sense in the circumstances? There is first the problem
of determining whether there can possibly be for human beings *any* messages

at all from God, or from any other supernatural source. Some might argue, for instance, that God does not move, does not change, and hence does not intervene in the affairs of human beings.[51] But this, I take it, has always been a minority view among peoples—and so means have had to be devised (along with standard checks for pathology) to help communities pass judgment, without the aid of direct divine guidance, on the kind of private revelation that the messenger claims. (It is reported in *Exodus* that an extraordinary witnessing of divine power was shared in the Sinai by all of the people of Israel together. But we, in assessing this event, must rely upon the report not by *those* multitudes but primarily by one author.)

Several tests suggest themselves (aside from the question of whether a purported manifestation for a messenger conforms to earlier *known* revelations, sacred texts, etc.):

1. the predictions conveyed by the messenger can be compared to subsequent events;
2. the miracles, and especially cures, induced by the messenger or her message, can be assessed;
3. the overall effects, especially the moral stance and the psychological state, of the messenger and her program can be evaluated;
4. the personal aggrandizement attendant upon the message can be taken note of;
5. the logical consistency and common sense of the messenger's report can be taken account of.

Various of these tests can be used to *eliminate* claims. None of them can be used to establish any particular claim definitively and unquestionably. Thus, the Roman Catholic Church does not guarantee private revelation, at least not after that found in the Old and New Testaments. The most that the Church can certify is, I understand, that particular private revelations are not contrary to faith or morals.[52]

An established insincerity on the part of the messenger can call her claims into question. Private aggrandizement, for example, can indicate insincerity, as when the transmitter of a message calling for sacrifice and penance accumulates or spends a personal fortune from the contributions of believers. On the other hand, it should be evident from what has been said that sincerity, even when it is obvious, cannot suffice to validate a claim.

That Joan was sincere it would be presumptuous of us to question.[53] Consider various of the other tests: It is difficult to establish that the predictions she made were particularly remarkable, that significant miracles have followed upon her career, or that the overall effects and success of her career cannot be explained in political terms (or as the result of fleeting chance).[54] The remaining test, that of the logical consistency and sensibleness of her messages, should take into account difficulties in what she stood for, especially in her resistance to Church authority. She did not proclaim general principles arrived at independent of, or in opposition to, the Church; rather, she simply selected a part of what the Church had taught her and made that primary. There is about this something naive and touching—and there is no doubt that it touched a responsive chord in a troubled France, just as has, say, national Marxism in many Third World countries in the twentieth century. If Joan had lived in a different village, some might suspect, her political as well as spiritual allegiances might well have been different. In addition, and perhaps more important for purposes of assessment, one can notice that chance seems to have affected the form of the supernatural encounters she had: she evidently communicated with the saints that had been dramatized in her part of the country in and through churches.[55]

Such are the considerations that one might well take into account in judging reports of divine revelation, especially if one has the duty to judge them for the sake of the community entrusted to one's care. It is not enough to say—as many of us today would be inclined to say—that such determinations are matters of faith, of taste, and of opinion and hence beyond the competence of any community or other institution to decide. To say this is to deny that we can begin to understand what does happen in such cases. One who would truly or fully understand these things must determine as best that one can whether such messages can ever come from God.

VIII.

No doubt, Joan seemed quite presumptuous. Perhaps she was. But, also, she was quite young—and mature men should have been able to make some of the assessments we have, to have recognized what she was drawing on and what she was influenced by, and to have acknowledged at least her gallantry and their own limitations. But those in authority were burning witches right and left, even in circumstances where pathetic hallucinations must have been suspected.[56]

Joan's judges were prisoners of their fears and expectations as well as of their immediate temporal interests. They should have known that enthusiastic aberrations from the teachings, including the rituals and art, of the Church should be expected periodically. Impressionable girls of little education, but of considerable passion and spirit, have especially to be watched out for. Boys of a comparable temperament are more apt to have respectable outlets for their aspirations and energy.

To say all this is to suggest that Joan's judges should have been prudent: after all, they *were* rulers. Her insistence upon God's will, as it was revealed to her, in preference to Church decrees might well have entitled them to recognize her as partially independent of, if not separated from, them. But should they have resorted to explicit excommunication in circumstances where they could foresee the immediate cruel consequences of such a ruling?

What, then, should they have done? The truly decent thing to do would have been to continue to hold her as a prisoner of war, perhaps shipping her to England.[57] The authorities should have recognized, well before the time Joan was executed, that they had in their hands a young woman who was not able to secure her physical release by supernatural (including diabolical) means.[58] This powerlessness, properly publicized, would have gone far to dissipate the adverse political, as well as spiritual, influence they feared.

It may well be that Joan had "peaked" in her political effectiveness months before she was captured. This may even have contributed to her fall. Charles and some of his advisors must have sensed how vulnerable she could be if captured. But they seem to have abandoned her to her fate, if not even permitted her to expose herself to the risk of capture, perhaps because they did not consider her any longer useful to them. Had her failure to continue to move them prompted her to take chances by trying to do things she should not have tried?

Still, it may *not* have been in Joan's enduring interest to have escaped execution. One can even argue that a favor was done her, that she might otherwise have deteriorated as her powerlessness became evident, especially if her supernatural encounters reflected deep psychic disturbances that she had been temporarily able to put to good use. Did her deliberate relapse represent an unconscious recognition of her inability to live in ordinary circumstances with the inherent psychic turmoil that war and adventure had mobilized and thereby sublimated?

But, it must be immediately added, one cannot kill another human being as a form of therapy—or to head off anticipated psychic anguish. After all, there was nothing wrong with Joan that burning could cure. The perhaps accidental glorification of Joan that resulted from the conduct of her judges is no excuse for that conduct, conduct that was rooted in what *they* were so imprudent as to believe.[59] I suspect that Joan's judges acted the way they did in her case more because of their passionate ignorance than because of deliberate reasons of state. And, I presume to add, the things they should not have been ignorant of were not divine things but rather human things, including the pitfalls that human beings are likely to encounter when dealing with divine things.

IX.

I have argued that even such private and perhaps divine phenomena as reported messages from Heaven can properly be subjected (at least in an exploratory way) to dispassionate judgment, a judgment that assumes a moral as well as a physical coherence in the universe.[60] I have also argued that those officials, ecclesiastical or secular, who undertake to render such judgments can and should be subjected to dispassionate judgment as well.

The decisive critique to be made of the treatment of Joan of Arc by her judges at Rouen is a critique that can be made as well of such recent conduct [I could say in 1977] as the unhappy American role in the Vietnam War and our sometimes excessive responses to the Watergate revelations.[61] I remind you of a salutary maxim for such situations: one should not do evil in the hope that good may come. One must take care, that is, lest "a certain and positive evil be produced for the purpose of effecting an uncertain, remote, and very doubtful good."[62]

I return, as I close, to the Odysseus of Sophocles' *Ajax*. Odysseus is, in some respects, superior to Athena herself. Certainly, he seems to instruct that goddess in compassion, drawing upon the humanity that she is not privileged to share.[63] It is Odysseus who persuades his vindictive fellow kings that honorable burial should be permitted the body of Ajax.[64] And it is Odysseus who can say of the insanely murderous Ajax, even while he is still alive,

> Yet I pity his wretchedness, though he is my enemy, for the terrible yoke of blindness that is on him. I think of him, yet also of myself; for I see the true state of all of us that live—we are dim shapes, no more, and weightless shadows.[65]

Perhaps it takes such manly compassion, grounded in an awareness of human limitations, if those in power are to be purged of that self-righteousness and other shortcomings that stand in the way both of thoughtfulness and of decent conduct.

NOTES

1. This talk was given in the Law Lecture Series at Rosary College (now Dominican University), River Forest, Illinois, February 3, 1977. I have found useful the cautions offered by Professor Françoise Meltzer, of the University of Chicago, upon reading this talk. See Françoise Meltzer, *For Fear of the Fire: Joan of Arc and the Limits of Subjectivity* (Chicago: University of Chicago Press, 2001).

2. See *Jeremiah* 28:1–17. See also Moses Maimonides, *The Guide of the Perplexed* (Chicago: University of Chicago Press, 1963), bk II, chaps. 32–48.

3. See William Shakespeare, *Henry VI, Part 2*, II, i. See also Plutarch, *Life of Numa*.

4. See *Hellenic Chronicle* (Boston, Massachusetts), January 6, 1977, p. 10 (taken, it seems, from the *Saturday Evening Post*).

5. See Sophocles, *Ajax* 14–17:

Voice of Athena, dearest utterance of all the gods' to me—I cannot see you, and yet how clearly I can catch your words, that speak as from a trumpet's throat of bronze!

This is in the John Moore translation, published in *The Complete Greek Tragedies* by the University of Chicago Press. See also chapter 7-B, Section XIII.

6. See *The Trial of Jeanne d'Arc*, Wilfred Phillips Barrett, ed. (New York: Gotham House, 1922; reprinted in The Notable Trials Library, 1991), pp. 131, 197–98; Wilfred T. Jewkes and Jerome B. Landfield, eds., *Joan of Arc: Fact, Legend, and Literature* (New York: Harcourt, Brace & World, 1964), pp. 6–9. See also *Exodus* 3:2–6; Augustine, *Confessions* (Mentor Edition, 1963), p. 456 ("Suddenly a voice reaches my ears from a nearby house. It is the voice of a boy or a girl [I don't know which] and in a kind of singsong the words are constantly repeated: 'Take it and read it. Take it and read it.'"); Ann Stafford, *Bernadette and Lourdes* (London: Hodder and Stoughton, 1967), pp. 43, 53–54, 59, 74, 76, 81–82 (1967). See as well *Chicago Tribune*, February 2, 1977, sec. 4, p. 1:

Margaret Court, one of the world's winningest professional tennis players, claims to have seen visions from heaven.

Court, a [34-year-old] Roman Catholic, wasn't pushing her religious beliefs. They just came out during questioning at the luncheon gathering.

"I had visions on and off for about three months," she said.

She said about 14 months ago "I saw Our Lady on the wall. The next day I was praying about it. I had a tremendous urge in the middle of the day to pray. I put my hands up to my face and I heard this voice say: 'Open the gate and you shall see on the other side.'

"And then I saw a child going to church. I was still confused and thought I might be seeing things. Then I went to prayer again. I put my hands up to my face and saw like a big window and I was looking down at earth. It was in a turmoil. I'll never forget it.

"And then I saw a cross on top of a hill. . . . Behind this cross there were brilliant flashing lights with all colors. And then an archway. It took me three days to really believe what I was seeing."

Her visions began shortly after her return home [to Australia in 1975], she said, soon after she read a book about the Holy Spirit.

Joan of Arc evidently did not usually expect any of her earthly companions to hear the voices she did, even if they were present when the voices spoke to her. See chapter 8, note 47. See also *Acts of the Apostles* 22:9, 26:14. Compare 9:7. See, on Augustine, George Anastaplo, "Rome, Piety, and Law: Explorations," 39 *Loyola of New Orleans Law Review* 2, 83 (1993); George Anastaplo, "Teaching, Nature, and the Moral Virtues," 1997 *The Great Ideas Today* 2 (1997).

7. See Sophocles, *Ajax* 18–20.

8. Sophocles, *Ajax*, 51–52. See also chapter 9, note 49.

9. Sophocles, *Ajax*, 22.

10. Sophocles, *Ajax*, 69–82.

11. Sigmund Freud, *New Introductory Lectures on Psychoanalysis* (New York: W. W. Norton & Co., 1965), p. 59. See also Abraham Lincoln's poem on the madness of Matthew Gentry, *Collected Works of Abraham Lincoln*, Roy P. Basler, ed. (New Brunswick, N.J.: Rutgers University Press, 1953), 1: 384–86; George Anastaplo, *Abraham Lincoln: A Constitutional Biography* (Lanham, Md.: Rowman & Littlefield, 1999), pp. 131, 139, 143–45, 298–300. See as well chapter 5, note 4.

12. *New Catholic Encyclopedia*, 7: 992–93 (New York: McGraw-Hill, 1967).

13. See Vita Sackville-West, *Saint Joan of Arc* (New York: The Literary Guild, 1936), p. 286.

14. See Georges Bernanos, *Sanctity Will Win Out: An Essay on St. Joan* (New York: Sheed and Ward, 1947), p. 11:

> There was the illustrious University of Paris, and more especially the Theological Faculty. The Popes themselves feared this Faculty; it was the sovereign arbiter of kings, made up as it was of almost all of the eminent theologians . . . of whom the Christendom of that day could boast.

I am reminded here of the eminent University of Chicago faculty and how they could be led in the 1960s by *their* "Bishop of Beauvais" to put down the presumptuous young of their own day. See, e.g., George Anastaplo, *Human Being and Citizen: Essays on Virtue, Freedom and the Common Good* (Chicago: Swallow Press, 1975), pp. 263 n. 9, 286–87 n. 10. See also George Anastaplo, "*In re* Allan Bloom: A Respectful Dissent," in Robert L. Stone, ed., *Essays on "The Closing of The American Mind"* (Chicago: Chicago Review Press, 1989), p. 267; George Anastaplo, "Legal Education, Economics, and Law School Governance: Explorations," 46 *South Dakota Law Review* 102, 304 (2001). See as well the appendixes to this collection.

15. See "Joan of Arc," 22 *Encyclopedia Britannica* 379–80 (1988). Compare Alan M. Dershowitz's Introduction, in *The Trial of Jeanne d'Arc* (Notable Trials Library, 1991), pp. ii–iii:

> It is in the nature of formal legal proceedings to often disguise substantive injustices. In reading through transcripts of trials that we now know were fixed, it is often difficult to spot the smoking guns. The fixing generally takes place outside of the glare of the official record. Judges know how—and knew how in the fifteenth century—to "due process a defendant to death." The writer of the essay that closes this volume tells us that we are reading not only the trial of Joan of Arc, but also the trial of her judges. Surely that is true, but as twentieth century readers, we are not privy to the worst crimes of the judges—the secret crimes, the unspoken crimes, the covered up crimes.

See, for a summary of the charges against Joan, chapter 8, note 28.

16. 7 *New Catholic Encyclopedia* 993.

17. See 22 *Encyclopedia Britannica* 380 (1988).

18. See 28 *Encyclopedia Britannica* (1988). She did manage to avoid being tortured. See also the text at note 35 of chapter 8 of this collection.

19. See 22 *Encyclopedia Britannica* 378–80 (1988).

20. See *Encyclopedia Britannica*, 22: 380.

21. Albert Bigelow Paine, *Joan of Arc, Maid of France* (New York: Macmillan, 1925), I, vi.

22. See Larry Weintraub, "The People Place," *Chicago Sun-Times*, February 1, 1977, p, 10.

23. Weintraub, "The People Place," I, vi. See, on Churchill's questionable suggestion about the disposition of the worst Nazis, the text at note 69 of chapter 12 of this collection.

24. The lively Churchill account is marred by several errors of fact.

25. Winston S. Churchill, *A History of the English-Speaking Peoples* (New York: Bantam Books, 1963), I, 305, 308–09. See also chapter 10, note 78. Both Churchill (in his *History*) and George Bernard Shaw (in his play, *Saint Joan*) make up, as stalwarts in the English language, for the somewhat unfriendly treatment of Joan of Arc by Shakespeare in his *Henry VI, Part I*. Shakespeare was, to some extent, a victim of his political and social circumstances. See, for another instance of this, chapter 9 of this collection. But in some ways Shakespeare's treatment of Joan is more respectful than it seems on the surface.

26. See 22 *Encyclopedia Britannica* 378 (1988).

27. *Encyclopedia Britannica*, 22: 378.

28. *Encyclopedia Britannica*, 22: 378. "When the trial proper began [on about March 26], it took two days for Joan to answer the 70 charges that had been drawn up against her. These were based mainly on the contention that her whole attitude and behaviour showed blasphemous presumption: in particular, that she claimed for her pronouncements the authority of divine revelation; prophesied the future; endorsed her letters with the names of Jesus and Mary, thereby identifying herself with the novel and suspect cult of the Name of Jesus; professed to be assured of salvation; and wore men's clothing. Perhaps the most serious charge was of preferring what she believed to be the direct commands of God to those of the church." *Encyclopedia Britannica*, 22: 378. See chapter 8, notes 33, 36, 42, 43, 53. See, on blasphemy, chapter 7, note 31.

29. 22 *Encyclopedia Britannica* 378 (1998).

30. See, e.g., chapter 8, note 15. See also Walter Sidney Scott, *Jeanne d'Arc* (London: Harrap, 1974).

31. See, for example, the report of an observer in Jewkes and Landfield, eds., *Joan of Arc*, p. 71: "And Joan said [to the Bishop of Beauvais], 'Oh, you write down everything that is against me all right, but you will not record anything in my favor.' And I do not believe that remark was written down, either, though it aroused a great uproar in the court." Consider also the temperament of Saint Hugh, Bishop of Lincoln, who can sometimes seem to be Joan's soulmate. See the text at note 29 of chapter 6.

32. The 1945–1946 Nuremberg Trial was similar in key respects, but that did not necessarily prevent a fair judgment. See chapter 12-A.

33. Compare chapter 5, note 37, chapter 8, note 51. It is helpful, in thinking about Joan, to consider not only the dreadful centuries-long European experience with witch trials but also the spectacular career of Antigone of Thebes. See chapter 1, note 95, chapter 4-B. See also chapter 8, note 44. Don Quixote, with his canny idealism, should also be instructive here. See chapter 5, note 1. See, on the European witch trials, George Anastaplo, "Church and State: Explorations," 19 *Loyola University of*

Chicago Law Journal 61, 65 (1987). See, on Don Quixote, George Anastaplo, "Lawyers, First Principles, and Contemporary Challenges: Explorations," 19 *Northern Illinois University Law Review* 353, 437 (1999).

Central to the challenge posed by Joan of Arc was her willingness to be guided by her voices in disregarding conventional authority: "Asked [during her trial] whether she thought she had committed a sin when she left her father and mother, she answered that since God commanded, it was right to do so. She added that since God commanded, if she had had a hundred parents, or had been the king's daughter, she would have gone nevertheless." *The Trial of Jeanne d'Arc*, Barrett, ed., p. 98. See chapter 8, note 44. See also chapter 8, note 65; the text at notes 25 and 47 of chapter 9 of this collection. Compare chapter 7, note 40.

34. See 22 *Encyclopedia Britannica* 379–80 (1998).

35. See chapter 8, note 18.

36. *The Trial of Jeanne d'Arc*, Barrett, ed., p. 343. See chapter 8, note 28.

37. See *The Trial of Jeanne d'Arc*, Barrett, ed., pp. 343–45.

38. *The Trial of Jeanne d'Arc*, Barrett, ed., pp. 350–51.

39. Joan was "introduced" to St. Catherine and St. Margaret by St. Michael. See *The Trial of Jeanne d'Arc*, Barrett, ed., p. 60. See also 22 *Encyclopedia Britannica* 377 (1988).

40. A (stolen?) bishop's horse is brought up from time to time. See, e.g., *The Trial of Jeanne d'Arc*, Barrett, ed., p. 116. See also A. Ernestine Jones, *The Trial of Joan of Arc* (London: Barry Rose, 1980), p. 97.

41. See, e.g., "Heresy," 6 *New Catholic Encyclopedia* 1063 (1967).

42. It was ultimately on the issue of submission that the great proto-Protestant leader John Hus had been burned in 1415. See chapter 8, note 28.

43. "To her judges [Joan] was guilty of what they called 'superbity,' by which they meant the enormity of knowing that she was right when they told her she was wrong." Scott, *Jeanne d'Arc*, p. 145. See chapter 8, note 33; chapter 8, note 65; chapter 10, note 66. See also chapter 7, notes 66, 101. The condemnation of Joan included these observations by her judges: "We, having Christ and *the honor* of the orthodox faith before our eyes, so that our judgment may seem to emanate from the face of Our Lord, have said and decreed that in the simulation of your revelations and apparitions you have been pernicious, seductive, presumptuous, of light belief, rash, superstitious, a witch, a blasphemer of God and His saints, a despiser of Him in His sacraments, a prevaricator of the divine teaching and the ecclesiastical sanctions, seditious, cruel, apostate, schismatic, erring gravely in our faith, and that by these means you have rashly trespassed against God and the Holy Church." *The Trial of Jeanne d'Arc*, Barrett, ed., pp. 364–65 (emphasis added). See chapter 8, notes 28, 33, chapter 8, note 44. See also chapter 7, note 63. See, on religious allegiances and honor, chapter 7, note 49.

44. Compare Antigone's opinions about the proper relation of politics to religion. See chapter 8, note 33. The European context of Joan's early fifteenth-century challenge to the established way is suggested by this account of intellectual developments:

In the eleventh and twelfth centuries a trickle of Greek learning, mostly Arabic redactions of Aristotle and Hippocrates, had touched off a remarkable but still ecclesiastically controlled burst of creativity by the much-maligned Schoolmen. By the fifteenth and sixteenth centuries, however, the trickle was a flood, and common life was being de-sacralized.

Charles R. Morris, "The Three Ages of the Catholic Church," *The Atlantic*, July 1991, p. 108. Joan of Arc, with her apparent independence of mind, anticipated in certain ways the "Americanism" heresy condemned by Roman Catholic Churchmen in the nineteenth century. See Morris, "The Three Ages of the Catholic Church," p. 110. See also appendix D, note 4. She refused to say that she would submit in all things to the authority of the Church: "What Our Lord told her and shall tell her to do she will not cease from doing for any man alive. It would be impossible for her to deny them [that is, the things she has said and done with respect to the visions and revelations she claimed to have from God], and in the event of the Church commanding her to do anything contrary to God's bidding, she would by no means undertake it." *The Trial of Jeanne d'Arc*, Barrett, ed., pp. 240–41. See chapter 8, note 33. See also chapter 8, note 65, chapter 10, note 66. See, on Antigone and her family, chapter 4.

45. See, on Henry VIII, chapter 10, Section III.

46. See 22 *Encyclopedia Britannica* 380 (1988).

47. See *The Trial of Jeanne d'Arc*, Barrett, ed., pp. 123–24; the text at note 38 of chapter 8 of this collection. Was not Joan's abjuration essentially *hypothetical*? See the text at note 37 of chapter 8 of this collection. It must have been evident to some of the men who dealt with Joan that she continued to believe that she had heard the voices of saints, etc. See *The Trial of Jeanne d'Arc*, Barrett, ed., pp. 349–51.

Why did not Joan expect her voices (1) to appear to her judges and tell *them* to leave her alone, and (2) to do other things on her behalf? (Would she not have been insane if she *had* believed that the voices had appeared to *them* when they had not?) What did Joan finally believe her voices "wanted" to happen to her? See chapter 8, note 65. See also chapter 12, note 5. See as well chapter 5, note 39, chapter 9, section IX.

48. See, e.g., chapter 10, section VIII of this collection; chapter 10, notes 75, 78; the text at note 75 of chapter 10 of this collection. See also Anastaplo, *The American Moralist*, pp. 345–48; Anastaplo, *Human Being and Citizen*, pp. 46–60; chapter 12-A.

49. See, e.g., Anastaplo, *Human Being and Citizen*, pp. 46–60.

50. The devilish connection would be regarded by some to be evident not only in the second of these possibilities (the visions sent by the Devil), but in the third and fourth as well (the hallucinations and the deliberate deceptions). It is instructive, in considering Joan's accounts of the coming of the visions and her initial responses to them, to consult Maimonides, *The Guide of the Perplexed*, pp. 385–86, 388, 390, 394, 402, 406, 409. See chapter 8, note 2.

51. Maimonides cautions his reader that, in interpreting accounts of prophecies, one should not confuse "the possible things with the impossible ones." *The Guide of the Perplexed*, p. 406. See chapter 3, note 4, chapter 10, note 26. See also George Anastaplo, "On Trial: Explorations," 22 *Loyola University Chicago Law Journal* 765, 1054 n. 344 (1991). See as well chapter 1, note 65, chapter 5.

52. See 14 *New Catholic Encyclopedia* 717 (1967). The Church's complicated experience with Bernadette of Lourdes is instructive. See chapter 8, note 6. See, on the credentials of Muhammed as messenger, George Anastaplo, *But Not Philosophy: Seven Introductions to Non-Western Thought* (Lanham, Md.: Lexington Books, 2002), chap. 6.

53. This we can assert even though she was denounced as being presumptuous herself. See chapter 8, note 43.

54. Consider, for example, the career of Charles de Gaulle. See Henri Bernstein, "Charles de Gaulle and Joan of Arc," *New York Herald Tribune*, May 7, 1943. The author, a French dramatist, wrote:

> Now that De Gaulle's powerful speeches and the consistency and dignity of his leadership have invalidated the suspicion of political commitments, mockery has become the chosen weapon. A titter circulates among smart and critical groups: "The man believes he is Joan of Arc!" This reminds me somehow of a famous squib on Victor Hugo: "The poor devil actually thinks he is Victor Hugo!"
>
> Perhaps some of De Gaulle's aides have used this historical parallel too freely as an argument in discussion. I am pretty sure, though, that the partisans of the Maid were not all cautious diplomats when it came to expressing their faith. But if those who liken the miracle of De Gaulle to that of Joan of Arc are fools, I am one of those fools.

Thereafter Bernstein wrote,

> De Gaulle is difficult. He is stubborn. He is grave. So was the Maid. Like the Maid, he has a mystic view of France's destiny and sacred rights.

De Gaulle did identify himself as fighting under the Cross of Lorraine. (The family of Jeanne d'Arc *was* from Lorraine.)

55. See Scott, *Jeanne d'Arc*, p. 133. Would Odysseus, if an Egyptian, have had special relations with Isis instead of with Athena? I have long found it intriguing that those people afflicted with Tourette's syndrome do not (cannot?) simply disguise their embarrassing outbursts by putting them in a foreign language (however else they do try to conceal those outbursts). That is, are not their circumstances determining the form that their "inspired" manifestations take? Do they somehow want to be noticed and "understood?" (Could they, today, disguise their outbursts by pretending to be talking on cell phones? What do they "really" want in their relations with others? See chapter 5, note 39.)

56. There *is* a problem with mental aberrations: they all too often do reflect underlying moral attitudes—and those who deal with such aberrations can sometimes sense those moral attitudes to be dubious. See, on the trials of witches in Europe, chapter 8, note 33.

57. This is what had been done with the Duke of Orleans. See Jewkes and Landfield, eds., *Joan of Arc*, p. 12.

58. See Anastaplo, "Church and State," pp. 80–82. See also chapter 12-B.

59. See Abraham Lincoln's Second Inaugural Address: "The Almighty has His own purposes. Woe unto the world because of offences! for it must needs be that of-

fenses come but woe to that man by whom the offence cometh!'" See George Anastaplo, *The Constitution of 1787: A Commentary* (Baltimore: Johns Hopkins University Press, 1989), p. 301; George Anastaplo, "Abraham Lincoln and the American Regime: Explorations," 35 *Valparaiso University Law Review* 39, 137 (2000).

60. See, for example, Subrahmanyan Chandrasekhar's observations:

[Consider] the following statement of Einstein: "The most incomprehensible fact about Nature is that it is comprehensible." This expresses a profound truth and it is echoed in the writings of other great men of science. Thus, Eugene Wigner has written of the two miracles: "the miracle of the existence of laws of Nature and the miracle of the capacity of the human mind to divine them"; and he has also written about "the unreasonable effectiveness of mathematics in the understanding of Nature." And Schrödinger considers that this latter capacity of the human mind to divine nature's laws may well be beyond human understanding.

Commenting on the discovery of Kepler [with respect to the orbits of the planets in our solar system], Einstein has written: "Our admiration for Kepler is transcended only by our admiration and reverence for the mysterious harmony of Nature in which we find ourselves. Already in antiquity, man had devised curves exhibiting the simplest forms of regularity. Among these, next to the straight line and the circle, the most important were the ellipse and the hyperbola. We see that the last two are embodied—at least very nearly so—in the orbits of heavenly bodies."

Einstein continues: "It seems that the human mind has first to construct forms, independently, before we can find them in things. Kepler's marvelous achievement is a particularly fine example of the fact that knowledge cannot spring from experience alone but only from a comparison of the inventions of the intellect with the facts of observation." Let me repeat the crucial part of this remarkable statement: "The human mind has first to construct forms, independently, before we can find them in things".

S. Chandrasekhar, "Science and Scientific Attitudes," 334 *Nature* 285 (1990). See Plato, *Gorgias* 507E-508A; Anastaplo, *But Not Philosophy*, pp. 272f. See also Anastaplo, *Human Being and Citizen*, pp. 252–53 n. 30; chapter 1, notes 3, 91; chapter 2, notes 30, 31; conclusion, note 3. See as well Anastaplo, "On Trial" (*Loyola Law Journal*), p. 1053 n. 337. See, on Professor Chandrasekhar, George Anastaplo, "Thursday Afternoons," in Kameshwar C. Wali, ed., *S. Chandrasekhar: The Man Behind the Legend* (London: Imperial College Press, 1997), p. 122.

See, on the perennial problem of "the stability of excellence," Leo Strauss, *Thoughts on Machiavelli* (Glencoe, Illinois: The Free Press, 1958), p. 295.

61. See, e.g., chapter 12, parts D and E. Still another excessive response was to the unjustified Iraqi invasion of Kuwait. See, e.g., Patrick E. Tyler, "Disease Spreads in Iraq as Embargo Takes Its Toll," *New York Times*, June 24, 1991, p. 1. See also chapter 12, notes 6, 28, 48, 56, 105. See, on the 1991 Gulf War, George Anastaplo, "On Freedom: Explorations," 17 *Oklahoma City University Law Review* 465, 589, 604 (1992).

See, for preliminary assessments of the responses to the fiendish attacks of September 11, 2001, George Anastaplo, Letters to Editors, *Chicago Tribune*, September 21, 2001, sec. 1, p. 26; *Chicago Daily Law Bulletin*, September 28, 2001, p. 2; *Chicago Sun-Times*, October 2, 2001, p. 38; *University of Chicago Maroon*, October 2, 2001, p. 8 (conclusion, note 3); *New York Times*, October 13, 2001, p. A22; *Chicago*

Sun-Times, November 20, 2001, p. 30 (chapter 10, note 78); *Chicago Weekly News* (The University of Chicago), Janaury 31, 2002, p. 13 (appendix A, note 15); *Chicago Sun-Times*, April 9, 2002, p. 26; *Chicago Daily Law Bulletin*, June 13, 2002, p. 2; *Chicago Sun-Times*, June 20, 2002, p. 30.

Consider as another assessment of these matters my Letter to the Editor about the John Walker Lindh matter (July 2002):

> Much, perhaps most, of our effort on behalf of Homeland Security has been, for some time now, woefully misdirected, thereby wasting tremendous resources (both spiritual and material) that could be put to much better uses for the common good.
>
> It will be a sign that we as a people have begun to recover our balance, morally as well as politically, when it comes to be generally recognized how unduly, if not even cynically, dramatized the conduct is which has evidently gotten a silly young man a twenty-year sentence for "providing service to the Taliban."
>
> Much more dubious "service" is routinely provided to evil-doing by the fearful and uninformed among us who invest would-be terrorists with far more power and enduring influence than they are ever likely to have.

See *Chicago Daily Law Bulletin*, July 22, 2002, p. 2; *Chicago Tribune*, July 24, 2002, sec. 1, p. 18. See also chapter 10, note 78. See as well chapter 11, note 12.

See, on the promotion of a sound moral order worldwide, Anastaplo, *But Not Philosophy*, p. 303; appendix A, note 15. Consider, on a salutary public piety, my Letter to the Editor of July 2002:

> It would be virtually impossible for the federal courts, even if they should want to do so, to keep the "under God" invocation out of routine recitals of the Pledge of Allegiance these days.
>
> An effort should be made to be clear about what the current controversy is, and is not, about. The President has proclaimed, to great applause in West Virginia, "No authority of government can ever prevent an American from pledging allegiance to this one nation under God." (July 4, 2002). That kind of talk, however, simply does not address the fundamental issue in this situation, which is whether governmental authority can properly require citizens (especially schoolchildren, it turns out) to affirm a particular opinion about the role of Divine Providence in the affairs of this most fortunate Country.
>
> Be that as it may, no one should question the right, perhaps on occasion even the duty, of our leaders to speak piously about grand matters of state, something heard so eloquently done in President Lincoln's Gettysburg Address and in his Second Inaugural Address. But Abraham Lincoln resisted throughout his life the demands of his more zealous fellow-citizens that he conform publicly to the creeds and devotional practices of the dominant religious movements of his day.

See *Chicago Daily Law Bulletin*, July 8, 2002, p. 2

62. See Anastaplo, *Human Being and Citizen*, p. 305 note 3 (quoting Lord Cockburn).

63. See Sophocles, *Ajax* 118–133.

64. See Sophocles, *Ajax*, 1315–1402. Ajax had killed himself when he discovered how deluded and hence ridiculous he had been in his slaughter of the helpless animals. See the text at note 7 of chapter 8 of this collection.

65. Sophocles, *Ajax* 121–126. I have suggested that Antigone of Thebes anticipates Joan of Arc in some ways. But does not the deluded Ajax, with his private "revelations" about the animals he slaughters, also anticipate Joan? See the text at note 8
of chapter 8 of this collection. If one believes, as Joan evidently did, that "Our Lord
Jesus Christ, when he ascended into Heaven, committed the government of His
Church to the apostle St. Peter and his successors," was not the Church prudent to insist upon more credentials than Joan offered? Did not Joan depend upon the Church
for *most* of what she believed about spiritual matters, including about the very saints
she relied upon in opposing the authority of the Church? See *The Trial of Jeanne
d'Arc*, Barrett, ed., pp. 336–40. See also chapter 8, notes 43, 47, chapter 10, note 26.
And yet was it not simply wrong to execute her? Her canonization, too, raises complicated questions—and perhaps helps explain why it took five centuries to do it?
(Did the Church finally come around to recognizing what the people of France had already done with Joan? Similarly, in 1950, did the Church formally recognize what her
people at large had long believed about the bodily ascension of Mary? See George
Anastaplo, "Liberation Pedagogy," 39 *Cross Currents* 463, 467 n. 6 [1989–1990]
[with numerous unauthorized editorial revisions].) See chapter 8, notes 33, 44. See
also the text at note 78 of chapter 10 of this collection.

Still, we can recognize that we hear *her* voice: She has captured our imagination,
just as something had captured hers? However self-regarding one's piety may routinely be in critical respects, Joan's piety *was* in the service of her *patria*. It is significantly (and cheerfully!) different from the emphasis upon self-expression (or self-
indulgence), without regard to consequences, that we have become accustomed to.
See chapter 13. See also Anastaplo, "On Trial" (*Loyola Law Journal*), pp. 880–81.

Consider as well this exchange between Anne Hutchinson and her Massachusetts
inquisitors in the middle of the seventeenth century:

Q. How do you know that was the spirit [of God]?
A. How did Abraham know that it was God that bid him offer his son, being a breech of
the Sixth Commandment?
Q. By an immediate voice.
A. So to me by an immediate revelation.

The Antinomian Controversy, 1636–1638, David D. Hall, ed. (Middletown, Conn.:
Wesleyan University Press, 1968). Compare chapter 5, note 39.

9

Shylock and Shakespeare[1]

I.

The ugliest play written by William Shakespeare may well be *The Merchant of Venice*. It is a play in which considerable hate and little generosity are exhibited, although there is in it much talk of love and mercy. Even some of the sacrifices made in the name of love, about which sacrifices one also hears much in the play, seem to be due at least in part to a hatred of one's life, if not of life itself. This may be seen in the career of Antonio, the merchant who ventures his life in securing the money needed by his friend Bassanio in order to court the wealthy Portia. (I, i, 1–7, 77–92; I, iii, 139–55; II, ix, 90; IV, i, 111–18)

There are, no doubt, other plays by Shakespeare that have ugly features, plays such as *Macbeth*, *Measure for Measure*, *King Lear*, *The Winter's Tale*, and *Troilus and Cressida*.[2] But these plays usually have redeeming characters or features that lighten the overall effect. Portia may be intended as such a character in *The Merchant of Venice* and the wholesale indulgence in love at her estate (Belmont) as such a feature. (V, i, 1f) But, I confess, these effects are largely lost on me. There is hardly anyone in the play whom I can *like*. Bassanio may be an exception; but he *is* a spendthrift, and it is silly for him, in the circumstances, to allow his friend Antonio to risk his life as he does in order to secure ready cash for Bassanio. (I, i, 126–34)

I have long found the play troubling and troublesome. At the root of the trouble may be the fact that the kind of conflict presented here, especially when grounded in religion, is likely to degrade everyone involved. Making matters even more troublesome is one's perhaps naive expectation that poetry should be a thing of beauty instead of the ugly exhibition that this play is. Especially ugly is how Jews—not just Shylock but all Jews who remain Jews—are meant to be portrayed in this play. I have been deeply puzzled for some forty years [I could say in 1983] about the passions that permitted, and even moved, the Germans to slaughter the Jews as they did during World War II—and about the passions that have contributed to other such massive persecutions of Jews over the centuries. One can see in this play something of what it was that permitted Jews to be regarded almost as a species apart. Shakespeare helps us see these things, perhaps in part because he himself may have shared (or at least remembered having shared) some of the sentiments, or passions, at the root of the vicious animus against Jews in Christendom.[3]

Still, it should at once be added, people do like the play, including various Jewish friends of mine whom I have consulted about it. (I will consider later some of their reasons.) One or two of Shylock's speeches do appeal to people generally, as does the celebrated "quality of mercy" speech by Portia. (III, i, 51f; IV, i, 182f) One must wonder, of course, whether Shakespeare intended at least these speeches to be remembered and to have a salutary effect, if anything of the play survived. Even so, I continue to find the play grating on the soul, even atrocious in some respects.

I remind you that this play is about a Jew-baiting merchant who, for the sake of his friend's courtship of Portia, borrows money from a wealthy Jew who hates him in turn and who requires of him the notorious "pound of flesh" bond. (I, iii,145–46) This bond turns out to be something that the lender, one Shylock, can foreclose on when the payment is not made in time, with the borrower being saved, at the last minute, only by the ingenuity of Portia disguised as a judge. (IV, i, 164f) I return to the ugliness of the play by also reminding you of various of its features:

1. the original bond, its terms and the terrible passions concealed in it (I, iii, 37f);
2. the hard-hearted way in which Shylock insists upon the execution of its monstrous forfeiture provision (III, i, 44f);
3. the callous way in which Jessica betrays her father Shylock, who, so far as we know, had always cared for her (II, iii, 1f);
4. the cynical way in which Portia sets aside the deadly bond, deliberately destroying Shylock in the process, when there were commonsensical ways available for nullifying the unconscionable contract in a more humane manner (IV, i, 319f);
5. the thoughtless way in which the unfaithful daughter of Shylock is received by Portia, Bassanio, and others, and her further betrayal of her father in their company (III, ii, 284f);

6. the unrelenting character of the way Shylock is humiliated, including his forced conversion to "Christianity" (IV, i, 331f);

7. Shylock's own hatred of Christians, especially of Antonio, and the hostility of others that provoked or at least fueled his hatred (I, iii, 37f).

It seems to be assumed in the play that Jews *will* be, perhaps even should be, treated hostilely by others so long as they remain Jews. (I, iii, 45–48) This is so even in a commercial society such as Venice, where Jews can be regarded as useful for the financial life of the city. In fact, Jews may be even more vulnerable in a place such as Venice, because there is much about that kind of community that encourages Jews to relax their vigilance and that permits citizens the liberty of expressing themselves.[4] Consider the significance of the title of this play, *The Merchant of Venice*. Can the kind of problem investigated here, depending upon both the status and the presumptuousness of the outsider, arise only in a community where largely impersonal commercial relations rule? A Jew such as Shylock would never have had either the opportunity or the effrontery to attempt in ancient Rome (that is, in ancient Italy) what he tries to do in Venice (in modern Italy). It is revealing that deliverance for Antonio comes from someone with a Roman name. (I, i, 165–66) There can be seen here a reassertion of the prerogatives of the political community and of a prudence of sorts.[5]

Thus, it can be said, the ugliness of the play comes, in part, from its laying bare the bones and sinews of a commercial society. One feature of such a society is suggested by the observation by a law school faculty colleague who has pointed out, "It is certainty in the enforcement of contracts that permits calculations of risk upon which commerce depends and thrives."[6] And he adds, "Antonio does default, and Shylock insists upon the forfeiture. This conflict is resolved by a judicial decision that not only saves Antonio's life, but also preserves inviolate the principles of the law of contract and the practice of certainty in their enforcement."[7] Something of this old-fashioned attitude, about the vital importance of "certainty in the enforcement of contracts," may be seen in a recent *New York Times* article describing the continuance in Hong Kong of imprisonment for debt. The article opens, "Not many places still put people in prison for owing money, but then not many places take money as seriously as does this outpost of unbridled capitalism."[8]

We must now consider how Jews are presented by Shakespeare and perhaps why, including the instructive insights he does have about the worldly shrewdness of Jews. Questionable features of the Jewish as well as of the Christian character, as presented by Shakespeare, will be touched upon. Also to be touched upon are those limitations in Shakespeare himself that his treatment of Jews may expose to view. Before venturing upon these delicate matters, however, it is well to remind ourselves of something that even the great Shakespeare himself seems not to have been properly aware of, the deep sense of humanity to be found in Judaism. For this purpose I draw upon a story told in materials I picked up at a Yom Kippur service I looked in on a fortnight ago:

> It was late in the afternoon on Yom Kippur. Rabbi Levi Yitzhak had been praying in the Berditchev synagogue all day.
>
> For a moment, he closed his tired eyes. Suddenly, he was before the Judgment Seat of God. The fate of humanity was being weighed in the great scales. Alas, the sins were heavy; the prospects for humanity were bleak.
>
> Rabbi Levi Yitzhak pleaded with God: "If you wanted us to be angels, You should have let us remain in the Garden of Eden. But You sent us out into the world! And the daily struggles often put us into the hands of sin."
>
> The Lord was moved and motioned the rabbi to a chair at His side. The rabbi continued. His appeal was sincere and convincing. The scales began to tilt in humanity's favor.
>
> Suddenly, the rabbi heard a piteous cry. He looked down to earth, into the tiny Berditchev synagogue. Haim, the washerman, fasting on this holiest day, had fainted from hunger. Levi Yitzhak rose to leave, to hurry back to earth to conclude the service—so that Haim could break his fast.
>
> A voice called after him: "Levi Yitzhak! Where are you going? You were on the verge of saving the world." Replied Levi Yitzhak: "Where is it written that the price of salvation must be the life of Haim, the washerman?"
>
> And he left. As he hurried on his way, a great chorus of angels sang: "Levi Yitzhak, you *are* saving the world!"[9]

II.

However all this may be, Shylock is no Rabbi Levi Yatzhak, exquisitely sensitive to the claims of humanity. The thing that Shylock proposes to do—deliberately to take a fatal pound of flesh from Antonio—is surely monstrous not only to do but even seriously to want to do. And, it sometimes seems to me, Shakespeare would have us understand that Shylock's monstrousness may be intimately related to Judaism. It is not accidental that *he* should be the one who wants to do this; it is not just the doing of one peculiarly demented Jew, but rather of a respected member of his community. We are shown the conversation between him and another Jew, who never counsels Shylock against what he proposes to do. (III, i, 109–12) It does seem that Shakespeare believes that the Jewish community in a city such as Venice might tolerate, if not approve of, this kind of conduct by one of its members.[10]

True, Shylock had been grievously provoked by Antonio's abuse of him. (I, iii, 44–47) He is angered as well by Antonio's insistence upon lending money without charge, which keeps interest down. (I, iii, 39–40; III, i, 112–13) It *is* a much-reviled, much put-upon man who strikes back as Shylock does. But whatever Antonio may have done, either by his calumnies or by his competition, he surely was not guilty of a capital offense.[11]

It should be noticed as well that there is also something monstrous in Antonio's desire for martyrdom. (IV, i, 262–79) After all, there *were*, as I have suggested, commonsensical responses nullifying the contract that Shylock was attempting to enforce. The very fact that a contract provision was entered into for "merry sport," as Shylock originally put his proposed forfeiture arrangement (I, iii, 141), could easily provide the basis for finding that forfeiture provision void as not having been truly agreed upon. It should have been enough for Antonio to say, "Man, you know that my witnesses and I never took this seriously, whatever you may have wanted or even believed in your heart of hearts!" On the other hand, if the forfeiture provision was indeed valid, then Portia's "drop of blood" exception (IV, i, 308) would not make sense, since a *valid* contract implies the likely means necessary for its execution.[12]

Aside from the question of whether there had been enough evidence of an agreement to warrant the finding that a "pound of flesh" contract had truly been entered into here, there is also the question of whether such an unjust and destructive arrangement is one that the law can countenance at all. (IV, i, 345–54)[13]

The monstrousness of Christianity in this play may be evident not only in the appetite for martyrdom in Antonio (a Christ-like figure) but perhaps also in the very monstrousness of Shylock. He is, in critical respects, a "reaction" to the Christianity of his time and place.[14] That there is something critically wrong with Judaism and Christianity alike in Venice may be suggested in what Jessica can do—both in that she does to her trusting father what she does and in that she is received as she is by the Christians who know what she has done.[15]

Various commentators have argued that Shakespeare "humanizes" Shylock, making him far less of a stock villain, much more a man of sensibilities, etc., than other playwrights of the era did with Jewish characters on stage.[16] But may it not make matters worse to have Shylock be as "human" as he is and still be monstrous?[17] True, there may be something noble in Shylock's preferring revenge to his money, even a threefold amount of money, but it is a peculiarly perverted nobility. He is shown reverting to a baser level, once the elation due to his desire for revenge is dissipated, when he asks for his money back after Portia pounces. (IV, i, 207–08)[18]

To say that Shakespeare humanizes Shylock is to say that he knew better than his contemporary playwrights how to *begin* to think about Jews. But is it not also to say that he should have known better than to leave matters as he did in this play, that he should, as a thinker, have been more astute and hence more just and reasonable in his presentation of a much-reviled and perennially persecuted minority?

III.

The unsurpassed skill of Shakespeare as an artistic thinker may be seen in the way he put his play together—and in what is merely pointed to as unsaid.

Shylock is one of the two or three major figures in *The Merchant of Venice*. Yet he appears in only five of the twenty scenes of the play.[19] He is assigned seventy-nine speeches in the play. Shylock, in his central speech in the play (his fortieth speech, a good Biblical number[20]), has this to say in response to his fellow Jew, Tubal, who had reported to him, "Your daughter spent in Genoa, as I heard, one night fourscore ducats" (III, i, 95–99):

> Thou stick'st a dagger in me. I shall never see my gold again. Fourscore ducats at a sitting, fourscore ducats!

Some might wonder that he makes so much of his ducats here, rather than of his daughter. But the daughter is lost—she is now almost as if she had never been for him—whereas he had had hopes of retrieving what *could* be retrieved, his ducats. We notice that twice in his speech, he makes much of fourscore, that is of *eighty*. Is it too speculative a suggestion to conjure up one additional speech for Shylock, to add to the seventy-nine speeches provided him by Shakespeare? Should Shylock's signing of the deed, which is to be sent to his house for that purpose, be considered his eightieth speech? (IV, i, 394–95) What might he, as someone saved from killing another in cold blood, have thought if not said on that occasion, or perhaps at the time for the confession of faith he is obliged to make? (IV, i, 396) My talk today is, in effect, a contribution to the missing speech by Shylock.

To speculate as I have, and to proceed as I now propose to do, does testify, of course, to my generally high opinion of Shakespeare as a thinker.[21] It is often easy to overlook how much deliberate control a skillful artist has over his subject, especially when fierce passions (whether or not shared by the artist) are allowed to be vented. One is tempted to see an artist's particularly effective presentations as the result of uncalculating "inspiration"—as a kind of effusion of the spirit.

The control of the artist is obvious, of course, in how the parts of *The Merchant of Venice* are fitted together. We need not pause on this occasion to point out the obvious—this has been done many times by students of theater—except to notice that the trial scene *is* crafted into the gripping theater that it is. Shylock is given more than enough rope, if not to hang himself, then to bind himself firmly ever after.[22]

What we will linger on, in our further investigation of Shakespeare's treatment of Jews, is how Shylock and his daughter are presented—how they are presented by someone who has thought about what Judaism is and means.

IV.

Shakespeare is quite astute in his descriptions of Judaism. Certainly, he himself does not seem to share the low passions of a Gratiano, Bassanio's friend, who abuses the fallen Shylock unrelentingly. (IV, i, 311f) In fact, Bassanio himself is one of the few Gentiles in the play, perhaps the only major one, who does not speak harshly to Shylock. Perhaps it is this moderation that makes him worthy of Portia's wealth and beauty.

Jessica has, on stage, only two speeches to her father. These are not long before she flees his house, taking away a casket of valuables. In her first speech to him she says, "Call you? What is your will?" (II, v, 10) It is in response to this that he tells her he is going out to supper that night, leaving her the keys to everything. (II, v, 12) Thus, we first hear her asking whether he has summoned her and what his will is. This emphasis upon the will of the father does seem to conform to what is indicated throughout the rest of the play about Judaism as very much concerned with the law, with *the* Law, a law that requires and secures obedience even when it is not understood by those who are called (as Moses was?).[23] Her second (and last) speech to Shylock finds her simply lying to him about what the servant has just said to her, a servant who had alluded to Jessica's imminent flight. (II, v, 43)

Are not these two speeches related? Does an undue emphasis upon will (in the domineering father, or in the domineering Divinity) lead to evasion, especially when love beckons one in a community that is characterized by considerable freedom and mobility? Portia too is bound, at least in her marriage arrangements, by the will of her father. We hear her lament, "[S]o is the will of a living daughter curbed by the will of a dead father." (I, ii, 23) Portia, however, does not openly defy that will; but she may well "deceive" her father also, in that she may signal Bassanio which choice to make among the three caskets. (III, ii, 63f) Still, she does appear to conform to her father's will in manipulating the disposition of *her* father's caskets of valuables. That is to say, the Christian daughter is more inclined to be hypocritical (or is it states-manlike?) than the Jewish daughter? The two speeches of Jessica to her fa-ther sum up their relationship: she must either conform to his will or she must deceive in order to rob and abandon him.[24]

We continue with Shakespeare's portrayals of Jews. None of the three Jews we hear on stage—neither Jessica nor Shylock nor Tubal—ever uses any form of the word *nature*. It *is* a word used by others—by Solanio, for in-stance, and by Portia. (I, i, 51; IV, i, 175) Is not Jessica herself somehow im-mune to distinctions between the natural and the unnatural? And so she can conduct herself most unnaturally toward her father.[25]

But there may be still another reason Jessica, like Shylock and Tubal, does not use *nature*: this may be the lingering influence of her ancient Jewish her-itage. An opinion about the universe in which everything is always due to God, directly or indirectly, has no need of *nature* (or of the related notion, *chance*?). This can be seen in the total absence of the word *nature* from the Hebrew Scriptures.[26] Thus, Shylock can refer to the act of generation in his fourteenth speech, as "the deed of kind," which contemporary editors some-times translate for modern readers as "acts of nature." (I, iii, 81)

The unavailability of nature as a guide does point up the significance of *law*, which is a kind of convention (even when the source is divine?). When Shylock, in his most famous speech, tries to *use* the idea of (but not the word) *nature* in insisting that Jews and Christians are in many ways alike, he is re-duced to invoking natural similarities that are put in physical terms: "Hath not a Jew eyes? Hath not a Jew hands, organs, dimensions, senses, affections, passions?" etc. (III, i, 51–57) When he "rises" above the physical, it is only to *revenge*, which may be the physical spiritualized. (III, i, 59–63)

And so the law becomes the decisive guide for Shylock, even though he uses it to serve his passions rather than to consider the proper ends of law. He has distorted the law, seeing it more as something personal to him rather than as a community concern and response. Still, he can be moved by a legal in-terpretation, as may be seen in his response to Portia's manipulations: "Is that the law?" (IV, i, 312) Portia deceives him, certainly as to her credentials,[27] perhaps as to what the law in fact is. Shakespeare seems to approve of her do-ings here.

An emphasis upon the Law, which governs so much of an observant Jew's everyday conduct, is related to still another difference between Christian and Jew: for the Jew, material possessions matter more because the world is sub-stantially here, and temporal happiness is vital. (IV, i, 372–75) Wealth is re-lated, too, to one's concern for the family.[28] Shylock can look down on Christian husbands who would sacrifice their families for a friend or for love, as Bassanio says he would do to save Antonio. (IV, i, 293f) Much is made of sexuality at the end of the play, between Portia and Antonio, between Jessica and her husband, and between Gratiano and his wife, but is not this in the context of a ratification of the dismantling of Shylock-style families? A concern for love, even love between spouses, is not simply the same as a concern for family.[29]

The Jewish obligation to take the temporal seriously means, among other things, that one must be careful with one's wealth. Of course, thinkers such as Aristotle evidently considered the charging of interest to be unnatural,[30] as distinguished from the practice of running risks and thereby making profits, or incurring losses, as merchants do. Shylock is not restrained by considerations of the unnatural. But then, neither are we, at least with respect to financial matters, since most of us now agree that it is not only legitimate but rather quite fair that those who take our money for their profitable ventures should pay us something for the use of our money. Do we, like Shylock, have no natural restraints upon us in these matters, without having that which the pious Jew *would* have, various divine restraints, including deeply-felt obligations of charity?[31]

Shylock, in attempting to justify the charging of interest, uses the Biblical story about Laban, Jacob, and the sheep to support the proposition that one *should* look out for oneself. (I, iii, 67f) Does Shylock fail, however, because he does not properly look out for himself? He allows his usual shrewdness to be suppressed as he is swept along by his hate.[32] In this he is a Jew who *is* somewhat liberated by the freedom of the Venetian republic. An old-fashioned Jew would have counseled him that it was reckless to go after Antonio as he does—that among Christians, too, blood would eventually tell. Or, as an Aristotle would say, nature will assert herself eventually, whatever the doctrines (whether about law, about gain, or about the divine) that people are captivated by from time to time.

V.

We have been looking, for the most part, at how Jews are presented in *The Merchant of Venice*—but, of course, these *are* Jews in a Christian society. It has been observed by Allan Bloom, a most instructive commentator on this play, "Shylock and Antonio are Jew and Christian, and they are at war as a result of their difference in faith."[33]

If one is to grasp fully Shakespeare's remarkable portrayal of Jews, something more should be said about the Christians in this play. Christians tend to be somewhat opposed to Jews with respect to the matters we have noticed about Judaism here, such as the status of the family and of law. This many be seen as well with respect to dietary restrictions, which Jews make much of and Christians little if anything of. (I, iii, 29f) This is not to deny that most Jews today are, in many respects, for better as well as for worse, much influenced by Christianity and by post–Palestinian developments.[34]

One critical difference in Shakespeare's play between Christian and Jew is that there does not seem to be in Judaism any *obligation* to martyrdom, certainly not to the extent that it is found in Christianity. This seems to be related to what we have already noticed about the importance of *this* world to the Jew. This also bears, no doubt, on Christian assessments from time to time of the sincerity of seeming conversions by Jews to Christianity. It should make us wonder what the enduring significance is of Shylock's own forced "conversion," especially after he has had time to reflect on what has happened to him. (IV, i, 385)[35]

Mercy overrides for the Christian that justice which is grounded in law, even though Portia and her colleagues do not seem to make much if any use, in dealing with the devastated Shylock, of the mercy they have extolled. Consider, for example, how different the play would have been if Portia had begun to suggest, in public, some understanding of how Shylock had become the monster he had tried to be on this occasion.

Does not Shakespeare himself ("Gentle Will," as he was sometimes known) seem to prefer mercy to law? This may be, in part, a Christian influence upon him. Even so, does he not implicitly criticize, if not repudiate, both Christianity and Judaism, preferring to them an ancient virtue rooted in nature?[36] Shakespeare proposes, in effect, to correct the Bible by leaving other stories and teachings for the English-speaking peoples, especially with respect to the relation between religious faith and statesmanship.

Still, one must wonder whether Shakespeare has himself grasped sufficiently the distinctive characteristics of relations between Christians and Jews. May not he, in his genius, have presented more than he himself fully understood, especially since he was, for one reason or another, never fully able to see Judaism for what it was and is?

VI.

It should go without saying that the reservations one may have about what Shakespeare does in *The Merchant of Venice* should not be taken to disparage the remarkable things the playwright does do, including the insights he displays into both Jews and Christians. One is reminded of what he does, also in a Venetian setting, for Moors and Christians in *Othello*. Thus, as Professor Bloom has observed,

Othello and Shylock are the figures who are the most foreign in the context in which they move and to the audience for which they were intended. In a sense, it is Shakespeare's achievement in the two plays to have made these men—who would normally have been mere objects of hatred and contempt—into human beings who are unforgettable for their strength of soul. For the first time in European literature, there was a powerful characterization of men so different. . . . Whether they liked these men or not, the spectators now knew they were men and not things on which they could with impunity exercise their vilest passions.[37]

Still, it seems to me, we are not induced by Shakespeare's presentation to despise Othello, and even to exult at, or at least to enjoy, his overthrow the way the typical audience is moved to do with what happens to Shylock. Nor do we have the epithet "Moor" rubbed in, the way "Jew" is. To such a response Mr. Bloom has this concession to make: "Shakespeare does not understand Judaism, for he saw it from the outside; he looked at it, as no man rightfully can, from a purely political point of view."[38] I shall have something to say about this soon, but we should consider first another caveat from the same source.

We are reminded, by Mr. Bloom, of the limits of toleration and of the Enlightenment. Thus he observes,

It is very well to tell [Antonio and Shylock] to live together, but in any confrontation of the two they are bound to quarrel. What is prudence for one is robbery for the other; what is kindness for one is mawkish sentimentally to the other. There is no middle ground, since they see the same objects as different things; common sense cannot mediate between them. If there is to be harmony, one must give in to the other.[39]

And again he observes,

[Shakespeare] was of the conviction that it was of the nature of man to have varying opinions about the highest things and that such opinions become invested in doctrine and law and bound up with established interests. When confronted with one another, these opinions must quarrel. Such is life, and that must be accepted with manly resolution.[40]

Thus, the limits of Enlightenment and toleration are here faced up to. About this, too, I shall have something to say soon.

VII.

Let us consider first the significance of the defense that Shakespeare did not understand Judaism, because "he saw it from the outside." Yet did he not have access to—indeed, did he not rely upon—the best that is available about Judaism, not individual Jews (who may be bad as well as good) but rather the Bible itself, with which he seems to have been quite familiar and upon which he draws in this play? One must wonder how anyone familiar with, say the book of *Isaiah* could characterize Jews as they are characterized in *The Merchant of Venice*. Besides, should Shakespeare not have been able, by talking to sensible people who had traveled, either in Europe or in books, to determine what Jews of his day were really like?[41] Certainly, one should know what has happened to Jews throughout Christendom—and that should move one to be particularly scrupulous about both seeing justice done and promoting a proper compassion. Instead, Shakespeare presents on stage a seemingly plausible version, in what Shylock attempts to do to Antonio, of the notorious "ritual murder" blood-libel that Jews had suffered from for centuries all over Europe.[42]

Another way of putting all this is to notice that although Shakespeare saw the ancient Greeks and the ancient Romans, as well as the modern Italians, also from the outside, he came closer than he did with respect to the Jews in depicting *them* in their highest form. True, Shakespeare's depiction of Jews may be better than that of most playwrights of his day—but his is bad enough and has the peculiar disadvantage of being more likely to endure because he tells a much better story. What endures is not only Shylock's memorable "Hath not a Jew eyes?" speech, but also an image of the Jew that cannot help but be both painful and harmful and hence ugly. Another indication of Shakespeare's failing here is the way that he treats Jessica, the unfaithful daughter, who is never criticized by the Christians in the play and is left in apparent prosperity, having been enticed to flee from the "hell" of her father's house to the "heaven" that Christian love and fellowship promise. (II, iii, 1f; V, i, 1f)

At the very least, it seems to me, Shakespeare should have been aware of the limits of his information—and should have conducted himself accordingly.[43]

VIII.

Let us now consider the warning that Enlightenment and toleration cannot be expected to do much good with respect to the kind of conflict seen between Christian and Jew in this play.

It is prudent to be cautious about the expectation of any enlightenment wherever longstanding prejudices and radically different allegiances are to be found. But the argument that attempts to excuse Shakespeare because he did not know Jews well enough, or in their highest manifestations, is an argument that depends (does it not?) upon the assumption that enlightenment *does* help correct one's misconceptions or prejudices.

Still, it can be added, although Shakespeare would have been helped had *he* known more about Jews, that is not likely to help moderate the *typical believer*. For the believer can be threatened, not reassured, when he perceives how deeply others differ from him with respect to what he considers the most important matters.

Should not this limitation of public opinion caution us in any use by us of talents that help shape public opinion? The more astute one makes Shakespeare in depicting Jews—and astute he is!—the more questionable can be regarded the way that he leaves Jews for his audience. I hope I never forget how much a sophisticated theater audience I once observed here in Chicago enjoyed the downfall of Shylock, a Shylock played very well by a distinguished Jewish actor.[44]

There may be limits, of course, to what one can do about the prejudices of one's countrymen if one is to retain one's reputation and influence among them in other matters. Perhaps, indeed, Shakespeare could not have simply praised the Jews in a play for the London stage. But nothing compelled him, so far as I know, to use them on that stage: he could simply have left them alone. Nor does it seem to me sufficient justification to suggest that he treats the Jews as openly as he does in order to better question (if not even to bind) Christianity covertly. I am reminded of, among other things, the remonstrance by the rabbi, "Where is it written that the price of salvation must be the life of Haim, the washerman?"[45] In any event, it is far from clear to me that the radical questioning of Christianity since Shakespeare's time has done mankind in general, and the Jews in particular, the good that some of those moved by what Leo Strauss called "antitheological passion" had once anticipated.[46]

IX.

The story about the rabbi and Haim the washerman with which I began is not altogether unsentimental. Another story, also culled from the recent Yom Kippur service I attended, is made of firmer stuff and is salutary to recall here as we bring our conversation to a close. It is a much older story, based on the Talmud, and goes like this:

During the Hadrianic persecutions, decrees were promulgated imposing the most rigorous penalties on the observers of the Jewish Law, and especially upon those who occupied themselves with the promulgation of that Law. Nevertheless

Hananiah ben Teradyon conscientiously followed his chosen profession; he convened public assemblies and taught the Law.

Once he visited Jose ben Kisma, who advised extreme caution, if not submission, saying "My brother, I hear that you occupy yourself with the Torah, even calling assemblies and holding the scroll of the Law before you."

To this Hananiah replied, "Heaven will have mercy on us."

Jose became impatient on hearing this, and responded, "I am talking logic, and to all my arguments you answer, 'Heaven will have mercy on us!' I should not be surprised if they burned you together with the scroll."

Shortly thereafter Hananiah was arrested at a public assembly while teaching with a scroll before him. Asked why he disregarded the imperial edict, he frankly answered, "I do as my God commands me." For this he and his wife were condemned to death, and their daughter to degradation.

His death was terrible. Wrapped in the scroll, he was placed on a pyre of green brush; fire was set to it, and wet wool was placed on his chest to prolong the agonies of death. "Woe is me," cried his daughter, "that I should see you under such terrible circumstances!" The martyr serenely replied, "I should indeed despair were I alone burned; but since the scroll of the Torah is burning with me, the Power that will avenge the offense against the Torah will also avenge the offense against me."

His heartbroken disciples then asked: "Master, what do you see?" He answered, "I see the parchment burning while the letters of the Torah soar upward."[47]

The dedication, pious resolve, and dignity exhibited in this story are also on display, of course, throughout the Bible—and again remind us of the unjustified and otherwise unfortunate shortcomings of *The Merchant of Venice*.[48]

It is sobering to recognize how and perhaps why Shakespeare went astray in failing to make explicit, however much he sensed, the enduring worth of Judaism. It is well for us to be aware of such limitations whenever we deal with strangers, either the strangers among us or those in other lands—strangers whom we do not know as well as our interests, our fears, and our natural flaws persuade us to believe we do.

We may have, however, one advantage over the most gifted artists. The artist as artist, in presenting things "as they are," must make much of the "outward shows" of particulars, of bodies, of this people or nation as against that people or nation. (III, i, 73) He must, in short, present things as either this way *or* that way. It may be possible for us lesser mortals, when properly instructed—that is, when properly questioned?—to be open, as perhaps the artist by nature cannot fully be, to the Socratic insistence that we should always be aware of what we do not know.[49]

NOTES

1. This talk was given at the Cultural Center, Chicago Public Library, Chicago, Illinois, October 3, 1983. The original title of this talk was "Shylock's Missing Speech: Shakespeare, the Jews, and *The Merchant of Venice*." An epigraph was provided from *Exodus* 25:8: "And let them make Me a sanctuary, that I may dwell among them."

The parenthetical citations in the text are to *The Merchant of Venice* as it appears in *The Complete Pelican Shakespeare* published by Penguin Books. An instructive introduction to the play is provided by David Bevington in his collection, *The Complete Works of Shakespeare* (New York: Addison Wesley Longman, 1997).

2. Another quite ugly play, but by a much younger Shakespeare, is *Titus Andronicus*. See, on that instructive play, George Anastaplo, *The Artist as Thinker: From Shakespeare to Joyce* (Athens, Ohio: Ohio University Press, 1983), pp. 29–61.

3. I draw, for observations about the animus against Jews in the Western world, upon Leo Strauss's 1962 lecture, "Why We Remain Jews":

> Our worst enemies are called (since I do not know how many years) "anti-Semites," a word which I shall never use, and which I regard as almost obscene. I think that if we are sensible we abolish it from our usage. I said in a former speech here that it was coined by some German or French pedant: I smelled them. But then I learned, a few weeks ago, it was coined by a German pedant, a fellow called [Wilhelm] Marr. The reason he coined it was very simple. "Anti-Semitism" means hatred of Jews. Why not call it as we Jews call it? It is *rish'us*, "viciousness"? "Hatred of Jews" is perfectly intelligible. "Anti-Semitism" was coined in a situation in which people could no longer justify their hatred of Jews by the fact that Jews are not Christians. They had to find another reason; and since the nineteenth century was almost as proud of science as the twentieth century, the reason had to be scientific. Science proves that the Western world consists of two races, the Aryan race and the Semitic race, and therefore, by speaking of anti-Semitism, our enemies could claim that they acted on a spiritual principle, not from mere hatred. The difficulty is that the Arabs are also Semites.

Leo Strauss, *Jewish Philosophy and the Crisis of Modernity*, ed. Kenneth Hart Green (Albany: State University of New York Press, 1997), p. 320. See also chapter 7, note 49, chapter 12, notes 78, 79.

4. On Jews in a liberal society, I again draw upon Leo Strauss's lecture, "Why We Remain Jews":

> Assimilation now does not mean conversion to Christianity, as we know, because assimilation now is assimilation to a secular society, a society that is not legally a Christian society, a society beyond the difference between Judaism and Christianity, and—if every religion is always a particular religion (Judaism, Christianity)—an areligious society, a liberal society. In such a society there are no longer any legal disabilities of Jews as Jews. But a liberal society stands or falls by the distinction between the political (or the state) and society, or by the distinction between the public and the private. In the liberal society there is necessarily a private sphere with which the state's legislation must not interfere. It is an essential element of this liberal society, with its essential distinction between the public and private, that religion as a particular religion, not as a general religion, is private. Every citizen is free to

adhere to any religion he sees fit. Now given this—the necessary existence of such a private sphere—the liberal society necessarily makes possible, permits, and even fosters what is called by many people "discrimination." And here, in this well-known fact, the "Jewish problem" (if I may call it that) reappears. There are restricted areas, and in various ways, . . . I do not have to belabor this point; any glance at journals of sociology or at Jewish journals would convince you of the fact if you have any doubt about its existence.

Therefore the practical problem for the individual Jew, on the low and solid ground, is this: How can I escape "discrimination"? [This is a] term that I beg you to understand as always used with quotation marks. I would not use it of my own free will). The answer is simple: By ceasing to be recognizable as a Jew. . . . [But] this solution is possible at most only for individuals here or there, not for large groups.

Strauss, *Jewish Philosophy and the Crisis of Modernity*, pp. 314–15. Compare, e.g., R. Gustave Niebuhr, "Keeping the Faith: Marriage and Family No Longer Are Ties That Bind to Judaism," *Wall Street Journal*, August 8, 1991, p. A1. But see chapter 9, note 24 below.

5. Ancient Rome and ancient Judaism shared one vital opinion: morality was largely citizen morality. See chapter 9, note 36, chapter 10, note 65.

6. William T. Braithwaite, then of the Loyola University of Chicago School of Law faculty, said this in a talk he gave earlier in 1983 in a Shakespeare series at the Chicago Cultural Center. See appendix C, note 48 below.

7. Two articles by Professor Braithwaite that bear on these matters are (1) "Poetry and the Criminal Law: The Idea of Punishment in Shakespeare's *Measure for Measure*," 13 *Loyola University of Chicago Law Journal* 791 (1982); (2) "Why, and How, Judges Should Study Poetry," 19 *Loyola University of Chicago Law Journal* 809 (1988). See on the law of contracts in Venice, Shakespeare, *The Merchant of Venice*, III, ii, 278–79, III, iii, 26–31, IV, i, 101–03. See also chapter 12, note 187.

8. *New York Times* (Midwest Edition), May 6, 1983, p. 4.

9. *Haim* itself means *life*. See chapter 1, note 91; the text at note 27 of chapter 1 of this collection.

10. It is highly unlikely, of course, that any sane Jew, in any Christian city in Europe, would ever have tried what Shylock tried—or that, if indeed demented, he would have gotten as far as Shylock did: his fellow Jews would surely have stopped him, perhaps even confining him as insane. But in this play Shylock seems to be in good standing in his synagogue even though at least two other male Jews knew what he intended to do to Antonio. He had this deadly intention before his daughter fled his household with his money, if she is to be believed. (III, ii, 282–90) These observations point up the anomalous character of the 1983 London production by the Royal Shakespeare Company of *The Tempest* in which the Shakespeare-like Prospero is presented as a Jewish Cabbalist. See chapter 1, note 99.

11. This is aside from the question of what it is that entitled Shylock to have any money at all in Venice, to regard it as truly his own, and to trade for profit. See, e.g., George Anastaplo, "Prudence and the Constitution: On the Year 2000 Presidential Election Controversy" (on Dick Cheney, as a self-made man), in Ethan Fishman, ed., *Tempered Strength: Studies in the Nature and Scope of Prudential Leadership* (Lanham, Md.: Lexington Books, 2002), p. 210 note 7.

12. Why was not the blood that would be spilled taken into account by Shylock? Was he thinking of a proper, that is Jewish, killing of animals for consumption, which routinely has the blood drained from the flesh? See, on the implication of the means necessary for the execution of a valid contract, Thomas Hobbes, *Leviathan*, chap. 14.

13. It is no worse, some would argue, than laws and contracts with respect to slavery, which Shylock reminds the Venetians they permit. Is there not a contract here that, if it is taken seriously, would easily be held to be against public policy in any well-ordered state?

14. It is odd that Shylock's forced conversion to Christianity (first suggested by Antonio) should be seen by Christians as a punishment. (IV, i, 385) (Is the resentment against Jews by some Gentiles a reflection of their having had to have been civilized by having been Christianized—that is to say, by having been Judaized?) See chapter 9, note 35. Compare Prince Hamlet, who is reluctant to kill King Claudius at prayers lest he immediately send his soul to heaven. See Shakespeare, *Hamlet*, III, iii, 73–95. See also chapter 4, note 29. See, on Hamlet, George Anastaplo, "Law & Literature and Shakespeare: Explorations," 26 *Oklahoma City University Law Review* 1, 220 (2001). See, on *The Merchant of Venice*, Anastaplo, "Law & Literature and Shakespeare," p. 163.

15. Is Iago, in Shakespeare's *Othello*, presented as a distinctively Christian monster (also associated with Venice)? But he is not presented as *the* Christian; if anything, he is Satanic. See chapter 9, note 37. See, on Iago, Anastaplo, "Law & Literature and Shakespeare," pp. 98–118.

16. Consider also *The Complete Works of Shakespeare*, George Lyman Kittredge, ed. (Boston: Ginn and Company, 1936), p. 258:

> The character of Shylock fascinates critics and has lured them into endless mazes of debate. One thing is clear, however: *The Merchant of Venice* is no anti-Semitic document; Shakespeare was not attacking the Jewish people when he gave Shylock the villain role. If so, he was attacking the Moors in *Titus Andronicus*, the Spaniards in *Much Ado*, the Italians in *Cymbeline*, the Viennese in *Measure for Measure*, the Danes in *Hamlet*, the Britons in *King Lear*, the Scots in *Macbeth*, and the English in *Richard the Third*.

This is a rather forced argument, to say the least. I have several times observed the shock of sophisticated Jews, in University of Chicago adult education classes, when they encounter *The Merchant of Venice* for the first time.

Compare the introduction by Brents Stirling to *The Merchant of Venice* in *The Complete Pelican Shakespeare*, pp. 211–12:

> Facts, however, do not always speak clearly. What these tell us is that our ancestors could find entertainment in Jew-baiting; the question they do not answer is whether Shakespeare catered to that taste fully or with interesting modifications. If the question has an answer, only Shakespeare's play can give it. . . .
>
> Shylock's self-styled "Christian" course of revenge condemns him as it would condemn any Christian. Even so, there is much in the play and its age which condemns and ridicules him simply because he is a Jew, and we should not try to explain it away. But Shakespeare, like Marlowe before him, makes it very plain that Jews can learn bad habits from the large family of Christian hypocrites. An Elizabethan dramatist could not have

gone much further in clear, unsentimental fair dealing without becoming, for his time, a prophetic visionary.

Would it be going even further to add that since Shylock was acting like the worst of the Christians, he might as well become "officially" a Christian? In any event, we do know that Shakespeare would have personally known few if any Jews: "Jews had been banished from England in 1290 and were not readmitted until 1655." *The Reader's Encyclopedia of Shakespeare* (New York: Thomas Y. Crowell Co., 1966), p. 797. See chapter 9, note 42. See, on Christopher Marlowe and the Jews, George Anastaplo, "Law & Literature and the Christian Heritage: Explorations," 40 *Brandeis Law Journal* 191, 357 (2001). See also *Jane Austen's Letters*, Deirdre Le Faye, ed. (Oxford: Oxford University Press, 1995), pp. 307. An American in Tom Taylor's *Our American Cousin* (first produced in London before the American Civil War) can refer to a moneylender as "Shylock."

17. This is like having the Nazi commandant of a concentration camp playing Beethoven and Bach in his quarters while men, women, and children under his command are being routinely slaughtered.

18. Others have been bloodthirsty before him. Consider, for example, Achilles' vehemence, in Homer's *Iliad*: "I could eat his heart." He is indeed monstrous in this passion—but he becomes more gracious in his mourning, especially in his encounter with Priam. Consider, however, the human sacrifices he thereafter insists upon for Patroclus' funeral.

19. The scenes in which Shylock appears are I, iii, II, v, III, i, III, iii, and IV, i.

20. See, e.g., *Genesis* 25:20; *Exodus* 16:35; *Numbers* 32:13; *Deuteronomy* 8:2; *2 Samuel* 5:4; *1 Kings* 11:42; *Psalms* 95:10.

21. See Anastaplo, *The Artist as Thinker,* pp. 15–28. See also chapter 9, note 49.

22. See, on how Abraham bound Isaac and thereby also bound ever after the people of Israel, chapter 5.

23. See on the primacy of the will, chapter 1, note 115; chapter 5, note 62; chapter 9, note 23; the text at note 67 of chapter 10 of this collection. See also chapter 8.

24. Are Jews generally suspected by Gentiles as unreliable converts, so deeply are they shaped by their faith? I again draw upon Leo Strauss's lecture, "Why We Remain Jews":

> I was still brought up in the belief, in a very old-fashioned country, that no Jew who ever converted to Christianity was sincere. That was what I learned and what I believed until I met, as a student, a professor who told me of his conversion to Christianity. (He was a son of a rabbi.) I must say I was not impressed by his story . . . But I would have to admit that he was subjectively sincere, and no calculation entered into it. I cannot say anything more about that. I know there is a real disproportion between my primitive feelings (which I learned from my wet nurse, as a much greater man put it), and my rational judgment. But I said at the beginning [of this lecture] that conversion was always possible.

Strauss, *Jewish Philosophy and the Crisis of Modernity*, pp. 341–42. Compare Anastaplo, *The Artist as Thinker*, p. 269.

25. This is reflected in Jessica's recourse to a boy's clothing when she flees her father's house, something that makes her ashamed. (II, vi, 33–39) Portia, too, dons male clothing for the Trial Scene (IV, i), but she does not seem to be ashamed in doing so. See, on setting aside one's duty to one's parents in the name of something higher, chapter 8, note 33. See also chapter 2. Compare chapter 6.

26. See chapter 1, note 91, conclusion, note 3.

27. See, on the need for appropriate credentials, chapter 9, note 49.

28. Compare Jesus' "un-Jewish" command that one's family and one's dead should be abandoned. See chapter 7-A, Section III.

29. One consequence of an emphasis upon love as decisive is that when a couple's love goes (as it all too often "naturally" does) any family ties that presuppose love are likely to be severely threatened.

30. Consider Kenneth Myrick's introduction to *The Merchant of Venice* in the *Complete Signet Classic Shakespeare* (1972), p. 601:

> The Elizabethan hatred of usury was sanctioned by Aristotle's theory that money cannot breed money; but far more important were the enormous interest rates and fraudulent contracts of clever scoundrels. Recognizing Shylock as a usurer, the Elizabethans must have been hostile to him, especially when they saw him plotting against Antonio's life.

31. See chapter 9, note 41. See, for a useful summary of several of these points, Allan Bloom (with Harry V. Jaffa), *Shakespeare's Politics* (New York: Basic Books, 1964), p. 18. See, on Jewish materialism, Bloom, *Shakespeare's Politics*, p. 22. See, on Mr. Bloom's best-known work, chapter 8, note 14.

32. Compare in this respect the shrewdness of Homer's Odysseus. See, e.g., chapter 8, Sections II and IX. And yet Odysseus can exact a revenge of the Suitors that Shylock cannot exact of Antonio and his colleagues.

33. Bloom, *Shakespeare's Politics*, p. 17.

34. See, for example, a letter from Leo Strauss in London to Alexandre Kojève in Paris (in the early 1930s):

> I am very thirsty in this moment and I have not the good and cheap French wine. But instead of it we have the wonderful English breakfast—the hams taste too good as to consist of pork, and therefore they are allowed by the Mosaic law according to atheistic interpretation.

Leo Strauss, *On Tyranny*, Victor Gourevitch and Michael S. Roth, eds. (New York: The Free Press, 1991), p. 222. Mr. Strauss, in his later years, would no doubt have preferred (in such a context) "aesthetic" to "atheistic."

35. Perhaps it is to this subject that Shylock's "eightieth speech" should be devoted. Among the things to be considered in such a speech is why the suggestion for Shylock's conversion came not from Portia (whom he knows as Balthasar) but from Antonio (who is evidently more hostile to Jews as such). (I, iii, 44: "He hates our sacred nation;" IV, i, 385) Should Portia's legal judgment be subject to revision if it is discovered how she was connected with Antonio? See, on Portia, George Anastaplo, *The American Moralist, Essays on Law, Ethics, and Government* (Athens, Ohio: Ohio University Press, 1992), pp. 352–54, 361–63.

36. Does the ancient virtue make more of what we call "personal responsibility"? See, on the personal responsibility of even Oedipus, chapter 4-A. Compare Taylor, "Don't Blame Me: The New Culture of Victimization," *New Yorker*, June 3, 1991, p. 27. See the Letters to the Editor in subsequent issues. See also chapter 9, note 5.

37. Bloom, *Shakespeare's Politics*, p. 14. See also Strauss, *On Tyranny*, p. 301; chapter 9, note 15.

38. Bloom, *Shakespeare's Politics*, p. 31.

39. Bloom, *Shakespeare's Politics*, pp. 19–20.

40. Bloom, *Shakespeare's Politics*, p. 31.

41. Should not Shakespeare have recognized what a long-established people had probably required or had become? I return to Leo Strauss's lecture, "Why We Remain Jews":

> Judaism is not a misfortune (I am back to my beginning) but, let us say, a "heroic delusion." In what does this delusion consist? The one thing needful is righteousness or charity; in Judaism these are the same. This notion of the one thing needful is not defensible if the world is not the creation of the just and loving God, the holy God. The root of injustice and uncharitableness, which abounds, is not in God, but in the free acts of His creatures—in sin. The Jewish people and their fate are the living witness for the absence of redemption. This, one could say, is the meaning of the chosen people; the Jews are chosen to prove the absence of redemption. The greatest expression of this, surpassing everything that any present-day man could write, is that great Jewish prayer that will be known to some of you and that is a stumbling block to many, *Aleinu leshabeiah*. It would be absolutely improper for me to read it now.

Strauss, *Jewish Philosophy and the Crisis of Modernity*, p. 327. The prayer referred to by Mr. Strauss is this:

> It is our duty to praise the Lord of all things, to ascribe greatness to Him who formed the world in the beginning, since He has not made us like the nations of other lands, and He has not placed us like other families of the earth, since He has not assigned to us a portion as to them, nor a lot as to all their multitude. (For they worship vain things and emptiness, and pray to a god that cannot save.) But we bend the knee and bow in worship and acknowledge thanks before the supreme King of kings, the Holy One, blessed be He, Who stretched out the heavens and laid the foundation of the earth, the seat of Whose honor is in the heavens, and the abode of Whose might is in the loftiest heights. He is our God; there is none else. In truth He is our King; there is none besides Him. As it is written in His Torah: "And you shall know this day, and lay it to your heart, that the Lord He is God in the heavens and on the earth: there is none else."
>
> We therefore put our hope in You, O Lord our God, that we may speedily behold the splendor of Your might, when You will remove the idols from the earth, and the false gods will be utterly cut off, when the world will be perfected under the kingdom of the Almighty, and all human beings will call on Your name, and when all the wicked of the earth will be turned toward You. Let all who dwell in the world recognize and know that to You every knee must bend, and every tongue must swear allegiance. Before You, O Lord our God, let them bend the knee and prostrate themselves, and to Your glorious name let them render honor. Let them all accept the yoke of Your kingdom, so that You may

reign over them speedily, and for ever and ever. For the kingdom is Yours, and You will reign in glory for all eternity. As it is written in Your Torah: "The Lord shall reign for ever and ever." And it is said: "And the Lord shall be King over all the earth: on that day the Lord shall be One, and His name One."

Strauss, *Jewish Philosophy and the Crisis of Modernity*, pp. 327–28. See the text at note 49 of chapter 9 of this collection. See also chapter 1, note 3. See as well chapter 5, note 75.

42. Consider George B. Harrison's introduction to *The Complete Works of Shakespeare* (New York: Harcourt, Brace & World, 1968), p. 581:

In writing or rewriting *The Merchant of Venice* Shakespeare had before him a recent and most successful play that also told of a Jew who hated all Christians. This was Marlowe's tragedy *The Jew of Malta*. . . . Barabas, the Jew of Malta, like Shylock had an only daughter and many ducats, but he was altogether a more monstrous and far less credible character than Shylock. In a few passages Shakespeare owed something to Marlowe in portraying Shylock as remorseless and vindictive; but Barabas was a monster of hate who did not hesitate to poison a whole nunnery because it contained the daughter who offended him. In comparison Shylock is a mild-mannered simpleton.

See chapter 9, note 16. See, on Marlowe, chapter 1-B. See also chapter 9, note 16.

43. Is not this critical to the virtue of prudence? See, e.g., chapters 4-A and 8, chapters 10, 11 and 12-B. See also chapter 7, note 69, chapter 9, note 49.

44. I visited with this actor, Morris Carnovsky, in his dressing room after that performance. (Rabbi Maurice Pekarsky, of the Hillel Foundation at the University of Chicago, had provided the link between us.) Mr. Carnovsky was quite distressed by the considerable laughter that the Trial Scene had provoked—but it was evident to me on that occasion that that laughter had been consistent with what the playwright had done, especially when Shylock is presented as someone quite capable of slaughtering Antonio in a more or less ritualistic manner. See, on this actor, James Barron, "Morris Carnovsky Is Dead at 94; Acting Career Spanned 60 Years," *New York Times*, September 2, 1992, p. A15. See, on Rabbi Pekarsky, George Anastaplo, "American Constitutionalism and the Virtue of Prudence," in Leo Paul S. de Alvarez, ed., *Abraham Lincoln, The Gettysburg Address, and American Constitutionalism* (Irving, Texas: University of Dallas Press, 1976), p. 170.

45. See the text at note 9 of chapter 9 of this collection.

46. See Leo Strauss, "Marsilius of Padua," in *History of Political Philosophy* (Chicago: University of Chicago Press, 1987), p. 294. See also Leo Strauss, *Natural Right and History* (Chicago: University of Chicago Press, 1953), pp. 31–32, 146, 163–64. See, on the evil doctrines that have replaced Christianity, chapter 12-A. See also chapter 9, note 3.

47. See *Talmud, Avoday Zarah* 17b sq. See, for a not-unrelated story, Hayim Goren Perelmuter, *Siblings: Rabbinic Judaism and Early Christianity at Their Beginnings* (New York: Paulist Press, 1989), pp. 187–88. See also chapter 8, note 33. Compare Moses Maimonides, *Letter on Apostasy*.

48. Hananiah's daughter can be usefully distinguished from Shylock's Jessica.

49. But we cannot deal properly with our awareness of what we do not know if we do not have a reliable sense of what we can and perhaps do know. See George Anasta-plo, "Freedom of Speech and the First Amendment: Explorations," 21 *Texas Tech Law Review* 1941, 1943 (1990). See the text at note 5 of chapter 10. See also chapter 1, note 46; chapter 7, note 101; appendix C, note 29.

10

Thomas More, the King, and the Pope[1]

I.

I put you on notice by reporting that my long-suffering wife observed to me just the other day that there is one serious fault with my lectures: I try to say too much. Audiences, she pointed out, don't really want to learn everything I try to tell them. To this only one answer can prudently be made, especially by an incorrigible husband, and that is, "You're right, my dear, you're right." But perhaps I can dare add, in the safety of this company, a useful correction: part of my audience *does* want to learn everything I try to tell them, that part of the audience that I myself represent. A lecture permits one to see what can be publicly said, and said in a salutary manner, about the subject under consideration. It permits one to learn something about both one's subject and the way that that subject may be discussed.

The subject on this occasion is the trial of Sir Thomas More. Serious as the subject is—for it *is* about an Englishman who was canonized in 1935, four hundred years after his execution as a traitor[2]—I believe it instructive to open and close what I have to say with stories. Thomas More himself, it should be remembered, jested even on the scaffold.[3]

Not too long ago [I could say in 1975] I was at a University of Chicago party where I found myself talking to a professor of law and to a criminologist about the problem of deterrence of criminal behavior. This led to the law professor's saying that he had seen deterrence work when applied clearly, firmly, and with dispatch. He cited the experience of the Army during the Second World War when the rule was promulgated that anyone Absent Without Leave for longer than a certain period (seventy-two hours, let us say) would be tried by a formal court-martial rather than be subjected (as had previously been the case) to the more informal (and generally less rigorous) company discipline. The immediate result of the new rule, the law professor continued, was a marked reduction in extended AWOLs. To all this the criminologist, who tends to be rather dubious about the effects of deterrents, replied, "Was this really a change in behavior or only a change in classification?" The law professor replied in turn that it was indeed a change of behavior, certainly not a change in classification alone. "How do you know that?" the criminologist wanted to know. "Because," the law professor explained, "I was in the legal office on an Army post at the time the new rule went into effect—and the number of long AWOLs dropped remarkably. People knew what the rule was—the Army had made an effort to make *that* clear—and men absent without leave made it a point to return just within the seventy-two–hour limit. It had become obvious to them that it was now too painful to stay away beyond that limit." To all this the criminologist answered in his gravelly voice, "Now I will tell *you* what really happened. I remember that rule very well. *I* was a top sergeant at the time—and I would say to my company clerk, when someone was missing, 'Don't put him down as AWOL until we see when he gets back.' If a sergeant had a man AWOL whom he didn't want to lose through a court-martial, he would protect him in this fashion. I remember a cook I had, a very good cook—but every once in a while he would take off with some woman, and when he did, you can be certain he didn't watch the clock. But he *would* come back eventually, and I would deal with him in my own way. He couldn't do me any good in the stockade. So, I don't believe the rule changed behavior at all, no matter what you people down at the post legal office thought, but it certainly changed the classifications."[4]

What in fact did happen? Was *this* intelligent top sergeant's manner of response to the regulation the typical response by noncommissioned officers? Or was the Army lawyer's impression correct? I believe I have said enough about this problem to remind you of the difficulty of determining how "facts" about human beings are to be interpreted. I do *not* mean to suggest that there is no correct answer to any question about human motivation and behavior, but only that it is often difficult to know when one has probed deeply enough into the evidence and the relevant arguments to arrive at the correct answer.[5] I conclude my report on this conversation by noting the only contribution I made to it—and that was to observe, at its conclusion, that deterrents were shown by the skeptical criminologist to have some effect after all, in that this particular Army regulation had affected, and in a rather marked way, the behavior of top sergeants! Top sergeants, it seems, *are* intelligent, restrained, and informed enough to be affected by rules and to know how to deal with them effectively: otherwise they are not likely to get to, and to stay, where they are. But what about the ordinary would-be criminal? *That* issue, of what shapes human conduct, remains with us. It is indeed an old issue, and one that we do deal with, if only indirectly, as we examine the 1535 trial of Sir Thomas More.

II.

Old issues never die, they only seem to fade away—and then they reappear, sometimes unexpectedly or disguised, in new forms and with renewed energy. The issues about which men differ, even unto death, are not trivial or transitory, whatever may be the case of the circumstances that occasion them. For the issues about which men do differ address themselves—sometimes more obviously, sometimes less so—to fundamental questions about how human beings should live and die, about how they should be governed, about what makes for happiness here and salvation hereafter. Contending opinions about justice are relied upon—and the prudent human being tries to do justice to all of them, to give each of them what is its due, and to promote and preserve thereby what is truly human.

A ruler issues a decree about family relations. Somebody conscientiously defies that decree, invoking religious teachings reinforced by age-old tradition. The issue is joined; passions are aroused; the ruler crushes his opponent, but not without sustaining a mortal wound himself.[6] This pattern, if pattern it can be called, is as old as an ancient tragedy; it is as new as yesterday's headlines.

It was only a few months ago [I could say in 1975] that the Vatican issued a declaration in which it reaffirmed, despite the trends of the day, some old teachings:

> Never, under any pretext, may abortion be resorted to, either by a family *or by a political authority* as a legitimate means of regulating births. . . . In reality, respect for human life is called for from the time that generation begins. From the time that an ovum is fertilized, a life is begun which is neither that of the father nor that of the mother; it is rather the life of a new human being with his own growth. . . . It may be a serious question of health, sometimes of life or death, for the mother; it may be the burden represented by an additional child, especially if there are good reasons to fear that the child will be abnormal or retarded . . . We proclaim only that none of these reasons can ever objectively confer the right to dispose of another's life, even when that life is only beginning.[7]

Thus, the proposition continues to be maintained by the Church that there *are* definite limits to what the community may do to regulate births, a proposition to which most advocates of extensive access to abortion would probably agree. Of course, both sides may be mistaken as to where those limits are to be found.[8]

It was only a few thousand years ago that Antigone declared herself in unalterable opposition to the decree of a ruler who would have left her brother's corpse for the birds and the dogs to devour. To the ruler's rebuke, "And still you dared overstep [my] laws?", she responded in words that can be revived every generation in one form or another,

> For me it was not Zeus who made that order. Nor did that Justice who lives with the god below mark out such laws to hold among mankind. Nor did I think your orders were so strong that you, a mortal man, could overrun the gods' unwritten and unfailing laws. Not now, nor yesterday's, they always live, and no one knows their origin in time. So not through fear of any man's proud spirit would I be likely to neglect these laws, draw on myself the gods' sure punishment.[9]

And yet, in such controversies, one must, if one wishes truly to understand and to judge responsibly, hear both sides of the question.[10] When the question is so vital as to keep reappearing in so many different forms, the prudent observer suspects that there is indeed something to be said on both sides. Take Antigone, for example. Her nobility is evident; less so, her possible injustice. That is, she is prepared to sacrifice the welfare of the city—for it is in the name of the city's welfare, and not altogether without reason, that the ruler decrees that the body of the "traitor" should be denied burial—she is prepared to sacrifice the welfare of the city for the sake of what we might today call someone's spiritual well-being. The ruler, on the other hand, proceeds as if family-feeling can be entirely subordinated to political concerns: he acts as if the city does not need families to sustain and nourish it, those associations that are linked by blood and that do not reason and organize themselves as cities do.[11]

Antigone neglects the interests of the city; the ruler neglects the interests of the family—and each turns out to be particularly vulnerable by virtue of that which is neglected. She is cast out of the city and takes her life, prematurely as it turns out;[12] he is immersed in the city and loses the family he had counted upon.

The family is today—perhaps it has always been—the natural habitat of what we now know as the individual, the private person, the self. The family does depend upon the city, not only for protection but also for instruction and guidance. But members of a family are bound together by attachments that the city, as such, cannot comprehend: they look inward to those of like blood; they thus invoke a standard that not only questions the city's prerogatives but that can even dismiss the city as essentially conventional or arbitrary in its origins. When one begins to challenge the city in the name of family and ties of common blood, one may well be on the way (if one is enlightened) to also challenging the city in the name of the universal human family and hence the ties of a common species. Thus, the city—the country, the political order—is threatened both from within and from without: in the name of the family from within, in the name of humankind from without.[13] The city tries to meet both of these threats, sometimes with "a bad conscience." It tries to meet these threats by insisting that the natural habitat of the human being is really the city, however much the determination of that city's boundaries and its ways may depend upon chance. The city insists as well, when it knows what it is doing, that an emphasis upon the sovereignty of the family means, in effect, anarchy, and that an emphasis upon the sovereignty of humankind means, in effect, a universal state, temporal or spiritual—that both the sovereignty of the family and the sovereignty of humankind are likely to men, in effect, tyranny.

Such tyrannies—the tyranny of anarchy and the tyranny of universalism—are, when established, pervasive: the man of free spirit has nowhere to go, nowhere to hide. Such tyrannies can make the tyranny of a particular city look pale, and even benevolent, by comparison.[14] Particular tyrants are far more likely to be temporary and circumscribed. It may also be argued that a particular tyranny may be little more than a desperate response to the threatened subversion of the community either by private will or by cosmopolitan pretensions.

III.

It is in these terms—or terms like these—that the case can be made for Henry VIII, Thomas More's demanding sovereign.[15] Such terms present Henry, for all his faults and for all his passions, as standing for a healthy political order, for a political order in which a people can run its own affairs both with the minimum of deference toward either unpredictable private consciences or mysterious foreign potentates and with the minimum of risk from either outworn forms or restless experiments.

Henry died January 28, 1547. He was, when he died, in his fifty-sixth year and had reigned for thirty-seven years and eight months.[16] Seventeen years later William Shakespeare was born—and grew to manhood in an England that permitted his genius to flourish, the England of Elizabeth for which the profligate Henry VIII and his canny penny-pinching father can be thought to have laid the foundations.

It must have been a great time to be alive—for it must have been a time when one could feel that one was fully a human being and hence *truly* alive.[17]

Such times are rare—and much must be endured both in their fashioning and in their preservation.

Sir Thomas More endured a great deal. He was beheaded as a traitor on July 6, 1535, a dozen years before the death of his king. He was, when he died, in his fifty-eighth year, having spent the last year and a half of his life as a prisoner in the Tower of London. He was, only two years before he was executed, Lord Chancellor of England.[18] He was as well the most learned man in England and perhaps her greatest lawyer. His book, *Utopia*, published in 1516, had made him one of the first men in Europe. It should go without saying that such a gifted and conscientious man should never have been killed, whatever his errors (or even crimes) may have been. Rather, such men should be cherished and argued with.[19]

Thomas More's troubles seem to have been generated by Henry's determination to leave a male heir to succeed him. The Wars of the Roses had taught England and her monarchs what civil war meant. Decades of war had ended in 1485 with the enthronement of Henry VII.[20] His son, Henry VIII, could never feel secure until the succession was assured. And for this, he thought, only a son would do. It was then far from certain that a woman could inherit the throne of England in her own right—and it would be irresponsible, some thought, to have to find out.[21]

Catherine of Aragon, the Spanish princess, the first of Henry's six wives (and mother of Mary), had not produced a son.[22] She had, after some twenty years of marriage, reached an awkward age for Henry: too old to bear children, too young to make him a widower. The solution that policy suggested—the replacement of one queen by another—sexual attraction confirmed in the form of the vivacious Anne Boleyn, who was to become the mother of the great Elizabeth. In most other places in the world and at most other times, the substitution of one royal consort for another, for dynastic purposes, would have taken place as a matter of course. Even in sixteenth-century Christendom this could have been arranged. It need not even have been called a divorce, but rather an annulment, a declaration that the marriage between Henry and Catherine had been invalid from the outset inasmuch as Catherine had been Henry's deceased brother's widow. Such a marriage, it was argued by some, was prohibited by Church law. But whatever prohibition there was had been dispensed with to permit this marriage in the first place—and the Pope (Clement VII) could not be prevailed upon (perhaps in part because Rome happened then to be at the mercy of Spanish troops) to revoke the dispensation and thus leave Henry free to remarry or, as the purists would have it, to marry for the first time.[23] In 1533 Henry replaced his first Catherine by his first Anne—and this in clear defiance of the Roman Church.

Had the Pope granted the requested annulment, there would probably have been in England no significant opposition voiced, except perhaps by the pious Catherine herself, to the new marital arrangements. Certainly, it does not seem that there would have been any troublesome domestic objection "on principle" to such an annulment—and devout Catholics would have been able to live with it. Certainly, also, it must have been evident that the Pope could have—and, in other circumstances, might well have—come down on Henry's side.

Did it make sense—*does* it make sense—for anyone to insist upon the defense, even unto death, of a decision that could, perhaps with as much canonical authority, have easily gone the other way? Is the pious man obliged to stand with the Pope, to the furthest extreme in matters of this sort, when he knows that the Pope need not have decided as he did? Besides, is a coerced Pope a reliable guide, a Pope who was probably subjected to far less coercion than the men who were sent to the Tower of London in his defense? Was it not likely that coercion far short of that applied to English dissidents would have induced the Pope and his advisors to see things as Henry did? Is a coercible Pope really to be regarded as the Vicar of Christ? What then, in such circumstances, does a man stand for when he stands with such a Pope against his own King?

IV.

These questions and their like must have occurred to More while he was confined in the Tower. Such questions must have constituted the real trial of Thomas More—for they would have put what he was doing and why to a severe test. The severest test of all may have been the suspicion that he was sacrificing his life for what was essentially a chance position. It is one thing to die for what one considers to be the truth; it is quite another to die for what another man has been persuaded to pronounce to be true when one senses that that pronouncement is essentially arbitrary.

More's formal trial took place five days before he was executed. Parliament had promulgated both an Act of Succession and an Act of Supremacy. The first provided for the substitution of the issue of Anne Boleyn for the issue of Catherine of Aragon as heirs to the throne. The second provided for the substitution of the king for the Pope as head of the Church in England.[24] Thomas More, one gathers, had no difficulty with the Act of Succession: Parliament could make whom it wished king of England, whether legitimate or illegitimate issue of Henry or somebody else altogether.[25] Royal succession was one thing; spiritual succession (or supremacy) was quite another—and

More was not prepared to say that Parliament, or anyone else on earth, could replace the bishop of Rome as head of the Church.[26]

But neither was More prepared to *say* that Parliament could *not* replace the bishop of Rome as head of the Church in England. He evidently believed that he would put his soul in peril if he should "accept" what Parliament had done and that he would put his body in peril if he should "deny" what Parliament had done.[27] It was bad enough, he knew, *not* to accept what Parliament had done, for offices and privileges depended upon taking the oath that recognized the king as head of the Church.[28] Further parliamentary and other maneuvers found Thomas More officially called upon (the only layman thus singled out) to subscribe the controversial oath. His refusal to do so led to his immediate confinement in the Tower.[29] But until he expressly dissented from what Parliament had done in the Act of Supremacy and thereafter—which dissent would be considered treasonous in that it would question the legally prescribed extent of royal power and, in effect, the titles of the King—he evidently could not (as the law was written) be tried, convicted, and executed as a traitor.[30]

Thomas More was, within the confines of his great indiscretion, remarkably cautious. He remained silent: everyone knew he did not believe in what Parliament had done; but no one could testify on oath that he had heard More say he did not so believe. His was a most eloquent and, for the king, a most exasperating and perhaps even dangerous silence—and, it seems, when *this* king became exasperated, his lieutenants became desperate, so desperate that they could eventually produce a witness who was willing to testify that More had indeed said that which everyone believed he believed—and which virtually everyone else in the country had also believed, or at least had said they believed, not too many years before.[31] Other charges were included in the indictment, but they did not count for much. This was the one that mattered, and it did turn upon the testimony of what might well have been a perjured witness.[32] Whether or not this witness perjured himself, however, More in effect confirmed what the witness had attributed to him by explicitly denying, *after* he had been convicted, that any Parliament could recognize anyone other than the Pope as head of the Church in England.[33]

It remains a nice question, for students of legal ethics, whether a lawyer is permitted to put on the stand a witness who will perjure himself in testifying to what is essentially true. No, some will say, it was not true that More had ever *denied* the king's titles. But was not the serious problem here that he did not *believe* the king to be head of the Church in England? Was it not the belief that was critical here, not the statement of the belief?[34] The *voicing* of a belief may be simply the best, perhaps the only practical, evidence as to the belief itself. But if a man in fact does so believe, and out of canniness *indi-*

cates that belief in every way but the one that would condemn him (and all this to the detriment of domestic tranquility), why should not he be obliged and helped to take the consequences of what he truly believes?[35]

The case against More that we *can* be sure of, in that it depends not upon possibly perjured evidence but rather upon an interpretation, mistaken or otherwise, of the evidence everyone would have conceded, may be found in the remarks addressed by a prosecuting attorney to him:

> Sir Thomas, tho' we have not one Word or Deed of yours to object against you, yet we have your Silence, which is an evident sign of the Malice of your Heart: because no dutiful Subject, being lawfully ask'd this question, will refuse to answer it.[36]

Is it not a tribute to the English deference to the rule of law that More could elude powerful enemies as long as he did? Should he, however, have driven foolish enemies to the extremity they did go?[37]

It seems that efforts were made, again and again, to persuade More to retreat from the lonely post to which he considered himself assigned.[38] Assume, for the sake of analysis, that More truly believed that the eternal fate of his soul depended upon not renouncing his opinion that the Pope (in spite of his inevitable human failings) was always the head of the Church, in England as well as everywhere else. Must not considerable credit be given to one who stands by what he believes in? But how much credit? What if that which is believed in should be utter nonsense? Or what if it should be socially disruptive?

Was it reasonable for More to believe that his soul would be perpetually condemned if he should acquiesce? Perhaps, one might say, if acquiescence was merely self-serving and clearly against his reason. But what *did*—what *does*— reason call for here? Could not—should not—a reasonable man have been able to figure out that eternal punishment would hardly follow because a man took one position rather than another in support of a pronouncement that was itself essentially arbitrary?[39] But, it will be said in defense of Thomas More, it was not the correctness of the Pope's pronouncement with respect to Henry's marital status that he defended but rather the right and duty of the Pope, and of the Pope alone, to make such a pronouncement, correctly or incorrectly. The presuppositions and implications of that papal right and duty obliged More to refuse to concede that the king could legitimately be regarded as head of the Church in England. Were not both the Pope and the king unreasonable, *the one* in refusing to grant what the other desperately believed he needed and perhaps in refusing to do so because of threats to his own principality, *the other* in not settling for what he had taken but insisting also upon verbal acknowledgment, not passive acquiescence, from every prominent man in his realm?

Could not—should not—the Pope have held back from acting publicly against the king? That is, a refusal to grant the annulment was one thing; public condemnation of the king was quite another. Should not the Pope have said, for the benefit of men such as More, that although he could not grant the annulment, he would depend upon God to deal in His own way with Henry? Had the Pope conducted himself more prudently, it can be argued that Henry might not have gone so far as to have had himself declared head of the Church in England or that that declaration would not have had the consequences it did. How far *is* a reasonable human being obliged to go in defending the unreasonable, or imprudent, decisions of others?

V.

We repeat a critical question for this occasion: *Was* it reasonable for More to believe that his soul would be perpetually condemned if he should acquiesce, if only for the time being, in what had been done by the Parliament of England? One answer to this question is provided in an assessment of Thomas More made in 1587, a half-century after More's death:

> God had in most bountiful sort poured his blessings upon this man, enduing him with eloquence, wisdom, and knowledge; but the grace of God withdrawn from him, he had the right use of none, no, not of reason as it should be rightly used.[40]

We have seen how someone might question the rationality or sensibleness not only of what More did but perhaps even more of what More allowed to be done to him.

Another answer to the question of More's reasonableness, and hence his correctness, in the circumstances in which he found himself is provided by the great European scholar, a friend of More's, Desiderius Erasmus, who said of More that he was the English Socrates.[41] What is the understanding of Socrates relied upon here? And what does such a comparison oblige us to notice about More?

The similarities between Thomas More and Socrates are apparent. Both men were witty and urbane and hence wonderful companions; both were intelligent and learned men who were considered impractical in some ways, but who were deeply practical in appreciating the power of persuasion and example in bringing out the best in people; and, perhaps most important for those who see a similarity, both were good men who are believed to have suffered death unjustly for the sake of the opinions they held.

The opinions they held, however, were quite different in appearance, and not only on practical questions. These differences can perhaps be summed up in the observation that More was a devote Christian while Socrates, of course, never had the opportunity to consider that faith. By noticing the differences between the two men, and the implications as well as the causes of those differences, one may be assisted in an effort to understand and fairly to pass judgment on More.

Thomas More made much more of this family ties and obligations than Socrates ever seemed to to. This, and several other features of More's understanding of things as well, may be seen in the epitaph More prepared for the tomb of Jane, his first wife, which tomb he intended also for Alice, his second wife, and for himself:

> My beloved wife, Jane, lies here. I, Thomas More, intend that this same tomb shall be Alice's and mine, too. One of these ladies, my wife in the days of my youth, has made me father of a son and three daughters; the other has been as devoted to her step-children (a rare attainment in a stepmother) as very few mothers are to their own children. The one lived out her life with me, the other still lives with me on such terms that I cannot decide whether I did love the one or do love the other more. O, how happily we could have lived all three together, if fate and morality permitted. Well, I pray that the grave, that heaven, will bring us together. Thus death will give what life could not.[42]

It is difficult to imagine Socrates not only able to please one wife, to say nothing of two, but also proclaiming his conjugal accomplishments to the world. More was cared for as he was, by his wives, his children and his step-children and foster-children, in large part because he sincerely cared for them (or at least seemed to)—because, that is, he *displayed* himself as taking most seriously his family ties and duties. Socrates, on the other hand, sometimes seemed to regard his marital connections as something of a joke.[43]

It is also difficult to imagine Socrates seriously believing what More said in his wife's epitaph, that "death will give what life could not." Socrates conducted himself, by and large, as if the only life a reasonable human being can really count upon is here on earth.[44] Certainly, one does not find in any reliable recollections of Socrates a lively expectation of personal immortality, whatever the arguments he might have made from time to time about the indestructibility of souls.[45] Thomas More, on the other hand, seems genuinely concerned, or at least allows himself to appear genuinely concerned, about what his fate will be "there" if he should falter "here."

What More's fate will be, he seems to believe, depends upon what he *believes* (the faith that he subscribes to), a notion that would sound strange coming from Socrates. Socrates does speak of a Delphic oracle having induced him to pursue his unpopular and sometimes dangerous life of inquiry, but that life can be understood as an effort to test the oracle rather than in unquestioning obedience to it.[46]

It is instructive to notice that Socrates was distinguished much more by the *questions* he asked than by the *faith* he espoused. Thomas More, on the other hand, can be said to have been characterized as believing himself to know the answers to the most important questions. Socrates pretended (or was it a pretense?) that his critical achievement had been to become aware of his ignorance,[47] while More professed to know things about which a Socrates simply could never be sure.

Thomas More also professed an allegiance to his sovereign of which Socrates would have been incapable. Would Socrates, in More's place, have tried to question the King, calling him to account for what he was saying about and trying to do to Socrates?[48] Only if he believed such an inquiry useful? Neither death nor the law would have mattered as much to Socrates as they seemed to matter to More. Thomas More *was* a subject; Socrates, somehow, was not. More was a political man; Socrates said that he knew better than to try to be that, observing that he would not have lived as long as he did had he devoted himself to public affairs.[49]

Thomas More, in his own exercise of political power, did things that one can hardly imagine Socrates doing. Thus, More could, when in power, persecute and prosecute religious dissenters—whether ever to the death remains a question for the scholars to settle.[50] He expressed, on more than one occasion (including in the epitaph that he prepared for himself), his hatred of heretics, and this at a time when a number of respectable men and even entire peoples in Europe *had* become "heretical."[51]

Socrates recognized, of course, the need for courts and executioners—but he was himself temperamentally incapable of supervising or performing such useful functions.[52] Would he not have said that no thoughtful man, of mature years, should have conducted himself with the apparent inquisitorial fervor of Thomas More, no matter what the temper and the opinions of the times? Socrates was once directed by the rulers of Athens to go, with others, to fetch a man for a questionable execution: the others went to fetch him while Socrates went home—and, he adds, had not those rulers fallen shortly thereafter, he himself probably would have been killed for this defiance of them.[53] On the other hand, perhaps More stood as firmly as he did in part because he had seen despised heretics stand firmly in defense of what he evidently regarded as false faiths. Did he, that is, learn from his victims? Did both the true faith *and honor* require that he be at least as steadfast as desperate heretics had been?[54]

These differences between More and Socrates should be pursued even further, perhaps down to the divergent opinions that are at the root of each man.

Consider, for example, their respective attitudes toward pleasure. Socrates, was, it is know, often unconcerned about various pleasures of the body; but he would never had said, as More is reported to have said, that "a perfect man should abstain not only from unlawful pleasures but from lawful."[55] That is to say, Socrates was not particularly attracted by many of the things others found pleasurable; More acknowledged their pleasurableness, but resisted them.

Thus, Socrates dressed simply and was remarkably oblivious of cold and heat. He required, in order to be comfortable, far less than most men do.[56] More, on the other hand, made deliberate efforts to render himself uncomfortable—and, we are told, wore a hairshirt much of his adult life.[57] There are reports as well that More deliberately scourged himself.[58] It is difficult to imagine Socrates either wearing a hair shirt or scourging himself—or considering sensible any doctrines that called for or countenanced such systematic mortifications of the flesh.

Their respective attitudes toward pleasure, then, bear thinking about and point to something even deeper, just as do their respective attitudes toward politics. Socrates, we have noticed, knew that he could not engage in politics and survive. More believed he could, and should, engage in politics. He was quite successful at it, and but for a couple of accidents would have survived and died as much in prosperity as he desired. Here, too, we find a key difference between the men: Socrates' estrangement from the city was more nearly necessary than More's.

Socrates' way of thinking called into question, and in an unavoidable manner, the things held most dear by the cities of the world. Socrates said he would have found accusers wherever he would have gone.[59] On the other hand, any one of a number of developments, all of them quite plausible, would have saved More, keeping him from his fatal encounter with a king who very much wanted to keep Thomas More in his camp: Catherine could have borne living sons to Henry; or Catherine could have conveniently died;[60] or Henry could have died; or the Pope could have been spared Spanish pressures; or More could simply have been out of the country when the troubles began.

All this suggests that the essential relations of Socrates and of More to political life were quite different. In short, no contemporary ruler would ever say of Socrates what Charles V (the Holy Roman Emperor and King of Spain, Catherine's nephew) is reported to have said to the English Ambassador upon learning of More's execution:

> My Lord Ambassador, we understand that the King, your master, hath put his faithful servant and grave wise councillor, Sir Thomas More, to death. . . . [I]f

we had been master of such a servant, of whose doings our self have had these many years no small experience, we would rather have lost the best city of our dominions than have lost such a worthy councillor.[61]

VI.

To say that More's troubles were probably accidental is not to suggest that he did not feel deeply the promptings of his conscience. With an invocation of *conscience* we come to what may be the foundation upon which More's trial is based.

Conscience is, it can be said, essentially a Christian term. The Greek word, *synderesis*, once meant, literally, *to know jointly*. By the time of the New Testament it seems to have meant *know with oneself.* Relatively few uses of this word may be found in pre-Christian Greek. For example, one can go through Aristotle's long *Nicomachean Ethics* without noticing either the word *conscience* or any places where it might naturally be used.[62] It is when one comes to the New Testament, particularly to the writings of St. Paul, that one finds important uses of *conscience*.[63] Where the Christian writer uses *conscience*, Aristotle might have used *knowledge of what is right* or simply *good habits*; where the Christian uses *guilt*, Aristotle might have used *shame*.[64]

It is virtually impossible for us today *not* to use the word *conscience*—even when we mean by it something more old-fashioned, that is, something pre-Christian. The contrast between conscience and a sense of shame is instructive: conscience is more private in its implications; shame, more community minded. This may be why there does not seem to be much made of any term like *conscience* in the Hebrew Scriptures. The pious Jew is not expected only to look into his heart, although he *should* do that, but rather he is expected to take his bearings for the most part from the Law that has been handed down to his people.[65] It is when one comes to the Greek Scriptures, and to the doctrines generated by them, that one finds the repeated insistence upon the obligation "to take a stand," often against the things and people of this world—an obligation to stand by one's faith, by one's beliefs. This is an obligation that recognizes one as essentially on one's own, as obliged as well as entitled first and foremost to save one's own soul, to look out for oneself. One is primarily a private man who should not care what others think about one.[66]

If one is not careful, such independence can degenerate into a disregard not only for what others think but also for thinking itself. That is to say, an emphasis upon steadfastness in one's conscience both depends upon and reinforces an emphasis upon an individual will and upon the sincerity of that will.[67] To make a virtue of sincerity is to mean, eventually, that there may be no standards to be invoked, no public discourse to which one may be responsible and in which one must participate. The more that Thomas More invoked his conscience, the less he said.[68] One of the things he did say, and this several times, was that he would be saved by following his conscience while his adversaries could be saved by following *theirs*. Socrates, I believe, would have found this paradoxical assumption in need of considerable investigation.

VII.

If sincerity is enthroned and if standards and argument are played down, there can come a time, and one sees this again and again in one's students, when it becomes fashionable to ask, whenever anyone tries to pass moral judgment, "Who is to say what is right?" This question does not merely recognize that it is often difficult to pass judgment because it is difficult to know the facts; rather, it says, in effect, that there are no truly knowable standards by which anyone should be bound. Among other developments that are likely to follow from the opinions generated by an emphasis upon private will and conscience are a legitimation of self-expression for its own sake and (in order that we might understand and perhaps shape, if only for the sake of therapy, the self that is being expressed) a concern for the unconscious, that chance constellation of psychic forces that determine *who* we are and *what* we do.[69]

There can be something admirable in steadfastness itself, unless the cause in which one is steadfast is simply odious.[70] But is not steadfastness something like courage, that virtue which Aristotle recognized as having so many dubious (or at least divergent) forms?[71] Steadfastness may be something like justice as well—but that virtue too has some dubious forms, as may be seen, for example, when it is regarded as essentially law-abidingness. Do not what is truly courageous and what is truly just depend upon wisdom? Do not they depend not only upon an awareness of the commands one has been given (the laws of one's city in the circumstances in which one finds oneself), but perhaps even more upon an understanding of what the simply best would consist of?[72]

An emphasis upon conscience tends to discount the primacy of wisdom, especially that wisdom which takes the form of prudence. In fact, if sincerity and steadfastness are what count, then that for which one stands becomes secondary. The important thing is to stand for *something*, to "commit" oneself to something—and this, it is presumed, everyone can do. "Who *is* to say what is right?" Why, the human being who knows, of course. It can be difficult to know who knows, just as it can be difficult to get *to* know. But neither effort will be made if it should be generally believed that there is a royal road to virtue and that that road is readily available to everyone, that there is nothing really to be *learned* but only something to be *felt* and *done*—and that what is important about what is done is that it *be* done and that it be done sincerely, that is to say, with a good conscience.[73]

Of course, More does not deny that there are standards. His conscience tells him that there *are*, and that the Roman Catholic Church is often the authoritative expositor of those standards. What More chooses and to some extent examines, then, are not the standards but rather the guardians of the standards. But since he grants, in his extremity, the right to others to follow *their* consciences, he ultimately seems to have no argument in support of one set of standards over another. It is indeed appropriate that perhaps the greatest martyr to conscience in the English-speaking world should (in that extremity) have spoken so little about what he was doing and why.

VIII.

If one does *not* consider the call of conscience sufficient guidance, one can begin to consider such questions as this: Is it better to be sincere but wrong or to be insincere but right? Clearly best, of course, would be to be sincere *and* right—that is, to enjoy performing the right action. Which, then, is worse, that Thomas More believed he would be eternally lost if he affirmed the king's supremacy or that he only pretended to believe that? Or, put another way, did More make as much as he did of conscience and the salvation of his soul, despite the risk of misdirecting people's moral attention, in order to do what he could to advance particular temporal, even political ends?[74]

Those ends, taking the best possible view of what More was attempting to do, may be reduced to one: wisdom should govern human affairs, not national interest, not the appetites of sovereigns, not partisan maneuvering, whether by laymen or by clergy. Did he believe, that is, that respect for natural right and international law, both of which recognize the primacy as well as the fragility of reason in human affairs, depended, in his time, upon a united Europe and *that* in turn depended upon the Roman Church as the only available long-established religious institution in the Western world?[75] Did the Church somehow stand for natural right (albeit in the form of "natural law"), for rules and limitations on the private desires both of individuals and of sovereigns, be they kings, parliaments, or revolutionary movements? Are invocations of "conscience" and of "the laws of God" a way, a then-popular way (just as reminders of the right of revolution can be today an instructive way) of talking about natural right?[76] Does such support of natural right as a united Church can provide require unquestioning public dedication to an established central institution that, in the nature of things, *is* subject to the caprices of particular men?

One price of such a unified moral authority—and unless moral teaching *is* unified it is not, for most people, likely to be authoritative—may be the risk of foolish, even cruel, campaigns against heretics. But the alternative to a unified moral authority, it may also be argued, is fragmentation of the human soul as well as of human communities, permitting the intensification both of futile pleasures and of national passions. Such fragmentation leads in turn to the unprecedented mindless yet highly systematized atrocities of the twentieth century, in the light of which the cruelties of even the Inquisition pale by comparison.

Thus, one must ask, which is the more significant in understanding the role of Thomas More's Church in the sixteenth century, the coercion that we can detect behind some Vatican decisions or the deliberative form in which such decisions were couched? Coercion comes and goes—but the deliberative form, drawing upon and leaving precedents and a body of moral standards, remains available for use by those who are dedicated to realistic efforts to subject human affairs to the restraints and guidance of practical wisdom.[77] All this apparatus *can* be repudiated and dismantled, in the name of the independence of individuals as well as of nations. But the alternatives may be the unleashing of private desires and the promotion of worldwide catastrophes— that is to say, anarchy within the human soul and ever more violent conflicts among nations. Both kinds of disturbances promote tyranny.

It is along these lines that a case can be made for Thomas More, a case that sees him using, in the name of a humane and unified Europe, the language and forms of his time. It was a Europe that would permit a Shakespeare to emerge, a Shakespeare who can be thought of as consolidating, at least for the English-speaking peoples, the moral legacy which More had stood for. To make such a case for More is to assume that he saw what we might be able to see as the evident difficulties with the public position he took. It is to recognize, that is, that there was indeed an urbane, intelligent, and learned man behind the mask of a sometimes troublesome piety. It is to recognize, as well, that More trusted us to make, in changed circumstances, the case he was not in a position to make explicitly himself.[78] A carefully orchestrated drama of trial and execution could be expected to interest people in More's enduring aspirations, even people who would have little patience with hairshirts and mortification of the flesh. Perhaps, in any event, More depended upon us to see him in the best possible light and thereby to cherish among ourselves both nobility of the human spirit and dedication to the rule of law.

IX.

I have, you will recall, promised you a concluding story. And one's debts should be discharged, at least when it is not clearly unreasonable to do so.

It is important, I have in effect argued on this occasion, to find out what can be said on all sides of serious issues. Only if one grasps and concedes the merits of each side, can one begin to understand what the issues are truly about and to engage the interest, resources, and good will of the contending parties for a sound resolution. This is the course of moderation, it seems to me, that moderation that partisan passions can make so unfashionable.

I have just given you the moral of the story I have promised. Now for the story itself:

There was a rabbi, with a reputation as a marriage counsellor, who had an outspoken wife. She managed on one occasion to overhear her husband's dealings with a contentious couple. First the woman came to the rabbi and laid out her complaints: her husband did not devote himself as much as she had once been led to expect he would to her and their children and that short-coming everyone could see. This she said and much more. To all this, the rabbi replied, "You're right, my good woman, you're right. Do what you can." She went home somewhat pacified.

Then the man came to the rabbi and told his side of the story: his wife was always trying to get her own way without making a serious effort to under-stand what was really important. This he said and much more. To all this, too, the rabbi replied, "You're right, my good man, you're right. Do what you can." He also went home somewhat pacified.

Thereupon the rabbi's wife upbraided him: "First the woman said thus and so, and you told her she was right. Then the man came and said thus and so, and you told him also that he was right. What kind of a rabbi are you anyway? Don't you know you are supposed to decide who's really right?" To which the good rabbi replied, "You're right, my dear, you're right."

NOTES

1. This talk was given in the Law Lecture Series at Rosary College (now Domini-can University), River Forest, Illinois, March 6, 1975. Its original title was "Politics and Piety: The Trial of Sir Thomas More." See chapter 12, note 189.

2. See "Sir Thomas More (1478–535)," 13 *Dictionary of National Biography* 876 (1917).

3. See 13 *Dictionary of National Biography*, p. 886; *The Trial of Sir Thomas More Knight, Lord Chancellor of England, for High-Treason in Denying the King's Su-premacy, May 7, 1535, the 26th of Henry VIII*, in Francis Hargrave, ed., *A Complete Collection of State-Trials and Proceedings for High-Treason, and Other Crimes and Misdemeanors* (4th edition; London: T. Wright, 1776), I, 59, 63–4 (1776) (cited here-after as *State-Trials*). One of More's more solemn jests was in response to the Duke of Norfolk who had warned him, "By the Mass, Master More, it is perilous striving with Princes. And therefore I would wish you somewhat to incline to the King's plea-

sure, for, by God's body, Master More, '*Indignatio principis mors est*' ['The wrath of the prince is death']." "Is that all, my Lord?" More asked. "Then in good faith is there no more difference between your Grace and me, but that I shall die today and you tomorrow." William Roper, *The Life of Sir Thomas More, Knight*, in Ernest E. Reynolds, ed., *Lives of Saint Thomas More* (London: Everyman's Library, 1963), p. 35. See chapter 10, note 61. Thomas More had had occasion, upon resigning the office of Lord Chancellor, to give advice upon how Princes should be dealt with:

> Master [Thomas] Cromwell, you are now entered into the service of a most noble, wise and liberal Prince. If you will follow my poor advice, you shall, in your counsel giving unto His Grace, ever tell him what he ought to do, but never what he is able to do. So shall you show yourself a true faithful servant and a right worthy Councillor. For if a lion knew his own strength, hard were it for any man to rule him.

Roper, *The Life of Sir Thomas More*, p. 28. See chapter 10, note 68. Compare chapter 4, note 17.

4. See, on this criminologist (Hans W. Mattick), George Anastaplo, *The Artist as Thinker: From Shakespeare to Joyce* (Athens, Ohio: Ohio University Press, 1983), p. 437 n. 183.

5. See, e.g., the text at note 43 of chapter 9 of this collection. See also chapter 9, note 49.

6. See chapter 4-B.

7. *Chicago Daily News*, November 25, 1974, p. 1 (emphasis added).

8. See, e.g., George Anastaplo, *Human Being and Citizen: Essays on Virtue, Freedom, and the Common Good* (Chicago: Swallow Press, 1975), pp. 46–50. See also George Anastaplo, "On Trial: Explorations," 22 *Loyola University of Chicago Law Journal* 765, 1113 n. 876, 1115 n. 882 (1991).

9. Sophocles, *Antigone* 449–59.

10. See, on Athena as a proper judge in Aeschylus' *The Eumenides*, chapter 2-D, section V.

11. See chapter 4-B, section II.

12. See the text at note 50 of chapter 4 of this collection. See also chapter 8, note 33, chapter 9, note 3.

13. See George Anastaplo, "Freedom of Speech and the First Amendment: Explorations," 21 *Texas Tech Law Review* 1941, 1980 (1990).

14. See Leo Strauss, *On Tyranny*, Victor Gourevitch and Michael S. Roth, eds. (New York: The Free Press, 1991), pp. 10–1. See also pp. 238–39, 255–56, 290.

15. See the text at note 45 of chapter 8 of this collection.

16. See, for a lively account of the reign of Henry VIII, Winston S. Churchill, *A History of the English-Speaking Peoples* (New York: Bantam Books, 1963), II, 22–27. See also J. J. Scarisbrick, *Henry VIII* (Berkeley: University of California Press, 1968), pp. 236, 305f, 498–99.

17. See, e.g., John Aubrey, *Brief Lives*.

18. See chapter 10, note 2.

19. Another great lawyer, Francis Bacon (1561–626), also published a "utopian" classic (*New Atlantis*). He, too, should probably have been treated more

considerately than he was by the legal system of his country when *he* stepped out of line.

20. "For a generation and more the English monarchy had been tossed on the rough waters of a disputed succession. On August 22, 1485, Henry Tudor, Earl of Richmond, had won a decisive victory near the small Midland town of Market Bosworth, and his rival, the usurper Richard III, was slain in the battle. In the person of Henry VII a new dynasty now mounted the throne, and during the twenty-four years of careful stewardship that lay before him a new era in English history begins." Churchill, *A History of the English-Speaking Peoples*, II, 13. See, for a dramatic account of the Wars of the Roses, Shakespeare, *History Plays*. See, on some of the constitutional implications of that development, George Anastaplo, *The Constitution of 1787: A Commentary* (Baltimore: Johns Hopkins University Press, 1989), pp. 74–78. See, on realism and the *History Plays*, George Anastaplo, "Law & Literature and Shakespeare: Explorations," 26 *Oklahoma City University Law Review* 1, 133 (2001).

21. The following observations by Winston Churchill are instructive: "It was still doubtful if a woman could succeed to the throne by English law. Would England tolerate being ruled by a woman? Might Mary [Henry's first daughter] not turn out very like her Spanish mother, narrow and bigoted, a possible queen perhaps in Spain, or France, or Austria, *countries full of soldiers*, but not acceptable to the free English, who had obeyed Henry VII and Henry VIII because they wished to obey, and although there was no central army except the Beefeaters in the Tower? Would Mary be able to rule in the Tudor manner, by favour and not by force? The long clash of the Wars of the Roses had been a nightmare to the nation that a disputed succession might revive. To the monarch these great questions of State were also questions of conscience, in which his sensual passions and his care for the stability of the realm were all fused together." *A History of the English-Speaking Peoples*, II, 36 (emphasis added).

22. Here, again, is Churchill: "Then there was Queen Catherine. In 1525 she was aged forty. . . . A typical Spanish princess, she had matured and aged rapidly; it was clear that she would bear Henry no male heir. Either the King's illegitimate son, the Duke of Richmond, now aged six, would have to be appointed by Act of Parliament, or perhaps England might accept Catherine's child, Mary, now aged nine, as the first Queen of England in her own right since Matilda." *A History of the English-Speaking Peoples*, II, 36.

23. The Beefeaters at the Tower of London are not purists in these matters. They provide curious visitors with a handy guide, in the form of doggerel, to the fate of the six wives of Henry VIII: "Divorced, beheaded, died; divorced, beheaded, survived." (Should *annulled* be substituted for *divorced* in this formula?) Both Henry's second wife, Anne Boleyn, and his fourth, Catherine Howard, were executed for adultery. See Churchill, *A History of the English-Speaking Peoples*, II, 52–54, 63. Henry VIII was succeeded by his children in this order: Edward VI, the son of his third wife, Jane Seymour; Mary, the daughter of Catherine of Aragon; and Elizabeth I, the daughter of Anne Boleyn. See Churchill, *A History of the English-Speaking Peoples*, II. 67.

See, on chance and the form that challenges and issues may take, appendix C to this collection.

24. See *State Trials*, I, 59–60; 13 *Dictionary of National Biography* 881–85. See also Quentin Skinner, "The Lessons of Thomas More," *New York Review of Books*,

October 12, 1978, p. 58. See as well the accounts of these Acts of Parliament and their consequences in the biographies of Thomas More by William Roper and Nicholas Harpsfield in Reynolds, ed., *Lives of Saint Thomas More.*

25. See the exchange between Thomas More and Richard Rich reported in *State Trials*, I, 59. Although Parliament could have appointed as a successor Henry's illegitimate son (see chapter 10, note 22), Henry evidently considered it politically sounder to rely upon a legitimate son—and this required a new marriage, but a marriage that the accepted religion of his people would sanction, both during his life *and long thereafter.*

26. Thomas More, after he was convicted for high treason, did say, "For as much as, my Lords, this Indictment is grounded upon an Act of Parliament, directly repugnant to the Laws of God and his Holy Church, the Supreme Government of which, or of any part thereof, no Temporal Person may by any Law presume to take upon him, being what of right belongs to the See of Rome, which by special Prerogative was granted by the Mouth of our Saviour Christ himself to St. Peter, and the Bishops of Rome his Successors only, whilst he lived, and was personally present here on Earth: it is therefore, amongst Catholic Christians, insufficient in Law, to charge any Christian to obey it." *State Trials*, I, 61–62. See also I, 59; 13 *Dictionary of National Biography* 882; chapter 10, note 66.

This kind of argument probably does not sound as persuasive today to most pious Christians as it might have seemed to Thomas More or at least to his supporters. How would Socrates, for example, have dealt with it? Perhaps in the spirit of the inquiry he might have made of a headstrong Antigone about the grounds of the confidence *she* had in her judgment as to the precise burial services required by the gods for her brother's corpse and about the basis of her opinion as to what would happen to her brother or to her if the prescribed burial services could not be safely provided in the circumstances confronting Antigone? See note 58 of chapter 10. See also chapter 4-B, chapter 8, note 65. See, on Socrates' relaxed opinion about the proper disposition of his own corpse, Plato, *Phaedo*. Did both Antigone and Thomas More happen, in effect, to consider long-established conventions to have been decreed by the divine and perhaps ratified by nature? Compare the text at note 41 of chapter 10 of this collection. What, indeed, is the proper relation between *prudence* and *piety*? See chapter 5.

Leo Strauss observed that "every Platonic dialogue is based on the deliberate disregard of something crucially important." *On Tyranny*, p. 292. May not the same be said (except perhaps for the deliberateness) about the "dialogue" that Thomas More fashioned in his fatal encounter with Henry VIII? See note 51 of chapter 8 of this collection, note 68 of chapter 10.

27. References were made to "a two-edged Sword." See *State Trials*, I, 59, 60.

28. But, it seems, the citizen as citizen did not yet have a duty to take such a "loyalty oath"—or any need to do so if he was content to forego public office and to mind only his own business. See Roper, *The Life of Sir Thomas More*, pp. 28–29. See also the text at note 26 of appendix B to this collection.

29. See Roper, *The Life of Sir Thomas More*, pp. 32–37; 13 *Dictionary of National Biography* 884–85. Similarly, More had been the first layman to be made Lord Chancellor. See chapter 10, note 38.

30. See Roper, *The Life of Sir Thomas More*, p. 885; J. Duncan M. Derrett, "The Trial of Sir Thomas More," *English Historical Review*, LXXIX (No. 312), 449, 353f (1964).

31. See *State Trials*, I, 62:

> Here the Lord Chancellor [Audley] took [More] up, and said, That seeing all the Bishops, Universities, and the most learned Men in the Kingdom had agreed to that Act, it was much wondered that he alone should so stiffly stickle, and so vehemently argue there against it.
>
> [More's] Answer was, That if the Number of Bishops and Universities were so material as his Lordship seem'd to make it, then, my Lord, I see no reason why that thing should make any Change in my Conscience: for I doubt not, but of the learned and virtuous Men now alive, I do not speak only of this Realm, but of all Christendom, there are ten to one of my mind in this matter; but if I should take notice of those learned Doctors and virtuous Fathers that are already dead, many of whom are Saints in Heaven, I am sure there are far more, who all the while they lived thought in this Case as I do now. And therefore, my Lord, I do not think my self bound to conform my Conscience to the Counsel of one Kingdom, against the general Consent of all Christendom.

This was said by More *after* he had been found guilty of high treason. See also chapter 10, note 66. See, on *conscience*, chapter 10, section VI. See, on the condition of those "that are already dead," the text at note 45 of chapter 10 of this collection.

32. It must be rare that a vital witness in major litigation has been so soundly attacked as to credibility as Richard Rich was attacked by Thomas More on this occasion. Thus, More could ask, "Can it therefore seem likely to your Lordships, that I should in so weighty an Affair as this, act so unadvisedly, as to trust Mr. Rich, a Man I had always so mean an Opinion of, in reference to his Truth and Honesty, so very much before my Sovereign Lord the King, to whom I am so deeply indebted for his manifold Favours, or any of his noble and grave Counsellors, that I should only impart to Mr. Rich the Secrets of my Conscience *in respect to the King's Supremacy, the particular Subject, and only point about which I have been so long pressed to explain myself?*" *State Trials*, I, 61 (emphasis added). See Derrett, "The Trial of Sir Thomas More," pp. 463–68.

33. See chapter 10, note 26. See also chapter 10, note 66. Is not More conducting himself as a patriot here in that he concedes the basis in fact upon which his king's action rests? That is, King Henry is allowed to *seem* less unjust than he might otherwise be taken to be by his subjects?

34. See chapter 10, note 28. See also chapter 12, note 118. Thomas More had this to say about the proper significance of silence: "[Neither] this Statute, nor no other Law in the World can punish any Man for his Silence, seeing they can do no more than punish Words or Deeds; 'tis God only that is the Judge of the Secrets of our Hearts." *State Trials*, I, 60. See chapter 10, note 36. See also the text at note 25 of appendix B to this collection. See as well chapter 10, note 68.

35. Still, More suggests that silence can be regarded as a form of consent, not as a form of opposition. See chapter 10, note 36. But does not this depend upon the circumstances, something that a court is bound to take into account?

36. *State Trials*, I, 60. This follows immediately after the speech just quoted in chapter 10, note 34. The prosecutor's rebuke here is followed by this suggestion by More:

Sir, my Silence is no sign of any Malice in my Heart, which the King himself must own by my Conduct upon divers Occasions; neither doth it convince any Man of the Breach of the Law: for it is a Maxim amongst the Civilians and Canonists, Qui tacet consentire videtur, he that holds his peace, *seems* to give his Consent.

State Trials, I, 60. (emphasis added). See chapter 10, note 35. See also Derrett, "The Trial of Sir Thomas More," p. 459.

37. See Anastaplo, *Human Being and Citizen*, pp. 12–1, 26, 238 n. 26.

38. Thomas More may have been the only layman to suffer as he did on this issue. All of the other martyrs in England at that time were priests and friars, including a bishop whose imprudent public elevation by the Pope to the College of Cardinals, while he was held in the Tower of London, sealed his fate with Henry. See Nicholas Harpsfield, *The Life and Death of Sir Thomas More, Knight*, in Reynolds, ed., *Lives of Saint Thomas More*, pp. 152–53. See also chapter 10, note 29, chapter 10, note 78.

39. See, e.g., chapter 8, sections VII, IX. See also the appendixes to this collection.

40. *Shakespeare's Holinshed*, Richard Hosley, ed. (New York: Putnam, 1968), p. 310.

41. See, on More's reputation abroad, 13 *Dictionary of National Biography* 886; Roper, *The Life of Sir Thomas More*, p. 3; Harpsfield, *The Life and Death of Sir Thomas More*, p. 169, p. 164 ("our noble, new, Christian Socrates"), 174 ("Christian English Cicero"). Compare chapter 10, note 26.

42. *The Latin Epigrams of Thomas More*, Leicester Bradner and Charles A. Lynch, eds. (Chicago: University of Chicago Press, 1953), No. 242.

43. Xenophon is instructive here. Leo Strauss is quoted as having said about Xenophon, "'But Xenophon, Xenophon is a pure joy to read.' (Raising his eyes to heaven.) 'It is not like reading authors like Thucydides and Plato. These are incomparably great and always formidable, but with Xenophon you are with an equal—a pure joy to read!'" Diskin Clay, "A Forgotten Kind of Reading," in Alan Udoff, ed., *Leo Strauss's Thought* (Boulder, Colorado: L. Rienner Publishers, 1991), p. 264 n. 7. See also Strauss, *On Tyranny*, p. 549, passim. See, on Xenophon's Socrates, chapter 6-B of this collection.

44. See Plato, *Apology* 40C sq. See also Strauss, *On Tyranny*, p. 264.

45. See, e.g., Plato, *Meno* 81C sq.; Plato, *Republic* 614B sq.; Plato, *Phaedo*.

46. One must wonder, as well, what it was that had prompted Socrates to do what he had been doing *before* someone was moved to go to the considerable trouble and expense of travelling to Delphi to ask Apollo whether any man was wiser than Socrates. See Anastaplo, *Human Being and Citizen*, p. 23; chapter 6, note 27.

47. See chapter 9, note 49.

48. See, e.g., Plato, *Meno* 100B-C; Plato, *Charmides*; Plato, *Apology* 21B sq. See also chapter 6 of this collection.

49. See Plato, *Apology* 32A.

50. See, e.g., John P. Roche, "Burying the Hatchet on Sir Thomas More," *Chicago Tribune*, October 26, 1974, sec. 1, p. 13:

[More] was not canonized for his labors as Lord Chancellor of England, where he succeeded his patron Thomas Cardinal Wolsey as the top "royal hatchetman." He was personally honest—the first Chancellor to refuse "gifts" from litigants—but when King Henry was out getting the papal designation "Defender of the Faith," his Chancellor was sending Lutheran heretics to their execution. While I believe in an historical statute of limitations, the execution of heretics does not in my book qualify one for sainthood.

See the text at note 145 of chapter 12 of this collection.

51. See 13 *Dictionary of National Biography* 882–83; J. McGee, "Thomas More and Henry VIII Delineated Too Narrowly," *The Center Magazine*, January/February 1979, p. 38. See also chapter 1, note 95. Even so, More's *Utopia* is ahead of its time with respect to the religious toleration *espoused* therein. See Roper, *The Life of Sir Thomas More*, pp. 18–19. Compare chapter 12-C.

52. See Plato, *Gorgias* 425E–53A, 455A, 468C, 469B-C, 473E–74B, 480A-C, 485B sq., 516C-D, 521D, 522D-E, 523A sq. See also Strauss, *On Tyranny*, p. 275; chapter 10, note 62.

53. See Plato, *Apology* 32B-D.

54. See the text at note 37 of chapter 8 of this collection. See also chapter 7, note 49.

55. Eva Brann, "'An Exquisite Platform': *Utopia*," *Interpretation*, Autumn, 1972, p. 4.

56. See e.g., Plato, *Symposium* 219E–20B. See also chapter 6, note 25.

57. See, e.g., Roper, *The Life of Sir Thomas More*, pp. 24–25. See also Churchill, *A History of the English-Speaking Peoples*, II, 40 (on the self-indulgent Cardinal Wolsey's hairshirt). There was even, we have been told, probably a hairshirt beneath the fine robes depicted in Holbein's famous portrait of More.

58. See, e.g., Roper, *The Life of Sir Thomas More*, p. 25. This fits in with More's repeated references to "this miserable World." See, e.g., *State Trials*, I, 60. See also chapter 10, note 61. Compare, e.g., Aristotle, *Politics* 1278b25–9 (on the natural sweetness of existence); Plato, *Protagoras* 534 sq.; Leo Strauss, *Natural Right and History* (Chicago: University of Chicago Press, 1953), p. 250; George Anastaplo, *The American Moralist: On Law, Ethics, and Government* (Athens, Ohio: Ohio University Press, 1992), pp. 596–601; chapter 10, note 61. Thomas More's spirit with respect to these matters seems to have been inherited by his daughter. Consider *State Trials*, I, 64:

[More's] head was taken off at one Blow, and was placed upon London-Bridge, where having continued for some Months, and being about to be thrown into the Thames to make room for others, his Daughter Margaret bought it, inclos'd it in a Leaden Box, and kept it for a Relique.

See chapter 10, note 26.

John Gormly observed several decades ago, about Aristotle's "sweetness of existence" passage, that Aristotle has a healthier mind than Thomas Hobbes, for whom there is no joy of life, but only terror of death.

59. See Plato, *Apology* 37C-E. It was not inevitable that Socrates be condemned and executed, but "only" that he should always live under a cloud. See chapter 6.

60. Catherine did die in 1536, less than a year after Thomas More was executed. By that time Henry had broken with Anne Boleyn and was interested in Jane Seymour. See Churchill, *A History of the English-Speaking Peoples*, II, 52. See also the text at note 130 of chapter 12 of this collection.

61. Roper, *The Life of Sir Thomas More*, p. 50. Compare the comment made by Thomas More about Henry at a time when the king was displaying great affection for him: "I find his Grace my very good lord indeed, and I believe he doth as singularly favour me as any subject within this Realm. However, son Roper, I may tell thee I have no cause to be proud thereof, for if my head could win him a castle in France (for then was there war between us) it should not fail to go." Roper, *The Life of Sir Thomas More*, p. 12. See chapter 10, note 3.

Underlying the differences between Socrates and Thomas More are those between reason and revelation. See Leo Strauss, *The Rebirth of Classical Political Rationalism* (Chicago: University of Chicago Press, 1989), p. 206:

Both the traditional and current interpretations of Plato may be said to bring out the tragic element in Plato's thought, but they neglect the comic element except where it hits one in the face. Many reasons can be given for this failure. I mention only one. Modern research on Plato originated in Germany, the country without comedy. To indicate why the element of comedy is of crucial importance in Plato I read to you a few lines from the only Platonist I know of who had an appreciation of this element, Sir Thomas More. I quote: "For to prove that this life is no laughing time, but rather the time of weeping we find that our saviour himself wept twice or thrice, but never find we that he laughed as much as once. I will not swear that he never did, but at the leastwise he left us no example of it. But on the other side, he left us example of weeping" (*Dialogue of Comfort Against Tribulation*, chap. 13). If we compare what More said about Jesus with what Plato tells us about Socrates, we find that "Socrates laughed twice or thrice, but never find we that he wept as much as once." A slight bias in favor of laughing and against weeping seems to be essential to philosophy. For the beginning of philosophy as the philosophers understood it is not the fear of the Lord, but wonder. Its spirit is not hope and fear and trembling, but serenity on the basis of resignation. To that serenity, laughing is a little bit more akin than weeping. Whether the Bible or philosophy is right is of course the only question which ultimately matters. But in order to understand that question one must first see philosophy as it is. One must not see it from the outset through Biblical glasses. Wherever each of us may stand, no respectable purpose is served by trying to prove that we eat the cake and have it. Socrates used all his powers to awaken those who can think out of the slumber of thoughtlessness. We ill follow his example if we use his authority for putting ourselves to sleep.

See chapter 10, note 58.

62. See also *On Tyranny*, p. 275, where Leo Strauss says (in a letter to Alexandre Kojève):

[T]here is no "conscience" in Plato; anamnesis is not conscience (see *Natural Right and History*, p. 150n. re Polemarchus). Indeed, misology is the worst, as you say; therefore, there is ultimately no superiority of the merely honorable man to the sophist (contrary to Kant) or for that matter to Alc[ibiades] (cf. *N. R. & H.*, p. 151). I do not believe in the possibility of a conversation of Socrates with the *people* (it is not clear to me what you think about this); the relation of the philosopher to the people is mediated by a certain kind of rhetoricians who arouse fear of punishment after death; the philosopher can guide these rhetoricians but can not do their work (this is the meaning of the *Gorgias*).

See chapter 10, note 52. Are the people at large much more impressed by the prospect of death than is the philosopher? See chapter 10, note 3. Is the relation of *conscience* to *understanding* somewhat like the relation of the *people* to the *philosopher*? Samples of Thomas More's use of *conscience* may be seen in chapter 10, notes 31, 32, chapter 10, note 66. See also chapter 10, note 34.

63. See, e.g., Rudolf Bultmann, *Theology of the New Testament* (New York: Charles Scribner's Sons, 1951), I, 71–72; and Bultmann (1955), II, 226.

64. The Hebrew Scriptures also prefer *shame* to *conscience*. In a standard translation of the Bible into English, I count some thirty uses of *conscience* in the New Testament and none in the Old Testament, and some ninety uses of *shame* in the Old Testament to a dozen or so in the New Testament. See, for an instructive use by Leo Strauss of *sense of shame* where others today would probably use *conscience*, Anastaplo, *The Artist as Thinker*, p. 475 n. 282. See also John A. Murley, "*In re* George Anastaplo," in Kenneth L. Deutsch and John A. Murley, eds., *Leo Strauss, the Straussians, and the American Regime* (Lanham, Md.: Rowman & Littlefield, 1999), p. 159; appendix C, note 58.

65. See chapter 9, note 5. See also the text at note 15 of chapter 1, at note 70 of chapter 5, and at note 89 of chapter 7 of this collection.

66. See, on the shift in status for *parresia* from Classical to New Testament Greek, George Anastaplo, *The Constitutionalist: Notes on the First Amendment* (Dallas: Southern Methodist University Press, 1971), pp. 275, 781–82 nn. 8, 9. The emphasis shifts from a questionable "license of tongue" to a praiseworthy "frankness of speech" (or even to "intrepid testimony to the Lord"). On the relation between praiseworthy frankness of speech and a properly informed conscience, consider this exchange between Thomas More and his judges:

> When [More] had received Sentence of Death, he spake thus with a resolute and sedate Aspect: Well, seeing I am condemn'd, God knows how justly, I will freely speak for the disburdening my Conscience, what I think of this Law. When I perceived it was the King's Pleasure to sift out from whence the Pope's Authority was deriv'd; I confess I study'd seven years together to find out the truth of it, and I could not meet with the Works of any one Doctor, approv'd by the Church, that avouch a Layman was, or ever could be the Head of the Church.
>
> *Chancellor.* Would you be esteem'd wiser, or to have a sincerer Conscience than all the Bishops, learned Doctors, Nobility and Commons of this Realm?
>
> *More.* I am able to produce against one Bishop which you can produce on your side, a hundred Holy and Catholic Bishops for my Opinion; and against one Realm, the Consent of Christendom for a thousand years.

Norfolk. Sir Thomas, you show your obstinate and malicious mind.

More. Noble Sir, 'tis no Malice or Obstinacy that makes me say this, but the just Necessity of the Cause obliges me to it for the Discharge of my Conscience; and I call God to witness, that nothing but this has excited me to it.

State Trials, I, 62. See chapter 8, notes 43, 44. Does this approach lead eventually to what we know as an emphasis upon *individuality*? See chapter 10, notes 31, 37. See, on the usefulness of studying certain matters "seven years together," chapter 3, note 20; chapter 6. See also chapter 10, note 26.

67. See, on resoluteness and the will, chapter 1, notes 115, 116; chapter 2, note 18; chapter 5, note 52, chapter 9, note 23. Notice the use of *resolute* with respect to Thomas More in chapter 10, note 66. See, on Martin Heidegger and a perverted "resoluteness," Anastaplo, *The American Moralist*, pp. 144–50.

68. Thomas More was informed, the morning of his execution, that it was "the King's Pleasure he shou'd not use many Words at the Place of Execution." *State Trials,* I, 63. Was this a grim jest on the part of a king who had been exasperated so long by More's silence with respect to the Act of Supremacy? See chapter 10, notes 3, 34, chapter 10, note 78. See also chapter 4, note 17, chapter 10, note 26.

69. See, on the *self*, Anastaplo, *Human Being and Citizen*, pp. 87–86.

70. A parody of steadfastness may be seen in the testimony by Hermann Goering during the Nuremburg Trial about how he maintained his loyalty to the Fuehrer in bad times as in good. See chapter 12, note 49.

71. See Aristotle, *Nicomachean Ethics*, bk. 3, chap. 6.

72. See e.g., chapter 1, note 91; chapter 2, note 31; conclusion, note 2. See also Strauss, *On Tyranny*, pp. 229–30.

73. See, on Existentialism, Anastaplo, *The American Moralist*, pp. 139–43, 144–50.

74. That is, what was the controversy with respect to "the King's Marriage" truly about? See chapter 10, note 78.

75. See the text at note 48 of chapter 8 of this collection. The significance of Delphi in the ancient Greek world is not generally appreciated today. See, e.g., chapter 4, note 15; chapter 10, note 46; chapter 6; chapter 10, note 78. See also George Anastaplo, *Human Being and Citizen*, pp. 18–9, 23–5, 245 n. 47; George Anastaplo, *The Thinker as Artist: From Homer to Plato & Aristotle* (Athens, Ohio: Ohio University Press, 1997), p. 93.

76. See Anastaplo, *Human Being and Citizen*, pp. 42–50. Consider also the 1953 observation by M. Kojève to Mr. Strauss upon receiving a Strauss discussion of "natural law" (probably *Natural Right and History*, published in 1953):

Regarding the issue, I can only keep repeating the same thing. If there is something like "human nature," then you are surely right in everything. But to deduce from premises is not the same as to prove these premises. And to infer premises from (anyway questionable) consequences is always dangerous.

Strauss, *On Tyranny*, p. 261. See also pp. 261–2, 266. What does M. Kojève's implicit (and natural?) condemnation of "a Chinese peasant's animal-like starvation existence (before Mao-Tse Tung)" concede about the existence of a human nature that has ethical implications around the world in a variety of circumstances? See Strauss, *On Tyranny*, p. 262. See also chapter 1, note 91, conclusion, note 2.

77. See Anastaplo, *The American Moralist*, pp. 161–70, 345–48.

78. Thomas More's case is made, in a politically robust way, in Churchill, *A History of the English-Speaking Peoples*, p. 50:

> [Bishop John] Fisher and Sir Thomas More, who both refused the oath, were confined in the Tower for many months. At his trial More offered a brilliant defense, but the King's former trust in him had now turned into vengeful dislike. Under royal pressure the judges pronounced him guilty of treason. While Fisher was in the Tower the Pope created seven cardinals, of whom one was "John, Bishop of Rochester, kept in prison by the King of England." Directly Henry heard the news; he declared in anger several times that he would send Fisher's head to Rome for the Cardinal's hat. Fisher was executed in June 1535 and More in July. For their fate the King must bear the chief responsibility; it is a black stain on his record. Shortly afterwards Henry was excommunicated and in theory deprived of his throne by the Pope.
>
> The resistance of More and Fisher to the royal supremacy in Church government was a noble and heroic stand. They realized the defects of the existing Catholic system, but they hated and feared the aggressive nationalism that was destroying the unity of Christendom. They saw that the break with Rome carried with it the threat of a despotism freed from every fetter. More stood forth as the defender of all that was finest in the medieval outlook. He represents to history its universality, its belief in spiritual values, and its instinctive sense of other-worldliness. Henry VIII with cruel axe decapitated not only a wise and gifted counsellor, but a system that, though it had failed to live up to its ideals in practice, had for long furnished mankind with its brightest dreams.

See also chapter 10, note 38; chapter 12, note 189; the text at note 25 of chapter 8 of this collection.

Some of the issues raised by the career and trial of Thomas More are touched upon in Shakespeare's *King John*. See the text at note 48 of chapter 8, and at note 75 of chapter 10 of this collection. The suspicion of "royal pressure [upon] judges" can be aroused whenever tribunals seem to be too much in the control of the executive. Thus, concerns were expressed about the military tribunals for "terrorists" announced in an Executive Order of November 13, 2001, tribunals that would be far more under direct Executive control than the standard court-martial judges usually are. Consider, for example, my Letter to the Editor of November 17, 2001:

> Concerns have been voiced about the November 13th Executive Order providing for trials by military tribunals, even in the United States, of foreigners accused of acts of "terrorism" anywhere in the world. Critics of the Justice Department's current campaign against "terrorism" should be heartened as it becomes generally apparent how ill-conceived even this vigorously-defended Executive Order really is.
>
> Although it has been objected that the concurrence of only two-thirds of any tribunal established by the order suffices for convicting and sentencing, it has not been noticed that the judges thus empowered need be two-thirds only of the tribunal members present, so long as a majority of the military officers designated for a tribunal is indeed present. If, for example, there should be eleven officers chosen for a tribunal, only six need be present to permit a final decision, which decision can then be made if two-thirds of those

six (that is, four) agree. This can mean that little more than one-third of all of the officers who have heard the evidence during a trial can suffice for convicting and sentencing, whatever the other two-thirds (who happen not to be present for the decision) may believe or prefer.

Such curious anomalies suggest that this and related, potentially shameful, experiments in the administration of American justice are not likely to endure—and for this we all, not just suspected terrorists, can be thankful.

See *Chicago Sun-Times*, November 30, 2001, p. 30. Some critics were particularly troubled by the resemblance between the (perhaps secret) tribunals contemplated and the perversions of judicial tribunals that the United States government has long criticized various dubious regimes abroad for using. See also chapter 8, note 61. Consider as well my Letter to the Editor as published in the *Chicago Tribune*, June 22, 2003, sec. 2, p. 10:

> Palestinians continue their campaign against an occupation; Israelis continue theirs against terrorism.
>
> President Bush urges restraint in responses to what are, for each side, massive provocations.
>
> After all, each side, in the current Holy Land conflict, has suffered the last three years casualties that are, in proportion to population, far greater than what the United States suffered on Sept. 11, 2001.
>
> An almost miraculous self-restraint does seem to be required of both Israelis and Palestinians in the months ahead if there is to be a reliable peace among them.
>
> Is it too much, then, to expect the President to show the way by requiring a salutary restraint by his Attorney General and his Defense Secretary in our own campaigns (at home and abroad) against terrorism?

See appendix C, note 58. See also chapter 11, note 12.

The Churchill concern about a recourse to "aggressive nationalism" that might destroy "the unity of Christendom" anticipated the concern some have today about an aggressive nationalism (even imperialism) that threatens respect for international law. See chapter 12, notes 6, 30, 34, 56. See also chapter 12, note 61. See as well appendix A, note 15; appendix C, note 58; appendix D, notes 32, 33.

11

John P. Altgeld and the Haymarketers[1]

I.

The student of law who comes to the *Haymarket Case*,[2] a century after the spectacular events of 1886–1887, confronts one surprise after another. One is reminded of how fascinating and yet inaccessible various combinations of particulars can be. If it is not one thing, it is another that can challenge us.

The Pardon Message by John P. Altgeld, of June 26, 1893 (a few months after he became governor of this state), opens with this summary of the facts:

> On the night of May 4, 1886, a public meeting was held on Haymarket Square, in Chicago: there were from 800 to 1,000 people present, nearly all being laboring men. There had been trouble, growing out of the effort to introduce an eight-hour day, resulting in some collisions with the police, in one of which several laboring people were killed, and this meeting was called as a protest against alleged police brutality.
>
> The meeting was orderly and was attended by the mayor, who remained until the crowd began to disperse, and then went away. As soon as Capt. John Bonfield, of the Police Department, learned that the mayor had gone, he took a detachment of police and hurried to the meeting for the purpose of dispersing the few that remained, and as the police approached the place of meeting a bomb was thrown by some unknown person, which exploded and wounded many and killed several policemen, among the latter being one Mathias Degan. A number of people were arrested, and after a time August Spies, Albert R. Parsons, Louis Lingg, Michael Schwab, Samuel Fielden, George Engel, Adolph Fischer, and Oscar Neebe were indicted for the murder of Mathias Degan. The prosecution could not discover who had thrown the bomb and could not bring the really guilty man to justice, and as some of the men indicated were not at

the Haymarket meeting and had nothing to do with it, the prosecution was forced to proceed on the theory that the men indicated were guilty of murder, because it was claimed they had, at various times in the past, uttered and printed incendiary and seditious language, practically advising the killing of policemen, of Pinkerton men, and others acting in that capacity, and that they were, therefore, responsible for the murder of Mathias Degan. The public was greatly excited and after a prolonged trial all of the defendants were found guilty; Oscar Neebe was sentenced to fifteen years' imprisonment and all of the other defendants were sentenced to be hanged. The case was carried to the Supreme Court and was there affirmed in the fall of 1887. Soon thereafter Lingg committed suicide. The sentence of Fielden and Schwab was commuted [by the then-governor] to imprisonment for life; and Parsons, Fischer, Engel, and Spies were hanged, and the [signers of a 60,000-name pardon petition] now ask to have Neebe, Fielden, and Schwab set at liberty.[3]

I have referred to "one surprise after another." There are various minor surprises, which I merely mention here: it was a time when men, including anarchists, routinely wore suitcoats and ties.[4] It was also a time when such radicals could counsel each other to sell their watches and chains, or other personal property, in order to buy guns and dynamite for the revolution; it was rarely suggested, at least in this country, that one should use theft or force in order to get the necessary weapons.[5]

I restrict myself to discussing on this occasion three particularly instructive surprises related to important statements by various parties to the *Haymarket* controversy. These are statements by the defendants and their associates, by the Supreme Court of Illinois in upholding the defendants' convictions, and by the governor in pardoning in 1893 the surviving defendants.

There was not much serious difference of opinion in the *Haymarket Case* as to the "facts," but only as to their implications. That makes our effort harder as well as easier. Particularly important was the question of whether men should have been held responsible in the way they were in this case for the public positions they had taken with respect to the labor unrest of the day.

II.

Our first instructive surprise. One is not accustomed today to hearing among us language as violent as that of the defendants and their associates when they attack the capitalists, the police as lackeys of capitalism, and the entire system of government (especially the courts along with the police). Some of this language must be "seditious," *if* anything ever is.[6] It is certainly far more impassioned than I expected it to be, reflecting perhaps both the intensity of the speakers' grievances and the extent of American liberty. Here are some samples (with their extensive italicizing omitted):

February 23, 1885—The already approaching revolution promises to be much grander and more terrible than at the close of the last century, which only broke out in one country. The common revolution will be general, for it makes itself already felt everywhere and generally. It will demand more sacrifices, for the number of those over whom we have to sit in judgment is now much greater than that of the last century.[7]

March 23, 1885—Yet one thing more. Although every day brings the news of collisions between armed murder-serfs of the bourgeoise with unarmed crowds of people, (strikers and the like,) we must ever and again read in the so-called workingmen's papers, discussions of the question of [whether] arming ought to be avoided in the associations of the proletarian. We characterize such pacifying efforts as criminal.

Each workingman ought to have been armed long ago. We leave it an open question whether whole [organizations] are able to completely fit themselves out in a military point of view, with all their numbers; but we say that each single one, if he has the necessary seriousness and the good will, can arm himself, little by little, very easily. Daggers and revolvers are easily to be gotten. Hand grenades are cheaply to be produced; explosives, too, can be obtained; and finally, possibilities are also given to buy arms on installments. To give an impulse in that direction one should never tire of. For not only the revolution proper, approaching with gigantic steps, commands to prepare for it, but also wage contests of today demand of us not to enter into it with empty hands.

Let us understand the signs of the times! Let us have a care for the present, that we will not be surprised by the future, unprepared![8]

October 8, 1885—All organized workingmen in this country, no matter what views they might have otherwise, should be united on one point—they should engage in a general prosecution of Pinkerton's secret police. No day should pass without a report being heard, from one place or another, of the finding of a carcass of one of Pinkerton's—that this should be kept up until nobody would consent to become the bloodhound of these assassins.[9]

These men (in various publications and speeches for months and years before the Haymarket explosion) indulged in the most intemperate talk, thereby playing with fire. At the very least, they ran the risk of exciting further the more excitable people among themselves. Their talk may not have moved "the masses" to action, but it evidently impressed the newspapers, the police, the state's attorney, the trial judge, and the Illinois Supreme Court.

We must wonder what these men thought that they, as intellectuals, were doing. They were both severely provoked and most provocative in this recourse by them to what was, in effect, the right of revolution. Some of you will remember the intensity of similar labor disputes here in the Midwest in the 1930s.

Much of the *Haymarket Case* turned then, and still turns, around the question of how much, or in what way, one should be held responsible for incendiary language, even if no direct connection can be shown between such language and violent action. A considerable display of that language is to be found in an unexpected place, the Illinois Supreme Court *Reports* from which I have taken my samples. The Court prefaces its Opinion with rather extensive selections that seem to have been representative of the exhortations that people encountered in the defendants' publications and speeches.

III.

Our second instructive surprise. The Illinois Supreme Court's Opinion is much more sober than I had anticipated. It is certainly far less impassioned than the defendants' language. The spirit of the Court's approach is reflected in this short Concurring Opinion by one Justice:

> Not intending to file a separate opinion, as I should have done had health permitted, I desire to avail myself of this occasion to say from the bench, that while I concur in the conclusion reached, and also in the general view presented in the opinion filed, I do not wish to be understood as holding that the record is free from error, for I do not think it is. I am, nevertheless, of opinion that none of the errors complained of are of so serious a character as to require a reversal of the judgment.
>
> In view of the number of defendants on trial, the great length of time it was in progress, the vast amount of testimony offered and passed upon by the court, and the almost numberless rulings the court was required to make, the wonder with me is, that the errors were not more numerous and more serious than they are.
>
> In short, after having carefully examined the record, and given all the questions arising upon it my very best thought, with an earnest and conscientious desire to faithfully discharge my whole duty, I am fully satisfied that the conclusion reached vindicates the law, does complete justice between the prisoners and the State, and that it is fully warranted by the law and the evidence.[10]

The Opinion of the Court ran to more than one hundred and fifty pages. That opinion was preceded by a dozen pages of syllabus, by almost eighty pages stating the case, and by a dozen more pages summarizing the briefs of the parties. Most of the pages that were used to state the case are given over to long quotations from the defendants and their associates.[11]

The space devoted to all of this by the Court reflects both the intensity of the public controversy at the time and the fact that eight defendants were involved. No one ever argued that any of the defendants threw the fatal bomb, but no one denied that the defendants had advocated possession and use of guns and bombs, albeit in self-defense. One of the defendants was shown to be an expert bomb-maker—and he himself was to use a small bomb to commit suicide in jail while he was awaiting execution.[12]

The Court's 150-page Opinion is not a mere harangue. Considerable care is devoted to a review of the evidence and of various legal issues.[13] In many ways, the Illinois Supreme Court's Opinion was like a solid closing argument by a prosecuting attorney. It is an informative, even conscientious, opinion, however much one might have to differ from it.

One cannot speak so kindly, however, of various police officers (especially Captain John Bonfield) and of the trial judge (Joseph E. Gary). All too many police were simply sadistic in their attacks on strikers, who sometimes provoked the police by their own attacks upon strike breakers. The trial judge is, however rare, all too familiar, for he is one of a tradition that goes back to the notorious hanging judge, Lord Jeffreys.[14] That tradition includes, in our own time, Harold R. Medina, of the *Dennis Case* (the trial of the Communist Party leaders in the late 1940s),[15] Irving R. Kaufman in the *Rosenberg Case* (the atomic espionage case a few years later),[16] and Julius J. Hoffman (in the Chicgao Conspiracy Trial from 1966 through 1970).[17] Each of these three American judges did have a good side to him as well.

Sadistic policemen and bad trial judges are bound to turn up from time to time. Chance distortions cannot be avoided here—and so there is especially the need for timely interventions by a responsible press and by sensible appellate courts. Perhaps this was too much to expect from the Illinois Supreme Court on that occasion, considering how violently the issues had been framed both by the defendants and by their enemies.

IV.

Our third instructive surprise. The Governor's Pardon Message, issued five and a half years after the trial and executions, is a remarkable state paper.[18] It, too, reflects considerable care with the record, but from a point of view obviously quite different from that of the Illinois Supreme Court.

The new governor had been under pressure from many respectable men to pardon the surviving defendants. He kept his own counsel, did his own research, and then issued a message that disturbed even some of those (of the more respectable type) who had sought the pardon.[19] What had been sought was an act of mercy for the guilty men ("they have suffered enough"). What the governor provided, instead, was a reassessment of the record that obliged him to find that the defendants had been innocent of the murder for which they had been convicted.

The governor says that he would not pardon these men if he thought them guilty: law and order must be upheld, the guilty must be punished. But he cannot find any evidence that connects in any significant way the admitted language of the defendants to the action of the unknown bomb thrower. In fact, he concludes (but there is no substantial evidence of this either) that the bomb was probably thrown by someone who had a personal grievance against the police for a brutal assault upon him in a labor disturbance elsewhere.

The governor is particularly concerned about the way the jury was selected and the way the trial was conducted. Critical to his decision, furthermore, was his assessment of the trial judge. Altgeld conducted himself more as an appellate court reviewing a record than as a governor considering whether to set aside the demands or the effects of the law. This is the Opinion, or at least the Dissenting Opinion, that should have come out of the Illinois Supreme Court in 1887. Or, to put it another way, it is the kind of opinion that could come out of the United States Supreme Court today, a Brennan-like opinion working from rule-of-law (or due process) principles.[20]

No doubt, it would have been politically prudent for the governor to have emphasized "mercy," whatever he privately thought of the record. But is it not salutary to have an occasional *established* public figure openly addressing vital issues and finding against official misconduct? This may have permanently damaged Altgeld's career—but there is much to be said for having on the record, here and there, such a manifestation of informed spiritedness in a political man. In calling spades spades, he gave everyone hope for an enduring law and order; in correcting "the Establishment" as he did, he implicitly rebuked the anarchists' condemnation of government. In fact, it can be said, Captain Bonfield and, to a lesser extent, Judge Gary were themselves somewhat anarchistic.

It is salutary that we have one American state paper that shows, in so dramatic a form, what *can* be said by men in authority against the abuse of authority. Of course, it can sometimes be "impolitic" to say such things—but politics is not everything; or rather, short-term politics must give way to a statesmanship that can illuminate and guide generations to come.

V.

I return briefly to the defendants. They were again and again irresponsible in what they said and how they conducted themselves, insofar as they had any effect. Various callous employers were also irresponsible, of course, but that is much more obvious to us and need not be stressed on this occasion.

One of the defendants (August Spies) testified "that he procured the cartridges of dynamite and coils of fuse and detonating caps found in his office [at his newspaper] for the mere purpose of experimenting, without explaining why he wanted to experiment. He stated that he showed these things, or some of them, to the reporters [from other newspapers]. . . merely to give them something sensational to write about in their newspapers.[21] In short, he wanted to be noticed—and he was!

Among the thoughtless consequences of what the defendants did with their agitation were the following:

The defendants helped promote the use of bombs. Even if the Haymarket bomb thrower was moved primarily by a desire for personal revenge, the social atmosphere to which the defendants as well as some employers and police contributed probably influenced the still unidentified bomb thrower's decision, if not also his ability, to act.

The defendants probably affected the labor movement adversely, at least in the short term, setting back the efforts to improve working conditions, whatever the long-term effects of the Haymarket martyrdoms.

Perhaps worst of all, the defendants helped provoke the community to commit, with its executions, a great injustice.[22]

The defendants made it more likely, that is, that innocent men would be executed, with perhaps the guiltiest of them all (in terms of immediate acts) being the one who committed suicide by explosive.

The defendants brought out the worst in the police, the trial judge, the prosecuting attorneys, and the press, thereby making the community uglier than it need have been.

The defendants helped undermine the political career (whatever it may have done for the "eternal glory") of a conscientious governor.

On the other hand, the defendants' thoughtlessness did give that governor an opportunity to vindicate the very system that they condemned.

VI.

It should be noticed that there was a commendable discrimination in the way that the State of Illinois conducted itself, despite the excitement of the time and the awfulness of hanging four men.

This discrimination may be seen, as I have indicated, in the way that the Illinois Supreme Court did face up to the record and arguments before it. It may be seen as well in the way three of the defendants were singled out to be spared hanging: the evidence does indicate that these three had not been as uninhibited as the others.

The Supreme Court is most guarded in what it says about Oscar Neebe, one of the defendants who survived to be pardoned. Notice what the court does, and does not, say about him: "We cannot say that the jury were not justified in holding him responsible, along with his confederates, for the murder on Tuesday night [May 4, 1886] of one of the very policemen, whose death he was urging and advocating on Monday night."[23]

The jury selection issue was probably not as critical as the defendants, or the governor, believed. Rather, the critical issue was, and still is, whether one should be held responsible for quite reckless talk. It may not be possible to establish cause and effect here—and yet it is only proper to discourage reckless talk. It remains a perplexing question what, if anything, can safely be done about that sort of conduct in our kind of regime.

VII.

One can put all of this still another way by observing that it is often difficult to know what one is doing. Surely it is not enough, in justifying oneself, to protest that it has not been proven that what one said or did was clearly connected to what somebody else did. Should not the defendants have recognized that if they constantly talked the way that they did, the community would naturally be apt to hold them accountable for dramatic misconduct by others?

We can be reminded of how difficult it is to know what one is doing by returning, if only briefly, to the Opinion of the Illinois Supreme Court. That court, in ruling firmly and at length against the defendants, did so with remarkable honesty: it set forth at great length the defendants' opinions—opinions about labor's grievances, about capitalistic exploitation, and about political corruption. Thus, the opinions of the defendants were given far more exposure in the *Illinois Reports* than they could otherwise ever have had through their insignificant newspapers.[24]

Thus, every lawyer or judge in this state, if his professional library is to be adequate, must find room on his shelves for some eighty pages of the most impassioned criticisms of the legal system he serves. Those attacks are preserved and easily made available to us all, a century later, by courtesy of the Illinois Supreme Court.[25]

The decisive refutation of those impassioned criticisms of our system of government is not found, however, in what the Illinois Supreme Court did but in what Governor Altgeld dared to say, and hence to teach us about the rule of law, in explaining why it was "clearly [his] duty" to act as he did.[26]

NOTES

1. This talk was given at the annual Clarence Darrow Memorial Meeting, The Museum of Science and Industry, Chicago, Illinois, March 13, 1987. This meeting, on the *Haymarket Controversy*, was organized by Arthur Weinberg.

2. *Spies et al.* v. *People*, 122 Ill. 1 (1887); petition for writ of error dismissed, 123 U.S. 131 (1887).

3. John P. Altgeld, *Reasons for Pardoning Fielden, Neebe & Schwab, the Haymarket Anarchists* (Chicago: Charles H. Kerr Publishing Co., 1986), pp. 10–11. Useful accounts of the Haymarket matter are to be found in Paul Avrich, *The Haymarket Tragedy* (Princeton: Princeton University Press, 1984); Harry Barnard, *"Eagle Forgotten": The Life of John Peter Altgeld* (Indianapolis: Bobbs-Merrill Co., 1938); Ray Ginger, *Altgeld's America: The Lincoln Ideal Versus Changing Realities* (New York: Funk & Wagnalls, 1958). Selections from the Pardon Message are printed in *The Annals of America* 11: 438–44 (Chicago: Encyclopedia Britannica, 1976).

Governor Altgeld's pardon message was issued the day after the unveiling of a Haymarket monument, on the site of the bomb throwing. See Avrich, *The Haymarket Tragedy*, p. 421. A memorial statue also put up in the area for the police killed in 1886 had to be moved in 1972 into the lobby of police headquarters at Eleventh and State Streets in Chicago: it had, over the years, been repeatedly the target of politically motivated vandals. See *The Annals of America* 11, pp. 430–31.

4. But, then, photos of hobos in the 1930s, a half-century later, show *them* riding freight-train cars with hats on. In addition, one notices, in the anarchists' materials reproduced in the 1887 Illinois Supreme Court Opinion, a number of Classical allusions, something that one would not expect to find in the works of radicals today. See, e.g., *Spies* v. *People*, 122 Ill., at 15, 18, 48, 188, 189. See also chapter 11, note 19.

5. See, e.g., *Spies* v. *People*, 122 Ill., at 57, 58, 125, 126, 184. Compare at 133. The Illinois Supreme Court observed,

> Law and government can not be abolished without revolution, bloodshed and murder. The socialist or communist, if he attempted to put into practical operation his doctrine of a community of property, would destroy individual rights in property. Practically considered the idea of taking a man's property from him without his consent, for the purpose of putting it into a common fund for the benefit of the community at large, involves the commission of theft and robbery. Therefore, the prejudice, which the ordinary citizen [who serves on juries], who looks at things from a practical standpoint, would have against anarchism and communism, would be nothing more than a prejudice against crime.

Spies v. *People*, 122 Ill., at 263.

6. See, on "sedition," Altgeld, *Reasons for Pardoning*, pp. 11, 16; the text at note 3 of chapter 11 of this collection. See also Altgeld, *Reasons for Pardoning*, p. 36:

> [T]he talk of a gigantic anarchistic conspiracy is not believed by the then Chief of Police . . . and is not entitled to serious notice, in view of the fact that, while Chicago had nearly a million inhabitants, the meetings held on the lake front on Sundays during the summer, by these agitators, rarely had fifty people present, and most of these went from mere curiosity, while

the meetings held indoors during the winter, were still smaller. The meetings held from time to time by the masses of the laboring people, must not be confounded with the meetings named, although in times of excitement and trouble much violent talk was indulged in by irresponsible parties; which was forgotten when the excitement was over.

Similar observations should have been made by our political leaders in the late 1940s, the 1950s, and the 1960s about the dangers posed in the United States by the minuscule American Communist Party. See chapter 11, note 15. See also chapter 12, parts C and D. See as well appendix A to this collection.

Whatever the seditious implications of the language indulged in by the defendants, there was no question but that much of the troublesome language that the Illinois Supreme Court was concerned about was foreign (mostly German). See, e.g., Altgeld, *Reasons for Pardoning*, pp. 30, 34, 55, 126. One suspects that some of the rhetorical excesses to which the defendants may have been accustomed did not translate safely into English. See George Anastaplo, *The Constitution of 1787: A Commentary* (Baltimore: Johns Hopkins University Press, 1989), p. 1.

7. *Spies* v. *People*, 122 Ill., at 11.

8. *Spies* v. *People*, 122 Ill., at 16. There is something wonderfully American in the prospect of "buy[ing] arms on installments." A lyrical passage in the anarchists' literature about dynamite is used twice by the Illinois Supreme Court:

> Dynamite! Of all the good stuff, this is the stuff. Stuff several pounds of this sublime stuff into an inch pipe, (gas or water pipe) plug up both ends, insert a cap with a fuse attached, place this in the immediate neighborhood of a lot of rich loafers who live by the sweat of other people's brows, and light the fuse. A most cheerful and gratifying result will follow.

Spies v. *People*, 122 Ill., at 40, 123. See chapter 11, note 22.

9. *Spies* v. *People*, 122 Ill., at 19. Is this the program of the Iraqi "insurgents" in 2004?

10. *Spies* v. *People*, 122 Ill., at 266–67 (Justice John H. Mulkey, concurring).

11. *Spies* v. *People*, 122 Ill., at 1–11 (Syllabus); at 11–89 (Statement of the Case); at 89–99 (Briefs of the parties); at 100–266 (Opinion of the Court, by Justice Benjamin D. Magruder).

12. This was Louis Lingg. See *Spies* v. *People*, 122 Ill., at 105–12, 137–39, 169–76. See also Avrich, *The Haymarket Tragedy*, pp. 375–78. William Dean Howells wrote, on hearing the news of Lingg's death, "Miserable Lingg! I'm glad he's out of the story, but even with his death, it seems to me that humanity's judgment of the law begins. All over the world people must be asking themselves, What cause is this really, for which men die so gladly, so inexorably?" *Spies* v. *People*, 122 Ill., p. 377. How should the Howells question be answered in the wake of the 2001–2003 suicide bombings in this country and abroad? See chapter 8, note 61, chapter 10, note 78.

13. Some of these issues, related to jury selection, to the fairness of the trial judge, and to the law of conspiracy, would no doubt be decided differently today either by the Illinois Supreme Court or by the United States Supreme Court. See chapter 11, note 5, chapter 11, note 15. One could even say that these defendants were decidedly unlucky, especially in their timing. Compare, e.g., *People* v. *Coughlin*, 144 Ill. 140,

33 N.E. 1 (1893). The same can be said of Julius and Ethel Rosenberg. See chapter 12-B, section V. See, on the law of conspiracy, George Anastaplo, "Human Nature and the First Amendment," 40 *University of Pittsburgh Law Review* 661, 688 (1979).

14. Lord Jeffreys (1645–1689) is remembered as an "English judge notorious for his cruelty and corruption. He presided over the 'Bloody Assizes' of 1685 following the failure of the Duke of Monmouth's rebellion and was in charge of executing the unpopular religious policy of the Roman Catholic king James II." 6 *Encyclopedia Britannica* 524 (1988). Governor Altgeld, in the closing pages of his Pardon Message, includes these remarks:

> It is further charged, with much bitterness, by those who speak for the prisoners, that the record of this case shows that the judge conducted the trial with malicious ferocity . . . [and] that the judge's magazine article recently published, although written nearly six years after the trial, is yet full of venom . . . It is urged that such ferocity or subserviency [toward the prosecution] is without a parallel in all history; that even Jeffreys in England, contented himself with hanging his victims, and did not stoop to berate them after they were dead.

Altgeld, *Reasons for Pardoning*, pp. 57–58. Compare chapter 11, note 19. See also chapter 10, note 78.

15. See *Dennis* v. *United States*, 341 U.S. 494 (1951). This case is discussed in George Anastaplo, *The Constitutionalist: Notes on the First Amendment* (Dallas: Southern Methodist University Press, 1971). See also chapter 11, note 6; chapter 12-C; George Anastaplo, "On Trial: Explorations," 22 *Loyola University of Chicago Law Journal* 765, 1031–32 (1991).

16. See chapter 12-B.

17. See chapter 12-D. In all three of these twentieth-century cases, the defendants were not without fault—but bad judging made matters far worse than they need have been.

18. "The historian Allan Nevins has called it 'one of the best state papers ever written in America.'" Avrich, *The Haymarket Tragedy*, p. 422. See also chapter 11, notes 19, 26. See, for a summary of the Pardon Message, Avrich, *The Haymarket Tragedy*, pp. 422–23.

19. Jane Addams, for example, said of the Pardon Message that it was "a magnanimous action [that] was marred by personal rancor, betraying for the moment the infirmity of a noble mind." Avrich, *The Haymarket Tragedy*, p. 511 n. 29. See, e.g., chapter 11, note 14. Benjamin Tucker described the Pardon Message "as probably the most merciless message of mercy ever penned." Avrich, *The Haymarket Tragedy*, p. 422. Clarence Darrow, who had once been dismayed by the language in which the Pardon Message was couched (ibid., p. 425), still included these sentences in his eulogy during the Altgeld funeral in 1902:

> In the days now past, John P. Altgeld, our loving, peerless chief, in scorn and derision was called John Pardon Altgeld by those who would destroy his power. We who stand to-day around his bier and mourn the brave and loving friend are glad to adopt this name. If, in the infinite economy of nature, there shall be another land where crooked paths shall be made straight, where heaven's justice shall review the judgments of the earth—if there shall be a great, wise, humane judge, before whom the sons of men shall come, we can

hope for nothing better for ourselves than to pass into that infinite presence as the comrades and friends of John Pardon Altgeld, who opened the prison doors and set the captive free.

Altgeld, *Reasons for Pardoning*, p. 62 (appendix). See conclusion, note 3. One can be reminded, by the Darrow invocation of "a great, wise, humane judge," of language used by Gotthold E. Lessing's Nathan the Wise. See George Anastaplo, "Law & Literature and the Moderns: Explorations," 20 *Northern Illinois University Law Review* 251, 288 (2000).

Altgeld himself, it seems, looked for guidance in the Classics, observing that "experience has taught that the reading and digesting each day of a half page or a page of some classic author, so as to imbibe his spirit and assimilate his words, will by degree give elegance of diction and purity of strength of expression." John P. Altgeld, *Oratory* (Chicago: The Public, 1915), p. 5. Pericles, "the greatest man of antiquity, and in some respects the greatest orator," supplied Altgeld "one mighty model." Altgeld, *Oratory*, p. 39. See chapter 11, note 3.

20. See, e.g., Anastaplo,"Justice Brennan, Due Process and the Freedom of Speech: A Celebration of *Speiser* v. *Randall*," 20 *John Marshall Law Review* 7 (1986); George Anastaplo, "Justice Brennan, Natural Right, and Constitutional Interpretation," 10 *Cardozo Law Review* 201 (1988). John P. Altgeld *had* served as a judge in Cook County, Illinois. "Altgeld's way was to do things circumspectly. He was determined not to act [on the pardon petition submitted to him] before making a thorough analysis of the trial and the circumstances surrounding it." Avrich, *The Haymarket Tragedy*, p. 418. One can be reminded here of the way that Lincoln proceeded in developing the Emancipation Proclamation. See chapter 3, note 9. The career of Justice Brennan is illuminated by the incident recorded in a Letter to the Editor I prepared in July 1997:

The obituaries of Justice William Brennan have rightly noticed the profound humanity of this self-deprecating jurist. His charming modesty is reflected in a report by a University of Chicago law school teacher of mine, the late Harry Kalven. Mr. Kalven told me about a lawyers' meeting he was to address at a fancy resort hotel in Virginia. When he got to the reception held before he was to speak, he found to his dismay that all of the lawyers there were in formal wear; he alone was in an ordinary business suit. His discomfort grew as he mingled with his audience, for they were indeed dressed most elegantly. As he circulated about the hall he came upon a group that was obviously gathered around someone of importance; he figured that it must be the other guest speaker, who was, on that occasion, Justice Brennan. Sure enough, when Mr. Kalven penetrated that crowd he did find Justice Brennan in the middle—dressed also in an ordinary suit. When the Justice saw the similarly dressed Professor, his face lit up as he said, "Boy, am I glad to see you!" (Justice Brennan authorized me to publish in my *American Moralist* book [at pages 280–81] his delightful 1984 letter eleborating upon this incident.)

See appendix C, note 53.

21. *Spies* v. *People*, 122 Ill., at 234.

22. "'To you, Sir,' wrote one lifelong Republican to [Governor Richard J. Oglesby in 1887], 'in free and civilized America belongs the distinction of having first used

the halter as a mode of punishment for political offenders." Avrich, *The Haymarket Tragedy*, pp. 378–79. See chapter 12-B.

The bomb thrower himself should be singled out here as a major contributor to a series of injustices, beginning with the deaths of seven policemen and an unknown number of civilians from the bomb itself and then the police gunfire at the Haymarket, setting off what has been called "the first major 'Red Scare' in American history." Avrich, *The Haymarket Tragedy*, pp. 208, 215. See, on the identity of this bomb thrower, Avrich, *The Haymarket Tragedy*, pp. 437–45. "Contrary to the general impression, most of the injuries had been caused by [police] bullets rather than by bomb fragments. In fact, of the seven policemen who died before the trial, only [one] can be accounted an indisputable victim of the bomb. . . . All or nearly all of the policemen who had suffered bullet wounds had been shot by their fellow officers and not by civilians in the crowd." Avrich, *The Haymarket Tragedy*, p. 208.

Also deserving of severe censure, of course, are those who spoke so cavalierly about the virtues of dynamite. See chapter 11, note 8.

23. *Spies* v. *People*, 122 Ill., at 227. The weakness of the case against Neebe seems to have been recognized all around, including by the state's attorney. See Altgeld, *Reasons for Pardoning*, pp. 11–12, 54–57. See also the text at note 59 of chapter 12 of this collection.

24. One wishes that Oliver Wendell Holmes Jr. had exhibited the same instructive courtesy in the unfortunate case of *Schenck* v. *United States*, 249 U.S. 47 (1919). The innocuous circular upon which Justice Holmes's devilishly mischievous Opinion for the court depends may be found in Anastaplo, *The Constitutionalist*, pp. 294–305. See Anastaplo, "On Trial" (*Loyola Law Journal*), p. 1032.

25. Also available in the Illinois Supreme Court reports are detailed instructions for the making of explosives. See, e.g., *Spies* v. *People*, 122 Ill., at 43–44, 60–69, 72–74, 124.

26. Altgeld, *Reasons for Pardoning*, p. 58. It had become apparent by that time to thoughtful men and women that the police themselves were very much in need of a reliance upon the rule of law. Police officers who had been critical in the Haymarket events, including Captain Bonfield, had been exposed as "receiving payments from saloon-keepers, prostitutes, and thieves, and had been trafficking in stolen goods." Avrich, *The Haymarket Tragedy*, p. 415. Thus, Altgeld's action liberated many more than the three men still in prison because of the Haymarket affair. Leon M. Despres, a Chicago lawyer long dedicated to the cause of civil liberties in the United States, reminds us of the shining Altgeld legacy:

> The 1893 Altgeld pardon message is a stirring document in the history of American freedom. It is also an impressive testimonial to a strong man's courage and social concern. The pardon of the three living Haymarket defendants . . . restored the innocence of all the defendants, laid bare the pretentious cruelty of the Haymarket judicial proceedings, and redirected Illinois government toward justice and fairness. When Altgeld pardoned the defendants, he knew that his pardon message would prevent his 1896 re-election as Governor. The message is one of the great documents in the annals of American legal justice. It stamped John Peter Altgeld with greatness.

Altgeld, *Reasons for Pardoning*, p. 5 (Introduction). See chapter 12, note 143. See also appendix C, note 41.

12

Notorious Defendants in Our Time

12-A. HERMANN WILHELM GOERING ET AL.[1]

I.

Almost a half-century has passed since twenty-two Germans, including the surviving leaders of the Nazi regime, were put on trial before an international military tribunal in Nuremberg, a city notorious in the history of the rise of the Nazi Party to power in Germany in 1933.[2] The trial opened in the bomb-damaged Palace of Justice on November 20, 1945, some six months after the surrender of Germany. "The Tribunal on September 30 and October 1, 1946, rendered judgment in the first international criminal assizes in history."[3] Interest in the Nuremberg Trial continues to this day, as testified to both by the very large enrollment in a course I have on the trial this term [in 1991] at the Loyola law school and by the size of the audience here today. That interest is intensified at times by such conduct as that associated with the [1991] Gulf War.

The student of the Nuremberg Trial should be reminded of the great puzzlement, if not even deep distress, that we have upon observing how callous, or at least how detached, people can sometimes be when exposed to conduct and suffering that naturally shock the sensibilities of a decent community. I myself was reminded of what the natural response can be in such circumstances while watching a Mexican-American reenactment last Friday of the Passion Story in the streets of San Antonio.[4] Much of that Good Friday presentation could be responded to as theatrical, especially since a raised platform in El Mercado was the site of much of the outdoor drama. But there was a moment, before the on-stage performance, which had a different effect, at least on me, partly because it caught me completely by surprise. It happened that the movement of the actors *to* the stage (where Pilate, Herod, and others would carry on) passed within a few yards of where I was standing, something that I had not expected. Not only that, but the actors were really playing their parts, and this included a Roman soldier whipping before him a bound and stumbling Jesus. It seemed so much like "the real thing," and was so little expected by me, that I could notice in myself a natural impulse to move forward and inter- vene, if only to protest the inhumanity I was witnessing.[5] Fortunately I stopped myself in time—or, perhaps I should say, *unfortunately*, for I suspect such a response by a naive *gringo* would have been salutary or at least memorable. In any event, I am intrigued by my impulse and recall my having wondered, upon seeing the German people close-up in Berlin and elsewhere at the end of the Second World War, what had happened to their natural sensibilities during the just-completed war in which horrible atrocities that defy description had been done on such a large scale in their name.

I also saw at that time how the major German cities had been flattened by aerial bombardment, so much so that one could stand in the center of Berlin, say, and not see an intact building in any direction. The damage done to the German cities was far worse than anything I saw at that time in either Paris or even London. (It was not until 1951 that I saw the devastated cities of Coventry and Rotterdam.) Few of us Americans who saw such devastation, and the misery of desperate Germans, were likely to recall, however, that de- liberate assaults upon civilian population centers were once "universally" condemned as contrary to the rules of war.[6]

My earliest personal recollection of the Nuremberg Trial goes back to my tuning in, while serving as a flying officer somewhere over Western Europe in a United States Army Air Corps plane, to a radio broadcast of the passing of sentences by the tribunal. This must have been on October 1, 1946. I do not recall that I had any reservations about what was being done on that oc- casion, which included the pronouncement of one death sentence after an- other.

One fact should be recognized at the outset of any account of the Nurem- berg Trial: the men who were responsible for deeds of the enormity docu- mented in that trial had to be dealt with somehow. Hanging was too good for various of them, even if they were, in a sense, insane.

The indefensibility of the Nazis' documented deeds of horror is evident from the way the defendants, including the most guilty among them, consis- tently presented themselves during the ten months of the trial. Particularly in- structive were their final statements, in which most of them attempted to put considerable distance between themselves and the monstrous deeds that had by that time become all too familiar.[7]

No doubt, the defendants were moved by a desire to save their skins. But there seems to be more than merely a concern for mere self-preservation evident in those statements. Personal self-esteem, if not even a troubled conscience, may also be exhibited there, especially by those who considered themselves doomed from the beginning of the trial. Thus, I do not believe that Hermann Goering was playacting when he expressed resentment upon hearing the British prosecutor refer to his "friend Himmler."[8] Heinrich Himmler was obviously so awful a man that none of the defendants wanted to be associated with him in any way. Various of the defendants were also concerned about their long-term reputations and the standing of their families. Almost all of them expressed as well a dedication, probably sincere in some cases, to the well-being of the German people.[9]

In addition, it seemed, most of the defendants did come to care for what the tribunal thought of them. The seriousness with which the tribunal conducted itself month after month contributed to this, as did the gravity and scope of the deeds that were marshalled against the defendants. This became a drama that naturally impressed itself upon all of its participants.

II.

The Nuremberg Tribunal conducted a trial based on an indictment in which each of the twenty-two defendants was charged on two or more of four counts.[10] The four counts have been summarized in this fashion:

> Count One charged the common plan or conspiracy to seize power, establish a totalitarian regime, prepare and wage a war of aggression. Count Two charged the waging of wars of aggression. Count Three charged the violation of the laws of war, and Count Four charged the crimes against humanity, the persecutions and exterminations.[11]

These four counts were grounded in the Charter of the International Military Tribunal, signed in London on August 8, 1945, by representatives of the United States, France, Great Britain, and the Soviet Union.[12] Count One (the conspiracy count) and Count Two draw upon the Crimes Against Peace provision in the Charter, Count Three upon the War Crimes provision, and Count Four upon the Crimes Against Humanity provision. These three provisions read:

> (a) CRIMES AGAINST PEACE: namely, planning, preparation, initiation or waging of a war of aggression, or a war in violation of international treaties, agreements or assurances, or participation in a Common Plan or Conspiracy for the accomplishment of any of the foregoing;

(b) WAR CRIMES: namely, violations of the laws or customs of war. Such violations shall include, but not be limited to, murder, ill-treatment or deportation to slave labor or for any other purpose of civilian population of or in occupied territory, murder or ill-treatment of prisoners of war or persons of the seas, killing of hostages, plunder of public or private property, wanton destruction of cities, towns, or villages, or devastation not justified by military necessity;

(c) CRIMES AGAINST HUMANITY: namely, murder, extermination, enslavement, deportation, and other inhumane acts committed against any civilian population, before or during the war, or persecutions on political, racial, or religious grounds in execution of or in connection with any crime within the jurisdiction of the Tribunal, whether or not in violation of domestic law of the country where perpetrated.[13]

The charter, "in order to ensure fair trial for the Defendants," directed that "the following procedures shall be followed":

(a) The Indictment shall include full particulars specifying in detail the charges against the defendants. A copy of the Indictment and of all the documents lodged with the Indictment, translated into a language that he understands, shall be furnished to the defendant at a reasonable time before the Trial.

(b) During any preliminary examination or trial of a defendant he shall have the right to give any explanation relevant to the charges made against him.

(c) A preliminary examination of a defendant and his trial shall be conducted in, or translated into, a language that the defendant understands.

(d) A defendant shall have the right to conduct his own defense before the Tribunal or to have the assistance of counsel.

(e) A defendant shall have the right through himself or through his counsel to present evidence at the Trial in support of his defense, and to cross-examine any witness called by the Prosecution.[14]

Critical to the way the trial was conducted and to its results were the following two directives in the charter:

Article 7: The official position of the defendants, whether as Heads of State or responsible officials in Government departments, shall not be considered as freeing them from responsibility or mitigating punishment.

Article 8: The fact that the defendant acted pursuant to order of his Government or of a superior shall not free him from responsibility, but may be considered in mitigation of punishment if the Tribunal determine that justice so requires.[15]

These directives were essential to the trial, especially since the Nazis, if not the Germans generally, made much of the Fuehrer Principle. That principle obliged one who had sworn allegiance to the Fuehrer to do whatever he was ordered to do by superiors who were part of a chain of command that led back to the Fuehrer.

III.

The International Military Tribunal was made up of a judge and his alternate from each of the four principal signatories.[16] Most of these judges were civilians, even though the tribunal sat under military auspices in the American zone of occupied Germany.

> The Indictment [prepared by the prosecutors of the four nations] was presented at the first public session of the Tribunal, held October 18, 1945, at Berlin. It had organized by choosing the Right Honorable Lord Justice Geoffrey Lawrence of Great Britain as its president. His patience and Britannic calm did much to impress Defendants, their counsel, and spectators with the fairness and dignity of the proceedings.[17]

These are the words of Robert H. Jackson, chief of the American prosecution team.[18]

One of the twenty-two defendants, Martin Bormann, was tried *in absentia*.[19] Two other defendants would have been tried: the senior member of the Krupp family, who was severed because of his senility,[20] and Robert Ley, who committed suicide before the trial began.[21] Several others would have been included if they had not died before the war ended: Adolf Hitler, Heinrich Himmler, Joseph Goebbels, and Reinhard Heydrich.[22]

Three of the twenty-two defendants were acquitted of all charges and released by the tribunal.[23] Four defendants received sentences ranging from ten to twenty years, three received life sentences, and twelve were sentenced to death.[24] One of these twelve, Bormann, was probably already dead; another of them, Goering, committed suicide in his prison cell while awaiting execution. The remaining ten were executed on October 16, 1946, a fortnight after the tribunal delivered its judgment.[25]

The "eminence" of the defendants and the scope of the deeds documented during the trial provided a testing of the principles and practices of a regime that was radically nationalistic and, in its own terms, deeply patriotic.[26]

IV.

The first of the set of crimes described by the charter of the tribunal are the Crimes Against Peace. These are drawn upon in the indictment for Count

One, the conspiracy count, as well as in Count Two.[27] Vital to these two counts, if not to all four, is the recourse by a government to wars of aggression. Justice Jackson, in justifying the first two counts, speaks of

> the re-establishment of the principle of unjustifiable war [as being] traceable in many steps. One of the most significant is the Briand-Kellogg Pact of 1928, by which Germany, Italy, and Japan, in common with ourselves and practically all the nations of the world, renounced war as an instrument of national policy, bound themselves to seek the settlement of disputes only by pacific means, and condemned recourse to war for the solution of international controversies.[28]

Serious questions were raised then, and have been heard since, as to whether a justiciable crime could be based on such an approach. Several of the defendants denied that Germany had incurred any guilt in the way she had conducted her foreign affairs, especially after what had been done to her through the Treaty of Versailles after World War I.[29] One difficulty here is that of determining where one starts in weighing the equities of a controversy.[30] The *status quo* at any particular time for one country may be partly the result of serious injustices visited upon it by other countries a generation or two earlier. It must be a rare country that does not have a plausible grievance against others. Even rarer, perhaps, may be countries with no questionable conduct in the way they have conducted their foreign affairs from time to time.[31]

The bitter grievances of the German people, as well as a general debacle, had been exploited by the Nazis in coming to power.[32] A sensible and just assessment of the foreign policy of the country, including its recourse to war, may depend too much on "history" to provide a reliable basis for judicial (as distinguished from political) decisions.

It is indicative of the difficulty of dealing properly with the Crimes Against Peace offenses (Counts One and Two) that although all twenty-two defendants were charged with Count One, only eight of them were convicted on that conspiracy count.[33] This suggests that such charges should be used with extreme caution hereafter, especially if a conspiracy charge permits saddling defendants with the intentions and deeds of others that they might have known little or nothing about.[34] As for the somewhat more restrained Count Two, sixteen of the twenty-two defendants were charged with that. Four of them were acquitted.[35] The twelve convicted on Count Two included the eight convicted on Count One. That is, barely half of all of the defendants were convicted of Crimes Against Peace.[36]

It is somewhat reassuring, considering the problems I have been noticing about the Crimes Against Peace, that only one defendant was convicted and sentenced on Count One and Count Two alone. That was Rudolph Hess,

Hitler's most intimate associate before he flew off to Scotland on a hare-brained mission in the middle of the war.[37] It is also somewhat reassuring that Hess's life sentence may not really have mattered much to him, considering the mental condition he was obviously in throughout the trial and, evidently, for some time before. It may have seemed to the tribunal that no meaningful freedom was available for him, no matter where he happened to be during the rest of his life.[38]

Far less questionable than the Crimes Against Peace charges were the War Crimes charges and the Crimes Against Humanity charges.[39] Hess aside, then, the defendants who were convicted were punished (at least in part) for offenses that do not require much in the way of historical investigation, political analysis, or legal argument to recognize as deserving of condemnation.

V.

It can be a matter of considerable dispute whether a country's grievances and circumstances call for, or at least excuse, a war on any particular occasion. But how a war should be conducted, once embarked upon, *is* guided by the Laws of War, a body of rules (some of them spelled out in treaties) that seem to be widely accepted, at least by and among the Western nations. These rules direct how prisoners of war should be treated, how conquered peoples are to be used, and how war itself is to be fought in a variety of circumstances.[40]

Not only were war crimes offenses generally known, so was the mode of punishing them, with national military tribunals usually relied upon. That was the practice well before Nuremberg. All but three of the wefendants who were convicted on any count were found guilty of war crimes.[41]

Crimes Against Humanity are at least as unambiguously reprehensible as war crimes. There was no question during the Trial but that terrible things had been done by the Nazis to millions of innocent people. None of the defendants tried to justify these offenses. In fact, all but three or four of them, in their closing statements, spoke against these offenses in the strongest terms.[42] So reprehensible were these offenses, which could be resorted to on this scale only under cover of war, that the Nazis never acknowledged them publicly during the war, even while they were winning and were still confident of ultimate success.[43]

The principal concern of most of the defendants was to establish that they had not even known of the Crimes Against Humanity, that those crimes had been the doings of Hitler and the men closest to him for this purpose (such as Himmler and Goebbels).[44] It is significant that all of the defendants who were sentenced to death were found guilty of Crimes Against Humanity.[45]

VI.

Most of the defendants, having insisted that they never knew of the atrocities of the concentration camps, described themselves as horrified upon learning about them, some of them for the first time (they said) during the trial.[46] I do not believe that anyone ever said during the trial, "I always knew about these things, approved of them, and even helped carry them out. They were harsh measures that were necessary for the purgation and salvation of Germany, etc., etc." No monuments had been erected during the war, either in words or in stone, in praise of these mammoth massacres. Defeat, it seems, unnerved even the most fanatical believers with respect to these deeds, the more so because the Nazi faith very much depended for its mystique upon assurances about the ultimate success of the overall Nazi program.

It was harder, of course, for the defendants to deny knowledge of the obvious foreign policy of the Nazi regime than it was for them to deny knowledge of the programs of hidden systematic killings in the camps. Those defendants who were involved in the formulation and execution of that foreign policy had to deal with it differently at trial from the way that they dealt with the Crimes Against Humanity and the war crimes. But then, I have argued, the rights and wrongs of foreign policy *are* much more difficult to sort out, especially when the observer steps back from immediate engagement in a war that threatens his country.[47] The enormity of the Crimes Against Humanity, on the other hand, becomes more and more obvious as they become better known: to know such crimes is, for most people, naturally to hate them.

It can be difficult to determine what to make of those defendants (if any there were) who were ignorant of the atrocities of the regime that they supported for a decade. Which is worse in such matters, to be cynical or to be gullible?[48] Cynicism consists here in supporting men whom one suspects to be ruthless, if not even evil, in the hope that from such support something good will come about for oneself, if not for one's country. Gullibility consists here in supporting men whom one does not really know, entrusting them with vast powers, in the irresponsible hope that one's country will benefit. Goering, who proclaimed that he remained loyal to Hitler to the very end, insisted that he had not known of the slaughter in the concentration camps.[49] He never seemed to appreciate what he was revealing about a regime, or about loyalty to the leader of a regime, in which the "Number 2 man at the time in all Germany"[50] was not informed about, or did not know of, atrocities of the scale systematically practiced by the Nazis for years.

This, almost as much as the atrocities themselves, points up the deep irrationality of the Nazi regime.

VII.

Almost all of the defendants agreed—some explicitly, others tacitly—that it was inexcusable to order, to perform, or to support the terrible things done in the concentration camps and elsewhere. They conceded, in effect, that somebody should be punished by someone for such conduct.

In speaking as they did, whatever some of them may have "really" believed, the defendants reflected what does have to be said publicly about such deeds. By speaking as they did, they repudiated in effect the principles of the Nazi regime. When they tried to describe these atrocities, they themselves could not help, it seems, but refer again and again to them as insane or mad.[51] The immediate perpetrators of these atrocities in the camps certainly exhibited madness in the way that they mistook the human beings they personally killed for vermin or for other deadly pests that had to be exterminated.[52]

The inability of the defendants after the war to speak on behalf of these deeds mirrored the inability of the Nazi government during the war to publicize the extermination "service" it was rendering the German people and the European community. The natural limits of what human beings can openly acknowledge doing to one another seem to be evident here. Despite years of virtually unchallenged control of their country, the Nazis still could not depend upon the German people at large to accept what was happening in the camps. In fact, if the defendants are to be believed, the leaders directly responsible for the systematic atrocities could not even depend upon most of their Nazi Party colleagues with respect to these matters.[53]

The madness of the overall Nazi enterprise was exposed to public view once the massive military defeat of Germany made people face up to reality. So grotesque were the atrocities that the most guilty among these defendants would have been in a bad way, even if they had never been captured, tried, and punished.[54] It is awful and deeply demoralizing to have done such things, whether one is exposed and dealt with. The sustained and disciplined evil of the Nazi regime has seemed to me, for more than four decades now [this was said by me in 1991], to be simply incomprehensible, which is perhaps another way of saying that it was indeed a mad enterprise.[55]

Perhaps we will see published some day memoirs of thoughtful Russian observers at Nuremberg who were aware of what Joseph Stalin and his minions had done back home. American observers were probably reassured that the Japanese Relocation Camps were significantly milder both in purpose and in effect, whatever might be said about the treatment of slaves and of Native Americans in nineteenth-century North America.[56]

It does make a difference in these matters whether a policy is publicly known. An effort to justify a questionable policy can, in an otherwise civilized community, contribute eventually to transforming that policy into something that is justifiable. In short, the systematic concealment by the Nazis of their worst crimes does reassure us that they were sufficiently aware of the terribleness of their deeds for the purposes of the criminal law.

VIII.

It was not only the defendants who were on trial at Nuremberg, but also the tribunal and, in effect, the victors in World War II. It was noticed several times during the trial that the defendants were given much more of a hearing then they had allowed, or had even pretended to allow, their victims.[57]

The tribunal conducted itself fairly well. It is not difficult, upon examining the record, to see why the tribunal acted as it did in the disposition of various cases. If the Russian judges and Justice Jackson, as the American prosecutor, had gotten their way, however, there would not have been the three acquittals.[58] That would probably have been unfortunate for the long-term effect of the proceedings.

The tribunal did what it did in full view and with a voluminous public record. It was taken seriously, which was reinforced by its sense of dignity, its orderliness, *and its evident discrimination among defendants* in its final judgment.[59] It perhaps helped, on this landmark occasion, that the defendants *were* Germans: their almost instinctive respect for authority permitted the proceedings to be carried on with the appropriate solemnity.[60]

It can be useful to lay down, or to reaffirm, rules and standards in this fashion. Governments, or men in government, may be guided by such things.[61] The law, from whatever source, does instruct us as to good and bad. It does not always need physical sanctions in order to make a difference in guiding us.

One way or another, that is, the exercise of power has to be moderated if the powerful as well as their victims are to be spared evil deeds. Particularly sobering here is the counsel given by a defendant, one of the three acquitted, in his closing statement:

> The prosecutors have expressed the horror of their nations at the atrocities which occurred. They did not expect any good from Hitler, and [yet] they are shattered by the extent of what really happened. But try for a moment to understand the indignation of those who expected good from Hitler and who then saw how their trust, their good will, and their idealism were misused. I find myself in the position of a man who has been deceived, together with many, many other Germans of whom the Prosecution says that they could have recognized all that happened from the smoke rising from the chimneys of the concentration camps, or from the mere sight of the prisoners, and so forth.

I feel that it is a great misfortune that the Prosecution has pictured these matters in such a way as if all of Germany had been a tremendous den of iniquity. It is a misfortune that the Prosecution is generalizing the extent of the crimes which are in themselves horrible enough. As against this I must say that if anyone once believed in Hitler during the years of peaceful reconstruction, he only needed to be loyal, courageous, and self-sacrificing to go on believing him until, by the discovery of carefully-hidden secrets, he could recognize the devil in him. That is the only explanation for the struggle which Germany carried on for 68 months. Such a willingness to sacrifice does not grow from crime, but only from idealism and good faith, and from clever and apparently honest organization.

I regret that the Prosecution has undertaken to generalize the crimes, because it is bound to add still more to the mountain of hatred which lies upon the world. But the time has come to interrupt the perpetual cycle of hatred which has dominated the world up to now. It is high time to call a halt to the alternate sowing and reaping of new harvests of hatred. The murder of five million people is an awful warning and today humanity possesses the technical means for its own destruction. Therefore, in my judgment, the Prosecution should not replace one hatred by another.[62]

IX.

I have noticed that war crimes, of which all but three of the convicted men were found guilty, had been long recognized and occasionally punished, at least in the Western world. I should also notice that the defendants complained that the Crimes Against Peace and the Crimes Against Humanity charges were ex post facto in that there had been no previous authoritative declaration that these were offenses subject to formal adjudication and punishment.[63]

The war crimes convictions do tend to soften the concern one might have here about anyone convicted as well for the two seemingly ex post facto offenses. And, to carry my somewhat technical response further, the use at Nuremberg of the Crimes Against Peace and the Crimes Against Humanity charges tends to legitimate *them* for possible use "next time." This can be considered to be a service to which the reluctant defendants contributed.[64]

Even so, the student of the Nuremberg Trial who might be moved by the *ex post facto* concern should be reminded that most of the defendants themselves did speak of the massive atrocities as deserving punishment. Further, the student should consider what the principal purpose is of a prohibition against *ex post facto* laws. Is not that prohibition relied upon to make sure that one is not caught by surprise, having to answer charges for acts that one could not have anticipated would ever be regarded as criminal?

None of the defendants, it seems, questioned that *someone* should be able to do something to the men responsible for the systematic atrocities for which the Nazis were responsible. No law or precedent was needed to alert men to the evil of such acts, acts that they diligently concealed from public view.[65] Besides, it is hardly likely that it would have made any difference to the instigators of those deeds if the well-known worldwide abhorrence of such deeds had been formalized in a treaty or other instrument.[66] Nor is it likely that the most evil of men hereafter will be deterred by what happened at Nuremberg, especially if they are confident of success in their projects. But this does not keep the judgment of Nuremberg from having salutary effects. It affirms civilized standards for the world at large, standards that can be invoked by those who want to arouse opposition in their own country to the doings of evil men amongst them. It provides some retribution, even if not deterrence, in the worst cases. And perhaps it even guides aright some of those who might hereafter be tempted or directed to do terrible things, especially if the tribunal's actions are properly explained.

There was, we have noticed, no serious doubt at Nuremberg that *someone* should be able to do something about the perpetrators of the worst Nazi atrocities during World War II. Whether anyone *would* be able to do so might depend upon chance, including both the chance of who was detected and apprehended and the chance of whether a tribunal was made available. When the Crimes Against Humanity are as elemental and extensive as they were here, shocking the entire world upon discovery (and even silencing their perpetrators), it would make a mockery of justice to pretend that the perpetrators of such deeds could not have known that they might be punished *one way or another* some day for what they did.[67]

It will hardly do, then, to defeat justice by invoking traditional rules, such as the *ex post facto* prohibition, on behalf of men who had repudiated in the most comprehensive way one elementary rule and standard after another. Those rules are made for human beings, not human beings for those rules: their spirit and purposes should not be forgotten. One end of law is justice, gross violations of which are subject to correction even in the absence of explicit promulgation of rules by a sovereign power. A dedication to justice helps legitimate the very existence of sovereign power.

X.

We should also notice that there may not be even a technical *ex post facto* problem when dealing with atrocities committed by the Nazis outside Germany, which is where most of them took place. The occupied countries, once liberated, did not need to recognize German laws and practices: the people of those countries had not invited the Germans; nor had they authorized the Germans to set aside their laws or to establish killing camps.

This particular argument might not seem to apply to the atrocities committed in Germany against German nationals, such as the Jews, before as well as during the war. But are not such domestic offenses, on the scale and with the intensity seen here, something like piracy? Pirates have long been regarded as the common enemy of the human race, to be summarily dealt with by their captors—and civilized victors should take this kind of response into account when dealing with the apprehended perpetrators of Crimes Against Humanity.[68]

Furthermore, the punishment of Germans for what they did in Germany, even when there was no German law explicitly forbidding what was done, may be a variation upon the exercise of the right of revolution. One's sense of humanity naturally reacts against what the Nazis did in their Crimes Against Humanity, no matter what nationality their victims happened to have. There is here a natural sense of revulsion, from which a right of revolution readily flows. Among the prerogatives of the victors in such circumstances is the right, and perhaps the duty, to deal with monsters one way or another. Prime Minister Churchill, for example, argued during the war that the worst Nazis should, upon being captured, simply be shot.[69]

XI.

The Germans, well before the Nazis came to power, made a lot of the state and of the authority of those acting for the state. Justice Jackson, in his opening statement for the prosecution, said that "the German people [are] accustomed to look upon the German State, by whomever controlled, with a mysticism that is incomprehensible to [the American] people."[70] One manifestation of their virtual worship of the state was the emphasis placed by them upon the oath of allegiance.

Most of the defendants at Nuremberg, we have noticed, made much of the German people, a people who did yearn for something higher and who could be appealed to on that ground.[71] The Germans' long-standing, and deeply ingrained, dedication to loyalty, justice and fellow-feeling could be drawn upon by their leaders—but in such a way as to strip them of any regard about how outsiders were treated.[72] Most Germans, whatever they suspected, may not have *known* that the Jews were being routinely slaughtered (mostly abroad) in the concentration camps[73]—but they *had* known for years that it had become very dangerous to be a Jew in Germany, and they had tolerated that corrupting state of affairs.[74]

Fundamental to the German, or any other, emphasis upon the state is a reliance upon legal positivism, with its reliance in turn upon the sovereignty of
the will. The most authoritative willing in these circumstances emanates from
the state. The principal ideologist of the Nazi Party, Alfred Rosenberg, put the
Nazi ideal in this way in his closing statement (shortly before he was convicted on all four counts and sentenced to death):

> Among other matters, the Soviet prosecutor stated that the entire so-called "ide-
> ological activity" had been a "preparation of crime." In that connection I should
> like to state the following: National Socialism represented the idea of overcom-
> ing the class struggle which was disintegrating the people, and uniting all
> classes in a large national community. Through the Labor Service, for instance,
> it restored the dignity of manual labor on mother earth, and directed the eyes of
> all Germans to the necessity of a strong peasantry. By the Winter Relief Work it
> created a comradely feeling among the entire nation for all fellow-citizens in
> need, irrespective of their former party membership. It built homes for mothers,
> youth hostels, and community clubs in factories, and acquainted millions with
> the yet unknown treasures of art. For all that I served.[75]

Rosenberg speaks here of creating "a comradely feeling among the entire
nation," of uniting all classes "in a large national community." But one highly
placed defendant after another reported that the most reprehensible programs
that we can recognize as characteristic of the Nazi regime had been thoroughly hidden even from the leadership for years. What sense of community
can there be when *that* can happen? One is reminded of Aristotle's insistence
that Babylon was not a *polis*: part of it had once fallen to the enemy without
that being known for days in some other parts of Babylon.[76]

XII.

The true believers among the Nazis, some of the defendants reported, were
particularly disturbed by the willingness of Hitler to see Germany destroyed
with him when the end came.[77] This revelation exposed to them the abyss that
had always been there.

To speak of an *abyss* here is to notice once again the profound irrationality
at the core of the Nazi regime. This led to—and depended upon—conduct
that could not be acknowledged or explained, highly destructive conduct that
could not really be understood by others. It could not even be truly understood by those immediately involved in such conduct.

Leo Strauss used to say that the only principle the Nazis had was hatred of
the Jews.[78] Is that what a fervent nationalism comes down to, then, a hatred

of *the other*? The Jews were, for the Nazis, "the other" par excellence (with the equally far-roaming Gypsies, perhaps, a runner-up). This was not, however, simply a matter of the Nazis' *using* the Jews in order to advance their interests. Rather, they would obsessively destroy Jews even when it did not serve their immediate wartime interests to do so.[79]

The Jews were perceived as a continuing threat, perhaps ultimately because the Nazis sensed that, however patriotically a German Jew might act from time to time (as during World War I), he looked to something higher than the state for his ultimate inspiration and guidance. And those things—both the Jew and that which he looked up to—the Nazi could not bear to contemplate.[80]

XIII.

Whatever their limitations, the Nuremberg proceedings deferred to forms and justice in ways that the Nazis never could.[81] No doubt, some hypocrisy could be detected there, not least because of what the Russians were being subjected to at home and what they were themselves doing at that very time in Eastern Europe.[82] Even so, the Nuremberg judges *were* acknowledging that others would someday be justified in subjecting *them* in turn to the same standards.[83]

Although serious differences were already developing elsewhere between the United States and the Soviet Union during the course of the trial, the prosecutors and judges of the four powers could pretty well agree about the substance of the crimes against humanity.[84] Nature was thus publicly reaffirmed by all the parties: that is, it cannot be too often pointed out that fundamental moral standards were invoked and acknowledged by everyone at Nuremberg, including by the defendants who had been loyal to Hitler and by the two judges who had been appointed by Stalin.[85]

What were these Nazi defendants entitled to at Nuremberg? That their trial and condemnation would be an affirmation of their humanity. They were, to some degree, redeemed by their trial, having been given an unearned opportunity to state their positions upon discovering the worst things about themselves. They were given an opportunity thereby to make a contribution to that vindication of humanity and natural right that the Nuremberg Trial does stand for in a relativistic age.

An opportunity was also given the defendants, which several took advantage of, to protest what was then being done to the Germans by their conquerors.[86] Among these critics was Hans Frank, who was executed for crimes committed by him as governor of occupied Poland. Frank had been so moved by the revelations of the trial, it seems, that he said on the witness stand that "a thousand years would not suffice to erase the guilt brought upon [the German] people because of Hitler's conduct in this war."[87] His closing statement included sentiments that could well have been endorsed by many of his fellow defendants:

> I am grateful that I was given the opportunity to prepare a defense and justification against the accusations raised against me.
>
> In this connection I am thinking of all the victims of the violence and horror of the dreadful events of war. Millions had to perish unquestioned and unheard. I surrendered my war diary, containing my statements and activities, in the hour when I lost my liberty. If I was really ever severe, then it was above all toward myself, at this moment when my actions in the war were made public.
>
> I do not wish to leave any hidden guilt which I have not accounted for behind me in this world. I assumed responsibility on the witness stand for all those things for which I must answer. I have also acknowledged that degree of guilt which attaches me as a champion of Adolf Hitler, his movement, and his Reich.[88]

I deferred until my trip downtown this morning the preparation of the conclusion of this talk in which I want to caution against the sentimental repudiation of all forms of strength, a repudiation to which all too many intellectuals may be inclined because of the dismal records of both the Nazis and the Stalinists in the twentieth century. But it should never be forgotten that it had required superior strength, physical as well as moral, to subdue the Nazis and bring them to justice. It does not bode well for civilization if the use of strength is repudiated by all but the wicked.[89]

I began today by recalling my experience last week in San Antonio with a Good Friday celebration. I had this morning, as I biked downtown along the Lake Front from Hyde Park on this Eastern Orthodox Good Friday, another instructive experience. I came upon a falcon that had just grounded a pigeon. Here, too, strength was very much in evidence, brought to bear on a mild-mannered victim by a bird of prey whose power and majesty excited attention, if not even admiration. And this I can say although I *am* one of that minority who find pigeons to be attractive birds.[90]

The Nazis fancied themselves the falcons, if not the eagles, of the world, entitled by the laws of nature to feast upon the pigeons they conjured up. There is indeed something natural, and hence in a sense proper, in the way that the falcon conducts itself. But we must never lose sight of the fact, providentially recalled for us by my falcon's display this morning, that what may be natural and acceptable in a fierce bird is not to be tolerated in human beings by anyone who truly understands the dictates of nature.[91]

12-B. JULIUS ROSENBERG, ETHEL ROSENBERG, AND MORTON SOBELL[92]

I.

Twenty-six years after Julius and Ethel Rosenberg were executed at Sing Sing Prison, a leading member of the Chicago bar recalled

> that the reaction of the Government attorneys involved to Justice [William O.] Douglas's stay [of execution, on June 17, 1953] [had been] one of "outrage." For "at that stage when everything had been thought to have been passed upon by the Supreme Court itself"—indeed a number of times—[Justice] Douglas "had blocked the normal course of judicial procedure."[93]

And so Chief Justice Fred Vinson was prevailed upon by the attorney general and this lawyer "to reconvene the Court, which had just adjourned for the summer."[94]

This recent recollection, by a lawyer who was at that time acting solicitor general, is rather curious. His "outrage" itself borders on the outrageous, unless it is assumed that he does not realize what he is saying. It is implied in the article that reports on an interview with this Chicago lawyer, that "everything" had been reviewed by the Supreme Court, when in fact very little had been, inasmuch as the Court had repeatedly refused to take the case for substantive review. [I remind the reader that this *Rosenberg-Sobell Case* essay was first published in 1979.] Justice Hugo L. Black concluded his Dissenting Opinion of June 19, 1953, seven hours before the execution of the Rosenbergs,

> It is not amiss to point out that this Court has never reviewed this record and has never affirmed the fairness of the trial below. Without an affirmance of the fairness of the trial by the highest court of the land there may always be questions as to whether these executions were legally and rightfully carried out.[95]

It is also implied in the solicitor general's recollections, as well as by other apologists for the way the Rosenberg case was handled by an indignant government, that Justice Douglas' stay of execution would have prolonged unconscionably what had already been unduly prolonged proceedings, when in fact the other two capital cases upon which the court issued opinions that very week in June, 1953, had been in the courts substantially longer.[96]

The circumstances of the Rosenberg case were such that, it seems to me, "the reaction of the government attorneys involved" should have been one of relief rather than one of "outrage." That is, whatever they thought as professionals of the technicalities either of the question raised before Justice Douglas or of the way that that question had been raised, they should have been relieved that there would indeed be time for further reflection, and especially that a new president would be given more time to consider executive clemency in the event that all judicial remedies invoked on behalf of the condemned couple failed.

One cannot pass responsible judgment on what happened then and how lawyers and others conducted themselves, however, without recalling how the Rosenberg-Sobell case seemed to us in June 1953.[97]

II.

I should state here at the outset of my necessarily incomplete review of this case that I am not an "expert" in the matter. I did read with some care, many years ago, the entire trial record. I have followed discussions of the case over the years. And I have long been intimately associated with Professor Malcolm Sharp, whom I first met in 1948 when I entered the University of Chicago Law School. He was one of the lawyers for the Rosenbergs in the last desperate weeks of the case in June 1953. This review of the Rosenberg-Sobell case is, in part, a recognition of the fair-mindedness of Malcolm Sharp as a resolute champion of lost causes—and especially those causes that seem to him to bear on the passions that account for war.[98]

I begin this review of the case by drawing upon an account in *New Times*, an account sympathetic to the Rosenbergs. This account was first called to my attention during a Chicago television appearance I made in 1975 with Michael Meeropol, the older son of the Rosenbergs.[99] The *New Times* article includes these observations that, I believe, would be generally agreed upon:

On July 17, 1950, a 32-year old engineer named Julius Rosenberg was arrested in his home, while his older son Michael listened to the Lone Ranger on radio, and was charged with participating in an espionage conspiracy. A little less than a month later, his wife, Ethel, 34, was arrested on the same charge. Ethel and Julius, both the children of poor Jewish immigrants, had grown up in poverty on New York's Lower East Side. Like many of the Depression generation in America, the couple had turned sharply to the Left; they probably were members of the Communist Party. Shortly after their marriage, Julius went to work as a junior engineer for the government's Signal Corps. Their first son, Michael, was born in 1943, the second, Robert, in 1947. In 1945 Julius was fired from the Signal Corps for Communist associations. He went to work for a private firm, and then became a partner in a small machine shop. One of the other partners was Ethel's younger brother, David Greenglass.

Julius and Ethel Rosenberg were charged [in an indictment of August 17, 1950] with masterminding an espionage ring that had spirited the atomic secret out of the United States and into the Soviet Union. On trial with them was another engineer, Morton Sobell, accused of being part of the espionage ring but not with participating in the atomic theft. . . . The trial [of Julius and Ethel Rosenberg, Morton Sobell and David Greenglass] opened in the U. S. District Court in New York City on March 6, 1951, under Judge Irving R. Kaufman—at age 40, one of the youngest men on the federal bench. Judge Kaufman now sits as chief of the United States Court of Appeals for the Second Circuit.[100]

On April 5, 1951, at the conclusion of their trial for conspiring to commit espionage in violation of the Espionage Act of 1917, the Rosenbergs were sentenced to death; Mr. Sobell was sentenced to thirty years in prison, the maximum for his more limited offense. The next day Mr. Greenglass was sentenced to fifteen years in prison. Mrs. Greenglass was never indicted.[101]

The principal criminal acts charged against the Rosenbergs and the Greenglasses were alleged to have taken place in 1944 and 1945 and to have taken advantage of Mr. Greenglass's (evidently chance) employment as a machinist on the atomic-bomb development at Los Alamos, New Mexico. Information about the atomic bomb collected by Mr. Greenglass was passed on, it was alleged, to the Russians. The atomic bomb was used, as we all know, at the end of the war with Japan in August 1945. In September 1949, President Truman announced that the Russians had set off a nuclear explosion of their own.

In February 1950, Klaus Fuchs, a prominent nuclear physicist who had worked on the atomic bomb in the United States as well as in Great Britain, was arrested in England. He was tried there and convicted on the basis of his confession that he had furnished considerable atomic-bomb information to the Soviet Union. He was sentenced on March 1, 1950 to fourteen years in prison. The arrest of Mr. Fuchs led to the detection and arrest in this country of Harry Gold, who had been Mr. Fuchs's courier in the United States. This in turn led to the detection and arrest (on June 15, 1950) of Mr. Greenglass, who thereupon implicated the Rosenbergs.[102]

In the meantime—that is, since June 1950—the United States had been engaged in the Korean War. In late 1950, the Chinese entered the war.

III.

The tenor of those ugly times is suggested by the following excerpt from the rather disturbed and disturbing remarks made by Judge Kaufman when he sentenced the Rosenbergs to death:

I believe your conduct in putting into the hands of the Russians the A-bomb years before our best scientists predicted Russia would perfect the bomb has already caused, in my opinion, the Communist aggression in Korea, with the

resultant casualties exceeding 50,000 and who knows but that millions more
of innocent people may pay the price of your treason. Indeed, by your betrayal
you undoubtedly have altered the course of history to the disadvantage of our
country.[103]

The words "your treason" suggest that the Rosenbergs may have been,
without due regard for constitutional limitations, sent to their death for "treason," an offense that was neither alleged *nor provable* by the Government.[104]
In effect, Judge Kaufman may have condemned the Rosenbergs either for a
mistaken prediction by "our best scientists" or for a mistaken judgment by the
Secretary of State who discounted publicly, before the North Koreans' move
south in 1950, the importance for the United States of the Korean Peninsula.[105] The Rosenberg case was, at least in part, a sedition case, as well as a
treason and an espionage case: the political opinions associated with the defendants affected both the judgment reached and the sentences pronounced by
the trial judge.

The tenor of the times is also suggested by what Gloria Agrin, who as a
young lawyer had helped Emanuel Bloch and his seventy-four–year-old father Alexander Bloch in the defense of the Rosenbergs, says now in response
to those who suggest that Mr. Bloch lacked sufficient trial experience and that
he was too polite and acquiescent during the trial:

> Bloch was an experienced trial lawyer, but he was working under tremendous
> handicaps. We had no way of even hiring investigators. He was improvising all
> the way through the trial. We couldn't even get a lawyer to come in to assist us
> at the trial. Bloch and I were isolated. Left-wing lawyers walked across the
> street when they saw us coming—they didn't want to be tarred by the spy brush.
> Bloch was working without fee. Both of us went broke. We lost our shirts.[106]

I have been told by several lawyers who knew Mr. Bloch (who died of a
heart attack in January 1954) that he felt "terribly isolated" from the bar during most of the time he had this case. He knew his limitations as a criminal
trial lawyer and recognized that he was risking mistakes that might prejudice
the case for his clients, but he could not get competent criminal lawyers to advise him, as an experienced and successful Chicago trial lawyer told me a
decade ago, "even to talk to him."[107]

The tenor of the times is suggested as well by the fact that both parents of
young children should have been executed the very day that the Supreme Court
vacated a stay of execution that had promised at least a summer of relief—and
this was for giving to a wartime ally "the secret" of "the A-bomb." Serious
doubts have also been raised from time to time about the propriety of the government having treated the Rosenbergs as if they were equally culpable.

The critical question in thinking about such a case as this is, it seems to me, a simple one, "Was justice done?" My own answer is today, as it was a quarter of a century ago, "No." I believe now [1979] as I did then, that the sentences exacted both of the Rosenbergs and of Mr. Sobell were grossly excessive—and this I say without assuming any of them innocent and without assuming that the death penalty is never proper. Thus, the excessiveness, even brutality, of the sentences in these circumstances was enough to make what happened unjust.

In some ways, what was done to Mr. Sobell was even worse than what was done to the Rosenbergs. One could attribute the killing of the Rosenbergs to the passions of the day. But keeping Mr. Sobell in prison for more than eighteen years, even if the evidence upon which he had been convicted had been far stronger than it was, was the product of bureaucratic callousness and political spinelessness.[108]

The evidence against the Rosenbergs, or at least against Mr. Rosenberg, was considerably more substantial than that against Mr. Sobell. But almost all of it came down essentially to the question of who was to be believed, the Rosenbergs or the Greenglasses. Mr. Greenglass, it will be remembered, was Mrs. Rosenberg's younger brother. The Greenglasses confessed to espionage and were backed up, in their claims about what *they* had done, by the erratic Harry Gold.[109] Mr. Gold testified to absolutely no personal contact with, and to little if any knowledge of, the Rosenbergs. The Greenglasses' confessions would have made about as much sense with the Rosenbergs out of the picture as with them in it. That is, either the Greenglasses made their own contacts with a critical Russian diplomat in New York or the Rosenbergs did. One account seems to me, working from the trial record alone, about as likely as the other.

Each couple had considerable interest in telling the story it did. The Rosenbergs thereby removed themselves from involvement in a serious matter; the Greenglasses thereby minimized their roles, portraying themselves as instruments of their elders, the Rosenbergs. It should be added that there seems to have been bad blood between the two couples, partly because of difficulties encountered in the small business they had operated together after the war. Who was to be believed? The jury evidently believed the Greenglasses as did the trial judge and the prosecutors, who included, among others, Irving Saypol and Roy M. Cohn.[110]

I add "the prosecutors" because it seems to me that the prosecution, as well as the government attorneys on appeal, firmly believed that the Rosenbergs were guilty. I have never believed that the current search through government files will turn up evidence that government attorneys were a knowing party to a frame-up. A frame-up theory is much less interesting and less instructive than what I suspect really happened. For one thing, frame-up (like conspiracy) theories make far too much of malice and deliberation and not enough of incompetence and passion, and hence chance, in human affairs.

To say, however, that "the government" was sincere is not to say that it behaved as it should have. It was, in various ways, unscrupulous and self-righteous; it made far more of the danger to the country resulting from the alleged espionage than it was entitled to do; and it did not take due account of the radically changed circumstances since 1944–1945.[111] In addition, it did not permit sufficient leeway for the possibility that the Greenglasses were lying about one or both of the Rosenbergs.

My impression has always been that neither couple was particularly believable, that both sides stretched the truth somewhat. But more critical is whether the Greenglasses should have been believed to the extent that they were, since the burden of proof in such cases *is* the government's. If both the Rosenbergs and the Greenglasses were involved in espionage, it need not have been quite as sophisticated and extensive as the Greenglasses described it. For one thing, David Greenglass seems to have been rather gullible. I suspect that he believed a lot of things that were not so—and then embroidered them somewhat to make his case even more persuasive with the authorities who were threatening his immediate family.

Thus, I *suspect* (assuming the guilt of the Rosenbergs) that David Greenglass might well have been told by Mr. Rosenberg that a console table—the notorious console table around which the newly discovered–evidence motions turned at the end[112]—had come from the Russians and that it had been fitted up for microfilming, when in fact neither statement by Mr. Rosenberg was true. It would not be beyond Mr. Greenglass or his wife to add (on this assumption) that they had even been shown a place hollowed out in the table for a camera.

On the other hand, the Greenglasses (assuming the Rosenbergs innocent of atomic espionage) could have figured that the Rosenbergs had really gotten them into all this trouble through ideological indoctrination and that the Greenglasses should not alone pay the penalty, with perhaps no one anticipating death sentences for anyone if the blame were thus spread out. That is, the Greenglasses (still assuming the Rosenbergs innocent of espionage) might have found themselves getting in deeper and deeper—and, with even younger children than the Rosenbergs had, they too were in a vulnerable condition. Later, they probably lost their nerve, as did the government officials who did not intervene to stop the executions. But all this *is* conjecture. The fact remains that the Rosenbergs were executed. The Greenglasses dropped out of sight once Mr. Greenglass was released from prison in 1960.[113]

IV.

In preparing this review of the case, I have been helped most of all by reconsidering Malcolm Sharp's book *Was Justice Done? The Rosenberg-Sobell Case.*[114]

It is significant that Mr. Sharp's book would not be published in the 1950s by any large commercial publisher. Nor was Mr. Sharp's book generally reviewed, even though he was widely respected as a Chicago-School "free market" law professor.[115]

The introduction provided for the Sharp book by the Nobel Prize chemist, Harold C. Urey,[116] is like a breath of fresh air for anyone familiar with the record of and discussions about the case. The common sense of a truly intelligent man can be refreshing. Thus Mr. Urey shrewdly observes, "What a bother console tables must have been to Yakovlev [the Russian diplomat]! Why not give your spies cash and let them buy their own tables?"[117]

Of the testimony about the hollowed-out table and the microfilming, Mr. Urey can say, "Now I wish to ask some simple questions of technically trained men. On what principle do you think this device worked? How would you design it? Whom would you get to do the cabinet work? How much would it cost? Why not buy an ordinary commercial device and keep it permanently in a locked closet? How would you prevent visitors from lifting the top and exposing this device to view? Well, ask your own questions. This is all obviously nonsense."[118]

Mr. Urey might well be right, even though I can see (as I have indicated) that this "nonsense" could have originated with the Rosenbergs themselves. But since this story about the table is on its face highly questionable, a fair-minded court would have responded to the proffer by the defense of the newly discovered table in a much different way from Judge Kaufman and the courts on appeal.[119] This reminds me of still another observation by Mr. Urey: "After considerable conversation with lawyers on this subject, including one who worked on the government side of the case, I conclude that lawyers are more interested in the law than in justice."[120]

The most important point that comes out in Mr. Urey's analysis is one I have already suggested: It is quite plausible to account for atomic espionage in this situation without the Rosenbergs being involved. In fact wherever one reads "Rosenberg" in the prosecution's account, the words "some Russian" would do as well. In addition, Mr. Urey points up the potential injustice in any case that depends almost exclusively on accomplice testimony: "One criminal accuses another who again accuses another until perhaps an innocent person is accused and then the chain is broken and we give the maximum punishment to the innocent person."[121]

Anyone interested in the Rosenberg case should look at Mr. Urey's analysis for a vivid statement of the case for the defendants. One should study as well Mr. Sharp's exposition, a most remarkable book that should be reprinted (but with an index). Although he has himself spoken highly of subsequent discussions of the case, I believe his account will remain the decisive one for thoughtful students of the case. *It soberly assesses all critical evidence available during the appeals and upon which the parties and the courts acted.* One way of stating the superiority of the Sharp book is to say that it draws on law and ethics more than it does on social science, history, and ideology.

Mr. Sharp is fair both in his statement of the case for and the case against the Rosenbergs and in his explanation of why he takes the calmly partisan position he does. It shows us how this sort of thing should be done. And so I could say a few years ago, to a gathering of University of Chicago graduate students in political science,

> One model I can hold up to you of a useful curbing of indignation without sacrificing one's dedication to virtue and the common good may be seen in Mr. Sharp's book, published in 1956, on the *Rosenberg-Sobell Case, Was Justice Done?* [*sic*]. Because of its disciplined examination of the complicated passions of others, it remains the best book written on that disgraceful episode in our history. Great harm was done because of the indignation that blinded our government at that time. But great harm can be done as well because of indignation evoked among the unwary upon learning of the callous deeds generated by the indignation of others.[122]

The careful reader, even though he may differ in his conclusions, comes away from Mr. Sharp's book reliably aware both of what the evidence was and what the issues were. It is too bad that this book was not available for the Supreme Court to read. It is a pity, that is, that the Rosenbergs were not kept alive long enough for such a masterly lawyer's brief to be written on their behalf.

Mr. Sharp is still convinced of the Rosenbergs' innocence. I never have been. But, I should at once add, his conclusion does not rest on the original trial record alone but rather on that record as supplemented by two additional things: (1) the 1953 "newly discovered evidence" and its significance (that is, the console table and how would-be witnesses with respect to *it* conducted themselves in his presences); (2) his considerable association with the defense attorneys who had known the Rosenbergs and their friends. He believes that these lawyers, people themselves of intelligence and sensitivity, were convinced of the innocence of their clients. He would grant that it is probably impossible to *prove* innocence, but he believes it highly significant that the people he knows to have been closest to the Rosenbergs were themselves convinced of their innocence. He is aware, of course, that clients can foolishly mislead their lawyers even in capital cases.[123]

When Mr. Sharp gives such reasons for his belief in innocence, he may tacitly concede that anyone such as an appellate judge, who limits himself to the record of the trial, could have believed that the jury's verdict was justified. Even so, Mr. Sharp does provide a valuable account of the case—both of the evidence and of interpretations of that evidence—and thereby points up once again the problems with recourse to the death penalty in such cases.

V.

It is important to notice that Mr. Sharp's book was written for the most part in the fall of 1953, in the months immediately after the execution of the Rosenbergs. It is based on the evidence, standards, and arguments then available. I have emphasized this because, in passing judgment on others, one is obliged to work primarily with what was known and knowable in their particular circumstances. This is the nature of practical judgment.

The decisive criticism to be made of what was done then need not, and indeed probably should not, depend upon what we have happened to learn since [I could write in 1979]. The critical considerations were then available for assessment: considerations with respect to what the Rosenbergs might have done, with respect to what others might have done, with respect to the quality of the admissible evidence brought forward and the standards being applied, with respect to the haste with which the proceedings were moved along at the end, and with respect to the behavior of various judges and lawyers.

For example, one need not deny that there were any atomic-bomb secrets to steal in order to be able to recognize that the secrets stolen could not have been as momentous as the prosecution, the judges, and the government's lawyers on appeal allowed themselves to believe. That is, I do not consider it sensible to argue, as some advocates for the Rosenbergs now do, that there were *never* any secrets to steal. Both the Russians and the Americans evidently thought there were. Besides, in these matters, one's intentions might be important.

That the secrets were not momentous—whatever the Greenglasses or the Rosenbergs might have thought in 1945—is indicated by an observation in Bertrand Russell's generous review of Mr. Sharp's book:

[Judge Kaufman] seems to have thought, as most non-scientific Americans apparently did, that there was something which could be called the "secret" of the bomb, which was thought of as analogous to a magic formula in medieval

necromancy. . . . This whole conception is quite wide of the mark. There was
very much less that was secret about the atom bomb after Hiroshima than was
popularly supposed.[124]

It is implied, in Lord Russell's insistence upon the mistaken notions about
atomic secrets held by "non-scientific Americans," that the scientific community knew better *at that time*. They knew that what Judge Kaufman and
people like him believed and said was woefully exaggerated—and yet that
fearful community, with a few honorable exceptions such as Mr. Urey, remained silent. The defendants could not draw upon the scientific community
for an informed defense, one that could have legitimately played down the seriousness of what the Rosenbergs were supposed to have done and that could
have led to much more effective cross-examination of government witnesses.

The passions of the Cold War, which were not unrelated to passions left
over from World War II and which had been intensified by the outbreak of the
Korean War, made it difficult for most Americans to remain moderate. Domestic anticommunism was at its worst in those days—and it was obvious to
everyone that the Rosenbergs *were* involved with Communism. Anticommunism was particularly virulent on the East Coast, especially in circles that included a number of ex-Communists.[125]

One cannot help but wonder, of course, what the role was in this case of
prejudice against Jews. Virtually all of the major figures in the case at the trial
level were Jewish, as were a number at the appellate level. What does that
prove? I repeatedly heard it suggested at the time that critical to this case may
have been a defensive Jewish vindictiveness toward, or at least ostracism of,
any Jews suspected of notorious misconduct that endangered the entire Jewish community. Is not this perhaps a natural, however unfortunate and ultimately self-defeating, response by some Jews to centuries of persecution?
The prospect of anti-Jewish prejudice does seem to have affected Judge Kaufman. It affected also the organized Jewish community that, by and large, laid
low during those desperate years, even though both parents of small children
were slated for execution.

In a sense, perhaps, the Rosenbergs were sacrificed to the welfare of Israel.[126] It is instructive in this connection to remember that Mr. Truman, who
had been so critical to the international legitimation of Israel, was the president who should have commuted the Rosenberg death sentences. That is, he
should *not*, as the retiring president, have left this problem for his successor
to deal with in his first months in office.

Dwight Eisenhower was unfortunate enough in those days to have as his
attorney general another impassioned New Yorker pressing him not to intervene.[127] Once the Rosenbergs were killed, it can also be said, Mr. Eisenhower
did begin to develop more sensible relations with the Russians.

VI.

Were both of the Rosenbergs involved in atomic espionage? We probably never will know, unless critical documents come out of Eastern Europe or the Greenglasses repudiate their confessions or people close to the Rosenbergs confess. Even so, a careful assessment would have to be made of whatever documents or confessions should be offered us hereafter. This points up the limits of historical research: the most critical information and arguments are, I have suggested, already available to us, and have been since 1953. A trial record is necessarily incomplete; gaps and discrepancies can always be found by those who have an interest in finding them.[128]

We can, in the years ahead, expect more and more critics of the Government to find and develop problems with the official version of the *Rosenberg Case*. The Government is far less likely to assign intelligent people to researching and making *its* case. Thus we can now expect, among intellectuals generally, the development of the opinion that one or the other, if not both, of the Rosenbergs must have been innocent. The principal argument will then be about whether the Rosenbergs were framed by the authorities or by the Greenglasses alone.[129]

One thing that always has been clear to me about the case is that the Rosenbergs were very unlucky people. Indeed, they seem to have been "born losers." (So, for that matter, were the Greenglasses, perhaps even more so, but that is not as evident.) The Rosenbergs were, despite their considerable posturing, far less sophisticated than they believed themselves to be—and they were chronically unlucky: in business, in their associates, in their relatives, in their politics, and in having had someone they knew assigned to Los Alamos.

Their bad luck is reflected also in their timing. They would have been far better off if they had been caught either much earlier or much later—either "in the act" (in 1944–1945) or much later (say, after 1960).[130] Instead, they were caught at the worst possible time, which meant that they suffered from an *ex post facto* effect in how they were treated. They were regarded as having intended far worse than they could have, even if guilty of the offenses charged.

Another thing that is clear to me is that there were people in the American government, the bar, the law school faculties, the scientific community, and the press who should have known better. These leaders simply should not have permitted the execution of those convicted spies, whatever their opinions about guilt or innocence. But far too many respectable people and organizations timidly remained silent. Legal and bureaucratic "momentum" does build up in such matters—and it can be very hard to resist. It should be evident, upon any conscientious review of the Rosenberg case, that rules and standards are important if justice is to be done by the government. But also important, perhaps even vital, are people of integrity and magnanimity, as well as of common sense, in high office.

I return to an earlier observation. Our need is not so much for more data as it is for a more sensible assessment of the data we have had for two decades. To fall into the habit of looking for more and more data can even be harmful, partly because it places the emphasis upon mere information rather than upon judgment and upon the standards to be applied in assessing the available information. The information usually available in such matters as the Rosenberg case, which information is always bound to be "incomplete," should be assessed in the light of what we know and should know about human nature and about the times we live in. Only thus can we have a proper confidence in our institutions and in our ability to make good use of those institutions from day to day.

No research should be needed to oblige one to say that the sentences imposed upon the Rosenbergs were barbaric and should never have been carried out as they were, even if they were guilty of the crimes charged.[131] Nor should research be needed to permit us to recognize the merit of Justice Black's complaint when the Supreme Court ("led" by an unfortunate Chief Justice) was panicked into vacating Justice Douglas's stay of execution:

> Surely the Court is not here establishing a precedent that will require it to call extra sessions during vacation every time a federal or state official asks it to hasten the electrocution of defendants without affording this Court adequate time or opportunity for exploration and study of serious legal questions.[132]

I should add that it is not a sufficient justification for what the American public permitted with respect to the Rosenbergs that there were among the Russians thousands of Rosenberg cases. That there *were* thousands is evident, as Mr. Sharp has recently pointed out, in reports from the Soviet Union.[133] The dreadful Russian experience, it seems to me—to say nothing of the Nazi experience—is a good reason for not sitting quietly by when the first such cases appear among us.

These developments must be challenged in their beginnings—for the sake of the would-be perpetrators of injustice as well as for the sake of their likely victims. Thus, Lord Russell could say, in review of Mr. Sharp's book, "Apart from the question whether the verdicts were right, there is something utterly horrifying about the indecent haste shown by all the authorities in the last stages of the [Rosenberg case]."[134] Or, as Malcolm Sharp has recently recalled, "It was an episode of governmental insanity"[135]—and this is so, he too would add, apart from the question whether the original verdicts were right.

VII.

How should a lawyer conduct himself in such a situation as was presented during the final days of the Rosenberg case? Should not the Government attorneys have considered Justice Douglas' stay of execution as a godsend, whatever the merits or the sources of the legal questions submitted to him?

The principal legal question at the end was whether the Atomic Energy Act of 1946, which provides that the death penalty cannot be imposed without the recommendation of the jury in certain cases, had superseded, for purposes of sentencing, the statute under which the Rosenbergs had been condemned.[136] One can agree with Justice Felix Frankfurter that the questions presented the court in the last days of the Rosenberg case were "complicated and novel."[137] It is difficult for me to determine, from the Opinions of the justices, what the proper answers to *these* questions should have been.

Does not this difficulty reflect the inferior quality of the Opinions that the justices were able to come up with on such short notice? Certainly there was undue, even "indecent haste" at the end. This is further indicated in the Opinions of the three dissenting justices, which make sad reading for anyone dedicated to the deliberative processes upon which the rule of law depends. Thus, Justice Black protested,

> It is argued that the Court is not asked to "act with unseemly haste to avoid postponement of a scheduled execution." I do not agree. I do not believe that Government counsel or this Court has had time or an adequate opportunity to investigate and decide the very serious question raised in asking this Court to vacate the stay granted by Mr. Justice Douglas. . . . Certainly the time has been too short for me to give this question the study it deserves.[138]

Justice Frankfurter was so rushed that he could not even file his Dissenting Opinion until three days after the executions. The Frankfurter Opinion includes these observations:

> Neither counsel nor the Court, in the time available, were able to go below the surface of the question raised by the application for a stay which Mr. Justice Douglas granted. More time was needed than was had for adequate consideration. . . . We have not had the basis for researching conclusions and for supporting them in opinions. Can it be said that there was time to go through the process by which cases are customarily decided here?[139]

Even the then-acting solicitor general seems to recognize the problem:

> Justice Black made some remark implying that I wasn't as well prepared as I usually was before the Court and, of course, he was correct. On the other hand,

although I knew perfectly well, due to the lack of time to prepare, that I hadn't the time to master all the legislative history or read all the cases, I thought that the main line of our argument was perfectly reasonable and correct.[140]

Compare, however, Justice Frankfurter's testimony on this very point:

In all matters of statutory construction, one goes, especially these days, to the history of the legislation and other illuminating materials. It is almost mathematically demonstrable that there just was not time within twelve waking hours to dig out, to assess, to assemble, and to formulate the meaning of legislative materials.[141]

But *why* did there have to be, for the solicitor general as for everyone else, this (unprecedented?) "lack of time to prepare"? All this is spoken of by the solicitor general almost as if there had been a necessity beyond human reflection and choice. Consider, also, how he speaks of his duty in these circumstances: "My job as the Government's lawyer was to defend the Government's position as long as I could do so in good conscience; and certainly the Government's position was more than respectable."[142] The "Government's position" is spoken of by him as if it somehow existed independently of the men who were defending it. But, in fact, the solicitor general and the attorney general were themselves determining the "Government's position," not merely defending it. In these matters, is not the "Government's position" to be determined, in large part, by what it should be? Is not what it should be something that responsible officers are obliged to be sensible and decent about, especially when simply dreadful acts are contemplated?

Why, then, was there such unlawyer-like haste? In order, it would seem, to attempt to stop the agitation, in this country and abroad, of the question, "What should be done with the Rosenbergs?" I have yet to hear any other explanation that makes any sense at all. That is, the executions were rushed, in the spirit of impassioned partisanship, in order to deprive us of the opportunity, sorely needed, to think about what was being done in our name.

It is difficult for me [I could say in 1979] to escape the conclusion that what the authorities did here was, however sincere, far worse than anything that we know to have happened in connection with Watergate. This kind of misconduct by the authorities is hardly likely to produce or to maintain a sensible and humane people dedicated to the rule of law.[143]

In such desperate circumstances, a lawyer (who is, after all, a member of a privileged class, trained to be "above the battle")—a lawyer should have the good sense and the fortitude to say to a client, even if that client should happen to be the government of the United States, "What you propose to do is simply wrong, and I for one am not going to help you do it."

12-C. THE COMMUNIST PARTY OF THE UNITED STATES[144]

Subversion has been defined as "a systematic attempt to overthrow or undermine a government or political system by persons working secretly from within."[145] The danger of subversion can seem particularly ominous to any constitutional regime defined as much as the United States has always been by dedication to a body of political principles. The heightened fear of subversion felt from time to time in the history of the United States has prompted a variety of repressive measures by both national and state governments in this country.

Perhaps the most revealing encounter with the issue of subversion by the United States Supreme Court was its review in 1961[146] of a challenge by the Communist Party to the Subversion Activities Control Board (S. A. C. B.) created by the Internal Security Act of 1950.[147] That board was obliged to determine, on request of the attorney general, whether a designated organization was to be stigmatized as a "Communist-action" or "Communist-front" organization for which various duties and disabilities were prescribed. Special attention was to be paid to whether the organization thus investigated with a view to its being virtually outlawed was dominated by a hostile foreign power. Harry Kalven has said of this legislation, "It was in a real sense the major government attack on Communism in the United States and hence a political development of high import. . . . [I]t is quite possibly the precedent which carries the greatest threat to political freedoms in the future."[148] Echoes can be heard in that 1950 legislation of the much-reviled Alien and Sedition Acts of 1798.[149]

The five to four decision of the Supreme Court in the 1961 case displayed the justices dividing along the lines quite common in civil liberties cases of that period. The Opinion of the court—a curious mixture of technical competence and foolish conjectures—was written by Justice Frankfurter. He devoted more than one hundred pages in support of the court's holding that Congress was entitled to establish a repressive regulatory program grounded in a series of elaborate legislative "findings."[150]

The first of these legislative findings, set forth in the Act, was,

There exists a world Communist movement which, in its origins, its development, and its present practice, is a world-wide revolutionary movement whose purpose it is, by treachery, deceit, infiltration into other groups (government and otherwise), espionage, sabotage, terrorism, and any other means deemed necessary, to establish a Communist dictatorship in the countries throughout the world.[151]

Congress also declared in its findings that although Communist-action organizations

usually designate themselves as political parties, they are in fact constituent elements of the world-wide Communist movement and promote the objectives of
such movement by conspiratorial and coercive tactics, instead of through the democratic processes of a free elective system or through the freedom-preserving
means employed by a political party which operates as an agency by which people govern themselves.[152]

The First Amendment authorities relied upon by Justice Frankfurter in 1961
began with the unfortunate 1919 opinion of his mentor, Justice Holmes, in
Schenck v. United States.[153]

Three of the four dissenting members of the court (Chief Justice Warren,
Justice Douglas and Justice Brennan) wrote Opinions in *Communist Party v.
S. A. C. B.* questioning the constitutionality of the Internal Security Act and
the propriety of its implementation by the S. A. C. B. on procedural, eviden-
tiary, self-incrimination, bill of attainder and other grounds.[154] Particularly
memorable was the counsel with which Justice Black began and ended his
own dissenting Opinion, which made much more than did the other three of
the First Amendment:

> I do not believe that it can be too often repeated that the freedoms of speech,
> press, petition and assembly guaranteed by the First Amendment must be ac-
> corded to the ideas we hate or sooner or later they will be denied to the ideas we
> cherish. The first banning of an association because it advocates hated ideas—
> whether that association be called a political party or not—marks a fateful mo-
> ment in the history of a free country. That moment seems to have arrived for this
> country. . . . This widespread program for punishing ideas on the ground that
> they might impair the internal security of the Nation not only sadly fails to pro-
> tect that security but also diverts our energies and thoughts from the many far
> more important problems that face us as a Nation in this troubled world. I would
> reverse this case and leave the Communists free to advocate their beliefs in pro-
> letarian dictatorship publicly and openly among the people of this country with
> full confidence that the people will remain loyal to any democratic Government
> truly dedicated to freedom and justice—the kind of Government which some of
> us still think of as being "the last best hope of earth."[155]

The influence of the complicated Frankfurter Opinion in this 1961 case has
thus far chanced to be slight, partly because it was even more tedious than his
opinions usually were by this time, partly because it evaded facing up to key
issues, and partly because relations improved considerably between the Soviet Union and the United States during the following decade. Also, it eventually became generally apparent that the Communist Party of the United
States had been inconsequential ever since, if not even before, the imprisonment of its principal leaders in 1951.[156]

Long before then, however, the various repressive measures sanctioned by the Supreme Court since World War II had significantly damaged healthy political discourse in the United States. Particularly insidious was the common practice, legitimated in Justice Frankfurter's 1961 Opinion, of considering any group suspect that dared to express too many of the opinions that the rulers of the Soviet Union were identified with. Such official subversion of republican institutions, which Justice Black had warned against, contributed perhaps to critical misjudgments in the 1960s with respect to genuine American interests in Indochina and thereafter to disturbing question, especially among the young, about whether the people of the United States truly govern themselves.

12-D.   DAVID T. DELLINGER ET AL.[157]

I.

The Chicago Conspiracy Trial of 1969–1970, *United States* v. *Dellinger et al.*, following upon the 1968 Democratic National Convention in Chicago, aroused considerable interest in both legal and lay circles.[158] A reconsideration of it, with special attention to the recently published recollections of perhaps the most thoughtful defendant in that trial, should be instructive, especially as other controversial politicized trials (such as those connected with the Iran arms-Contra aid dealings) engage public attention.[159]

It will be remembered that American involvement in the Vietnam War escalated after the election of Lyndon Johnson in 1964. This proved particularly disturbing to many young people who had gotten the impression that the president was the "peace candidate" during the 1964 election campaign. Mr. Johnson's troubles, in Vietnam and consequently at home, became so oppressive that he announced, in early 1968, that he would not run for reelection. This was after he had been effectively challenged by Eugene McCarthy in several Democratic Party primaries.

The Democratic nomination was then left to Eugene McCarthy, Hubert Humphrey, and Robert Kennedy to sort out. After the murder of Mr. Kennedy, it became apparent that the administration and the Democratic Party regulars would throw their support behind Mr. Humphrey, the then vice president. The Convention in Chicago was destined to be the place where this decision would be sealed, but not without last-ditch resistance from supporters of Mr. McCarthy and from opponents of Mr. Humphrey and the Johnson Administration. That same summer the Republican Party nominated Richard Nixon for the presidency.

Highly publicized disturbances during the convention issued both from various antiwar groups and from the Chicago police force.[160] The Chicago Conspiracy Trial, following upon the convention, collected in the dock eight men who were alleged to have been primarily responsible for the disturbances that had marred the nomination of Mr. Humphrey. This trial, which began during the first year of the Nixon Administration, ran between September 1969 and February 1970. The United States attorney for the Northern District of Illinois who had been appointed by the Democratic Administration was held over, evidently so that he could conduct the Conspiracy Trial prosecution.

Five defendants were found guilty by a Chicago jury of having crossed state lines with the intention of inciting a riot during the August 1968 convention. Each of the five convicted defendants was sentenced to five years imprisonment and fined $5,000 (as well as the costs of prosecution, assessed at $41,748.60). Eight defendants and their two lawyers in this federal trial were sentenced for contempt of court after having been pronounced guilty by the trial judge of courtroom behavior intended to disrupt the orderly administration of justice. The contempt sentences ranged from two months and eighteen days (for one of the defendants) to four years and thirteen days (for one of the lawyers).[161]

II.

Tom Hayden, one of the defendants, has recently [1998] published a memoir that includes an extended account of the Chicago Conspiracy Trial.[162]

I looked in upon an average of two to three sessions a week during the five months that the 1969–1970 trial was going on. (I had press privileges that permitted me to avoid the lines of people almost always waiting for admission to the crowded courtroom in the Federal Building in downtown Chicago.) Mr. Hayden's account of the trial is interesting, providing a quite instructive addition to the many descriptions already published of that legal monstrosity.

Mr. Hayden is one of the more remarkable figures of his generation to have come out of the civil rights and antiwar struggles in this country after World War II. He does not report anything of note about the trial that I recall *not* to have happened the way he tells it. His account of the trial, as of much else in the book, is considerably better than I thought twenty years ago that he or any of his colleagues would ever be able to write about those events. My concluding remarks, in the account of the trial I published in 1971, assessed in this fashion the conduct of the principal participants:

It should be noticed, before concluding this survey of the Chicago Conspiracy Trial, that there was (on the part of the Government, the judge, and the defendants alike) much about this months-long encounter which was contrived, shallow, and hence tiresome. . . . It should also be noticed—and this is attested to by the bickering in court between defense counsel and prosecutors and between the defendants and the judge as to who among them had really been closest personally to Martin Luther King and to Robert F. Kennedy—that this trial was, just as had been the 1968 Democratic National Convention, a "civil war" among American "liberals." . . . All that was proved by such "civil war" was that everyone embroiled in both the Convention and the trial should have known better.[163]

One can see from the Hayden account how the civil rights movement, and the distrust of authority that that legitimated, led into the antiwar movement. One can also see the hopes that had been nurtured by Martin Luther King and the Kennedy brothers before their untimely deaths, hopes that tended to induce rebellious youth to enlist in public-spirited endeavors of a more or less respectable character.

III.

After the Democratic National Convention, with Mr. Nixon elected (not without their help), Mr. Hayden and those of like mind considered themselves badly beaten. The Hayden account of the 1968 struggles ends with these observations:

> Rarely, if ever, in American history has a generation begun with higher ideals and experienced greater trauma than those who lived fully the short time from 1960 to 1968. Our world was going to be transformed for the good, we let ourselves believe not once but twice, only to learn that violence can slay not only individuals, but dreams. After 1968, living on as a ruptured and dislocated generation became our fate, having lost our best possibilities at an early age, wanting to hope but fearing the pain that seemed its consequence. As Jack Newfield wrote, after 1968, "The stone was at the bottom of the hill and we were alone."[164]

In short, these young people were defeated and demoralized.

But they were not destined to be "alone" for long, thanks to the miscalculations of President Nixon, Mayor Daley (acting through the United States attorney in Chicago), and others who decided to prosecute. Why? To discourage further protests? To teach the young a lesson, meting out the punishment that they deserved? Or simply because they could? It is hard to be sure.[165]

Chapter 12

Mr. Daley felt humiliated, for he was astute enough to appreciate that he had helped defeat Mr. Humphrey, a candidate who had not been resolute enough to impress upon the mayor what should *not* happen on the streets of Chicago. Particularly galling for Mr. Daley was his awareness that he had dirtied up his liberal credentials and, even so, had failed in his effort to protect his city from looking bad.[166]

Mr. Daley and his lieutenants could not bear facing up to the fact that they had lost control of the situation. One of the sillier decisions of the city administration during convention week in 1968 had been its refusal to allow demonstrators to march to the amphitheater where the convention was meeting, a march that would have required several miles of walking in the August heat, an exertion that probably would have calmed down everyone.

Even sillier was the refusal to allow the demonstrators to stay in Lincoln Park, three miles from the downtown area around the Hilton Hotel where the celebrities and cameras were. Instead, the demonstrators were, in effect, driven into the Grant Park area, across from the Hilton—and that proved to be an explosive situation.[167]

The trial judge too had had some liberal credentials, having successfully presided over the first desegregation hearings in a northern school district. But he had always been autocratic in court—and at times he could be almost unbelievable in his arbitrariness and nastiness.[168]

Then there was the United States attorney, who gambled. This case, some believed, was going to make his public career—but it ended up derailing it. Even so, he has evidently been successful since then as a respected litigator.

Mr. Daley, too, never fully recovered from his 1968 ordeal. It is appropriate to return to these matters during the very week [in 1998] that his son has been elected mayor of Chicago—and as something of a reform candidate at that!

IV.

The "overkill" resorted to by the authorities, local and federal, permitted the antiwar movement to have a cause, or occasion, around which to regroup. It became easier to see how the United States government was misbehaving against the defendants in Chicago than against the Vietnamese in Southeast Asia. Months of extensive mass media coverage followed the indictments. The Nixon Administration allowed itself to be saddled with the mistakes of the Johnson Administration in more ways than one.

The Chicago Conspiracy Trial defendants (originally eight of them) figured from the outset that they would be convicted, and that they would be packed off to jail for five to ten years. It was not for them a happy prospect. But because they believed they had nothing to lose, they exploited the situation with verve. They became quite astute here, more so than they had been during 1968. The United States attorney and the trial judge played right to the defendants' strength. After a while, these authorities did not seem to be able to do anything to extricate themselves from the mess they were in.

The defendants were thus rehabilitated with the help of their enemies. They were offered a challenge that permitted them an opportunity to respond nobly. They managed in their response to capture the imagination of youngsters across the country, which was testified to by the dozen or so people camped out night after night on the sidewalk outside the Federal Building, even in the bitterest winter weather.[169]

At times, the trial judge and the United States attorney were astonishingly misguided, as when they resorted to the public shackling and gagging of one of the defendants, the only man of color among them.[170] One could not help but wonder at that time what the authorities could have been thinking—and how the legal community could have permitted that sort of thing to be done on several occasions. This spectacle, perhaps more than anything else, suggested a weakening, if not a breakdown, in the sense of community in the country at large.

Why the "overkill"? Partly because the president, the attorney general, and their advisors evidently believed their own propaganda. This susceptibility is related to that hollowness that makes much of power, or ambition, for its own sake. One must wonder whether this spiritual emptiness led, perhaps necessarily, to the Watergate debacle within a few years.

V.

The extent to which the defendants were able to exploit the opportunities thrust upon them by the authorities during the 1969–1970 trial is remarkable. It is revealing also to see, upon learning now the way the defendants spoke among themselves then about their trial, how threatened and sometimes even desperate they often felt. They did manage, however, to conceal their anxiety from public view and conducted themselves with bravado and even with wit. The Hayden account is particularly instructive in that it exposes to view the "human dimension" of such events.[171]

One tends to see such notorious people as facades only. Mr. Hayden indicates how the defendants did differ from one another, how their personal lives mattered, and what shambles their private affairs sometimes were in.[172]

The actions and sentiments of the defendants were all too often dubious. This is acknowledged in the Hayden account. But also recognizable is a certain decency about them, as well as an openness (behind the public scenes) to argument and to moral appeals, more so than one could be sure of as one watched their antics during the Chicago Conspiracy Trial.[173]

VI.

The best as well as the worst of the legal system could be seen at work during that trial and its aftermath.

The worst is suggested by an observation made in my 1971 account of the Chicago Conspiracy Trial:

> None of the participants in this prosecution conducted themselves as they should have. The Government was the victim of its unbridled indignation, the defendants of their sentimental self-indulgence, and the judge (like Mayor Daley during August, 1968) of his injudicious vanity. But a fairminded critic of the defendants would have to recognize in them at least a perverse gallantry. Thus, there was in the Conspiracy Trial much that seemed a replay, in slow motion, of what happened in Chicago during Convention Week, with the same questionable behavior on the part of all the principal parties involved in both "confrontations."[174]

The worst in the antiwar movement could be seen in the "crazies" who resorted to senseless violence in their exhibitionism and desperation. The weathermen phenomenon is a case in point, something that is repudiated in the Hayden account, as is the willingness of some of the more rebellious to identify themselves with the likes of Charles Manson and his barbarities.[175]

The worst on the government side could be seen in the way that the trial judge routinely conducted himself, in the way that the Justice Department carried on, and in the way that the Federal Bureau of Investigation was used (and was itself using the political and judicial system). It was evident at the time, and is referred to in my 1971 account,[176] that there was another "conspiracy" at work here: the chief judge, the trial judge, the United States attorney, and the Federal Bureau of Investigation coordinated various moves in a highly improper manner. This is now confirmed by several F.B.I. documents reprinted in the Hayden account. It also seems that the government had an informer among the defense attorneys' staff.[177]

It is still something of a mystery to me why the police ran amok the way they did during convention week in Chicago in August 1968. The ultimate responsibility for that must rest with the city administration, however provocative the antiwar demonstrators may have been.

The best in the legal system can be seen in the way the United States Court of Appeals (in Chicago) corrected what the trial judge had done, reversing all of the convictions on the substantive charges. Thus, it was recognized in a 1981 opinion by the Court of Appeals what had been done by that court a decade before:

> Prosecutorial and judicial misconduct have been acknowledged and fully reflected in radical reductions and nullifications of the earlier sanctions in this proceeding.[178]

Both the trial judge and the United States attorney have been repeatedly, sometimes harshly, criticized over the years by the Court of Appeals sitting in Chicago.[179]

These criticisms were anticipated, in effect, by what the jury did at the trial itself. All of the defendants were acquitted by the jury of conspiracy charges. Two others were acquitted of all other charges as well. Without the conspiracy counts,[180] and the relaxation of the rules of evidence thereby permitted, there would not have been either the kind of trial there was or any conviction of a serious felony. Even as it was, one of the jurors is quoted as saying, "I just voted five men guilty on speeches I don't even remember."[181] The most that could be said against various of the defendants' August 1968 conduct in Chicago is that they did indulge in highly irresponsible speeches.[182]

Also a credit to the legal system was the way that the trial on the contempt charges was eventually conducted by a federal judge brought in from Maine to review all of the evidence. He found, properly enough, that there had indeed been some instances of contempt—far fewer than the trial judge had tallied—but he added that no useful purpose would be served by sentencing to jail any of those he found guilty of contempt.[183]

The way that judge handled the contempt hearings won the respect of the defendants. What is particularly remarkable is that this "imported" judge managed to get, from the record and testimony, a reliable "feel" for what we had observed in the courtroom several years before.[184] Thus, the federal courts refused to permit the original trial judge to impose criminal-like contempt penalties without permitting defendants a proper criminal trial.

VII.

It is heartening to see that "the system" did work, not only in the courts but also in the community at large, with the political institutions of this country finally managing to come to grips in a sensible way with the problems of the

Vietnam War. Mr. Hayden's own career is illustrative, with his successes as an elected (and reelected) member of the California legislature.[185]

It is instructive to see what the limitations, as well as the aspirations, of the young rebels were—and how ill-equipped their elders were in dealing with them. One has to make an effort to be generous to the authorities who, either because of the arrogance of power or because of an unreasonable and unreasoning fear, conducted themselves so foolishly. No doubt, some of them might have conducted themselves better if the attorneys for the defendants had been able in turn to restrain their own self-righteousness.[186]

A common phenomenon in the repressive episodes in this country during the 1950s and 1960s was that the victimizers could regard themselves as the victims, which could lead them, years afterwards, to become sullen, embittered, and silent. This, too, suggests that the authorities never understood what was going on. On the other hand, the Chicago Conspiracy Trial defendants and some other defendants elsewhere were made better by their experiences. They at least could be prouder of how they had conducted themselves than could their opponents, who all too often hardened into caricatures of themselves.[187]

By and large, the young among the Left had their sympathies enlarged and their understanding deepened by their experience, not least by their eventual recognition of those mistakes of theirs that also had authoritarian, destructive tendencies. All too many of the Right, on the other hand, had their worst tendencies legitimated by the Reagan Administration and by the money and influence temporarily available to them.[188]

Perhaps the most heartening thing about this return to the Chicago Conspiracy Trial is the observation that the truth, more often than not, does manage, eventually, to see the light of day and is more likely than not to be recognized as such. Perhaps we are also seeing this, on a much grander scale, in the revelations coming these days [this was written in 1988] out of the Soviet Union, a regime that for more than half a century made all of the participants in the Chicago Conspiracy Trial seem rather tame, if not even civilized, by comparison.[189]

12-E. RICHARD M. NIXON ET AL.[190]

I.

Our press has, with a handful of exceptions, responded with outraged protest to the September 8 [1974] announcement of a presidential pardon for Richard M. Nixon. In this respect the press reflects the attitude in political matters of all too many intellectuals today.

The thoughtful political man asks, when confronted with an irrevocable development such as this pardon, "Now that that's done, how can it best be lived
with?" That is, one should ask, "What response on my part does the common
good call for?"

Of course, vigorous protest may be what is clearly called for if the action
announced is so unjust—in that it is harmful to the community or to innocent
parties—as to require immediate correction or, at least, measures insuring that
it cannot happen again. Is that the case here?

What would have been the effects of Mr. Nixon's trial? Some say that it
would have been shown thereby that men in high office cannot "get away"
with misbehavior. But has it not long been the opinion of the country that Mr.
Nixon should not be jailed for his conduct in office? Besides, it is a rather low
view of humankind that assumes that a man who has been obliged to resign
the presidency in disgrace will be "getting away" with something if he is not
actually brought to trial and convicted of a criminal offense. Has not Mr.
Nixon's dismal fate sufficiently warned all future presidents and their subor-
dinates against conduct that can be fatal to an administration? We should also
consider, in defence of the pardon, what the effect would have been among
the public of an *acquittal* of Mr. Nixon after a trial. Should we have run that
risk once he was forced out of office?[191]

II.

Some say that the most unfortunate aspect of the Nixon pardon is that it de-
prives the American people of the opportunity to learn "the full story" about
Watergate and other presidential misconduct. But are not the essential facts
already known to us? Indeed, have not the most important facts long been
known by everyone who has carefully followed Mr. Nixon's career of the past
quarter century? What of importance remains to be learned either about him
or about his most recent misconduct? When does the need for essential information degenerate into a desire for mere scandal?[192]

There are, of course, still ways of learning even more than we have already
about the Nixon Administration if we are so minded. Congressional investigations come to mind, for instance. But are further probings worth the inevitable turmoil in Washington, if not in the country at large? Should not we
take due account [I could ask in 1974] of the risks run by permitting even
more of what we have had so much of the past two years? Do we not have
enough genuine problems to concern ourselves with in the months ahead?

One unfortunate effect of the outcry against the presidential pardon is that
it probably has made the president reluctant to clear the docket completely of

the Watergate and related offenders. Such comprehensive pardoning would probably be healthy for the country, especially if coupled with immediate amnesty for everyone (not just draft evaders) who has acted in conscientious opposition to our misconceived involvement in Indochina. (The harassed nurse, Jane Kennedy, comes to mind, as does another victim of the Cold War, Gordon Liddy.[193]) Is it not at least plausible that both the presidential misconduct and the illegal war resistance are legacies of the Cold War? Should not all that be put behind us in a mature manner?

One can even add to the catalogue of failings of the Nixon Administration that the president did not, before resigning his high office, relieve his successor of the burden of granting blanket pardons with respect to both Watergate and war resistance. But he seems to have been too distraught to perform this valuable service for the country—if not unduly concerned to nurture public sympathy that would protect him upon his return to a vulnerable private life.

This failing by Mr. Nixon should remind us of the serious mistake made by Harry S. Truman on leaving the White House in January 1953—the mistake of not commuting the death sentences of Julius and Ethel Rosenberg upon conviction for wartime espionage on behalf of an ally. Within six months the Rosenbergs were dead. President Ford can be understood not to want a similar blot on his record.[194]

Perhaps the most important effect of the presidential pardon, despite the initial outcry it has provoked, is that it reduces the unpredictable effects of a continued pursuit of Mr. Nixon. The anti-Nixon people, although they sometimes do not seem to recognize it, have won a remarkable victory. Is not this the time for them to exhibit generosity, the kind of generosity that Mr. Nixon himself, to his detriment, was rarely capable of in his days of triumph toward *his* enemies? Would not generosity now make it less likely that Mr. Nixon's supporters will harbor a divisive bitterness? Is there not serious danger of turning Mr. Nixon and his inept associates into martyrs? The further we push with investigations, trials and punishment, the more likely we are to oblige the ordinary citizen to consider the awkward question, "What did the Nixon people do anyway to warrant this much suffering?"

III.

The most serious criticism one can make of the Nixon pardon may be that it prematurely risked the much-needed "credibility" of a new president. But was it not best for Mr. Ford to act quickly, if at all? Why should he have played games with Mr. Nixon, the prosecutors, the courts, and the American people? Besides, the damage incurred by Mr. Ford depends in large part upon how the pardon is seen—and here we return to the conduct of the press.

The immediate public response is rarely decisive in such matters, except among the timid or the superficial. That response may yet turn into a general sense of appreciation for forthright decency on the part of the president, especially if the press should now be mature enough to recognize its duty to moderate the volatile public passions that are inevitable in a democracy.[195]

That is, the press (and intellectuals generally) should take care lest the spectacular usurp among us the place of the thoughtful. Is it not partly because of journalistic addiction to the spectacular—at the expense of careful examinations of problems and character—that someone such as Mr. Nixon was permitted to survive and prosper as long as he did in American public life? Even so, his talents and his accomplishments should not be lost sight of—for these, too, contributed to his remarkable career.[196]

NOTES

1. This talk was given in the First Friday Lecture Series, The Basic Program of Liberal Education for Adults, The University of Chicago, at the Cultural Center, Chicago Public Library, Chicago, Illinois, April 5, 1991. The original title of this talk was "Natural Right and the Nuremberg Trial."

I have found very helpful the suggestions that have been made by Laurence Berns of St. John's College, Annapolis, Maryland, by William T. Braithwaite then of the Loyola University of Chicago School of Law, and by Bernard D. Meltzer of the University of Chicago Law School. Professor Meltzer was formerly Trial Counsel, Office of the United States Chief of Counsel for Prosecution of Axis War Criminality. See chapter 12, note 18 . I have also found helpful Professor Meltzer's comment, "A Note on Some Aspects of the Nuremberg Debate," 14 *University of Chicago Law Review* 455 (1947).

I have found helpful as well what I learned by taping, for many hours, my interviews in 2000–2001 of Simcha Brudno's recollections of his dreadful experiences with the Nazis in Lithuania and in Dachau. I hope to be able, some day, to publish these conversations in book form. I was initially drawn to Simcha Brudno, a gifted mathematician and a remarkably resilient human being, when I learned that we are virtually the same age: it was intriguing to explore the radically different effects upon us, as youngsters, of the Second World War. See, e.g., appendix C, note 1 (on "the blessings of good fortune").

2. The record of this tribunal is found in *Trial of the Major War Criminals Before the International Military Tribunal*, which was published in 1947 at Nuremberg, Germany (cited here as *Trial Record*). This record includes almost three dozen volumes of trial transcript and documents. I have drawn upon a dozen of these volumes. See chapter 12, note 91. Also useful are the reports by the most articulate survivor of

the Nuremberg Trial defendants. See, e.g., Albert Speer, *Spandau: The Secret Diaries* (New York: Macmillan, 1976). Compare Dan van der Vat, *The Good Nazi: The Life and Lies of Albert Speer* (London: Weidenfeld & Nicolson, 1997).

Twelve trials were conducted between 1946 and 1949 in Nuremberg before American military tribunals after the conclusion of the great trial in Nuremberg of the Major German War Criminals. See Max Rheinstein, "Preface," in August von Knieriem, *The Nuremberg Trials* (Chicago: Henry Regnery Co., 1959), pp. ix, xii, xv. My references in this talk to the Nuremberg Trial are to the major trial of 1945–1946, the only international military tribunal that sat in Germany after the Second World War. The judges for that trial were supplied by the United States, France, Great Britain, and the Soviet Union. See chapter 12, note 12.

3. Robert R. Jackson, *The Nürnberg Case* (New York: Cooper Square Publishers, 1971), p. xii. See, on the disposition of the defendants, the text at notes 23–26 of chapter 12 of this collection. See also chapter 12, note 45.

4. See J. Michael Parker, "Churches Re-enact Trial, Death of Christ," *San Antonio Express-News*, March 30, 1991, p. 1-B. Compare "Killing Plays to Audience; 5 Teens Charged," *Chicago Tribune*, August 8, 1991, sec. 1, p. 2.

5. Skillful dramatization makes a difference in these matters. See Edward Gibbon, *The Decline and Fall of the Roman Empire* (Modern Library edition, 1932), I, 390–91: "The mind of Clovis was susceptible of transient fervor: he was exasperated by the pathetic tale of the passion and death of Christ; and instead of weighing the salutary consequences of that mysterious sacrifice, he exclaimed with indiscreet fury, 'Had I been present at the head of my valiant Franks, I would have revenged his injuries.'" See also chapter 8, note 47 and chapter 12, note 46. It can be said that Clovis and his Franks were indeed present at the Crucifixion—that is, as Roman soldiers (without the benefit of the later dramatization of what they, the Romans, were witnessing).

6. See, e.g., Frederick J. P. Veale, *Advance to Barbarism: The Development of Total Warfare from Sarajevo to Hiroshima*, in *The Veale File* (Torrance, California: Institute for Historical Review, 1979), vol. 1. All too often, the victims "ask for it," as Iraq can be said to have done by her treatment of Kuwait in 1990–1991. Even so, the coalition (principally American) response has to be weighed. See, e.g., David Evans, "Study: 'Hyperwar' Devastated Iraq," *Chicago Tribune*, May 29, 1991, sec. 1, p. 5; Patrick E. Tyler, "U. S. Officials Believe Iraq Will Take Years To Rebuild," *New York Times*, June 3, 1991, p. 1; William W. Arkin, "The Gulf Hyperwar—An Interim Tally: The Horrific Costs are Becoming Invisible," *New York Times*, June 22, 1991, p. 15; Barton Gellman, "Gulf Air War's Broad Aim: Disabling Iraqi Society," *Chicago Sun-Times*, June 23, 1991, p. 8; Patrick E. Tyler, "Disease Spirals in Iraq as Embargo Takes Its Toll," *New York Times*, June 24, 1991, p. 1. See also chapter 8, note 61, chapter 12, notes 28, 48, 56, 105. If sustained guerilla warfare is encountered by occupation forces in 2003 and thereafter, it is likely to be fueled in part by what the Iraqis suffered between 1990 and 2003.

It remains to be seen what the long-run effects will be, in Iraq as well as in the Middle East (if not also on the Korean peninsula and elsewhere), of our 2003 "preemptive war" with its remarkably flexible rationale. Are such unilateral actions by the powerful apt to promote the sound moral order worldwide that seems to be needed?

See chapter 10, note 78, appendix A, note 15 . See also chapter 12, notes 28, 20, 61. See as well appendix C, note 58, appendix D, note 33.

    7. See *Trial Record*, XXII, 366–410.

    8. See *Trial Record*, IX, 612: Goering said, "I do want to object to your reference to my 'friend Himmler.'" The British Prosecutor, Sir David Maxwell-Fyfe, then said, "Well, I will say, 'your enemy Himmler,' or simply 'Himmler' whichever you like. You know whom I meant, don't you?" To this Goering replied, "Yes, indeed." See, on Himmler, Michael Kater, "The Fuehrer's Disciple," *New York Times Book Review*, May 5, 1991, p. 7. See also chapter 12, note 44.

    Goering could be fastidious about other matters as well. Thus, he preferred the translation "total solution" to that of "final solution" with respect to "the Jewish question." *Trial Record*, IX, 519. He had been offended by the recourse of the French to guerilla warfare: "Bombs were even thrown in places where there were women." *Trial Record*, IX, 321. And he could describe the shooting of some English fliers who had tried to escape as "the most serious incident of the whole war." *Trial Record*, IX, 593. (See, on the cross-examination of Goering about these murders, chapter 12, note 18.) This "incident" was for him somehow more serious, it seems, than the deliberate slaughter of millions of civilians in the camps: what mattered to him here was his honor as a distinguished flying officer of World War I. The loss of all sense of proportion is perhaps a symptom of the madness that Nazism turned into, if it was not that from the beginning. See, for thoughtful reflections on these matters, *The Jewish Thought of Emil Fackenheim: A Reader*, ed. Michael L. Morgan (Detroit: Wayne State University Press, 1987). See, on Himmler, *The Jewish Thought of Emil Fackenheim*, pp. 141f, 153. See also appendix A, note 2.

    9. See, e.g., *Trial Record*, XII, 368, 373, 375, 378, 384, 387, 390, 405.

    10. Seven Nazi and military groups or organizations were charged as well. Four of those organizations were declared to have been criminal in character. See *Trial Record*, I, 257–78. I will not concern myself with any of them on this occasion. See Airy Neave, *On Trial at Nuremberg* (Boston: Little Brown, 1978), pp. 306f.

    11. Jackson, *The Nürnberg Case*, p. xiii. See chapter 12, note 27 .

    12. See *Trial Record*, I, 10–16. This charter was in pursuance of an agreement of the same date. That agreement was adhered to by the governments of Greece, Denmark, Yugoslavia, The Netherlands, Czechoslovakia, Poland, Belgium, Ethiopia, Australia, Honduras, Norway, Panama, Luxembourg, Haiti, New Zealand, India, Venezuela, Uruguay, and Paraguay. *Trial Record*, I, 8n.

    13. *Trial Record*, I, 11. Consider, for what "military necessity" can mean, President Lincoln's Emancipation Proclamation. See chapter 3, note 9.

    14. *Trial Record*, I, 14. Doubts can be raised as to whether the indictment did include "full particulars specifying in detail the charges against the defendants." On the other hand, the defendants did seem to have a fairly reliable notion, over the months of the trial, of what each of them was being called to account for. This may be seen in the judgment as well. See *Trial Record*, I, 171–341.

    15. *Trial Record*, I, 12. The use here of *justice* reminds us that the tribunal, and the nations (if not the world) on whose behalf the tribunal was understood to be acting,

did have a standard of justice to look to independent of the charter. See chapter 12, note 32. See also the conclusion.

16. The members and alternate members of the tribunal were identified as "Lord Justice Lawrence, Member for the United Kingdom of Great Britain and Northern Ireland, President; Mr. Justice Birkett, Alternate Member; Mr. Francis Biddle, Member for the United States of America; Judge John J. Parker, Alternate Member; M. le Professeur Donnedieu de Vabres, Member for the French Republic; M. le Conseiller R. Falco, Alternate Member; Major General I. T. Nikitchenko, Member for the Union of Soviet Socialist Republics; Lieutenant Colonel A. F. Volchkov, Alternate Member." *Trial Record*, I, 1. See, on the awkward position of the Russian judges, Neave, *On Trial at Nuremberg*, pp. 308–09, 316. See also chapter 12, notes 40, 47, 48, 60, 82, 83, 85 .

17. Jackson, *The Nürnberg Case*, p. xvii.

18. Robert H. Jackson was on leave for the year from his post as an Associate Justice of the United States Supreme Court. See George Anastaplo, *The Constitutionalist: Notes on the First Amendment* (Dallas: Southern Methodist University Press, 1971), p. 458, note 34.

Justice Jackson had the following men as Executive trial Counsel: Colonel Robert G. Storey and Mr. Thomas J. Dodd; he had as Associate Trial Counsel: Mr. Sidney S. Alderman, Brigadier General Telford Taylor, Colonel John Harlan Amen, and Mr. Ralph G. Albrecht. He had as well sixteen Assistant Trial Counsel. See *Trial Record*, I, 3. See also chapter 12, note 1.

It seems to be generally agreed among observers of the trial that Justice Jackson (as the American prosecutor) failed in his cross-examination of Goering. See *Trial Record*, I, 417f. The much more experienced British prosecutor put Goering on the defensive, especially with questions about the murder of English fliers. See Neave, *On Trial at Nuremberg*, pp. 258f. See also chapter 12, note 8. "Cross-examination, at its best, discomfited Goering in a way that no political duel with Jackson could ever have done." *Trial Record*, p. 263. "Goering repeated his denials [about the murdered fliers]. He became alarmed and blustering. He lost his self-control. He shouted that he knew of no 'atrocities.' Neither he nor Hitler, he cried, knew anything about the extermination of the Jews! This last assertion was so preposterous that among those who were inclined to cheer the week before, Goering had lost the battle. This straightforward cross-examination saved the face of the Allied prosecution. *It marked Goering down for the death sentence* as I can witness from my conversation with those judges who had been impressed by his defense." *Trial Record*, p. 264 (emphasis added). See chapter 12, note 8, chapter 12, notes 43–44, 46, 53. See also the text at note 76 of chapter 12 of this collection.

19. See *Trial Record*, I, 102–103, 338–41.

20. See *Trial Record*, I, 118–47. See also Robert E. Conot, *Justice at Nuremberg* (New York: Harper & Row, 1983), p. 77. Questions were also raised about the mental competency of Rudolph Hess and of Julius Streicher. See *Trial Record*, I, 148–54, 155–67, 284, II, 156. See as well chapter 12, note 38 below.

21. See *Trial Record*, I, 115.

22. Hitler, Himmler, and Goebbels committed suicide as the war drew to an end. Heydrich had been killed by the Czech Resistance in 1942. See *Trial Record*, XIX, 598. See also *Fackenheim Reader*, p. 148.

23. The three acquitted defendants were Hjalmar Schacht, Franz von Papen, and Hans Fritzsche. See *Trial Record*, I, 307–310, 325–27, 336–38. They remained subject to proceedings before other postwar tribunals in Germany and elsewhere in Europe. Lynching was also a concern for them. See Neave, *On Trial at Nuremberg*, p. 311.

24. See *Trial Record*, I, 366–67. See also chapter 12, note 45.

25. See Jackson, *The Nürnberg Case*, p. xiii.

26. See, e.g., the text at note 62 of chapter 12 of this collection.

27. The conspiracy alleged in the indictment extended to War Crimes and to Crimes Against Humanity as well as to Crimes Against Peace. See, e.g., *Trial Record*, I, 29, 42–43, 65. During the trial, however, conspiracy seems to have figured most critically in the Crimes Against Peace, which depended upon a showing of the planning and execution of wars of aggression. See, e.g., the text at note 11 of chapter 12 of this collection.

28. Jackson, *The Nürnberg Case*, p. 15. The Kellogg–Briand Peace Pact of 1928 has these critical provisions:

Article I. The High Contracting Parties solemnly declare in the names of their respective peoples that they condemn recourse to war for the solution of international controversies, and renounce it as an instrument of national policy in their relations with one another.

Article II. The High Contracting Parties agree that the settlement or solution of all disputes or conflicts of whatever nature or of whatever origin they may be, which may arise among them, shall never be sought except by pacific means.

Treaties, Conventions, International Acts, Protocols, and Agreements Between the United States of America and Other Powers, 1923–1937, IV, pt. 2, p. 5132 (1938). The High Contracting Parties surely cannot have meant to say what they seem to have said here, that there could be no recourse to war even in self-defense or to punish or to correct a defiant aggressor. See, e.g., chapter 12, note 6, chapter 12, note 30.

29. The Treaty of Versailles, which had been emphasized in Hitler's original appeal to the Germans, was repeatedly referred to. See, e.g., *Trial Record*, IX, 237–38, XVII, 546, 551, XXII, 373. Compare, e.g., XIX, 437, where the chief prosecutor for the United Kingdom said, "The so-called injustice of Versailles, so cunningly exploited to provide a popular rallying point under the Nazi banner, had succeeded in uniting behind the Nazis many Germans who would not otherwise have supported some of the rest of the Nazi program." But consider what Justice Jackson observed:

The Germans of the 1920's were a frustrated and baffled people as a result of defeat and the disintegration of their traditional government. The democratic elements, which were trying to govern Germany through the new and feeble machinery of the Weimar Republic, got inadequate support from the democratic forces of the rest of the world, including my country. It is not to be denied that Germany, when worldwide depression was added to her other problems, was faced with urgent and intricate pressures in her economic and political life which necessitated bold measures.

Trial Record, II, 109. See also Winston S. Churchill, *Great Contemporaries* (London: Odhams Press, 1947), pp 19–29, 203–210; Milton S. Mayer, *They Thought They Were Free: The Germans 1933–45* (Chicago: University of Chicago Press, 1955); chapter

12, note 71. Even so, it should be noticed, "The Scottish-Catholic historian Malcolm Hay asks why what happened in Germany did not happen in France forty years earlier, during the Dreyfus affair. He replies that in France there were fifty righteous men." *Fackenheim Reader*, p. 136. On the other hand, should intelligent Jews have sensed, long before the Nazis came to power, how deeply they were hated by many if not by most Germans—and hated more for their virtues then for their vices? Friedrich Nietzsche seems to have recognized this. He may even have warned his fellow Germans against the evil of which they were capable. See Milton S. Mayer, *What Can a Man Do?* (Chicago: University of Chicago Press, 1964), pp. 136–45. See also chapter 12, notes 75, 79, 80.

30. The question remains, of course, whether "aggressive war" is the proper way to deal with an equitable claim. See chapter 12, note 6. See also chapter 10, note 78. Goering complained that the four signatory powers conducting this trial "call more than three-quarters of the world their own." *Trial Record*, IX, 263. Joachim von Ribbentrop, in his final statement, argued,

> History will believe us when I say that we would have prepared a war of aggression immeasurably better if we had actually intended one. What we intended was to look after elementary necessities of life, in the same way that England looked after her own interests in order to make one-fifth of the world subject to her, and in the same way that the United States brought an entire continent and Russia brought the largest inland territory of the world under hegemony. The only difference between the policies of these countries as compared with ours is that we demanded parcels of land such as Danzig and the Corridor which were taken from us against all rights, whereas the other powers are accustomed to thinking only in terms of continents.

Trial Record, XXII, 374. The opening paragraphs of Adolf Hitler's *Mein Kampf* (1924) exhibit the moral stance assumed by the Nazis from the outset of their movement with respect to the colonial entitlements of the Germans:

> Today it seems to me providential that Fate should have chosen Braunau on the Inn as my birthplace. For this little town lies on the boundary between two German states which we of the younger generation at least have made it our life work to reunite by every means at our disposal.
>
> German-Austria must return to the great German mother country, and not because of any economic considerations. No, and again no: even if such a union were unimportant from an economic point of view; yes, even if it were harmful, it must nevertheless take place. One blood demands one Reich. Never will the German nation possess the moral right to engage in colonial politics until, at least, it embraces its own sons within a single state. Only when the Reich borders include the very last German, but can no longer guarantee his daily bread, will the moral right to acquire foreign soil arise from the distress of our own people. Their sword will become our plow, and from the tears of war the daily bread of future generations will grow. And so this little city on the border seems to me the symbol of a great mission.

One can see again and again, both in what the Nazis said *and in what they concealed*, that they somehow knew the difference between good and evil as commonly (and naturally?) understood. See chapter 12, note 76, appendix A, note 15. See also chapter 2, note 31.

31. See, e.g., Leo Strauss, *Thoughts on Machiavelli* (Glencoe, Illinois: The Free Press, 1958), pp. 13–14.

32. Elements of the standards drawn upon in what came to be known as Crimes Against Humanity (Court Four) could be seen as well in the sense of injustice, mistreatment, misery, and vulnerability of the German people themselves between the two world wars. See chapter 12, note 15, chapter 12, note 80. See also chapter 12, notes 65, 69.

33. See chapter 12, note 45.

34. See, on a conspiracy theory and its pitfalls, George Anastaplo, "Human Nature and the First Amendment," 40 *University of Pittsburgh Law Review* 661, 688 (1979). See, on the problems that Europeans had with Anglo-American conspiracy notions, Neave, *On Trial at Nuremberg*, pp. 307f. The European response should help us see ourselves better than we otherwise might.

35. Of the four defendants charged but acquitted on Count Two charges, two were convicted on Count Three and Count Four charges. See chapter 12, note 45.

36. See chapter 12, note 45.

37. There have recently [I could say in 1991] been speculations in the press about what prompted Hess to make his May 1941 flight to Scotland. These speculations include the suggestion that he was hoping to arrange a separate peace between Germany and Great Britain before Germany became engaged in a war with the Soviet Union. See, e.g., Alexander Cockburn, "Column Left," *Los Angeles Times*, July 4, 1991, p. B5; George Lardner Jr., "The KGB, Rewriting the Book on Rudolf Hess," *Washington Post*, June 25, 1991, p. D4; Wolf Rudiger Hess, "British Files Hide Truth About Hess Plot," *New York Times*, June 21, 1991, p. A26; James Douglas-Hamilton, "Hess and the Unanswered Truth," *The Times*, London, June 15, 1991, Features Section; Charles Bremner, "KGB says Hess Was Duped by British," *The Times*, London, June 10, 1991, Overseas News Section; "Hess Lured to Britain, Paper Says," *Chicago Tribune*, June 9, 1991, p. 10; Craig R. Whitney, "Rudolf Hess's Daring Flight: K.G.B. Files Tell New Tales," *New York Times*, June 8, 1991, sec. 1, p. 1; Lisa Anderson, "Sins of the Fathers," *Chicago Tribune*, June 5, 1991, p. 1. See also Speer, *Spandau*, p. 60; chapter 12, note 101.

38. Hess spent forty-six years in Berlin's Spandau Prison, until his death, at age 93, in 1987. His death was deemed a suicide. See Anderson, "Sins of the Fathers," *Chicago Tribune*, June 5, 1991, p. 1. He evidently remained a very odd man to the end of his life. At times, he faked a loss of memory. See Conot, *Justice at Nuremberg*, pp. 158–60; Speer, *Spandau*, pp. 20–21. At other times, the loss of memory, or the loss of a realization of where he was, seems to have been genuine enough. "We [prisoners, in Spandau Prison] do not know what Hess is up to. Every chance he gets he asks us about things that need doing; he recently questioned [Walter] Funk about the strengths and weaknesses of each one of us [prisoners]. 'All his remarks suggest that he is putting together a new government,' Funk commented. 'What craziness! Just imagine a list of cabinet members being found under his mattress!'" Speer, *Spandau*, p. 42 (February 16, 1947). "Talked with Hess. He keeps to his cell while the rest of us go walking. Like

Hitler when things started to go badly, he has built up an escapist world. . . . Sometimes I have the impression that being a prisoner was always his destined role. Ascetic in appearance, his eyes sometimes wild in their deep, dark sockets, as a prisoner he can again be the total eccentric he was when he moved so strangely in the sphere of power. Now at last he can play the martyr and the buffoon, thus fulfilling the two sides of his personality." Speer, *Spandau*, p. 59 (April 24, 1947). See also Speer, *Spandau*, pp. 11, 90, 119, 121, 147, 151–52, 165–66, 167–68; chapter 12, note 58. It does seem that Hess was treated most like a political prisoner of all of the defendants at Nuremberg, with the possible exception (in some respects) of Goering. See chapter 12, note 18. One British observer of the trial, who had himself been held as a prisoner of war by the Germans, has said, "I could not help feeling that the sentences passed on Speer, Sauckel, Jodl, and Rudolf Hess were open to question." Neave, *On Trial at Nuremberg*, p. 312. "From the beginning, [Speer] was the most cultivated of the Nazis who made Hitler's doctrines respectable in his own professional circle." Neave, *On Trial at Nuremberg*, p. 313; chapter 12, note 71. "[Hess] was plainly mad by any but the most exacting legal standards of the time." Neave, *On Trial at Nuremberg*, p. 315.

39. To what extent did the tribunal, because of concerns about the breadth and seeming technical retroactivity of the Crimes Against Humanity tend to blend them with the more traditional-seeming war crimes? All but two of the defendants who were found guilty of Crimes Against Humanity were found guilty as well of War Crimes; and all but two of the defendants who were found guilty of War Crimes were found guilty as well of Crimes Against Humanity. See chapter 12, note 45. In both cases, obvious (indeed horrendous) mistreatment of human beings is at the heart of the conduct condemned. The critical character of war crimes is suggested by an observation by Justice Jackson in his opening argument, "The fact of the war and the course of the war [is] the central theme of our case." *Trial Record*, II, 103.

40. It is true that the victors tend to overlook such offenses when done by their own men. Or, rather, they tend to resort to a "cover-up," even as they may be careful not to rely upon the particular offending officers again. A "cover-up" does recognize the dubious character of the conduct dealt with. See also chapter 12, notes 44, 60–61, 82–83.

41. See chapter 12, note 45.

42. See *Trial Record*, XXII, 366, 370, 375, 378, 378–79, 380–82, 384, 386–87, 389, 393, 396–97, 400, 402.

43. Consider, e.g., Goering's observation: "Repeatedly we have heard here how the worst crimes were veiled with the most secrecy. I wish to state expressly that I condemn these terrible mass murders to the utmost, and cannot understand them in the least." *Trial Record*, XXII, 366. Goering distinguished these crimes from other questionable actions he did try to justify, such as the preventive arrests of people who had been considered enemies of the state. See chapter 12, note 18.

44. See chapter 12, note 8. Consider, also, this diary entry from Spandau Prison:

> The thought inevitably recurs that of course the other side committed many war crimes too. But we cannot and may not use those as justifications for the crimes on our own side—that I firmly believe. Crimes are not open to that kind of balanced bookkeeping. Moreover, the National Socialist crimes were of a nature that cannot be compared to anything the other side

may have done. After Rudolf Hess, the Auschwitz commander, had given his extensive testimony, even Goering turned irritably to Raeder and Jodl, exclaiming, "If only there weren't this damned Auschwitz! Himmler got us into that mess. If it weren't for Auschwitz we could put up a proper defense. The way it is, all our chances are blocked. Whenever our names are mentioned, everybody thinks of nothing but Auschwitz and Treblinka. It's like a reflex." Once, after such an outburst, he added: "How I envy the Japanese generals." But that has since proved a wrong conclusion; the Japanese generals received as harsh a verdict as we.

Speer, *Spandau*, pp. 52–53. See also Neave, *On Trial at Nuremberg*, p. 265; chapter 12, note 18. As for the Japanese leaders, did not Pearl Harbor, the Bataan Death March, and other such atrocities serve for Americans as the Japanese "Auschwitz and Treblinka"? Compare chapter 12, note 111. See, on the Pearl Harbor attack and its repercussions, George Anastaplo, "On Freedom: Explorations," 17 *Oklahoma City University Law Review* 465, 645 (1992).

45. The following table, taken with corrections from Justice Jackson's *The Nürnberg Case*, records what each of the twenty-two defendants was charged with, whether he was convicted or acquitted on the charges he faced, and the sentences imposed upon those found guilty:

	Count 1	Count 2	Count 3	Count 4	Sentence
Hermann Goering	G	G	G	G	Hanging**
Rudolf Hess	G	G	I	I	Life
Martin Bormann	I		G	G	Hanging***
Joachim von Ribbentrop	G	G	G	G	Hanging*
Wilhelm Keitel	G	G	G	G	Hanging*
Ernest Kaltenbrunner	I		G	G	Hanging*
Alfred Rosenberg	G	G	G	G	Hanging*
Hans Frank	I		G	G	Hanging*
Wilhelm Frick	I	G	G	G	Hanging*
Julius Streicher	I			G	Hanging*
Walther Funk	I	G	G	G	Life
Hjalmar Schacht	I	I			Acquitted
Karl Doenitz	I	G	G		10 years
Erich Raeder	G	G	G		Life
Baldur von Schirach	I			G	20 years
Fritz Sauckel	I	I	G	G	Hanging*
Alfred Jodl	G	G	G	G	Hanging*
Franz von Papen	I	I			Acquitted
Artur Seyss-Inquart	I	G	G	G	Hanging*
Albert Speer	I	I	G	G	20 years
Constantin von Neurath	G	G	G	G	15 years
Hans Fritzsche	I		I	I	Acquitted

G—guilty; I—innocent; Blank—not accused of that crime.
*Death sentences carried out October 16, 1946, at Nuremberg.
**Suicide by poison.
***Tried in absentia (probably already dead).

"[G]enerally Count One charged the common plan or conspiracy to seize power, establish a totalitarian regime, prepare and wage a war of aggression. Count Two charged the waging of wars of aggression. Count Three charged the violation of the laws of war, and Count Four charged the crimes against humanity, the persecution and extermination." Jackson, *The Nürnberg Case*, pp. xii–xiii. See also *Trial Record*, I, 366–67.

46. See chapter 12, note 42. Goering's counsel observed, "A cunning system of secrecy insured that the plans and aims of the Fuhrer remained unknown to his associates as long as at all possible, so that his most intimate assistants time and again were taken by surprise by the events, and, in fact, were shocked to learn some of them only at the present trial. This system of secrecy also insured an isolation of the individual collaborator, since one person was not allowed to know what the others did." *Trial Record*, XVII, 513–14. See *Trial Record* XXII, 379, 387, 397. Compare chapter 12, note 18.

Even those who do terrible things can be said to aim at the good. See chapter 2, note 31, chapter 12, note 30. They are, however, often in need of authoritative guidance, such as that which the law (including the penalties it prescribes) *can* provide, as to what the good is in particular circumstances. (The significant influence of the law could be seen in the successful resistance put up against the August 1991 coup in the Soviet Union.) Perhaps, it can also be said, even those defendants intimately involved in the mass murders of the Nazi regime did not truly see what they had been doing until it was all brought together and *publicly* presented the way it was during the trial. See chapter 12, note 5. That is, until the defendants were obliged to view the atrocities as organized by and through the moral consciousness of ordinary people, they may never have truly known what they had done. Consider, for example, the effects upon the defendants of the showing (early during the trial, on November 29, 1945) of a film depicting the atrocities of the concentration camps:

> The screen filled with images of skeletal men and women, crematoria and gas chambers, the scarred and disfigured bodies of women who had survived medical experiments, mound upon mound of cadavers whose sticklike arms and legs gave the appearance of jumbled piles of driftwood, displays of human lampshades, Germans holding their noses as they were compelled into sightseeing tours through the camps and impressed into burying details, and tractors pushing the dead into mass graves like contaminated jetsam. The juxtapositioning of the motion picture with the levity that had preceded it heightened the effect and horror.
>
> The accused were graphically confronted with the product of the regime whose leaders they had been. Funk, biting his knuckles, cried like a baby; Sauckel shuddered; Schirach gasped; tears welled in Ribbentrop's eyes; Hess appeared bewildered. None watched the movie in its entirety. Schacht turned his back and later exploded: "How dare they make me sit there with those criminals and watch a film on concentration camp atrocities!"
>
> In his cell that evening Fritzsche exclaimed: "No power in heaven or earth will erase this shame from my country—not in generations—not in centuries!" Frank, similarly emotional, burst out: "To think we lived like kings and believed in that beast! Don't let anybody tell you they had no idea! Everybody sensed that there was something horribly wrong with this system, even if we didn't know all the details. They didn't want to know! It was too comfortable to live on the system, to support our families in royal style, and to believe that it was all right. May God have mercy on our souls!"

Sauckel and Ribbentrop were still trembling and shaking hours afterward. Hess kept muttering over and over, "I don't understand, I don't understand." Goering, deflated, shook his head: "It was such a good afternoon, too—and then they showed that awful film, and it just spoiled everything!"

Conot, *Justice at Nuremberg*, p. 149. See chapter 12, note 60. Another such film, shown in the courtroom on December 11, 1945, drew these responses:

Keitel muttered, "Furchtbar! "Furchtbar!" ("Frightful! Frightful!") Goering, later pacing up and own in his cell, pretended bewilderment: "I still cannot see how he [Hitler] was capable of ordering those mass murders. I keep thinking—it is such a mystery—the whole thing!" Hess had a simple, resigned explanation: "I suppose every genius has a demon in him. You can't blame him—it is just in him."

Schirach shrugged. "It's all over. I wouldn't blame the court if they just said, 'Chop off all their heads!' Even if there are a couple of innocent ones among the twenty, it wouldn't make a bit of difference among the millions who were murdered."

Conot, *Justice at Nuremberg*, p. 199. See also chapter 12, note 67. Compare chapter 12, note 111.

After the deaths of the defendants sentenced to execution, "[Their] bodies were loaded into two lorries that left the prison under heavy guard. . . . The lorries continued to Dachau concentration camp near Munich where the death ovens were alight. The bodies were cremated and the ashes thrown in secret into a river. There are no shrines to their evil memory." Neave, *On Trial at Nuremberg*, p. 318. See chapter 12, note 91.

47. Consider, for example, the complications that the Russians faced in distinguishing their foreign policy maneuvers from those of the Germans. See Conot, *Justice at Nuremberg*, pp. 350–52. See chapter 12, note 16.

48. Have not similar questions been asked in recent years about the National Administration in the United States with respect to such matters as the Iran Arms-Contra Aid scandal or the irresponsible (if not even cynical) encouragement by the United States in 1991 of the ill-fated uprisings by the Shiites and the Kurds against Saddam Hussein? See chapter 8, note 61, chapter 12, note 6. See also chapter 12, note 105. Was it cynicism or gullibility that permitted the Russian prosecutors to attempt to blame the Germans for the Katyn Forest massacre of Polish officers? See chapter 12, note 82. See also chapter 12, note 60.

49. See, e.g., *Trial Record*, XVII, 366. See also chapter 12, note 46. See, on Goering's proclaimed loyalty to Hitler, *Trial Record*, IX, 418, 428, 431–32, 615, 651; XVII, 549–50; XXII, 368. See as well chapter 10, note 70.

50. *Trial Record*, XXII, 427.

51. Even the badly disturbed Hess can speak, in his final statement, of "the hitherto inexplicable actions of the personnel in the German concentration camps, including the scientists and physicians who made these frightful and atrocious experiments on the prisoners":

But this is also of equally great significance in connection with the actions of the persons who undoubtedly gave the orders and directions for the atrocities in the concentration camps and who gave the orders for shooting prisoners of war and lynchings and other such things, up to the Fuhrer himself.

I recall that the witness Field Marshall Milch testified here that he had the impression that the Fuhrer was not normal mentally during the last years, and a number of my comrades here have told me, independently of each other and without having any knowledge of what I am saying here now, that during the last years the Fuhrer's eyes and facial expression had something cruel in them, and even had a tendency towards madness.

Trial Record, XXII, 370. A few minutes later, however, Hess exposed his chronically disturbed psyche to full view by saying,

I was permitted to work for many years of my life under the greatest son whom my people has brought forth in its thousand-year history. Even if I could, I would not want to erase this period of time from my existence. I am happy to know that I have done my duty to my people, my duty as a German, as a National Socialist, as a loyal follower of my Fuhrer. I do not regret anything.

Trial Record, XXII, 373. Not to "regret anything" is to reveal, in effect, that he did not truly understand what had happened. See chapter 2, note 31, chapter 12, note 46.

See, for a contrasting assessment of Hitler, chapter 12, notes 71, 79.

52. Some students of Nazism have said that the concentration camp officials seemed to need to reduce their captives to a subhuman condition in order to make such officials feel right about exterminating them. See, e.g., *Trial Record*, I, 287, 302; IX, 619; XIX, 506–07, 543. See also *Fackenheim Reader*, pp. 136-37; chapter 12, note 67; the text at note 69 of chapter 12 of this collection. Consider as well "the unfortunate statement in an obscure unpublished lecture on technology in which [Martin] Heidegger compares the extermination technology of the concentration camps to various forms of agricultural technology." Victor Farias, *Heidegger and Nazism* (Philadelphia: Temple University Press, 1989), p. xi. See, on Heidegger and Nazism, chapter 1, note 110. See, on proper agriculture or cultivation, conclusion, note 2.

53. The British prosecutor addressed the defendants' insistence that others were responsible, not they:

When one considers the nature and the immensity of the crimes committed, the responsibility of those who held the highest positions of influence and authority in the Nazi State is manifest beyond doubt. . . . These men, with Hitler, Himmler, Goebbels, and a few other confederates, were at once the leaders and the drivers of the German people. It was when they held the highest positions of authority and of influence that these crimes were planned and perpetrated. If these men are not responsible, who are? If minions who did no more than obey their orders, Dostler, Eck, Kramer, and a hundred others, have already paid the supreme penalty [after having been tried and convicted before other tribunals], are these men less responsible? How can it be said that they and the offices of state that they directed took no part?

Let them now, accused murderers as they are, attempt to belittle the power and influence they exercised how they will, we have only to recall their ranting as they strutted across the stage of Europe dressed in their brief authority, to see the part they played. They did not then tell the German people that they were merely the ignorant, powerless puppets of their Fuhrer. . . . Had the war been won by Germany is it to be supposed that these men would have retired to the obscurity and comparative innocence of private citizenship?

Trial Record, XIX, 435-36. Earlier that day (July 26, 1946) Justice Jackson had said,

The defendants have been unanimous, when pressed, in shifting the blame on other men, sometimes on one and sometimes on another. But the names they have repeatedly picked are Hitler, Himmler, Heydrich, Goebbels, and Bormann. All of them are dead or missing. No matter how hard we have pressed the defendants on the stand, they have never pointed the finger at a living man as guilty. It is a temptation to ponder the wondrous workings of a fate that has left only the guilty dead and only the innocent alive. It is almost too remarkable.

Trial Record, XIX, 429. See also ibid., II, 142; XIX, 574. Were not the worst men among the leaders, however, more apt than others to resort to suicide (as did Hitler, Himmler, and Goebbels) when defeat became imminent? See chapter 12, note 90.

54. See, e.g., Plato, *Gorgias* 480A-E. See also chapter 10, note 62; chapter 12, note 46; the text at note 88 of chapter 12 of this collection.

55. See chapter 12, notes 8, 51, chapter 12, notes 71, 81. If the Nazis were the worst in the twentieth century, we may well wonder, were their principal victims among the best? See the text at note 78 of chapter 12 of this collection. See also chapter 12, note 78. Compare, on the shortcomings of any perennially victimized people, Machiavelli, *The Prince*, e.g., chapter 26. Consider, for example, the afflictions endured (if not even "asked for") by the Gypsies and by the modern Greeks. Consider also chapter 12, note 29, chapter 12, note 80. This bears on the case for supporting Israel. See chapter 12, note 126. See also chapter 12, notes 73, 79. See, on the Gypsies, George Anastaplo, "Lessons for the Student of Law: The Oklahoma Lectures," 20 *Oklahoma City University Law Review* 19, 159–60 (1995). See, on modern Greek affairs, appendix C, note 16.

56. See, on slavery, George Anastaplo, "Slavery and the Constitution: Explorations," 20 *Texas Tech Law Review* 677 (1989); George Anastaplo, *Abraham Lincoln: A Constitutional Biography* (Lanham, Md.: Rowman & Littlefield, 1999). Slave owners, it should be noticed, usually have a considerable interest in keeping their slaves healthy.

The Indians, on the other hand, were often regarded as fierce enemies against whom Europeans in North America had to defend themselves. Americans (like all too many other people) *can* do destructive things in pursuit of what they consider their national interest. See, e.g., chapter 10, note 78, chapter 12, note 6. See also George Anastaplo, *But Not Philosophy: Seven Introductions to Non-Western Thought* (Lanham, Md.: Lexington Books, Rowman & Littlefield, 2002), p. 225 (on North American Indian thought).

57. See *Trial Record*, II, 102 (Justice Jackson's opening statement) (emphasis added):

If these men are the first war leaders of a defeated nation to be prosecuted in the name of the law, *they are also the first to be given a chance to plead for their lives in the name of the law*. Realistically, the Charter of this Tribunal, which gives them a hearing, is also the source of their only hope. It may be that these men of troubled conscience, whose only wish is that the world forget them, do not regard a trial as a favor. But they do have a fair opportunity to defend themselves—a favor that these men, when in power, rarely extended to their fellow countrymen. Despite the fact that public opinion already condemns their acts, we agree that here they must be given a presumption of innocence, and we accept the burden of proving criminal acts and the responsibility of these defendants for their commission.

See also *Trial Record*, IX, 508, XIX, 570; the text at note 69 of chapter 12 of this collection; chapter 12, notes 63, 66, 69.

58. See *Trial Record*, XXII, 342–64; Jackson, *The Nürnberg Case*, p. xiv. It is to be regretted, however, that the tribunal did not permit Hess to talk as long as he wanted to when he finally decided to explain himself during his final statement, after having declined to testify earlier. It would have been instructive to hear him out, at whatever length, however improper that might have appeared according to the rules. Instead the presiding judge said,

> The Tribunal has made its order that the defendants shall only make short statements. The Defendant Hess had full opportunity to go into the witness box and give his evidence upon oath. He chose not to do so. He is now making a statement, and he will be treated like the other defendants and will be confined to a short statement.

Trial Record, XXII, 372.

59. See chapter 2, section VI.

60. The formality with which the defendants referred to each other is from the Old World. Consider, also, how one of the acquitted defendants spoke of the proceedings:

> To the credit of the Nuremberg bench it must be said that, despite this undoubted defect in its construction [that is, that many points of the indictment filed against the accused could have been brought forward against the Russians themselves], the way in which it conducted the trial was exemplary. Admittedly, both the evidence and the pleadings had to be limited to some extent. As it was the proceedings lasted eleven months. But they were limited in practice as reasonably and justly as possible. The whole tone of the proceedings was deliberately kept dignified. And the accused themselves must be given credit for behaving accordingly.

Dr. Hjalmar Schacht, *Account Settled* (London: George Weidenfeld & Nicolson Ltd., 1949), p. 234. See also George Anastaplo, *The American Moralist: On Law, Ethics and Government* (Athens, Ohio: Ohio University Press, 1992), pp. 541–44 (on German law abidingness); chapter 12, note 88. Compare chapter 12, note 56.

Another assessment of these proceedings, this time by a defendant who was sentenced to twenty years of imprisonment, includes the observation, "Despite all the mistakes, the Nuremberg Trial was a step in the direction of recivilization." Speer, *Spandau*, p. 50.

61. General Norman Schwarzkopf, for example, has been quoted as saying that he would refuse to obey an immoral order, such as the killing of the Jews. See *San Antonio Light*, March 24, 1991, p. L-4. The influence of the Nuremberg Trial may have

been evident in the comment just quoted. "Army lawyers are holding classes with front-line units to avoid a repeat of the My Lai massacre when ground troops are committed to battle. . . . The lawyers' warning, and their admonition to respect the laws of war, conclude: 'You will be angry. You will see fallen comrades. You will want to seek revenge. You've got to control yourself.'" David Evans, "Lawyers Tell Troops: 'Control Yourself,'" *Chicago Tribune*, February 15, 1991, sec. 1, p. 5. See also chapter 12, note 40.

It is fashionable, but perhaps misleading, to make much of the place in *law* of *sanctions*. This misleading approach may be seen in a column by George Will, "The Perils of Legality":

> Before congeries of customs, habits, norms, and arrangements can properly be called law, questions need answers. If international law is really law, who enacts, construes, adjudicates and enforces it? The phrase "international law" often is virtually an oxymoron. Law without a sword is mere words; lacking an enforcement mechanism, *soi-disant* "law" is merely admonition or aspiration. Law must be backed by coercion legitimized by a political process. The "international community" has no such process. Indeed, the phrase "international community" is metaphoric and misleading.

Newsweek, September 10, 1990, p. 66. For many people the law provides guidance as to what is right. It often suffices, for this instructive purpose, that people know that this is what the community, or people of common sense and good will, believe should be done, without a concern about the sanctions that apply. If sanctions are as decisive here as Mr. Will believes, then why should one obey a law that one is confident that one can disobey (perhaps even to one's profit) without the authorities becoming aware of such disobedience? See James Lehrberger, "Crime Without Punishment: Thomistic Natural Law and the Problem of Sanctions," in John A. Murley, Robert L. Stone, and William T. Braithwaite, eds., *Law and Philosophy: The Practice of Theory* (Athens, Ohio: Ohio University Press, 1992), I, 237. See also chapter 12, notes 6, 48; chapter 12, notes 183, 196. See as well chapter 10, note 78; chapter 13, note 9.

62. Hans Fritzsche, *Trial Record*, XXII, 409.

63. See, on the maxim, *Nulla Poena Sine Lege*, *Trial Record*, I, 168–170, 731, Robert A. Taft, "Equal Justice Under Law: The Heritage of the English-Speaking People and Their Responsibility," 13 *Vital Speeches of the Day* 44–48; also in Russell Kirk and James McClellan, eds., *The Political Principles of Robert A. Taft* (1967), p. 103; chapter 12, note 111. Compare *Trial Record*, II, 144f; XVII, 506f; XIX, 410, 440, 464; chapter 12, note 57. Compare also Anastaplo, *The Constitutionalist*, pp. 683 n. 21, 800 n. 35; Meltzer, "A Note on Some Aspects of the Nuremberg Debate," pp. 456–59. Do not those who argue against the Nuremberg Trial on *ex post facto* grounds draw upon principles of justice that may not themselves be incorporated in any body of written, or formally promulgated, law? See George Anastaplo, *Human Being and Citizen: Essays on Virtue, Freedom, and the Common Good* (Chicago: Swallow Press, 1975), p. 651 n. 24.

64. This is aside from what the United Nations has done in formally adopting the principles of the Nuremberg Trial.

65. Consider, also, the existence of Common Law crimes in the Anglo-American tradition, including the crime of murder. The concealment of the worst Nazi atrocities is revealing here. Also significant are the repeated warnings given by the Allied Powers during World War II about the justice that would be meted out to the perpetrators of atrocities. See, e.g., *Trial Record*, XIX, 576, 609–610. See also chapter 12, note 82. Justice Jackson asked, in his opening statement, "The fourth Count of the Indictment is based on Crimes Against Humanity. Chief among these are mass killings of countless human beings in cold blood. Does it take these men by surprise that murder is treated as a crime?" *Trial Record*, II, 145. Compare chapter 12, note 111.

66. War crimes did have such instruments dealing with them, with the results that we have seen. In fact, the invocation of an *ex post facto* guarantee in these circumstances is not truly serious. See chapter 12, note 111.

67. I have recently [1991] been told by a Greek-American who lives in Chicago of what he witnessed when an American Army unit liberated Buchenwald: the monstrous things they came upon there drove some of the G.I.'s to such a frenzy that they gunned down at once as many of the S.S. men who had been running the camp as they could find. This, too, may have been a war crime, but with significant mitigating circumstances that a tribunal would have to take into account in allocating punishments. The inmates too, it seems, did some S.S. killing of their own in those last days. See Ray Moseley, "Buchenwald Haunts Muses' Valley," *Chicago Tribune*, June 23, 1991, sec. 1, pp. 1, 14. See also *Fackenheim Reader*, pp. 279, 366. Accounts of the atrocities at Auschwitz by its commandant should suffice to condemn the entire Nazi system. See, e.g., Jadwig Bezwinska and Danuto Czeck, eds., *KL Auschwitz Seen by the SS* (New York: H. Fertig, 1984), pp. 95–100, 134–37. See also James-Claude Pressac, *Auschwitz: Technique and Operation of the Gas Chambers* (New York: Beate Klarsfeld Foundation, 1989); chapter 12, note 52. See also chapter 12, note 44.

68. See *Trial Record*, II, 149f. Is it not likely, however, that the worst atrocities committed by the Nazis in Germany were committed without formal legal authorization, if not even against the recognized law of the land? But the German courts had been so corrupted by the Nazis that they could not be relied upon to do what was needed to punish German offenders after the war. See, e.g., Volker Berghahn, "The Judges Made Good Nazis," *New York Times Book Review*, April 26, 1991, p. 3. The post–World War I experience did not encourage the Allies to believe that the Germans would effectively judge themselves if left alone. See *Trial Record*, II, 101. Compare Speer, *Spandau*, p. 43.

69. See Neave, *On Trial at Nuremberg*, pp. 24, 46, 321–23. ("In August 1944, Churchill was still urging the publication of a list of fifty to a hundred Nazi leaders who were to be shot on the spot." Neave, *On Trial at Nuremberg*, p. 322.) See also Conot, *Justice at Nuremberg*, pp. 13–14; chapter 12, note 62. Compare Veale, *The Veale File*, II, 47. Compare also the text at notes 23–25 of chapter 8 of this collection. The British prosecutor said, in his closing argument,

> Twelve million murders! Two-thirds of the Jews in Europe exterminated, more than 6 million of them on the killers' own figures. Murder conducted like some mass production industry in the gas chambers and the ovens of Auschwitz, Dachau, Treblinka, Buchenwald, Mauthausen, Maidanek, and Oranienburg. . . .

For such crimes these men might well have been proceeded against by summary executive action and [if] the treatment, which they had been parties to meting out against so many millions of innocent people, [had] been meted out to them, they could hardly have complained. But this Tribunal is to adjudge their guilt not on any moral or ethical basis alone, but according to law—that *natural justice* which demands that these crimes should not go unpunished, at the same time insists that no individual should be punished unless patient and careful examination of the facts shows that he shared the guilt for what has been done.

Trial Record, XIX, 434 (emphasis added). See Meltzer, "A Note on Some Aspects of the Nuremberg Debate," pp. 467–69. Compare chapter 12, note 111.

70. *Trial Record,* XIX, 131.

71. Consider Speer's observation at the conclusion of the Nuremberg Trial:

[T]he Himmlers, Bormanns, Streichers, and their ilk cannot explain Hitler's success with the German people. Hitler was sustained by the idealism and devotion of people like myself. We who actually were least inclined to think selfishly were the ones who made him possible. Criminals and their accomplices are always around; they explain nothing. Throughout the trial, all the talk was only of those misdeeds that are judicially tangible. But at night in my dimly lit cell I often ask myself whether my real guilt did not lie on an entirely different plane.

Speer, *Spandau,* p. 8. Three years later Speer asked himself, "If I remember rightly, during the past few months I have not mentioned [in my diary entries] a single engaging trait of [Hitler's], and in fact I no longer feel a trace of loyalty to him. Is that betrayal?" Speer, *Spandau,* p. 133. Thirteen years later Speer recalled:

I think of my own father, and of [Thomas Mann's] father. For them there were still wholly unassailable values. They had no doubts whatsoever about right and wrong, good and evil. It is unimaginable to think of my father or grandfather with Hitler and his cronies at Obersalzberg on one of those dreary movie nights. How brittle all aesthetic and moral standards must have grown before Hitler became possible. I still recall my father's reaction after he had intensively studied, with the architect's eye, our [Hitler's and Speer's] plans for the new capital of the Reich. After some moments of silence he said merely, "You know you've all gone completely crazy." And left.

Speer, *Spandau,* p. 370. See van der Vat, *The Good Nazi,* p. 79. See also Peter Schjeldahl, "Hitler as Artist," *New Yorker,* August 19/26, 2002, pp. 170–71. See chapter 12, note 29, chapter 12, note 79. See also chapter 12, note 68. Compare Farias, *Heidegger and Nazism,* p. 118: "[Karl] Jaspers asked Heidegger during a conversation in June 1933, 'How do you think a man as coarse as Hitler can govern Germany?' Heidegger answered, 'Culture is of no importance. Look at his marvellous hands!'" See, on Heidegger, chapter 1, note 110. See, on Heidegger's students (such as Hans-Georg Gadamer and Leo Strauss), George Anastaplo, "Constitutionalism and the Good: Explorations," 70 *Tennessee Law Review,* 738, 783 (2003). Curiously enough, students of Leo Strauss (who loathed what Heidegger, his teacher, had done with the Nazis) could themselves think of Mr. Strauss's hands as marvelous.

72. See, for the Roman distinctions in civic status, chapter 7, note 74.

73. Some have suggested that the viciously dehumanizing treatment before the slaughter was worse than the slaughter itself. But much of that preparatory aspect of the conduct of the Nazis was shared by the entire country, whereas the slaughter itself was reserved for the victims, whatever the corrupting effects of these deeds upon the slaughterers themselves and upon their fellow countrymen. See, for the crippling effects of hatred, chapter 12, note 79. See also chapter 12, note 52.

74. Goering said, in 1933, "I would like to say again that I would not like to be a Jew in Germany." *Trial Record*, IX, 544. The British prosecutor, in his closing argument of July 26, 1946, said, "It is a measure of the wickedness and effectiveness of [their] domestic policy that, after 6 years of rule, the Nazis found little difficulty in leading *a perverted nation* into the greatest criminal enterprise in history." *Trial Record*, XIX, 439 (emphasis added).

75. *Trial Record*, XXII, 383. A sympathetic resonance with Martin Heidegger's thought is evident here. See Anastaplo, *The American Moralist*, pp. 144–60; chapter 1, note 110. See also chapter 12, note 29. See, on the will, chapter 1, notes 110–15, 116.

76. See Aristotle, *Politics* 1276a 28–31, Anastaplo, *The American Moralist*, pp. 459–61. We have noticed that Goering testified to his belief that even Hitler had the worst systematic atrocities concealed from him. See chapter 12, note 18. We have recently noticed that even the official apologists for the monstrous Saddam Hussein regime in Iraq knew which of their atrocities to deny. See appendix A, note 15. See also chapter 12, note 82.

77. See, e.g., *Trial Record*, XXII, 383.

78. I draw (as in chapter 7, note 49) upon Leo Strauss's 1962 lecture, "Why We Remain Jews" (emphasis added):

I want to show that [our enemies] recognize that we are not from the gutter. Let us take the latest and crudest and simplest example, the Nazis. The Nazis' system was based on the notion of the Aryan. I mean, it was no longer a Christian Germany, it was to be an Aryan Germany. But what does "Aryan" mean? The Nazis were compelled, for example, to give the Japanese the status of Aryans, and quite a few others. In a word, "Aryan" had no meaning but "non-Jewish." The Nazi regime was the only regime of which I know which was based on no principle other than the negation of Jews. It could not define its highest objective except by putting the Jews into the center; that is a great compliment to us, if not intended as such. I take more serious cases: first the anti-Judaism of late classical antiquity, when we (*and incidentally also the Christians*) were accused by the pagan Romans of standing convicted of hatred of the human race. I contend that it was a very high compliment. And I will try to prove it.

This accusation reflects an undeniable fact. For the human race consists of many nations or tribes or, in Hebrew, *goyim*. A nation is a nation by virtue of what it looks up to. In antiquity, a nation was a nation by virtue of its looking up to its gods. They did not have ideologies at that time . . . At the top there were the gods. And now, our ancestors asserted *a priori*—that is to say, without looking at any of those gods—that these gods were nothings and abominations, that the highest things of any nation were nothings and abominations. . . . In the light of the purity which Isaiah understood when he said of himself, "I am a man of unclean lips in the midst of a nation of unclean lips," the very Parthenon is impure.

Leo Strauss, *Jewish Philosophy and the Crisis of Modernity,* ed. Kenneth Hart Green (Albany: State University of New York Press, 1997), p. 321. See *Fackenheim Reader,* pp.131, 274–76, 284, 360. See also chapter 9, note 3; chapter 12, note 55; chapter 12, notes 79–80. See as well chapter 7, note 43.

79. Speer again and again notices "how absolutely essential the figure of the Jew was for Hitler—as an object of hatred and at the same time an escape." Speer, *Spandau,* p. 213. "Again the central problem. Everything comes down to this: Hitler always hated the Jews; he made no secret of that at any time. By 1939 at the latest I might have foreseen their fate; after 1941 I ought to have been certain of it." Speer, *Spandau,* p. 27. This was noted by Speer in his diary during the first few months of his twenty-year sentence. A decade and a half later he said,

When I consider it, Eichmann precisely sums up the problem. . . . Desire for power and lack of scruple cannot surprise anyone really acquainted with conditions on this continent. Even the [Nazi] regime's antisemitism was nothing unusual; throughout the nineteenth century the governments in St. Petersburg and Vienna provided many examples of antisemitism, and in Paris the Dreyfus affair revealed that something like "official" antisemitism existed even in Western Europe. In all these matters Hitler remained within the norms of European tradition.

Where he did really go beyond the norms was the way he took seriously his insane hatred of Jews and made that a matter of life and death. Like almost all of us, I thought Hitler's antisemitism a somewhat vulgar incidental, a hangover from his days in Vienna. God only knows why he can't shake it off, we thought. Moreover, the antisemitic slogans also seemed to me a tactical device for whipping up the instincts of the masses. I never thought them really important, certainly not compared with the plans for conquest, or even with our vast projects for rebuilding the cities.

Yet hatred of the Jews was Hitler's central conviction, sometimes it even seems to me that everything else was merely camouflage for this real motivating factor. That perception came to me in Nuremberg when I saw the films of the death camps and became acquainted with the documents; when I learned that Hitler was even prepared to risk his plans of conquest for the sake of that mania for extermination.

Going over it all in Spandau, I have gradually understood completely that the man I served was not a well-meaning tribune of the masses, not the rebuilder of German grandeur, and also not the failed conqueror of a vast European empire, but a pathological hater. The people who loved him, the German greatness he always talked about, the Reich he conjured up as a vision—all that ultimately meant nothing to him. I can still recall the astonishment with which I read the final sentence of his testament. In the midst of an apocalyptic doom it attempted to commit us all to a miserable hatred of the Jews.

Perhaps I can forgive myself for everything else: having been his architect is excusable, and I could even justify my having served as his armaments minister. I can even conceive of a position from which a case could be made for the use of millions of prisoners of war and forced laborers in industry—even though I have never taken that position. But I have absolutely nothing to say for myself when a name like Eichmann's is mentioned. I shall never be able to get over having served in a leading position a regime whose true energies were devoted to an extermination program.

Speer, *Spandau,* pp. 353–54. See chapter 12, note 29, chapter 12, note 90. "Only Streicher remained faithful to his and Hitler's lifelong obsession; he maintained that the trial was a triumph of world Jewry. . . . Streicher's last words [at his execution] were: 'Heil Hitler! This is the Purim festival of 1946!'" Speer, *Spandau*, pp. 13–14. Consider also the perverse reminiscence of the Auschwitz commandant, Rudolph Hess: "Jewish gold was a catastrophe for the camp." Bezwinska and Czeck, eds., *KL Auschwitz Seen by the SS*, p. 132. See, on the effects of hatred, Farias, *Heidegger and Nazism*, p. 210: an evidently respectable German academician, in response to a political denunciation of a colleague by Heidegger during Nazi times, dismissed it as "not usable, filled with hatred." See, on the traditional hatred of Jews, chapter 9, note 3.

80. It should be noticed, however, that Germany had many Christians about whom this could also be said, but the Nazis did not go after them in the way or to the extent that they went after the Jews. The Jews, a distinguishable *minority*, were especially useful for serving the Nazis' interests as focal points for hatred, thereby helping to unify otherwise antagonistic social forces. (Something of this may be seen in how various Arab regimes today, in their domestic propaganda, depict Jews.) Hitler could say, in effect, "I am not opposed to labor unions, only Jewish-led labor unions; I am not opposed to capital, only Jewish capital." Jews had been liberated and enfranchised by antitraditionalist political movements and could easily be identified with those modern liberal movements. The Jews were few enough and weak enough to be vulnerable at the hands of those who resented disturbing social changes in Germany and elsewhere. Furthermore, traditional Christian (and especially German) anti-Jewish hatred could be exploited to make the Germans receptive to Nazi lies about not only the Jews. Rapid industrialization seems to have made many Germans particularly nostalgic for old-fashioned village and small-town community feelings. (It is prudent for traditionalists and their sympathizers to be aware of the vices that tend to accompany the virtues promoted by community feeling.) Besides, there were many Jews in high professional and academic positions, whose successes inspired envy in people who could believe that aliens were taking over. The commercial successes of European Jews made matters worse, partly because the man of commerce (Gentile and Jew alike) tends to consider the entire world as his sphere of action, rather than any particular country. Consider how the wily Goering put these matters at the trial:

> After Germany's collapse in 1918 Jewry became very powerful in Germany in all spheres of life, especially in the political, general intellectual and cultural, and, most particularly, the economic spheres. The men came back from the front, had nothing to look forward to, and found a large number of Jews who had come in during the war from Poland and the East, holding positions, particularly economic positions. It is known that, under the influence of the war and business concerned with it—demobilization, which offered great possibilities for doing business, inflation, deflation—enormous shifts and transfers took place in the propertied classes.
>
> *There were many Jews who did not show the necessary restraint* and who stood out more and more in public life, *so that they actually invited certain comparisons* because of their numbers and the position they controlled in contrast to the German people. In addition there was the fact that particularly those [political] parties which were avoided by nationally minded people also had Jewish leadership out of proportion to the total numbers of Jews [in Germany]. . . . At that time, there thus ensued a continuous uninterrupted attack on everything national, national concepts and national ideals. I draw attention to all

the magazines and articles which dragged through the mud things which were holy to us.
I likewise call attention to the distortion which was practiced in the field of art in this direction, to plays which dragged the fighting at the front through the mud and befouled the
ideal of the brave soldier.

Trial Record, IX, pp. 272–73 (emphases added). See also chapter 12, notes 29, 55.
However this may be, the systematic atrocities visited upon so profoundly civilized a
people as the Jews in the twentieth century oblige us to notice serious failings both in
Christianity and in modernity, and perhaps also in Islam. See chapter 9, note 3, chapter 12, note 126. See, on Islam, Anastaplo, *But Not Philosophy*, chap. 6; conclusion,
note 3. (I no longer recall the source[s] for much of what is said in this note 80.)

81. See chapter 12, note 57.

82. Consider, for example, the efforts made by the Stalinists to attribute to the
Nazis their own murder of thousands of Polish officers in the Katyn Forest. See Veale,
The Veale File, II, 25–27, 38–51. See also *Trial Record*, XVIII, 497, 539f, XIX,
606–607; chapter 12, notes 16, 48. On the other hand, the eagerness of the Nazis during the war to expose to world view, and hence to exploit for propaganda purposes,
what the Russians had done in the Katyn Forest confirms that they knew that what
they themselves were doing in systematically killing millions of people was widely
(if not universally) regarded as clearly reprehensible. See chapter 12, note 40. See
also chapter 12, note 76. Compare chapter 12, note 111.

Consider, also, this report about *postwar* activities by the Soviets: "[T]he Soviets
interned more than 30,000 people at Buchenwald and about 100,000 more in other
camps throughout eastern Germany. Of the total, possibly 40,000 died." Moseley,
"Buchenwald Haunts Muses' Valley," p. 14.

83. See William Shakespeare, *Measure for Measure*, II, ii, 162–85. Various of the
prosecuting (and judging) countries were culpable also. But just as the "unworthy
minister does not invalidate the sacrament, so Nuremberg should not be evaluated by
the character of the judges but rather by the justice or injustice of their verdicts."
William J. Bosch, *Judgment on Nuremberg: American Attitudes Toward the Major
German War-Crime Trials* (Chapel Hill: University of North Carolina Press, 1970),
p.125. See chapter 12, note 16. The atrocities of which European colonial powers
have been capable, even in the twentieth century, are suggested by the African film,
Camp de Thiaroye. It has been virtually impossible, however, to subject offenses of
this kind to judicial examination. In such situations, therefore, the right of revolution
has had to be invoked, sometimes to good effect. Compare Alan Riding, "They Now
Stand Divided for France," *New York Times*, July 17, 1991, p. A7. See, on the tribu-
lations of "colonial exploiters," Alex Waugh, *My Place in the Bazaar* (London: Cas-
sell, 1961), e.g., p. 51.

84. See chapter 12, note 39.

85. Whatever the questionable acts done elsewhere by the governments responsible for the trial, the judging was done by particular men who did give reasons for
their judgments after hearing the evidence (including the extended defenses) presented on this occasion. Does not the acknowledgment paid by vice to virtue in the
form of hypocrisy attest to the power of fundamental moral principles in normally

decent souls? See Anastaplo, *The Constitutionalist,* pp. 643 note 77, 681–82 note 18. See also chapter 12, note 40, chapter 12, note 91. Compare chapter 12, note 51.

   86. See, e.g., *Trial Record,* IX, 422; XXII, 375–76, 400, 404.

   87. *Trial Record,* XXII, 385. See also XIX, 406, 433.

   88. *Trial Record,* XIX, 384–85.

   89. This is one of the lessons for which Machiavelli has been honored by his countrymen. See Anastaplo, *The American Moralist,* pp. 516–22.

   90. See Natalie Angier, "Pigeons Fight for Survival as Falcons Make Comeback," *New York Times,* July 8, 1991, p.1. Even so, falcons are not suicidal, whereas the Nazis were ultimately self-destructive. See, e.g., chapter 12, note 79. Compare Churchill, *Great Contemporaries,* p. 29: "When the final collapse came [for Germany] on the Western Front [during World War I], tempters had urged [the Kaiser] to have an attack prepared, and fall at the head of his last remaining loyal officers. He has given us his reasons for rejecting this pagan counsel. He would not sacrifice the lives of more brave men merely to make a setting for his own exit. No one can now doubt that he was right. There is something to be said after all for going on to the end." See chapter 12, note 53. See also chapter 6. (The considerable work by Robin S. Oggins on falconry, which is soon to be published by the Yale University Press, should be most instructive.)

   91. From the point of view of the most sophisticated opinion about nature today, we rational animals are basically domesticated animals. But is there not still something in all of us that can understand decent reasonability *as a fulfillment of nature*? See Anastaplo, *The Constitutionalist,* pp. 642–43 n. 77; Anastaplo, *Human Being and Citizen,* pp.113–14. See also chapter 12, note 78, chapter 12, note 117, and the conclusion.

The voluminous records, both official and unofficial, of the Nuremberg Trial should be most instructive when thoroughly reviewed by a thoughtful student. A proper study of the worst can teach us, and perhaps even reassure us, about the best. See chapter 12, note 46. See, on nature as a reliable guide to the best, Anastaplo, *But Not Philosophy,* p. 303.

   92. This discussion is adapted from my article, "Speed Kills: The Rosenberg Case and the Perils of Indignation," *Chicago Lawyer,* July 1979, p. 19. I have had the benefit of a review of my *Chicago Lawyer* article by the late Malcolm P. Sharp, who had not seen it before publication in that journal. The text remains substantially what it was in 1979, except that some sentences originally in the text have been put in the notes. Most of the notes for this discussion (as is true for much of this book) were prepared in 1990–1991.

   93. Robert L. Graham, "Landmark Cases: Rosenberg Case," *Chicago Lawyer,* June 4, 1979, p. 28 (quoting a former acting solicitor general). See chapter 12, note 142. See chapter 12, note 120. See, on the usefulness of the Supreme Court practice manual of the former acting solicitor general, the text at note 12 of appendix B to this collection.

   94. Graham, "Landmark Cases," p. 28 See chapter 12, note 142.

   95. *Rosenberg* v. *United States,* 346 U.S. 271, 300–01 (1953). The case is described in the text at note 100 of chapter 12 of this collection. See also appendix A.

96. One was *Burns* v. *Wilson*, 346 U.S. 137 (1953), an appeal by two defendants from sentences of death, after trial by court-martial for rape and murder. See also *Burns* v. *Wilson*, 346 U.S. 844 (1953). The other was *Stein* v. *New York*, 346 U.S. 156 (1953), an appeal of three defendants from sentences of death, after trial in a state court for murder. See, for further proceedings with respect to these defendants, 348 U.S. 878 (1954), 348 U.S. 922 (1955).

97. Morton Sobell's part in the case is indicated in the text at note 100 of chapter 12 of this collection. See, for a conversation with Mr. Sobell, appendix A, section IV. See, for other discussions by me of the Rosenberg case, Anastaplo, *The Constitutionalist*, pp. 188, 459, 542, 620, 632–39, 700, 703; chapter 12, note 99.

98. See, e.g., Malcolm P. Sharp, "Aggression: A Study of Values and Law," 57 *Ethics* 1 (1947). See, on Mr. Sharp himself, my tributes to him: *University of Chicago Law Alumni Journal*, Summer 1975, pp.18–24 (reprinted in 121 *Congressional Record* H12486 [1975]); Anastaplo, "Lessons for the Student of Law," p. 133; Anastaplo, "On Trial" (*Loyola Law Journal*), p. 1117 n. 897; appendix B, note 9. See also Sharp, "Crosskey, Anastaplo and Meiklejohn on the United States Constitution," *University of Chicago Law School Record*, Spring 1975, p. 3. Mr. Sharp's bibliography, as of 1966, is set forth in 33 *University of Chicago Law Review* 221–28 (1966). Mr. Sharp died in 1980. See George Anastaplo, "Mr. Crosskey, The American Constitution, and the Natures of Things," 15 *Loyola University of Chicago Law Journal* 181, 228 n. 68 (1984).

99. Part of the transcript of that television discussion and my comments on it are set forth in George Anastaplo, "The Occasions of Freedom of Speech," 5 *Political Science Reviewer* 390–94 (1975). See also Anastaplo, *The American Moralist*, pp. 199–213. I have the impression, from the little that I have personally seen and heard of the two Rosenberg children, that they have turned out much better than it was feared among their parents' friends in 1953 than they would. Much of the credit for this seems to belong to their adoptive parents. The children do seem to be genuinely interested in learning the truth about their parents. See, e.g., Sam Roberts, "The Rosenbergs: New Evidence, Old Passions," *New York Times*, September 23, 1983, p. B1.

100. Daniel Yergin, "Victims of a Desperate Age," *New Times*, May 16, 1975, p. 22. This article provides a quite useful introduction to the case, whatever reservations one might have about some of its assessments.

101. It has been suggested, because of bank deposits made by the Greenglasses in New Mexico, that Mr. Greenglass "was deeply involved in a theft ring at Los Alamos, was entrapped by government authorities, and either voluntarily or under pressure implicated the Rosenbergs." Yergin, "Victims of a Desperate Age," p. 26. I do not know anything about this, but such talk does indicate the bitterness that this case has provoked among the parties, even within the extended Rosenberg-Greenglass family. It remains to be seen what the troubling revelations in 2001 about David Greenglass really mean. See chapter 12, notes 111, 113, 115.

102. Did Mr. Fuchs identify Mr. Gold as his courier? There seems to be some question about this. See Yergin, "Victims of a Desperate Age," p. 26.

103. *Rosenberg* v. *United States*, 346 U.S. 271, 312 (1953). See, on Judge Kaufman, chapter 12, note 143.

104. The Russians, it should be remembered, were not, at the time of the criminal actions alleged, our enemies in the sense evidently required for "treason" by section 3 of Article III of the Constitution. (This is aside from the question of whether a formal declaration of war is usually needed for the crime of treason against the United States.) Compare chapter 12, note 111.

105. One is reminded here of what the American ambassador to Iraq evidently said to Saddam Hussein in the summer of 1990 (before the invasion of Kuwait). See chapter 12, note 48.

106. Yergin, "Victims of a Desperate Age," p. 23.

107. Compare chapter 12, note 123. Mr. Sobell told me in 1987 that some of the regular counsel for the Communist Party did offer help to the Rosenberg-Sobell defense counsel behind the scenes. See appendix A, section IV.

108. I prepared in 1954, at the request of one of Mr. Sobell's attorneys (Stephen Love, a Roman Catholic lawyer in Chicago), a memorandum on the administrative order consigning Mr. Sobell (a well-behaved, nonviolent prisoner) to Alcatraz. There was *then*, I discovered from my legal research, little to appeal to in any attempt to secure a reversal of the Alcatraz order but the good faith and the sense of honor of people in the Department of Justice and the Bureau of Prisons. The fee that Mr. Love insisted on paying me on that occasion I donated to charity, principally I believe to the Salvation Army and to a Catholic Worker settlement house. See appendix A, note 8.

109. See, on Mr. Gold, Yergin, "Victims of a Desperate Age," pp. 24–26; Augustus S. Ballard, "Letter," *Juris Doctor*, November 1975, p. 8.

110. See, on the business relations between the Rosenbergs and the Greenglasses, Yergin, "Victims of a Desperate Age," p. 25. See, on Mr. Cohn's business ventures, Anastaplo, *The Constitutionalist*, p. 311.

111. Consider this observation from Francis Bacon, *Maxims of the Law*:

> The law construeth neither penal laws nor penal facts, but considereth the offence in degree as it standeth at the time when it is committed, so as if any circumstances or matter be subsequent, which laid together with the beginning should seem to draw it to a higher nature, yet the law doth not extend or amplify the offence.

Compare chapter 12-A, sections IX and X of this collection.

Consider, also, this observation made in the light of revelations in the 1980s about the Rosenbergs and espionage (see chapter 12, note 115):

> The martyr status of the Rosenbergs has been seriously diminished now, but the equivocators are making the most of FBI irregularities, the harshness of the sentence, the lesser guilt of Ethel, and so forth. Julius's legal guilt is conceded, but the moral category "traitor" has been for the most part avoided. Liberals who stressed substance over process in the Nuremberg and Eichmann trials are reordering their priorities for the Rosenbergs, giving process priority, at least, with substance. In short, even when guilt is proved, liberals see no reason for outrage against Communist traitors to this nation.

"The Rosenbergs, Cont'd," *National Review*, September 16, 1983, p. 1120. See chapter 12, note 63. Compare chapter 12, notes 66, 104, 101; chapter 12, note 143. Compare also chapter 12, notes 44, 46, 65, 67–69, 81; chapter 12, note 116.

112. See section IV of this discussion of the Rosenberg case.

113. One hears reports [I could say in 1991] that David Greenglass has been deeply troubled since his release from prison. This would be consistent, I suppose, either with his having told the truth and thereby having helped to kill his sister or with his having lied in order to protect his wife and to save his own skin. See chapter 12, note 101, chapter 12, note 115.

114. Mr. Sharp's book was published in 1956 by the Monthly Review Press.

115. Several books on the Rosenberg-Sobell case have been published in recent years, including books by Mr. Sobell and by the Rosenberg children. The passions that can still be aroused by this case [I could say in 1991] are evident in the responses, pro and con, to Ronald Radosh and Joyce Milton, *The Rosenberg File: A Search for the Truth* (New York: Holt, Rinehart & Winston, 1983). Alan M. Dershowitz, in his review of this book by authors who have studied extensive government files, has endorsed what he describes as the book's "six major conclusions":

> Julius Rosenberg played a central role in the Soviet espionage ring and transmitted material that he believed contained important atomic secrets.
>
> Klaus Fuchs had already given those secrets to the Russians, but David Greenglass's amateurish sketches provided some confirmation of his information.
>
> Ethel Rosenberg was not deeply involved in her husband's espionage activities but she knew about them and may have typed the notes he passed on.
>
> The F.B.I. was aware of Mrs. Rosenberg's limited role but deliberately exaggerated it and insisted that Federal prosecutors demand the death penalty for her in order to increase the bureau's leverage on her husband to cooperate in the investigations.
>
> Some of the evidence against the Rosenbergs was highly questionable and probably false.
>
> Nearly all those involved—from the Soviet intelligence agency K.G.B. to the F.B.I. to some of the Rosenbergs' own "defenders"—were willing to see the Rosenbergs die so their case could be used to serve partisan interests.

"Spies and Scapegoats," *New York Times Book Review*, August 14, 1983, p. 1. Compare chapter 12, note 123. See chapter 12, note 101. A seventh major conclusion, relating to the misconduct of Judge Kaufman in the case, is neglected by Professor Dershowitz. (His explanation for this neglect, when called upon it, is rather lame. See Dershowitz, *New York Review of Books*, December 8, 1983, p. 53. See also chapter 12, note 143, chapter 13, note 19.) See, on Judge Kaufman, chapter 12, note 143. Among those critical of the Radosh-Milton book are Walter and Miriam Schneir, who had prepared the most influential book in the Rosenbergs' defense, *Invitation to an Inquest* (first published in 1965). See *New York Review of Books*, September 29, 1983, p. 55.

An updated and expanded version of the Schneir book, *Invitation to an Inquest* (New York: Pantheon, 1983) has been reviewed by Ronald Radosh and Joyce Milton, who are quite critical of it. See "Were the Rosenbergs Framed?" *New York Review of Books*, July 21, 1983, p. 17. Those of us who, although *not* insisting on the Rosenbergs' innocence, have always been disturbed about what was done to them, can find considerable *support* in the Radosh-Milton findings, which are reflected in their concluding remarks on July 21, 1983 about the Schneir book:

It is true that the FBI files released so far by no means vindicate every aspect of the government's case. They reveal, for example, that even J. Edgar Hoover was well aware that the dangers to national security of the Rosenbergs' espionage ring had been greatly exaggerated. They show also that Ethel Rosenberg was arrested and prosecuted on the slenderest of evidence, so that she could be used as a hostage to pressure her husband into confessing. *One of the most shocking documents in the FBI files shows that among the questions the FBI agents at the death house planned to ask Julius Rosenberg if he decided to talk was this: "Was your wife cognizant of your activities?"*

The FBI documents also reveal deeply improper behavior on the part of Judge Irving Kaufman. . . .

It is a long way from these revelations, however, to the Schneirs' claim that the files prove the existence of a frame-up. They do not. The Schneirs apparently believe that a witness's inability to remember certain details of an incident during his first interrogation renders his entire testimony invalid. Their understanding of police procedure, and of the limitations of human memory, seems at best naive. . . .

Painful as it may be for those who have long held the Rosenbergs innocent, the evidence available today makes it clear that they did indeed take part in an espionage conspiracy— and that Julius Rosenberg, in particular, was deeply involved. To recognize this in no sense validates Judge Kaufman's reasoning in condemning them to death. Nor does it contradict the conclusion that the Rosenbergs died essentially for political reasons. They were—as the critics charge—made the scapegoats for American insecurity over the loss of its nuclear monopoly. Three decades after their execution, we know that the Rosenbergs were not the archtraitors Judge Kaufman accused them of being. They did not give away "the secret" of the atomic bomb, although the Russians may conceivably have used Greenglass's inadequate sketches to confirm the expert information of Klaus Fuchs—who went to jail for only nine years. They certainly did not cause the Korean War. They were shamefully treated by the court and by some of the officials responsible for protecting them. But they were not blameless martyrs.

Radosh and Milton, "Were the Rosenbergs Framed?" pp. 20–21 (emphasis added). See also chapter 12, note 101, chapter 12, notes 125, 143.

Recent reports on the Rosenberg case controversy (I could add in 2003) include Clyde Haberman, "50 Years and Many Spies Later, the Executions Linger," *New York Times*, June 20, 2003, p. A 23; Jim Fitzgerald, "After 50 Years, Rosenbergs' Executions Evoke Memories," *Chicago Tribune*, June 20, 2003, sec. 1, p. 14 ("A year and a half ago [David] Greenglass announced that he lied about the typewriter—and some other matters—to save himself and his wife.")

116. Mr. Urey, like Mr. Sharp, was on the faculty of the University of Chicago at that time. A charming and informative recollection of Mr. Urey was prepared by Clyde A. Hutchison, also of the University of Chicago, for a volume of memoirs of distinguished professors prepared for the University's Centennial Celebration in 1991–1992. See Edward Shils, ed., *Remembering the University of Chicago* (Chicago: University of Chicago Press, 1991), p. 575.

117. Urey, "Introduction: A Layman's View of the Case," in Sharp, *Was Justice Done?*, p. xxi. It is prudent to emphasize here the point I made (some years ago) in the text at note 112 of chapter 12 of this collection. That point appears more and more plausible over the years. Central to the assessment of any trial, it seems to me, is not truth

but justice. Thus, whatever the truth about the precise involvement of the Rosenbergs in espionage activities in 1944–1945, the critical question remains whether they should have been executed in 1953—and scholarly research is not likely to help us much in answering that kind of question. See chapter 12, note 91, chapter 12, notes 118, 128.

118. Urey, "Introduction," p. xxi. The government might have figured that however nonsensical this sort of talk was, it did serve to persuade the jury to convict someone whom the government "knew" to be both guilty and cunning. See the text at note 34 of chapter 10 of this collection. See also chapter 12, note 117.

119. See, on the then newly discovered evidence and its significance with respect to Mr. Greenglass's credibility, Sharp, *Was Justice Done?*, pp. 111–20. See also the text at note 112 of chapter 12 of this collection. Mr. Sharp describes in some detail the experiences that led him, a thoughtful and perceptive man, to conclude, "I can only say . . . that I saw the witnesses on this matter, and found them convincing." Sharp, *Was Justice Done?*, p. 112. See also pp. xxvii–xxviii. See, on Judge Kaufman, chapter 12, note 143.

120. Urey, "Introduction," pp. xxvi–xxvii. See George Anastaplo, "Bork on Bork," 84 *Northwestern University Law Review* 1142, 1154 n. 46 (1990). Consider also the concluding paragraph of the Graham *Chicago Lawyer* article upon which I have commented in this discussion of the Rosenberg case:

> Reflecting a quarter century later on the *Rosenberg* case, [the former acting solicitor general] recognizes, of course, the continuing public interest in the political aspects of the controversy. From a legal perspective, however, [he] believes that the significance of the *Rosenberg* decision goes well beyond the narrow question of how the Espionage Act and the Atomic Energy Act of 1946 should be reconciled. "The much more important part of the decision from the viewpoint of the administration of justice" is the Court's general disapproval of the practice of granting standing to argue to any lawyer in the country who could say he was appearing for anyone on behalf of the accused, especially after judicial remedies had been exhausted by the accused's own counsel. For that practice, if it had been approved, "would have presented a threat to orderly and responsible representation of accused persons" and would have made for "disorder in the administration of justice. Our policy must be that, eventually, even criminal cases must end."

Graham, "Landmark Cases," p. 28. Compare, on the use by a lawyer of his skills in the best tradition of public service, my commentary on President Lincoln's Emancipation Proclamation, chapter 3, note 9.

121. Urey, "Introduction," p. xxviii. See also Anastaplo, "Human Nature and the First Amendment," pp. 688f, which includes a discussion of conspiracy prosecutions and the use of accomplice testimony. It is not that accomplices cannot provide useful information, but rather that their motives for minimizing their own role and maximizing that of others can distort both what they recall and what they say.

122. Anastaplo, *The American Moralist*, pp. 588–90.

123. I believe that Mr. Sharp, who was a mild-mannered man, would have been vehement in challenging those who, on the basis of the Radosh-Milton book, have suggested that Emanuel Bloch might have been "willing to see the Rosenbergs die so their case could be used to serve partisan interests." See chapter 12, note 115. I, too,

find this hard to believe, especially since I know how highly Mr. Sharp came to esteem both Mr. Bloch and his devoted associate in the Rosenberg case, Gloria Agrin. See, e.g., chapter 12, note 143. I believe such personal assessments should count for something in these matters.

124. Bertrand Russell, Book Review, 24 *University of Chicago Law Review* 589 (1957).

125. One is reminded of the East Coast feverishness with respect to these matters by the intensity of the response, both in print and in public meetings, to the Radosh-Milton book, *The Rosenberg File*. See, e.g., Michiko Kakutani, "Books of the Times," *New York Times*, August 12, 1983, p. C24; Walter Goodman, "The Rosenberg Case," *New York Times*, August 14, 1983, p. 31; R. Z. Sheppard, "Invitation to a Bad Time," *Time*, August 22, 1983; Alan Brinkley, "A Story Without Heroes," *Washington Post Book World*, September 4, 1983, p. 1; Curt Suplee, "The Rosenbergs: The Press for Answers," *Washington Post*, September 10, 1983, p. F1; Jim Miller, "The Executioner's Song," *Newsweek*, September 12, 1983, p. 79; "The Rosenbergs, Cont'd," *National Review*, September 16, 1983, p. 1120; Letters, "Reactions to The Rosenberg File," *Nation*, September 18, 1983, p. 16; Sam Roberts, "The Rosenbergs: New Evidence, Old Passions," *New York Times*, September 23, 1983, p. B1; Ethel Rosenberg Appel, "Replaying the Rosenbergs," *Time*, September 26, 1983, p. 9; Michael and Robert Meeropol, "Some Evidence Left Out of Recent Rosenberg Case Accounts," *New York Times*, October 14, 1983, p. 28; Walter Goodman, "For a Spirited Audience at Town Hall, 'The Rosenberg File' Remains Open," *New York Times*, October 22, 1983, p. 25; Jerry Schwartz, "The Rosenberg Showdown: Authors' Sold-Out Debate Brings Cries & Hecklers," *Washington Post*, October 22, 1983, p. C9; Erie Brendel, "Rosenbergs Redux," *New Republic*, October 31, 1983, p. 6; Peter McGrath, "The Debate That Will Not Die," *Newsweek*, October 31, 1983, p. 94; Alexander Cockburn, "The Rosenberg Debate," *Voice*, November 1, 1983, p. 18; "An Exchange on the Rosenbergs," *New York Review of Books*, November 10, 1983, p. 59; Michael Meeropol, "Refuting `The Rosenberg File'," *Nation*, December 10, 1983, p. 586; "Letters," *Nation*, December 31, 1983, p 682. (I have not tried to collect post-1983 responses to the Radosh-Milton book.) See also chapter 12, note 115, chapter 12, note 173.

The Hiss case was critical to these developments. If Alger Hiss, a well-established figure, could be believed by the public to have committed espionage, why not the lowly Rosenbergs as well? See, on the Hiss case, David Gates, "Hiss: Still Innocent After All These Years," *Newsweek*, November 28, 1983, p. 23; Anastaplo, "The Occasions of Freedom of Speech," pp. 387–90. See also "Those Who Served," *Wall Street Journal*, August 26, 1991, p. A10.

126. See, on an American case for supporting Israel, Anastaplo, *Human Being and Citizen*, pp. 155–59; Anastaplo, "On Freedom," pp. 604–29; appendix A, note 15; chapter 7, note 99; chapter 12, note 55. See also *Fackenheim Reader*, pp. 283–84:

> What is the upshot of these somber recent developments? Despite all protestations to the
> contrary, the post-Holocaust transfiguration of antisemitism is "anti-Zionism." A qualitative
> change has once again occurred, of course, but it is the same reality. For pre-Holocaust
> antisemites, Jews, and Jews only, have no right to exist—or, at any rate, their right to exist

is debatable. For post-Holocaust antisemites the Jewish state, and that state alone, has no right to exist—or, at any rate, in its case alone the right to exist is debatable. . . .

That is why, in the minds of Jewish people, the pope's recent meeting with Yasser Arafat was a shocking episode and one, indeed, that may have caused a severe setback in Catholic–Jewish relations. For if in this meeting the pope asked Arafat to abrogate the PLO's Palestinian National Covenant (which clearly calls for Israel's destruction through "armed struggle"), the media did not report it. . . .

In my view, one element of that meeting was worse even than the meeting itself. The pope used the occasion to express, once again, the Vatican's wish for the internationalization of Jerusalem. That, of course, may seem a humane, universalistic gesture. However, after 2,000 years of Christian antisemitism, much of it institutionalized, one must ask a few tough questions. The late King Saud of Saudi Arabia lamented that he could not worship in the al-Aksa Mosque because Jerusalem was in Jewish hands; yet he never bothered to go there even once in the nineteen years that it remained in Muslim hands. This is only one striking piece of evidence indicating that Muslim anti-Jewishness is not dead, that it is Jewish Jerusalem that must be negated. So I must ask this question: Why, in the nineteen years that Jerusalem was in Jordanian hands, did the Vatican never once call for the internationalization of Jerusalem?

The Christian theologian Krister Stendahl of Harvard University has noted that in the view of Muslims and Christians Jerusalem has holy sites, but that for Jews Jerusalem itself is holy. That is why the present rebuilding of Jewish Jerusalem is of religious as well as secular significance—almost 2,000 years after the Jewish Jerusalem was destroyed.

See chapter 12, note 80. See also chapter 7, note 42.

127. See, e.g., Nathan Glazer, "Verdicts of History," *Commentary*, October 1983, p. 69:

J. Edgar Hoover argued against the death sentence for Ethel [Rosenberg] not only because of extenuating circumstances but because he saw that it could become, as it did, the basis of international propaganda against the United States. Others argued against both death sentences, also on pragmatic grounds. Douglas Dillon, then Ambassador to France, sent an "eyes-only" dispatch to John Foster Dulles: "The fact . . . is that even those who accept the guilt of the Rosenbergs are overwhelmingly of the opinion that the death sentence is unjustifiable punishment for offenses as revealed at the trial, particularly when compared with prison terms meted out to British scientists Alan Nunn May and Klaus Fuchs. . . . We should not (repeat not) deceive ourselves by thinking that this sentiment is due principally to Communist propaganda. . . ." This telegram was sent to the White House but was not allowed to reach President Eisenhower.

See also Yergin, "Victims of a Desperate Age," p. 28:

On the morning of June 19 [the day of the executions], during a Cabinet meeting, Eisenhower said, "I must say I'm impressed by all the honest doubt about this expressed in the letters I've been seeing." "Who's going to decide these points—pressure groups or the Supreme Court?" retorted Attorney General [Herbert] Brownell. Eisenhower retreated. "My only concern is in the area of statecraft, the effect of the action," he said.

Compare Anastaplo, *The Constitutionalist*, pp. 634–35. See the text at note 194 of chapter 12 of this collection.

128. The arguments we have had since 1953 are related, in large part, to what we were entitled to believe and to do *on the basis of the information we then had available*. See chapter 12, notes 37, 117. I would tend to be skeptical [I could say a generation ago] about any additional information coming out of the Soviet Union, whether inculpating or exonerating the Rosenbergs. Were the leaders of the Soviet Union, for example, any more reliably informed about these matters than Mr. Eisenhower was? See chapter 12, note 127. Compare "Khrushchev's Secret Tapes," *Time*, October 1, 1990, p. 75; Robert D. McFadden, "Khrushchev on Rosenbergs: Stoking Old Embers," *New York Times*, September 25, 1990, p. A3; Michael and Robert Meeropol, "Doubts on Khrushchev's Rosenberg Comment," *New York Times*, December 11, 1990, p. A18. See chapter 12, note 37.

129. Although the United States government has not been doing much in recent years with the *Rosenberg Case*, independent researchers of intelligence *have* been tending to support the proposition that some Rosenberg espionage was involved. See, e.g., chapter 12, note 125. A deliberate frame-up will be hard to establish—and for this we, as citizens, can be grateful.

130. See, on Sir Thomas More's bad luck, the text at note 60 of chapter 10 of this collection. See, on the chance timing of bar admission challenges, the appendixes to this collection.

131. See chapter 12, notes 115, 127, chapter 12, note 143.

132. *Rosenberg* v. *United States*, 306 U.S. 271, 289 (1953).

133. See, e.g., Roy A. Medvedev, *Let History Judge: The Origins and Consequences of Stalinism* (Nottingham: Spokesman Books, 1971).

134. Bertrand Russell, Book Review, 24 *University of Chicago Law Review* 588, 590 (1957). See Anastaplo, *The Constitutionalist*, pp. 633–34, for an analysis of the perhaps botched and certainly unseemly effort by the government to have the Rosenbergs executed before the Jewish Sabbath began. See also Sharp, *Was Justice Done?*, pp. 170, 172 (on the attorney general's sensitivity to criticisms about rushing the executions to avoid the Sabbath).

135. Another such episode for Mr. Sharp was the run-up to the outbreak of World War I. See George Anastaplo, *The American Moralist*, p. xix. See also George Anastaplo, *Campus Hate-Speech Codes, Natural Right, and Twentieth Century Atrocities* (Lewiston, New York: Edwin Mellen Press, 1999), p. 49 ("Did Anyone 'In Charge' Know What He was Doing? The Thirty Years War of the Twentieth Century").

136. See Sharp, *Was Justice Done?*, pp. 5, 109–10, 164–68.

137. *Rosenberg* v. *United States*, 346 U.S., 289.

138. *Rosenberg* v. *United States*, 346 U.S., 296.

139. *Rosenberg* v. *United States*, 346 U.S., pp. 308–09. One wonders if the case brought back for Justice Frankfurter memories of the Sacco-Vanzetti case in which he had been involved as a young law professor. See Felix Frankfurter, *The Case of Sacco and Vanzetti: A Critical Analysis for Lawyers and Laymen* (1927).

140. Graham, "Landmark Cases," p. 28.

141. *Rosenberg* v. *United States*, 346 U.S., 307.

142. Graham, "Landmark Cases," p. 28. Was it indeed "respectable" to hasten the executions thus of both parents of quite young children, considering the reservations

people had as to what had been done by them which really helped the Russians? See, on conscience, chapter 10, section VI. It should be noticed that Mr. Sharp recorded that defense counsel's relations with this acting solicitor general had been "excellent." See Sharp, *Was Justice Done?*, p. 170. See also chapter 12, note 93; the text at note 12 of appendix B of this collection.

143. Nathan Glazer, who reported that he was satisfied upon reading the entire trial transcript in 1952 that the Rosenbergs were guilty of espionage, endorsed the Radosh-Milton book. See "Verdicts of History," *Commentary*, October 1983, p. 66. Even so, Mr. Glazer, in the course of his review of the book, passed this judgment on the trial judge in that case:

> [Ethel Rosenberg] was arrested and indicted . . . as a way of putting pressure on Julius [Rosenberg] to confess. Once set in motion, the strategy moved to its grim conclusion in execution. This despite the fact that Deputy Attorney General Peyton Ford, acting for the Department of Justice, opposed her execution, and that J. Edgar Hoover (who . . . presumed her to "to be acting under the influence of her husband") also opposed it.
>
> Why then was Ethel executed? This brings us to the most disturbing part of the case— the role of Judge Irving Kaufman. Kaufman sought the views of the FBI and the Department of Justice on the sentencing. *When he learned that both were against Ethel Rosenberg's being sentenced to death, he asked the prosecutor to refrain from making any recommendation, and then sentenced them both to death.*
>
> There was more to Kaufman's role. While he could not be faulted in his public capacity as judge, his commitment to his sentence of death—and his concern that it would not be carried out rapidly—led him into contacts with the FBI which seem to me incompatible with the judicial office. We may allow a senior colleague, Justice Felix Frankfurter, to pass judgment on him: "The individual that Frankfurter held most responsible for the courts' less than dispassionate handling of the Rosenberg case was Judge Irving Kaufman. Writing to Judge Learned Hand in 1958, Frankfurter said of Kaufman,' I despise a judge who feels God told him to impose a death sentence,' and he vowed, 'I am mean enough to try to stay here [on the Supreme Court] long enough so that K will be too old to succeed me.'" . . .
>
> Some explanation of [Judge Kaufman's] distinctly non-judicial behavior still seems to be called for. Even if it is from the point of view of law beyond challenge, from the point of the kind of judgement we are called upon to make on the character of public persons, he must be condemned.

"Verdicts of History," p. 68 (emphasis added). Professor Glazer added here a note: "I am mystified as to why Professor Alan Dershowitz has not a word to say about Judge Irving Kaufman in his lengthy review of this book in the Sunday *New York Times Book Review*, August 14, 1985." "Verdicts of History," p. 68. See chapter 11, note 6, chapter 12, note 115. See, on the "pretentious cruelty of the Haymarket judicial proceedings," chapter 11, note 26. See also chapter 12, note 177.

We will probably never know what personally moved Judge Kaufman to resort to, *and to persevere in*, the extreme measures that he did in the Rosenberg case. Consider how one reviewer of the Radosh-Milton book dealt with the matter:

> It was widely wondered whether the death penalty would have been levied against a Gentile. But if none of the jurors was Jewish, the judge, the chief prosecutor and the Rosenbergs' defense attorney were. And the harshest cries of anti-Semitism came from Europe

(France especially) and the Soviet Union, which found propaganda value in the charge. In the United States, a few voices claimed persecution. But the American Jewish Committee openly advocated the death penalty, Radosh and Milton write, preferring to "disavow the victims as in no way typical of the patriotic and anti-Communist Jewish community." Similarly, they write, many believed that the ferocity of Judge Kaufman's sentence derived from "a deep psychological animosity toward the couple whose actions had thrown into question the patriotism of 'respectable' Jews such as himself and his family."

Suplee, "The Rosenbergs," p. F2. Compare Sharp, *Was Justice Done?*, pp. xxxv–xxxvi:

> Mr. Bloch's heart attack and death on January 30, 1954, may well have been the result of his long labors on behalf of his friends, the Rosenbergs, and their sons. During the last two and a half weeks of the case, working with Miss Agrin and Mr. Emanuel Bloch, I came to think of them, with Mr. Justice Black and Mr. Justice Douglas, as symbols of justice in a time of difficulty. It is an exceptional honor and a source of deep satisfaction to have been associated with them, however briefly and modestly, in the defense to which they gave so much.

144. This discussion has been developed from my memorandum on Subversion prepared for (but not used by) *The Oxford Companion to the Supreme Court of the United States*, January 1990. An appropriate epigraph here is supplied by Montesquieu's *The Spirit of the Laws:* "The corruption of each government almost always begins with that of its principles."

145. *Webster's Ninth New Collegiate Dictionary* (1985), p. 1177. See chapter 7, note 30; chapter 8, notes 28, 43; the text at note 41 of chapter 8; and at notes 50–51 of chapter 10 of this collection. See also the account of European witch trials in George Anastaplo, "Church and State: Explorations," 19 *Loyola University of Chicago Law Journal* 61, 65–86 (1987). See as well appendix A.

146. *Communist Party of the United States* v. *Subversive Activities Control Board*, 367 U.S. 1 (1961). "This litigation has a long history. On November 22, 1950, the attorney general petitioned the Subversive Activities Control Board for an order to require that the Communist Party register as a Communist-action organization." *Communist Party of the United States* v. *Subversive Activities Control Board*, 367 U.S. 1, 19 (1961). By November 1950, the Korean War passions had begun to distort patriotic impulses across the land. See, e.g., Anastaplo, *The Constitutionalist*, p. 334. See also chapter 12, note 158. See as well the appendixes to this collection.

147. The Subversive Activities Control Act was Title I of the Internal Security Act of 1950, 64 Stat. 987, 50 USC sec. 781 et seq. It was amended, principally by the Communist Control Act of 1954, 68 Stat. 775 and some of its provisions were carried forward in sections of the Immigration and Nationality Act adopted in 1952, 66 Stat. 163, 8 USC secs. 1182, 1251, 1424, 1451. See *Communist Party* v. *S.A.C.B.*, 367 U.S. 1, 4 (1961).

148. Harry Kalven Jr, *A Worthy Tradition: Freedom of Speech in America* (New York: Harper & Row, 1988), pp. 264–65.

149. See *Encyclopedia of the American Constitution*, I, 43–48 (New York: Macmillan, 1986).

150. Justice Frankfurter's Supreme Court performance could be dismal at times. See, e.g., Anastaplo, "On Trial" (*Loyola Law Journal*), p. 1113 n. 866, for what he did in the *Flag Salute Cases*. Compare the text at note 141 of chapter 12 of this collection. See also chapter 12, notes 141, 143; Anastaplo, *The Constitutionalist*, p. 364. The dismal side of Justice Frankfurter is caught in his argument, "It is thus impossible to say now what effect the provisions of the Act affecting members of a registered organization will have on the Party. . . . To pass upon the validity of those provisions would be to make abstract assertions of possible future injury, indefinite in nature and degree, the occasion for constitutional decision. If we did so, we would be straying beyond our judicial bounds." *Communist Party* v. *S.A.C.B.*, 367 U.S. 1, 81 (1961). See also chapter 12, note 156. Compare *N.A.A.C.P.* v. *Alabama*, 357 U.S. 516 (1960); *Bates* v. *Little Rock*, 361 U.S. 516 (1960). On *those* occasions, the court (including Justice Frankfurter) was sensibly willing, if not even eager, "to make abstract assertions of possibly future injury" that might follow because of registration requirements.

Would it have been better for American political morale in the late 1940s, the 1950s, and the early 1960s if the Supreme Court had simply said that it recognized that it could not exercise any effective power of judicial review of Congressional legislation regulating the Communist Party, thereby warning everyone that Congress should proceed cautiously? What it did, instead, was to reassure both Congress and the public that what Congress was doing was undoubtedly constitutional. Even without the power of judicial review, however, the Supreme Court *is* obliged to consider whether the Congress, by "legislative fiat," is usurping the judicial power. See *Communist Party* v. *S.A.C.B.*, 367 U.S. 1, 84 (1961).

151. *Communist Party* v. *S.A.C.B.*, 367 U.S. 1, 5 (1961)

152. *Communist Party* v. *S.A.C.B.*, 367 U.S. 1, 5 (1961)

153. 249 U.S. 47 (1919). See *Communist Party* v. *S.A.C.B.*, 367 U.S. 1, 91 (1961). See, on *Schenck*, Anastaplo, *The Constitutionalist*, pp. 294–305. See also chapter 11, note 24.

154. See *Communist Party* v. *S.A.C.B.*, 367 U.S. 1, 115–37, 169–202 (1961).

155. *Communist Party* v. *S.A.C.B.*, 367 U.S. 1, 137, 168–69 (1961). The quotation with which Justice Black ends is taken from Abraham Lincoln. See, on Justice Black, appendix C, note 53.

156. See *Dennis* v. *United States*, 341 U.S. 494 (1951). See also Anastaplo, *The Constitutionalist*, p. 824 (Index). By the mid-1960s, the Supreme Court finally began to place severe limitations upon the operations of the S.A.C.B. In 1974 the board's Congressional funding ceased, effectively putting the board out of business. See Kalven, *A Worthy Tradition*, pp. 263–89, 639–40; *Encyclopedia of the American Constitution*, IV, 1803 (1986). Compare Justice Frankfurter's equivocating language, *Communist Party* v. *S.A.C.B.*, 367 U.S. 1, 95 (1961). We must wonder what he believed the court might properly do to moderate what even he recognized to be "an ugly public temper." *Communist Party* v. *S.A.C.B.*, 367 U.S. 1, 102 (1961) See chapter 7, note 101. See also chapter 11, note 6.

157. This talk was given at the Law and American Culture Panels, American Culture Association, St. Louis, Missouri, April 7, 1989. The original title of this talk was "The Chicago Conspiracy Trial —Twenty Years Later."

158. The trial was recalled in this systematic way in 1981 by the United States Court of Appeals for the Seventh Circuit:

The criminal contempt convictions which the defendants seek to set aside arose directly from their conduct during *the celebrated 1969–70 "Chicago Seven" conspiracy trial . . .* at which five defendants were found guilty of violating the Anti-Riot Act of 1968, 18 U.S.C. sec. 2101 (1976), in connection with their participation in events surrounding the August 1968 Democratic National Convention in Chicago, Illinois. *United States* v. *Dellinger*, 68 CR 180 (N.D.Ill.1969). [Note 1: This court subsequently reversed the convictions on the substantive charges against the five defendants and remanded for retrial. *United States* v. *Dellinger*, 472 F.2d 340 (7th Cir. 1972), *cert. denied*, 410 U.S. 970, 93 S.Ct. 1443, 35 L.Ed.2d 706 (1973). The government thereafter elected to dismiss the substantive charges.] [David] Dellinger, [Abbie] Hoffman, and [Jerry] Rubin were defendants in that case, and [William M.] Kuntsler was one of the two trial counsel for the defendants. After the Anti-Riot Act charges had been submitted to the jury, the presiding judge, the Honorable Julius J. Hoffman of the United States District Court for the Northern District of Illinois, summarily convicted all seven defendants and both trial counsel on a total of 159 specifications of criminal contempt of court, in violation of 18 U.S.C. sec. 401(1) (1976). These contempt convictions were subsequently reversed by this court and 141 of the specifications were remanded for retrial before another judge. *In re Dellinger*, 461 F.2d 389 (7th Cir. 1972). [Note 2: In a companion case, this court also reversed the contempt convictions of Bobby G. Seale, an eighth defendant who had been severed and summarily held in contempt by Judge Hoffman. *United States* v. *Seale*. 461 F.2d. 345 (7th Cir. 1972). Subsequently, the government dismissed both the substantive charges and the contempt charges against Seale.]

The Chief Justice of the United States . . . then designated the Honorable Edward T. Gignoux, District Judge of the United States District Court for the District of Maine, to hear the contempt specifications on remand. After granting the government's motion to limit the maximum sentences of any of the defendants to 177 days and to dismiss 89 of the remaining 141 specifications of contempt, the court, sitting without a jury, heard the case. *In re Dellinger*, 357 F.Supp. 949, 955 (N.D.Ill.1973) At the conclusion of the government's case-in-chief, which consisted solely of the introduction of the Anti-Riot Act trial transcript and tape recordings, the court acquitted two of the defendants and dismissed a number of the contempt specifications against the other defendants. *In re Dellinger*, 370 F.Supp. 1304, 1307 (N.D.Ill.1973). At the end of the trial, three more defendants were acquitted of all charges and judgments of acquittal were entered as to several specifications against the remaining defendants. Hoffman, Rubin and Kuntsler were each then convicted on two specifications of criminal contempt and Dellinger on seven specifications, although no sentences or fines were imposed. *Ibid.* at 1323–34. These convictions were affirmed by this court and certiorari was denied by the United States Supreme Court. *In re Dellinger*, 505 F.2d 813 (7th Cir. 1974), *cert. denied*, 420 U.S. 990 (1975).

United States v. *Dellinger et al.*, 657 F.2d 140, 141–423 (7th Cir. 1981) (emphasis added in the opening sentence). In effect, I elaborate or comment in my 1989 talk upon various of the points made in the 1981 opinion from which I have just quoted. That opinion was issued in support of a denial of the defendants' motion for vacation and expungement of their 1974 contempt convictions. *United States* v. *Dellinger et al.*, 657 F.2d 146 (7th Cir. 1981). See, on the 1968 events, Anastaplo, *The Constitutionalist*, p. 312.

159. See, e.g., David Rogers, "[Robert] Gates, Named to Lead U.S. Intelligence Efforts, Is Haunted by Pledges to the Senate 5 Years Ago," *Wall Street Journal*, July 23, 1991, p. A18. See also chapter 12, notes 165, 172.

160. See Anastaplo, *The Constitutionalist*, pp. 313, 315. "The relevant events during [Convention] week are summarized" in *United States v. Dellinger*, 472 F.2d 340, 350–52 (1972).

161. *United States v. Dellinger*, 472 F.2d 312–13 (1972).

162. Tom Hayden, *Reunion: A Memoir* (1988), pp. 25lf. "[In his book] he's pompous, but he means to be honest. . . . Certain errors Mr. Hayden takes as his own responsibility. He regrets not criticizing the drug culture and has come to appreciate differences between Communism and democratic radicalism. . . . [H]is book [is not] a vendetta against rivals, unusual among 60's autobiographies. Abbie Hoffman, in his own memoir, pummeled Tom Hayden mercilessly, but Mr. Hayden confines his comments about Mr. Hoffman to a quiet knife-thrust about being frozen in the past." Paul Perman, "At the Center of the 60's," *New York Times Book Review*, June 12, 1988, p. 7. See chapter 12, note 188. See also L. Wright, "A Born-Again Tom Hayden Looks Back—Distantly—to the Barricades," *Chicago Tribune*, June 12, 1988, sec. 14, p. 7; P. Galloway, "Tom Hayden," *Chicago Tribune*, July 19, 1988, sec. 5, p. 1. See, for other articles on the 1988 events, Anastaplo, *The Constitutionalist*, pp. 322–23.

163. Anastaplo, *The Constitutionalist*, p. 323. See chapter 12, note 168.

164. Hayden, *Reunion*, p. 326.

165. A much more sensible approach to such controversies is suggested in reflections by David Broder in his column, "We Should Have Shunned Oliver North, Not Put Him on Trial." *Chicago Tribune*, April 5, 1989, sec. 1, p. 15. See also chapter 13, note 8. See as well as part E of chapter 12 of this collection.

166. See, on Mr. Humphrey and the Chicago Convention, chapter 12, note 193. See, on Richard J. Daley's concern that *his* city not be mishandled by federal authorities, Hayden, *Reunion*, p. 295.

It is not generally known that, also in the 1960s, Mr. Daley was instrumental (behind the scenes) in making sure that city employees with radical associations not be harassed, and that his administration not be criticized, by investigators from the House UnAmerican Activities Committee. What happened in Chicago at that time can be said to have accelerated the decline of that House Committee. The story has been told in an unpublished account by Richard Orlikoff, a Chicago attorney, who (with Harry Kalven Jr.) represented Milton M. Cohen on that occasion. Albert Jenner Jr. and Thomas Sullivan represented Jeremiah Stamler and Yolanda F. Hall, who were employed by the city. (This arrangement was, I understand, in accordance with Mr. Daley's desire.) See *Stamler et al. v. Willis*, 287 F.Supp. 734 (N.D. Ill. 1968), 371 F.2d 413 (7th Cir. 1966), 415 F.2d 1365 (7th Cir. 1969), 393 U.S. 407 (1969), *cert. den.* 399 U.S. 929 (1970).

Another Chicago lawyer, Bernard Weisberg, who is now a United States Magistrate Judge, recalled recently [I said in 1989] that the late Stanley A. Kaplan, "as a member of the [Chicago] Bar Association was instrumental, along with the father of our present mayor [Richard M. Daley], in ending its longstanding exclusion of black lawyers."

167. This anticipated the folly of collecting eight volatile characters and their spirited lawyers in one courtroom for the Chicago Conspiracy Trial the following year.

See Anastaplo, *The Constitutionalist*, p. 314, Anastaplo, *Human Being and Citizen*, pp. 141–42, 302.

168. The northern school district was in South Holland, Illinois. Judge Hoffman, who had been appointed to the federal bench in 1953 and who died at age 87 in 1983, elicited "mixed reviews" in his obituaries. See, e.g., Faward Baumann and J. Houston, "Judge Julius Hoffman Dies: Famed Jurist Presided Over 'Chicago Seven' Trial in 1969," *Chicago Tribune*, July 1, 1983, p. 1; J. Warren, "Judge Julius Hoffman Dies: Tried Chicago 7," *Chicago Sun-Times*, July 2, 1983, p. 1. "His oldest colleague, Senior District Judge Abraham Lincoln Marovitz, expressing sorrow, underlined Judge Hoffman's 'impact,' but pointed to a two-sided facet of his personality and career that baffled many and created constant controversy. Engaging and often delightful off the bench, Judge Hoffman could be badgering, cold and even a touch cruel in the courtroom. 'He had a dual personality,' Marovitz said. 'He was sociable and most affable off the bench. He was different on the bench. But he did have a full and eventful life.'" Warren, "Judge Julius Hoffman Dies," p. 36. See also Anastaplo, *The Constitutionalist*, pp. 317–18.

Ruth G. Bergman, a student for many years in an adult education program in which I have taught in Chicago, was a longtime anonymous speechwriter for Judge Hoffman. She, a lady of talent and integrity, spoke of him with respect.

169. Sensible government officials would have permitted these spectators to wait in the lobby of the building. Such sensibleness could have been exhibited elsewhere as well, to the government's advantage. See the text at note 193 of chapter 12 of this collection. See also chapter 11, note 6.

170. I was present for these ugly episodes. See *United States* v. *Seale*, 461 F.2d 345 (7th Cir. 1972); Anastaplo, *The Constitutionalist*, pp. 320–21; chapter 12, note 158. See also K. Koshner, "Bobby Seale at 41; Revolutionary Minus Rage," *Chicago Sun-Times*, January 31, 1978, p. 13.

171. What is the significance of Sidney Lens's recollection, which I once heard from him, that Jerry Rubin had been concerned lest he *not* be indicted? See Steve Neal, "Tearful Eulogies Wasted on a Bum—Abbie Hoffman," *Chicago Sun-Times*, April 21, 1989, p. 38. See also chapter 12, note 193. One can get a reliable sense of each of the defendants and their counsel by studying the transcript portions relating to each of them (selected by Judge Hoffman) which are quoted in the appendixes to the court opinion dealing with the contempt convictions. See *United States* v. *Bobby Seale*, 461 F.2d 345, 373f (1972); *In re Dellinger*, 401 F.2d 389, 404f (1972); *In re Dellinger*, 370 F.Supp. 1324 (1972). See also chapter 12, note 184. Compare chapter 12, note 188.

172. We can expect to learn someday from Reagan Administration memoirs how disturbed the powerful and glamorous figures of the 1981–1988 period could be at times. Consider, for example, the testimony by Attorney General Meese about the fear of presidential impeachment because of the Iran-arms, Contra-aid situation. See chapter 12, note 159.

173. A suggestion of what may be behind the facade of "notorious people" may be seen in a Rosary College press release prepared by Mary Gorman and Ruth G. Wahlgren, September 27, 1972:

Daniel Ellsberg will never spend a single day in jail, said two Rosary College professors, George Anastaplo and Dr. Malcolm P. Sharp. The two talked recently with Ellsberg in a Chicago panel discussion.

Ellsberg, accused of violating the Espionage Act, stealing classified government documents (The Pentagon Papers), and entering into a conspiracy to undermine the classification system, has been traveling around the country during the temporary suspension of his trial in Los Angeles. He seemed astonished when Professor Anastaplo offered 3-to-1 odds against a conviction that would stand up on appeal.

"This is the first time anyone has said this to me," he observed. "I wish my wife could hear it."

The professors reviewed their conversation with Ellsberg recently in a Current Issues seminar for Rosary students. . . . "We think there is really no law which Ellsberg has broken," Prof. Sharp said, "thus we feel his chances of going to jail are slim." Dr. Anastaplo added that he would not want to say this publicly in the jurisdiction where the trial is being conducted.

In the professors' judgment the existence of the case is due to the very size of the security leak—more than 40 volumes of classified documents. It must have been felt by the Justice Department, they said, that if Ellsberg cannot be convicted in a case of such massive proportions, it is extremely doubtful that they can ever convict anybody. The question of how and why documents are classified is raised by this prosecution. If they were classified unnecessarily or improperly, that could have some effect.

Both professors were surprised by Ellsberg's demeanor. From his writings they expected an aggressive . . . attitude, but in conversation they found him interesting, sensitive and restrained.

Dr. Anastaplo suggested that if by some chance Mr. Ellsberg should go to jail, he could do wonders "exposing" the problems of prison life and contributing to much-needed reforms in that area. Ellsberg was barely consoled by the prospect.

When Mr. Ellsberg asked us why he had not been given such an encouraging appraisal by his New York and California lawyers, I suggested that we in the Midwest tend to be more moderate about such matters than people on the East and West Coasts. See chapter 12, note 125.

Our prediction about Mr. Ellsberg's fate proved sound. See George Anastaplo, "Law & Literature and the Christian Heritage: Explorations," 40 *Brandeis Law Journal* 191, 290 note 383 (2000–2001) ("He still owes me a dinner.").

See, on the Pentagon Papers, George Anastaplo, "Preliminary Reflections on the Pentagon Papers," 118 *Congressional Record* 2490 (July 24, 1972); George Anastaplo, *The American Moralist*, pp. 250–54. See also George Anastaplo, "'Racism,' Political Correctness, and Constitutional Law: A Law School Case Study," 42 *South Dakota Law Review* 108, 154–55 (1997).

See, for another collaboration by Mr. Sharp and me, our memorandum on the promises that presidents make, in Leo Paul S. de Alvarez, ed., *Abraham Lincoln, the Gettysburg Address, and American Constitutionalism* (Irving, Texas: University of Dallas Press, 1976), pp. 136–37.

174. Anastaplo, *The Constitutionalist*, p. 313. See also Anastaplo, *Human Being and Citizen*, p. 223: "The occasion for the 1967 usurpation [in Greece] was provided the Colonels by prolonged constitutional turmoil to which virtually every prominent

Greek leader contributed." See as well George Anastaplo, *Human Being and Citizen*, pp. 3–7; George Anastaplo, *The American Moralist*, pp. 501–515; appendix C, note 16.

175. See, e.g., Hayden, *Reunion*, pp. 310, 359, 360–62, 378–79, 419–20.

176. See Anastaplo, *The Constitutionalist*, pp. 320–21.

177. This is insisted upon in the Hayden book and is referred to in the 1981 appeal. See, e.g., *United States* v. *Dellinger*, 657 F.2d 140, 142, 145 (1981). See also chapter 12, note 178. Judge Hoffman's misconduct here was anticipated, in a far grimmer mode, by Judge Kaufman's in the Rosenberg case. See chapter 12, note 143.

178. *United States* v. *Dellinger*, 657 F.2d 140, 146 (1981). The Court of Appeals adds here, "The documents submitted at this time suggest additional improprieties [Note 15: We have little doubt that the wrongdoing suggested by the FBI documents would have required reversal of any convictions obtained in the 1969 conspiracy trial [if they had not already been reversed]. The government's alleged acquiescence in the surveillance of private meetings of the defendants and their counsel appears particularly egregious in this regard.]" *United States* v. *Dellinger*, 657 F.2d 446.

179. See, e.g. *United States* v. *Dellinger*, 472 F.2d 340, 386 ("The district judge's deprecatory and often antagonistic attitude toward the defense is evident in the record from the very beginning. It appears in remarks and actions both in the presence and absence of the jury."), 389 ("Remarks made by the prosecutors in considerable number, and before the jury, were not called for by their duties, and whatever contribution the defense conduct may have made to the deficiencies of this trial, these remarks were not justified thereby and fell the standards applicable to a representative of the United States.").

180. See, on the effects of conspiracy charges, Anastaplo, "Human Nature and the Criminal Law," p. 688. See also chapter 12, note 34.

181. Hayden, *Reunion*, p. 407.

182. See Anastaplo, *The Constitutionalist*, p. 315. Compare the anarchists' speeches and writings quoted in the Illinois Supreme Court's Haymarket case Opinion in 1887. See chapter 11.

183. See *In re Dellinger*, 370 F.Supp. 1304, 1321 (1973). Judge Gignoux observed,

> Present government counsel urge that substantial jail sentences for these defendants are necessary to vindicate the judicial process and to deter other defendants and defense counsel from similar misbehavior. After a careful evaluation of the record, however, this Court is convinced that, in the particular circumstances here present, the affirmation of the integrity of trial proceedings and the goal of deterrence have both been achieved by the findings of guilt. . . . The condemnation of [Mr. Kuntsler's] conduct and the potentially grave consequences of a criminal contempt conviction to a member of the bar should serve as adequate deterrents to other lawyers who may be disposed to similar misbehavior.

In re Dellinger, 370 F. Supp. 1321–22. Compare George Will's argument, chapter 12, note 61. See George Anastaplo, *The Constitutionalist*, pp. 317, 319. See, on Mr. Kuntsler, George Anastaplo, *The Constitutionalist*, pp. 324–30.

184. See, on the original contempt findings, Harry Kalven Jr., *Contempt* (Chicago: Swallow Press, 1970). See also Hayden, *Reunion*, p. 358; chapter 12, note 171. Compare chapter 12, note 186.

185. Mr. Hayden ran unsuccessfully for the United States Senate in 1976. See Hayden, *Reunion*, pp. 467–71. It is sad to notice that the marriage of which he spoke

so warmly in his book fell apart not long after the book was published. Consider the comment made by Grey Gowrie upon reviewing Sylvia Plath's career: "Whenever I read her, I feel as if I were living with her and wanting a divorce." See Harvey Porlock, "On the Critical List," *Sunday Times*, London, July 7, 1991, Features section. I had felt, upon reading Mr. Hayden's book, that some of the intimate relations he described should not have been expected to survive public display. See, e.g., Hayden, *Reunion*, pp. 447–48. Compare Anastaplo, *The Constitutionalist*, p. 547: "When Siminov, the popular author of *Days and Nights*, published a volume of moderately passionate love poems a few years ago, Stalin was said to have remarked that only two copies should have been printed—one for the writer and the other for the lady." A reviewer, in the *London Daily Mail*, has condemned Janet Morgan's recent biography of Edwina Mountbatten as "Too nice," saying that the author lacked "the killer instinct [that] great biographers possess. She seems to think that her subjects have a right to emotional privacy." See Porlock, "On the Critical List." *Is* there not something, indeed much, to be said for tact in these matters, especially considering the expectations and jaded tastes of our time? See Anastaplo, "On Trial" (*Loyola Law Journal*), pp. 1113–15 n. 881. Unfortunately, however, those who write about the tactful are sometimes not as tactful as their subjects. See, e.g., Angela Lambert, "The Polymath and the Viceroy's Wife," *The Independent*, London, June 20, 1991, Living section, p. 14.

186. It can be salutary to study the oral arguments in *Somerset v. Stewart*, 98 Eng. Rep. 499 (K.B., 1772), where the highest stakes, having to do with the fate of slavery in Great Britain, could be argued on both sides in a most elevated fashion. See *Encyclopedia of the American Constitution*, IV, 1710 (1986). Also instructive are Lord Mansfield's statements in that case, dealing in a technical, even prosaic manner with issues that have profound consequences for human liberty. See George Anastaplo, ed., *Liberty, Equality & Modern Constitutionalism: A Source Book* (Newburyport, Massachusetts: Focus Publishing Company, 1999), I, 249.

A similar constructive craftsmanship may be seen in the subsequent judicial assessments of the record in the Chicago Conspiracy Trial. See chapter 12, note 158. See also Anastaplo, "On Freedom," p. 715 (on *Somerset v. Stewart* [1772]).

See, on self-restraint and effectiveness, George Anastaplo, *The Artist as Thinker: From Shakespeare to Joyce* (Athens, Ohio: Ohio University Press, 1983), pp. 323, 329–30. Janet Morgan has observed, "Nehru was a tremendously honorable man with very good manners. Some people may laugh at this, but good manners can see you through almost anything. They constrain you." Lambert, "The Polymath and the Viceroy's Wife," p. 14. See also chapter 12, note 189.

187. I touch upon this kind of deterioration in my review of Allan Bloom's *The Closing of the American Mind*. See chapter 8, note 14. See also chapter 12, note 188.

188. Consider my comments on Robert H. Bork's career, Anastaplo, "Bork on Bork." These comments apply as well to some of the Chicago Conspiracy Trial defendants and counsel. Perhaps the most talented, certainly the wittiest, of the lot was Abbie Hoffman. *Did* he, after the 1960s, become "frozen in the past"? See chapter 12, note 162. Mr. Hoffman apparently committed suicide in 1989, at age 52. See "Abbie Hoffman, Chicago Seven Defendant and Yippie Founder," *Chicago Tribune*, April 13, 1989, sec. 2, p. 11; "How Yippie Hoffman Led the Radical Surge of '68," *Chicago*

Sun-Times, April 14, 1989, p. 35; James Yuenger, "Hoffman at the End: 'Movie Not Over Yet,'" *Chicago Tribune*, April 14, 1989, sec. 2, p. 10; Anthony M. Casale and Phillip Lerman, "Rebel with Too Many Causes," *Chicago Tribune*, April 28, 1989, sec. 5, p. 1; "Hoffman Gave Up a Fortune," *Daily Times*, Ottawa, Illinois, May 6, 1989, p. 3. Compare "No Weepy Nostalgia," *Chicago Sun-Times*, April 14, 1989, p. 32 (editorial); chapter 12, note 171, chapter 12, note 193. In any event, Mr. Hoffman had the knack for apt descriptions. Thus the surgeon general of the United States has recently observed, "Remember Abbie Hoffman said, 'Violence has become as American as apple pie.' I believe the time has come for us to say [that] we have to make violence un-American." Michael L. Millenson, "Warning: New Surgeon General Has Pet Causes," *Chicago Tribune*, July 24, 1991, sec. 1, p. 2.

189. See the text at note 133 of chapter 12 of this collection. See also Anastaplo, *The Constitutionalist*, p. 322; Anastaplo, *The American Moralist*, pp. 556–59.

We return to Judge Gignoux and his humane opinion in the 1973 trial on the contempt charges:

> Trials which proceed in accordance with the law, the rules of evidence and the standards of demeanor not only reaffirm the integrity and viability of the judicial process, but also serve to insure the ability of each one of us to protect the rights and liberties we enjoy as citizens. The point is well made by the following dialogue which comes, not from a judicial opinion or a legal treatise, but from Robert Bolt's play, "A Man For All Seasons." The dialogue [at pp. 37–38 of the 1962 edition] is between Sir Thomas More and his son-in-law, William Roper, a young lawyer:
>
> *Roper*: So now you'd give the Devil benefit of law!
>
> *More*: Yes, What would you do? Cut a great road through the law to get after the Devil?
>
> *Roper*: I'd cut down every law in England to do that!
>
> *More*: Oh? And when the last law was down, and the Devil turned round on you—where would you hide, Roper, the laws all being flat? This country's planted thick with laws from coast to coast—man's laws, not God's—and if you cut them down—and you're just the man to do it—d'you really think you could stand upright in the winds that would blow then? Yes, I'd give the Devil benefit of law, for my own safety's sake.

In re Dellinger, 370 F.Supp. 1304, 1322–23 (1973). See chapter 12, note 186. See also chapter 2, note 10, chapter 12, note 61. See, on Thomas More, chapter 10 of this collection. See, on the Devil, chapter 1, parts A and B.

190. This discussion of September 15, 1974, was published in an abridged form in the *Chicago Tribune*, September 30, 1974, sec. 2, p. 6. The original title of this discussion was "In Defense of Forthright Decency, Now and Then." See also *Hyde Park Herald*, Chicago, Illinois, October 9, 1974, p. 5. See, on Spiro T. Agnew and Richard M. Nixon, chapter 13, note 27.

191. See, on the impeachment of Mr. Nixon, Anastaplo, *Human Being and Citizen*, p. 160; Anastaplo, *The American Moralist*, pp. 431–32. See also chapter 12, note 172.

192. See Anastaplo, *The American Moralist*, pp. 291–94. See also chapter 12, note 165.

193. See George Anastaplo, "Passion, Magnanimity, and the Rule of Law," 50 *Southern California Law Review* 350, 363–69 (1977). "Truth be told, [Abbie] Hoffman was the forerunner of Watergate operatives Donald Segretti and G. Gordon Liddy. But neither Segretti nor Liddy was nearly as effective as Hoffman in sabotaging the Democratic Party and boosting the fortunes of Richard M. Nixon. Hoffman helped elect Nixon. . . . 'I was a victim of [the Chicago Convention],' [Hubert H.] Humphrey recalled not long before his death in 1977. 'I felt when we left that convention, we were in an impossible situation. Chicago was a catastrophe. My wife and I went home heartbroken, battered and beaten.' Humphrey's loss was a win for Abbie." Neal, "Tearful Eulogies Wasted on a Bum," p. 38. Compare, on Mr. Humphrey's lack of the necessary resoluteness, the text at note 166 of chapter 12 of this collection. See also Anastaplo, *Human Being and Citizen*, p. 142.

194. See the text at note 126 of chapter 12 of this collection.

195. Consider, for example, how the mass media allowed themselves to be used in the shameless "Willie Horton" campaign run against Governor Michael Dukakis in 1988, thereby contributing to the corruption of the American people. (Much the same can be seen today in how fear of "terrorism" is exploited.) Father Andrew Greeley has observed, "Gov. Michael Dukakis of Massachusetts had an excellent idea for an education program—grants to students that are paid back later in life by an extra tax on the students' income—which would have lifted a huge burden from the shoulders of middle-class parents. But the plan was obscured by such really important national issues as Willie Horton, the Pledge of Allegiance and the American Civil Liberties Union." Andrew Greeley, "The Democrats Can Win In '92," *Chicago Sun-Times*, August 18, 1991, p. 42. See Carl Rowan, "Bush Signals a Rerun of Politics of Racism," *Chicago Sun-Times*, August 18, 1991, p. 42: "It is fair to point out that Nixon, Reagan and Bush have presided over the streets, and the law enforcement machinery, for 19 of the last 23 years, but they have nothing to show for their [racist] promises of law and order. Many cities will see all-time record numbers of murders this year. The nation's prisons and jails bulge with record numbers of inmates, and Mr. Bush's Justice Department wants billions of dollars for new prisons to hold an expected horde of new criminals." See also Anastaplo, "On Trial" (*Loyola Law Journal*), pp. 1113–15 n. 881. See as well appendix C, note 57.

It now seems to be generally recognized that President Ford's pardon of Mr. Nixon was sensible.

196. "[Richard Nixon] takes a surprisingly relaxed view of flag burning. 'If the day comes when [people] refrain from desecrating [the flag] only because of the law or some dimly remembered custom, it will have truly become an empty symbol,' he says.'" "Nixon Sorry His Swearing Was on Tape," *Chicago Tribune*, March 29, 1988, sec. 1, p. 6. See George Anastaplo, "Bork on Bork," p. 1165 n. 71. See also Anastaplo, "Constitutionalism and the Good: Explorations," 70 *Tennessee Law Review* 737, 828 (2003). Governor Mario Cuomo, in 1991, identified Mr. Nixon as the smartest politician in the country. See Sherry Henry, "Are These the Smartest People in America?" *Parade*, August 4, 1991, p. 7.

See, on television in the United States, appendix C, note 21.

13

From Spiro T. Agnew to O. J. Simpson[1]

I.

Spiro T. Agnew and O. J. Simpson have exhibited in our time the perils inherent in the career of the modern celebrity with its tendency toward a self-destructive overreaching. My first extended commentary on the O. J. Simpson case was on June 30, 1994, in the last session of a month-long course for American law students I was teaching in Rome—that is, among a people who tend to be gentler and less color conscious than Americans are apt to be. The Simpson case killings had occurred a fortnight before, on June 12, 1994. My next extended commentary on the case was, in effect, in the footnotes prepared (in March 1995) upon the publication of my June 1994 talk in the spring of 1995.[2] This talk today, my third commentary on the case, has been prepared for this occasion, the last session (in 1995) of our semester-long Jurisprudence course on problems of evidence and proof at the Loyola University of Chicago School of Law.

Our point of departure at this time can be taken from the talk I gave in Rome on June 30, 1994:

> The distressing facts of the nightmarish Simpson case are, unfortunately, already well known. They include a history of serious spousal abuse by the principal suspect (with the *possibility* of the murdered ex-spouse having herself been somewhat provocative), remarkably violent attacks by someone upon the ex-spouse and her friend, and the principal suspect's bizarre efforts at postponing his arrest thereafter. (Not that the pursuit of Mr. Simpson by the authorities and the mass media was not also somewhat bizarre on that occasion.) The fatal attacks upon the two victims were evidently such that they could be depicted in the press as "a pair of unimaginably savage and bloody crimes." One need not

know the people who may have been involved here to recognize that something is dreadfully wrong with the man or men who did what is reported here, whoever he or they may be.[3]

Immediately to be added to this account is the fact that a long-suffering jury, on October 3, 1995, acquitted Mr. Simpson on all criminal counts after nine months of trial and five hours of deliberation.

The Simpson case cannot be discussed sensibly without at least a provisional opinion as to what the truth is about who killed the two victims. An inquiry into any matter has to work from premises. The sounder those premises, the better an inquiry is likely to be. Soundness here includes an awareness of what one's provisional opinion is and what the limitations are of that opinion. The perspective from which we approach such matters is not that of the professional investigator, but rather is that of the citizen who assesses the information that happens to have been made available by investigators and others.[4]

My provisional opinion as to the truth in this matter is reflected in my expectations about the outcome of the criminal trial. First, there was my expectation in March 1995, at the time that I prepared my June 1994 talk for publication. I say in the final footnote for that article:

> My own guess is that if the trial does happen to end in a hung jury (an outright acquittal seems highly unlikely), the prosecution will probably consider itself obliged to try the defendant again, especially if the State's evidence has been revealed to be as strong as it now appears it will be. By then the defense, with its material (and perhaps spiritual) resources depleted, may be disposed (if Mr. Simpson *is* physically responsible for the killings) to enter into a plea bargain on an insanity-related manslaughter charge.[5]

Thereafter, the state's evidence was shown to be quite strong indeed. But, at the same time, various other factors, such as one police officer's obvious racism and the appearance of incompetence among some technicians used by the police, permitted a plausible questioning of what the evidence meant. Even so, when we learned last month that the jury had decided as quickly as it did (after having asked to hear again only the limousine driver's testimony), I believed that conviction was likely. It seemed to me, that is, that the kind and amount of evidence provided by the state would have impressed at least a few on the jury, requiring some time for *them* to be argued into an acquittal by those disposed to acquit for whatever reason.

Still, it should be noticed that most lawyers evidently did *not* expect a conviction. Thus, in late February 1995, this report was published:

> As the trial of O. J. Simpson moves into its fourth week, 70 percent of the nation's lawyers have come to believe the celebrity defendant will [because of

racial differences among the jurors] not be convicted of killing his ex-wife, Nicole Brown Simpson, and her friend, Ronald Goldman—an increase of nearly 10 percent from five months ago.[6]

On the second day of the state's closing argument (September 27, 1995) I polled my Constitutional Law II students by secret ballot. Of the 35 students who responded, only three of them registered the belief that Mr. Simpson had not done the killings; 32 said he did them. Of these 32, eight said he would be convicted; nine said there would be a hung jury; and fifteen said he would be acquitted. Thus, of the 32 who believed he had done the killings, only one-fourth believed he would be convicted. (This was even before defense counsel played the "race card" in closing argument.) After the students had voted, they asked me for my opinion. I replied that I believed both that Mr. Simpson had done the killings and that he would be convicted. Perhaps the most significant fact about all this is something that I have not seen referred to elsewhere: few if any of our fellow citizens (whether "pro-Simpson" or "anti-Simpson") believed that an innocent man would be convicted on this occasion. That could be interpreted as a sign of some progress in race relations in this country. Another such sign is the general impression that if Mr. Simpson is not responsible for these killings, they were not done by *any* African American. The savagery unleashed here strongly suggests a "personal" relation between the killer or killers and at least one of the victims.

No one seems to dispute the opinion that in an ordinary murder trial, the kind and amount of evidence produced by the state in the Simpson trial would have secured a conviction, regardless of the race either of the defendant or of the jury. Circumstantial evidence can be very strong; sometimes it can be superior to more direct evidence (such as eye-witness testimony). We rely upon circumstantial evidence all the time. Indeed, we would be virtually paralyzed in our everyday activities if we did not.

We have become so accustomed to, if not corrupted by, disparagements of government that we fail to appreciate what an elaborate, and hence highly vulnerable, chain of acts would have been required to establish and maintain the anti-Simpson conspiracy suggested by defense counsel in the Simpson case. Such an effort would have had to start quite early after discovery of the killings, without knowledge of what Mr. Simpson would be able to provide in the way of an alibi or other evidence in his defense. And it would have had to have been done with considerable skill, and at considerable risk to their careers, by people otherwise condemned by defense counsel as generally incompetent.[7] If such a conspiracy was ever engaged in, any "repentant" participant could now make himself wealthy by exposing the plot. After all, fortunes have already been promised in contracts for other "inside stories" about the case.

We should be clear, in any event, what a criminal trial jury verdict does and does not mean in this country. An acquittal does mean—and virtually everyone agrees that it should continue to mean—that a defendant can never be prosecuted again by the same government for the same crime. Thus, Mr. Simpson is now "free" of any liability (in a California state court) for murder, whatever evidence may turn up hereafter. (Could he be tried for soliciting murder or a related crime if it should ever be learned that he had gotten someone else to do a killing, or that he had helped him do it, or that he had helped him to escape detection?)

An acquittal in a case does *not* mean that a defendant did not do it. Nor does it mean that the community at large should regard an acquitted defendant as not having done the crime of which he has been acquitted. There are standards with respect to truth and falsity that a jury verdict may help us apply, but with respect to which such a verdict cannot be conclusive. Truth, in short, is not something that "automatically" results from an operation or a method.[8]

However much the purpose of a trial may be furthered by seeking the truth about the matter under consideration, a trial is not primarily a search for truth but rather a search for justice. That is, it is an effort, in accordance with established and known rules, to find the best way of dealing with a disputed matter of a legal character. It can be ominous when it is believed, as may be seen in my classroom poll, that the guilty (when skillfully represented) will not be convicted of a grave criminal offense. But whatever problems we may have with the verdict in the Simpson murder case, perhaps all this can still be put to good use, especially if we try to understand the various participants and what they were thinking.

II.

What *were* the jurors in the criminal case thinking? Were they angry, frustrated, bamboozled—or were they simply doing what has traditionally been expected of them? Some have argued that this jury "sent a message," exercising the power (if not the right) of "nullification" long available to determined juries. Precisely what the "message" was in this case may not be clear. The experts who predicted an acquittal placed special emphasis upon the "racial dynamics" in the situation and upon the deep sense of grievance among African Americans about how they are routinely treated by the police and the criminal justice system. There is certainly something to this explanation.

Other experts, commenting on the verdict, have been critical of the way that the state conducted its investigation and presented its case.[9] Even so, as

I have noticed, it seems to be generally recognized that a defendant confronted with "the mountain of evidence" available in this case, and with no alibi evidence, will usually be convicted.[10] Typically, in fact, such a situation will find conscientious defense counsel negotiating a plea bargain with a view to avoiding a death sentence. That is, prosecutors who are far less prepared than the state was in the Simpson case routinely prevail in such cases—and there is not much doubt in the community at large about the guilt of almost all those who are currently imprisoned for crimes of violence in this country.

The verdict in the Simpson case raises questions about what "reasonable doubt" can mean in the typical case where circumstantial evidence is critical. Related to this are questions about what has been happening to the popular judgment, inundated as the public is by fanciful stories in the mass media about conspiracy theories, pseudosciences, abductions by aliens in UFOs, and the like. The general sense of the *probable* seems to need strengthening, even as sloppy thinking needs to be questioned.[11]

The Simpson jury might have been more tough-minded if it had been "qualified" for the death penalty. Certainly, a better-educated jury is needed in cases where racial prejudice may be a problem and where scientific evidence has to be relied upon [12] There is much to be said, on the other hand, for the English mode of selecting juries, which can produce competent juries within hours. Much is also to be said against extended sequestration of a jury, which is likely to affect adversely the mental balance of those subjected to such abuse.[13]

It is likely that some of the defects of the Simpson trial and of this jury can be attributed to the way that the judge ran his courtroom. (This is aside from concerns that observers have had about the corrupting effects upon participants, as well as upon the general public, of televising the trial of a celebrity.)[14] This entire matter should have been disposed of, at the trial level, before the end of 1994, rather than stretching out as it did to October of 1995. The tighter the trial run by a fair-minded judge, the more likely it is that the verdict will be rendered promptly and that it will be generally accepted as sensible. The way that the judge in the Simpson criminal case permitted himself to be overwhelmed by high-powered lawyers was anything but reassuring.

Much can be said for continued reliance upon trial by jury in this country, however more disciplined everyone involved in a trial such as this should be. A properly supervised jury trial tends to assure people that only the guilty are likely to be convicted and that the state is likely to be held in check when it relies upon inadequate evidence or upon political prejudices. It is hard, therefore, to overestimate the social value of reliance upon trial by jury in contested cases.[15] It is easy, but not sensible, to attribute to the criminal law system in general the social and other failings exposed by this bizarre case.

Whatever reservations one may have about the caliber of the jury in the Simpson criminal case, it is prudent to keep in view the extent to which ordinary citizens are being led astray by irresponsible people of influence who should know better. Consider, for example, the conspiracy theory, self righteously insisted upon by well-financed partisans (month after month), which seems to question whether an unfortunate presidential aide, Vincent Foster, really committed suicide. One can be reminded, by our own irresponsibility, of what has been happening in Israel in recent years:

> At a gathering in Jerusalem of national religious parties [after the assassination of Prime Minister Yitzhak Rabin], one repentant leader, Rabbi Yuhuda Amital from the Meimad Party, remarked that the assassin may have been following overzealous religious-Zionist teaching. Amital called for rabbis to stop mixing politics and religion: "We are guilty of educating an entire generation to primitive thinking through cliches."[16]

III.

We turn now from the jury and the judge to the lawyers in the Simpson case. What were those lawyers thinking? One could well wonder how much such sentiments as the following apply to their calculations about how they should conduct themselves:

> Generally speaking, a community's dignity and self-respect would be best served if the obvious and the obviously just were acted upon promptly. Would not everyone be usefully shaped and properly restrained by such an approach? Instead, . . . the most celebrated lawyers in our country are licensed to practice systematic distortion of the truth and avoidance of the just dispositions of cases. Should we not be almost as vigilant about defense counsels' misconduct here as about prosecutors' misconduct?[17]

One suspects that the prospects of multimillion-dollar book deals and other means of self-enrichment made much more sense to the lawyers in this case than the kind of "moralizing" evident in the sentiments just quoted.

A serious rebuke for the prosecuting lawyers is implicit in their inability to secure a conviction, or at least a hung jury, despite the considerable evidence they had available to them. The use they made of a racism-vulnerable detective was, to say the least, imprudent, especially after they elected to try the case where they did. The detail that the prosecutors insisted upon in making their case probably contributed to the deadening of the sensibilities, including the moral sensibilities, of the jury.[18]

The defense lawyers may be, by far, the most interesting of all the "players" in this drama. They may also be the furthest from what they should have been, coming closest to the "rogue" status assigned by them to a few members of the Los Angeles Police Department. In a sense, the conduct of defense counsel has to be more self-regulated than that of any other officer in the criminal justice system. Defense counsel, if "successful" at the trial level, are less subject to correction on appeal than are judges, juries, or prosecutors: if they should secure an acquittal from the jury, the criminal case is almost certainly over. One consequence of this is that defense counsel may "safely" resort to sophistry and other abuses in the service of their client. This observation invites a question that is remarkably difficult for both law students and experienced lawyers to understand, let alone take seriously: If Mr. Simpson did the savage things that were done to the victims in this case, did his counsel act in his interest by securing his acquittal? It is easy, in the excitement of a case, to be caught up by the apparent goodness of "winning." We repeatedly heard references to "the Dream Team" of lawyers engaged for the Simpson defense, as if this trial had been a basketball game. (The original "Dream Team," contrived for the Olympic Games, was also misconceived. NBA professionals have no business competing in those Games—or, rather, basketball is too much of a business for them to be there. It is hardly sporting thus to insist upon exhibiting what everyone already knows about their preeminence.)

What did Mr. Simpson's lawyers really believe about his guilt? Did they tend to believe that one is guilty only if a judge or jury so rules? This would be a peculiar way to define "justice," however practical it may be for a decent community to rely considerably upon what the criminal justice system happens to produce on any particular occasion. If lawyers do come to be seen as having no standards aside from what happens to be arrived at in court, then respect for the system itself is apt to suffer:

> Whenever lawyers conduct themselves in questionable ways it is not likely to be good for the community, or for the lawyers' clients (whether individuals or the State), or for the lawyers themselves. Such conduct tends to promote cynicism, self-centeredness, and eventually the feeling among lawyers (as well as among others) that the legal profession, if not life itself, is meaningless. Particularly worrisome here is that the legal profession, which should be and should appear to be made up of reliable ministers of justice, is steadily demeaned, even as there is radical disaffection in the subverted community.[19]

I have the impression that only a very small minority of informed people in this country considers Mr. Simpson innocent. Do the Simpson lawyers now truly believe that he is innocent? That is, do they know something that most of us do not know? Or are they themselves deluded because of their calling, perhaps becoming thereby the most serious victims of the legal system as it has developed? And yet these lawyers appear the most successful and the most sophisticated of lawyers. If the Simpson lawyers believe him to have done the killings, what good do they see for the community, *as well as for him*, in his "vindication"? All this is a sad state of affairs for practitioners who were probably first drawn to the law because of their high-minded dedication to the cause of justice and the common good.

IV.

I have considered what the jurors, and to some extent the judge, in the Simpson case were thinking. I have also considered what the lawyers in the case were thinking. What about Mr. Simpson himself? If he did do the two killings, it could not have been altogether on impulse. That is, there are indications that the killer made preparations, if only with respect to the knife, clothing, and schedule relied upon. If Mr. Simpson did the killings, what did he believe would happen? Did he wonder whether he, a "likely" suspect, would have an adequate alibi? How could Mr. Simpson, if he set out to kill, be sure that no one would see him in the neighborhood? The thoughtlessness evident here may be seen as well perhaps in the spousal abuse episodes connected to him, episodes that would immediately make him a suspect when his ex-wife was slaughtered.

Those episodes testify to passions that may be hard either to predict or to control altogether. Certainly there were intense passions exhibited in the killings themselves, especially in the extension of the violence against what seems to have been an innocent bystander, the companion of the apparently targeted woman. Even so, it is becoming evident that Mr. Simpson is not of much consequence "personally," however sincerely he could once be described by a veteran sportswriter as one of "the most genuinely good-natured people I've ever met."[20]

If Mr. Simpson did the killings, he is (in a layman's terms) probably crazy.[21] Symptoms of craziness may be seen in his evident expectation that he would once again be able to hobnob with the rich and powerful upon his release from custody, whereas the only people who now support him in sizable numbers are among the poor or alienated of his race, the very people with whom he has had little to do since he became a celebrity. How did Mr. Simpson, if a savage killer, get to be the way he is? He can be accounted for by a peculiar combination of natural talent and early mistreatment, mistreatment of which we have had only glimpses thus far. (In more ways than one he seems to consider himself "abused." There may be something to this.)

Has this man, if indeed a killer, also come to consider himself truly innocent? However that may be, he probably is not so innocent even in his own estimation that he can admit to the deeds and still be able to justify them. O. J. Simpson is, in critical respects, a contrived figure, pointing up for us problems with the modern celebrity phenomenon. Unless there is a profound religious conversion, he can be expected to deteriorate in the years ahead, especially since there does not appear to be anything solid or enduring inside. He said, shortly after his acquittal, that he would devote himself to the pursuit of the killer of his ex-wife and her companion. He may have spoken more truly than he realized: one way or another he may be pursuing—that is, he may be trying to come to terms with—the killer within himself.

I return here to observations made in my June 1994 talk in Rome and published in my 1995 article on the Simpson case:

> Thus, would it not be better for someone in O. J. Simpson's situation (*if* that situation is indeed what it appears to be) simply to acknowledge what he did and thereafter to accept the appropriate punishment *and treatment*? It should now be obvious that Mr. Simpson himself, whether or not guilty on this occasion, was not served well by the legal system (and perhaps by his counsel) when he was questioned about severe attacks upon his wife over the years. Did he, with the aid of skillful counsel, really "get away with it" on *those* occasions? Perhaps he was encouraged to believe that *he* was the victim, that there was a conspiracy against him, etc. It is natural for the perpetrator of awful deeds to try to blame them upon, if not even physically to assign them to, someone else. Intense guilt can often lead one to desperate efforts to wish away, to deny, indeed to blot out of one's memory, what has been done. But in whose interest is it that one should be allowed to live a lie in this way for the remainder of one's years? Certainly, a healing and enduring peace of soul is not to be secured thus.[22]

What, then, would be truly good for a man in Mr. Simpson's dreadful circumstances? True repentance and facing up to what he has done and why, the old-fashioned moralist would have said. The recent NBC-interview fiasco is revealing: it is probably becoming apparent even to Mr. Simpson that there are limits now to the manipulation by him that can work in the conduct of his life. Brutal, even cruel, jokes about him suggest the hopelessness of the efforts that might now be made to rehabilitate him, jokes that began at once on the airwaves.[23]

V.

The key issue never has been, it seems to me, whether Mr. Simpson serves time in prison. He is, if the killer, already a prisoner of his past and of his passions.

For most of us, it is as if he is already put away. For some, however, it remains vital that he be "officially" recognized as a killer.[24] The civil suits brought against him offer hope to some. They are looked to as a way of clarifying matters, as well as a way of keeping him from profiting financially from his notoriety. (There does not seem to be, unlike what happened to the police officers exposed on videotape in the 1991 Rodney King matter, also in California, the possibility of a federal criminal trial to begin to make up for what was not done in the state criminal trial.) But what more is there to learn from what is likely to be said by Mr. Simpson or by anyone else in court at this time? Perhaps the civil suits can at least help persuade impressionable people that to escape conviction in a criminal trial does not mean that one has "really gotten away with it." People also need to be persuaded that the rich and the powerful do not readily escape the consequences of murder in this country. The convictions of businessmen, Congressmen, and judges on lesser charges remind us that influence is not always enough to protect one in criminal proceedings. We can see as well that influential men and women can be trapped by the illusions spun around them. (Perjury prosecutions, of the type that some hope may follow in a criminal court upon Mr. Simpson's testimony in a civil suit, seem to be rare.[25])

It will be interesting, in any event, to see what happens to Mr. Simpson's support, such as it is, once a long-term opinion about him becomes settled. The degree of support for him in the African-American community is instructive. Part of that support is an instinctive "closing of ranks" by a people behind "one of their own." This sort of response was seen, for example, on more than one occasion during the notorious political career of James Michael Curley in Boston, with the Irish-American community coming to *his* support again and again. Once, indeed, he was elected to office while serving time in jail.[26]

Then there was the way that the Greek-American community closed ranks behind Spiro T. Agnew, even after it became evident that he had been accepting bribes (still "due" to him from his years as governor of Maryland) while vice president of the United States. It had not seemed to bother most of the Greek-American community that Mr. Agnew (who preferred to be called "Ted" rather than "Spiro") never showed much interest in the Greek community, except as a source of campaign contributions. Even worse was what the Greek-American community did, between 1967 and 1974, in supporting the colonels' coup in Greece, a coup that led eventually to the subjection (ever since 1974) of a significant portion of Cyprus to Turkish rule. Without pressure from the Greek-American community, the American State Department would probably have conducted itself more sensibly in dealing with the colonels, including their irresponsible policy with respect to Turkey.[27]

Unlike the bulk of Greek-Americans, many others in this country could easily see the Greek colonels for what they were: incompetent usurpers who were good for neither Greece nor the United States. It was not surprising that Americans at large were without the illusions that the more influential Greek-Americans had about the colonels who flattered and appealed to them.[28] The same can be said about the large majority of whites who appreciated the considerable case that had been mounted against Mr. Simpson during his trial. Thus, African-American support for O. J. Simpson is, in part, rooted (how deeply rooted remains to be seen) in the same kind of allegiance exhibited by Greek-Americans when they supported Spiro Agnew and the colonels and by Irish Americans when they supported James Curley. This sort of thing, it can be said, is "natural."

VI.

But there is even more to the African-American show of ethnic allegiance in the Simpson case than there is to how Irish Americans and Greek Americans have conducted themselves from time to time. The responses of African Americans to the Simpson cause, I have noticed, testify to depths of alienation, if not even to the profound despair, that the other minority groups in this country (except perhaps for Native Americans) have not fallen into. (Both African Americans and Native Americans do seem to be in need of whatever help can be provided them by sensible affirmative action programs.) There *is* something desperate about the African-American situation, as may be seen in the kind of man that can be turned (albeit temporarily) into a "hero." (It may be significant that Colin Powell does not stir up the same degree of passion among African Americans that various other leaders of their race do, even though it should be evident that the more strident leaders in any minority group, not being apt to arouse much general support among the majority, will be of limited influence in the community at large.)

It is sometimes recognized that whites do not see what African Americans routinely experience and see. That experience includes the kind of things accidentally exposed in the vicious treatment of Rodney King by his arresting policemen in Los Angeles. Even worse may be what a largely white jury did in acquitting those policemen. But a critical difference should be noticed (in addition to the successful, however questionable, effort we have seen to get at those policemen in a subsequent federal *criminal* trial). It has been reported that groups of African-American students all over this country responded with "jubilation" upon learning of the Simpson acquittal.[29] Perhaps such students could not "help themselves," a weakness that their teachers should try to remedy. But it should at least be recognized that there evidently was not such jubilation expressed by mainstream students of any color when Rodney King's assailants were acquitted. Would we not have been deeply troubled upon learning that any group of, say, white Loyola law students had publicly responded in this fashion on that occasion?

One hopeful sign in all this is that those African Americans who defend the Simpson verdict do *not* usually put it simply in terms of "payback time." Rather, they talk about "police conspiracy" and "reasonable doubt" in justifying the jury's refusal to defer to the considerable case evidently made against Mr. Simpson. That is, they do not want to seem, or indeed to be, unprincipled or arbitrary on this occasion. They should be taken at their word as we try to assess what happened and why.

Two sets of opinions, from the sidelines so to speak, should be noticed here. There is one set of opinions about the Simpson case that I have heard from several African Americans during the past year. They have now and then expressed the conviction that although Mr. Simpson did not do the killings himself, he knows who did them. This bears thinking about, perhaps as a partial recognition of Mr. Simpson's role in all this. Another set of opinion that bears thinking about may be found in a letter of October 10, 1995, from a white police officer I know and respect, written to me from a Northern California city:

> When the verdict was read I was struck by a nearly overwhelming sense of despair. As a police officer, I thought I was familiar with the vagaries of our justice system, but still felt optimistic about the ability of the jurors to do what was right.
>
> It was difficult to go to work the day of the verdict. We had lost our credibility. I realized that our effectiveness was not a function of our uniforms or guns, but rather was derived from our position in a larger scheme of justice: if there is no justice the police are merely an occupying army.
>
> Several experiences that I have had since the verdict have revealed its meaning, I think. Shortly after the verdict my partner and I stopped a car driven by a black man. A group of people came out of their houses to heckle us. A woman yelled, "You're just mad because we won!" . . .
>
> At the station yesterday, I overheard a black officer angrily tell a white officer that even though O. J. had committed the murders, "white America got what they deserved."
>
> Despite working everyday in the black community, I vastly underestimated the racial divide. It seems clear to me now that the verdict was an expression of deep resentment.

This letter records the dismay and then the self-examination displayed by many whites in this country upon confronting what was for them the stunning verdict in the Simpson criminal case.[30]

VII.

There are, I have suggested, truths about legal controversies that do not depend upon what a jury happens to say. We need, in assessing such matters, a sense of what is knowable and of how it is to be known. Some have argued that the Simpson trial dramatizes defects in our criminal law system. No doubt, various aspects of jury selection, trial management, and attorney conduct can be improved. But what we have seen in Los Angeles since June 1994 is much more an indictment of our popular culture than of our legal system. Our criminal law system works fairly well, usually, making it highly unlikely that those now found in prison did not do either what they were charged with or something very much like it. (This does not rule out the practice sometimes resorted to by police, and not impossible in the Simpson case, of enhancing or perhaps even creating evidence in order to reinforce the case that the authorities themselves are certain of already.[31])

What does not work very well is how we treat both those who are more likely to become criminals and those who have been identified as criminals. Something is dreadfully wrong, for which we shall all have to suffer for decades to come, when there is (as now) large-scale chronic unemployment in our inner cities (a decade-long depression) and when there are so many African-American young men (one third, it is said) who are enmeshed by the criminal law system, numbers that have been rising steadily.

A social system in which such appallingly wasteful things become routine is deeply flawed. Does not the responsibility for this state of affairs rest with all of us? This is not to deny that the way all too many of these young men, and their own people, respond to their deprivations can make matters worse, including for themselves. (We have long seen this kind of desperation in Sicily, where violent crime sometimes seems a "natural" way of life.) Nor is it to deny that the young criminal must be firmly dealt with, for his own good as well as for the good of the community, when he steps out of line. But that is only the beginning of a challenge that is ignored by those who believe that our salvation lies in building more and more prisons (corrupting though they may be) and then throwing their keys away after they are filled up.

I argued, in my June 1994 talk on the Simpson case, "Particularly harmful is the teaching, all too common among us these days, that it is fitting and proper to evade having to face up to what one has done."[32] This teaching applies not only to desperate defendants and their single-minded lawyers. It applies even more to the community at large, which sometimes seems blithely unaware of what it is doing to cripple, to enrage, and otherwise to damage so many of its youth. I have long believed that one useful place to begin, in an effort to remedy things in this country, would be with a massive public works project, along with first-rate schools and intensive job training, for our inner cities.[33] After all, we were willing to undertake and sustain for a decade such a humane and morale-repairing experiment on an even larger scale, sixty years ago, when the Great Depression (unlike the persistent depression in our inner cities today) was color blind.

NOTES

1. This talk was given in a Jurisprudence course, The School of Law, Loyola University of Chicago, Chicago, Illinois, November 21, 1995. See George Anastaplo, "The O. J. Simpson Case Revisted," 28 *Loyola University of Chicago Law Journal* 461, 463 note 5 (1997).

The principal texts for this 1995 Jurisprudence course were Aristotle's *Physics* and Francis Bacon's *Novum Organum*. In the following two semesters the principal texts in my Jurisprudence courses were the Bible and Shakespeare, See George Anastaplo, "On Freedom: Explorations," 17 *Oklahoma City University Law Review* 465, 724–26 (1992).

It should be noticed that unanimity was required for a verdict in the O. J. Simpson criminal trial, but not in the civil trial. Both the 1995 criminal trial verdict and the 1997 civil trial verdict *were* unanimous. (The civil trial, touched upon in the notes to chapter 13 of this collection, was held after this 1995 talk was given.)

2. See George Anastaplo, "On Crime, Criminal Lawyers, and O. J. Simpson: Plato's *Gorgias* Revisited," 26 *Loyola University of Chicago Law Journal* 455 (1995).

My fourth commentary on the Simpson case may be found, in effect, in the notes to this 1995 talk in this collection.

See, on Spiro T. Agnew as an unfortunate model of extremism in politics, chapter 13, note 27.

3. Anastaplo, "On Crime, Criminal Lawyers, and O. J. Simpson," p. 458. The "bizarre efforts" referred to include the notorious Bronco chase with which the prosecution did little, if anything, during the criminal trial, but which the plaintiffs' attorneys used in the civil trial. See chapter 13, notes 9, 18.

4. This double-murder case is considered closed by the Los Angeles Police Department. See Anastaplo, "On Crime, Criminal Lawyers, and O. J. Simpson," p. 465 note 23. See also chapter 13, note 30 and the accompanying text.

5. Anastaplo, "On Crime, Criminal Lawyers, and O. J. Simpson," p. 470 note 33.

6. Anastaplo, "On Crime, Criminal Lawyers, and O. J. Simpson," p. 470.

7. See Gale Holland and Jonathan T. Levitt, "Jurors Detail the Thinking That Went into Their Ruling," *USA Today*, February 11, 1997, p. 1A: "Most jurors said the defense put on a strong case [in the civil trial] of possible police contamination of evidence and conspiracy. But in the end [defense] theories were too speculative, too much of a reach, jurors said." Professor Albert Alschuler, of the University of Chicago Law School, has observed, "The American justice system often gets it right the second time around," Ken Armstrong and Flynn McRoberts, "Civil Case Meant 2nd Trial

Was in Different League," *Chicago Tribune*, February 5, 1997, sec. 1, p. 20; chapter 13, note 30. See also "The Second Simpson Verdict," *Chicago Tribune*, Editorial, February 6, 1997, sec. 1, p. 26. Compare Yale Kamisar, "Call It Double Jeopardy," *New York Times*, February 14, 1997, p. A23.

8. Much the same can be said, for example, about what Oliver North's successful criminal conviction appeal does and does not mean. See chapter 12, note 165. Consider also how physicists work—as, for example, when they look to a mechanical operation to create or to identify what they call a "vacuum." But must there not be a standard (of what a vacuum would truly be) that helps them see what operation or method does a better job in developing (or, rather, approaching) a vacuum? Also, I note in passing, it may not be possible to have a true vacuum anywhere in the universe if there are gravitons that are responsible for gravity: the pull of gravity is everywhere, however tiny it may be in some places. See, on the mystery of being and nothingness, George Anastaplo, *The Thinker as Artist: From Homer to Plato & Aristotle* (Athens, Ohio: Ohio University Press, 1997), p. 301.

9. The same experts (such as Philip Corboy and Scott Turow) have spoken with more respect about how the civil trial against Mr. Simpson was conducted. See Bob Kurson, "Bottom Line for O. J.: He's Going to Suffer," *Chicago Sun-Times*, February 6, 1997, p. 6. See also chapter 13, note 3, 18.

See, for a vigorous condemnation of the way the Simpson criminal trial was conducted, Vincent Bugliosi, *Outrage: The Five Reasons Why O. J. Simpson Got Away with Murder* (New York: W.W. Norton & Co., 1996). It remains to be seen what "got away" means. See, e.g., chapter 13, notes 17–18, 23, 30. See also chapter 12, note 61 (the George Will problem).

10. Among the advantages that the plaintiffs' lawyers had in the civil trial, with its lower standard of proof to meet, was the damaging testimony of Mr. Simpson himself. See, e.g., Ken Armstrong and Flynn McRoberts, "Civil Case Meant 2nd Trial Was In Different League," p. 20 (quoting Professor Jamie Carey of the Loyola University of Chicago School of Law); Jonathan T. Lovitt and Richard Price, "Plaintiff's Best Witness Was O. J.," *USA Today*, February 5, 1997, p. 1A. "Christopher Darden, [an African-American] member of the unsuccessful criminal trial prosecution team, said the difference in the civil case was that Simpson had to testify. 'O. J. lied in front of this jury, he lied to the black community, and he lied to the American public. This jury focused on the evidence, not on race or politics,' he said." Patrick Brogan, "Civil Defeat Has Simpson Facing Ruin," *Glasgow Herald*, February 6, 1997, p. 13. See chapter 13, note 18.

What safeguards would be needed if defendants in nonpolitical criminal cases were required to testify? Defense attorneys are sure, in any event, that juries do take into account the lack of testimony from defendants in criminal proceedings. See chapter 13, note 18.

11. See George Anastaplo, "Lessons for the Student of Law: The Oklahoma Lectures," 20 *Oklahoma City University Law Review* 17, 187 (1995). See also chapter 13, note 16.

12. See, on capital punishment, George Anastaplo, *The American Moralist: On Law, Ethics, and Government* (Athens, Ohio: Ohio University Press, 1992), p. 422.

See also "A Lawyerly Cry of Conscience," *New York Times*, February 22, 1997, p. 16 (Editorial); "Reality Check on the Death Penalty," *Chicago Tribune*, March 3, 1997, sec. 1, p. 14 (Editorial). See, on the American jury, Anastaplo "On Crime, Criminal Lawyers, and O. J. Simpson," p. 168 n. 33.

13. Our extended jury sequestrations are resorted to partly because of the considerable leeway usually allowed both to the mass media in covering a trial and to counsel in publicly commenting upon it daily. See, e.g., James Brooke, "Newspaper Says McVeigh Told [His Lawyers] of Role in [Oklahoma City] Bombing," *New York Times*, March 1, 1997, p. 1. No extended sequestration was required in Mr. Simpson's civil trial. Is not a jury somewhat like the fox in a fox hunt, defining the course that the chase is to follow?

14. Mr. Simpson's civil trial was not televised. See, on the salutary abolition of broadcast television in this country, Anastaplo, *The American Moralist*, p. 245; appendix C, note 21.

15. See, for an account of the woman with "second sight" in my parents' village in Greece, Anastaplo, *The American Moralist*, p. 388.

16. Storer H. Rowley, "As Crackdown Looms, Settlers Tone Down," *Chicago Tribune*, November 10, 1995, sec. 1, p. 20. See also Arthur Schlesinger Jr., "The Worst Corruption," *Wall Street Journal*, November 22, 1995, p. A10. See as well George Anastaplo, "On Freedom," pp. 622–25; George Anastaplo, *Human Being and Citizen: Essays on Virtue, Freedom, and the Common Good* (Chicago: Swallow Press, 1975), pp. 155–59. See, on Vincent Foster and related matters, Robert L. Bartley, "Whitewater Reconstructed," *Wall Street Journal*, March 22, 1996, p. A12; "Pattern of Obstruction," *Wall Street Journal*, June 19, 1996 (Editorial), p. A20; "Mr. Foster to Mr. Livingstone," *Wall Street Journal*, July 12, 1996 (Editorial), p. A12; Trude B. Feldman, "The President at 50," *Wall Street Journal*, August 1, 1996, p. A14; "Privileged First Lady," *Wall Street Journal*, August 3, 1996 (Editorial), p. A10; Eugene H. Methvin, "Justice Without Fear or Favor," *Wall Street Journal*, September 30, 1996, p. A18; "The White House Conspiracy," *Wall Street Journal*, January 13, 1997 (Editorial), p. A18; Clarence Page, "Paranoia Rules," *Chicago Tribune*, February 16, 1997, sec. 1, p. 21; Anthony Lewis, "Ken Starr's Problem," *New York Times*, February 21, 1997, p. A19; Anthony Lewis, "Closure on Vince Foster," *New York Times*, February 24, 1997, p. A15. See also chapter 13, note 11.

17. Anastaplo, "On Crime, Criminal Lawyers, and O. J. Simpson," p. 468. See also Anastaplo, *The American Moralist*, p. 185. See, on how defendants and their lawyers should conduct themselves, Anastaplo, *Human Being and Citizen*, pp. 8, 203. See also p. 105. The work of Harrison Sheppard with the California Bar is instructive here. Consider, as well, how attorneys for tobacco companies should conduct themselves. See, for indications of Mr. Simpson's lifelong vulnerability, Dana Canedy, "O. J. Simpson's House Searched in Drug Case," *New York Times*, December 3, 2001, p. A16.

18. See, for a preliminary account of the way that the plaintiffs' case in the civil trial was presented, Elaine Lafferty, "The Inside Story of How O. J. Lost," *Time*, February 17, 1997, p. 29. See, also, Christopher Darden, "Justice Is in the Color of the Beholder," *Time*, February 17, 1997, p. 38. Mr. Darden, a prosecutor in the Simpson criminal trial, concludes his article thus, "Given the wealth of evidence against Simpson, the fact he remains free while others are convicted on one-tenth the evidence is

fundamentally unfair. I don't expect that he'll ever pay for his crimes," Darden, "Justice Is in the Color of the Beholder," p. 39. Compare R. Bruce Dodd, "An Amazing State of Affairs," *Chicago Tribune*, February 7, 1997, sec. 1, p. 27; chapter 13, notes 3, 10. Compare, also, the quotation in the text at note 22 of chapter 13 of this collection; chapter 13, notes 24, 30. Compare as well chapter 13, note 9.

19. Anastaplo, "On Crime, Criminal Lawyers, and O. J. Simpson," p. 468. See also Anastaplo, "Individualism, Professional Ethics, and the Sense of Community: From Runnymede to a London Telephone Booth," 28 *Loyola University of Chicago Law Journal* 285 (1996); Anastaplo, "Teaching, Nature, and the Moral Virtues," 1997 *The Great Ideas Today* 2 (Encyclopedia Britannica, 1997); "Natural Law or Natural Right?" 38 *Loyola of New Orleans Law Review* 915 (1993) (reprinted in appendix B of George Anastaplo, *But Not Philosophy: Seven Introductions to Non-Western Thoughts* [Lanham, Maryland: Lexington Books, Rowman & Littlefield, 2002], p. 303). "It's that mixture of sophistry with conformity that frightens me about most lawyers. Perhaps it's because they're closer to the moral vacuum of our times than anyone else. The O. J. spectacle might not be law's embarrassment, but [rather] its true and empty core." Pat Kane, "Smooth Talkers Who Know the Score," *Glasgow Herald*, February 6, 1997, p. 19. The well-meaning sophistry of Professor Alan M. Dershowitz, as a commentator on the Simpson cases, has been instructive. See chapter 12, note 115. (His defenses of the state of Israel are much more sensible.)

20. Anastaplo, "On Crime, Criminal Lawyers, and O. J. Simpson," p. 464 n. 25 (quoting Bob Costas). See, on Mr. Simpson as a witness, chapter 13, note 10.

21. See Anastaplo, "On Crime, Criminal Lawyers, and O. J. Simpson," p. 464 (a comment upon the John Wayne Gacy case). See, on psychiatry and the law, Anastaplo, *The American Moralist*, p. 407.

22. Anastaplo, "On Crime, Criminal Lawyers, and O. J. Simpson," pp. 466–67.

23. Particularly rough was the "humor" about Mr. Simpson on *Saturday Night Live* the first weekend after his criminal case acquittal (NBC televison broadcast, October 7, 1995). See, on the aborted television interview, Bill Carter, "Simpson Cancels TV Interview, But Talks of Life Since Verdict," *New York Times*, October 12, 1995, p. A1; David Margolick, "Late Meetings Led to Cancellation," *New York Times*, October 12, 1995, p. 87; Frank Rich, "The Second Wind," *New York Times*, October 14, 1995, p. 19; Lawrie Mifflin, "NBC Confronts the What If's of Simpson Coup That Wasn't," *New York Times*, October 16, 1995, p. D7.

24. See *Genesis* 4:15; chapter 13, note 18, 30.

25. See, e.g., "The Simpson Finale" (Editorial), *Wall Street Journal*, February 6, 1997, p. A14.

26. See Jack Beatty, *The Rascal King: The Life and Times of James Michael Curley, 1874–1958* (Reading, Massachusetts: Addison-Wesley Publishing Co., 1992), pp. 77–91. One can be reminded here of the recent career of Mayor Marion Barry in Washington, D.C.

27. See, for an unfortunate resemblance between Vice President Agnew and President Clinton, George Anastaplo, Letters to the Editor, *Chicago Daily Law Bulletin*, September 10, 1998, p. 2; *New York Times*, September 11, 1998, p. A26 (abridged); *Hickory Daily Record* (Hickory, North Carolina), September 1998, p. A-8; *Chicago*

Sun-Times, September 13, 1998, p. 38A. See, on Cyprus and the Greek colonels, George Anastaplo, "Bloodied Greece: No Way Out?" *Baltimore Sun*, April 19, 1974 (reprinted in 120 *Congressional Record* 14371 [May 13, 1974], 120 *Congressional Record* 15597 [May 20, 1974]). See, also appendix C, notes 16, 64.

A commentary on Spiro T. Agnew, relevant to our inquiry in this collection, is my Op-Ed page article about him ("The Education of Spiro T. Agnew—and of Us All," *Chicago Tribune*, October 12, 1973, sec. 1, p. 18), the text of which follows (with modifications):

The vice president, before his resignation [on October 10, 1973], took a constitutional position which still requires, and even invites, a respectful assessment. Something more than what we have already heard should be said for, as well as against, the former vice president in his recent difficulties, especially since those difficulties are to some extent ours as well.

The immediate cause of the Agnew difficulties was the investigation by a Baltimore Federal grand jury into what may have been routine shenanigans in Maryland politics. But, as is still true as well of our beleaguered president [who was to resign on August 9, 1974], there were deeper causes of the vice president's vulnerability.

It is instructive to notice, in any attempt to understand the fascinating unraveling we have witnessed since January [1973] of the Nixon Administration, that much of the trouble of the president and his former vice president stems from their tendency to associate themselves primarily with devoted "organization men" rather than with irreverent politicians. Politicians usually develop more of the human touch than do partisan technicians who have never had to run for office and who are more apt to be extremists.

Experience teaches seasoned politicians to be restrained in their public behavior and to be tolerant of opponents and of criticism. An understandable desire for political self-preservation does incline politicians to "straddle the fence" rather than to "tell it like it is." Such caution reflects an appreciation of the limits of public opinion and helps promote a moderating "give-and-take" attitude among political "enemies."

Except in the gravest of circumstances, things do have a way of working themselves out in a healthy community. Compare the behavior in 1969 and 1970 of a politically inexperienced vice president [Mr. Agnew], a spirited man who probably rose to national prominence too fast for his own good. He permitted himself to be so used for bitterly partisan attacks upon the media and upon political opponents that he could expect no help either from the press or from Congress when he in turn became vulnerable.

The vice president did not seem to realize in his days of rhetorical excesses and hence of a notorious celebrity what practical politicians learn through years of observation, that the "outs" all too often become the "ins," that few of us are so nearly perfect as to be completely invulnerable to a reversal of fortune or to an *ex post facto* tightening up of everyday standards.

It is not useful to assume, however, that it was only the desire for political retaliation which moved the politicians in the House of Representatives to disregard the vice president's recent desperate claim of Executive Privilege against judicial processes (prior to impeachment and removal from office). This is a claim about which the Constitution of the United States has little to say explicitly. But it is a claim which may be understood to have been anticipated and decisively repudiated by what was said more than three centuries ago in Shakespeare's *Henry IV, Part 2*, a play in which the playwright expressed and thereby reaffirmed in an authoritative manner the significance of the rule of law for the English-speaking peoples.

In that *History Play*, a "constitutional" claim similar to that recently made by the former vice president was advanced on behalf of the heir apparent to the English throne, an even more privileged character than a mere American vice president. Thus, the new King (Henry V) confronted the apprehensive Chief Justice who had dared to imprison Henry while he was still (as Prince Hal) the heir apparent. Their instructive conversation went like this (Act V, Scene 2):

King:
> You are, I think, assured I love you not.

Chief Justice:
> I am assured, if I be measured rightly,
> Your Majesty hath no just cause to hate me.

King:
> No? How might a prince of my great hope forget
> So great indignities you laid upon me?
> What? rate, rebuke, and roughly sent to prison
> The immediate heir of England? Was this easy?
> May this be washed in Lethe and forgotten?

Chief Justice:
> I then did use the person of your father,
> The image of his power lay then in me.
> And in the administration of his law,
> Whiles I was busy for the commonwealth,
> Your Highness pleased to forget my place,
> The majesty and power of law and justice,
> The image of the King who I presented,
> And struck me in my very seat of judgment;
> Whereon, as an offender to your father,
> I gave bold way to my authority
> And did commit you. . . .
> Question your royal thoughts, make the case yours;
> Be now the father and propose a son,
> Hear your own dignity so much profaned,
> See your own dreadful laws so loosely slighted,
> Behold yourself so by a son disdained,
> And then imagine me taking your part
> And in your power soft silencing your son.
> After this cold considerance, sentence me
> And, as you are King, speak in your state
> What I have done that misbecame my place,
> My person, or my liege's sovereignty.

King:
> You are tight, Justice, and you weigh this well.
> Therefore still bear the balance and the sword;
> And I do wish your honors may increase,
> Till you do live to see a son of mine
> Offend you and obey you as I did.

Thus the rule of law was recognized and dramatically reaffirmed by the new King's self-restraint, a lesson in moderation and in constitutionalism which is particularly salutary for troubled times such as ours. It would seem, on the basis of this thoughtful precedent, that a good-faith judicial proceeding may properly be conducted against any vice president of the United States and, in most circumstances, against a president as well. It would also seem that, under a republican form of government, impeachment proceedings (in public or in private) may be conducted independently of ordinary judicial proceedings.

It should be immediately added, however, that a responsible respect for republican government and the rule of law includes the obligation by us and by our Congress to reexamine and to correct from time to time the laws by which we are governed. A serious question remains whether the bribery and extortion laws which were applied to the former vice president's Maryland conduct are indeed laws which should be on the Federal books at all or which should be used as they have been in recent years.

A serious question remains, that is, whether federal power should continue to be used to supervise suspected financial corruption on the part of State officials. Federal supervision of such conduct is likely to mean, in effect, a second-guessing of local electorates and of local practices by the Washington bureaucracy of the Department of Justice. (This means ever more meddling by technicians in the political life of the country.)

Should not the people of "Sovereign States" served by a free and robust press be permitted to deal, pretty much as they decide, with the local misconduct of duly elected public officials, except when Federal funds are involved? This, too, reaffirms the rule of law—the higher law of our long-established and moderating constitutional arrangements. It is too bad, both for the former vice president and for a public in need of repeated reminders of the principles and conditions of American federalism, that he was not heard to make such arguments as these when greedy Democratic politicians began [after the Republican ascendency nationally in] 1968 to come under systematic attack in the Federal Courts.

However that may be, it is heartening that a compromise could be found which permitted an unfortunate vice president the option of retiring to the relative anonymity of a private station with as much dignity as possible in the circumstances. Would not his replacement by the sixty-four-year-old Barry Goldwater reassure partisans on all sides? That is, conservatives could thus be more easily persuaded that the vice president's resignation was not due to a "radical conspiracy"; liberals could see that no emerging and vigorous Republican candidate was thereby being given special advantage for the 1976 presidential election.

Prudent relaxation of political excitation is the order of the day if we are to continue to keep divisive passions in check. Do not both compassion and self-interest counsel moderation? Or must we all learn the hard way the lessons that an exploited vice president, transformed into a celebrity, had to learn about the perils of extremism?

Some of the observations made here (in 1973) bear upon the abuses of the Office of the Independent Counsel during the Clinton Administration. See, on Shakespeare's *History Plays* and American constitutionalism, George Anastaplo, *The Constitution of 1787: A Commentary* (Baltimore: Johns Hopkins University Press, 1989), pp. If, 74f.

28. See Anastaplo, *Human Being and Citizen*, p. 3; Anastaplo, *The Artist as Thinker: From Shakespeare to Joyce* (Athens, Ohio: Ohio University Press, 1983), p. 331; Anastaplo, *The American Moralist*, p. 501.

29. One such group seems to have been at the Howard University School of Law, Washington, D.C. See *The Independent* (London), October 6, 1995. See, also, David K. Shipler, "Living Under Suspicion: Why Blacks Believe Simpson and Not the Police," *New York Times*, February 7, 1997, p. A17.

30. My Northern California police officer, Harry S. Stern, supplied me, on February 11, 1997, the following comment on the 1997 verdict in the Simpson civil trial:

The end of the criminal trial [in October 1995] was preceded by a big buildup. The verdict was intentionally announced the morning after it had been reached in order to give the police and others time to prepare. The public knew what time it would be read and thus could tune in at the appropriate time. My narcotics unit was placed on alert. We were to wear regular blue uniforms, have our helmets with us, and we were divided into squads. The conclusion of the [1997] civil trial was not as climactic. There was no anticipation of unrest. The verdict was read shortly after it had been reached.

My wife and I watched the reading of the verdicts on television. A friend called from Chicago and told me that a local station had information that there had been a defense verdict. This was upsetting news. I had never doubted that Simpson had stabbed Ron Goldman and Nicole Brown to death. There was no other explanation for their brutal deaths. So I was relieved when the rumors proved false; the jury had determined that Simpson was the killer.

The black people that I spoke with about the civil trial seemed resigned rather than angry. My sense is that, despite the results of so many polls and surveys, the belief by blacks in Simpson's innocence was not deeply held. Rather, blacks chose to support Simpson from what they deemed an attack from white institutions.

Thus, my view as a police officer is that the civil verdict was not a vindication of the justice system. The civil trial was in essence a dispute between private parties. The Goldman and Brown family brought their own cases against the man that they believed had killed their relatives.

In the criminal trial the most often repeated description of the police (and hence by association, the District Attorney and the State of California) was that they were "racist" and "bungling." From my perspective these enduring assessments represented the criminal defense's complete success in replacing Mr. Simpson with the police as the defendants. The police were put on trial, not O. J. Simpson.

The effects of this strategy, not unique to the Simpson case, are far-reaching and quite disastrous, I believe. A criminal trial is not merely a clinical inquiry; it has the potential to offer a moral lesson for both the accused (who must come to terms with his actions if responsible) and the community at large.

Although, I did not follow the civil trial closely, I gathered that the plaintiffs prevailed, in part, because of their ability to distance themselves from the institutions that Simpson's criminal defense team had done so much to discredit. As I stated, the plaintiffs were private parties seeking a private remedy. Furthermore, in the civil arena the apparatus that places such a premium on ferreting out alleged police misconduct, the exclusionary rule, is not present. Accordingly, the civil defense could not delve into the "conspiracy theory" to the extent that their criminal [defense] counterparts had.

It seems to me, then, that for black people much less was at stake in the civil trial; they did not feel the same animosity toward the Goldman and Brown families that they felt toward the police. And in turn, the civil verdict did little or nothing to restore the reputation of California law enforcement.

(Both of the letters of Mr. Stern, who is now a lawyer practicing in the San Francisco area, are printed here with his permission.) See, on the exclusionary rule, George Anastaplo, "Constitutional Comment," in Gera-Lind Kolarik, *Freed to Kill: The True Story of Larry Eyler* (Chicago: Chicago Review Press, 1990), p. 367. See also Akhil Reed Amar, "A Second Chance at Justice," February 6, 1997, p. A21.

If Mr. Simpson did not do the killings but knows who did them, this could mean that Mr. Simpson is protecting a dangerous killer who is likely free to move around. See chapter 13, note 4. On the other hand, if Mr. Simpson *is* the killer, he is hardly likely to kill anyone else again, whatever he may do to himself spiritually or otherwise. See chapter 13, notes 17, 18, 24.

31. See, e.g., Eric Zorn, "Maybe O. J. Did It and the Cops Tried to Frame Him, Too," *Chicago Tribune*, February 5, 1997, sec. 2, p. 1.

32. Anastaplo, "On Crime, Criminal Lawyers, and O. J. Simpson," p. 469.

33. See, e.g., George Anastaplo, "What Is Still Wrong with George Anastaplo? A Sequel to 366 U.S. 82 (1961)," 35 *DePaul Law Review* 551, 627 (1986); Anastaplo, *The American Moralist*, p. 454. The Simpson case can be expected to remain a substantial "public works project" for lawyers and journalists, with considerable litigation and many revelations yet to come. "The criminal case prompted many to say that Simpson was acquitted because he is wealthy, . . . Simpson's money gave him the best lawyers and the best possible chance. This is nothing new, but we hope the Simpson trials will prompt public discussion of the quality of legal representation available to the poor." "Important Lessons from Simpson Circus," *Chicago Sun-Times* (Editorial), February 5, 1997, p. 37.

See, on the complexities of race relations in this country, my April 21, 2002, Letter to the Editor (unpublished):

> The ethnicity conflicts reported at Harvard University threaten many other schools of higher education as well. ("Comments About Ethnicity Divide Harvard Law School," *New York Times*, April 20, 2002, p. A14) Particularly troubling is a widespread condition which discourages both faculty and students from saying anything "insensitive" about race-related issues which might offend the racial pieties of our day. These pieties often rely upon questionable history and unsound data, sometimes even promoting addiction to a paralyzing victimology.
>
> All this means that long-standing deficiencies in the preparation and morale of minority students cannot be candidly examined and vigorously dealt with. This makes it difficult in turn to develop efficiently and to assess properly the affirmative action programs which may still be needed if deep divisions in our country are to be healed.
>
> The self-inflicted crippling we are witnessing here can remind older observers of the respect for Cold War pieties which stifled the much-needed political discourse that might have spared us our Vietnam debacle.

See also the text at note 43 of appendix C of this collection. See as well appendix C, note 15.

Conclusion

A vital question again and again noticed in the talks and essays collected here has to do with the bearing of *nature* upon the legal, moral, and political judgments we make and upon how we should conduct ourselves with respect to the kinds of controversies reviewed in this collection. The significance and yet ambiguity of *nature* is suggested by this description of a spectacular bird by an English naturalist a century and a half ago:

> It is scarcely possible for the imagination to conceive anything more rich and gorgeous than the golden-green color which adorns the principal part of the plumage of this splendid bird; or more elegant and graceful than the flowing plumage, which sweeps pendant from the lower part of the back, forming a long train of metallic brilliancy. *Nature appears to have ordained* that birds possessing unusual brilliancy of plumage should be inhabitants of retired and obscure situations; and *in strict conformity with this law* the Resplendent Trogon, by far the most beautiful of its tribe, is only to be found in the dense and gloomy forests of the southern state of Mexico, remote from the haunts of civilized man.[1]

Much of what I have done in this book can be considered an attempt to clear ground and lay down seed for the proper cultivation (by others, if not by me) of the idea of nature and of that sense of right and wrong (or natural right) upon which people somehow or other naturally draw.[2] Critical to much of what I have said, and to the way I have conducted my inquiries and made my preliminary assessments in one "situation" after another, is the proposition that the *principles and standards* relied upon in my inquiries *can indeed be thought about*. Particularly important here can be the nurturing of that prudence that permits one to sense when one knows enough to be able to judge and to speak responsibly in a variety of circumstances, circumstances that can be very much shaped by chance. The reader is reminded that the date of composition of each chapter in this collection can be critical.

It is one thing to figure out what natural right calls for in any particular situation. It is, unfortunately, quite another thing to be able to share one's conclusions effectively with one's less thoughtful or more passionate fellows. The helpful uses here of divine signs, and of other forms or revelation, should be apparent. Consider for example this episode, as recalled by a nineteenth-century preacher in Kentucky:

> During the late struggle of the Greeks to regain their liberty, a body of Turks were, in 1824, encamped in a part of Greece, and committed every kind of excess upon the inhabitants. One of these barbarians, an officer, had pursued a Greek girl, who took refuge in the house of a widow. The widow met him at the door, and mildly attempted to dissuade him from forcing his way in to seize the girl. Enraged, he drew his saber, but when in the act of attempting to cut down the widow, it snapped in two pieces before it reached the victim. The wretch paused, but drew a pistol to accomplish his purpose in that manner, but it missed fired; and when in the act of drawing a second [pistol], *he was forcibly dragged away* by one of his companions, who exclaimed, "Let her alone! Do you not see that her time is not yet come?"[3]

Thus, it is most instructive to notice in this story, a barbaric officer's humane comrade—a fellow Muslim in need of an argument to accompany his own salutary recourse to force—could usefully draw upon Providence in promoting the dictates of justice.

NOTES

1. "Trogon Resplendens," in John Gould, *A Monograph of the Ramphastidae, or Family of Toucans* (London: Taylor and Francis, 1854) (emphasis added). This book has beautiful illustrations.

It is the privilege of the artist to help us discern, through graphic particulars, that which is universal. See George Anastaplo, *The Artist as Thinker: From Shakespeare to Joyce* (Athens, Ohio: Ohio University Press 1993), p. 144. Whatever interest the typical reader is likely to have in this collection of mine probably depends, for the most part, upon the individual cases themselves or the stories I tell about them, not upon any general statement by me about such cases. Since controversies depend upon *facts* to a considerable extent: one does have to get the facts straight in order to begin to understand the issues in a controversy. A gifted artist can give his audience the impression that the facts are indeed grasped.

2. I hope to do, on other occasions [I could say in 1991], more of the cultivation called for here. See, for bibliographies of my work, George Anastaplo, "Law & Literature and the Moderns: Explorations," 20 *Northern Illinois University Law Review* 251, 581–710 (2000); George Anastaplo, "Constitutionalism, The Rule of Rules: Ex-

plorations," 39 *Brandeis Law Journal* 17, 219–87 (2000–2001). See also appendix C, note 60, appendix D, note 12.

See, on culture and cultivation, Leo Strauss, *Liberalism Ancient and Modern* (New York: Basic Books, 1968), pp. 1f. Compare chapter 12, note 52. See, on nature and natural right (or, as some say, natural law), chapter 6, section V. See also the text at note 16 of chapter 4; at note 62 of chapter 5; at note 94 of chapter 7; at note 26 of chapter 9; and at note 76 of chapter 10 of this collection; introduction, note 3; chapter 1, notes 3, 20, 53, 91, 113; chapter 3 notes 3, 46; chapter 5, notes 33, 67; chapter 7, notes 49, 101; chapter 8, note 60; chapter 10, notes 20, 62; chapter 12, notes 15, 32, 46, 70, 91, 114. See as well George Anastaplo, *The American Moralist: On Law, Ethics, and Government* (Athens, Ohio: Ohio University Press, 1992), pp. 412–16. Compare the caution, by Alexandre Kojève, recorded in chapter 10, note 76. Is there a "natural" movement (a decline?) from Adam and Eve to Doctor Faustus, just as there is from, say, Shylock to O. J. Simpson?

It has been sad to notice how exercised some sophisticated legal scholars can become at the prospect of a single "believer" in "natural law" being added to the United States Supreme Court. See, e.g., Lawrence Tribe, "Clarence Thomas and 'Natural Law,'" *New York Times*, July 15, 1991, p. A15. Compare Michael McConnell, "Trashing Natural Law," *New York Times*, August 16, 1991, p. A13. See, on the limitations of Justice Thomas, George Anastaplo, "'McCarthyism,' the Cold War, and Their Aftermath," 43 *South Dakota Law Review* 103, 138–56 (1998). See, for an instructive introduction to natural right teachings in literature, Catherine H. Zuckert, *Natural Right and the American Imagination: Political Philosophy in Novel Form* (Savage, Md.: Rowman & Littlefield, 1990); Book Review, 47 *Review of Politics* 172 (1993). See also George Anastaplo, *But Not Philosophy: Seven Introductions to Non-Western Thought* (Lanham, Maryland: Lexington Books, Rowman & Littlefield, 2002), p. 303.

3. J. W. Kasey, *The Young Man's Guide to True Greatness* (Big Springs, Kentucky, 1859), p. 95. One can see in this story the combination of persuasion and force evident in the way Athena deals with the Furies in Aeschylus' *Oresteia*. See chapter 2, note 18. Consider also my Letter to the Editor of September 2001:

> Among the innocent victims of the monstrous assaults last month on the World Trade Center and the Pentagon are the multitudes of decent Muslims worldwide who must endure the shame, for years to come, of the shocking abuse of American hospitality by their demented co-religionists, the kind of hospitality that Islam and its Prophet have always cherished. Is it not the duty of prudent Muslims everywhere to remind their peoples of what is truly noble in their great tradition?

See *University of Chicago Maroon*, October 2, 2001, p. 8. See also *Chicago Tribune*, September 21, 2001, sec. 1, p. 20. See as well chapter 8, note 61; chapter 12, note 80; appendix A, note 15.

It is sometimes argued that the laws of nature get their efficacy from God. See, e.g., Kasey, *The Young Man's Guide*, pp. 77–94. If one asks what gives God *His* efficacy, the answer is likely to be that that is just the way He is. That is, it is *His* nature? Should the same be said, therefore, about "the laws of nature" (or even about the nature of matter and its awesome multitude of productive manifestations and combinations)? But do not most people want the guiding principles of the universe to be intelligent as well as intelligible? What does this virtually universal yearning suggest about the nature of things? Consider, for example, the status and role of the ideas in Plato's *Republic*. See George Anastaplo, *The Thinker as Artist: From Homer to Plato & Aristotle* (Athens, Ohio: Ohio University Press, 1997), pp. 303f. Compare Aristophanes, *The Clouds*; Anastaplo, *The Thinker as Artist*, pp. 199f; chapter 5, notes 31, 71, chapter 7, note 44. See also chapter 1, note 101, chapter 8, note 60. See as well the text at note 1 of the Introduction to this collection; chapter 2, note 31; chapter 3, notes 6, 21.

Leo Strauss has suggested that "the only question which ultimately matters" is whether "the Bible or philosophy is right." See chapter 10, note 61. *Is* this so? It may depend partly upon what one takes the Bible, or revelation, to be, and whether any other (that is non-Biblical) revelation is to be taken seriously. Certainly, the Strauss position here depends both upon his extraordinary interest in theoretical pursuits and upon his personal grounding in Judaism. See, e.g., Anastaplo, *The Artist as Thinker*, pp. 249f; George Anastaplo, "Leo Strauss at the University of Chicago," in Kenneth L. Deutsch and John A. Murley, eds., *Leo Strauss, the Straussians, and the American Regime* (Lanham, Md.: Rowman & Littlefield, 1999), pp. 3f; George Anastaplo, "Willmoore Kendall and Leo Strauss," in John A. Murley and John Alvis, eds., *Willmoore Kendall: Maverick of American Conservatives* (Lanham, Md.: Rowman & Littlefield, 2002); George Anastaplo, "Constitutionalism and the Good: Explorations," 70 *Tennessee Law Review* 737, 780, 843 (2003).

What is the significance of the fact that much of revelation has to do with what seem to be quite mundane matters? Consider George Anastaplo, *The Constitutionalist: Notes on the First Amendment* (Dallas: Southern Methodist University Press, 1971), pp. 30–32: "'Twere to consider too curiously, to consider so." See, on the relation between reason and revelation, chapter 1, notes 15, 65; chapter 5, notes 31, 39; chapter 7, notes 49, 101; chapter 10, notes 61, 75; the text at note 36 of chapter 5 of this collection. Should genuine prudence and true inspiration direct one to the same *action* (if not to the same thoughts) in any particular situation? See, e.g., chapter 1, note 65, chapter 8, note 51. Even so, one may have to emphasize different things to different peoples with respect to the same matter. See, e.g., chapter 7, parts A and B. See also Anastaplo, *But Not Philosophy*, *passim* (e.g., pp. 373–74).

See, on the relation of Providence to justice, chapter 1, note 3; chapter 10, note 36; chapter 11, note 19. See also chapter 7, note 101. See as well appendix C, note 65 of this collection.

Appendixes

In re George Anastaplo

The reader might well wonder how an author who reviews notable cases and controversies, fictional as well as actual, might conduct himself in a controversy of his own. One might even hope to see, in that author's case, how issues look "from the inside," so to speak. It can be hard for "the outsider" to be certain about what happened and why in a controversial matter. Nuances and qualifications are apt to be set aside as an attempt is made to get down to the heart of a matter. But may "the insider" not fully grasp what he was really doing—or why he was doing it?

My bar admission litigation began in 1950, before a Committee on Character and Fitness in Chicago. It ended, in 1961, when the United States Supreme Court ruled against my effort to have my exclusion from the Illinois bar reversed. Thereupon I announced my "retirement" from the practice of law.

Contrasting assessments of my controversy were offered by the leaders of the contending factions in my 5 to 4 decision in the United States Supreme Court. (See 366 U.S. 82 [1961].) These differences are suggested in an article about Supreme Court proceedings published in the *Washington Post*, April 25, 1961.

That front-page article, by James E. Clayton ("Court Deeply Divided on Controversial Cases") introduced my own case in this way:

> The first indication that [the] tempers [of the justices] were frayed came when Justice John M. Harlan announced the Court's decision to affirm Illinois' refusal to license George Anastaplo to practice law.
>
> Justice Hugo L. Black, who led the dissenters in that five to four decision, said Anastaplo's troubles came because he "made the mistake of saying he believed

fully in the Declaration of Independence." Anastaplo first got in trouble with the Illinois courts because he insisted he believes in a theoretical right of revolution.

When Justice Black finished, Justice Harlan said, "It is clear from the opinion of the Illinois Supreme Court that he was denied admission not because he believes in the Declaration of Independence but because he refused to answer questions about his Communist Party membership."

Further on, in this *Washington Post* article, long-standing differences between these two justices were developed:

In three cases involving the power of a state to bar a man from practicing law, Justice Black attacked what has become known as the Court majority's "balancing test."

This is the test which the Court has adopted when it confronts a claim that a governmental power conflicts with an individual right. Five Justices, led by [Felix] Frankfurter, approve the test. Four, led by Black, oppose it.

Justice Harlan defended it yesterday [April 24, 1961], saying that when the Court faces a claim of a violation of free speech, it must weigh the claim against the governmental interest involved.

In the cases of the lawyers, he said, the Government's interest in having lawyers devoted to the law are "clearly sufficient" to outweigh any effect on freedom of speech or association which might be abridged when a man is asked if he has belonged to the Communist Party.

Justice Black, who contends the First Amendment guarantees are absolute, said the cases take their place in an "ever-lengthening" line in which individual liberty is abridged "in a manner precisely contrary to the explicit commands of the First Amendment."

One of the cases decided involved Raphael Konigsberg of California. There was some evidence in the record that he had once joined the Communist Party. The other involved George Anastaplo of Chicago about whom there is nothing but favorable reports in the record. Both refuse to answer on principle.

The third lawyer case involved the refusal of Albert Martin Cohen of Brooklyn to answer questions about ambulance chasing on the grounds of self-incrimination. The Court said he could be disbarred because he blocked the inquiry. The dissenters said the same principle applied as in the other two cases.

(The dissenters did not add an observation suggested by this array of bar-related cases: Mr. Cohen was unfortunate to have had his garden-variety disciplinary dispute decided along with our much more highly publicized issues.)

The Harlan-Black assessments were judicial responses "from the outside" to my controversy. An insider's views, provided by me at different times, sketch my impressions of the same matter in varying circumstances. I suggest in the preface to this book how the four accounts collected in these appendixes can be said to suggest Aristotle's "Four Causes": the Material Cause, the Efficient Cause, the Formal Cause, and the Final Cause.

The first of these accounts, the 1987 talk found in appendix A, was given a quarter century after my litigation ended. An attempt is made to suggest the background of opinion and controversy, including Cold War passions, against which my case developed. The following three appendixes (B, C, and D) collect talks given by me in 2001 to 2003, almost two decades after the 1987 talk. My bar admission case is returned to again and again in these four talks as I look at different aspects of the matter.

My bar admission case may itself still be of some interest. Certainly, all this has affected substantially my academic, as well as on my legal, career down to this day. Perhaps even more important, on this occasion, is what is suggested in these appendixes about the temperament and perspective of an author who discusses the matters reviewed in this book.

Many have long been convinced that I have been remarkably, if not even improperly, imprudent all my life, at least since my Army Air Corps days. In recent years however, more and more people (but still a minority?) have suspected that I may have really been rather prudent all along, especially as our Cold War, if not even our imperialistic, follies have become more apparent. Certainly, it is a study of prudence to which many, if not all, of the "situations" reviewed in this book are devoted.[1]

NOTE

1. An essay by Abner J. Mikva in a Chicago newspaper usefully supplements my introduction to the four appendixes that follow in this book. This essay, by the exemplary public servant who provides the foreword for this book, anticipated a talk I gave at the Hyde Park Historical Society of Chicago, November 16, 2003, "If You're as Good as You Look, Why Aren't You a University of Chicago Professor?" (http://hydeparkhistory.org) The text of Judge Mikva's essay, "Anastaplo: A Teacher Who Never Stopped Learning," *Hyde Park Herald*, Chicago, Illinois, November 12, 2003, p. 4, follows:

George Anastaplo has been described as an iconoclast, and the description covers part of his makeup. He does not like idols—especially false ones—and he does not like to follow the crowd if there is no reason to. When the new dean of our law school decided in 1950 that it would be a good idea for students to start getting used to wearing the lawyer's uniform, he suggested that a coat, if not a coat and tie, would be the acceptable garb. Most of us took the suggestion—at least most of the time. Not George. He continued to wear a sweatshirt or sport shirt as he had always done. He wasn't defiant; he just could not see any reason to change his style.

He ended up first in his class, not because he was the most competitive, but because he was the smartest. He liked the pedagogy of the time, and he has always thought that educating and being educated are what people do with their brainpower. His interests and intellectual appetites are enormous. He has written books and articles analyzing the influence of Greek literature on American politics, on the Thinker as Artist, and the Artist as Thinker, on the O. J. Simpson trial, on lights at Wrigley Field, on McCarthyism, on hate speech, on lawyers, on judges, on the Bible, on ethics, on Abraham Lincoln, on the remodeling of Soldier Field, and I have only touched the surface of his eclecticism.

He received his Ph.D. from the University of Chicago more than a decade after he finished law school. It confirmed his commitment to teaching rather than to practicing all of the arts that he has learned. He has taught constitutional law, history, political science, literature, ethics. He has interests, and he will teach. But unlike some teachers who have been at it as long as he has, he has never lost his interest in learning. You can see him at public lectures, at seminars, even at political rallies. (Although I had difficulty in getting him to take on a precinct when I ran in Hyde Park.) He was kicked out of the Soviet Union in 1960 and the Greece that was run by the dictatorship of the Colonels in1970. I thought he went overboard on literalism when he opposed Richard Nixon's impeachment because the Congress could not establish the necessary "high crimes and misdemeanors." But it serves as one more example that George Anastaplo has not limited himself to ivy towers.

He stood up for principle when he challenged the Illinois bar authorities in the 1950s and 1960s—not because he was (or is) pugnacious, but because it was important to him not to trade those principles for a license to practice law. The practice of law has been the poorer for it, but education and scholarship have been the richer.

Len Despres, everybody's alderman, called George Anastaplo the Socrates of Chicago. Fortunately the local hemlock has not been as lethal and George Anastaplo remains a live and vital thinker and activist right here in Hyde Park.

Appendix A

Subversion, Then and Now (1987)[1]

I went into a theatre as sober as could be,
They gave a drunk civilian room, but 'adn't none for me;
They sent me to the gallery or round the music-'alls,
But when it comes to fightin', Lord! They'll shove me in the stalls!
  For it's Tommy this, an' Tommy that, an' "Tommy, wait outside";
  But it's "Special train for Atkins" when the trooper's on the tide,
  The troopship's on the tide, my boys, the troopship's on the tide,
  O it's "Special train for Atkins" when the trooper's on the tide.

—Rudyard Kipling

I.

Who were the Americans that were feared and hunted down as subversives in the 1950s? It was easy to see them as agents of Joseph Stalin, a man responsible for great evils. Many in this country were intimidated by the threat of Stalinism, especially after the shackling of Czechoslovakia in 1948. The threat posed by the Russians to the United States after World War II seemed even worse because it confronted here a people who had endured one crisis after another since 1929, if not since 1914. It had seemed, at last, that Americans could relax after their deprivations during the Great Depression and their sacrifices during the war. It took some time, after 1945, for us to get used to living in a world in which the Russian menace had unexpectedly become so critical.

Even so, Americans had few domestic Stalinists whom they could know well enough either to like or to dislike. American Communist Party members were hard to get to know at all in the late 1940s and early 1950s. One did not go around asking one's acquaintances whether they were Communists. (A decade or two earlier Communist Party membership had evidently been less of a disability and hence was more open.) I do not recall ever having personally met anyone in those days that I could be sure was a Communist Party member at the time that I knew him.

There was, however, one known Communist Party member whose public career left me somewhat sympathetic to him, in human terms. That was Robert G. Thompson, one of the Communist Party leaders who was convicted in 1949 under the Smith Act. He went into hiding for a few years in order to escape the imprisonment he was eventually subjected to. What made his career rather sad was that he had distinguished himself in the Army during World War II, having been awarded the Distinguished Service Cross for his heroism. I did not believe then, nor do I believe now, that the activities he was charged with by our government outweighed his gallantry as a patriot during the war. He should never have been required to serve time in prison, whatever his political folly may have been.[2]

II.

I knew about the Thompson career only what I had read in the press.[3] I believe it can be instructive, in order better to assess what did and did not happen in the 1950s, to recall for you a Chicago Leftist I did chance to know personally, a somewhat politically harassed man who died two months ago [in 1987] in his late sixties, Charles G. Bloom. He, too, was a patriot, a man who had, as a navigator with the Eighth Air Force in England, flown two full tours of bombing missions over German-occupied Europe during World War II. I believe he was decorated for his tours of duty, but these were not matters he ever talked much about in my presence.

Chuck Bloom became a loving father and a good husband, however difficult to live with he may have been at times. He was rather shy, despite his bluff manner and tough talk about the class struggle and the impending revolution. All this was consistent with his marrying off a daughter in fine style a few years ago at the South Shore Country Club, which was by then being run by the Chicago Park District.

He earned his living as an English teacher in one of Chicago's junior colleges. Earlier he had worked on the railroad. His union membership was something he reveled in, not least because of his New York state upbringing in the wealthy family he was chronically rebelling against.

His principal political activity, so far as I personally knew, was in local politics. He worked hard for Democratic Party candidates for the Chicago City Council and for the Illinois General Assembly. He could be counted upon to put in long hours as a volunteer in keeping Chicago organizations such as the Hyde Park Coop Supermarket and the Hyde Park Neighborhood Services Club socially useful.

Perhaps most of all he yearned for the just treatment of racial and other minorities and of the poor. All in all, I remember him as a civic-minded man who served conscientiously wherever he recognized a call from the community.

III.

Much of Mr. Bloom's local community service was during the last two to three decades. Our earlier encounters featured arguments during parties in his apartment, going back to the late 1940s on the University of Chicago campus, in which the respective merits of the United States and of the Soviet Union were debated. These were the kind of arguments—for hours at a time into the early hours of the morning—that only graduate students have either the time or the passion for. One sometimes felt trapped by such engagements; and, of course, they could become dull. But since I often found myself virtually the only one among the guests defending the American regime, this kind of challenge could also be very instructive, especially as one was obliged to collect reports and data of one's own in order to counter those offered by intelligent opponents.

It was only in one sense that it should be said that I was the only one among us defending the American regime—for the others were doing so also, but much more in terms of what it had once been or (even more likely) in terms of what it promised to be. Besides, various of my opponents in those late-night arguments had indirectly, if not directly, endured mistreatment, such as the vicious abuse of Jews, that I had not, mistreatment that had embittered them or at least had made them particularly sensitive to flaws in the American regime. This kind of experience, or response to such experience, is reflected in the record made in the bar admission controversy of Raphael Konigsberg in California.[4]

Be that as it may, the "militant" leftists I have personally known have tended to be idealists and even romantics. Sometimes that kept them from noticing obvious truths, including the truth about ugly regimes around the world, even as it made them unduly critical of the American regime that had nurtured them and that had continued, in its way, to inspire them. Still, they could be understood as dreamers who yearned for the fulfillment of American aspirations.

A key question during our extended debates in the Bloom apartment was about how Stalin was to be understood. The deaths of hundreds of thousands, if not even millions, of Russians at his hands, or at least because of his policies, could be cavalierly overlooked. Much could be made instead both of the vital "Great Patriotic War" against the horrible Nazi menace and of the supposedly color-blind ethnic policies of the Soviet Union.

At times, in my defense of the United States, I no doubt refused to acknowledge American defects that my opponents, who were not unintelligent, could point out. Much more could have been made than we as young people were inclined to make of the economic systems of the United States and of the Soviet Union, and of how a market economy can contribute to political freedom.[5]

One thing I did insist upon was the much greater political freedom in the United States, as exemplified by our ability to discuss these issues as openly as we did. This repeated insistence on my part led one night to a challenge from Chuck Bloom: "Do you believe the country to be so free that you would dare subscribe to the *Daily Worker*?" If I thought so, he added, he would pay for the subscription. I forget now how many months were offered me, but probably no more than a year. I accepted his challenge, adding (with the bravado of youth) that I would not only take whatever he gave me but that I would also write to the Director of the Federal Bureau of Investigation to inform him that I had become a subscriber. I remember little about the *Daily Worker* during my months as a subscriber. After the subscription ran out, I would see it from time to time in libraries. Nor do I remember whether I received an acknowledgment from the F.B.I. (I do recall that my letter to the Director turned up as an item in the rather tame F.B.I. file on me that I inspected decades later by invoking the Freedom of Information Act.)

It must have eventually become evident to both Chuck Bloom and me that neither one of us was going to convert the other—and so we tacitly agreed to differ. Whenever we talked about political matters during the last two to three decades of his life, it would be about local politics and what he was doing in immediately practical ways to organize this or that precinct and to get out the vote in favor of candidates who supported racial brotherhood and welfare programs.

I do not know what influence I ever had on Chuck Bloom. My arguments may have obliged him to consider his own more carefully—and my bar admission difficulties did win a certain respect from him, although I do not now recall ever discussing it with him.[6] Perhaps, indeed, my response to the inquisitorial character committee of the Illinois bar was in part influenced by our long arguments as students: I was again insisting upon the virtues of the American regime. That is, I continued to act as one does who lives in a free country.

IV.

This "ancient history" was recently dramatized for me [I could say in 1987] by a meeting with Morton Sobell, the man sentenced to thirty years imprisonment upon being convicted as a codefendant with Ethel and Julius Rosenberg in 1951.[7] I introduced myself to him after a lecture appearance he made on the University of Chicago campus last month. He remembered that I had worked on a brief prepared by one of his lawyers, Stephen Love, who had asked me in 1954 to help him try to get Mr. Sobell out of Alcatraz, where he had been vindictively exiled by the Bureau of Prisons. Mr. Sobell remembers my efforts now more kindly than he had responded to them then—for I had heard that he had not been pleased by the line of argument I had developed in my memorandum, which had appealed to the good faith and the professional integrity of the Bureau of Prisons personnel.[8] (There was not then the case law to support the administrative law review that might be available in comparable circumstances today.) Also, he associated me with Malcolm Sharp, of the University of Chicago Law School, whose efforts on his behalf he remembered fondly.[9]

I invited Mr. Sobell to breakfast in our home on October 10, 1987, which I believe was the following morning. It was a long and lively conversation, which I rather enjoyed (as did, I believe, my wife). It is remarkable how "American" and good-natured this convicted Soviet spy is. One would expect someone who has protested his innocence for three decades to be embittered, if he was innocent, or to be devious, if guilty, neither of which does he appear to be.

Whatever Mr. Sobell had been guilty of, it had clearly been done for "ideological" reasons. Certainly, he is appalled by what is happening in contemporary espionage, as we learn from periodic exposures of Americans who are willing (even eager) to betray their country merely for money, with no pretense of any cause being served by them.

The willingness of Americans to spy for money reflects, for Mr. Sobell as for me, a general corruption. Consider the Navy communications expert who has betrayed his country *by selling* military secrets to the Russians.[10] He engaged in seventeen years of profitable (and even tax-free!) espionage, initiated by himself, evidently recruiting members of his family for his enterprise.[11]

I found Mr. Sobell to be a decent man, however ingenuous he can be when he deals with political things. In fact, I suspect it was his ingenuousness that got him mixed up in the early 1940s with people who were so vulnerable to charges of subversion, if not also of espionage. It should be noticed that serious spies have always, or so it is said, steered clear in this country of identification with the Communist Party. And, I recall, the American Communist Party was very much disturbed initially by the Rosenberg-Sobell indictments, not wanting to be publicly associated with such deadly business. This contributed to the lack of availability of experienced criminal defense counsel for these defendants, although (Mr. Sobell told me) some of the regular counsel for the Communist Party did offer the Rosenbergs and him help behind the scenes.

A change in times is reflected in the fact that such a relaxed conversation could be carried on by my wife and me with someone with Mr. Sobell's record, and carried on with no efforts at concealment. The considerable change is reflected also in the fact that a respectable law journal such as the *DePaul Law Review* could devote as much of a recent issue as it did to a collection of documents related to my bar admission case.[12]

This is to be contrasted to the suppression in 1951 of an article of mine about my bar admission case at the insistence of the dean and a leading professor of the University of Chicago Law School (from which I had recently graduated), an article that had been commissioned and accepted for publication by the *University of Chicago Law Review*.[13]

Those were the days also when almost all of my classmates, understandably enough, ran for cover when my bar admission troubles began in 1950. But then, all too many law school professors and established members of the bar were doing the same.

V.

But however improved the climate of opinion is in critical respects, a troubling deterioration may be seen in that pervasive materialism of which one particularly ugly manifestation *is* the espionage that is carried on solely for personal gain.

Still, the conduct of my character committee very much depended upon its taking material considerations seriously. For one thing, the committee discouraged any dedication to principles on the part of applicants for admission to the bar. It in effect said to such applicants, "If you insist upon standing by principles, we will deprive you of your livelihood as a lawyer."[14] This approach does teach that principles should be sacrificed to personal interest, that the common good should be sacrificed to mere self-preservation and individual aggrandizement.

Young people notice such lessons and conduct themselves accordingly, either by knuckling under with a view to calculated self-interest or by mindlessly resisting all authority, legitimate as well as illegitimate.

The ascendancy of a deference to self-interest may also be seen in the current respectability of a jurisprudential approach that makes much—I believe too much—of the marketplace in the development, understanding, and application of legal principles.

VI.

The extent of the political and moral consequences of Cold War suppression in the United States has yet to be generally appreciated. There can no longer be any question about the enormity of the crimes of Stalin—but it remains to be seen whose efforts, Stalin's or those of the much milder American repressors, did more harm to the United States itself.

Our sacrifices in Korea, and even more (and to far less good effect) in Vietnam, were in large part due to the crippling in the United States of free and full discussion of vital public issues, discussion that might have helped us to see better what truly threatened this country. Certainly, this country is healthier when it faces up honestly to what is wrong, as well as to what is right, about it. The true subversives among us were those Americans who discouraged their fellow citizens from serious political discussion, all in the name of hunting down subversives.

Be that as it may, Communist Party spokesmen were driven out of American public life in the late 1940s and early 1950s—and they have still to return in an open and direct form. And yet they do have a significant set of opinions that should be taken seriously in the modern world, however discredited they may be in most places. Such opinions need to be put in forms that only Americans are likely to be able to present them for proper assessment by the American people.[15]

VII.

I return now to Chuck Bloom. Perhaps I never saw him clearly—but if so, that may be because I could never forget how we first met on an air base in California. He had recently come in, as a First Lieutenant, from his service in Britain and I from flying around (also as a navigator) over the Pacific.

He was drawn to me, he often reported for decades thereafter, because he saw me sitting at the bar in the officers' club drinking a glass of milk and reading *Alice in Wonderland*. Even then, Lt. Bloom was open to good literature, which reflected what was best in him. We had good conversations out there, mostly about books, with little if anything at all said about politics.

I believe I had decided, before we met, that I would like to attend the University of Chicago upon returning to civilian life. I do not know whether I had any influence on his decision to go to school there also. I recall no further contact, after our few days in California, until we looked up each other on the Chicago campus where Mr. Bloom drifted toward a radical political position.

I am not sure how that happened. I suspect that his troubled domestic relations of that period, rooted perhaps in his upbringing, had something to do with his willingness to assert himself by running risks. (A sense of superiority could even be sought as the noble champion of obvious underdogs.) His second marriage was a steadier partnership, evidently providing him more personal security than he had ever known before. By then, also, he was a middle-aged man, and much of the wildness of his youth had been tamed.

Chuck Bloom could always be impressed by those who read good books— and good books were not limited for him by any Marxist categorization. I suspect that he would have done better with the books he respected if the almost obsessively rigorous English Department of his day at the University of Chicago had been more humane than it was.

Even so, his respect for art meant that he recognized that there *were* standards of the beautiful and the good to be guided by. A sensible approach to things was thereby encouraged, whatever his political ideology may have tried to teach him.

Chuck Bloom's openness to art finally found expression in photography, which proved in some ways a more productive, perhaps also a safer, form of expression for him than either philosophy or politics had been. He earned a reputation as a photographer, so much so that he could be called upon regularly by the local press. I prize a *Hyde Park Herald* portrait he did of me in front of the large "St George and the Dragon" painting that hangs over the mantel in our living room.[16]

This then, is my tribute to a fellow aviator, a patriot who loved his country deeply despite both his and his country's failure to understand what he meant and why.[17]

NOTES

1. This talk was given in a Constitutional Law seminar conducted by Professor Rodney Blackman at the DePaul University College of Law, Chicago, Illinois, No-

vember 4, 1987. See also "Subversion and Legislative Investigations," in George Anastaplo, "Freedom of Speech and the First Amendment: Explorations," 21 *Texas Tech Law Review* 1941, 1975 (1990). See, for the original publication of this 1987 talk ("Subversion, Then and Now"), 21 *Texas Tech Law Review* 2041–51 (1990).

The epigraph is taken from Rudyard Kipling's "Tommy." See *Collected Verse of Rudyard Kipling* (London: Hodder & Stoughton, 1910), p . 277. See also George Anastaplo, "What Is Still Wrong with George Anastaplo? A Sequel to 366 U.S. 82 (1961)," 35 *DePaul Law Review* 551, 628–29 (1986). See as well appendixes B, C, and D.

2. The 1949 Smith Act convictions were confirmed in *Dennis* v. *United States*, 341 U. S. 494 (1951). I could write in 1965, "It was sad to observe recently the public reaction to the sentimental request of Robert G. Thompson—aWorld War II hero (Distinguished Service Cross) who was subsequently imprisoned under the Smith Act as a Communist Party leader—the request that he be buried in Arlington Military Cemetery. Much of our patriotism these days is characterized by a lack of grace and of generosity, to say nothing of gratitude." George Anastaplo, *Human Being and Citizen: Essays on Virtue, Freedom, and the Common Good* (Chicago: Swallow Press, 1975), p. 266 n. 20. See Anastaplo, "Freedom of Speech and the First Amendment," pp. 2065–73. See also chapter 12, note 8 (on Hermann Goering's concern about his reputation as an honorable World War I aviator).

A happier career than Mr. Thompson's was enjoyed by Harry Bridges, the Leftist leader of the International Longshoreman's and Warehouseman's Union, after he avoided deportation in the 1940s as a subversive. See *Schneiderman* v. *United States*, 320 U.S. 118 (1943). Thus, a top management official eventually praised this notorious labor union leader in these terms: "He was the single most powerful and most stabilizing influence in the West Coast maritime industry, and you cannot say enough to honor this man who has never, never broken his word." Harry Bernstein, "Marxist Harry Bridges, 88, Led Longshoremen's Union," *Chicago Sun-Times*, March 31, 1990, p. 36. See also Wolfgang Saxon, "Harry Bridges, Docks Leader, Dies at 88," *New York Times*, March 31, 1990, p. 11. See, on Cephalus and justice, Plato, *Republic*, bk. I.

3. See, for a poignant note about the sacrifices by American Leftists in the Spanish Civil War, Harry Kalven Jr., *A Worthy Tradition: Freedom of Speech in America* (New York: Harper & Row, 1988), p. 295.

4. See *Konigsberg* v. *State Bar of California*, 366 U.S. 36 (1961). See also Anastaplo, *Human Being and Citizen*, p. 261 n. 6. See as well Anastaplo, *Human Being and Citizen*, p. 105; appendix B, note 6.

5. See, e.g., Milton Friedman, "Political Freedom Depends Upon Economic Freedom," in George Anastaplo, ed., *Liberty, Equality & Modern Constitutionalism: A Source Book* (Newburyport, Massachusetts: R. Pullins Co./Focus Publishing, 1999), II, 138. See also I, xiii.

6. One can never anticipate the influence one may have in such matters. See, e.g., Anastaplo, *Human Being and Citizen*, pp. 109–110.

See, on my bar admission case, *In re George Anastaplo*, 366 U.S. 82 (1961). See also Anastaplo, "Freedom of Speech and the First Amendment," pp. 2071–81; appendixes B and C.

I should note "for the record" that the only covert activity that I personally ever knew Chuck Bloom to engage in was when he spent most of a winter day helping me move into "veterans' housing" on the University of Chicago campus. He and I did this while my wife, who was then midway in her first pregnancy, was downtown for the day, unaware that a long-awaited student-housing apartment had become available for us. He took a childlike delight in anticipating how surprised and relieved she would be upon discovering what had been done without her having had to lift a finger. (This must have been in late 1949 or early 1950.)

7. See *Rosenberg v. United States,* 346 U.S. 273 (1953). See also George Anastaplo, *The Constitutionalist: Notes on the First Amendment* (Dallas: Southern Methodist University Press, 1971); George Anastaplo, "The Occasions of Freedom of Speech," 5 *Political Science Reviewer* 390–94 (1975); Anastaplo, "Freedom of Speech and the First Amendment," p. 2002.

8. Stephen Love, a prominent Roman Catholic layman in Chicago, had been the only member of the seventeen-member Committee on Character and Fitness to support my original application for admission to the Illinois bar in 1951. (The vote against me in a 1954 rehearing was 11–6.) See appendix A, note 6. The report I prepared in 1954 for Mr. Love was entitled, "Memorandum with Respect to the Imprisonment of Morton Sobell on Alcatraz." See chapter 12, note 108.

9. See, on Mr. Sharp, George Anastaplo, "Lessons for the Student of Law: The Oklahoma Lectures," 20 *Oklahoma City University Law Review* 19, 133 (1995); chapter 12, note 98. See, for the best discussion I know of the *Rosenberg-Sobell Case*, Malcolm P. Sharp, *Was Justice Done?* (New York: Monthly Review Press, 1956). See also appendix C, note 57, and the text at note 22 of appendix B and at note 8 of appendix D.

I now have the impression [I could say in 1990] that I might have met Mr. Sobell once before; that is, we may have been on a Chicago television discussion program together with two or three others, perhaps in the course of a book promotion tour by him some years before. If so, we did not see anything more than that of each other on that occasion, so far as I now recall. [That earlier television occasion was in 1974.]

I did hear from Mr. Sobell in 2002, after many years of no contact. He wondered whether I might be of help with a study he wanted to make of various papers in the Rosenberg-Sobell litigation of the 1950s and thereafter, a study related to recently renewed interest in that matter. I suggested that he try to enlist the help of law professors in the places where the papers are stored, professors who might have students interested in working on such a project.

10. See, e.g., Christopher Lehmann-Haupt, Book Review, *New York Times,* October 8, 1987, p. 24; Smith, Book Review, *Chicago Sun-Times Book Week*, p. 17; Wood, "Spy Drama Compelling," *Christian Science Monitor*, February 2, 1990, pp. 10–11. Compare George Anastaplo, "Clausewitz and Intelligence: Some Preliminary Observations," *Teaching Political Science: Politics in Perspective*, vol. 16, p. 77 (1989); William Safire, "Spies of the Future," *New York Times*, March 16, 1990, sec. 5, p. 15. See, on Socrates' warnings about money-making, Anastaplo, "Freedom of Speech and the First Amendment," pp. 1957–58.

11. Consider also the sales of military secrets by French and Japanese officers to the Soviet Union. See Engelberg, "Jury Hears Tale of Spy Who Did It Out of Greed,"

New York Times, July 19, 1989, p. 7. See also Wines, "Spy Reported in Soviet Hands was a Top Agent, U.S. Says," *New York Times*, January 16, 1990, p. 10.

There have recently been imprisoned, in this country, additional trusted employees of the United States government (including an agent of the Federal Bureau of Investigation) who evidently made considerable money spying for the Soviet Union for years, even contributing thereby (it seems) to the deaths of American agents in Eastern Europe. One's reservations about capital punishment are put to a severe test upon encountering such cynical wickedness. See, on capital punishment generally, George Anastaplo, *The American Moralist: On Law, Ethics, and Government* (Athens, Ohio: Ohio University Press, 1992), p. 422.

12. See George Anastaplo, "What Is Still Wrong with George Anastaplo? A Sequel to 366 U.S. 82 (1961)," 35 *DePaul Law Review* 551–647 (1986).

13. See Anastaplo, "What Is Still Wrong with George Anastaplo?," pp. 602–07. See also "Edward Hirsch Levi (1911–2000)," in George Anastaplo, "Legal Education, Economics, and Law School Governance: Explorations," 46 *South Dakota Law Review* 102, 304 (2001). See as well chapter 8, note 14, appendix D, section II.

14. See Ralph S. Brown, Jr. and John D. Fassett, "Loyalty Tests for Admission to the Bar," 20 *University of Chicago Law Review* 480 (1953). See, for an instructive interview a decade ago with the leader of the American Communist Party, "New Climate for Communism in USA," *USA Today*, March 5, 1990, sec. A, p. 7. See also "An Advance for American Free Speech," *New York Times*, February 6, 1990, sec. A, p. 16; "Time to Bury a Red Scare Relic," *Chicago Tribune*, February 3, 1990, sec. 1, p. 10 (editorials supporting repeal of a provision of the McCarran-Walter Immigration Act of 1952).

15. Consider a recollection by Lloyd Barenblatt (of the *Barenblatt Case*, 360 U.S. 109 [1959]): "The Communist Party at that time [in the late 1940s and the 1950s] served as a familial and emotional support system for many people, for good or bad." Peter Irons, *The Courage of Their Convictions: Sixteen Americans Who Fought Their Way to the Supreme Court* (1988), p. 99. My review of the Irons book may be found in, George Anastaplo, "On Trial: Explorations," 22 *Loyola University Chicago Law Journal* 765, 1022 (1991).

Now, a half century later, the overriding fear among us seems to be of "terrorism." A proper discussion of this threat (whatever it may mean) should help us develop sensible notions about how to respond to it. The excessive security measures resorted to recently (anticipated by how the president's plane was handled on September 11, 2001) should make us wonder how many "demented Arabs" we really believe are "out there." In the long run, our best security is grounded in the promotion of a sound moral order worldwide. See, e.g., chapter 8, note 61, conclusion, note 3. See also chapter 12, note 6. See as well appendix D, note 32.

Consider, in this connection, two of my Letters to the Editor after the September 11 assaults. The first Letter, in September–October 2001, is reprinted in note 3 of the conclusion. The second letter, of January 24, 2002, reads:

It can be dismaying to learn that many "informed" Arabs insist that the September 11 attacks were really the work of the C.I.A., or of the Israelis, or of anyone else they happen to hate. (Thomas Friedman column, *New York Times*, January 23, 2002) There is, however, a heartening aspect to such absurd accusations, for they do recognize that such attacks are monstrous and hence to be repudiated. Thus, Arabs everywhere can be understood to consider themselves morally, as well as politically, obliged to condemn the perpetrators of the September 11 attacks, whoever they may be.

See *Chicago Weekly News* (The University of Chicago), January 31, 2002, p. 13. See also George Anastaplo, Letter to the Editor, *Chicago Tribune*, June 22, 2003, sec. 2, p. 10. See as well chapter 8, note 61; chapter 10, note 78; chapter 12, note 76.

16. See Anastaplo, "What's Still Wrong with George Anastaplo," pp. 643–45 (incorporating Judith Colp, "Anastaplo Still Has More Dragons to Kill," *Hyde Park Herald*, Chicago, Illinois, December 7, 1983). See, on St. George and his dragon, George Anastaplo, "Law, Education, and Legal Education: Explorations," 37 *Brandeis Law Journal* 585, 744 (1998–1999).

17. See, on the Americanization of both the Roman Catholic Church and the American Communist Party, Anastaplo, *The Constitutionalist*, pp. 508–509 n. 31. See, for a discussion of the beguiling proposition that freedom should not be permitted to those who, were they to gain power, would not in turn permit freedom to others, George Anastaplo, *The Constitutionalist*, pp. 109–111. See also Anastaplo, "Freedom of Speech and the First Amendment," pp. 1958–75 ("The Nazi Speaker on the University Campus").

Appendix B

On Representing Oneself (2001)[1]

[Neither] this Statute, nor no other Law in the World can punish any Man for his Silence, seeing they can do no more than punish Words or Deeds; 'tis God only that is the Judge of the Secrets of our Hearts.

—Sir Thomas More

I.

When I mentioned to the editor of the Law Review a couple of hours ago that I would be speaking about bar admissions to your Dean's Professional Responsibility class, he responded that he regarded my bar admission case as an "epic."[2] "What particularly interests you about it?" I asked. "That you argued it *pro se*," he answered. So, let me say a little about that, cautioning you as I do so that much of what may be said here can be debated.

The decision to handle the case entirely on my own was one of the three best decisions I made in the course of that decade of litigation (from 1950 to 1961).[3]

The first of these was my decision not to acquiesce to the hazing, if not the bullying, that members of the Character and Fitness Committee in Chicago would indulge in from time to time. That hazing seemed to me to reinforce, in the 1950s, the prevailing spirit of repression that I considered harmful to our country. Besides, I had, only a few years before, finished more than three years of service during and after World War II as an aviation cadet and as a flying officer—and I was in no mood to be bullied by men who (because of their age) had probably not served as I had.[4]

The second of my "three best decisions" was to walk away from my bar admission case when the United States Supreme Court finally decided against me in 1961, five to four, leaving me without a license but with a marvelous dissenting opinion by Justice Hugo Black.[5] Retiring from the practice of law as I did in 1961 freed me up for other pursuits that I could develop without the distractions of continued efforts with the bar.[6] This has meant, during the forty years since then, that I have never reapplied for admission to the bar, which some members of the Illinois Supreme Court are said to have indicated that I could have if I did reapply. It has long seemed to me that my own experience with the Illinois bar would remain most interesting, and hence most instructive, if I remained a conspicuous nonmember of that bar. (If, however, the United States Supreme Court should ever consider properly my application for direct admission to *its* bar—which I submitted with my appeal in the 1960–1961 case—then I would be disposed to consider with favor an invitation to join *its* bar.[7])

This brings us to the third of my "best decisions" as an applicant for admission to the bar—the decision early on to handle completely, including to finance completely, my entire bar admission litigation. This meant, among other things, that I could shape the controversy in the best possible way, with a view more to defining the issues properly than to simply winning (which any lawyer of mine would have naturally been much more concerned about).

This self-representation also meant that I learned a lot from the experience, especially since it was considered likely from the outset that I *would* lose in the courts. It turned out that a lawyer acting on my behalf would almost certainly have gotten, in 1961, the same division of the court in Washington as I did, since this was the way a series of "National Security" cases were being decided at that time, including the companion bar admission case from California, which a very good lawyer ran.[8] One observer who recognized, early on, that self-representation, at least in this instance, was a very good idea was Milton Mayer, a Quakerish radical who was close to Robert Maynard Hutchins. He recognized, that is, that this experience would be good for my education.[9]

Defining the issues properly included both shaping the record in the detail I wanted and drafting the petitions and briefs necessary in my two efforts in the Illinois Supreme Court and my two efforts in the United States Supreme Court.[10] One of my best efforts was the brief I prepared in support of my final Petition for Rehearing in the United States Supreme Court. This proved to be a nice transition to the work I would do later in classical literature and political philosophy.[11]

I did learn a good deal about bar admissions, about the now somewhat-obsolete right/privilege distinction, and about the distortions in First Amendment and other law dictated by the national security concerns of the day. I also learned much more than I would ever have learned otherwise about Supreme Court practice, using the standard, and quite helpful, manual of that day.[12] It was gratifying to be able to do all that needed to be done that would get me before the Supreme Court for oral argument in December 1960. This charting of my course reminded me of the navigating I did in the Air Corps. (It was with some regret, years later, that I had to take issue with one of the authors of the Supreme Court practice manual, when there was published an unfortunate article about him and the Rosenberg case.)[13]

II.

The hardest part about the effort to appear before the Supreme Court proved to be the trip *to* Washington. My wife and our children (the oldest, who is now herself a lawyer, was then ten) drove out for the argument—and we had a difficult time, in our Volkswagen Microbus, getting over roads in the West Virginia mountains that were covered by a recent snowstorm. Only after we purchased snow chains were we able to manage. (We had, earlier that year, driven that Microbus for six months and some seventeen thousand miles in a camping trip across Europe.[14])

I allowed my family to watch the argument, but only on condition that they be as unobtrusive as possible, one or two of them slipping in for a few minutes at a time to *see* (not really to hear) what was going on. I was never aware of their presence in the courtroom. (Two of our children, much later, were to attend Justice Black's funeral in Washington Cathedral. He and I had corresponded for several years after the decision in my case.[15])

I had previously argued before the Character and Fitness Committee, of course, which conducted, over the years, dozens of hours of hearing in my matter. I had also appeared, at one stage of these proceedings, before the Illinois Supreme Court, which led in 1954 to a unanimous decision against me. That was the first time around.[16] One consequence of this encounter was the very interesting conversation I had, with the Illinois Supreme Court justice who wrote that 1954 unanimous opinion against me, a conversation that took place when he chanced to enter the taxicab I was driving in downtown Chicago.[17]

In the second round of the appellate process I waived oral argument before the Illinois Supreme Court because I believed it would be advantageous for me to get up to the United States Supreme Court as soon as possible, that Court having refused to take my case the first time around. It is quite a story in itself, told to me and others thereafter by one of the justices of the Illinois Supreme Court and also by his longtime clerk, about how (in 1959) the Illinois Supreme Court decided four to three against me the second time around.[18] Perhaps I might have done better then if I *had* asked for oral argument—but, who knows? Perhaps I look better on paper than in person.

The oral argument in Washington was, of course, dramatic. After all, *pro se* appearances *are* rare in the United States Supreme Court. Justice Black, in his dissent, was gracious enough to commend my oral argument.[19]

What could one see in the court when I appeared before them? Justice Douglas was busy working on his next book (and Robert F. Kennedy, designated that December 1960 as the next Attorney General, attended part of my argument, for he evidently had a lunch date with Justice Douglas that day). Justice Brennan, another of my votes, was also quiet. He wrote a short dissenting opinion in my matter—and he and I, years later, had a nice exchange of letters about one of my few University of Chicago Law School faculty supporters.[20] And the Chief Justice, my fourth vote, was both benign and magisterial as he presided over the court during the oral arguments in the three bar-related cases that stretched over two days.[21]

As for the other five: I do not remember anything about either Justice Stewart or Justice Clark during the argument. Justice Frankfurter was somewhat bad-tempered, but I could not take that personally, considering the way he often conducted himself during oral arguments. Justice Whittaker dozed off during much of the proceedings, afflicted as he was (I believe) by some kind of neurological disorder. And Justice Harlan, who had earlier registered his disapproval of cases such as mine simply glowered throughout my argument—and a few months later he wrote the Opinion for the court in my case (as well as in the two other bar-related cases heard with mine).[22]

III.

The key question at that time was, of course, where one's fifth vote would come from. Justice Stewart was one possibility, because he would shift occasionally. Justice Frankfurter was another, if only because he might be moved to examine a case more carefully that one of his favorite students from his Harvard Law School days had identified himself with.[23] And Justice Clark was still another, if only because he might be moved to look at my matter with interest, if not with sympathy, because I had been a law school classmate of his son (who later became Attorney General, and with whom I have been on good terms over the years). And, in fact, a nun I know, who was then doing research for her doctoral dissertation in the Supreme Court building, reported to me that she had run into Justice Clark in the halls shortly after my oral argument—and that he had had a most benevolent expression on his face. Well, perhaps he did—and if that *was* inspired by me, it evidently wore off once the conference deliberations began. His son and I have never discussed his father's vote. (I did have a very good visit with his son when I arranged for him to speak at the Loyola School of Law early in my tenure on that Chicago faculty.)[24]

Perhaps the most significant thing that could be observed during my oral argument happened (or rather did *not* happen) when the Illinois Assistant Attorney General, representing the Supreme Court of Illinois, was pressed about a fact in the record, a record that he really did not know. In effect, he had to tell the inquiring justice that *I* could be asked about this during my rebuttal— and, he assured the justice, the court would be able to rely upon whatever I said. *That* should have been the moment for someone such as Justice Frankfurter or Justice Clark to have expressed amazement, if not even anger, that the Illinois bar authorities would say *this* about an applicant who, they claimed, they were not *able* to certify for his character because of his refusal to answer all the questions that the committee had been moved to ask him and *only* him. But nothing like this was said—and later, in my oral argument, if I remember correctly, I *was* able to supply the information needed.[25]

A few months later, as I have said, the court decided the case. A *Chicago Tribune* reporter then called me for any comment I might have. I replied that I would try, thereafter, to mind my own business. Whether I have succeeded in doing even *that* can of course be debated.[26]

NOTES

1. This talk was given in a Professional Responsibility course conducted by Professor Barry H. Vickrey at the University of South Dakota School of Law, Vermillion, South Dakota, April 6, 2001.

The Thomas More epigraph is taken from *A Complete Collection of State-Trials and Proceedings for High-Treason, and Other High Crimes and Misdemeanors*, Francis Hargrave, ed. (London: T. Wright, 1776), I; 60. See also chapter 10, note 34; the text at note 25 of appendix B of this collection.

2. See *In re George Anastaplo*, 366 U.S. 82 (1961). See also appendix A above, appendixes C and D below.

3. See, on this bar admission litigation, George Anastaplo, "What Is Still Wrong with George Anastaplo? A Sequel to 366 U.S. 82 (1961)," 35 *DePaul Law Review* 551 (1986); George Anastaplo, "Freedom of Speech and the First Amendment: Explorations," 21 *Texas Tech Law Review* 1941, 2065 (1990).

4. See appendix A, section VII above, appendix C, section II (end) below.

5. See *In re George Anastaplo*, 366 U.S. 82, at 97 (1961); George Anastaplo, *The Constitutionalist; Notes on the First Amendment* (Dallas: Southern Methodist University

Press, 1971), pp. 367–79. See also Roger K. Newman, *Hugo Black: A Biography* (New York: Pantheon Books, 1994) pp. 503f; the text at note 53 of appendix C to this collection. See as well Irving Dilliard, "Mr. Justice Black and *In re Anastaplo*," 9 *Southwestern University Law Review* 953 (1977); George Anastaplo, "Mr. Justice Black, His Generous Common Sense, and the Bar Admission Cases," 9 *Southwestern University Law Review* 977 (1977). See on Irving Dillard, appendix B, note 26 below.

6. See *Konigsberg* v. *State Bar*, 366 U.S. 36 (1961). I contributed, by talking to lawyers in California, to the eventual admission of Mr. Konigsberg to their bar, something for which he very much yearned for years.

7. See, on direct admission to the bar of the United States Supreme Court, *In re Anastaplo*, 366 U.S. 82, 97 n.20 (1961). The use there of "of course" is curious, especially when *Revised* Rules are cited. That is, cannot rules always be further revised in the interest of justice?

8. Raphael Konigsberg was ably represented by Edward Mosk. Mr. Mosk's brother later served on the California Supreme Court.

9. See, for Mr. Mayer's work, chapter 12, note 29 above. See, on his relations with Mr. Hutchins, George Anastaplo, "Legal Education, Economics, and Law School Governance: Explorations," 46 *South Dakota Law Review* 102, 212 (2001).

10. See, for a chronology of developments in my bar admission litigation, Anastaplo, *The Constitutionalist*, pp. 334–35. See also Anastaplo, "What Is Still Wrong With George Anastaplo," p. 588.

11. See Anastaplo, *The Constitutionalist*, pp. 380f. Part of this Petition for Rehearing has been reprinted in John A. Murley, "In re George Anastaplo," in *Leo Strauss, the Straussians, and the American Regime*, Kenneth L. Deutsch and John A. Murley, eds. (Lanham, Md.: Rowman & Littlefield, 1999), pp. 178–79. See also appendix C, note 58 below.

12. See Robert L. Stern and Eugene Gressman, *Supreme Court Practice* (Washington, D.C.: BNA Incorporated, 1954). See the text at note 93 of chapter 12 of this collection. See also chapter 12, note 142 above.

13. See Robert L. Graham, "Landmark Cases: *Rosenberg* Case," *Chicago Lawyer*, June 1979, p. 28; George Anastaplo, "Speed Kills: The *Rosenberg* Case and the Perils of Indignation," *Chicago Lawyer*, July 1979, p. 19 (adapted for use in chapter 12-B above).

14. This trip had included my expulsion from the Soviet Union midway through a two-week visit to that country. A decade later I was expelled from Greece by the colonels who had hijacked the government of that country. See George Anastaplo, *Human Being and Citizen: Essays on Virtue, Freedom, and the Common Good* (Chicago: Swallow Press, 1975), pp. 1–7, 223–33. See also appendix C, notes 16, 64, appendix D, note 33 below.

15. See, on that correspondence, 408 U.S. xxvi–xxviii (1972). See also appendix C, note 33 below. See as well the text at note 3 of appendix D to this collection.

16. See *In re George Anastaplo*, 3 Ill. 2d 471, 121 N.E. 2d 826 (1954).

17. See, for an account of that conversation, Anastaplo, *The Constitutionalist*, pp. 377–440. See also the text at note 44 of appendix C to this collection.

18. The Illinois Supreme Court Justice was George W. Bristow; his longtime clerk was Thelma Brook Simon. See Anastaplo, *The Constitutionalist*, pp. 337, 414–15.

19. See 366 U.S., at 107 (1961).

20. That faculty supporter had been Harry Kalven Jr. See Kalven, *A Worthy Tradition: Freedom of Speech in America* (New York: Harper & Row, 1988), pp. 570–74. See also appendix C, note 53 below. See, on Mr. Kalven, George Anastaplo, "A Little Touch of Harry,"43 *University of Chicago Law Review* 13 (1975).

See, on Justice Brennan's career, chapter 11, note 20 above.

21. See Anastaplo, *The Constitutionalist*, p. 364 (quoting Laurence Berns).

22. I had hoped that the generous spirit of his remarkable grandfather might somehow be revived on this occasion. See Anastaplo, *The Constitutionalist*, p. 824 (the Harlan entries, where "current" might well read "imitation").

23. That student had been Malcolm P. Sharp, one of the few members of my law school faculty to support me. See appendix A, note 9 above. See also the dedication of this book.

24. The nun was Sister Candida Lund. See the text at note 47 of appendix C to this collection. See, for my eulogy of her, George Anastaplo, "Sr. Candida Lund, O.P. '42 (1920–2000)," *Dominican University Magazine*, 15: 18 (Winter 2002). The eulogy includes these observations that bear upon the prudential judgments examined in various chapters in this collection:

> Her establishment of a Jewish Studies Department at Rosary, perhaps the first in a Catholic institution of higher learning in this country, led to another crisis. She called me one evening, as her Chairman of the Political Science Department, for advice in her dealings with the Chairman of the Jewish Studies Department, an observant Jew whom I had been the first to recommend to her. He was, as she would say, "a dear," but there was one exasperating matter she had to share with me. College problems do come up on weekends, she explained, but she could not telephone her Jewish Studies chairman during his Sabbath. And, although she was not normally *this* observant herself, she felt honor-bound to be as observant as *he* was—and so she could not telephone him on *her* Sabbath. Thus the weekend would be lost for the pressing College business at hand. "Sister," I suggested, "you will simply have to call him between sundown on Saturday and midnight [that is, before Sunday begins]." She was enthusiastic about this solution, which led to her inordinate praise of me as a political scientist.

See, e.g., chapters 4 and 10 of this collection.

Ramsey Clark has had occasion to draw on my bar admission controversy in this way:

> As individuals we can find ways to pursue justice, to share justice, to spread justice among people for whom it has been a rare quality. In doing so, we find freedom for ourselves as well. Fear will be the enemy, as it is of every human act that defies cultural norms. I would leave you with Justice Black's admonition from a glorious case we should all remember, *In re Anastaplo*: "We must not be afraid to be free."

Ramsey Clark, "The Lawyer's Duty of Loyalty: To the Client or to the Institution," 16 *Loyola University of Chicago Law Journal* 459, 469 (1985). See, for a discussion of this "glorious case," Ronald K. L. Collins and Sam Chaltain, *We Must Not Be Afraid to Be Free: First Amendment Law Stories* (Oxford University Press, forthcoming), chapter 1.

25. See, on this episode, Anastaplo, *The Constitutionalist*, p. 363. See, on the legal significance of silence, the epigraph for appendix B of this collection. See also chapter 10, note 68 above. appendix D, note 1 below.

26. See *Chicago Tribune*, April 25, 1961, p. 1; Anastaplo, *The Constitutionalist*, p. 417; chapter 10, note 28 above; the text at note 2 of appendix C to this collection. See also appendix D, note 1 below. Compare *Chicago Tribune Magazine*, November 26, 2000 (Cover).

I had occasion to provide, as a dedication to a University of Chicago talk of mine on Euclid, March 7, 2003, the following remarks about the newspaperman cited in note 5 of this appendix, a public servant who was always conscientious in representing himself:

Irving Dilliard (1904–2002)

Good night, sweet prince and flights of angels sing thee to thy rest!

—Horatio

We celebrate, on this occasion, the work of Euclid, an ancient mathematician who taught the Western world how his discipline could be most beautifully and hence most effectively organized. It is fitting, therefore, to invoke here by way of a dedication another venerable figure, a fellow Illinoisan, who died recently at the age of ninety-seven: Irving Dilliard, one of the great journalists of the twentieth century, taught his fellow citizens what is solid and hence lovable in the tradition they have inherited.

It is particularly appropriate to remember Mr. Dilliard here, in the old public library building of Chicago. He was, for many years, on the board of the public library in Collinsville, his hometown. He was a man who had an instinct for associating himself with institutions that would bring out the best in him and through which he (like Euclid) could most effectively serve to elevate others as well as himself.

He, as citizen journalist, graced the editorial pages of the *St. Louis Post-Dispatch* for decades. It was a great newspaper, which, like all great newspapers, stoutly reflected the character (including the "prejudices") of its publisher. The *Tribune* here in Chicago and the *Courier-Journal* in Louisville were other such regional newspapers with considerable national influence. It was the *Post-Dispatch*, which aspired to be "a people's university," that our family read regularly in the southern Illinois town in which I happened to grow up.

Irving Dilliard was old fashioned in his loyalties, just as in his habits. He could also be idiosyncratic, as in his practice of collecting the stationery of the hotels in which he stayed all over the world, stationery that he would use thereafter to "dress up" his personal correspondence. His ability to reach beyond the mundane could also be seen, in a more august form, in the books he put together about distinguished jurists—one on Louis Brandeis, another on Learned Hand, and still another on Hugo Black. It has even been said of him, by a long-serving Justice of the United States Supreme Court, that he was "the finest writer to ever cover" the Court.

Our paths first crossed when he contributed an article on Congressional investigations to a symposium on that subject that I, as a student, had helped organize for the *University of Chicago Law Review*. I believe we met for the first time when he invited me to lunch here in Chicago. I was surprised to learn that the luncheon party in which I found myself was really a meeting of the board of trustees of the University of Illinois, the board on which Mr. Dilliard was then serving. It might even be said that he permitted me (with this luncheon) to share his experience as a board member, just as he permitted many others (with his stationery) to share his experience as a guest in the best hotels.

Mr. Dilliard was quite sophisticated in the ways of the world—and he could lead sustained editorial charges against his own governments in the cause of justice. (He, as a lieutenant colonel, could also be awarded the Bronze Star medal for his military service during the Second World War.) Even so, it is rare to see, in a man as worldly wise as he was, both the show of affection that he could exhibit regularly and the affection he could, in turn, inspire in others.

It may even be said of Irving Dilliard, as perhaps of the great Euclid, that what you saw is what you got, someone who was both sound in his principles and reliable in the application of those principles in a variety of circumstances. He was always asking, in the mode of the thoughtful citizen, "What do we really know about this situation—and what should *we* do about it?"

Appendix C

Chance and the Good Life (2001)[1]

Socrates: We are, by Zeus, on the verge of omitting the greatest of the goods,
Cleinias: What is that?
Socrates: Good fortune, Cleinias, a thing that all men, even the worst fools,
refer to as the greatest of goods.
Cleinias: You are right.

—Plato

PROLOGUE

I have been asked to speak about "my call" as an academician, with an emphasis upon my research and writing. The subjects I investigate have been quite varied, with that variety making it likely that my discussion in print of any particular subject will be different (for better or for worse) from conventional discussions of that subject.[2]

Even more important than *what* I do is, of course, *why* I do it. Still more important, it can be argued, is the question of whether academicians should be encouraged, or even permitted, to work as I have for the past half-century.

The invitation to which I respond here does encourage me to look at my career, thereby giving me an opportunity to come to know myself better by examining what I have done, especially as I attempt to work out the overall sense of what I have been studying and saying. I can hope, that is, to learn something more about myself (and to make appropriate corrections in my life) by preparing this account.

It should soon be evident that my circumstances, from time to time, have very much affected what I have investigated and written about. I have been

inspired, therefore, even to notice the peculiar circumstances of this February 14 meeting. This is, of course, the day "officially" dedicated to love and
lovers—and love, or *Eros*, has long been believed to be critical to the richest life of the mind. But when I say "peculiar" I am moved by the special
meaning for us Chicagoans of St. Valentine's Day. I was only three years
old, and living in St. Louis (where I was born in 1925), when there was carried out, not far from where we are gathered here on the North Side of
Chicago, that "well-planned" operation known as the St. Valentine's Day
Massacre. The date: February 14, 1929; the place: a warehouse at 2122
North Clark Street; the agents of the massacre: five mobsters, disguised as
uniformed and plain-clothes policemen making a routine raid on a bootleg-
ger's delivery station; the targets: the "Bugs" Moran gang, seven of whom
were "arrested" by the "police," easily disarmed, and then riddled by ma-
chine-gun fire on the spot, after which the uniformed "police" with drawn
guns marched off the "plainclothesmen," hands up (or, perhaps, "hand-
cuffed"), to a waiting "police car." It was observed at the time, "Only
Capone kills like that!"[3]

It remains to be seen how our own encounter, on this occasion, should be
characterized. What kind of Valentine's Day greetings are being exchanged,
here on the North Side of Chicago, this time around?

I.

My investigations over the years can be distributed (with some overlapping)
among the topics used for arranging the three-score contributors to a two-
volume Festschrift published in my name in 1992, *Law and Philosophy: The
Practice of Theory*.[4]

These topics, seven in all, were given the following designations by the editors of the Festschrift:

1. Mathematics and the Natural Sciences
2. Political Theory and Political Practice: Ancient
3. Political Theory and Political Practice: Medieval and Modern
4. George Anastaplo: Human Being and Citizen
5. American Politics
6. Constitutional Law
7. Literature, Language, and Poetry

My own efforts, often quite amateur efforts in the fields listed here, have
been recorded in the bibliography included in this Festschrift.[5] That list has

been brought up to date by the bibliography appended to my article, "Law & Literature and the Moderns: Explorations," in the *Northern Illinois University Law Review*.[6] All this has been supplemented by "Tables of Contents for [George Anastaplo's] Books and Published Collections (1950–2001)," a compilation appended to my article, "Constitutionalism, The Rule of Rules: Explorations," in the *Brandeis Law Journal*.[7]

II.

My published books can be organized according to three (somewhat overlapping) categories. This is a different principle of organization from that used by the editors of the *Law and Philosophy* Festschrift.

First, there are the books in which Constitution-related issues are addressed. My interest in these issues, first developed as a student in law school, were deepened by my inability to secure admission to the Illinois bar, after having finished my legal studies in 1950. I can say more about those difficulties later, if that should be desired. It suffices to notice here that the motivation for my First Amendment-based refusal to act in the way demanded of me by the bar admission authorities was both personal and political: I did not believe that the capitulation demanded of me would be good either for the country or for me. My law school dean and teachers (for the most part), as well as the courts, believed otherwise.[8]

My bar admission litigation ended in 1961, by which time I had returned to school with a view to earning a Ph.D. A few years later my University of Chicago dissertation, *Notes on the First Amendment*, was finished.[9] That dissertation was published seven years later as *The Constitutionalist: Notes on the First Amendment*.[10] Had its publisher been able to move promptly to publish my manuscript when it was first accepted, that book would have been less than half of its more than eight-hundred pages. The longer that publication was delayed, the more notes I could prepare for the book. Not a few readers have been rather taken by the scope of those wide-ranging notes, which can still be dipped into here and there with some profit. Now, three decades after its initial publication, this book is scheduled for reissue by another publisher.[11]

Intimately related to *The Constitutionalist* have been two commentaries published by me: *The Constitution of 1787*[12] and *The Amendments to the Constitution*.[13] I did not discover, until after I had almost finished *The Constitution of 1787*, that mine would be the first systematic commentary on the Constitution itself. Other, much more important expositions of the Constitution have been done by others, of course—such treatises as the *Federalist* (which presents an extended, powerfully argued case for the ratification of the Constitution in New York) and such texts as the nineteenth-century-multi-volumed commentary on the Constitution by Joseph Story and the Twentieth Century annotations of the Constitution (all of which depend far more than I do upon judicial and other official interpretations of the Constitution). My two-volume commentary deals, instead, primarily with the text of the Constitution and its Amendments more or less in the sequence of the provisions that we have.

Critical to my bar admission litigation of 1950–1961 was a dispute, in effect, as to the status of the Declaration of Independence and its right of revolution.[14] A faint echo of that Character and Fitness controversy of a half-century ago has been the bizarre "racism" charges I was obliged to refute at our law school here at Loyola in 1995 to 1996. One consequence of this recent controversy was my development and publication of a series of memoranda investigating the temptations and perils of political correctness today, even as I continued to defend recourse in this country to affirmative action programs. Of course, the adverse consequences for me personally this time around have been far less severe—after all, I had nothing at all like academic tenure when I first ran afoul of the Illinois bar. But there *have* been some unfortunate consequences the past few years, which I have been able to describe and, to some extent, counteract. One response is highly likely in such situations, which I have encountered decades apart: if one does not choose to ignore the challenge by which one happens to be confronted, especially when it is believed by one's associates that one could "safely" do so, then one should not expect much if any support, or even sympathy, from colleagues who are otherwise quite decent and well-meaning. There can be about this sort of experience something both instructive and liberating, as well as disappointing.[15]

In any event, it can be added, some people never seem to learn: in between these two exposures of me as a troubling nonconformist, there have been still other challenges that have proved difficult for me to ignore. One of them led to my being expelled from the Soviet Union in 1960; another of them led to my being declared persona non grata by the Greek colonels in 1970. These adventures, along with the difficulties with the Illinois bar that began in 1950, are described in various books and articles of mine.[16]

All of this was preceded by challenges that can be considered to have been decisive in preparing me for the encounter I have more or less happened upon since. One was the near-death experience with diphtheria when I was in the second or third grade; the other was the experiences I had, for more than three years in the United States Army Air Corps during and immediately after World War II, where I learned (as an eighteen-year-old) to fly an airplane before I ever drove an automobile, where I navigated aircraft all over the world, and where I accepted and at times even enjoyed risks that have made the threats posed by subsequent inquisitors (whether of the Right or of the Left) seem rather trivial by comparison, something for which I am truly thankful.

III.

I continue with the categorization of my published books, having begun with those that address Constitution-related issues.

The second category encompasses my books on political matters and on American studies. I make use in those books of my studies in political philosophy, ancient and modern, touching here and there upon the problems of lawyering and judging.

These books include the following: *Human Being and Citizen: Essays on Virtue, Freedom, and the Common Good*;[17] *The American Moralist: On Law, Ethics, and Government*;[18] *Campus Hate-Speech Codes, Natural Right, and Twentieth Century Atrocities*;[19] and, most recently, *Abraham Lincoln: A Constitutional Biography*.[20] Critical to all of these efforts has been the study of *prudence*. (The *American Moralist* book, too, is quite long, running to more than six-hundred pages, but, unlike *The Constitutionalist*, it has only forty notes, one at the head of each of its essays.)

Related to these books are the things I have published on foreign affairs, including a number of articles on the colonels' foolish regime in Greece (between 1967 and 1974) that could well be collected as a book some day. On the fringes of these activities have been the Letters to the Editor that I have produced over the years: these, too, could make a useful book some day, chronicling as they do the series of responses of a busybodyish citizen to the events of his time.[21] The earliest such letter that I recall was to a Greek-American newspaper in New York (I must have been a freshman or sophomore in high school): the merits of the American regime were extolled by me on that occasion, which was about the time that World War II began in Europe.

The books in this second category, on political matters and American studies, have been backed up by a two-volume collection I have put together, *Liberty, Equality & Modern Constitutionalism: A Source Book*.[22] I use these readings in my Jurisprudence course in the law school. These volumes include a number of things not readily available elsewhere, including a remarkable 1774 attack upon slavery by John Wesley, an 1835 proposal by Andrew Jackson for the removal of "the Aboriginal People" "to the country west of the Mississippi river," and a Roman Catholic priest's 1944 moral condemnation of the obliteration bombing of German cities.[23] Father Raymond

Baumhart [formerly president of Loyola University of Chicago] has told me that he remembers this priest, another Jesuit, John C. Ford, as tall, lively, and handsome. Certainly, Father Ford conducted himself handsomely in his article, making arguments that I never heard among those of us who were training, at the same time, for such obliteration bombing, arguments that probably would not have had much effect on us if we *had* heard them. It is hard to overestimate the degree to which the 1941 attack on Pearl Harbor, and earlier attacks on Rotterdam and London, made most of us single-minded in our determination to crush the enemy, so much so that even the Hiroshima and Nagasaki atom bombings were, initially, generally well received among us.[24] In the decades following, however, the authorities in this country squandered, especially in Vietnam, much of the trust that a people naturally, and properly, has in its government.[25]

IV.

My remaining books can be gathered under the category, "General Studies." I draw there upon what I have learned from the political philosophy courses I took at the University of Chicago as well as the courses I have given at Rosary College (now Dominican University), at the University of Dallas, at The Clearing in Door County, Wisconsin, and here at Loyola (including at its Rome Center, the programs at which can be quite good when properly run). Also critical here have been the seminars I have conducted for four decades in the Basic Program of Liberal Education for Adults at the University of Chicago, seminars in which we have discussed again and again many of the greatest texts in the Western tradition.[26] There were also the irregular seminars in political philosophy for University of Chicago graduate students that I chaired for almost a decade.[27]

Much of one's concern in these inquiries is with what is true, good, and beautiful—and how, if at all, these may be served by a proper political order.[28] That prudence that is essential to an understanding of the American regime is further explored in these inquiries. What understanding itself means, and does not mean, has been illuminated for me by the weekly Physics Department Colloquium that I have been attending at the University of Chicago for decades.[29]

My "General Studies" publications include two books, *The Artist as Thinker: From Shakespeare to Joyce*[30] and *The Thinker as Artist: From Homer to Plato & Aristotle*.[31] Along with these has been a collection of mine, "Law & Literature and the Bible: Explorations," in the *Oklahoma City University Law Review*.[32] These inquiries have been reinforced by work I have done on paintings, on operas, and on scientific texts. The scope of my "General Studies" work is suggested by the title of another book, *But Not Philosophy: Seven Introductions to Non-Western Thought.*[33] There, as elsewhere, I presume to offer to the public the investigations of an amateur, a not-uninformed amateur with some practice in the art of reading. Also there, as elsewhere, I clarify and reinforce what I try to say by citing freely to other things I have published, compensating thereby for the obscurity of many of the journals in which I have appeared.

V.

All of the work I have described is part of a long-standing attempt by me to understand the whole of things, even while I try to have a salutary (however limited) effect upon the everyday affairs of the communities in which I happen to find myself.

The role of chance in this development has sometimes seemed central, beginning with an initial inclination (however begun and nourished) to be curious about the things I do happen upon. I have been fortunate in having always been fairly good in all of the subjects offered to schoolchildren from early on. I have also been fortunate in having had very good health and modest appetites for quite a long time. It is not reasonable, however, to expect such good health to continue much longer, no matter how much bicycling I do. (After all, my two brothers, born after me, have already died.)

I have been pretty much on my own in the work I have done, even in preparing my dissertation (which, it happened, was officially accepted before it was either finished or submitted).[34] Precisely what I have studied (and with whom) and what I have written about have been much influenced by chance. I have happened upon interesting things and have looked into them. (A minor example of this may be seen in my ruminations about St. Valentine's Day, once this date was given to me for this talk.)

Thus, much of what I have done has been self-generated. I do not depend much, if at all, upon others to validate what I have done. Indeed, it can be difficult these days to know who does read what one writes. Even so, I am confident that a few of my things are likely to be read a century from now, including my explications of Plato's *Apology of Socrates*,[35] of the Declaration of Independence and the Constitution, [36] of the Emancipation Proclamation,[37] and of some literary (including Biblical and Shakespearean) texts (if not also the mathematical exercise at the very end of *The Constitutionalist*).[38]

Another way of putting what I have just said is to observe that I have been influenced relatively little by academic needs and ambitions. I have been fortunate in never having had any academic appointment or promotion that depended immediately upon any publications I might arrange. The subjects I delve into are, at least for me, intrinsically interesting, challenging, and rewarding. Much of the best teaching I have done was teaching for which I was paid little or nothing. On the other hand, I am glad to accept whatever the going rate is for whatever teaching or lecturing I am asked to do, even when (as in the case of law school teaching) we often happen to be paid far more than we are "really worth" when compared to other teachers in the same university who work at least as hard as we do and who publish far more than most of the law faculty do.[39]

VI.

I should now say more about the role of chance in my career, that element with which one has to come to grips (or to transform, as some are tempted to do, into the Providential) if one is indeed to try to understand the whole of human things.

This may most obviously be seen in what happened with the Illinois bar, beginning in November 1950, three days after my twenty-fifth birthday.[40] That encounter, which very much affected my career, could easily have been otherwise—if, for example, a different two-member panel of the seventeen-member Character Committee had been in charge of my routine fifteen-minutes hearing for applicants for admission to the bar.[41] Also, that initial encounter could easily have been otherwise, with nothing adverse following from it, if I had been wilier in my responses to the panel I did happen to draw.[42]

I have already referred to the importance of my Air Corps career in preparing me to deal with the Character Committee, a career that had included considerable service as a flying officer who was not inclined thereafter to allow himself to be bullied by self-proclaimed patriots who had been, for the most part, too old to serve (except perhaps behind desks) during the great war of our time, that war for which I had been eager (despite apparent physical disabilities) to volunteer as a seventeen-year-old. Chance affected, in critical ways, the experiences I had in the Air Corps, as well as later in the Soviet Union and in the Greece of the colonels.

Also quite accidental was our 1995–1996 "racism" controversy (generated by reckless charges from misinformed students in the law school), a controversy that should never have been allowed by our administration and faculty to develop as it did—and this very much needed to be faced up to (and identified as the irresponsible nonsense that it was) for the good both of the school and of our wrongheaded students. This, like the bar admission controversy almost a half-century earlier, opened up some opportunities even as it closed down others.[43]

VII.

All of us, I suspect, are very much aware of how much chance affects the employment we secure from time to time. On the other hand, it is highly likely, in our social circumstances, that *some* employment will always be available for people like us.

Someone I happened to serve with in the Air Corps suggested to me (I believe it was while we were stationed on Guam, and this was reinforced during my service thereafter in the Middle East)—it was suggested that the University of Chicago was the school to which I should go upon my return to civilian life. This I did do, beginning in the College of the University, where I carried a double load of courses and established the lifelong habit of attending a couple of public lectures a week on the campus.

A short career as a taxicab driver proved to be useful during my transition from my aborted legal career to my decades-long academic career. The highlight of my taxicab service was the chance pickup in the Loop of the Illinois Supreme Court justice who had written the opinion confirming my exclusion from the Illinois bar. My published recollection of our conversation (the accuracy of which has been sworn to under oath by me) has been a source of delight to some, including (I understand) to some of that justice's colleagues.[44]

Each of the academic appointments I had thereafter came with the help of friends with "connections," which is not at all unusual in these matters. First, there was a management–consultant position with the Industrial Relations Center at the University of Chicago;[45] then a seminar-leading position with the Basic Program of Liberal Education for Adults, also at the University of Chicago;[46] then a political science and philosophy professorship at Rosary College when a nun who had been a fellow graduate student became president of the school;[47] and then my current position (since 1981) in the Loyola School of Law after a distinguished trial lawyer, who had been in my Basic Program seminars, joined that faculty.[48] Loyola, it should be added, has been the unsung hero of my legal career, having been the only law school ever to take me seriously once my bar admission troubles began.

Chance may also be seen in the development of the lecture series that led to my two volumes of constitutional commentary. All this began with an invitation to give a series of Bicentennial Lectures at the Rochester Institute of Technology. This was upon my nomination by a faculty member there who recalls fondly how I had befriended him decades ago when he was a young Ph.D. without prospects or connections of his own.[49]

Chance may be seen as well in the development of the essays in my book of introductions to non-Western thought. I had, after a Basic Program seminar on Confucian thought, given a lecture and then published an article on that subject in the University of Chicago alumni magazine.[50] Mortimer Adler, upon reading that article a few years later, recommended it to the executive editor of the Encyclopedia Britannica's *The Great Ideas Today* for publication in his 1984 volume.[51] There followed in the next decade the essays that have been reworked for publication as the book, *But Not Philosophy*, whose very title suggests that there are vital differences between the philosophical tradition that we in the West happen to have inherited and the vital, quite influential schools of thought found elsewhere in the world. The Britannica executive editor, with whom I worked, John Van Doren, has provided a lovely foreword for this collection.

VIII.

Even more critical, of course, than the chance associations and experiences one might have in the shaping of one's career are likely to be the influences that may be fundamental in shaping the kind of human being one is. These influences, too, may be very much governed by chance developments.

The material worked upon by such influences is provided early on in one's life, obviously beginning with one's heredity. Intimately linked to that heredity, so much so as to seem almost natural, is the training provided in the family, including the religious instructions and associations in one's youth. Also significant here, but harder to be sure about (at least in public), is the marriage one embarks upon and its consequences. When one has been married as long as I have (more than a half-century) it can become hard to see the situation as other than natural. (Also natural, it can be said, is my wife's lack of serious interest in what I write. Much the same can be said about our children. Perhaps both my wife and our four children can be understood, considering how much I might impose upon them, to be acting in self-defense. On the other hand, I have been the one primarily responsible for the preservation and publication of my wife's poems across several decades.) In my youth, in any event, our primary religion was Greek Orthodoxy, which was as much political as spiritual, and which was overlaid, so to speak, by the Baptist mores with which I became quite familiar from fifth grade through high school in Carterville, the Southern Illinois town to which we moved from St. Louis, and thereafter overlaid further by the Presbyterianism of my wife's Southern family, a family that numbers both Sam Houston and the founder of Davidson College among its ornaments. (Many an hour was spent by me, while growing up, behind the counter of my father's restaurant [often on my own] in Carterville.)

In any survey of influences, one's teachers become important. Elbert Fulkerson and Fred and Georgia Lingle in the Carterville Community High School; Henry Rago, Robert H. Hutchins, Richard Weaver, and Donald Meiklejohn (and through him, his father, Alexander Meiklejohn) in the College of the University of Chicago; Malcom P. Sharp and Harry Kalven, among others, in the Law School of the University of Chicago; David Grene, Yves Simon, Friedrich von Hayek, and Edward Shils, among others, in the Committee on Social Thought at the University of Chicago; and C. Herman Pritchett in the Political Science Department.[52] In the background, in a way, has been Hugo L. Black, because of the remarkable Dissenting Opinion he wrote in my case, the concluding passage of which he later designated to be read at his funeral.[53]

Perhaps most critical, in any attempt to understand the work I have done, have been two men whose influence upon me personally very much depended upon personal contact over several years: William Winslow Crosskey, of the University of Chicago Law School, and Leo Strauss, of the University of Chicago Political Science Department. (I have published articles suggesting the influence of these men.[54]) Both men were able, in their fields (constitutional law and political philosophy, respectively), to impress upon receptive students three critical lessons: (1) there are texts that are vital to a proper understanding of the most important matters; (2) there is a way of reading such texts that is most apt to convey what was originally intended by their authors; (3) there are not apt to be, at any particular time, many scholars who are truly serious in what they do and say.

I do not believe that either of these men would have had anywhere near the influence upon my work that they have had if I had chanced to know them only through their publications. Perhaps that reveals a serious limitation in me, at least with respect to my ability to make use of my contemporaries, as distinguished from my use of ancient texts. Nor do I believe I would have been able to do much with the teachings either of Mr. Crosskey or of Mr. Strauss if I had ever started practicing law, thereby getting caught up with the escalating demands and the seductive rewards of "the real world," where spiritual massacres abound. Here, indeed, I consider *Fortuna* to have been very kind to me.[55]

IX.

Still another way of putting most of what I have said on this occasion is to confess that I have always been very much an opportunist. Particularly important here have been my Basic Program assignments, especially since I have long been known to be available to conduct seminars on any of the texts in our list, texts that range across the social sciences, humanities, and the natural sciences.

I am also known to be available, not unlike perhaps some of the Sophists depicted by Plato, to talk publicly on whatever subjects need to be discussed in the academic institutions with which I have been associated. The last such talk, in the noontime First Friday Lecture Series of the Basic Program at the Chicago Public Library's Cultural Center, was on Friedrich Nietzsche's *The Genealogy of Morals*. That was on February 2, when I was asked to fill in at the last minute for the scheduled speaker on Nietzsche. (This proved a fitting topic for a Ground Hog's Day talk, dealing as it did with a remarkably gifted thinker who fled "the real world" upon really seeing its shadows.) The next such talk by me, in the same Lecture Series, is to be on March 2, with the rather presumptuous title, "How to Read a Platonic Dialogue."[56]This is to be followed, later in the month, by a briefing paper on Sigmund Freud's *The Interpretation of Dreams* for the Basic Program Staff. I am known as well, and here I do deviate from the Sophists—I am known to do whatever work is needed to make a proper presentation, whether or not there is any money involved. It is in this spirit that I have campaigned for more faculty workshops in our law school.[57]

There are two conditions I have tried to adhere to when I speak. The first is that I do not simply repeat what I have said elsewhere; the second is that I try to leave the manuscript I prepare in fairly good shape so that it can be readily returned to later for incorporation in a publication. My considerable use of *talks* as my point of departure for publications borrows of that dialogue form that animates what might otherwise be lifeless prose.

Some nine hundred talks and papers have been developed pursuant to this mode, many of which have been circulated by me in typewritten form.[58] (This mode of distribution was a practice of mine that Leo Strauss endorsed many years ago, pointing out that I did have a list of good people with whom I was sharing my work.) Of those talks and papers, probably half of them have already been included in books and articles.

I have even developed a literary genre of my own, the "Explorations" articles published in law reviews. These began with a "Church and State" collection in 1987.[59] There are now almost a score of these collections already or almost in print, ranging from one-hundred to four-hundred pages in length. Law review editors have been receptive to these offerings—not the most prestigious journals, or course, which tend to be hidebound, but that does not really matter much these days with the easy access provided to all journals by the Internet. No doubt, it helps that a much-published (and intermittently notorious) *law school* professor is offering law review editors such things, things that appear (at least on the surface) to be of more enduring interest than most of the things published in law reviews. (I myself *do not* try to keep up with what may be found these days in the more prestigious law reviews and political science journals. Citations to these "Explorations" and other articles of mine may be found in the bibliographies to which I have referred.[60])

Some of these "Explorations" collections are scheduled to be issued in book form.[61] Eventually, others of them, if they are of more than passing interest, should also find their way into book form. If and when that happens, the peculiarities of the standard law review format can be modified. Fortunately, I have enough material already in print that the sensible reader can readily distinguish what I meant to say from what has been sometimes done, by enterprising student editors, to what I have said. Even so, I continue to be impressed by how much useful work is done by conscientious law review editors, including the filling in of gaps (in references, quotations, and data) that I have had to leave open. I have also been helped, over the years, by the generous secretarial services that have been available to faculty in our law school.[62]

EPILOGUE

I return to the heart of the original assignment given me by asking, *Why does one do all this?* What is one "called" by or to? All this is, among other things, a way of *learning* and hence of *being.* My experience with the top-flight physicists I have long associated with has been instructive, for one can come to see both what it is that they do know (which *is* quite a bit) and what it is that they neither know nor sense that they do not know (which is quite important). It is also instructive to watch the best of them work, just as it is to watch top-flight musicians work, who can sometimes be equally incomprehensible.[63]

I return as well, as I prepare to close, to the 1929 St. Valentine's Day Massacre of the Moran gang. The ultimate target of that massacre was the leader of the gang, George Moran. (I use here the name by which he was christened, rather than "Bugs," in order to associate thereby my fortunes with his.) George Moran escaped being murdered on February 14, 1929, which permitted him to outlive Al Capone by a decade. He escaped simply because he overslept that morning, which got him to the fateful site to see the "police raid" in progress. Naturally, he stayed outside, which permitted him to escape the executions hidden from public view.

I, too, have been fortunate enough to have missed out on the action that my fellow law students were "on time" for, ever so many years ago.[64] Of course, from their point of view, as eminently successful practitioners who have done much good work, I have not been realistic, having slept through the "wake-up call" that would have permitted me to share their fate.[65]

NOTES

1. This talk was given to the Lilly Faculty Research Group, Loyola University of Chicago, Chicago, Illinois, February 14, 2001. The Group was convened by John Haughey, S. J. See appendix C, note 65. The original title of the talk was "Chance and the Good Life: An Autobiographical Sketch." The epigraph is taken from Plato, *Euthydemus* 179C. Compare George Anastaplo, *The Thinker as Artist: From Homer to Plato & Aristotle* (Athens, Ohio: Ohio University Press, 1997), pp. 182 ("On the Noble and the Just"), 303 ("On the Doctrine of the Ideas").

See, on "the blessings of good fortune," Mortimer J. Adler, *A Second Look in the Rearview Mirror* (New York: Macmillan Publishing Co., 1992), pp. 287–99. I have happened to benefit personally, directly and indirectly, from Mr. Adler—partly from various programs that he developed, partly from association with him (and with his longtime colleague John Van Doren). See, e.g., George Anastaplo, "Law & Literature and the Bible: Explorations," 23 *Oklahoma City University Law Review* 515, 865–66 (1998) (on *The Great Ideas Today*). See also George Anastaplo, *But Not Philosophy: Seven Introductions to Non-Western Thought* (Lanham, Md.: Lexington Books, 2002), p. v. See as well chapter 12, note 1.

2. The Lilly Faculty Research Group was provided, along with these remarks of mine, two published accounts of my career. One official account is taken from the Loyola University of Chicago School of Law's *Catalogue 1998–1999:*

> George Anastaplo, B.A., 1948, J.D., 1951, Ph.D., 1964, University of Chicago. Prof. Anastaplo is also a lecturer in the liberal arts at the University of Chicago and professor *emeritus* of political science and of philosophy at Dominican University. Between 1950 and 1961 he conducted his own bar admission litigation, 366 U.S. 82 (1961). He was nominated annually between 1980 and 1992 for the Nobel Peace Prize. There has been issued in his honor a two-volume Festschrift, *Law and Philosophy: The Practice of Theory.* Six articles were devoted to his scholarship in the 1997 volume of the *Political Science Reviewer.* He is the author of (1) *The Constitutionalist: Notes on the First Amendment*; (2) *Human Being and Citizen: Essays on Virtue, Freedom, and the Common Good*; (3) *Title I Funds, Church-Sponsored Schools and the First Amendment* (an HEW study); (4) Notes Toward an "Apologia pro vita sua"; (5) *The Artist as Thinker: From Shakespeare to Joyce*; (6) *The Constitution of 1787: A Commentary*; (7) "What is Still Wrong With George Anastaplo? A Sequel to 366 U.S. 82 (1961)"; (8) " Slavery and the Constitution: Explorations;" (9) *The American Moralist: Essays on Law, Ethics, and Government*; (10) *The Amendments to the Constitution: A Commentary*; (11) "Lessons for the Student of Law: The Oklahoma Lectures"; and (12) *The Thinker as Artist: From Homer to Plato & Aristotle.* Professor Anastaplo teaches constitutional law and jurisprudence [at the Loyola School of Law].

The other official account of my career is taken from the Association of American Law Schools, *Directory of Law Teachers 2000–2001:*

> Anastaplo, George, (M) Prof. Loyola, Chicago. b.1925. B.A., 1948; J.D., 1951; Ph.D., 1964, Univ. of Chicago. Lect., Liberal Arts, Univ. of Chicago, since 1956; Prof., Pol. Sci., Dominican Univ., River Forest, IL, 1964–84; Vis. Prof., Loyola, Chicago, 1981–83; Prof.,

since 1983; Prof. Emer., Pol. Sci. & Phil., Dominican Univ., since 1984. *Subjects*: Constitutional History; Constitutional Law; First Amendment; Jurisprudence; Law & Literature; Supreme Court History. *Publications*: The Artist as Thinker: From Shakespeare to Joyce, 1983; The Amendments to the Constitution: A Commentary, 1995; The Thinker as Artist: From Homer to Plato & Aristotle, 1997; Abraham Lincoln: A Constitutional Biography, 1999. *Member*: Phi Beta Kappa; Order of the Coif. Res. Dir., Gov'rs Comm. on Personal Privacy, St. of IL, 1974–76; Consult., Paideia Prog., Chgo Public Schs., since 1984.

3. See, on Chicago crime and the careers of "Bugs" Moran, Al Capone and others, William Gaines, "Bad Guys . . . ," *Chicago Tribune*, April 14, 2002, sec. 14, p.1 (reviewing Gus Russo, *The Outfit: The Role of Chicago's Underworld in the Shaping of Modern America* [Bloomsbury, 2002]).

4. John A. Murley, Robert L. Stone, and William T. Braithwaite, eds. (Athens, Ohio: Ohio University Press, 1992). See appendix C, note 7.

5. See Murley, Stone, and Braithwaite, eds., pp. 1073–1146.

6. 20 *Northern Illinois University Law Review* 251, 581–710 (2000).

7. 39 *Brandeis Law Journal* 17, 219–87 (2000–2001). See, for the table of contents of the two-volume *Law and Philosophy* Festschrift, 30 *Brandeis Law Journal* pp. 281–86.

8. See *In re George Anastaplo*, 366 U.S. 82 (1961). See also appendixes B and C (especially section VI), appendix D.

9. The table of contents of this Committee on Social Thought dissertation (*Notes on the First Amendment to the Constitution of the United States*) may be found in "George Anastaplo: Tables of Contents for His Books and Published Collections (1950–2001)," 39 *Brandeis Law Journal*, 277–79.

10. (Dallas: Southern Methodist University Press, 1971).

11. The publisher of the reissue is to be Rowman & Littlefield. See, on the notes of *The Constitutionalist* as "a little university, a second University of Chicago," George Anastaplo, "Notes Toward an 'Apologia pro vita sua,'" *Interpretation*, 10: 321 (1982) (quoting Laurence Berns).

12. (Baltimore: Johns Hopkins University Press, 1989).

13. (Baltimore: Johns Hopkins University Press, 1995).

14. See, on the Declaration of Independence and its right of revolution, George Anastaplo, *Abraham Lincoln: A Constitutional Biography* (Lanham, Md.: Rowman & Littlefield, 1999), pp. 1–38.

15. A series of articles by me, in volumes 42, 43, and 46 of the *South Dakota Law Review* (1997, 1998, and 2001), describe and comment upon the Loyola School of Law "racism" controversy and its aftermath. See appendix C, note 43. See also chapter 13, note 33. See, as well, appendix C, note 64.

The late Gerald Gunther, of the Stanford Law School (the leading constitutional law casebook editor of his time), commented in this way (in an August 4, 1997 letter to me) upon the first of my *South Dakota Law Review* "racism" collections (see chapter 7, note 49):

I'm only partly through the most powerful piece [you sent me], your collection of statements, speeches, and memoranda regarding your school's "racism" controversy.

I think you have done a real service to the profession in collecting all these in one piece, for I don't know of a single university that has not encountered this kind of problem in recent years. Your collection is instructive in the best sense of the word. I think it is the ultimate irony that you, of all people, should have been a target of such charges, and I am really glad that you have continued to speak up about the issues.

I write, for now, in haste and just briefly. . . . [We] are about to take a vacation in Europe . . . but I thought I would acknowledge receipt and, especially, to express my enthusiasm about the "racism" piece.

The consequences of the Loyola School of Law "racism" controversy are commented on in the following letter to the *Bulletin of the Atomic Scientists,* December 2000, by John A. Murley, Professor of Political Science, Rochester Institute of Technology:

I read with interest your profile of George Anastaplo (*Bulletin of the Atomic Scientists,* November/December 2000). You are correct. It was not only well-known scientists and members of the Arts and Letters community who were forced either to kowtow to McCarthy anti-Communism hysteria or to lose their careers. We will never know how many young men and women just beginning their careers in the 1950s were thus affected.

Today a similar danger is posed by the McCarthyism of the Left. Political Correctness regarding race, gender, and class intimidates education and professional decision-making throughout Academia in this country. Anastaplo has continued his refusal to be intimidated, this time by the reckless charges of racism that were leveled against several members of the Loyola law faculty in 1995–1996. (This is reported in the *Chicago Tribune Magazine,* November 26, 2000.)

The most recent consequence of Anastaplo's resistance to intimidation may be seen in the elevation last spring of two other faculty members in the Loyola School of Law to the newly created positions of Research Professor. This was done at a time when George Anastaplo was likely the only member of that faculty with a national reputation as a legal scholar. It sometimes seems that he had published as much as, if not more than, all of the rest of the then-active faculty of that law school combined.

George Anastaplo demonstrated how one responded properly to McCarthyism in the 1950s. He has now shown us how men and women of good will in Academia might properly respond to the threats posed by Political Correctness today.

Your readers may be interested in the collections compiled by George Anastaplo about these matters for Volumes 42 and 43 of the *South Dakota Law Review* (1997, 1998). There is also the article about him in *Leo Strauss, the Straussians, and the American Regime,* Kenneth L. Deutsch and John A. Murley, eds. (Rowman & Littlefield, 1999)

See Gerorge Anastaplo, "Legal Education, Economics, and Law School Governance: Explorations," 46 *South Dakota Law Review* 102, 300–301 (2001). See also my November 16, 2003, talk for the Hyde Park Historical Society, Chicago, Illinois, "If You're as Good as You Look, Why Aren't You a University of Chicago Professor?" See for the text of this talk: http://hydeparkhistory.org.

16. See appendix B, note 14. C. Herman Pritchett, Past President of the American Political Science Association, opened his review of my first book, *The Constitutionalist,* with these observations:

On 24 April 1961 the Supreme Court of the United States, by a vote of five to four, affirmed the action of the Illinois Supreme Court which, by a vote of four to three, had upheld the decision of the Committee on Character and Fitness of the Illinois bar which, by a vote of eleven to six, had decided that George Anastaplo was unfit for admission to the Illinois bar. This was not Anastaplo's only such experience with power structures. In 1960 he was expelled from Soviet Russia for protesting harassment of another American, and in 1970 from the Greece of the Colonels. As W. C. Fields might have said, any man who is kicked out of Russia, Greece, and the Illinois bar can't be all bad.

Law and Philosophy: The Practice of Theory, p. 539 (reprinted from 60 *California Law Review* 1476 [1972].) See appendix B, note 14, appendix C, note 64.

17. (Chicago: Swallow Press, 1975).

18. (Athens, Ohio: Ohio University Press, 1992).

19. (Lewiston, New York: Edwin Mellen Press, 1997, 1999).

20. (Lanham, Md.: Rowman & Littlefield, 1999).

21. See the text at note 26 of appendix B of this collection. Sometimes the subjects are fairly prosaic, as may be seen in the following letter (in which I identified myself as "Frequent cyclist"):

As we grow older, we naturally scale down our expectations. Thirty years ago, I began campaigning for the abolition of broadcast television in this country. The campaign itself, I believed, could help us recognize how corrupting television, with its intense promotion of self-indulgence, has been in our community.

Now I settle for much more modest goals. One such is the suppression of bicycle riding on city sidewalks by adults when pedestrians are present. This is an atrocity we see more and more of these days. Cyclists who are afraid to ride in the streets feel entitled to shift the risk to pedestrians who have no reason to expect a vehicle to race by them at close quarters.

Such bikes ought to be impounded on the spot by police, leaving it to their owners to explain to judges why they "had" to endanger pedestrians as they did. A campaign against this atrocity can not only contribute to the public safety but may also remind us of the duties we all owe to the community.

See *Chicago Tribune*, July 17, 2001, p. 16; *Hyde Park Herald*, Chicago, Illinois, August 1, 2001, p. 4. See also George Anastaplo, "Terror in the Skies," *Chicago Sun-Times*, September 1, 1998, p. 22. See, on the case for the abolition of television, Anastaplo, *The American Moralist*, p. 245. Is the substantial rise in the riding of bicycles on sidewalks related to the prevalence of television, a medium that tends to make the self-indulging viewer oblivious of others?

The installation of a former student of mine as president of the Chicago Transit Authority has "licensed" me to make to him both prosaic and elevated suggestions about changes in the system: (1) that public transportation in the Chicago area be free, supported by taxes; (2) that an occasional bus on a route be equipped as "a singing bus," permitting passengers to sing their way through long runs; (3) that emergency measures be developed in case a subway tunnel has the Chicago River accidentally emptied into it where a rail line runs under the river. See chapter 6, note 26.

See, for the text of other Letters to the Editor in the notes to this collection, chapter 8, note 61; chapter 10, note 78; chapter 13, note 33; conclusion, note 3; appendix A, note 15; appendix C, note 21; appendix C, note 57.

22. (Newburyport, Massachusetts: R. Pullins Co./Focus Publishing, 1999). This publisher has issued a translation of Plato's *Meno* that Laurence Berns and I have prepared. See, on the *Meno*, Anastaplo, *Human Being and Citizen*, p. 74; George Anastaplo, "Teaching, Nature, and the Moral Virtues," *The Great Ideas Today*, vol. 1997, p. 2 (Encyclopedia Britannica, 1997); chapter 6-A, above.

23. See Anastaplo, *Liberty, Equality & Modern Constitutionalism*, I, 252, II, 172, 199.

24. See "The Vices of Treachery and of Revenge," in George Anastaplo, "On Freedom: Explorations," 17 *Oklahoma City University Law Review* 465, 645 (1992).

25. See, e.g., Anastaplo, *The American Moralist*, p. 225.

26. See, for the reading list of the Basic Program, Anastaplo, *The Artist as Thinker*, pp. 299–300.

27. See, e.g., Andrew Patner, "George Anastaplo, Human Being and Citizen," 26 *Political Science Reviewer* 3, 16.

28. See, e.g., Anastaplo, *The Artist as Thinker*, p. 275.

29. See, e.g., Anastaplo, "Thursday Afternoons," in Kameshwar C. Wali, *S. Chandrasekhar: The Man Behind the Legend* (London: Imperial College Press, 1997), p. 122. See also George Anastaplo, Review of Subrahmanyan Chandrasekhar, *Newton's "Principia" for The Common Reader, The Great Ideas Today*, vol. 1995, p. 448 (Encyclopedia Britannica, 1995). See as well George Anastaplo, "The Forms of Our Knowing: A Somewhat Socratic Introduction," in Douglas A. Ollivant, ed., *Jacques Maritain and the Many Ways of Knowing* (Washington, D.C.: Catholic University Press, 2002), p. 1; chapter 1, note 65; chapter 3, note 8; chapter 9, note 49; the text at note 31 of appendix D to this collection.

30. (Athens, Ohio: Ohio University Press, 1983).

31. (Athens, Ohio: Ohio University Press, 1997).

32. 23 *Oklahoma City University Law Review* 515 (1998). See also George Anastaplo, "Law & Literature and the Christian Heritage: Explorations," 40 *Brandeis Law Journal* 191 (2001).

33. (Lanham, Md.: Lexington Books, Rowman & Littlefield, 2002). I have been reassured, after presuming to stray so far from my accustomed intellectual paths, by the observations about *But Not Philosophy* provided for the cover of the paperback edition by Stanley N. Katz, Kenneth Hart Green, and William H. McNeill.

34. The Committee on Social Thought acted on David Grene's advice that the way to get me to put my dissertation in final form would simply be to announce that it had been approved by the Committee. And that is what happened. See, on David Grene, George Anastaplo, "'McCarthyism,' the Cold War, and Their Aftermath," 43 *South Dakota Law Review* 103, 170 (1998).

35. See Anastaplo, *Human Being and Citizen*, p. 8.

36. See appendix C, notes 12, 13, 14.

37. See Anastaplo, *Abraham Lincoln*, p. 197.

38. See Anastaplo, *The Constitutionalist*, pp. 806–808 n. 39.

39. The "reality" here, of course, is that law faculties do have to compete with law firms for the services of their teachers. See appendix C, note 57.

40. See appendix C, note 8.

41. I have recently been given, by chance, the program for a 1947 meeting celebrating the career of Governor John P. Altgeld (see chapter 11 of this collection). That meeting included remarks by Carl Sandburg, by the mayor of Chicago, by the governor of Illinois, by Cardinal Stritch, and by Justice William O. Douglas of the United States Supreme Court. This meeting of December 30, 1947, honoring a man who had once taken a quite controversial stand that cost him his reelection as governor, was introduced by Stephen A. Mitchell, a Chicago lawyer. Three years later Mr. Mitchell was to be one of the two-member subcommittee of the Character and Fitness Committee that blocked (in November 1950) my admission to the Illinois bar because of my apparently unorthodox opinions about the Declaration of Independence and the right of revolution. Decent, well-meaning men such as Mr. Mitchell need at least a half-century before they can begin to judge controversial situations sensibly. (Mr. Mitchell served, in 1952, as chairman of the Democratic National Committee during Adlai Stevenson's first campaign for the presidency. The defects in judgment that he had exhibited in dealing with me in Chicago proved even more serious when he went "national.") Indeed, at my initial character hearing (in November 1950), I knew nothing at all about the two men I was immediately dealing with, probably not even their names. But then, of course, one might wonder what I truly knew about myself. See appendix C, note 1, appendix C, note 58. See also appendix C, note 65.

42. Thus, I could have said something to the subcommittee that may well have been true, that I simply did not know enough about the controversial matters that had been raised to have an opinion worth sharing with the committee. See chapter 6, note 27.

43. Among the opportunities were those developed, with the help of Professor Jonathan Van Patten, in the *South Dakota Law Review*. See appendix C, note 15. See also George Anastaplo, "Law & Literature and the Austen-Dostoyevsky Axis: Explorations," 46 *South Dakota Law Review* 712 (2001). See as well chapter 13, note 33.

44. See appendix B, note 17.

45. Critical here were the responses of Jeremiah J. German and Nicholas J. Melas (who later became the president of the Metropolitan Water Reclamation District of Chicago).

46. Critical here were the responses of Laurence Berns and Maurice F. X. Donohue (dean of the adult education program at the University of Chicago). See Maurice F. X. Donohue, "Making a Living, Making a Life," in *Law and Philosophy: The Practice of Theory*, I, 597.

47. Critical here was the response of Sister Candida Lund. See appendix B, note 24.

48. Critical here were the responses of William T. Braithwaite, Charles W. Murdock (then dean of the Loyola School of Law), and Father Raymond Baumhart (then president of Loyola University). See chapter 9, note 6.

49. See also appendix C, note 4.

50. See George Anastaplo, "One Introduction to Confucian Thought," *University of Chicago Magazine*, Summer 1974, p. 21.

51. See George Anastaplo, "An Introduction to Confucian Thought," *The Great Ideas Today*, vol. 1948, p. 124 (Encyclopedia Britannica, 1984).

52. I have published recollections of various of these men, most of which can be gleaned from my bibliography. See conclusion, note 2.

53. See George Anastaplo, "Mr. Justice Black, His Generous Common Sense and the Bar Admission Cases," 9 *Southwestern University Law Review* 977 (1977), especially note 1. See also appendix B, note 5. Consider as well these observations by Harry Kalven Jr.:

> In the end, what is moving about Justice Black's dissent is its special generosity toward Anastaplo personally. He comes very close to embodying Black's idea of what a lawyer should be. Black quotes at length and with evident approval Anastaplo's statements to the committee about the proper role of the bar in American democracy. Black sees him as rejected in reality because he believed too much in the principles of the Declaration of Independence. His final praise is put ironically: "The very most that fairly can be said against Anastaplo's position in this entire matter is that he took too much of the responsibility of preserving that freedom upon himself." Thanks to the dissent of Justice Black, the *Anastaplo* case has in a very real sense a happy ending, although Anastaplo is still not a member of the Illinois bar. He earns the distinctive reward of being enshrined in the pages of the United States Reports in a living opinion by one of the most cherished of justices.

Kalven, *A Worthy Tradition*, p. 574. See, for Justice Brennan's generous comment on the Black opinion, Roger K. Newman, *Hugo Black: A Biography* (New York: Pantheon Books, 1994), p. 507. See also chapter 11, note 20; the introduction to these appendixes. See, as well, Willmoore Kendall, Book Review, *American Political Science Review*, September 1967, p. 783 (reprinted in John A. Murley and John E. Alvis, eds., *Willmoore Kendall: Maverick of American Conservatives* (Lanham, Md.: Rowman & Littlefield, 2002), pp. 263–65); appendix B, note 11; appendix C, note 15.

54. See, e.g., George Anastaplo, "Mr. Crosskey, the American Constitution, and the Natures of Things," 15 *Loyola University of Chicago Law Journal* 181 (1984); George Anastaplo, "Leo Strauss at the University of Chicago," in Kenneth L. Deutsch and John A. Murley, eds., *Leo Strauss, the Straussians, and the American Regime* (Lanham, Md.: Rowman & Littlefield, 1999), p. 3; Anastaplo, "Constitutionalism and the Good: Explorations," 70 (3) *Tennessee Law Review* 737, 780, 843 (2003).

55. This is not to suggest that my life has not been, on the whole, fairly comfortable. A useful resiliency is encouraged by our family name, which can be translated as "Son of the Resurrected One."

56. My readiness and longevity have combined to induce the Basic Program staff to announce, on my seventy-fifth birthday, that the annual November lecture in the venerable Works of the Mind Series at the University of Chicago would be presented in my name "in perpetuity." The first such lecturer was John Van Doren, with whom I had had many happy collaborations while he was, on behalf of the Encyclopedia Britannica, the eminently sensible executive editor of *The Great Ideas Today*. (His lecture was titled, "The Poet and the World.) The second such lecturer was Christopher A. Colmo, of Dominican University, drawing on his pioneering study of Alfarabi. The third was Albert W. Alschuler, of the University of Chicago Law School, drawing on his work on Oliver Wendell Holmes Jr.

57. I have made these suggestions about faculty salaries in a February 2002 Letter to the Editor:

The tuition increases now being resorted to by American schools threaten to make college education even more difficult to pay for than it already is for those middle-class families who do not have access to the financial aid that poorer families may have. ("Trend of small tuition increases ends at universities," *New York Times*, Feb. 22, 2002, sec. 1, p. 18) Robust cost-cutting is needed throughout higher education, including in the considerable amenities that students have been allowed to expect.

One major mode of cost-cutting by schools is rarely relied upon these days: the substantial reduction of full-time faculty and administrative salaries until economic conditions improve. Some of this effect can also be secured by raising teaching loads.

I have long believed that law schools, too, should do this kind of thing when financially troubled. Perhaps I reflect here what I learned from Professor Malcolm Sharp at the University of Chicago Law School many years ago. It is salutary to be reminded from time to time of his insistence that a man who would not teach for nothing should not be teaching at all.

See *New York Times*, February 26, 2002, p. A20; *Chicago Tribune*, March 13, 2002, sec. 1, p. 20. See also appendix C, note 39. Something *is* to be said for providing free higher education in this country for all students who agree to an appropriate adjustment in their federal income tax rate ever after. See chapter 12, note 195.

58. See appendix C, note 6. It should be noticed (as suggestive of the pitfalls of the scholarly life) that my wife and children do seem to believe in *Immaculate Conception*—in that they do not seem to appreciate why I have had to accumulate the dozens upon dozens of boxes of materials I have in preparing various publications. The curators of the University of Chicago Special Collections Library have asked for all of my papers that I am willing to give them. My wife was delighted to see a large van filled up from our attic for the first consignment a few years ago. See, for a generous appraisal of my career by a regular Army officer, Ollivant, ed., *Jacques Maritain and the Many Ways of Knowing*, p. xii. Consider as well, this two-sentence letter to me of June 22, 1961 (under the letterhead of the Center for Advanced Study in the Behavioral Sciences):

> Dear Mr. Anastaplo:
>   This is only to pay you my respects for your brave and just action. If the American Bench and Bar have any sense of shame, they must come on their knees to apologize to you.
>   As ever yours,
>   Leo Strauss

John A. Murley concluded his 1999 chapter, "*In re* George Anastaplo," in this fashion:

> I have, in the opening section of this chapter, quoted the letter written by Leo Strauss to George Anastaplo after receiving the June 1961 *Petition for Rehearing* filed by him in the United States Supreme Court. It is fitting to conclude my account of this somewhat unusual Straussian by reprinting here the opening and closing paragraphs of that 1961 *Petition for Rehearing*, passages in which (it can be said) Leo Strauss must have recognized his influence.

Deutsch and Murley, eds., *Leo Strauss, the Straussians, and the American Regime*, p. 177. Mr. Strauss also "must have recognized his influence" in the article on Plato's

Apology of Socrates that I contributed to his 1964 Festschrift, an article to which he responded generously. See Anastaplo, *Human Being and Citizen*, p. 8. See also appendix C, notes 53, 54. See as well chapter 1, note 64.

Precisely what Leo Strauss' influence was has recently become a matter of public debate. See, e.g., Jenny Strauss Clay, "The Real Leo Strauss," *New York Times*, June 7, 2003, p. A29. My unpublished letter to the *Times*, of June 9, 2003, drew upon the Strauss letter already quoted and commented upon in this note:

> Leo Strauss's daughter has reported that she does not recognize her father in the recent news stories about him as the mastermind behind the neo-conservative ideologues who control American foreign policy today. Some of us, who were Mr. Strauss's students at the University of Chicago, also fail to see him as the reactionary guru that some would like him to be.
>
> I recall, for example, what he said to me after I lost my Bar Admission "loyalty-oath" case in the United States Supreme Court. (366 U.S. 82 [1961]) That is, his two-sentence letter to me, of June 22, 1961, was hardly that of a rightwing ideologue: "This is only to pay you my respects for your brave and just action. If the American Bench and Bar have any sense of shame they must come on their knees to apologize to you."
>
> I suspect that Leo Strauss, upon confronting those Administration adventurists who now claim to find in his teachings support for their presumptuous imperialism, would recall (as he often did) the Dutch grandmother's advice: "You will be surprised, my son, to learn with how little wisdom this world of ours is governed."

See also Ron Grossman, "How an Academic Came to Dominate Foreign Policy," *Chicago Tribune*, June 22, 2003, sec. 1, pp. 1, 6; George Anastaplo, Letter to the Editor, *Chicago Tribune,* June 22, 2003, sec. 1, p. 10 (chapter 10, note 78).

59. See George Anastaplo, "Church and States: Explorations," 19 *Loyola University of Chicago Law Journal* 61 (1987). Other "Explorations" collections are introduced in the following notes (and cited many times elsewhere in this collection): introduction, note 4; chapter 1, note 7; chapter 1, note 14; chapter 1, note 15; chapter 1, note 51; chapter 1, note 91; chapter 2, note 24; chapter 4, note 17; chapter 4, note 29; chapter 6, note 11; chapter 7, note 39; chapter 7, note 49; chapter 8, note 6; chapter 8, note 35; chapter 8, note 59; chapter 9, note 49; chapter 11, note 19; appendix D, note 32; appendix A, note 16.

60. See appendix C, notes 6 and 7. Professor John A. Murley is developing an Internet website that should try to keep up to date the bibliographies of a number of scholars interested in political philosophy. (This massive compilation should be first published by Lexington Books.) See also conclusion, note 2, appendix D, note 12.

61. Thus, this *On Trial* volume has been developed from the "On Trial: Explorations" collection first published in volume 22 of the *Loyola University of Chicago Law Journal* (1991).

62. Budgetary concerns have at times threatened curtailment of all kinds of services, but we have managed somehow. See, e.g., Anastaplo, "Legal Education, Economics, and Law School Governance," p. 118.

63. See Anastaplo, "Thursday Afternoons," p. 124.

64. Among my classmates were two who became members of the House of Representatives, Abner J. Mikva and Patsy T. Mink. They were most helpful, in that ca-

pacity, by entering things of mine in the *Congressional Record* from time to time. Indeed, the frequency of my commentaries on the regime of the colonels in Greece, making me seem much more important than I have ever been, contributed to my being declared *persona non grata*. See appendix C, note 16. See, for Professor Mikva's remarks about my bar admission case to a University of Chicago Law School graduating class on June 8, 2001, *University of Chicago Law School Record*, Fall 2001, p. 13. See also the foreword to this collection. See, for appropriate "closure" with respect to the Greek case, George Anastaplo, "What Is Still Wrong with George Anastaplo?" 36 *DePaul Law Review* 551, 574 note 87 (1986). See also chapter 13, note 27. (Little, of anything, was made, in the course of my litigation, of the fact that I refused on several occasions to answer committee questions about possible membership in the Ku Klux Klan and various fascist organizations. See appendix C, note 15.)

Abner J. Mikva, along with Bernard Weisberg, Alexander L. Polikoff, and Leon M. Despres filed an amicus brief (for the American Civil Liberties Union) on my behalf in the Illinois Supreme Court in 1954.

65. See conclusion, note 3. The following comment on this February 14, 2001 talk was made by John Haughey, S. J., chairman of the Lilly Faculty Research Group, Loyola University of Chicago, in "Research Autobiographies" (*Connections Association of Jesuit Colleges & Universities*, May 2000, p. 6):

> It has been interesting to find out how many heard "the call" to go in one direction rather than another by having a door slammed on their ambitions. The angelic whisper in the ear was rare. For example, one of our participants has achieved much national attention because of his work in the area of jurisprudence. The door to practicing attorney was slammed on him by those judges who were to credential him but who saw their gatekeeper function as [obliging them to insist upon questions which he considered] inappropriate and which he refused to answer on the basis of their impropriety. Refused permission to practice law, he turned to a life of jurisprudential scholarship. When asked whether he saw this as the hand of providence, he demurred from giving a positive answer on grounds that he was far too insignificant for such exalted self-understanding.

See the text at note 1 of the introduction to this collection. See also appendix C, note 41 (on not knowing oneself). Here, as elsewhere, one can wonder what the freedom of the will could mean. Is there a knowable (and self-knowing) "I" with some discernible control of events? This inquiry should be advanced by a study of the work of Jonathan Edwards (whatever limitations there may be in his [political?] insistence upon the anger of "God"). See, on truly knowing oneself, Anastaplo, *Human Being and Citizen*, pp. 8f.

I have had occasion to comment on Jonathan Edward's famous sermon, "Sinners in the Hands of an Angry God" (1741). My comment, in a talk of November 6, 2003, for the Episcopal Center at the University of Chicago, "God in the Hands of an Angry Preacher," includes these observations:

> The fierce anger of God that is described by Edwards has long been lavished on the already dead. There are in his sermon at least a half-dozen references to the wrath of God for every reference to his mercy. Indeed, it is hard to imagine the divinity of this Edwards sermon as "a loving God."

It can be argued that the expression of anger is often intimately related to the perception of injustice. Even so, there can seem, to the modern reader, a remarkable lack of proportion between the fierceness of the eternal punishment threatened and what has been done (or not done) by the sinner. Such disproportion can even seem monstrous and ugly, unless it is simply dismissed as ludicrous.

We have long known that anger is a problem. After all, it is the word with which the first great secular text in the Western world opens. Anger among human beings is usually recognized, especially in the Bible, as at least a problem: It tends to distort judgment; it is not usually good for social order. Compilers of Bible dictionaries recognize the problem here, as may be seen in their assurances that the wrath of God referred to from time to time in the Bible should not be mistaken for that wrath of human beings, which is usually disparaged.

Questions can be raised here about how the divine may properly be portrayed. Authors as diverse as Plato, Aristotle, and Maimonides can agree that the truly divine should not be considered to be moved by passions. Care must be taken here lest the divine be depicted in such a way as to suggest that it is little more than a projection of human passions. . . .

One suspects, that is, that what we see displayed in something like the "Sinners" sermon may not be the character and passions of God but rather the soul of the Preacher. . . .

It is only just, before concluding this critique of Edwards's remarkable sermon, to notice (however briefly) what can be said for this portrayal of "an angry God."

God, if not the universe itself, *is* shown as *caring*, as fundamentally *meaningful*, for human beings. We creatures are substantial enough to be taken seriously, whatever may happen to such assurances when we "learn" of innumerable galaxies of unimaginable scope elsewhere in the universe. Nihilism is contradicted by the scheme of things offered by Edwards, whatever may be considered questionable either about his intimidating harangues or about the people who submit themselves to them.

In a perverse way, the kinds of threats issued by Edwards do argue for the immortality of the human soul. The risk of unending torment assures us that a blissful perpetuity is also available.

Compare Paul Tillich, *Systematic Theology* (Chicago: University of Chicago Press, 1951–1963), I, pp. 61, 217, 283–84; II, pp. 76–78, 172.

Appendix D

Why Did You Do It? (2003)[1]

If you don't say anything, you won't be called on to repeat it.

—Calvin Coolidge

I.

The convenor of this meeting has put to me the fateful question, "Why did you do it?" I have thus been asked to try to explain why I, in my last term in this law school—at age twenty-five, married, with a six-month-old daughter—why I chose in November 1950 not to answer critical questions put to me (and, evidently, only to me) by the Committee on Character and Fitness for the Illinois Bar. Indeed, one might even wonder, upon delving into issues of temperament, whether I had actually done much in the way of *choosing*.

Certainly, it can sometimes be hard to say, with confidence, why I responded as I did to the inquiries that the committee had been moved to make. In those days, military veterans in this state could take the bar exam while still in law school. An appearance before a two-member panel of the seventeen-member Character Committee was the last step in the bar's testing process. The questions asked of the applicant during that appearance, which was typically scheduled to run about fifteen minutes, depended upon the interests of the panel members one happened to draw.

Sometimes questions would be asked that reflected Cold War concerns, for this was a few months after the beginning of the Korean War. One question asked now and then, which did come up in my inquisitorial lottery, was whether the applicant believed that a member of the Communist Party should be considered eligible for admission to the bar. Others besides me, it seems, were asked that kind of question.[2] There was never any suggestion by the committee that there had been a basis for singling me out for such an inquiry. (I notice this point because Justice Black, in his dissenting opinion in my case, suggested that answers on my application form had alerted the committee to watch out for me.[3] I believe he was simply mistaken about this, having failed to appreciate how haphazard all this really was. One can see here how misleading historical conjectures may be.)

The typical applicant who happened, in the early 1950s, to be asked *this* question about the eligibility of Communists evidently did not have much difficulty determining what the inquiring committee member wanted to hear— and that would be the end of that line of inquiry, if it did chance to come up. I, however, must have been a slow learner about such matters: I said that I did not see why a Communist would not be eligible. I was informed by one of the subcommittee members that Communists believed in revolution. I responded that we all did.[4] This led to exchanges that culminated in the decisive question, because of what I was saying—the question whether I myself was a member of the Communist Party.

No one on the committee—either then or during the many hours of hearings through the following decade[5]—ever suggested that there was anything adverse to me in the record then available to them or thereafter compiled by them about me. At the heart of hundreds of pages of hearings were two issues: the right of revolution and a possible Communist Party membership. At the time that all this started I was being interviewed for employment by one of the leading law firms in the Loop.[6] This initial November 1950 encounter was followed in January 1951 by my appearance before the full (seventeen-member) committee. Shortly thereafter the three of us (my wife, our daughter, and I) sailed for France, where I was able to use up at the Sorbonne some of the rest of my eligibility under the G.I. Bill.

It was not until June 1951 that the committee could act. It had been less than candid theretofore in explaining its delay. When I read in the *International Herald-Tribune* in Paris that the United States Supreme Court had decided the *Dennis Case*, upholding the first convictions of the Communist Party leaders under the Smith Act,[7] I knew that I would be hearing from the committee soon. The original vote against me was evidently 16 to 1. During the decade following, as committee membership changed, the vote became unanimous against me; but finally, after an extended 1958 rehearing, it became 11 to 6 against me. The ringleader of that eleven was an alumnus of this law school who is distinguished enough (at least as a benefactor) to have the faculty lounge named after him in this building.

Perhaps, on another occasion, I can say more than I already have this afternoon about why *they* did it. But it is to why *I* did it that I can finally turn, having provided you some of the background needed to begin to understand what happened.

It can be, in such matters, hard to say *why*. Much depended upon that first encounter with two commissioners who were even more unknown to me than I probably was to them. One of them was, from the outset, obviously rather decent (he later became prominent, however ineffectual, in Adlai Stevenson's first run for the presidency); the other was something of an impetuous fool, which (some might say) made two of us.

Why then? A simple answer is that I was resisting hazing, and hazing that came in a form that was not good for the country at that time. (I believe it was Malcolm Sharp, of the faculty of this law school, who first used that term.[8] He and Harry Kalven were my principal supporters among the faculty. Mr. Kalven wrote generously about my case in his First Amendment book.[9]) The kind of thing that the committee was doing—when done by others on a grander scale and with far more publicity—this kind of thing probably contributed to such profound miscalculations as our campaign in Vietnam. It is not likely, however, that what I did immediately affected in any way, for good or for ill, what was happening in the country—or even what was happening at that time here in Chicago (except for my family), whatever effect it may happen to have in the long run (partly because of the writings of others).

Resistance to hazing, without regard for consequences, *was* critical in the opening stages of my career at the bar. Perhaps other "psychological" factors can be unearthed, including a kind of pride, which meant among other things that I would not ask others for help. After all, I had been, only a few years before, on active duty as a flying officer in the Army Air Corps. In fact, I still held in 1950 a commission in the Air Corps Reserve—and I could even wonder, in the early months of 1951, who would act on me first: the Air Corps by recalling me to active duty (in the Korean War, which I more or less supported) or the Character Committee by rejecting me for admission to the bar.[10]

Be all this as it may, I was then young enough to believe that I was too old to be pushed around by a bunch of "old men." My sense of it all—about what happened and why—has shifted from time to time. One thing I have always been aware of, however, is how much the element of chance did play in all this.[11] Certainly, it can be hard to be clear about one's motives, especially when one's entire being is engaged.

Chance has even affected what I am saying on this occasion: the chance of the inquiry put to me as it has; the chance also of reminders that have surfaced, so to speak, as I have thought about what I should say here. I do not like, when offered an opportunity to speak, simply to repeat what I have said elsewhere. Much of what I have said thus far *has* been said by me at greater length, and much better, elsewhere. I have repeated myself to the extent I have on this occasion in order to provide the background for what I might usefully add at this time.[12]

II.

A recent chance revelation has contributed to my recollection of how naive I must have been a half-century ago. (This was exhibited in other fateful decisions of that period than that seen in my bar admission experience, but those, too, can be reserved for other occasions.)

That naiveté was recalled for me as I worked on these remarks. For it was in the course of this preparation that I happened upon intriguing information that I had never had before, information about a distinguished lawyer (indeed, one of the most distinguished in the history of the Illinois bar), a lawyer who turned out to be critical in what happened to me. He was someone who was, to say the least, decidedly unsympathetic to the stance I took toward the committee's inquiries.

Had he, and only one or two others like him, been sympathetic, I probably would have been admitted to the Illinois bar, certainly in the late 1950s, if not at the very outset of my first encounter with the committee in 1950 to 1951.

I have long sensed that many, if not most, of the men critical to my fate as a would-be lawyer—men both in the bar and in this law school—I have long sensed that many of them had been too old to serve as I had during World War II and immediately thereafter. I have believed, for some time, that it was somewhat disgraceful that a youngster in my circumstances (difficult as I may have been) could be treated as I was by such men.

This belief has been reinforced by what I stumbled upon just this weekend. One of those I had to contend with—the intelligent lawyer of noteworthy accomplishments to whom I have just referred—had been born only a decade or so before I was. I chanced a few days ago upon his account of his desire, as a civilian, to leave government service in order to resume his career in Illinois. This was at the height of the Second World War.

It seems, from the account I now have, that this man had been willing to remain in government service, for which he was evidently deferred from conscription, until it was determined that he was not physically fit for military service. He was thereafter somewhat troubled lest it be thought that he should *not* leave government service in these circumstances—but it is obvious that he did not personally consider it his duty to stay on in that government service if he did not *have* to. Nor did he seem to have any regret that he could not himself undertake military service, whatever regret he might have had, of course, for whatever physical disability he might have had. I do not know what he finally decided to do—but knowing him to have been a very cautious, if not even a timorous, man, prudence (if not also patriotism) might have dictated staying on in government service.

III.

The engaging thing about this revelation is that it nicely points up my naiveté, something that the realists among us (and not only those of the Law and Economics variety) could have fun with.

The lawyer I have been describing openly conducted himself as he did in the latter half of 1943. What makes this particularly intriguing for me is that it was at this very time (within a couple of months) that I was making repeated efforts at Chanute Field to enlist in the Air Corps. I say "repeated" because I was rejected more than once because of a heart murmur and high blood pressure. Nor did it help that I was underweight. I was finally able, however, to persuade a flight surgeon to take a chance on me. Perhaps he figured that I would be "washed out" before I could do either myself or the Air Corps any harm. All this took place seven years before I misstepped just as I was about to be admitted to the bar.

We need not concern ourselves further about the lawyer with a career parallel to mine, but in the opposite direction. It is hard enough for me to be clear about my own motivation from time to time. I do not know enough about *his* circumstances to say much more than what I have already said about a lawyer generally regarded as an honorable man of considerable talent. Even so, the juxtaposition of these two 1943 experiences can serve to dramatize the shamelessness of what was done to me, however foolish I was then.[13] All this was long enough ago that I can look back at what is, in some ways, another person, someone clearly "idealistic," with no adverse evidence against him, on good terms with his law school classmates,[14] and with an honorable military record—someone, in short, who was far younger than he realized he was.

Was I naive in not making more than I did of the kind of disparity in military records that I have noticed this afternoon? And, even earlier, had I been naive in struggling as I had to get into the Air Corps? Was I even more naive— that is to say, too proud—in not making more of this sort of thing (not just military records) than I did? No doubt, a lawyer representing me, especially a lawyer of mature years, would have done much more with all this than I was ever inclined to do. Perhaps he might even have asked that the military biographies of the committee members be entered into the record, having first taken the precaution of making sure that there were no genuine heroes among them. Perhaps, also, *he* might have let it be known to the United States Supreme Court, during the December 1960 oral argument, that I had been expelled from the Soviet Union the preceding summer.[15]

I notice in passing that one unfortunate result of our Vietnam debacle was to discourage spirited youngsters from wanting to have the kind of experience I had had during World War II. At times, I almost felt that that war was being conducted for my benefit. This, too, suggests how naive I was.

IV.

Another encounter, this time in the form of a reminder of something I have written, also has helped me appreciate how much chance *can* matter in our lives. A conservative scholar I know recently happened to tell me that he was much taken by a note in an article of mine about Willmoore Kendall, the political scientist who had most influenced William Buckley at Yale. I report in that note:

> I sketch, in part C of this chapter, the fundamental alternatives for Leo Strauss. . . .
> It is, in large part, a matter of chance that I was able to become as interested in the
> Straussian endeavor as I have been. Much the same can be said about my acquaintance with, and interest in the work of, William W. Crosskey. . . . Such a dependence upon chance reminds us of our mortality and hence of our vulnerability.[16]

Chance can be both reassuring and intimidating: reassuring—in that I did happen upon Mr. Crosskey and upon Mr. Strauss while a student in this University more than four decades ago (first in this law school and thereafter in the Committee on Social Thought); intimidating—in that those scholars, who have been so important for me, would never have become as important as they have been for me if I had not known them personally. This dependence upon personal contacts reveals, I suspect, a deep inadequacy in my makeup. Certainly, one's limitations, grounded in one's mortality, are thus displayed.[17]

Be that as it may, both of these teachers made much of reading carefully whatever was most worth reading. And they were instructive about what the most rewarding texts were.

V.

William Crosskey's reading of the Constitution still seems to me vital to any serious reading of that and like texts.[18] Most legal scholars, even those at this law school, do little with him these days. In fact, not much has ever been done with him.

Constitutional law, one learned from him, was something to be reasoned about, with the study of the fundamental documents of our regime critical to one's inquiry. He did not regard as serious much of what passed as constitutional law in his day. He recognized, that is, that much of constitutional law is merely history, an account mostly of what the United States Supreme Court has happened to say from time to time.

And what the Supreme Court has had to say has been much moved by political considerations. This may be seen in such "celebrated" cases as *Marbury* v. *Madison*,[19] *Dred Scott* v. *Sandford*,[20] and *Bush* v. *Gore*.[21] In each case judicial usurpation may be seen, which can be matched, in a way, by judicial suicide in *Erie Railroad Company* v. *Tompkins*.[22]

Suggestive of what the Crosskey approach can mean in practice is what I said in the opening paragraph of the preface to my 1989 commentary on the Constitution of 1787:

> I was surprised to discover, upon preparing these lectures for publication, that there evidently has not been, since the Ratification Campaign of 1787–1788, any other book-length, section-by-section commentary upon the United States Constitution proceeding primarily from the original text itself. Even during the Ratification Period, the longer expositions, as in the *Federalist* and in the State Ratification Conventions, were not systematic but rather were tailored, properly enough, to local interests and concerns. There have been, of course, many instructive systematic accounts of constitutional law in our own time, but these have relied far more than I want to do here upon judicial and other official interpretations and applications of the Constitution.[23]

Much the same can be said about my 1995 commentary on the Amendments to the Constitution.[24]

VI.

Leo Strauss's reading of classical texts, both ancient and modern, still seems to me vital to any serious reading of those texts.[25] I was fortunate to be able to audit his classes for more than a decade.[26] This was one happy consequence of the obstacles to my career that kept me from going anywhere. Those classes have been supplemented by the more than forty years I have had teaching in this university's Basic Program of Liberal Education for Adults.[27] Thus, I am conducting in that program this year a three-hours-a-week seminar on the thirteen books of Euclid; last year that seminar was on the Bible;

next year that seminar should be on the "history" of Greece, using Homer, Hesiod, Herodotus, Socrates, Thucydides, and Xenophon.

I have noticed my commentaries on the Constitution and on its Amendments as work that has been influenced by Mr. Crosskey. That work of mine influenced by Mr. Strauss included the discussion of Plato's *Apology* first published in his 1964 Festschrift[28] and the translation of Plato's *Meno*, which I am helping to prepare for publication later this year.[29] The most recent work exhibiting Straussian influences is my 2002 book, *But Not Philosophy: Seven Introductions to Non-Western Thought.*[30]

One happy consequence, then, of the totally unexpected difficulty I had securing admission to the bar was my liberation from the temptations and demands of a conventional career. This liberation is symbolized by my having been able to attend, for decades now, the weekly colloquium in the physics department of this university, meetings in which I understand little but from which I believe I have learned a lot.[31]

The careers of both William Crosskey and Leo Strauss at this university have been, in a perverse sort of way, somewhat reassuring to me as I contemplate my ambiguous status on the fringes of this institution. Neither of these men is considered conventional enough to be made much of today by their faculties (the law school and the political science department, respectively).

I can only hope that the work I have done will remain as vital, albeit on a much lower level, as theirs has continued to be.

VII.

Perhaps, then, part of the answer to the question, "Why did you do it?", is that I might have sensed that I would have to conduct myself as I did in order to be, and in order to do, what I may have instinctively wanted to be and to do.

Another way of answering this question is to suggest something about myself by examining what I have been thinking and saying about the September 11 attacks during the past eighteen months. Perhaps we can talk about this during our discussion, working from my evidently justified expectation early on that we would suffer far more damage materially and spiritually from the way we responded to those monstrous attacks than we had originally suffered from the attacks themselves.[32]

A sense of proportion is sadly lacking in the lavish security measures in which we have indulged ourselves. This is consumerism with a vengeance. I suspect that we will come to recognize our follies here sooner than we did during the Cold War, partly because our adversaries this time are nowhere near as formidable as the Soviet Union once was.[33]

Still another way of answering the "why" question put to me on this occasion is to suggest that I did not want to become like those lawyers and teachers of law who were "on the other side" during my encounter with the bar admission authorities. That is, I was fortunate enough to shy away, perhaps instinctively, from what they deemed to be realism and success. Perhaps it can even be said that each side in this half-century–long encounter has somehow gotten what it deserves.

NOTES

1. This talk was given in an Older Students Seminar, University of Chicago Law School, Chicago, Illinois, February 5, 2003.

The epigraph can bring to mind the significance of silence in the career of Sir Thomas More. See chapter 10. Consider also the significance of a May 1930 observation by Calvin Coolidge, "I should like to be known as a former President who tries to mind his own business." Burton Stevenson, ed., *The Home Book of Quotations* (New York: Dodd, Mead & Co., 1964), p. 1553. See the text at note 26 of appendix B of this collection.

2. See, e.g., Ralph S. Brown Jr. and John D. Fassett, "Loyalty Tests for Admissions to the Bar," 20 *University of Chicago Law Review* 480 (1953).

3. See *In re George Anastaplo*, 366 U.S. 82, 98–100 (1961). See also Supreme Court Proceedings in Honor of Hugo L. Black, 405 U.S. xl, xxvi–xxviii (1972). See as well appendix B, note 5.

4. Consider, for example, a constitutional amendment proposed, in 1788, by the Virginia Convention that ratified the Constitution of 1787: "[G]overnment ought to be instituted for the common benefit of, protection, and security of the People; . . . the doctrine of non-resistance against arbitrary power and oppression is absurd, slavish and destructive to the good and happiness of mankind." See George Anastaplo, *The Amendments to the Constitution: A Commentary* (Baltimore: Johns Hopkins University Press, 1995), p. 299. See, on the Declaration of Independence and the right of revolution, George Anastaplo, *Abraham Lincoln: A Constitutional Biography* (Lanham, Md.: Rowman & Littlefield, 1999), pp. 11–38. See also James E. Clayton, "Court Deeply Divided on Controversial Cases," *Washington Post*, April 25, 1961, p. A-1 (drawn upon in the introduction to these appendixes). See, for the "Americanism" heresy, chapter 8, note 44.

5. See, on this decade-long litigation, appendixes A, B, and C to this collection. See also George Anastaplo, "What Is Still Wrong with George Anastaplo?: A Sequel to 366 U.S. 82 (1961)," 35 *DePaul Law Review* 551 (1986).

6. Nothing more was heard by me from that quite good law firm, D'Ancona & Pflaum, after my bar admission troubles began.

7. See *Dennis v. United States*, 341 U.S. 494 (1951). See, on the Dennis case, George Anastaplo, *The Constitutionalist: Notes on the First Amendment* (Dallas: Southern Methodist University Press, 1971), p. 824 (index).

8. See, on Mr. Sharp, appendix A, note 9.

9. See appendix C, note 53.

10. See, on my military service, appendix A. See also appendix B, section II, section III of appendix D to this collection.

11. See, for example, appendix C.

12. Bibliographies of my work may be found in 20 *Northern Illinois University Law Review* 581–710 (2000); 39 *Brandeis Law Journal* 219–87 (2000–2001). See conclusion, note 2. See also *The Legacy of Leo Strauss,* a massive bibliography in political philosophy, compiled by John A. Murley of the Rochester Institute of Technology, to be published by Lexington Books; appendix C, note 60.

13. See, e.g., Andrew Patner, "The Quest of George Anastaplo," *Chicago,* December 1982, p. 185.

14. I was recruited by Harry Kalven, early in my study of law, to take notes (financed by the Veterans Administration) for a fellow student who had lost his hearing in the service. This got me in the habit of making, and thereafter typing daily, detailed notes of all my classes, a habit that continued throughout my career as a law student. (Our afflicted fellow student died at the end of his first year in law school.) It was known, among my classmates, that those notes were available (without charge) to anyone who wanted to borrow them—and it seemed to me that one third to one half of my classmates must have made use of my notes at one time or another. They *were* quite good notes.

15. See, e.g., George Anastaplo, *Human Being and Citizen: Essays on Virtue, Freedom and the Common Good* (Chicago: Swallow Press, 1975), p. 3; appendix C, note 16.

16. George Anastaplo, "Willmoore Kendall and Leo Strauss," in John A. Murley and John E. Alvis, eds., *Willmoore Kendall: Maverick of American Conservatives* (Lanham, Md.: Lexington Books, 2002), p. 184 n. 53.

17. See, e.g., "The Accidental Leo Strauss," in George Anastaplo, "Constitutionalism and the Good: Explorations," 70 *Tennessee Law Review,* 738, 780 (2003); appendix D, note 26. See also appendix C, note 58.

18. See William W. Crosskey, *Politics and the Constitution* (Chicago: University of Chicago Press, 1953). See also Malcolm P. Sharp, "Crosskey, Anastaplo and Meiklejohn on the United States Constitution," *University of Chicago Law School Record* (1973), p. 3; appendix C, note 54.

19. 5 U.S. (1 Cranch) 137 (1803). See, on *Marbury* v. *Madison,* George Anastaplo, *The Constitution of 1787: A Commentary* (Baltimore: Johns Hopkins University Press, 1989), p. 335 (index). See also an article of mine on this case that is to be published in *Thémis* (Montreal, Quebec) ("On the Sometimes Salutary Illusions of Judicial Review").

20. 60 U.S. (19 How.) 393 (1857). See on *Dred Scott* v. *Sandford,* Anastaplo, *Abraham Lincoln,* p. 363 (index).

21. 531 U.S. 98 (2000). See, on this case, George Anastaplo, "*Bush* v. *Gore* and a Proper Separation of Powers," 34 *Loyola University Chicago Law Journal* 131 (2002).

22. 304 U.S. 64 (1938). See, on *Erie Railroad Company* v. *Tompkins,* Anastaplo, *The Constitution of 1787,* pp. 128–37, 320; George Anastaplo, "Constitutionalism, The Rule of Rules: Explorations, " 39 *Brandeis Law Journal* 17, 179 (2000–2001).

23. Anastaplo, *The Constitution of 1787*, pp. xiii–xiv.

24. George Anastaplo, *The Amendments to the Constitution: A Commentary* (Baltimore: Johns Hopkins University Press, 1995).

25. See, e.g., Leo Strauss, *Natural Right and History* (Chicago: University of Chicago Press, 1953). See, for another seminal text published in 1953 by the University of Chicago Press, appendix D, note 18.

26. See George Anastaplo, "Leo Strauss at the University of Chicago," in Kenneth L. Deutsch and John A. Murley, eds., *Leo Strauss, the Straussians, and the American Regime* (Lanham, Md.: Rowman & Littlefield, 1999), p. 3; appendix D, note 17. See also appendix C, note 58.

27. See, for the Basic Program reading list, George Anastaplo, *The Artist as Thinker: From Shakespeare to Joyce* (Athens, Ohio: Ohio University Press, 1983), p. 284.

28. See Anastaplo, *Human Being and Citizen*, p. 8.

29. See appendix C, note 22.

30. See appendix C, section VII.

31. See appendix C, note 29. See also Hellmut Fritzsche, "Of Things That Are Not," in John A. Murley, William T. Braithwaite, and Robert L. Stone, eds., *Law and Philosophy: The Practice of Theory: Essays in Honor of George Anastaplo* (Athens, Ohio: Ohio University Press, 1992), I, 3.

32. I have prepared for publication a collection of my talks and Letters to the Editor about these matters, titled, *September 11: The ABC's of a Citizen's Responses*. See, e.g., conclusion, note 3, appendix A, note 15. My *September 11* collection is to be published by the *Oklahoma City University Law Review* and thereafter (it is hoped) in book form.

33. See, on our Cold War miscalculations, George Anastaplo, *The American Moralist: Law, Ethics, and Government* (Athens, Ohio: Ohio University Press, 1992), pp. 161 (on George Orwell's *1984*), 225, 245, 319, 555. It was evident during our July 1960 family visit to the Soviet Union (as part of a six-month, seventeen-thousand mile camping trip across Europe), both how oppressively regimented the Russians were and how deteriorating the regime was. Our recent "success" in Iraq may conceal, at least for a while, how misguided and hence truly vulnerable we are, spiritually if not yet physically. See chapter 10, note 78, chapter 12, note 6. See also appendix D, note 32. See as well appendix C, note 58.

Index

About the Author

George Anastaplo was born in St. Louis, Missouri, in 1925 and grew up in southern Illinois. After serving three years as an aviation cadet and flying officer during and just after World War II, he earned A.B., J.D., and Ph.D. degrees from the University of Chicago. He is currently lecturer in the liberal arts at the University of Chicago (in the Basic Program of Liberal Education for Adults), professor of law at Loyola University of Chicago, and professor emeritus of political science and of philosophy at Dominican University. See http://hydeparkhistory.org. See also http://www.cygneis.com/Anastaplo.

His publications include a dozen books and two-dozen book-length review collections. His scholarship was reviewed in seven articles in the 1997 volume of the *Political Science Reviewer*. A two-volume Festschrift *Law and Philosophy* was issued in his honor in 1992 by the Ohio University Press. Between 1980 and 1992 he was nominated annually for a Nobel Peace Prize by a Chicago-based committee that had as its initial spokesman Malcolm P. Sharp (1897–1980), professor emeritus of the University of Chicago Law School.

Professor Anastaplo's career is assessed in a chapter in *Leo Strauss, the Straussians, and the American Regime* (Rowman & Littlefield, 1999). A bibliography of his work is included in the 1992 Festschrift *Law and Philosophy* (v. II, pp. 1073–145). See also "George Anastaplo: An Autobiographical Bibliography (1947–2001)," 20 *Northern Illinois University Law Review* 581–710 (2000); "George Anastaplo: Tables of Contents for His Books and Published Collections (1950–2001)," 39 *Brandeis Law Journal* 219–87 (2000–2001). See as well the massive bibliography in political philosophy compiled by John A. Murley, Rochester Institute of Technology, *Leo Strauss: A Bibliographical Legacy* (Lexington Books, forthcoming).